DEMOCRACY AND THE PARTY

MOVEMENT IN PREWAR JAPAN

DEMOCRACY AND THE PARTY

MOVEMENT IN PREWAR JAPAN

THE FAILURE OF THE FIRST ATTEMPT

ROBERT A. SCALAPINO

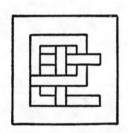

BERKELEY, LOS ANGELES, LONDON

UNIVERSITY OF CALIFORNIA PRESS

UNIVERSITY OF CALIFORNIA PRESS
BERKELEY AND LOS ANGELES, CALIFORNIA
UNIVERSITY OF CALIFORNIA PRESS, LTD.
LONDON, ENGLAND
COPYRIGHT, 1953, BY
THE REGENTS OF THE UNIVERSITY OF CALIFORNIA
CALIFORNIA LIBRARY REPRINT SERIES EDITION, 1975
ISBN: 0-520-02914-3
MANUFACTURED IN THE UNITED STATES OF AMERICA
DESIGNED BY JOHN B. GOETZ

To DEE

PREFACE TO THE THIRD PRINTING

It comes as a shock to realize that this work was first written nearly twenty years ago, although its publication took place a few years later. Since that time, many excellent English-language studies of modern Japan have appeared, studies which use new data and new methodological techniques. We may well be on the threshold of an even more significant advance in the Japanese field, particularly in the social sciences, for young scholars now combine excellent linguistic training with ample opportunities for field research.

Some of us have come to believe that the concept of "modernization" is a useful means whereby to assess Japanese political development after the mid-nineteenth century. In a recent essay, I suggested that there were at least five central aspects to the modernization process in Japan, each of which had certain applicability to that process elsewhere.[1] Japanese modernization involved first the creation of a nation-state, and the successful adjustment of loyalties to that state, together with the substantial increase of centralized political power at the sacrifice of local autonomy. Clearly, the nation-state has been the most important political unit of our times, the unit around which both economic and political institutions in their highest forms have taken shape.

Japanese modernization involved also the replacement of an hereditary officialdom, recruited out of the military class and fixed in status by birth or adoption, with a differentiated civil and military officialdom, the former recruited via the civil service system after higher education, and the latter given technical training in specialized institutions, with merit playing an increasing role in

---

[1] See my essay, "Environmental and Foreign Contributions—Japan," in Robert E. Ward and Dankwart A. Rustow (eds.), *Political Modernization in Japan and Turkey*, Princeton University Press, Princeton, New Jersey, 1964. I have used essentially the same language here in describing the features of Japanese modernization as I used in that essay.

selection and promotion for both groups. No one can doubt that the relatively efficient and reliable bureaucracy of modern Japan was a major factor in the successful evolution of that society.

Modernization in Japan also involved the establishment of a comprehensive legal system, one capped by a national constitution; the universalization and standardization of law and procedures, with the abolition of legally privileged classes; and the movement toward equal rights under the law for all citizens of the state. Yet this aspect of the process created problems. The considerable tension between *borrowed* political institutions and indigenous socio-economic proclivities was an omnipresent factor in modern Japan, as this study indicates. Perhaps that strain was increased, moreover, because of the relatively inelastic character of twentieth-century written constitutionalism versus the extraordinary rapidity of social change in a society like Japan. And clearly, the tension was easy to discern in the 1920's and 1930's, in the zenith period of "Taisho Democracy," and its aftermath.

Finally, Japanese political modernization involved the participation of the citizen in the political process—at first through the unfolding of parliamentarism, followed by a brief and abortive effort at mass-mobilization politics of an authoritarian type, and finally, after total military defeat, a return to competitive politics involving free elections, rival political parties, and the balancing of interest groups.

For most societies, political modernization involved one other central feature, namely, the movement from a religious to a secular ideology—the evolution from a supernatural, mythological rationalization of power toward a "scientific," secular defense of the legitimacy of the state and its leaders. In the case of Japan, as is well known, this change was blocked by the availability—and enormous utility—of the Emperor myth, one of the numerous indications of the usefulness of selected traditional elements to the Japanese modernization process.

The themes set forth above could easily be superimposed upon much of the data and conceptualization presented in the study that follows. Immediately after World War II, however, many of us were naturally interested in the question of whether a democratic political system imported from outside would work in Japan. It seemed appropriate, therefore, to ask the question as to why parliamentarism had failed in the era before 1945—and it was to this question that I addressed myself.

viii

Some scholars have doubted the validity or appropriateness of the question, others have expressed reservations concerning the conclusions which I reached. To both groups, I would like to make a brief response. Let me begin by asserting that I still consider it completely valid to ask the question, "Why did democracy fail in prewar Japan?" It has been suggested that such a question betrays a certain ethnocentrism, since it assumes that Western-style democracy *should* have worked, or *could* have worked, and it seeks to look at Japanese politics through Western eyes. For any scholar, asking any question, the danger of remaining culture-bound and interpreting another political society through the prism of one's own political values and institutions is a constant one. Some portions of this study may well reflect that danger, although I was conscious of the problem and ended the manuscript by asserting that if democracy were to prove meaningful in Japan, it could not be "burdened with provincialism or an inelastic historic reference," but must encompass "the indispensable essence of the democratic system."

In any case, it is important to make a distinction between the error of ethnocentrism and the legitimacy of inquiring why a political system borrowed from abroad failed to perform adequately and was ultimately abandoned or drastically altered. The question which I asked relating to Japanese politics between 1890 and 1945 could be asked with equal validity about many non-Western societies after 1945. To ask this question, moreover, is not to argue that Western-style democracy either can or should be the system adopted. The critical evidence, indeed, may point in the opposite direction. It is merely to seek out the central reasons as to why such a system failed in a given society at a given point in time.

Some have argued that it is unfair to assert that democracy failed in prewar Japan because it was never truly attempted. It is sometimes asserted that the modernizing oligarchy of Japan had no desire to establish "democracy," and that this was also true of the subordinate bureaucracy, civil and military. It is true that within the oligarchy there was both opposition and ambivalence to concepts like parliament and parties. Nevertheless, the thrust of Japanese politics for some decades was in the direction of both. The era of "Taisho democracy" was not a complete mirage. Thus, to assert that democracy in prewar Japan did not fail because it was never really tried is to beg the question. It received the only trial its society was equipped to give it—and after World War I, even the elite generally paid lip service to democracy, using that term as I have defined it in my original preface.

Another school of thought—and currently a more significant one, I suspect—insists that the failure of democracy in prewar Japan has been overemphasized. There is some merit in this contention, particularly as it relates to the professional pessimism of Japan scholarship, a scholarship which in turn influenced American writers including myself. A number of recent writers have emphasized *the democratic legacy* which prewar Japan bequeathed to the postwar era. A certain revisionism is probably beneficial in this score, but it is also essential to reiterate one cardinal fact: democracy, as I have used the term, did *fail* in the prewar era. It was in sharp decline after 1930, both in ideological and in institutional terms. As I suggest in this work, moreover, it failed in a context of broader, international failure. It is impossible to know what precise political theories and institutions would have developed had Germany and Japan won World War II—or even had they avoided it—but there is no reason to assume that such theories and institutions would have been democratic ones. One must never forget that democracy in Japan got its second chance under the aegis of American tutelage and in the aftermath of a total defeat which irreparably smashed certain crucial aspects of the old order. The thesis of a democratic legacy must be used with these facts in mind, and probably is more valid if advanced as part of a broader concept—namely, that Japan already had a considerable legacy of modernization, enabling democracy in its second attempt to have a much greater chance of success.

R.A.S.

Berkeley, California
June, 1967

PREFACE TO THE FIRST PRINTING

History leans heavily upon success, but often the failures of the past provide the greatest insights into the real nature of a society. Democracy and the political party movement failed in Japan before World War II. But to understand the nature, causes, and results of that failure is to progress toward an understanding of the whole nature of modern Japan, and perhaps to shed some light on the problems of all late-developing societies.

The failure of democracy in Japan was not due to trivial causes. Its causal factors were fundamental, and they were not confined to Japan alone. If they are to be discovered and analyzed, therefore, it is important to examine most of the major facets of Japanese society and at the same time constantly relate that society to its contemporary world. I have attempted this difficult task because I have felt that no lesser analysis could possibly convey the full bearing which the failure of democracy in Japan, in all its implications, has on the problems of our time. If the study, despite its shortcomings, makes some small contribution toward outlining the future task of democracy, I shall be content.

An author's introduction is not the place in which to anticipate the evidence or the conclusions, but it is important at the outset to make clear my own usage of the term "democracy," which is the theme of this work. I have used "democracy" with two criteria in mind: (1) adherence to the concept of the innate dignity of man and recognition of his total development as the ultimate goal of the state; and (2) acceptance of choice as the fundamental qualification of democratic institutions, with positive protection for civil liberties, a competitive party system, and the other necessities of an "open society." In omitting economic qualifications, I am not ignoring the supreme importance of the economic structure in determining whether democracy in these terms can be made meaningful, or even attempted. The above definition, however, acknowledges the necessity for experimentation in economic forms, insisting only that the term "democracy" cannot be applied to governments or societies that fail to meet these two criteria. It is also my opinion that the time has come to release the term "liberalism" for broader uses; it should not be restricted in meaning merely to the "classical liberalism" of the nineteenth century. Consequently, the reader will find that on occasion I have used the term "liberalism" as a synonym for "democracy" under the above definition; with this explanation, the context should make clear the usage intended.

Some explanation concerning the use of Japanese words should be offered. I have followed the customary fashion of presenting Japanese names with the family name first. For the convenience of those who read Japanese, the Glossary contains the characters for all words and names presented in the book. The Japanese section of the Bibliography includes the Japanese characters. The Index may also require a word of explanation. Most items have been listed under their Japanese romanized forms rather than under their English translations. This seemed desirable, since translations have rarely been standardized and will undoubtedly appear differently in other works. In the case of a few very common terms such as "cabinet," however, such a practice appeared to be unnecessary. I trust that the system used in the Index of listing footnote as well as textual references will serve those readers who wish to use it.

I could not close this brief introduction without expressing my appreciation to the many individuals who have rendered advice and assistance. This manuscript was first completed in 1948. In the period immediately afterward, Dr. Edwin Reischauer kindly offered to read the manuscript and provided valuable comment and criticism on matters of both interpretation and fact. To such colleagues in the Far Eastern field as Mr. T. A. Bisson, Dr. Delmer Brown, Dr. Nobutaka Ike, Dr. Marius Janson, Dr. John Maki, and Dr. Donald Shively, I am also extremely grateful for suggestions rendered at various stages. In addition, it has been my good fortune to have become personally acquainted with many Japanese scholars in the course of several trips to the Far East. I should like to take this opportunity to express my deepest appreciation to Professors Horie Yasuzo, Maruyama Masao, Oka Yoshitake, Royama Masamichi, and Tsuji Kiyoaki, who were very generous in their personal assistance. The citations contained in this work seem completely inadequate acknowledgment of my debt to modern Japanese scholars whose works I have used profusely. Three individuals whose special field is not Japan have also aided me in many ways. During the period 1947–1948, I had the encouragement of Dr. Rupert Emerson, and his comments were much appreciated. In the final stages of the manuscript, major sections were read by Dr. Lloyd Fisher and Dr. Leslie Lipson, and our discussions were invaluable to me. I should also like to mention the assistance given me by Mr. Akira Wakasugi and Mr. Leo Rose. If this is a rather lengthy acknowledgment, it is actually much too short, a fact which I know can be appreciated by all authors. For errors of fact or judgment, of course, I am solely responsible.

While this work was being prepared for publication, I was again in the Far East. Naturally, the burdens placed upon the University Press were greatly increased, and I am most appreciative of the unfailing coöperation of its staff. My gratitude goes especially to Miss Helen Travis of the Editorial Department, who labored for many hours over the manuscript in my absence. Her services were both valuable and exceedingly generous.

R. A. S.

Berkeley, California

CONTENTS

ABBREVIATIONS

IMTFE International Military Tribunal for the Far East. "Proceedings" and "Exhibits"
JC *The Japanese Chronicle*
JGD McLaren, Walter W. (ed.). *Japanese Government Documents, 1867–1889.* Part I of Vol. XLII of *Transactions of the Asiatic Society of Japan.* Tokyo, 1914
JM *The Japan Mail*
KC *The Kobe Chronicle*
TASJ *Transactions of the Asiatic Society of Japan*

I

THE TOKUGAWA
BACKGROUND

THE CENTRAL PROBLEM confronting Japanese democracy in its
various attempts to find expression has lain in the difficulty of
surmounting the obstacles of timing. A solution to this problem
contained from the beginning the only real hope of challenging
effectively an overwhelmingly hostile tradition. To place the problem of timing in perspective and to explore the nature of Japanese tradition, some understanding of the Tokugawa era is indispensable. The Tokugawa period, spanning the years between 1603
and 1867, reflects the chasm which separated the mind and structure of nineteenth-century Japan from that of the contemporary
liberal societies of the West. The Japanese political party movement, which emerged only a few short years after the close of
the Tokugawa era, was fundamentally dedicated to Western liberalism and therefore dependent for its success upon the bridging
of this gulf.

Before this problem is placed in its Japanese context, it might
be well to recall briefly the historic process through which Western politics passed before such instruments as modern democratic
parties were well established. The growth and acceptance of
democratic parties in the West came only as a by-product of the
highest development of representative government. Centuries
after the first impact of the Renaissance and Reformation had
forecast the doom of Western feudalism, political power was still
accessible to a very few and authority was held or captured
largely by armed might. Only as the full tide of the industrial
revolution swept on in wave after wave of economic, social, and
political changes was the narrow channel leading to political
power widened. With the middle class as its initial vanguard, the

1

system of representative government, in places where it was triumphant, gradually expanded to include even the lower economic stratum of society as this group manifested its strength and readiness.

Then and only then could political parties in the liberal pattern flourish and become powerful, for, as Lord Bryce pointed out, they were dependent upon two major factors: the size of the group participating in government and the acceptance of liberal techniques.[1] Public participation in government had to grow to the stage in which some organization was necessary to avoid a complete fragmentation of the popular will. As long as the few held absolute political control over the many, there was little need for an organized division of the public mind. Moreover, the acceptance of parties involved an acceptance of the ballot as the final determinant in internal political decisions. Vying parties could become a stable part of the political structure only when the rights of each were assured. To establish such assurances, it was necessary to put limitations on the power which any victorious party could wield. Allegiance to rule by one's political opponents —indeed, the very concept of political opposition within a society —was made palatable only after the community had erected a framework of inalienable individual rights on which no triumphant party could trespass.

Long after the first limited acceptance of popular government as a theory, these prerequisites for democratic party growth were attained, slowly and in varying degree. They were predicated upon the underlying assumption that political disagreements were inevitable and, within limits, beneficial to the growth of a good society. The core of classical liberalism was the theory that progress could come most quickly from the free play of ideas—as well as goods—in the open market. The democratic community of the late nineteenth century had succeeded, in theory at least, in enthroning each man as a part of the ruling class and in making him the

---

[1] James Bryce, in his introduction to M. Ostrogorski, *Democracy and the Organization of Political Parties*, New York, 1922, Vol. I, p. xl.

I have used the phrase "political parties in the liberal pattern" to avoid the implication that the criteria set forth here are prerequisites for all parties. Certainly the term "party" can be applied to various groups seeking political power without recourse to such techniques. Indeed, this very fact suggests one of the central problems with which this work is concerned in terms of the Japanese parties. It is important at the outset, however, to establish qualifications for a democratic party movement against which Japanese politics can be measured.

2

supreme *raison d'être* of the state. Political parties were conceived as the instrument through which each man might align himself with others of similar persuasion and exert his voice in affairs of government. It must be remembered that of the important Western communities, only in England, the United States, and possibly France had political parties of this type assumed a commanding position in the governmental structure by 1870.[2]

In the West as a whole, the struggle to establish the procedures of liberalism had achieved only a modicum of success, in spite of the support of powerful forces and the long, arduous battle which had been waged. In Japan, that struggle was just beginning, greatly complicated by a cultural background offering little support for liberal principles, and also by the particular requirements of modern Japanese evolution. To review the Tokugawa era with these factors in mind is to point up many genetic weaknesses of a movement yet unborn.

Japanese feudalism is divisible into several periods, but the last era of so-called "centralized feudalism"[3] under the Tokugawa family (1603–1867) is one of those transitional periods that are of the greatest interest to the students of any society. It was the role of this era to transmit to modern Japan many essentially

---

[2] Even in these countries, party supremacy was of recent vintage and still the subject of acrimonious debate. Speaking of England, Bryce said: "Down to 1832, the number of voters in nearly all the boroughs was so small, and the control of one person, or a few persons, was so effective in most of these boroughs, that no organization of the voters was needed, while in the counties, the influence of a few great landowning families supplied the necessary leadership when an election arrived." Bryce, Introduction to Ostrogorski, *op. cit.*, p. xi.

With regard to the United States, it will be remembered that a part of Washington's "Farewell Address" carried these words: "The common and continual mischiefs of the spirit of party are sufficient to make it in the interest and duty of a wise people to discourage and restrain it. It seems always to distort the public councils and enfeeble the public administration."

[3] There are many reasons for exercising great care in using the term "feudal" with reference to the Tokugawa period. Indeed, since "feudalism" has come to be used as a term for a total system of social organization, one must not overlook the important distinctions, as well as similarities, between Japanese feudalism and European feudalism as a whole. This is all the more necessary since Communists currently equate the terms "feudal" and "reactionary."

Japanese scholars continue to discuss the proper boundaries of their feudal period. Professor Imanaka would divide Japanese feudalism into four eras and two types: the Kamakura and Muromachi eras come under what he refers to as the *kajin hoken seido* (family feudal system), and the Azuchi-Momoyama

"feudal" characteristics, while at the same time giving rise, in its middle and latter stages, to the great upheavals that made possible the rapid modernization from the Meiji era onward.

When the lord Tokugawa Ieyasu received the title *Sei-i Tai Shogun* (Barbarian-subduing Generalissimo) and the control of the country from the Emperor in 1603, he was reaping the reward for a great military victory over his last important rivals, and he was soon to apply his political genius in leading Japan out of a period of intermittent civil warfare comprising nearly three hundred years. The military feudalism of the earlier period, dating from the fall of the court nobility in the twelfth century, had disintegrated into internecine war and near anarchy. Owing to the military capacities of his two immediate predecessors, however, Ieyasu inherited a country once again welded together, to a considerable degree, by the power of the sword, but desperately needing effective centralized political machinery if it were to hold and augment its military gains. Before 1600 the Throne had lost all real power; its sole function had become that of authenticating the rule of the leading warrior. By acquiring their original appointment from the Throne, the military shogunates sought to establish a legitimacy equal to that of the Imperial Household itself. This protective device probably helped to preserve the Emperorship as an institution, but the Throne, in its very helplessness, begat violence among those seeking its hand. Ieyasu, together with his political subordinates, was shrewd enough to fashion a realistic program aimed at perpetuating himself and his heirs.

His immediate success is best demonstrated by the fact that for more than two hundred and fifty years Japan enjoyed a period of almost unmarred peace under a ruling family that secured greater recognition than had ever been afforded its predecessors in power. Ieyasu's chief objective of creating a stable political structure was achieved largely by keeping in mind two essential goals: unity under centralized power and an undeviating perpetuation of the status quo. Nothing was to be feared and hated more than what

---

and Edo (Tokugawa) eras are called *hochi hoken* (fiefal feudalism). Imanaka Tsugimaro, *Nihon seiji shi taiko* (*Outline of Japanese Political History*), Tokyo, 1936, p. 133. For a discussion of various Japanese theses on feudal boundaries, see *ibid.*, pp. 133–140.

Many Japanese writers have classified the Tokugawa period by the phrase, *shukenteki hoken seido* (centralized feudal system), to make clear its hybrid nature. The adequacy of even this term is questioned, however, especially if the time span is intended to embrace the *Bakumatsu* (shogunate twilight period).

were known as *toha* (factions), the first character of which term came to be used for the Western word "party." This term was applied along with *jashu* (heretical sects) to signify the opponents of the government.[4] Some indication of the strong influence which this particular aspect of Japanese heritage had on the later political parties can be judged from the following words of Itagaki Taisuke, cofounder of the first embryonic party:

With regard to the naming of our party the *Aikokukoto* [Public Party of Patriots], . . . the reasons that we deliberately put the term *"koto"* [Public Party] into our new political organization was so as to make clear in this way the distinction of our party. For in the feudal government, party factions were strictly prohibited, and for the people to join such a faction was in itself equivalent to treason. Moreover, we are not yet too far separated from the world of feudalism of that time, and popular sentiment has not yet been able to discard those old traditions of the time when opposition was merely called *toha* [factions]. We are fearful lest we invite misapprehensions, such as if it were felt that this was in the nature of a private party. Hence, in naming the new party, we specifically chose the name *"koto."* [5]

In seeking to combat factionalism and make strong the fabric of the new order, Ieyasu and his successors nurtured powerful philosophic allies. Confucianism, with its emphasis upon the *dotoku kokka* (ethical state), in which rulers were benevolent and people obedient, rapidly replaced Buddhism as the central stream of Tokugawa thought. Certain doctrines of Confucianism that had proved very valuable to the ruling class in China were now utilized by the *bakufu* (military administration), through its encouragement of Confucian learning and the rise of such scholars as

---

[4] From Okuma Shigenobu, "Meiji kensei keizai shiron" (A Historical Treatise on Meiji Constitutionalism and Economics), in *Nihon no seito* (*The Political Parties of Japan*), quoted in Osatake Takeshi, *Nihon kensei shi taiko* (*An Outline of Japanese Constitutional History*), Tokyo, 1939, Vol. II, p. 440.

A study of the derivations of modern Japanese political terminology yields a clue to one of the problems confronting the political parties. The characters assigned to approximate new Western concepts naturally retained some measure of their older connotations. In the case of the word "party" these connotations were universally bad. For instance, the Chinese term *p'eng tang* (Japanese pronunciation: *hoto*), meaning "faction" or "clique," was often used in the sense of bandit or pickpocket groups. "Political party" was later translated by the term, *seito*, which was formed by the addition of the character for "government" or "politics" in front of the old "faction" character. See *ibid.*, pp. 439–440.

[5] Quoted from *ibid.*, p. 446.

Hayashi Razan, Nakae Toju, and Yamaga Soko.[6] Under these savants and others, the central Confucian themes were woven into the fabric of Tokugawa society, intertwined on occasion with strands of earlier Buddhism and Shintoism.[7]

Two interrelated reasons for the triumph of Confucian philosophy over competing ideologies in ancient China were its prescription for social order and the utility of this prescription for the ruling class. Dismissing sheer power as a justification of rule, the Confucianists evoked the highest ethical concepts as the proper basis for political relationships. Viewing society as the giant prototype of the family, they sought to transfer familial ethics to society by making these the moral basis for government. Whether practiced or not, Confucianism could serve as a powerful myth on behalf of the ruling elite.[8]

It was asserted that the necessity of government came from the nature of man and society. To the Confucianists, men were, of course, unequal—in birth, in capacities, in occupation, and in a host of other ways. When the inconvenience of anarchy required the institution of government, it was logical that the morally and

[6] These scholars were themselves sharply divided into the two schools of neo-Confucianism and classicism. As Japanese Confucianism grew in importance, the philosophic battles of Sung China were reproduced in Japan, after the appropriate time lag. With the rise of Hayashi, pupil of Fujiwara Seika, the Chu Hsi school became the official one, but the writings of such classicists as Nakae were still influential. See Nomura Kentaro, *Tokugawa jidai no shakai keizai shiso gairon* (*An Introduction to the Social and Economic Thought of the Tokugawa Period*), Tokyo, 1949 ed., pp. 88–89.

[7] Although the predominance of Confucianist thought among early Tokugawa philosophers is clear, the continuing influence of Buddhism and Japanese primitivism in the form of *Shinto* (Way of the Gods) is often apparent. Indeed, during this period, a popularizing of Buddhism was undertaken, primarily as an antidote to Christianity. Each person in every class of Japanese society was forced to belong to a Buddhist temple. But perhaps, as Professor Nomura suggests, this "popularization" policy contributed to the decline of intellectual interest in Buddhism. See Nomura Kentaro, *Gaikan Nihon keizai shiso shi* (*A General History of Japanese Economic Thought*), Tokyo, 1949, p. 66.

[8] Note the following famous and oft-quoted passage from the "Analects": "Chi K'ang asked Confucius about government, saying, 'What do you say to killing the unprincipled for the good of the principled?' Confucius replied, 'Sir, in carrying on your government, why should you use killing at all? Let your evinced desires be for what is good and the people will be good. The relation between superiors and inferiors is like that between the wind and the grass. The grass must bend when the wind blows across it.'" From "Confucian Analects," Book XII, chap. xix, in Vol. I of James Legge (trans.), *Chinese Classics,* 1893 Oxford ed., reprinted in China, 1939, pp. 258–259.

intellectually superior should rule their inferiors. The inferiors however, should expect the justice due them if, content with their status, they rendered the same type of unswerving obedience as was to be expected from children to their parents. The position of the governed was thus essentially dependent, not upon legal safeguards, but upon the virtue of the ruling class.[9] It was the ruler's duty to reward or discipline with the attitude of a father watching over his children. In theory, moreover, the scope of power was coextensive with the society itself; there was no area of society into which the "educational" force of the state could not move.

The Confucianist emphasis was, of course, upon man, not upon men. The individual could never be considered as an end in himself; he was important only as he completed the unity of his society. In a vast patriarchal family, he played a very small role, dependent upon his sex, age, and position in life. If Confucianism emphasized introspection, it was for the purpose of helping the individual to identify that role. And that aspect of Confucianism known as *min-pen-chu-i* (Japanese, *mimponshugi;* principle of the people as the basis [of the state]) should never be equated to democracy. Mimponshugi signified the importance of the people to the wealth and power of the state. In this concept was contained a reminder that without popular support, no ruler could long survive, and that for internal stability and external power, there was a compelling necessity to regard the general welfare of the people. Should any ruler cease to heed this injunction, Chinese (but not Japanese) Confucianism contained its famed "right of revolution" concept, for toleration of the overthrow of a tyrant (who had ceased to be a king) was at once a corollary of Confucian ethics, a safeguard for the bureaucracy, and an excellent rationalization for dynastic change.

These general principles of Confucianism were naturally molded to fit the contours of Japanese society. At the hands of the *samurai* (warrior) scholars, Confucianism became the vehicle whereby warrior ethics were elevated and transmitted as the political code of the state. The main tenets of Tokugawa political philosophy were spelled out in the *buke sho hatto* (Regulations for the Mili-

---

[9] It is true that the vast body of custom, much of it encased in written code, served in ordinary times as a type of protection, prescribing as it did the relations between rulers and ruled. For its enforcement and interpretation, however, it depended upon the character of the rulers, just as familial custom depends upon the character of the parents.

tary Class) and in various private family codes, of which Ieyasu's "Legacy" to his heirs is probably the most famous.[10]

But Confucian values depended for their effectiveness on the political and economic techniques of the new shogunate. The interaction of ideas and social forces is brilliantly portrayed in the early Tokugawa era. In its political aspects the Tokugawa system was based on a tripod of centralized checks upon feudal fiefdoms, the maintenance of social staticism, and the preservation of national isolation. Each of these policies had a heavy impact on the nature of Tokugawa society and the legacy which it passed on to the Meiji era.

The key to the control of any feudal structure lies in the control of the regional lords, who in turn command the obedience of their vassals, attendants, and commoners. In Tokugawa Japan, this meant a control of the less than three hundred *daimyo* (feudal lords) whose *han* (fiefs) marked the political divisions of the country.[11] The Tokugawa system for retaining the allegiance of the daimyo was essentially one of rewards and punishments and one that required a skillful use of checks and balances. The great battle of Sekigahara in 1600, which had assured Tokugawa supremacy, marked the dividing line in determining political patronage. Those lords who had supported Ieyasu before his victory were known as *fudai daimyo* (hereditary lords) and were rewarded with most of the high offices and responsible positions, but shared the posts of honor and authority with the *hatamoto* (bannerets), who were the immediate vassals of the Shogun, and also with the branches of the Tokugawa family itself.[12] Those lords

[10] For an English translation of this, see James Murdoch, *A History of Japan*, Vol. III, London, 1926, Appendices, p. 802.

[11] The number of daimyo varied somewhat, but it remained close to three hundred during the Tokugawa period. See Honjo Eijiro, *Meiji ishin keizai shi kenkyu* (*A Study of the Economic History of the Meiji Restoration*), Tokyo, 1930, p. 20.

The word *han* in Japanese is usually translated "clan," but, as Western writers have frequently mentioned, it does not imply necessarily a blood relationship, since it is used to designate a fiefdom ruled over by a daimyo and hence has a geographic connotation. References to "clan cliques" and "clan government" should be read with this fact in mind.

[12] The branches of the Tokugawa family came to be known as the *sanke sankyo;* the *sanke* were the Tokugawa branches of Owari of Nagoya, Kii of Wakayama, and Hitachi of Mito; the *sankyo* were the families of Tayasu, Hitotsubashi, and Shimizu. Together these constituted the whole of the Tokugawa family. See Oka Yoshitake, *Kindai Nihon no keisei* (*The Foundation of Modern Japan*), Tokyo, 1947, p. 5.

acknowledging the suzerainty of the new shogun only after his victory were termed *tozama daimyo* (outer lords), and their relationship to the shogunate was substantially different from that of the fudai daimyo. The latter were more like true vassals and became, increasingly with the passing years, the officials for the national administration. The tozama lords, although owing the Shogun tribute, military levy obligations, and obedience to his call to guard duty, had a marked degree of local autonomy and generally conducted important administrative, judicial, and military affairs in their own name like sovereigns.[13] Their independent power was often great. At the same time, because of the potential threat which they represented, they were frequently the targets of such discriminations as the shogunate had the power to effect. The tozama daimyo were ineligible for high positions in the central government, and in the redistribution of han they were generally the ones who suffered most. The Tokugawa family itself controlled about one-fourth of the rice-income land directly, and the outer lords probably controlled not more than one-third of the production.[14] Moreover, the tozama daimyo were strategically checkmated whenever possible by strong Tokugawa supporters who controlled most of the main arteries of communication and transit.[15]

Having thus sought to segregate potential opponents and reduce their power, the bakufu put into effect an ingenious system which would go far toward rendering difficult any organized or wide-

[13] See Kawashima Takeyoshi, *Nihon shakai no kazokuteki kosei* (*The Familial Structure of Japanese Society*), Tokyo, 1949, pp. 120–121.

[14] Land revenue figures are necessarily approximate, since land distribution varied with the period. Tokugawa household figures are given by Tsuchiya Takao in English in his *An Economic History of Japan*, Vol. XV of the 2d series of *Transactions of the Asiatic Society of Japan* (serial hereinafter cited in the notes as *TASJ*), Tokyo, 1937. See also James Murdoch, *op. cit.*, Vol. III, pp. 21–24.

[15] Imanaka, *op. cit.*, pp. 165–166. There were practically no tozama daimyo in the *Kinki* (Osaka) or *Naichi* (Home Provinces) areas; they retained fiefs in Kyushu, Shikoku, and other areas isolated from the heart of the country. *Ibid.*, p. 166. To be sure, this also constituted a source of strength in some respects, and it was from the "outside han" of the southwest (the extremity of Honshu, Kyushu, and Shikoku)—namely, the Choshu, Hizen, Satsuma, and Tosa han—that the successful opposition to the bakufu finally arose.

It should also be pointed out that the bakufu occasionally followed conciliatory policies toward the tozama daimyo when desirable. In some cases, it increased the rice-income acreage and promoted marriages between tozama daimyo and shogunate families. Oka, *op. cit.*, p. 8.

spread opposition among dissident daimyo. In the first place, with the aid of the fudai daimyo, an efficient centralized administration was established. As the centralized bureaucracy developed, groups of officials and inspectors of provincial administration were sent out from the capital to carry forth the edicts of the Edo (present-day Tokyo) government. Local autonomy remained very strong, especially in areas far removed from the central administration, but this enforcement procedure gave the government an opportunity to observe han activities. In this capacity, the *metsuke* (censors) held a key position. Charged with an inspection of provincial administration, as well as serving as circuit judges, they were in an excellent position to observe the effects of Tokugawa edicts and to ferret out unrest. When a menacing lord arose, he could often be transferred to an insignificant and isolated han, or be deprived of his land completely.

In addition, the central administration elaborated upon a policy that came to be known as *sankin kotai* (alternate trips for service).[16] Under this system, the daimyo were required to spend part of their time in the capital, Edo, under the watchful eye of the bakufu. During the time spent in their han, they were required to leave their wives and children in the capital as hostages for their good conduct. This served both to disrupt potential plans for revolt and to keep han resources low, especially when public works expenditures were added to these expenses. Such assessments for national upkeep were a most convenient mechanism to impoverish potentially hostile daimyo. Although the general economic maxim was frugality, it was politically expedient for the bakufu to encourage certain types of ostentation. This encouragement did not include approval of expenditures for military purposes, such as those for castle and moat repairs, which were carefully supervised and limited.[17]

To minimize further the dangers of collusion and plots, the bakufu built up an intricate network of road barriers to check

---

[16] Details of this system are discussed in Professor Yoshimura's book: Yoshimura Miyao, *Kinsei seiji shi* (*Modern Political History*), No. 16 in Shin Nihon shi (History of New Japan Series), Tokyo, 1936, pp. 55–56.

[17] The rule of *ikkoku ichijo* (one country, one castle) was adopted. The bakufu also established restrictions on the number of han troops, and on alliances, marriage arrangements, and temple construction; their all-pervasive paternalism even extended to prohibitions on stays of visitors, frivolous amusements, and gambling. Imanaka, *op. cit.*, p. 166. It is small wonder that acceptance of governmental restriction was so thoroughly ingrained in modern Japan.

travelers on the roads leading to Edo. The following sign appeared on a notice board at Hakone in 1711:

All persons passing through the barrier must remove their head-coverings [straw hats and *"zukin"*]. The doors of palanquins must be opened on entering. Women travellers must be strictly examined in relation to their passports, and those riding in carrying chairs must be taken to the lodge of the barrier guards for examination. Passports are required for wounded persons, dead bodies or other suspicious burdens.

Court Officials and Daimyo need not be inspected if they have previously given notice of their arrival, but if anything seems suspicious, any person, whatever his rank, is subject to inspection.

These rules shall be strictly obeyed.

1711 5th Month   Magistrate of the Shogun.[18]

Visits between daimyo were discouraged, and some roads and communications were deliberately allowed to fall into disrepair to prevent the lords of different han from fraternizing.[19]

Another important link in the Tokugawa chain around the feudal lords needs to be noted. In carefully circumscribing the relationships among the han, the bakufu did not overlook the potentialities of the Emperor and the Imperial Court at Kyoto. For convenience, the fiction of Imperial supremacy was studiously maintained, as a cloak under which moved the living tissue of military power.[20] The Tokugawa, however, were fully aware of the latent jealousies of court officials who might hope to revive past power, and of the danger of any alliance between slighted daimyo and the Imperial House. Every precaution was taken to continue the impersonalization of the Emperor, who was thus relegated to the misty realm of spiritual existence, completely separated from political affairs.[21]

---

[18] Translated in Neil S. Smith (ed.), *Materials on Japanese Social and Economic History: Tokugawa Japan* (1), London, 1937; Koda Shigetomo, *Edo and Osaka*, 1934, p. 57.

[19] Bridge building in particular was often regulated by political considerations. Tsuchiya Takao, *op. cit.*, p. 15.

[20] The role of the Emperor in legitimizing power in a given family that was struggling against many rivals for the shogunate had a long historic tradition and, as has been pointed out, was one reason for the continuation of the Imperial line. Probably of equal importance is the fact that control of land and rice income was the real measure of power and the real concern in the feudal state; the acknowledgment of the Emperor's superior social position and of his theoretic power of investiture of office were of little moment, especially since, in matters of business, the tone of bakufu orders to the Throne left no doubt about who was the master.

[21] Some Japanese historians have referred to the shogunate policy toward the Throne as a policy of *gai-son nai-atsu* (outward respect, inner oppres-

Kyoto remained a shrine, but one closely watched. For the daimyo to enter the city, even on a sight-seeing tour, required permission and consequent supervision on the part of bakufu officialdom; only fudai daimyo were made local officials. Court nobles and even court ladies surrounding the Imperial Household were stringently limited in the visits which they could make to outside areas.

To this entire system of bakufu controls was drawn the support of Confucian principles properly interpreted in accordance with Japanese society. Loyalty to one's superior in the hierarchical scale was extolled as the chief virtue. A strenuous attempt was made to place this loyalty in precedence even over one's familial obligations, so far as the samurai class was concerned; the code of the warrior was to desert his family before deserting his lord. If this represented a certain transposition of the values of Chinese Confucianism, it was a logical attempt to meet the needs of a largely feudal society.

When one analyzes this entire aspect of Tokugawa policy with respect to its influence on Meiji politics and on the emergence of political parties, certain interesting factors are revealed. In the first place, under such a system, key political relationships were chiefly vertical, not lateral. Contacts in political life were made on an ascending or descending scale in the hierarchical structure, but the han themselves were isolated and half-foreign to one another. In recognizing that the road to continued power lay in keeping potentially discontented elements segregated, the bakufu had striven to separate the tozama daimyo and to surround them, whenever possible, with trusted subordinates of the central government officials. The whole program of travel permits, Imperial Court isolation, and restrictions on trade among the han was designed to separate the han lords from one another and also from the officials surrounding the Throne.[22]

The fact that the early Meiji parties developed in some measure from the rivalries and jealousies among the four powerful han

---

sion). In 1615, a series of regulations relating to the Imperial Household were promulgated by the bakufu. These made clear the fact that Imperial powers were to continue to be restricted largely to matters of art and culture. Yoshimura, *op. cit.*, pp. 66–67.

Except in emergencies such as a fire, the Emperor spent his life in the confinement of the Imperial Palace, carefully guarded.

[22] It is true that frequent contact was possible while the daimyo were in residence at Edo, but such meetings were often in an atmosphere of competition for bakufu support, and of suspicions due to the possibility that reports might be carried to the shogunate.

in positions of leadership is connected with this background. Close coöperation among the emergent elements of the Restoration period was, of necessity, poorly grounded and precarious. The mutual suspicions of these groups had been skillfully fostered under a system based upon keeping them apart or pitting them against one another as rivals for bakufu favors. The problem of factionalism and sectionalism in modern Japanese politics had many of its source springs in this setting. At the same time, however, it should be noted that the central emphasis upon loyalty to superiors laid the groundwork for a transference of this loyalty to the larger unit —the nation—and thus enabled Japan to approach modern nationalism with much greater ease than China. This interesting counterplay of factionalism and nationalism has assumed a remarkable role in shaping the nature of modern Japanese politics, including the parties, and both forces will receive further attention later in this study.

In the second place, the bakufu policy of bleeding the potential enemies of the administration through a heavy drain on han finances had important consequences in the financial difficulties of the han and of the *bushi* (warrior) class as a whole. This, together with the more important rise of commercial capitalism, will be examined subsequently, but it is proper to point out here that the economic dislocation of the han—and most particularly, the samurai class—contributed a strong economic motivation for political parties in the early Meiji era, a repercussion, in part, from Tokugawa political policy.

Nor should one overlook a third important outcome of the bakufu program to control the han. In its striking success and long continuance, the system provided an excellent pattern of action for successors to power, especially since these were to be from the same bushi class—samurai whose concept of power was molded by the past actions of their supreme leaders. When political parties finally arose to struggle against the government, they found themselves confronted with many of the same tactics to which the bakufu had resorted in seeking to avoid han factionalism and build more securely their own political position. In expanding the drive for centralization, the Meiji government was disposed to use many of the successful and well-established Tokugawa methods. The Meiji oligarchs followed the familiar techniques of "divide and conquer" and "rewards and punishments." They sought to segment the parties, just as the Tokugawa had segmented the han. When force was necessary, they did not hesitate to use it, but whenever inducements in the form of governmental positions would suffice to buy off party leaders, these Meiji oligarchs were as proficient as the bakufu had been in rendering lucrative fiefs to deserving supporters. To be sure, the parties themselves, led by men from a similar background, often betrayed these same characteristics.

The Tokugawa policy of daimyo and court control was, as noted earlier, only one part of the system of political controls. The shogunate was equally desirous of strictly maintaining the social and economic status quo, and of actually increasing the rigidity of the social caste system to the point where birth and occupation would be the final determinants in life.[23] The strong desire to perpetuate class distinctions was clearly stated in the famous "Legacy":

"The *samurai* are the masters of the four classes. Agriculturists, artisans, and merchants may not behave in a rude manner towards *samurai*. The term for a rude man is 'other than expected fellow'; and a *samurai* is not to be interfered with in cutting down a fellow who has behaved to him in a manner other than is expected." [24]

At the top of the social pyramid was thus the samurai, warrior and administrator, who held in his hands the affairs of government and, as can be seen from Ieyasu's proscription, the fate of his fellow man. It was the duty of the samurai to teach the other classes, to impart to them the higher morality and selflessness which were supposed to characterize his code. The *nomin* (farmers) came a poor second on the social scale, and the main reason they fared even this well was that they were producers of rice, key to the feudal economy.[25] It was they who were to be considered the "treasure of the country" and therefore honored, in the abstract; but in reality, they were treated usually as foolish animals who had to be constantly guided and watched. Below the third class, *konin* (artisans), came the *chonin* (merchants), at the bottom of the

---

[23] For an excellent discussion of the Tokugawa Confucianist approach to social class theory, see Nomura, *Gaikan Nihon keizai shiso shi*, pp. 67–82. Professor Nomura points out the fact that although certain writings by Hayashi and others would imply an equality in men, these were but passing abstractions and that the central theme was an emphasis on the fate of birth and the relative importance of each occupational group to the state.

[24] From "The Legacy of Ieyasu," chap. xlv, translated in Murdoch, *op. cit.*, Vol. III, Appendices, p. 802.

[25] See the section, "The Theory of Honoring Agriculture," in Nomura, *Gaikan Nihon keizai shiso shi*, p. 82–94.

14

social register.[26] The social contempt heaped upon the merchants was the result of the "unproductive" life they led and the fact that they put "profit" above "duty." As their real position improved, the members of the merchant class became, increasingly, the target for hatred and abuse.

With all the power and knowledge at its command, the Tokugawa bakufu, abetted by the daimyo-samurai class, sought to freeze the class system into these fixed categories. From the administration of justice to the prescribing of clothing, the pattern was the same; all was dependent upon the individual's place in the social hierarchy. From birth to death, with a way station at marriage, the path was marked with the proper signposts, each written in the language of the class but clear to the individual, whose duty it was to follow in the prescribed course.[27] The thesis

---

[26] The four classes were known as *shi-no-ko-sho,* in which term the characters represented the occupation of each category. Below these, of course, were the *eta* (outcasts), a group distinguished by occupations considered most repulsive, such as butchering and tanning. Actually, certain Confucian scholars made other divisions. Nakae, for example, lumped all the *shomin* (common people) into one category, his fifth. Preceding them, in order of their importance, were the Emperor, the *shoko* (lords), *kyodaifu* (major officials), and samurai. Indeed, the difference between the *bushi* (military) class as a whole and the other classes was so great that there was considerable justice in lumping the shomin together.

[27] The numerous restrictions placed upon the commoners rested largely on two interrelated desiderata: first, the maintenance of class divisions with a clear preëminence for the bushi class; second, the protection of a static, agrarian society. In connection with the first, it was natural to make innumerable distinctions in food, dress, and customs among and even within the various classes. The 1648 Osaka law directed toward the chonin is an excellent example of the prohibitions extended to shomin groups. See Nomura, *Tokugawa jidai no shakai keizai shiso gairon,* p. 81. That these restrictions extended even to language is well known to the students of Japanese.

In connection with the second aim, the bakufu of course desired to emphasize an increase in agrarian production, and especially, the highest possible rice payment to the treasury. Hence it sought to prohibit the peasant from producing bean curd, vermicelli, and other products which would interfere with rice production; it also prescribed that he should eat cereals other than rice, denied him certain amusements calculated to encourage idleness, and forbade him to move without authority. With staticism desired, it was natural to emphasize a theory of frugality—a concept of "no desire in our hearts"—and to seek to prevent the rising monetary economy from disrupting class relationships or agrarian emphasis. Thus, the theory on wealth was that it was to be used in accordance with one's social position. Moreover, to whomever given, wealth was not for purposes of ostentation,

that the common people were to be pitied and should not be made to suffer was an integral part of the ethics preached by the Confucian scholars, and served a useful purpose in building up the folklore, but it could scarcely mask the haughty and superior attitude of leadership taken by the members of the Tokugawa ruling class toward those beneath them.

To the privileged samurai class went almost all the benefits of education, military training, and political tutelage—those accouterments necessary to feudal control. The early Tokugawa leaders strove with great success to turn the bushi class from men who despised learning into men honoring it; as a leisure class in a period of long-enduring peace, the samurai turned to intellectual pursuits largely denied other groups. In samurai schools, their children learned the Chinese classics, bushi ethics, and in some measure, the art of war—although the training for war became increasingly formalistic as the need for it ceased. Concomitantly, the bushi, and especially the samurai, by controlling the han governments were acquiring experience as practical administrators. The bureaucratization of the military class was one of the most interesting phenomena of the early Tokugawa period.[28]

Whatever political movement should arise out of the collapse of the bakufu, it could scarcely be led by any class other than the samurai, whose political acumen and experience were the product of exclusive privileges. Although the samurai constituted less than 8 per cent of the population, they were, politically speaking, "the people" of Tokugawa Japan.[29] The peasantry were long

but to aid the poor; the *gimu* (duty) of the wealthy was great. If this philosophy was violated for political expediency in the case of encouraging some daimyo extravagance, it became increasingly important to be used against the rising chonin and to provide some solace to the troubled bushi class. The haughtiness of the bushi did not abandon them, even when they stood before the door of a rich merchant, requesting a loan.

[28] In this connection, the absolutism of the daimyo was often a façade behind which samurai, often of a low status, conducted the real affairs of government. Within the samurai class, numerous divisions were maintained; in Tosa han, for instance, samurai were divided at one time into nine categories, with distinctions made even down to the color of the *haori* (Japanese coat) to be worn. Nevertheless, Professor Osatake states, within the samurai class itself, ability played a fairly important part in determining political position and influence in the han, despite these divisons. See Osatake, *op. cit.*, Vol. II, p. 25.

[29] During the Tokugawa period there was a very large increase in the samurai population; by the time of the Meiji Restoration the samurai, to-

inured to a blind obedience interrupted only by periodic outbursts of an animal passion to survive, and it was quite natural for them to accept the leadership of their feudal mentors. Nor could the rising chonin lead an opening political party movement in which they had had no practical experience.[30]

Such a static system as that devised by the early Tokugawa might not have survived so long as it did had not the bakufu utilized another powerful weapon for resisting change—the well-nigh complete isolation of Japan from the outside world. When the Portuguese first landed in the southern part of Kyushu soon after 1540, they began a series of Western contacts with sixteenth-century Japan which were to end in disaster for many of the "red-haired barbarians." Inevitably the Bible followed the cargo ship, and proselyting the Japanese became the great goal of the Jesuits.

The Japanese, unusually tolerant in matters of faith, were at first generally unconcerned, but with the arrival of Spanish traders and Franciscans, the implications of foreign religious and commercial strife took on a serious aspect. The foreigners were not loath to denounce each other in front of the shogunate, and the spectacle of foreign aggression in the Philippines and elsewhere was disconcerting. Moreover, the political and commercial uses to which the "Christian" daimyo put their new religion were clearly in the mind of Hideyoshi when he decreed, in 1587, that all Christian missionaries must go.[31] At first unenforced for the most part, the decree was finally executed with a vengeance that left death and confiscation in its wake.

When Ieyasu established the Tokugawa dynasty, there was an

---

gether with their families, probably numbered between 1,500,000 and 2,000,000, or about one-sixteenth of the population.

[30] It is true that an increasing number of merchant families provided themselves with education, and that chonin culture reached new heights, accounting for such splendid periods as that of the Genroku era (1688–1704). Chonin schools, however, emphasized, for the most part, "chonin learning," which did not include the art of government. Moreover, as Professor Nomura points out, the chonin assimilated the bushi philosophy, rather than developing one of their own, and this greatly retarded their capacity to rise to political power. See Nomura, *Tokugawa jidai no keizai shiso gairon*, pp. 167–173.

[31] It was alleged that at the time of the Shimizu uprising (1587) one of the rebel leaders had borrowed a large sum of money from the Portuguese missionaries, offering as security a year's tribute from the Nagasaki region. Shortly thereafter, Hideyoshi issued his proclamation. Imanaka, *op. cit.*, p. 206.

attempt to modify earlier severities and make a place for foreign trade, but the inevitable intrusion of Western religious and commercial ideologies into a precariously balanced internal structure was fraught with too great a risk of disunity.[32] Although the Dutch and English arrived in the early seventeenth century with less converting zeal than their earlier predecessors, the die had been cast and the challenge of Westernism was met by more and more rigorous exclusion policies. By 1639, the year in which the Portuguese were excluded, a cycle had ended, and the inroads of the "barbarians" had been checked. Only with the Chinese and Dutch at Nagasaki did Japan continue to retain commercial ties, and these on such a limited scale as to preclude significant political effects. In the main, the foreigner left a heritage of suspicion and fear that was never to be completely dissipated. Certainly the events of the early nineteenth century did little to reverse previous convictions that foreigners were dangerous people, especially when armed.

The effects of this long period of withdrawal on subsequent political developments can hardly be overrated.[33] The national isolation policy shut Japanese society off from a rapidly changing world. Although this could not prevent changes from taking place within the country in the Tokugawa period, it did have a remarkable effect upon the type of response made to these changes and upon the over-all time schedule for change. And these were factors which molded the basic structure of modern Japan. As an initial result of isolation, the earliest ideological reactions against the bakufu were perforce cast largely in traditionalist terms. Deprived of contemporary foreign stimuli, the samurai scholars and savants thumbed through the pages of their own history, as well as that of ancient China, to find the answers to the perplexing problems that were beginning to emerge. The rise of the commercial revolution in Japan was itself greatly retarded by the imposition of isolation, but as the revolution slowly picked up momentum, orthodox Confucianism seemed inadequate to provide solutions for the transitional period. In the resultant confusion, the classicists re-

[32] In 1612, a secret Dutch report to the shogunate stated that Portugal and Spain were plotting the overthrow of the government. *Ibid.*, p. 207. Moreover, the political theories of the West were influencing certain elements, especially the *ronin* (masterless samurai). For an interesting interpretation, see *ibid.*, pp. 206–207, and also Yoshimura, *op. cit.*, pp. 83–104.

[33] For one study which emphasizes the influence of isolation on Japanese thought and politics, see Inobe Shigeo, *Ishin zenshi no kenkyu* (A *Study of Pre-Restoration History*), Tokyo, 1935.

opened the ancient Japanese texts and began to portray the era of Imperial rule as the golden age. A contradiction had long rested uneasily in samurai intellectual circles: the preponderant influence of Chinese thought had produced a renewed reverence for Chinese culture, but at the same time it was not easy to accept the contemptuous manner in which the Chinese dismissed Japan as a barbarian country, and there were many Japanese who stubbornly insisted that Japan, quite as much as China, should be considered *chung-kuo* (the central state). With the inadequacies of Confucianism increasingly displayed, there was an ever greater tendency to portray the differences between the two states, attack subservience to China, and glorify Japan's own heritage. Isolation no doubt contributed to the concept that Japan was the most important, most sacred country of a world which, to the Japanese mind, existed only in vague form.[34] Thus a political and religious revival was produced which rediscovered the position of the Emperor in primitive Japanese society, resurrected Shintoism, and elevated it to a key position. This renaissance of traditional values and atti-

---

[34] The Tokugawa nationalist movement is one of basic importance and would constitute a very fertile field of research for Western scholars. Only an inadequate suggestion of its course can be given here. It is clear that the rise of nationalism in Tokugawa Japan was closely connected with the commercial revolution taking place, but the relationship was different from that obtaining in the West. Since Chinese theories had always been assimilated only with considerable difficulty, because the environment was very different from the Chinese environment, the ground had been previously cultivated for such men as Hayashi Shihei and Honda Toshiaki. These men emphasized the differences between China and Japan and played up the concepts of wealth and power which, under the phrase *fukoku kyohei* (literally, wealthy country, powerful soldiery), became a guidepost for the modern period.

Closely interrelated was the deep division in Tokugawa economic thought which produced two main schools: those who decried the commercial trend and sought a return to pure agrarianism, the premise of the Tokugawa state; and those who accepted commercialism as inevitable, or even beneficial. In a period when learning was chiefly in the hands of the bushi class, the first school was generally more powerful. The fruit of its efforts contained the same paradox, in greater degree, that had marked Tokugawa aims. Although feudalist in intent, its creed built up Imperial centralization and high-lighted the unique qualities of the Japanese, Shintoism, and the other paraphernalia of nationalism. This was the true school of *sonno-joi* (Revere the Emperor—Oust the barbarians [Westerners]). With the end of isolation, however, the second school was able to build on this substantial foundation, and, without destroying it, amend it by substituting the concept of a modern industrial state, expressed in its early form by the term *kaikoku* (Open the country). We shall have occasion shortly to examine these economic aspects more closely.

tudes was to set the whole tone of the Restoration, providing the basis for a nationalism which was not to come to fuller fruition until the Restoration era, but which had its roots in the center of the Tokugawa period.

Curiously enough, it was under the direction of one of Ieyasu's grandsons, Mitsukuni, Prince of Mito (not a shogun), that traditionalism received its first great impetus. Through his efforts, a number of scholars compiled the monumental *Dai Nihon shi* (*History of Greater Japan*) in 1715. Though it remained unpublished because of bakufu opposition, its detailed study of the ancient polity was a guidepost to succeeding works. Later histories, such as those of Rai Sanyo (1780–1832), steadily built up the historical case for direct Imperial rule and had great influence on the young samurai.[35] The revival of Shinto studies was led by such scholars as Kamo no Mabuchi, Motoori Norinaga, and Hirata Atsutane in the eighteenth and nineteenth centuries.[36] It was these movements which together justified the original designation of the Restoration—*fukko* (return to antiquity).

The samurai leaders of political parties, along with all other members of the intellectual class, were connected intimately and

[35] Rai Sanyo's *Nihon seiki* and *Nihon gaishi* had a tremendous influence on certain key figures of Restoration politics. Prince Ito, one of the leading Meiji figures, once stated to a colleague: "Even since I was a child, I have read Rai Sanyo's *Nihon seiki* [*Political Records of Japan*] with delight and appreciation. Not only was I deeply impressed by his discourse on royalism; I particularly took note of the fact, deep down in my heart, that the system of government which prevailed at the height of the Imperial regime was the prefectural type now in existence in the modern world, and that this constituted the vital source of the Imperial authority." Hamada Kenji, *Prince Ito*, Tokyo, 1936, p. 57.

[36] The revival of pure Shintoism keynoted the nationalistic spirit. Its pioneer, Kada Azumamaro (1669–1736) was followed by Kamo (1697–1769), Motoori (1730–1801), and Hirata (1776–1843). The writings of these men were attempts to reassert traditional values in religion and politics. Holtom says of their works:

"The contents of the old literature are so interpreted as to furnish the means of a nationalistic propaganda and, more particularly, as an instrument of attack on the Tokugawa usurpation. The growing consciousness here relies on an exegesis of history in order to develop the twofold thesis of a *jure divino* sovereignty in an imperial line unbroken from divine ages and a divine Japanese race which, by virtue of the intimacy of its genealogical connection with the gods, was braver, more intelligent and more virtuous than all the other races of the earth." Daniel C. Holtom, *The Political Philosophy of Modern Shinto*, Part II of Vol. XLIX of *TASJ*, Keio University, 1922, pp. 10–11.

inextricably with this panorama of the past, and hence they could not avoid being prisoners, in some degree, of the forms that Japanese nationalism took. Their original opposition to the bakufu had stemmed from the teachings of men like Yoshida Shoin, the fiery Imperial patriot who, by the age of twenty-nine, had been lecturer, writer, and martyr to the cause of Imperial restoration.[37] Executed for his treachery to the bakufu in 1859, he had preached the doctrines of restoration of the ancient system, foreign expansion, and hatred of the "barbarians." It should not be surprising that when it came to writing party programs and philosophies, the leaders would liberally, and often incongruously, mix the old with the new.

Thus far I have attempted to point out the ways in which the main lines of Tokugawa policy and thought served to influence the practical pattern of future politics in Japan. I have indicated that the bakufu method of controlling potential opponents assured divisions in Meiji politics, despite the goals of feudal philosophy. No single man or han was allowed to become strong enough to overthrow the shogunate and take over its scepter of absolutism; no combination could long remain united when segregation and suspicions had been fostered so long and skillfully by the Tokugawa regime and when the philosophic tides were increasingly running at crosscurrents. In seeking a weapon with which to strike back at the victorious clique, the dissident elements were certain to discover belatedly the contemporary liberalism of the West, hitherto unknown to them. On the one hand, political parties of the Western type, properly interpreted, would appear as heaven-sent to groups that were seeking expression for their economic and political discontent, and yet were not strong enough to win a contest of arms. The ruling oligarchy, on the other hand, would quite naturally find in the policies of the bakufu some guidance, both philosophical and practical, in dealing with factions.[38] The leaders

---

[37] For an English study of Yoshida Shoin, see Horace E. Coleman, "The Life of Shoin Yoshida," in *TASJ*, Vol. XLV, Part I, pp. 119–188.

[38] Suzuki Yasuzo comments as follows on the feudal influence in the Meiji government:

"Because the officials of the Government were themselves feudal samurai or court nobles, however much one may say that they absorbed the new learning, there were both ideological and practical limitations. From their special psychology as governors, there was a strong feeling that they should try to maintain the present system and discipline of the time; even though they saw and heard of various new systems and took certain ideas and theories, when it came to a pinch, they could not cast off a preservation of the old

of both the government and its opponents would be from the only politically conscious group of the semifeudal society, the samurai class. No class of the *shomin* (common people), not even the rising merchants, possessed the proper education, experience, or social respectability to take the political helm.

The great influence of the Tokugawa political and social forces on modern Japanese politics, however, can be better appreciated if the nature of the transformation from Tokugawa to Meiji Japan is made clear. In 1853 the Tokugawa family had lost few of the visible signs of political absolutism, and the political structure seemed relatively intact; by 1867 the bakufu had been overthrown and new samurai leaders were striving to bring order out of chaos by a series of startling innovations. There is a significance in these facts that must not escape our attention. The external political forms of the Tokugawa period had tremendous resiliency, and, surviving the vicissitudes of great social changes, were able to cast a long shadow over the new era. Indeed, this staticism of political forms has caused some Western writers to err by conveying the impression that the Tokugawa era was one in which the hands of time stood still. In reality, however, this is far from true. Indeed, the final overthrow of the bakufu was attributable to profound economic and social changes which had been under way since the early part of the Tokugawa administration. It was these changes which carried within their development the real nature of the transformation taking place—a fact which the destroyers of the Tokugawa dynasty themselves could not fully comprehend, and which was therefore to cause certain vital economic and political cleavages in the new era.

Undoubtedly, the focal point of change was the rise of capitalism, which undermined feudal agrarianism and the rigid class structure that had been the basis of the status quo.[39] The rise of commercial capitalism in Tokugawa Japan stemmed from a variety

---

discipline and a viewpoint which in its essentials was basically feudal thought." Suzuki Yasuzo, *Jiyuminken kempo happu* (*Civil Rights and the Promulgation of the Constitution*), in Kindai Nihon rekishi koza (Modern Japanese History Series), Tokyo, 1939, p. 7. Although this may not do complete justice to all members of the new oligarchy, it has a considerable element of truth.

[39] Among the Japanese writers on Tokugawa capitalism, those to whom I am particularly indebted for their research are Professors Hirano Yoshitaro, Honjo Eijiro, Horie Yasuzo, Nomura Kentaro, and Tsuchiya Takao. Their works, together with certain other studies on this period which have been of value, are given in the Bibliography and will be cited frequently in the text.

of sources. There can be no doubt that the imposition of national isolation seriously retarded the commercial activities which had been given great momentum in the relatively brief period of Western trade. Commercial development was both restricted and molded by the fact of isolation; however, it received increasing impetus as the Tokugawa period progressed. An era of peace facilitated production and the expansion of internal markets. Despite political obstacles, trade barriers were gradually removed, surplus produce within the han found its way to markets outside the han, and the flow of commerce became remarkably free.[40] Communications were gradually improved—another contributory factor. Moreover, the *sankin kotai* (alternate trips for service) system and the general rise of castle towns established great consumer centers, providing the need for distribution centers like Osaka.[41] Urbanized bushi acquired luxury tastes which necessitated the selling of large amounts of rice to obtain commercial articles. These large-scale operations were facilitated by the establishment of a coinage system, and the result was the gradual transformation from an economy based on rice to one based on money.

The signs of this general trend were abundant from the middle Tokugawa era onward. The great merchant houses of Osaka and Edo were acquiring control over the price and distribution of agrarian products; capital was accumulating in their hands, and some of this capital was invested in land, urban capitalism and agrarian landholding thus becoming interrelated. Of equal importance was the fact that in the various han, conditions were also opportune for a rising commercialism. An enforced self-containment of the han had produced a strong impetus to develop district enterprise to satisfy local needs.[42] As the Tokugawa period

---

[40] See Horie Yasuzo, *Nihon shihonshugi no seiritsu* (*The Establishment of Japanese Capitalism*), Tokyo, 1939, pp. 28–32.

[41] Edo, product in part of the sankin kotai system, was the great city of the Tokugawa period. At its peak, it had a population of between 1,300,000 and 1,400,000, and between the beginning of the eighteenth century and the beginning of the nineteenth century it was probably the largest city in the world. About one-half of its population was of the bushi class. Osaka, the greatest commercial center, probably had a population of more than 400,000; and Kyoto, both a cultural and a commercial center, about 500,000. See Tsuchiya Takao, *Ishin keizai shi* (*Economic History of the Restoration*), Tokyo, 1942, p. 19. Also Horie Yasuzo, *op. cit.*, pp. 39–40.

[42] Since the system of han isolation had originally permitted only limited trade among the han, a flourishing productive system had arisen within the han, resulting in a type of self-sufficiency. This district commercialism was marked by a considerable amount of regional specialization and a close rela-

progressed, many han were caused to promote this commercial activity and actively participate in it in order to meet the increasing financial difficulties with which they were plagued. Thus capitalism was growing in the districts, as well as in the great urban centers, and particularly in the districts with access to raw materials and with trade possibilities.

As these trends continued, capitalist techniques were refined and showed remarkable advancement, especially in the great urban centers. The merchants, through their organizations, were not only controlling prices and establishing coördinated policy; they were also selling shares, dealing in futures, and becoming highly adept at many practices of interest and exchange capitalism.[43]

Such an economic transformation naturally had a drastic impact upon the Tokugawa class structure. The bushi class as a whole was sustaining a very heavy assault on its economic and social position. Many of the daimyo had new masters in the merchants who controlled their prices, loaned them money at high rates of interest, and thus helped to sustain the antiquated feudal structure. With the decline of the agrarian economy, which was almost continuous after the Genroku era (1688–1704), the position of the bushi for the most part steadily worsened. As financial problems grew, numbers of samurai were released by feudal lords who could no longer afford to keep them; others left because of their own debts. Many of these became *ronin* (masterless samurai) and broke the placid surface with periodic waves of a violence symptomatic of the depth of unrest. At the same time a considerable exchange was taking place between the bushi and chonin classes. Han commercial activities were converting a number of daimyo and samurai into merchants. Some merchants were buying samurai rank, and marriage alliances between the merchant class

---

tionship to raw materials coming from the area. Thus textiles, lacquered ware, pottery, rice wine, and similar products became the produce of small handicraft and agricultural village industry. Carried on by the family system, this small-scale industry produced a growing rural commercial class; gradually, by means of merchants engaged in coastal shipping, or by the system of sankin kotai, surplus produce began to find its way to other parts of the country. This trend was accelerated when the han governments themselves began to undertake commercial activities in order to make up fiscal deficits. See Hirano Yoshitaro, *Nihon shihonshugi shakai no kiko* (*The Mechanism of Japanese Capitalist Society*), Tokyo, 1934, pp. 246–247; also Horie Yasuzo, *op. cit.*, p. 38.

[43] For this development, see Tsuchiya Takao, *Ishin keizai shi*, pp. 16–18.

and the samurai class made honor more honorable for the latter by giving it sustenance.

Equally important changes were occurring in terms of the land and the farmers.[44] A "capitalistic" accumulation of land was progressing during the latter Tokugawa period; city merchants and, most especially, district entrepreneurs were buying or developing land with their capital accumulations. Thus a landowner class was being created which received tenant income, and this shift, in turn, created marked divisions in the old *nomin* (agrarian) class and increased the plight of the bushi class as a whole by reducing its income and separating it further from land production.[45] Landowner exactions, together with the oppressively harsh treatment meted out by a desperate bushi class, ground down the peasant and produced an increasing number of riots and revolts.[46]

All these changes in class structure and relationship signified the fact that a commercial class was rising, in both the urban centers and the districts, which had monetary power and prestige out of all proportion to its social rank. The original aims of Ieyasu to maintain an agrarian economy and the supremacy of the bushi class were being irretrievably lost. The bakufu and han governments had long been aware of the serious nature of the problem. At first, to be sure, little attention was paid to the challenge of growing commercialism. The bakufu, despite its political ingeniousness, failed to grasp the significance of the commercial revolt, and indeed during the whole of the period, government economic policy continued its paradoxical features. In early Tokugawa times, a policy of noninterference was the general rule, and this enabled the merchants to establish their own organizations and expand rapidly in spite of the obstacle of limited markets. Gradually, however, as such problems as the rise of the ronin, the fiscal difficulties of bakufu and han, and the power of the chonin began to make themselves felt, much attention was paid to the economic

[44] For an excellent account of agrarian class changes, see Ono Takeo, *Ishin noson shakai shiron* (*An Historical Treatise on Agrarian Society at the Restoration*), Tokyo, 1932, pp. 281–317.

[45] Professor Tsuchiya, in discussing this development, states that at the end of the Tokugawa period the ratio of tenants to independent cultivators was probably near one to three. Tsuchiya, *Ishin keizai shi*, p. 14.

[46] For an excellent account, in English, of Tokugawa peasant revolts, see Hugh Borton, *Peasant Uprisings in Japan of the Tokugawa Period*, Vol. XVI of 2d series, *TASJ*, Tokyo, 1938. For a recent Japanese study, see Tamura Eitaro, *Kindai Nihon nomin undo shiron* (*An Historical Treatise on the Modern Japanese Agrarian Movement*), Tokyo, 1948.

questions. In the polemic tracts which followed, two broad divisions are to be seen. On the one hand, there were the advocates of a return to agrarian primitivism, the reidentification of the bushi class with the soil, and the crushing of the merchants. On the other hand, there were those who found reality denying the possibility of any such course and who were willing to take up the gauntlet for a commercialization of the bushi class and an expansion of commercial enterprise. This division was of great significance for modern Japan. The former group, as the chief exponents of *joi* (Oust the barbarians!) were essentially agrarian, and a part of their heritage has been a continuous factor in modern Japan, especially with respect to nationalism and extending into Japanese Fascism, as is noted in a later chapter. The latter group, who were a definite minority at that time, were intellectual forerunners of exponents of the concept of *kaikoku* (Open the country) and presaged the application of the industrial revolution in Japan.[47] Among the members of this group, however, the main emphasis was naturally upon a commercialism strongly controlled by state policy and designed to foster state interest. The dominant Confucian philosophy was almost wholly on the side of state control,

---

[47] For this vital debate in Tokugawa thought, see, among other sources, Honjo Eijiro, *Nihon keizai shiso shi gaisetsu* (*A General Summary of the History of Japanese Economic Thought*), Tokyo, 1946, pp. 8–147. As has already been indicated, the original premises of Tokugawa economic theory were largely contained in the concepts of emphasizing agriculture, adhering to a rice economy rather than a monetary economy, propounding frugality, and opposing change in any form. When the increasing commercialism began to shake the very foundations of these premises, Tokugawa savants were thrown into confusion. Such early Tokugawa writers as Ogyu Sorai proclaimed that the crime lay in the trend toward a monetary economy which could be corrected only as the bushi returned to the soil, identified themselves with the peasants, practiced frugality, and returned to the self-sufficient economy of old. It is extremely interesting to note the connection between this thesis and that of one wing of the Japanese "Fascist" movement many decades later. Other leading Tokugawa exponents of this thesis included Motoori Norinaga (1730–1801), whose role in the revival of Shintoism has already been mentioned; and this points to the original close relationship between these common factors of primitivism, and to their relationship with the ultranationalist movement of modern Japan.

At the same time, however, there was a gradual realization on the part of a few Tokugawa writers that the only means of continued supremacy for those of the bushi class lay in their active participation in the commercial revolution rather than in a futile resistance to it. One of the earliest writers to drive home this point was the famed Dazai Shundai (1680–1747), who was followed by many others.

26

and the practical necessities of revenue raising contributed also to this policy.[48] The practices of the various han in setting up semi-monopolies were the practical application of the state-control theory and set an ample precedent for the political-commercial relationships of the early Meiji era in Japan.

As internal economic changes were producing an upheaval which bakufu regulations were powerless to control, the tide of Western commercialism was lapping ever closer to the shores of Japan. The expanding commercial empires of Europe and America, having leveled many an isolated citadel in the Far East, appeared as an ominous spectacle to a country already sorely troubled by indigenous problems, a spectacle regarded as ever more ominous after the dawn of the nineteenth century. The Nagasaki trade with the Chinese and Dutch, periodic and scanty though it was, had served as a crack in the dike built against foreign infiltration, a crack through which trickled exciting news of Western science and industry, but disquieting reports of Western aggression.

As early as 1721 the bakufu authorities had rescinded the absolute prohibition on Western books, leaving only works on Christianity in the "forbidden" category, and a small group of native scholars arose, attempting to master the complexities of the Dutch language. Through prodigious effort on their part and help from Dutch traders, they managed to convey a small part of Western scientific and industrial knowledge to their incredulous countrymen. Indeed, the cultural benefits of contact with the Dutch were sufficiently great to constitute one of the chief reasons for continuance of the trade. Long before the arrival of Perry in 1853, moreover, as we have noted, there were a small group of bakufu councillors, a few daimyo, and assorted writers who were desirous

---

[48] The strongest theory of commercialism was the theory of a controlled economy. If one recalls that theory was largely in the hands of bushi scholars rather than of chonin, this is understandable. Confucianism, with its emphasis upon the "ethical state" and its repudiation of private gain, antisocial action, and individualism, naturally bolstered theories emphasizing regulatory rights. In general, however, as has already been mentioned, Confucianism was wholly inadequate to cope with commercialism, since it had mainly emphasized the agrarian state and hence was of more meaning and value to the feudalists.

The rise of the chonin in the Tokugawa period also produced a very subordinate theory of noninterference; this indicated that at least some seeds of laissez faire were carried with the growing commercial revolution. These, however, could not take root in a society which was dominated by another philosophy and in which the timing of the capitalist emergence was so long retarded.

of greater communications and trade with the Western world.[49] The great majority of the members of officialdom, however, were skeptical, because of their general antipathy to commercialism and in the light of past experience with foreigners; this skepticism increased with the threatening events of the early nineteenth century.

As early as 1795, the expanding Russian Empire had planted a colony on an island off Yezo (Hokkaido). In 1804 the governor of the Russian Fur Company attempted to present his credentials as an envoy, and this was followed two years later by a Russian attack on certain northern Japanese settlements in Saghalien and Iterup, creating widespread panic in the area. The menace of the Russians was complicated by a British intrusion in 1808; with Britain and Holland at war, the British ship *Phaeton* sailed into Nagasaki harbor and seized certain Dutchmen, and this caused the distraught governor of the area to commit suicide.[50] A climax was finally reached in 1824, when another British ship, reportedly foraging for provisions in a highhanded manner, robbed the Japanese inhabitants near Kagoshima. To combat these predatory activities the bakufu authorities issued a notable expulsion edict in 1825 which provided that foreign vessels should be driven away and landing parties arrested or killed. The Dutch residents, through their yearly reports to the bakufu, were providing the authorities with a far more current and accurate picture of world events than is generally realized, and undoubtedly the Chinese were adding to the store of information. Thus the news of the Opium War of 1840 had profound repercussions. The shogunate, panic-stricken by the dangers of foreign aggression and awe-struck by the fate

---

[49] The early debate over the advisability of foreign trade is interesting in respect to the general economic arguments used and the types of controversies after Perry's visit. Arai Hakuseki and Honda Toshiaki are noted representatives of early protagonists in this debate. Arai argued that, with the possible exception of medicine, there was no need for foreign products and that great harm would result from trade and its expansion. Honda contended that the concept of self-sufficiency was injurious and that an expansion of foreign trade was indispensable for the sake of building up the wealth of the country and meeting the demands of the people. See Honjo, *Nihon keizai shiso shi gaisetsu*, pp. 18–20; Horie, *op. cit.*, pp. 90–93; and Inobe, *op. cit.*, pp. 289–295.

[50] For detailed accounts, see Oka Yoshitake, *op. cit.*, pp. 18–21; also Inobe, *op. cit.*, pp. 260–262. For an account of this and other episodes, related from a British point of view, see M. Paske-Smith, *Western Barbarians in Japan and Formosa in Tokugawa Days*, Kobe, 1930, especially chaps. v and vi, pp. 123–140.

of a country whose culture they had always respected, showed the greatest concern. Antiforeignism gained in strength. Though the strict provisions of the 1825 edict were modified out of fear, flat rejections were given to a Dutch attempt to place an envoy of diplomatic status in Edo, and new restrictions were placed on Dutch books and the study of Dutch in Japan. As the spirit of nationalism rose, the demands for coastal defenses and a defiant attitude toward the insolent barbarians grew apace. However, with ships still limited to 500 *koku* in capacity, to prevent adventurous wayfaring (a *koku* equals 4.96 bushels), with internal economic conditions critical, and with much difference of opinion concerning the means of solving the Western threats, the bakufu drifted helplessly before overwhelming odds.

When Commodore Perry and his "black ships" arrived at the very doorstep of the Shogun with a thinly veiled ultimatum in 1853, the curtain parted on the final act of the Tokugawa dynasty. The complicated political events of the next fifteen years were marked by two important and interrelated trends.[51] The first was the progressive weakening of bakufu absolutism and the rise of powerful competing forces, ultimately led by the southwestern han of Choshu, Satsuma, Hizen, and Tosa. The second was the gradual intrusion of the long-quiescent court nobility and Throne into active politics. The bakufu, greatly bewildered by the dilemma of Perry's demands, consulted both a group of assembled daimyo and the Imperial Court at Kyoto, thus establishing important precedents.[52] Moreover, although the attempt was made to confine

---

[51] For an excellent recent study of this whole period, see Professor Oka's work, *Kindai Nihon no keisei*, already cited. Oka's documentation and interpretations have been of great aid to me.

[52] The bakufu hoped that the daimyo would agree to the foreign demands, lessening the pressure upon the administration, but a great number of the daimyo opposed such a move, even at the risk of war, and even among those agreeing, most did so only as a temporary expedient to give themselves a breathing spell for military preparation. Actually, the bakufu group itself used this latter argument, partially as a matter of political expediency, but also out of the conviction of many bakufu officials. Probably the chief cause of the difference between the bakufu and many of the han opponents to trade was the fact that the bakufu were responsible for policy execution and knew more about Western power. Some information concerning the outside world was available to the daimyo, but most of them were in the dark about actual world conditions, and taking an adamant stand was considered supporting the honor of their han, especially since they did not have to negotiate directly with the "barbarians."

The important thing is that a system of consulting the daimyo concerning

the issue to the matter of American ships, this move on the part of the bakufu oligarchs made inevitable a division into pro- and antiadministration forces on much broader issues, intensifying the factionalism which the government had for so long feared. An additional threat to bakufu security was contained in the serious dispute which had emerged within the bakufu itself by 1857 concerning a successor to the Shogun. One party was supporting Tokugawa Keifuku, from the Kishu han; the other faction was backing Tokugawa Keiki (Yoshinobu), from the Hitotsubashi branch of the Tokugawa family. In the political intrigue that followed, court support was enlisted on behalf of Keiki, and despite the final designation of Tokugawa Keifuku by the bakufu, a close relationship between the Imperial House and bakufu had been attempted on two issues of treaty permission and shogunate succession, thus giving ground to those attempting to restore the prerogatives of the Throne.

Meanwhile, debate was growing on the question of policy vis-à-vis the West. The opening of ports and the rapid expansion of foreign trade to which the bakufu had been forced to agree were wreaking havoc with an already shaky economic structure. The currency system became chaotic because of a heavy export of gold; price inflation was rampant; and groups dependent upon fixed incomes, such as the samurai, were in a miserable condition. It is no wonder that the slogan, *sonno joi* (Revere the Emperor— Oust the barbarians!) appealed to a large percentage of the bushi class.[53] In these two ideas most of them envisaged a new align-

---

important policies was gradually being established, and this indicated at once the weakness of the bakufu and the rise of a *reppan kaigi* (powerful han conference) concept, both of which had important implications for the future.

Likewise, the bakufu felt obliged to consult with the Imperial Court and get Imperial permission for the treaties. This process was a constant struggle, in which persuasion, pleading, and threats all were used; the fact of consultation, however, was the opening wedge of the Imperial Court and the Throne in politics, and soon their influence was a force of some importance. See *ibid.*, p. 25.

[53] Gold currency outflow was due to the fact that the internal gold-silver ratio made it advantageous for foreign traders to bring in foreign silver, convert it to Japanese silver coins, buy gold coins, and thereby make a profit of from 50 to 140 per cent. This practice ceased only when the bakufu revised the ratio, in line with that of the West. Before such action was taken, the excessive introduction of silver dollars and the heavy exportation of such items as raw silk, tea, and silk paper created currency unbalance and great price inflation. The inflation in rice prices was also very severe. For some statistics

ment of power in which the landed aristocracy would remain dominant, with the feudal system strengthened by a greatly centralized administrative structure and made secure by the perpetuation of isolation. It was the inability of the Tokugawa shogunate to maintain its original lines which produced most of the early opposition it had to face.

Increasingly, however, the impossibility of carrying out this program in its entirety was made clear. As we have noted, there had long been a minority who were prepared to grant the inevitability and benefits of the commercial trend. The bakufu group in a position of authority had finally had to accept foreign trade and the necessity of opening the country, and was placed somewhat unwillingly in the position of leading this movement. To strengthen its position it attempted to develop a court-bakufu coalition with the support of as many han as possible, on the principle of *sabaku-kaikoku* (Support the bakufu—Open the country), to counteract the principle of sonno-joi. Within and among the han there were serious divisions, products of genuine political differences on the central subject, political expediency, and the long-festering rivalries cultivated so assiduously by the bakufu itself. For a time it appeared as if the government might succeed, but gradually the forces opposed to the bakufu gained control in several of the important han, and a coalition of idealistic young samurai and *kuge* (court nobles) finally completed the overthrow of Tokugawa rule.[54]

---

on this and a general discussion of the impact of foreign trade on the Tokugawa economy, see Tsuchiya, *Ishin keizai shi*, pp. 39–52.

Foreign trade also disrupted the Tokugawa commercial structure. For the most part, those engaged in foreign trade were merchants of the port cities, who had hitherto been trading on a very small scale, and not the great merchant houses, which betrayed an excessive conservatism toward the new venture. These *nouveaux riches* did not conduct their transactions through the tonya and other organizations, and in this way they were steadily breaking down the influence of these protective associations.

Meanwhile, bakufu and han finances continued to deteriorate. Despite the added revenues from trade and the rice inflation, costs mounted, and the general inflation caused poverty to rise among the members of the bushi class, especially those trying to live on fixed rice incomes. Since necessaries were often being shipped out by the foreigners and only luxuries were coming in, it is easily understandable why the samurai and ronin classes were leaders in the "Oust the barbarian" movement.

[54] The two trends which characterized this entire period were especially marked by 1860. The locus of real power lay more and more in the hands of Satsuma, Choshu, and the court, and the Imperial prestige grew increas-

The final mode of transfer was shaped by three significant events. First, with the death of the Shogun, Iemochi, in September, 1866, Hitotsubashi (Tokugawa) Keiki finally received the wobbly title of Shogun. As has been noted, his house, that of Mito, had long included strong supporters of Imperial power, and he himself did not intend to defend his authority strenuously. At almost the same time (February, 1867), the old Emperor Komei died, and a young boy, Mitsuhito—the Emperor Meiji—came to the throne, not

---

ingly stronger. The bakufu class strove desperately after 1860 to mend its relations with the Throne by abandoning hostility and marrying the new shogun to an Imperial Princess, but the signs of its growing weakness were omnipresent. In 1862, the sankin kotai system was modified to require the tozama lords to spend only one hundred days in residence at Edo in the course of three years, and the hostage system was abandoned. This personal surveillance had been the cement which had held the bakufu together. Subsequently, the scramble among the western daimyo for quarters in Kyoto was spectacular, and all presented themselves at court, something long since prohibited.

Slowly, powerful forces were emerging to challenge bakufu absolutism. In 1862, Choshu han policy was in control of the probakufu faction, and han leaders sought to join the court and the bakufu in a policy of opening the country; in 1863, Satsuma made a similar attempt, urging that the matter be settled by "public opinion." Although neither of these attempts was successful, they reveal the breaking of the traditional policy against negotiations between the han and the court. In the latter year, moreover, the Imperial Household requested Satsuma to provide troops to accompany the Imperial Envoy carrying rescripts to Edo—a striking indication of the changing role of the Throne.

In the same year, a change of policy had occurred in Choshu in favor of exclusion of foreigners and overthrow of the bakufu; with Satsuma men gone, Choshu reigned supreme in Kyoto, and, as a result, a court rescript was sent to Edo demanding that the matter of exclusion be settled by means of a reppan kaigi (strong han conference). Now, the court, in combination with either Choshu or Satsuma, was seeking to play an active role, and all the han were becoming aware of the new locus of power. From this point until the summer of 1864, more than seventy han sent representatives to Kyoto; finally the Shogun himself, accompanied by about 3,000 troops, came to Kyoto in an attempt to offset the sonno-joi movement, thereby breaking a precedent of more than two hundred years' standing.

Soon thereafter, the rash of antiforeignism brought Western retaliation. Choshu hostility led to the bombardment of Shimonoseki straits by Westerners, and, similarly, Satsuma soldiers' killing of a British subject led to the British attack on Kagoshima. On both occasions, the Emperor appeared before the shrine to pray for a strengthening of arms to chastise the "barbarians," thereby symbolizing the role of Sei-i Tai Shogun (Barbarian-subduing Generalissimo) formerly held by the Tokugawa. Satsuma policy continued to be one of compromise and opening the country, and when Choshu at-

32

shackled by a tradition of Imperial timidity or by old-age reservations, and an excellent subject for the ambitions of the court and han factionalists. Finally, at a strategic moment, a letter was sent to the unhappy Shogun under the leading signature of an ex-daimyo of Tosa, asking him to resign for the sake of a strong and unified nation, allowing the young Emperor to be restored to his ancient powers. Keiki, in his letter of acceptance, wrote the finale to Tokugawa power:

Now that foreign intercourse becomes daily more extensive, unless the government is directed from one central authority, the foundation of the state will fall to pieces. If, however, the old order of things be changed, and the administrative authority be restored to the Imperial Court, and if national deliberations be conducted on an extensive scale, and the Imperial decisions be secured, and if the empire be supported by the efforts of the whole people, then the empire will be able to maintain its rank and dignity among the nations of the earth.[55]

tempted to "free" the Emperor by marching troops into Kyoto in the seventh month of 1864, the bakufu group was able to count upon Satsuma to help put down the revolt.

Late in 1864, however, the antibakufu faction of Satsuma, headed by Saigo Takamori and Okubo Toshimichi, came to power. Meanwhile, the antibakufu faction of Choshu recouped strength, and Choshu's attitude toward peace terms with the bakufu stiffened. When the bakufu attempted to strike down Choshu again, in 1866, an alliance had already been effected between the Satsuma and Choshu forces, thanks to the efforts of Saigo and Okubo (S) and Kido Koin (C), with the aid of certain ronin formerly from Tosa han. As a result, the coalition was too powerful for the bakufu, and it was humiliated in the struggle. The Choshu-Satsuma-court coalition against the bakufu now reigned supreme. For details of this whole period, see Oka, *op. cit.*, pp. 39–100.

[55] Translation taken from Walter W. McLaren (ed.), *Japanese Government Documents, 1867–1889*, Part I of Vol. XLII of *TASJ*, Tokyo, 1914, p. 2. (*Japanese Government Documents* is hereinafter cited in the notes as *JGD*.) The reference to national deliberations will be discussed in the next chapter. Professor Oka points out that the idea of the letter was actually to save the Shogun from imminent overthrow by the Sat-Cho-court forces. Yamanouchi, ex-daimyo of Tosa and from a family that had been highly rewarded by the Tokugawa, sought to preserve the Shogun's dignity and if possible some of his prerogatives. The letter was written by Goto Shojiro and was based upon the ideas of Sakamoto Ryuma. Yamanouchi's apprehensions concerning the future were completely justified. In the interval since its foundation, the Sat-Cho alliance had garnered strength from many sources, including dissidents from Tosa such as Itagaki Taisuke. Moreover, at the time Keiki accepted the Tosa letter, the court, under Iwakura Tomomi and Sanjo Saneyoshi, had already arranged for a secret edict to be delivered to the Sat-Cho for the overthrow of the bakufu. See Oka, *op. cit.*, pp. 103–109.

Once the resignation was forthcoming, the antibakufu forces insisted on exceedingly harsh terms from the Tokugawa, and a moderately short civil war ensued. Aided by the financial support of certain leading commercial merchants, the court-han alliance emerged victorious.[56] A new oligarchy was formed, the real control of which rested in the hands of a few court nobles (notably Iwakura Tomomi and Sanjo Saneyoshi) and young samurai from the han of Satsuma, Choshu, Hizen, and Tosa—the powerful southwest han. The new era of Meiji Japan was thus inaugurated, presaging a spectacular period of far-reaching adjustment, the culmination of the great economic and social cur-

---

[56] Although this work cannot go into detail on the role of the commercial merchants in the Restoration and its immediate aftermath, the broader aspects merit some comment. The merchants of Osaka and Kyoto were indispensable to the Imperialist cause in the beginning. Not only did they finance the Imperial campaigns against the bakufu forces, but in the very early period of reconstruction, they helped to underwrite the ambitious plans of a poverty-stricken government by donations and loans.

Despite this immediate importance, however, there were many reasons why the commercial class could neither assume any real leadership in the Restoration or, with few exceptions, become the pillars of the new industrial capitalism. We have already noted that the merchants, as a class, lacked the political self-confidence and experience, the social respectability, and, for the most part, the proper educational background to become the dominant leaders of the new period. Connected with this is the fact that the merchant class did not seek to strike down the feudal system by means of a concerted movement. Some of the economic reasons for this are given in Mr. E. H. Norman's excellent treatment of the subject, based upon materials from the works of Professors Honjo, Tsuchiya, and Takigawa. In the first place, the merchant was inextricably tied to the feudal land system. The daimyo were his best sources of revenue (there was little foreign trade) and also his debtors—factors that made their demise rather painful. Moreover, some of the merchant capitalists had invested their surplus capital in land and had thus assumed an additional role of landowner under the old order. It should also be remembered that in the closing half-century or so of the Tokugawa era many of the merchant class had bought or married their way into samurai status. See E. H. Norman, *Japan's Emergence as a Modern State*, New York, 1940, pp. 49–62.

All these factors militated against the possibility of an immediate "bourgeois revolution"; and in the aftermath of the Restoration it became clear that the Tokugawa merchants as a class lacked both the *desire* and the *resources* to transform Japan into a modern industrial capitalist state. For all the aid this class gave in the opening stages, commercial resources were puny in comparison with the task of modernization which lay ahead. This fact, which is discussed in some detail in a later chapter, is one key to understanding the political implications of modern Japanese capitalism.

34

rents abroad in the Tokugawa era which had finally broken loose under the impact of the West.

These were some of the salient features of the Tokugawa era and of the transitional period which led to the Restoration. It is now important to attempt some brief generalizations on the inter-relationship between Tokugawa and Meiji Japan and to capture, if possible, the true significance of the former period in terms of its great influence on modern Japan. The most obvious factor of interrelationship was the considerable degree of continuity in the ruling class. The Restoration was marked by a transition of power from the higher to the lower ranks of the bushi class, but this was a transition which in terms of han and even bakufu politics had long been under way, and in the new era, the bushi elite still held undisputed sway of political leadership. Given the timing of the Restoration, this was inevitable, in view of the structure and development of Tokugawa society, as has previously been noted. Thus the Meiji Restoration differed greatly from a bourgeois revolution on the Western model. The Tokugawa merchants as a class, despite their economic power, had not been able as yet to convert this power into a struggle for political representation or leadership. At the same time, however, it is extremely important to remember that a part of the bushi class was itself becoming commercialized, combining trade and primitive manufacturing with agrarian interests to escape the poverty of a declining agrarian economy. Indeed, the nature of the Tokugawa society, with its partially enforced internal isolation and its nearly complete na-tional isolation, favored the early rise of decentralized, relatively small district enterprises closely connected with the immediate landed interests, and the division between urban and district enterprise was one substantial characteristic of Japanese capital-ism. We have previously noted the heightening controversy among the Tokugawa bushi scholars, over the utility of com-mercialism. The lower samurai who became leaders of the Meiji era had for the most part been participants—consciously or uncon-sciously—in the commercialization trend. As han administrators or private venturers, they had seen the utility of commerce and some had participated in it. The significance of this lies in the fact that the leadership of the Meiji era was vested in the hands of a group who would transmit many of the traditional values of their class and their culture, which were basically agrarian-militarist, while at the same time blending with these the products of their own economic transformation and the necessities implicit in the transitional nature of their society and its new role in the world.

This is certainly not to deny that most of the bushi forces who participated in the overthrow of the Tokugawa did so with the intention of defending—not destroying—the feudal system as they knew it. As we have already remarked, it was the inability of the bakufu to keep in repair the salient defenses of the traditional economic, social, and political structure and the resultant plight of the bushi class which led to the opposition. In the heated theoretical controversies of the middle and late Tokugawa period, the dominant note sounded by samurai scholars was a return to the original ground of bushi supremacy; only a minority could understand that this outmoded approach was not feasible. Consequently, the bulk of the Tokugawa dissidents were the unwitting and unwilling sitters at the wake of the old order. They had participated in a movement whose true significance they could not understand and whose subsequent course met with their violent disapproval. Indeed, their awakening to the trends of the early Meiji era was one of the causes of the political cleavages which followed.

These facts can also be summarized through a recapitulation of the philosophic interrelationship of the two periods. The original designation of the Restoration as *fukko* (return to antiquity) was the succinct statement of the aims of a majority of the samurai class. Depicted in terms of the slogan *sonno-joi* (Revere the Emperor—Oust the barbarians), it reflected the earnest desire to return to the ancient system of Imperial rule, a feudal economic-social structure, and a maintenance of isolation. This slogan remained the dominant one during the chaotic period preceding the Restoration. However, as has been noted, its sponsors were unwittingly involved in the same striking paradox as the Tokugawa in even greater degree; they were seeking to use the weapon of centralization—in this case through the symbolism of the Emperor—to protect feudalism. The nature of Japanese nationalism has been deeply colored by the fact that its cultivation lay initially in the hands of the agrarian classes, who sought to rely on the primitivist society of their own ancient world as a possible source of protection from the inroads of modernization. The paraphernalia of Imperial divinity, Shintoism, and the whole mythology of the Japanese race were the result. We have already noted the role that isolation played in making this development as deep and lasting as it was. The Western impact, however, was sufficient to

separate sonno from joi in the minds of some of the more enlightened bushi elements, as a disintegrating economy and open foreign
assault dinned into them the impossibility of a return to the old
order. The good judgment of those Tokugawa pioneers who had
in some measure foreseen this fact was being demonstrated. The
release of sonno from joi and its fixation to *kaikoku* (Open the
country) symbolized the final nature of the Meiji Restoration and
forecast the whole character of the new era. Nationalism was partially united with capitalism, and an intense study of Westernism
in all its aspects was inaugurated. This transformation was first
realized in the minds of a part of the bushi class just before the
Restoration, and although the great majority of the bushi of this
era never fully accepted it, the important fact is that leadership
in the Meiji era fell largely to those who did. As a part of the bushi
class themselves, however, these new leaders found acceptable
the symbolisms of a nationalism which had been cultivated for other
purposes, and indeed, with minimal alterations they proceeded to
push forward much of the primitivism incipient in it at the same
time that they urged technological modernization. In this they
were abetted by the fact that there was little natural science or
Western humanism in their own background or that of their society
which would restrain them.

Thus when one reviews the differences between the Japanese
society of 1867 and that of such contemporary liberal communities
as England and the United States, the contrasts are startling. Politically, it was the difference between a society advancing an unqualified theory of divine right, limited by tradition but not by
law, and one seeking to practice popular government. The former
was buttressed by a philosophy of complete social integration, the
inequality of men, and a personal rather than legal concept of
political institutions. The liberal community had been produced
over a long evolutionary period through the atomization of society,
an emphasis on the individual over the state, a theoretical acceptance of equal rights, and the use of law to define and constrict
governmental prerogatives in a very different fashion from that
of the East. The great gulf between the two societies mirrored
the substantial differences in traditions and in the timing of development. In the background of Japan lay the traditions of a
semifeudal society, grounded in samurai ethics and lacking the
type of social or economic structure to support the liberal creed.
In the future lay the necessity of building a modern state as rapidly
as possible, to make up for the time gap between Japan and the

advanced Western world. The most natural instruments for this project were the rapid creation of an industrial capitalism and an emphasis upon nationalism.

It was into this era that the Japanese political parties were born. The stage had been set for their introduction, for although the political philosophy and leadership of the Meiji era bear true witness to the lasting power of the previous period, the Tokugawa regime also left to the Meiji period the scattered wreckage of its inner disintegration. There were certain currents of friction abroad which a philosophy of harmonious absolutism under the rising nationalist star could not overcome. These, too, were a heritage of the past. The age-old rivalries of the han and the classes, together with economic chaos amidst the collapse of the feudal economic structure, made political factions almost inevitable. The political factionalism of disillusioned samurai was latent only until it could find a means more successful than warfare by which to express itself; it was to find this means in the world of John Stuart Mill, Rousseau, Bentham, and a host of other Western writers. The end of isolation brought some curious remedies to antiforeign Japan. As Western industrial capitalism was to come to the aid of a nation threatened by internal collapse and foreign imperialism, so Western democratic theory was to come to the aid of those seeking a way in which to attack the trends and governors of the time. An explanation of the ways in which the democratic parties, led by ex-samurai, sought to reconcile the newly discovered creed with their own past and with the goals of Meiji society, belongs to the next section.

The twofold task of this chapter has been to attempt an understanding of the import of the Tokugawa era and an appreciation of how deeply the significant characteristics of it persisted in all phases of Meiji society. We have sought to study the Tokugawa background of Meiji politics in order to provide a basis for understanding the true nature of the emergence of political parties and the problems inherent in it. When Japanese parties sought to base their attack against the ruling oligarchy on liberal principles, they would be working in opposition to the background of their society as well as to the current trends which were its product. How far they could diverge from the main bent of their society and how far that society could move toward the democratic creed were the principal questions which lay ahead. In Meiji Japan the hope of democracy and the party movement lay in the capacity of Japanese society to reach the broad social premises upon which these were based and in the ability of the parties to make democratic issues and goals clear. For this reason the opening phases of political party development merit close attention, encompassing as they do the first stages of this struggle.

II

PARTY EMERGENCE AND THE PHILOSOPHIC STRUGGLE WITH THE GOVERNMENT

A SPLIT in the samurai oligarchy controlling the new government over issues of power and policy gave rise to the first political associations in Meiji Japan. Antagonized by han favoritism and by certain economic and political trends, a dissident minority resigned from their posts determined to rally the growing external opposition around them. By 1873, when the first of these defections took place, Western political techniques had already made a sufficient impression upon some of the antigovernment leaders to suggest the utility of peaceful opposition via political parties. A genuine enthusiasm for certain new concepts embedded in Western liberalism was combined with a shrewd appraisal of its value as a technique for obtaining personal power. Western political ideas enabled the opposition to revise earlier vague concepts of han assemblies by bringing forth the Western model of representative government, underwritten by a philosophy of popular rights. Under this banner, political associations led by men of Tosa and Hizen sought to enlist wider support for their cause and break the Satsuma-Choshu monopoly of power.

The resultant battle between the "liberal" party spokesmen and the government focused largely on what was the most effective means of strengthening and unifying the nation.[1] That nationalism

---

[1] The use of such terms as "liberal," "conservative," "radical," and "reactionary" is hazardous enough in the context of Western politics; it is even more dangerous to affix them without definition to Japanese movements and

40

was to be a central objective was implicit in the broad challenge which Meiji society faced. The manner in which the liberal philosophy was oriented around this objective by its spokesmen was of crucial importance, revealing as it did many of the significant weaknesses of early Japanese democracy and of the party movement. Despite their emphasis upon popular rights and self-government, a sizable portion of the "liberals" were impelled by their background and by contemporary events to emphasize liberalism primarily as a means of building a strong state. Never fully appreciating the vital importance of the individualism inherent in the liberal creed, they had a strong tendency to dwell upon the benefits which liberalism would confer on the state rather than those it would grant to the individual. The individual was still treated as a means rather than an end. Few adherents of liberalism in the Meiji period could so far escape the context of their times as to avoid this pattern of interpretation.

The opposition to liberalism and the creed of party government took many forms and was compounded of many forces. It was foremost in the indifference of an unprepared society, and it lay strong in the purely traditionalist elements who viewed any Western creed as an anathema. The immediate political opposition which the liberal parties faced, however, was in the hands of different men, for it was the Sat-Cho oligarchy [2] that stood athwart the path of party power. These men were not purely traditionalists, but men who were themselves espousing in greater or smaller degree the cause of Europeanization and championing its influence in the new Japan—men who were taking up the cudgels for modernization along the lines of the Western industrialized state. Indeed, in the opening years of the Meiji era, these men permitted a remarkable degree of freedom, reflective in part of their own intellectual and political insecurity. They themselves participated in an exhaustive study of Western politics and philosophy, and the divergence of opinions concerning the proper course for Japan within their own group was considerable. The passage of time and events, however, augmented their self-confidence and power, in

men. We shall therefore seek a description of the political forces before attaching any Western label to them; when, for the sake of convenience, it is desirable subsequently to refer to them as "liberal" or "conservative," such labels must be understood in the light of the previous descriptions.

[2] Sat-Cho is the abbreviation used by Japanese historians to designate the oligarchy of Satsuma and Choshu men who constituted the supreme governing power of Meiji Japan.

addition to making far more clear the basic philosophic concepts which would accord with their goals. With a bolder hand they moved to attack the ideas and actions of their political enemies. The era of relatively free debate and disputation gave way increasingly to the reimposition of stern controls on political opposition, many of which showed a strong likeness to bakufu techniques. The rising tide of a nationalism which had as its foremost symbol Imperial absolutism strengthened this trend, and the inconsistencies of the parties on this score could be used as clubs with which to batter them down.

The climax to these developments was the Meiji Constitution of 1889, a fundamental law superbly timed and written to fit the oligarchic cause. It is true that the Constitution granted some important concessions to Western liberal theory, but they stood as shaky superstructures on unsound foundations. It was a document written largely for the oligarchs, high-lighting their own political concepts. By it, they succeeded in riveting upon the nation a status quo which was more strongly oligarchic than representative and one which perpetuated and strengthened the myth of Imperial absolutism, thus making party control of government extremely difficult. In the Constitution of 1889, the liberal party spokesmen acquiesced with a remarkable complacency, to be explained in part by their inability and unwillingness to challenge the central philosophic barriers to the democratic creed. We must now turn to the details of these significant trends.

The Meiji oligarchy remained united only six years. By 1873, discontent both within the Sat-Cho-Do-Hi group and among other elements had reached a high pitch. It was a discontent produced by a variety of causes, but centering largely around the samurai and other agrarian groups. Within each han there was a conservative element, composed largely of the old daimyo and their close protégés, who resented the rapid abolition of the feudal system they had hoped to rebuild. The young leaders of Japan were taking bold and swift action.[3] The chaos of the transitional

---

[3] In 1871 the han system was abolished and a system of prefectures was established. Previously, in 1869, the daimyo had been appointed governors of their han to ease the transition. With the inauguration of the prefectural system, the daimyo were allotted an annual pension amounting to one-tenth of their former revenue, and the samurai also were given a small pension. This served to minimize opposition temporarily, but these pensions were paid off in a reduced lump sum beginning in 1873. The fact that this move coincided with growing samurai distaste for the government indicates the powerful economic motivations for antioligarchy movements.

period made unrest rife at all levels among the agrarian classes. In addition, there had long been a deep-seated suspicion among the men of Tosa, Hizen, and other han that the men of Satsuma and Choshu were aspiring in an even more absolutistic fashion to the laurels of the Tokugawa.[4] A powerful opposition containing the heart of the old aristocracy was arising, needing only a concrete issue and active leadership to give it voice. An issue was provided by 1873, over the question of whether to attack Korea. Japan had been seeking to reëstablish the old pattern of commercial and diplomatic relations, but with negative results. The friction reached a climax in 1872 and war seemed imminent. It was natural that there would be a strong prowar faction among the samurai. The impetus of the nationalist spirit and the teachings of such expansionists as Yoshida Shoin were well implanted in the warrior class. A war, moreover, would provide employment and honor to a group rapidly falling into serious straits.

The whole question of the Korean campaign divided the leaders and intellectual classes into two groups, known as the *Shimpo ha* (Progressive [prowar] Faction) and *Hoshu ha* (Conservative [antiwar] Faction).[5] For a time the prowar group was in the ascendancy, for in December, 1871, a mission headed by Iwakura, and including such important leaders as Kido Koin, Okubo Toshimichi, and the young Ito Hirobumi, had gone abroad to seek treaty revisions, and in their absence the expansionist party held

Moreover, with the institution of military conscription also occurring in 1871, the samurai found their social as well as their economic status undermined. For an account of these developments, in Japanese, see Oka Yoshitake, *Kindai Nihon no keisei (The Foundation of Modern Japan)*, Tokyo, 1947, p. 179; and for one in English, see E. H. Norman, *Japan's Emergence as a Modern State*, New York, 1940, pp. 194–195.

[4] In the light of both historical and contemporary trends, this fear had a substantial basis. The time-honored method of attaining power in feudal Japan had been to raise the standard of the Emperor for the purpose of succeeding the current ruling group. By 1873 the Sat-Cho clique was in a clearly dominant position, controlling not only the important positions in the civil administration, but the army and navy as well. See Osatake Takeshi, *Nihon kensei shi taiko (An Outline of Japanese Constitutional History)*, Tokyo, 1939, Vol. I, p. 75.

[5] For details of this episode, in Japanese, see, among other sources, Otsu Junichiro, *Dai Nihon kensei shi (A Constitutional History of Greater Japan)*, Tokyo, 1927–1928, Vol. I, pp. 330–331. This monumental work of eleven volumes, although weak in interpretation, is rich in political documents of the modern period and has frequently been used as a reference in the present study. See an article in English, by Nobutaka Ike, "Triumph of the Peace Party in Japan in 1875," *The Far Eastern Quarterly*, Vol. II, May, 1943.

the upper hand in state councils. However, the powerful statesmen returned to Japan in September, 1873, and, having failed
to accomplish their mission, they had clearly seen the futility of
attempting to bargain on equal terms with any colossus of the
West until the tremendous backwardness of their country was
remedied. Consequently, they set themselves against any immediate war which would dissipate the energies of a yet unrecon-
structed and unprepared Japan.[6]

After a seesaw struggle, the Iwakura faction emerged victorious.
Defeated within administration circles but believing that public
opinion was behind them, the prowar faction resigned from the
government. The composition of the "progressive" faction indicates
that the Korean issue was but a surface manifestation of much
deeper currents of dissent. The leaders included Saigo Takamori,
Itagaki Taisuke, Soejima Taneomi, Goto Shojiro, and Eto Shimpei,
all of whom, except Saigo, were formerly from the Tosa and Hizen
han. Saigo, the great military hero and commander of the Imperial
forces against the shogunate army in 1869, was not an implacable
feudalist, but his strong sympathies for the agrarian groups, and
particularly the bushi classes, led him to cast his lot with these
elements in his own han, that of Satsuma. He was subsequently
to lose his life in the last major revolt against the Meiji government
in 1877. Goto and Itagaki were the leading Tosa representatives
in the oligarchy and were soon to lead the first political association.
Soejima and Eto were Hizen men. The Sat-Cho-Do-Hi coalition
was broken and an open political opposition had emerged.[7] Though
the minority han continued to have some representation in the
government (notably Okuma Shigenobu, a Hizen leader) and
from time to time Tosa-Hizen strength would be somewhat aug-

---

[6] One of the arguments advanced by the antiwar faction was the danger
of becoming involved in a war with Russia. At the time, there was a controversy over Karafuto (Saghalien), and Iwakura argued that a Korean adven-
ture might have disastrous repercussions unless the Russian problem were
settled first. The Formosa issue with China was also pending. See Otsu, *op. cit.,*
Vol. I, pp. 635–636, for excerpts from Iwakura's speeches.

[7] Even before the break the Sat-Cho group had the real power of the
oligarchy. The three principal leaders had been Saigo and Okubo (Satsuma)
and Kido (Choshu). After the break, Okubo was to become the central
figure in the oligarchy, for Kido soon resigned in opposition to the Formosan
expedition, an expedition which was undertaken in part to alleviate the
samurai unrest engendered by the Korean controversy and other matters.
See *ibid.*, pp. 465–466.

mented, a new period of more or less complete domination by the powerful Sat-Cho clique had been inaugurated.

The decision to initiate a political association was not made without some difficulties. The opponents of the bakufu likely to be attracted to Saigo had, as a rule, no interest in Westernism and no desire to emulate it; their desire was a resort to arms in the true tradition of the warrior. However, Goto, Itagaki, and other members, who had been greatly influenced by the currents of Westernism, sought recourse in the adaptation of liberalism.[8] In October, 1873, this group tried to set the issues before a wider circle by organizing a club called the *Kofuku Anzenkai* (Happiness-Security Society) in Tokyo. Their position was to urge an elected national assembly and the formation of political parties. Finally, on January 12, 1874, the *Aikokukoto* (Public Party of Patriots) was established under the leadership of Itagaki.[9] In the preface to the party pledge, the political philosophy of the movement is outlined:

When men were created by heaven, there were attached to them certain fixed, inalienable rights [*tsugikenri*], and these rights, having been bestowed upon men equally by heaven, cannot be usurped by human power. But when the [political] movements of the time have not yet been opened [to the people], even if there is a public [*jimmin*] movement, the main essentials of these rights cannot be protected. No, since we have not yet completely erased from our country the excessive crimes of several hundred years of the feudal militarist system and the making of our people into slaves, even if we cannot correct these factors, those of us who are desirous of somehow raising our national prestige and enriching our people, stimulated greatly by our extremely sincere

---

[8] Goto, who had drawn up the petition to Tokugawa Keiki and had long been active in promoting the assembly idea, initiated the move, then secured the support of Itagaki and the others. According to Itagaki, Saigo approved the move, but he did not join the group. Osatake Takeshi, *Meiji seiji shi tembyo* (*Sketches in Meiji Political History*), Tokyo, 1938, p. 76. See also Oka, *op. cit.*, pp. 184 ff.

[9] In its beginning, this very small association of samurai did not consist of more than fifteen men; its leading members, other than Itagaki, Goto, Eto, and Soejima, were Furuzawa Uro, Kataoka Kenkichi, Hayashi Yuzo, Yuri Kosei, Okamoto Kensaburo, and Komuro Shinobu.

Furuzawa is believed to have written the first draft of the Aikokukoto platform. He and Komuro had recently returned from England, tremendously impressed with the British Parliament, and their enthusiastic reports had a substantial effect on the minds of men like Itagaki. See Hayashida Kametaro, *Nihon seito shi* (*History of Japanese Political Parties*), Tokyo, 1927, Vol. I, pp. 16–17; also Otsu, *op. cit.*, Vol. I, p. 786.

patriotism, desire to protect those heavenly bestowed gifts by mutually pledging ourselves with a common will and championing the universal principles of rights for our people. For this is the path of loving our sovereign and our country.[10]

Thus did a small group of samurai intellectuals introduce the ideas of human equality and popular rights, two basic tenets of Western liberalism, into the main stream of Meiji politics. It has been observed that nothing could indicate the novelty of this doctrine in Oriental political thought more than the fact that it required a compound word composed of four characters, *tsugi-kenri,* to express the concept of rights or privileges. The abbreviated form *kenri* had not yet appeared.[11]

Having established their embryonic party, the Aikokukoto leaders proceeded to issue a memorial to the government in which the basic arguments for a popularly elected assembly were presented. Taken together, the Aikokukoto pronouncements form the first expression of liberal polemics in a Japanese setting. The shock of thrusting theories of popular rights and human equality into the Japanese political system, however, was mitigated by an earnest effort on the part of the liberals to reconcile their doctrine with the concept of Imperial sovereignty and to make the liberal creed a useful handmaid to nationalist aspirations. In the memorial, these two important trends are already discernible. On the subject of the Emperor it is very interesting. This memorial, which was probably drawn up by Furuzawa, originally contained a passage urging the overthrow of *kunshu sensei* (monarchical absolutism) and the substitution of parliamentarism; in the ensuing discussions, however, it was argued that it was perfectly proper to consider Aikokukoto supporters loyal to the Emperor, and opposed only to his use of absolute power. Moreover, "If our Emperor has selected the cultivated path of Jimmu Tenno [the mythical first Emperor of Japan] for his own person, he is probably desperately anxious to submit to the popular will." [12]

Consequently, the original memorial was changed by the substitution of the phrase *yushi sensei* (official absolutism) for *kunshu sensei* (monarchical absolutism), and the center of attack was here,

---

[10] From the "Aikokukoto hensei" (Aikokukoto Pledge), reproduced in full in Aono Kondo, *Nihon seito hensen shi* (*A History of Changes in Japanese Parties*), Tokyo, 1935, pp. 7–8.

[11] Osatake, *Nihon kensei shi taiko,* Vol. II, p. 448.

[12] For this quotation, and the whole episode, see Otsu, *op. cit.,* Vol. I, pp. 786–787.

as the following passage makes clear: "When we humbly reflect upon the quarter in which the governing power lies, we find that it lies not with the Crown [the Imperial House] on the one hand, nor with the people on the other, but with the officials alone." [13]

Actually, this was a far more natural vantage point of attack for the liberal spokesmen. The Emperor Meiji was still little more than a boy, and the real power did lie in the hands of the oligarchy. Of equal importance was the fact that Japan lacked a history of recent Imperial absolutism suitable to attack in the fashion of Western polemics.[14] The historic position of the Japanese Emperor had often been one of prestige, but seldom of power. And from this position it was all the easier to weave around him the Confucian fable of a benevolent father. As nationalism centered its centripetal force on his person, this myth became overpowering and influenced even the liberals, as can be seen by the *Aikokukoto* statement cited above and other examples to be given later.

Having attacked the inadequacies and injustices of official despotism, the Aikokukoto writers proposed their cure:

"We have sought to devise a means of rescuing it [the nation] from this danger, and we find it to consist in developing public discussion in the empire. . . . The means of developing public discussion is the establishment of a council-chamber chosen by the people." [15]

And how was the liberal creed to benefit the nation? In the following passages, the memorialists presented a powerful case for popular rights, and in doing so, maintained that it was the only path toward unified action and national strength.

Between the arbitrary decisions of a few officials and the general opinion of the people, as ascertained by public discussion, where is the balance of wisdom or stupidity? We believe that the intelligence of the officials must have made progress as compared with what it was previous to the Restoration, for the intelligence and knowledge of human beings

---

[13] "Memorial on the Establishment of a Representative Assembly," January 17, 1874, document translation from *JGD*, pp. 427–428.

[14] Even Ueki Emori, whose brilliant defense of the liberal creed places him as probably the foremost intellectual of the liberal movement, and concerning whom we shall have more to say, picked his examples of Imperial absolutism from China, Rome, and England, but with regard to Japan, discussed the Tokugawa, which was only natural. See his "Minken jiyu ron" (Treatise on Popular Rights and Liberty), in *Meiji bunka zenshu* (*Collected Works of Meiji Culture*), edited by Yoshino Sakuzo, Tokyo, 1928–1930, Vol. V, pp. 183–195, especially p. 185.

[15] *JGD*, p. 428.

increase in proportion as they are exercised. . . . The duty of a government and the object which it ought to promote in the fulfillment of that duty is to enable the people to make progress. Consequently in uncivilized ages, when manners were barbarous and people fierce, turbulent, and unaccustomed to obey, it was of course the duty of the government to teach them to obey, but our country is now no longer uncivilized, and the tractableness of our people is already excessive. The objective which our government ought therefore to promote is by the establishment of a council-chamber chosen by the people to arouse in them a spirit of enterprise, and to enable them to comprehend the duty of participating in the burdens of the empire and sharing in the direction of its affairs, *and then the people of the whole country will be of one mind.*[16]

The last clause is important to an understanding of the early Meiji liberals, for it represented more than a mere pattern of speech; it was made an integral part of the liberal argument. To reinforce their stand, the memorialists continued:

How is the government to be made strong? It is by the people of the empire becoming of one mind. We will not prove this by quoting ancient historical facts. We will show it by the change in our government of October last [reference to Coalition split]. How great was the peril! What is the reason of our government standing isolated? How many of the people of the empire rejoiced or grieved over the change in the government of October last? Not only was there neither grief nor joy on account of it, but eight or nine out of every ten in the empire were utterly ignorant that it had taken place, and they were only surprised at the disbanding of the troops [for the Korean campaign]. The establishment of a council-chamber chosen by the people will create community of feeling between the government and the people, and they will mutually unite into one body. Then and only then will the country become strong.[17]

We have quoted at length from this historic document because it reveals so clearly the forces at work in the minds of the authors. They had grasped the Western liberal view of J. S. Mill and others, that an active and free people could produce a state in which progress and strength were unlimited. Fascinated by this prospect, the early Japanese liberals, for the most part, minimized or ignored the concomitant factors in liberalism from the individualistic point of view. Indeed, it is obvious that although they approved of popular rights as an instrument in building up the power and prestige of the state, they were by the same token contradicting liberalism

---

[16] *Ibid.,* pp. 429–430. (Italics mine.—R. A. S.)
[17] *Ibid.,* p. 430.

48

by making the individual the means rather than the end. The concept of the people becoming "of one mind" indicates the degree of subserviency to which liberalism was subjected by the prior claims of nationalism.[18]

One can search here in vain to find any reference to such indispensable prerequisites of liberalism as minority rights, toleration of the opposition, or indeed, the suggestion of an opposition as a natural part of governmental machinery. Their emphasis was rather on the unanimity with which the people, being fortified by knowledge and political experience, would act, and on the power and prestige which would accrue to the state when it skillfully utilized that unanimity. The house that the liberals were seeking to build was one in which neither liberalism nor the political party movement could live. If it was an unwitting contradiction and one implicit in the times, it was none the less disastrous.

The emerging political associations were using their popular rights theories to justify their demands for an elected assembly. Actually, the position of the Sat-Cho leaders could hardly be one of outright opposition to the idea of an assembly, for, as has already been suggested, the idea—if not the practice—of some sort of representation had played a part in the overthrow of Tokugawa rule and subsequently in the pronouncements of the Emperor himself. In order to make the philosophic battle lines clear, we must revert to the background of government policy and thought.

The first national meetings of han representatives had been called at the instigation of the shogunate itself, "for the sake of the nation," at the time of Perry's arrival. These assemblies were supposedly temporary in nature and were no more than various daimyo assembled and given lectures by authorities, who allowed them to ask questions. According to an account of one such meeting held at the time of the American-Japanese Treaty ratification in 1858, although the daimyo were permitted to present their points of view, they were sternly warned not to spread antigovernment propaganda outside the meeting—which, of course, they nevertheless proceeded to do.[19]

---

[18] Itagaki, the great leader of the early liberals, expressed his point of view on liberalism when he said, bind the people together, give them political power, and you will create a *fukoku kyohei* (wealthy country, powerful soldiery).

[19] This account is taken from *Bakumatsu seijika* (*Political Records of the Close of the Bakufu*), pp. 62–63, quoted in Osatake, *Nihon kensei shi taiko*, Vol. I, p. 10.

The idea of regular rather than merely temporary assemblies grew rapidly with the opposition to the bakufu.[20] It is important to note that these early ideas of assemblies did not depend primarily upon Western prototypes for their stimulus, for they were sanctioned philosophically by the Chinese scholars and their theories of the benevolent sovereign listening to his people. This, indeed, formed a philosophic basis for the proposal of *reppan kaigi* (powerful han conference) which the bakufu's opponents raised, and there had been a precedent of local han assemblies in all except two or three of the han governments.[21] With the growth of scholarship among the samurai, the idea of elitist discussion had gained in popularity. There was, however, a vast difference between the Chinese concept of "listening to the voice of the people," allowing them to question or suggest, and the emerging Western concept of assemblies for legislative decision. The Western ideas were perceived, even though dimly, during the last days of the shogunate, but they made little headway until later.[22]

In many quarters, however, the political exigencies of the late *Bakumatsu* (shogunate twilight period) heightened the movement for an assembly of some sort. The bakufu officials themselves were considering several plans in an effort to stabilize their declining power, and, as we have previously noted, both Satsuma and Choshu at various times brought forth such concepts as that of a "powerful han conference," or decisions based upon *kogi yoron*

[20] Professor Osatake says that the germination of the idea was contained in the famous three plans proposed by the Choshu han in 1862. These were mainly concerned with organized measures to be taken with regard to foreign affairs and national defense; though not adopted, they became a pattern for the more far-reaching proposals of the Tosa han in 1867. See *ibid.*

[21] Without exception these local assemblies were composed of the samurai classes only and were forums for discussion.

[22] As early as 1827 the shogunate had ordered a translation of a Dutch book published as *Yochi shiryaku* (*A Short Record of the World*), which included a discussion of the British Parliament. This was probably one of the earliest introductions to modern Western politics. Osatake, *Nihon kensei shi taiko,* Vol. I, pp. 15–16. For a list of some early books on Western politics, see *ibid.,* pp. 16–28. Some of these books included discussions of elections and representative government, and of course there were also Chinese writings on the West.

Naturally, only a very few samurai were acquainted with these works, but Sir Ernest Satow found that when he visited the Tosa han, Goto Shojiro had a surprising knowledge of English institutions. Actually, the southwest han, with their trade relations, were in a good position to acquire such information. For interesting contemporary observations, see Ernest Satow, *A Diplomat in Japan,* London, 1921.

(public opinion). But when the fall of the bakufu appeared imminent, it was the men of Tosa who took up the cudgels for an assembly most strongly. Among them there was already some anxiety concerning what persons should fill the vacuum of power, since few were naïve enough to believe that direct Imperial rule would become a reality in the hands of a fifteen-year-old boy. Consequently, on the eve of the Restoration, Tosa men had not only suggested an assembly in the letter written to Tokugawa Keiki, but also, somewhat earlier, they had included among eight proposals a concrete suggestion for a two-house assembly, the upper house to be organized by various han under the leadership of the Emperor and the lower to be composed of han samurai and "the people." This suggestion was obviously intended to make it difficult for any one han to control the new government; indeed, the fear that this might happen made the Tosa men instrumental in throwing off the older concept of a subservient han assembly and in basing the idea of an assembly on a public-military alliance under the Emperor.[23] The term "people" or "public," however, must be taken to mean the lower samurai classes and only the wealthiest *heimin* (commoners), as selected by the han daimyo; it most certainly did not refer to the peasantry, urban workers, or the greater part of the merchant class. Moreover, the Tosa men, envisaging the continuation of the old pattern, promulgated the idea that the unit of representation should be the han.

Whatever the Tosa proposals implied, there was no broad representation in the new centralized administration, which was set up in the first month of 1868. The new structure bore a remarkable resemblance to the prefeudal system of Japan, as developed after the great Taika reform of the year 645 A.D.[24] Moreover, the ap-

---

[23] This era constitutes the best evidence of the central motivation of early Japanese liberalism and illustrates the background of the Tosa liberals. For other details, see Osatake Takeshi, *Ishin zengo ni okeru rikken shiso* (*Constitutional Theories in the Period Around the Restoration*), Tokyo, 1929, especially pp. 8–9.

[24] The new structure was planned late in 1867, mostly by Saigo and Okubo, from the Satsuma antibakufu faction, and Iwakura, representing the court. Shortly before it was inaugurated, Tosa support was sought and obtained. Under the plan, three offices of central administration were created, chief of which was the *Sosai* (Office [or Officer] of Supreme Control), aided by the *Gijo* (Legislature) and the *Sanyo* (Council), which were to serve in an advisory capacity. Prince Arisugawa, high-ranking court official, was made Sosai, but the real court powers were Iwakura and Sanjo. Membership in the Gijo was limited to certain Princes of the Blood, court nobles, and daimyo from the han of Satsuma, Tosa, Echizen, Owari, and Geishu; and the Sanyo

pointments to office made it clear that only important court nobles and a few han, chiefly from the southwest, were to have any power. It soon became evident that changes would be necessary if the new government were to gain stronger support and stem the tide of growing resentment among those who had been ignored. The first significant step in this direction occurred in April, 1868, when the famous "Imperial Oath" was issued in the name of the young Emperor, proclaiming the goals of the new era. This oath, purporting to represent the sovereign himself, was tremendously important, and over its interpretation raged many a subsequent battle between the parties and the government. On April 6, 1868, before the shrine of his ancestors, the Emperor proclaimed:

1. An Assembly shall be widely convened and all issues shall be resolved by public opinion [*banki koron*].
2. Those above and below (the governing and the governed) shall be of one mind and the administration shall be conducted on the highest plane.
3. It is desirable that the officials, the military men, and the common people as well shall all attain their desires.
4. All absurd customs of former times shall be abandoned and actions shall instead be based upon the just and equitable principles of nature [*tenchi no kodo*].
5. Knowledge shall be sought for all over the world and thereby the Imperial Foundations shall be greatly advanced.[25]

The articles of the Oath were reflective of many things, including the impact of Western ideas, the emphasis upon national unity and centralization, the transition away from the rigidly hierarchical class lines, and the abandonment of joi. It must be emphasized, however, that this pronouncement was essentially directed at the alliances of han lords and samurai and the wealthy merchants, whose support and assistance were crucial, not at the masses.[26]

was composed of three samurai from each of these han. In both the Gijo and the Sanyo, places were also reserved for Choshu. See Oka, *op. cit.*, p. 114. In a very short time, seven, then eight departments were established, among which the administrative duties were divided.

[25] This document is included in almost every Japanese work dealing with Meiji history or politics. The above translation is mine. For another English translation, see *JGD*, p. 8.

[26] An analysis of the motivations behind the Imperial Oath is a revelation of current political and economic forces. It was indispensable that the various han fearful of Satsuma-Choshu domination hear the purposes and ideas of the new era voiced by the person who symbolized it, the Emperor. The continuous insistence for more representation could not be ignored.

Thus the reference to *banki koron* (all issues by public opinion), which was to provide the great rallying cry of the political parties, was qualified in the minds of its authors both in interpretation and in extent. A confusion between the classical Oriental concept of taking account of popular desires and the Western concept of an assembly with supreme legislative powers was still strong. Moreover, any assembly idea at this point was certain to pay homage to social class distinctions and the han system.

Nevertheless, the governmental reform of June, 1868, which followed, marked a high tide of movement toward Western models from which the government was subsequently to recede. The new structure mirrored the groping of the young and as yet uncertain Meiji leaders in a bewildering but enticing world. Western ideas had already begun to flood into Japan from a variety of sources.[27] The desire to hold off Western power by emulating it and to broaden support for the rather shaky government were widely held objectives among the oligarchs. The result, in terms of the new organic law, or *Seitaisho*, was an interesting mixture—one might say confusion—of traditional and Western principles. The central government, or *Dajokan* (Chief Administrative Office), showed the influence of the American division-of-powers concept, but the divergence was great.[28] Moreover, although the concept

Moreover, both the Imperial Household and the loyal han were poor in resources, and the military commanders in the field were clamoring for money to use in defeating the bakufu forces; the civil war did not end until the summer of 1869. If the government were to obtain coöperation and funds from the wealthy landowners and merchants, it had to adopt a policy which would coincide with some of their wishes and instill in them confidence in the new order. It was with these groups, and primarily the former, and not the peasantry and urban masses, that the government was concerned. See Osatake, *Nihon kensei shi taiko*, Vol. I, pp. 111–113; also Suzuki Yasuzo, *Jiyuminken (Civil Rights)*, Tokyo, 1948, pp. 4–5.

[27] American sources were particularly prominent at this time. Elijah C. Bridgman, an American missionary, had written a history of the United States which had been translated from Chinese into Japanese; a copy of the United States Constitution was made available by Guido Verbeck, a Dutch-American missionary who was using it as a text in teaching English at Nagasaki; and use was made of Fukuzawa Yukichi's *Seiyo jijo (Conditions of the Western World)*, a work based on his earlier visit to America.

[28] For details, see Oka, *op. cit.*, pp. 152 ff., and Ishii Ryosuke, *Nihon hosei shiyo (An Historical Summary of Japanese Law)*, Tokyo, 1949, pp. 246–247. Under the Dajokan there were seven offices or departments, including those for the administrative, judicial, and legislative subdivisions; however, only the legislative office was in any degree separate from the others in its membership and powers.

of voting was introduced through the establishment of an elective lower house of the two-house *Gijokan* (Legislative Office), the powers of this house were strictly subordinate, and the legislative branch as a whole was dominated by the administrative oligarchy.[29] Later in the same year, slight modifications were made in the legislative branch and its name was changed to the *Kogisho* (Public Deliberation Chamber).

From this point onward, however, controlling elements in the oligarchy began to retrench, turning away from legislative assembly concepts. Professor Oka has suggested that some of the reasons for this were the gradual strengthening of oligarchic authority, the relatively poor representation in the Kogisho due to preference given han leading families and daimyo under the appointive system, and the increasing desire for unhampered power on the part of the dominant Sat-Cho group.[30] In truth, there had been no intention to establish an elected assembly coequal in power with the administration. In the important reform of 1869, the trend away from "all state affairs by public opinion," in the sense of a representative assembly, was clear.[31] The Kogisho was replaced by the *Shugi-in* (Assembly Chamber). Even though membership was the same, the Shugi-in retained no legislative powers whatsoever, being only a questioning organ supposed to reflect public opinion.[32] After the abolition of the han in 1871, another

---

[29] The upper house of the Gijokan was composed of the old Gijo and Sanyo; the lower house was composed of taxpaying gentry elected from the han, *fu* (metropolitan districts), and *ken* (prefectures). (At this time the fu and ken consisted only of former Tokugawa areas.) Discussion in the lower house was limited to matters referred to it by the upper house, and in no case were decisions of the two houses any more than recommendations to the administration.

[30] Oka, *op. cit.*, pp. 172–173.

[31] As is pointed out by Professor Oka, this reform clearly demonstrated the establishment of bureaucratic supremacy based on the premise of Imperial prerogative. Separation of powers was completely abandoned in favor of a highly centralized, bureaucratically controlled structure. The Dajokan was to have general control of all affairs, assisting the Emperor; below this were the Ministers of the "Right" and the "Left," and under these were the Councillors; the departments were under the direct supervision of the Dajokan. In this connection, the desired supremacy of Shintoism and the union of Shinto with the state was sought through placing the *Jingikan* (Office of Deities) in the highest position among the governmental departments. See *ibid.*, pp. 174–175.

[32] Earlier in 1869, the government had established a bureau to which people could bring their ideas and suggestions, with the promise that these would reach the proper authorities; this system, which had a long Oriental

important structural change was made in the national government, and the Shugi-in, which had been based upon han representatives, gave way to the *Sa-in* (Chamber of the Left), whose powers were not only limited to questioning, but whose members were appointed and dismissed by the Central Chamber, or *Sei-in*, the administrative organ of the oligarchy.[33]

Thus the Aikokukoto could boldly assert in the first of its planks that it only desired the sincere application of the Imperial Oath, and the government was placed in an awkward position. With the split in 1873, power had been clearly narrowed down to the Sat-Cho group, and there was nothing remotely resembling a representative body in the governmental structure. The oligarchy's reply to the Aikokukoto proposals has been aptly summed up by some Japanese historians in the phrase *Gikai shoso* (too soon for a representative assembly). Though the Sa-in "adopted" the Aikokukoto memorial and promised to recommend that it be considered, the only immediate result was the establishment of the *Chihokan Kaigi* (Assembly of Prefectural Governors), neither elected nor representative, and in the traditional convention. Almost immediately, spokesmen for the oligarchy attacked the program and memorial of the Aikokukoto as an unrealistic proposal, "in our present stage of progress toward civilization." Kato Hiroyuki, early contributor to liberal thought who had already begun to recant, succinctly expressed the official position in a published letter of January 26, 1874:

"It is no doubt true that our nation is gradually moving towards enlightenment, but the peasant and merchant classes are still what they have always been. They rest satisfied in their stupidity and ignorance, and it has not yet been found possible to rouse in them the spirit of activity. The soldier class alone is far in advance of

---

tradition, was the government's way of honoring *kogi yoron* (public opinion). *Ibid.*, p. 153.

[33] Under the reform of 1871, the central government was composed of three main branches—the Sei-in, *U-in* (Chamber of the Right), and Sa-in. The Sei-in, or Central Board, was to be the over-all Imperial "assistant"; headed by Sanjo, it included as Councillors Saigo, Kido, Okuma, and Itagaki. The U-in was in charge of administrative matters, and under it came the various departments; and the Sa-in was designated as the legislative branch. With two exceptions the department chiefs were all from the Sat-Cho-Do-Hi group, as were all the important posts except those held by Sanjo and Iwakura. With the strengthening of controls, the han daimyo and outsiders had been cast off, and the nucleus of power greatly narrowed. See *ibid.*, p. 176; also Ishii, *op. cit.*, p. 247.

them, but still how few there are in it who understand the principles of things." [34]

Kato continued his argument with a heavy reliance upon the Prussian system, of which he was a serious student and an ardent admirer:

"The self-reliant and active character of the Prussian nation at the present day which has at last raised it to the position of the most powerful nation in Europe, has not been due to the establishment of a deliberative assembly, but to the fact that since the time of Frederick II, the Prussian Government has devoted itself to the cultivation of the people's minds." [35]

The duel of Western philosophies in a Japanese setting had already begun. In attempting to answer these salient objections, the assembly spokesmen further revealed their proposals. Quoting and paraphrasing J. S. Mill's *On Liberty* extensively,[36] Soejima, Goto, and Itagaki replied to Kato on February 20. (Eto, in the interim, had already been executed for his part in the Saga Rebellion against the government.) With regard to public participation, they said:

"Now if this council-chamber be established, we do not propose that the franchise should at once be made universal. We would only give it in the first instance to the samurai and the richer farmers and merchants, for it is they who produced the leaders of the revolution of 1868." [37]

The term "people" was to be limited for the time being to these groups, and was not intended even by the liberals to include the obviously unequipped lower classes.

Despite its use of the term *koto* (public party), the Aikokukoto was nothing more than an association of a few samurai, without

[34] "Objections to the Establishment of a Deliberative Assembly Chosen by the People," letter of Kato Hiroyuki, translated in *JGD*, p. 136.

[35] Translation from *JGD*, p. 438. Kato was an extremely important figure in the introduction of Western ideas to Japan, as is noted later in this study. Some of his early writings included substantial defenses of the liberal creed, but these he afterward disavowed with vigor. At this time he was serving as Imperial Lecturer on Politics and Law; subsequently, he became President of Tokyo Imperial University. An interesting study of Kato's political philosophy has been made by Tabata Shinobu in his *Kato Hiroyuki no kokka shiso* (*Kato Hiroyuki's Theory of the State*), Tokyo, 1939.

[36] Mill's *On Liberty* had appeared in Japanese translation in 1871; it was quoted in this letter no less than six times; eventually, however, the Tosa school of liberals were to use Rousseau to a much greater extent.

[37] Letter of Soejima, Goto, and Itagaki, translation from *JGD* (pp. 440–448), p. 445.

popular support or organizational structure. The boldness of their new philosophy was offset by many weaknesses of both theory and practice. Among the latter was the fact that Meiji society was by no means equipped to accept a philosophy of peaceful change. Violence lay very close to the surface of all political action. The bushi traditions, the desperate nature of the times, the intransigency of leading oligarchs, and the impossibility of translating liberalism into immediate practice all had an interactive effect. Those ancient twins of terrorism and suppression were the inevitable result. The liberal movement was a magnet drawing toward it the dissident elements of Meiji society, including extremists of many types. In the confusion of a transitional era, issues and personalities cut across logical philosophic lines and this unsteady force of discontent underwrote some of its demands with blood. To protect their power and their lives, the government leaders refurbished the traditional weapons of suppression, and the spiral of matching force against force had begun. Although its zenith in the early Meiji period was not reached until later, as we shall note, it was already under way. Early in 1874 an attack was made upon Prince Iwakura by nine samurai of the prowar faction, led by a Tosa man. Increasing hostility on the part of the government was the immediate result. The dissident samurai soon saw that little could be accomplished on a national scale under the watchful eye of the Tokyo officials, and they began to return to the provinces, where a number of associations similar in feeling and aim to the Aikokukoto were being organized.[38]

Itagaki returned to Kochi, capital of what had formerly been Tosa han, and, in conjunction with a local society, organized a political and education association known as the *Risshisha* (The Society to Establish One's Ambitions), in April, 1874. For several years the liberal movement was transmitted by this Tosa association, and the first genuine national party, the *Jiyuto* (Liberal Party), stemmed mainly from its exertions.[39] In political philos-

---

[38] The advantage of the districts, from the standpoint of party development, was not only in their distance from the seat of oligarchic authority, but also in the fact that they were natural harboring grounds for those who had failed to make good in the central administration. Returning to their native areas, these samurai formed a pool of malcontents available for almost any antigovernment movement. See Osatake, *Meiji seiji shi tembyo*, p. 82.

[39] We have already noted, in the main, the reasons for Tosa leadership of the liberal movement. Professor Suzuki lists them in three categories: (1) Among the discontented groups, Tosa was preëminent in power and men of ability. (2) By this period Tosa men had been definitely frozen out

57

ophy, the Tosa samurai followed a pattern similar to that of the Aikokukoto. In the prospectus of their organization, they railed against Sat-Cho monopolization, announced as their goal the establishment of a *minkai* (people's assembly), and promised to work for this so as to advance the prosperity of the Empire.[40] Reflective of the deteriorating economic position of the samurai and the desire to broaden the popular base of the movement, they denounced special privileges, social or economic, and proclaimed that all people were equal. The first step for those who desired to protect the rights of the people was *jishu* (self-government); only in this way could Japan become strong.

If the spirit of independence in a people is damaged, the spirit of the nation thereby declines, and that is the reason why the people of Europe and America alone predominate over the world and cannot be compared in trade with the peoples of China and India; for this reason, if we sincerely wish to raise our Empire, we should endeavor to raise ourselves by beginning to govern ourselves.[41]

The identification of liberalism with national defense and dreams of commercial and political expansion struck an even more strident note in the Risshisha literature than in that of the earlier Aikokukoto. And in analyzing the crimes of the Tokugawa, the Risshisha writers commented that the overthrow of the Tokugawa rulers was caused by their despising the Emperor above and oppressing the people below, and by their conducting affairs through two or three all-powerful ministers; [42] in drawing the parallelism with the Sat-Cho forces, the Risshisha was powerfully abetting the "Emperor-people united" theme.

Schools and associations similar to the Risshisha began to spring up throughout the country, and in February, 1875, a general meeting of popular assembly factions was held in Osaka. The outcome of the gathering of some forty samurai representatives was the

by the Sat-Cho group. (3) Western ideas had been introduced more in Tosa than in any other area. See Suzuki Yasuzo, *op. cit.*, p. 90.

[40] "Risshisha soritsu shuisho" (Prospectus on the Establishment of the Risshisha), document reproduced in Aono, *op. cit.* (pp. 9–12), p. 9. For other vital documents relating to the Risshisha, see Itagaki Taisuke, *Jiyuto shi* (*History of the Jiyuto*), Tokyo, 1913, Vol. I, and Suzuki Yasuzo, *op. cit.*, pp. 91–97.

[41] "Risshisha soritsu shuisho," in Aono, *op. cit.*, p. 10.

[42] "Risshisha kempaku" (Risshisha Memorial), in Suzuki Yasuzo, *op. cit.*, pp. 91 ff.

establishment of the *Aikokusha* (Society of Patriots).[43] Its avowed ambitions were expressed in the preamble to its resolutions:

Now opening this conference, we desire to exert the obligations of our duties as human beings to the utmost and spread various privileges by studying and deliberating together; and by protecting each person and each household in small, thus maintaining the national state in large, in the end, we desire to increase the prosperity and happiness of His Majesty by causing our Empire to be raised to the lofty peaks with the countries of Europe and America.[44]

By the time of the Aikokusha the government was exceedingly anxious to come to some agreement with opposition forces. The power base of the oligarchy had been seriously weakened and was mainly controlled by Okubo, a very strong conservative leader from Satsuma. Kido, the chief Choshu spokesman, had been lost, and the decline of Choshu power was disconcerting to such young Choshu participants as Ito Hirobumi and Inoue Kaoru. In many circles of the government, moreover, it had been felt wise for some time to compromise with the liberal forces, lest the dangerous ideas of liberty lead to open civil war and possibly republicanism. Thus, in February, 1875, after preparations by Ito and Inoue, Okubo met with Kido and Itagaki in the famous Osaka Conference.[45] As inducements to return to the fold, the government leaders agreed to push forward the constitutional idea by replacing the Sa-in with a *Genro-in* (Elder Statesmen's Council, or Senate) [46] and by establishing a *Daishin-in* (Supreme Court) to act as a judiciary. On the basis of these concessions, which were finally promulgated in April by Imperial proclamation, Kido and Itagaki returned to the government.

Three paragraphs of the Imperial order, however, are of particular interest:

It is Our desire not to restrict Ourselves to the maintenance of the five principles which we swore to preserve, but to go still further and enlarge the circle of domestic reforms.

With this in view We now establish the *Genro-in* to enact laws for the

---

[43] For a detailed account of this convention, see Osatake, *Nihon kensei shi taiko*, Vol. II, pp. 456–458.

[44] "Aikokusha kaigisho" (Aikokusha Convention Report), document reproduced in Aono, *op. cit.* (pp. 13–14), p. 13.

[45] See Oka, *op. cit.*, pp. 196–199.

[46] The membership of the Genro-in, however, was still chosen in the same way as had been that of the Sa-in.

Empire and the *Daishin-in* to consolidate the judicial authority of the Courts. By also assembling representatives from the various provinces of the Empire, the public mind will be best known and the public interest best consulted, and in this manner the wisest system of administration will be determined.[47]

We hope by these means to secure the happiness of Our subjects and Our own. And while they must necessarily abandon many of their former customs, yet must they not on the other hand, yield too impulsively to a rash desire for reform.[48]

Besides the clever interpretation of the "Five Oaths" incorporated in this proclamation, certain spokesmen for the oligarchy had also contrived to turn retreat into victory by adding a word from the Emperor, damning those who were demanding "rash reforms" in his name. Imperial absolutism was a potent weapon against political agitators. If the parties had to pattern their philosophy within its general confines, they would always be bound by the words of the Throne.

As the conservatives in the oligarchy moved to bring the pressure of the Throne to their side, they also sought to curtail the effectiveness of the opposition in other ways. The extraordinary degree of freedom characterizing press and speech was now seriously reduced. On June 28, 1875, a new Press Law was promulgated which rigorously limited permissible political attacks and held over the head of each editor heavy fines, imprisonments, and suspensions.[49]

The strenuous efforts of the government to obtain solidarity were doomed to failure. In October, 1875, Itagaki withdrew from the government for an interesting combination of reasons. He

---

[47] An assembly of prefectural governors had also been agreed upon in the Osaka Conference; that this was to be interpreted as a system of consulting the public mind is reflective of oligarchic sentiments.

[48] "Imperial Proclamation Announcing the Creation of the *Genro-in* and the *Daishin-in*," April 14, 1875, translated in *JGD* (pp. 41–42), p. 42.

[49] An earlier law had been promulgated in October, 1873, at the time of the split in the coalition, but the 1875 law was far more rigorous. Under its provisions, more than two hundred writers were punished in the succeeding five years; in July, 1876, new provisions were added to it. The government, which at first had encouraged the press as an agency through which to expound their views to the people, found that with the advent of the party movement it acted as the most vocal source of opposition; consequently the government moved to curtail it. For provisions of the laws of 1873 and 1875, and a discussion of their effects, see Suzuki Yasuzo, *op. cit.*, pp. 64–69; for a similar discussion in English, see Kawabe Kisaburo, *The Press and Politics in Japan*, Chicago, 1921, especially pp. 65–66.

was dissatisfied with Japanese pusillanimity toward Korea, and he felt that internal reforms in the direction of liberalism were far too weak. While the popular assembly factions were seeking to regroup their forces, Saigo and his followers among the Satsuma han revolted in 1877.[50]

Despite a severe test of strength and great apprehension lest other samurai elements join the movement, the government defeated the feudal die-hards completely, and the tragic Saigo died in the struggle. In a very real sense the Satsuma defeat marked the beginning of a new epoch in Japanese political history, for it solved the dilemma of those who sought to oppose the oligarchy. Henceforth, it was clear that one could not use the name of the Emperor in a resort to arms against the government. Centralization of power by means of taxation and conscription rendered rebellion well-nigh impossible; violence shifted, for the most part, from a mass to an individual basis. Itagaki and the other adherents to opposition by means of political parties who had astutely seen this were more than vindicated in their judgment.

The Satsuma Rebellion, however, cost the embryonic political associations heavily. The government imprisoned hundreds of "dangerous opponents," including some from party ranks,[51] severely curtailed the press and speech, stopped work on reform measures, and came out of the rebellion more strongly entrenched than ever. Despite these new handicaps, the assembly faction had certain advantages. Their plea for representative institutions remained basically unmet, and although the beginnings of this political agitation had been in the hands of samurai, the economic and political unrest of the old heimin classes, especially among the agrarian groups, was growing. In every district, political societies were organized to express the prevailing discontent. The Risshisha, both as a source of political leadership and as a prior organization, began "electioneering" throughout the whole country. In April, 1878, members went into various districts carry-

[50] This revolt climaxed a series of agrarian uprisings between 1869 and 1877, led largely by displaced samurai. The significance of these in terms of later political party movements was very great, as we shall later note; in their economic aims and antigovernment policy, they were laying the groundwork for a large-scale agrarian political movement. See Osatake, *Meiji seiji shi tembyo*, pp. 91–92, and see especially Ono Takeo, *Ishin noson shakai shiron* (*An Historical Treatise on Agrarian Society at the Restoration*), Tokyo, 1932.

[51] This action by the government was not without justification; within the Risshisha there were many who favored joining the Saigo forces.

ing a petition for the reëstablishment of the Aikokusha.[52] Because of obstacles engendered by a suspicion of Tosa motives and fear of government retaliation, progress was slow at first. Okubo, the pillar of the government, was assassinated by an assembly zealot in May, 1878, and many prospective supporters of the assembly movement feared that joining would implicate them and make them targets of a repressive government campaign of reprisals.[53] Nevertheless, by the time of its fourth general meeting, the Aikokusha had become a formidable opponent. Meeting in Osaka in March, 1880, the fourth general convention numbered 114 delegates, who claimed to represent some 87,000 people in organizations scattered among two *fu* (metropolitan districts) and twenty-two *ken* (prefectures).[54]

It is clear that in spite of this national growth the "civil rights movement" was still predominantly in the hands of the southwest ex-samurai, more especially the men of the Risshisha; not only did they hold the majority of high offices, but their views were the determinants in policy.[55] Under their direction it was decided to change the name of the association to *Kokkai Kisei Domeikai* (Association for the Petitioning for a National Assembly), and two men, Kataoka Kenkichi, president of the Risshisha, and Kono Hironaka, were sent to Tokyo with a petition for an elected assembly. In this interesting document, the prevailing philosophy of the proponents of *jiyuminken* (civil rights), is excellently revealed.[56] In outlining their reasons for desiring an assembly, the petitioners make it clear that they do not desire "to disparage the great labors of Your Majesty"; some compensation, however, must be made for the unrest which has vexed the government and caused it much effort, and this can be done by broadening the scope of

---

[52] For an account of this and other episodes of the period, written in English, see A. H. Lay, "A Brief Sketch of the History of Political Parties in Japan," *TASJ*, Vol. XXX, Tokyo, 1902 (pp. 363–662), pp. 379–380.

[53] Okubo's murder marked a definite tightening in governmental policies toward political activities, as was only natural. For reaction on the Risshisha, see the quotations from *Risshisha shimatsu kiyo* (*Factual Record of the Risshisha*) in Suzuki Yasuzo, *Jiyuminken kempo happu* (*Civil Rights and the Promulgation of the Constitution*), in Kindai Nihon rekishi koza (Modern Japanese History Series), Tokyo, 1939, pp. 29–30.

[54] Hayashida, *op. cit.*, Vol. I, p. 102.

[55] Suzuki Yasuzo, *Jiyuminken kempo happu*, p. 34.

[56] "Kokkai wo kaisetsu suru inka wo negaiage suru sho" (Petition Requesting the Establishment of a National Assembly), document reproduced in Aono, *op. cit.*, pp. 26–34.

responsibility. Even the tranquillity and strength of the Imperial Household is being jeopardized by the arbitrariness of the officials. The only way to rectify the deplorable conditions is to establish a *teiritsu no seiji* (government of law).[57] This means the establishment of representative institutions.

Again, the petitioners advert to the "Five Oaths"; these are taken up in detail, with the attempt to show that only through a national assembly can the Emperor's desires be achieved. By such a move "the patriotic hearts of the people will be developed, and the whole nation will be made one." [58] To leave the despotism of the present government unchanged is to invite a hundred years of grief, and it will result in the scorn of all nations and the misery of all the citizenry.

By following through the most important changes in recent years, the petitioners seek to show the increased responsibilities of the people through conscription, revision of land taxes, abolition of the han system, and leveling of the social classes. With increased duties, should not rights proceed also? When people pay taxes and bear such obligations, can government still be a private affair? [59]

This petition represented the most forthright statement of the civil rights movement up to that time. The authors had even been bold enough to suggest that the Imperial Household would be "jeopardized" if oligarchic tyranny were not checked. Such orthodox arguments on behalf of liberalism as the classic "no taxation without representation" theme were mustered, and the document as a whole showed to an extraordinary degree the influence of Western writings. Nevertheless, in terms of their philosophic argument, the petitioners did not surmount the old obstacles which still blocked the way to formulating any coherent pattern of Japanese liberalism. Recognizing that Imperial prerogative was the base of oligarchic absolutism, adherents of liberalism still sought to rest their cause on the *Imperial will* almost as much as their opponents did. Popular rights arguments, moreover, were distorted by the strongly chauvinistic demand for absolute unity; a warrior spirit shone through the liberal garment.

The effort of the Kokkai Kisei Domeikai met with a complete rebuff as far as immediate action was concerned; both the *Dajokan* (Council of State, or Chief Administrative Office) and the Genro-

---

[57] *Ibid.*, p. 27.
[58] *Ibid.*, p. 28.
[59] *Ibid.*, p. 31.

in refused to accept the petition, maintaining that there was no basis for receiving political petitions. In the aftermath of the Saigo revolt, however, the government had again moved in the direction of reform. In July, 1878, immediately after the revival of the Aikokusha and only two months after Okubo's assassination, the oligarchy established regulations for *fu* (metropolitan) and *ken* (prefectural) assemblies, laws of local taxation, and regulations for city and county districts. As with any mainly authoritarian regime, the Meiji oligarchy was dependent upon a combination of power and strategic compromise to retain its position. The ratios of power and compromise used were dependent, in the main, on the current stability of the government, but they were also dependent upon the degree to which a particular compromise fitted the general framework of Sat-Cho designs for the future of Japan. Naturally, there were within this framework fairly large areas of disagreement in the oligarchy itself, but there was basic agreement upon the concept of bureaucratic supremacy under Imperial prerogative.

Consequently, the government officials were not prepared to allow opposition political associations to grow unchallenged, and hence, on April 3, 1880, they struck hard with the "Law of Public Meetings." Justified to some extent by the violence in the liberal movement, this measure nevertheless showed all the predominant characteristics of the background from which the nation had so recently emerged. All meetings on political matters had to be sanctioned by the police authorities, and prior approval had to be obtained, not only for the speakers and subjects under discussion, but also for the lists of members and rules of the association. Articles v and vi gave police authorities the right to send officials to any meeting and disband it "when the warrant of official sanction is not produced on demand; when the lecturers or deliberators go beyond the subjects mentioned in the information; when discourses are found to have any tendency to lure or tempt people into crimes or delicts, or may be deemed prejudicial to public tranquillity; or when those who, from their positions, are prohibited from attending such meetings, do not obey the police when ordered to leave." [60]

In article vii, the political associations were struck a heavy blow, and one which would prove most telling:

"All military and naval men now on active service or in the first

[60] "Regulations for Public Meetings and Associations," April 5, 1880; translated in *JGD* (pp. 495–499), p. 496.

or second reserves; police officers, teachers and students of government, public, or private schools, agricultural or technological apprentices, must not attend any meeting where politics form the subject of address or deliberation. Neither may they become members of any political association." [61]

The importance of this particular clause can hardly be overestimated, for it excluded from party participation some of the ablest and most articulate members of Japanese society.

Thus, by 1880, the Sat-Cho oligarchy had determined to wipe out the threat of political parties by supervising and regulating their every move, by controlling their membership, and by making it impossible to maintain national organizations. According to article viii, "No political association, intending to lecture or deliberate upon politics, may advertise its lectures or debates, persuade people to enter its ranks by despatching commissioners or issuing circulars, *or combine and communicate with other similar societies.*" [62]

This was a direct answer to the endeavors of the Aikokusha to create a nationally coördinated movement, and it threatened to convert parties into segmented and impotent district groups, isolated from any main headquarters and incapable of intercourse with fellow thinkers. Indeed, the law was reminiscent of the Tokugawa edicts prohibiting daimyo activities.

The indirect result of the law, however, was to help produce the first genuine national party, the *Jiyuto* (Liberal Party).[63] As the realization of their impotence dawned upon them, the ex-samurai, who had often been reluctant to draw the common people into their organizations, began to realize that victory could come only through a movement coördinating press and public opinion against the oligarchy and fighting back. As one Risshisha writer put it, after the failure of Kataoka and Kono in Tokyo and the severity of the government, "we reflected and there were many who favored changing the *Kokkai Kisei Domei* and forming a Liberty Party which would appeal broadly to public sentiment." [64]

---

[61] *Ibid.*, pp. 496–497.

[62] *Ibid.*, p. 497. (Italics mine.—R. A. S.)

[63] The accurate translation of *Jiyuto* is "Liberty Party," not "Liberal Party." The latter term, however, is accepted universally now by both Western and Japanese writers. This is very unfortunate, in a sense, for it was as a "Liberty Party" that the founders of the Jiyuto thought of themselves, and the true connotations of the term are not quite the same as are those of a "Liberal Party."

[64] Quoted from *Risshisha shimatsu kiyo* by Suzuki Yasuzo, *Jiyuminken kempo happu*, pp. 166–167.

Leading members of the Domeikai proceeded to draw up a covenant for the Jiyuto, and this was published on December 15, 1880. It consisted of four short articles, proclaiming in vague terms that the new party proposed to work for an extension of civil rights, national advance and prosperity, equality of rights, and constitutional government.[65] With the drawing up of this covenant, the organization stopped, for the time being. It was practically impossible to build a political party in the midst of strict government repression. Two unexpected events, however, soon came to the liberals' rescue. The most important development involved a split between Okuma Shigenobu and the government,[66] over the issue of the timing and nature of a constitution for Japan. There had been scarcely a year since the Restoration when this problem had not occupied the attention of the oligarchic leaders, and countless proposals had come forth.[67] In March, 1881, Okuma, Hizen repre-

---

[65] For the document, see Hayashida, *op. cit.*, Vol. I, pp. 137–138.

[66] Professors Oka, Osatake, and Suzuki all have detailed accounts of this episode in their works previously cited.

[67] In the beginning, as we have noted, the desire for a fundamental law had stemmed from many sources, principally, from the desires to increase centralization, to capture the secret of Western strength, and to stabilize relations between the government and the people. The validity of this reasoning was not damaged by the abandonment of early timorous experiments in Western ideas. As Miyajima Seiichiro, member of the Sa-in, said regarding his proposal for a constitution in 1872, the danger of present thoughts of liberty, freedom, and republicanism could only be curbed by a fixed fundamental law which would regulate the relations between the people and the Emperor. See Suzuki Yasuzo, *Jiyuminken*, pp. 24–25. Pursuing this objective, the government made numerous studies, and various leaders submitted proposals. Kido, who was the most "constitution"-minded among the chief leaders, came back from Europe in 1863 enthusiastic over the idea and subsequently submitted to the Emperor a brief draft which had been drawn up while he (Kido) was in London. Although it made the Imperial position and powers paramount, it was still a very enlightened document. Even Okubo submitted a proposal, but there was a widening gulf between the desires of the liberals and proposals like those of Okubo, which relegated the legislature to an inferior position.

Finally, in 1876, the Genro-in was given an Imperial rescript ordering it to investigate and draft a Constitution, and had actually been given a copy of Todd's *Parliamentary Government of England* by the Emperor. The conservative draft which the Council reported back was finally shelved, on the plea of Iwakura and others that it was too early, and the Satsuma Rebellion interrupted efforts for some time thereafter. See Osatake Takeshi and Hayashi Shigeru, "Seiji" (Politics), in *Gendai Nihon shi kenkyu* (*Studies of Contemporary Japanese History*), Tokyo, 1938, pp. 89–92. However, the government leaders soon resumed their constitutional studies, made more urgent by a rising tide of public opposition which mere suppression would not stop.

sentative who had remained with the government, submitted a proposal for the Constitution directly to the Emperor. Although Okuma had remained a member of the oligarchy, he had been much influenced by the parliamentary ideas of his young followers, and the proposal which he submitted actually came from the pen of Yano Fumio, one of these. Previously, Okuma, Ito, and Inoue, as the more enlightened of the younger statesmen, had conferred on numerous occasions; the latter two, however, were greatly antagonized by Okuma's unilateral action, and the conservative members of the oligarchy not only thought the plan far too radical and rapid, but also sensed a plot to bring down Sat-Cho power. Consequently, in October, 1881, Okuma finally left the government.

In the summer of 1881, as the tensions between the Okuma forces and those of the Sat-Cho were growing, a second major storm broke, in the form of a great scandal. The Hokkaido colonization project, which had cost more than ¥14,000,000, was proposed for sale to a private group at a ridiculously low figure. The project was headed at the time by Kuroda Kiyotaka, a Satsuma militarist. Connections between proposed buyers and the government made the loss of money look extremely suspicious, particularly when approval was rushed through in record time. A wave of indignation swept most of the press and the vocal political groups, finally forcing the government to rescind approval.[68]

These two events, taken together, augmented the antigovernment forces and lifted them from abstractions to realities on which they could campaign. Those of the Sat-Cho group were tremendously alarmed by the rise of popular opposition and the serious defections from their own ranks. Shaken from their reluctance to grant a national assembly, they determined to take an immediate stand to stem the tide of revolt.[69] On October 12, 1881—only a day

---

[68] See Hayashida, op. cit., Vol. I, pp. 139–145; Suzuki Yasuzo, Jiyuminken, p. 374.

[69] At about this time, Inoue Kowashi, in response to a request for a plan, submitted some proposals to Iwakura regarding the course of action which the government should follow. Among them, three are of particular interest. First, decisions by the Council must be set forth as the correct interpretations of the Imperial desires (this, to counteract the party endeavors to separate the government from the Emperor). Secondly, Satsuma and Choshu men must show their complete unity. Thirdly, "if there is no Imperial Mandate [on a national assembly and a Constitution], it is doubtful whether the public mind can be quieted." See Suzuki Yasuzo, Jiyuminken kempo happu, p. 159; and Jiyuminken, p. 375.

after Okuma's resignation—the Emperor announced that plans should be perfected for a national assembly which would be convened nine years later, in 1890. Shortly thereafter, Ito Hirobumi, the great Choshu statesman, was sent to Europe for study, from which he was to return to head a Constitutional Committee composed wholly of government personnel, charged with drawing up the new document.

The public commitment of the government to a constitution which would include some provisions for an elected national assembly changed the complexion of the party movement. Henceforth, the movement for the establishment of a representative government became a party movement to prepare for such a government.[70] In most senses, however, the emerging parties still existed in the political demimonde. They had no present function in government, and the actual preparations for the Constitution were carefully guarded secrets, placed beyond party control or supervision. The old antifaction laws still existed and were soon to be bolstered by more stringent regulations. The governmental leaders had accepted neither the inevitability nor the desirability of political parties in the new Japan. Organized before they had any legal or practical position in political affairs, the parties naturally continued to be surfeited with a philosophy of violence, and when they shouted *"seifu wo tempuku"* (Overthrow the government!), it was in terms of bullets that the majority of the people thought. The same philosophic conflicts, moreover, still plagued the liberal movement; the new parties were torn between a glorification of the state and an emphasis on the individual, between obeisance to the Imperial symbolism and service to popular government.

In the short space of a year, 1881 through part of 1882, three major parties were to make an active appearance—the Jiyuto, previously mentioned, the *Rikken Kaishinto* (Constitutional Progressive Party), and the *Rikken Teiseito* (Constitutional Imperial Party). The first two were to survive by means of various changes throughout the whole of Japanese party history before 1940 as the two dominant parties in Japan.[71] With the background of the Japanese liberal movement in mind, it is essential to state briefly the fundamental political philosophy on which these parties stood.

The Jiyuto, as we have noted, was the culmination of the organ-

---

[70] Suzuki Yasuzo, *Jiyuminken kempo happu*, p. 160.

[71] Indeed, in a sense, they still survive, for the two conservative parties in postwar Japan are closely related to the two dominant prewar parties.

ized opposition movement up to its time. Led by Itagaki, Goto, and Kono Hironaka, its greatest intellectual spokesmen were Ueki Emori and Nakae Chomin. The party prospectus indicates clearly what a great debt the party owed to Rousseau and his *Social Contract*. The document begins:

Liberty is the natural state of man and the preservation of liberty is man's great duty; but if the power of human authority moves so as to oppress divinely bestowed liberty and injure that natural state, then this right cannot be maintained. And even the maintenance of the security of our most precious lives and properties has been unreasonably entrusted to the dictates of the political leaders [*shujisha*]. Knowing this perilous situation to be indeed like treading on thin ice, when we have reached this point, we cannot help shuddering with shame as never before. . . .

To make clear the truth to the nation by spreading liberty as the natural state is the duty of each person; there are some who do not know the great road for which they should work, and consequently through the power of authorities, our area of liberty has been shrunk, liberty of speech and publication prevented, political theories, on the act of advancing have been suppressed, and they have attempted to misconstrue the unity of society. . . .

By establishing a political party called Jiyuto and developing a united spirit, we will spread the heavenly bestowed liberty and control the power of the authorities; from above, we will correct the government, and at the lower level, we will cause a spirit of self-government to be developed . . .[72]

It seems incontrovertible that the liberal movement was being used partly as a tool with which to bring personal power to certain ex-members of a warrior class who could no longer rely upon military force or social and intellectual prestige. We have noted this in terms of the leadership and background of the party movement. To deny, however, that there was a large measure of sincerity and idealism in the awakening of these men to Western ideas would be very wrong. One cannot read Ueki's "Minken jiyu ron" (Treatise on Popular Rights and Liberty) without being struck by the author's conviction and erudition.[73] The sparks from Ueki's

---

[72] "Jiyuto soshiki shuisho" (Prospectus of the Establishment of the Jiyuto), document reproduced in Aono, *op. cit.*, pp. 42–43. This work was written mainly by Nakae Chomin.

[73] This work is included in Yoshino (ed.), *op. cit.*, Vol. V, pp. 183–195. See Ueki's equally famous "Tempu jinken ben" (Understanding Natural Rights), *ibid.*, pp. 463–482. "Minken jiyu ron" had been published in separate form in 1879, and was written in very popular style so that it would reach the

pen set men's minds afire with new visions and ideas. We Japanese are dead, he said to those who could read his words, for living without understanding is death.[74] Men must use the intelligence and power which they were given by nature; otherwise, they remain always children. They should use these faculties to set up a state and employ officials, correcting mistakes and punishing evils.[75]

Out of his wealth of knowledge of world history, Ueki drew examples of bad governments and their fate. *L'Etat, c'est moi*, he said, is fundamentally wrong, because the state is the people—it is not the government, "nor even the monarch," for, as Mao Tze wrote long ago, a state can exist without a monarch, but never without people. Absolutism, said Ueki, is the certain means toward internal disorder, revolution, and weakness; and to prove it, he cited instances, from Rome to China. Liberty is indispensable to the strength and power of the state. This should be guaranteed by a constitution established by a conference between the people and their rulers, drawing up a division of rights which are not to be transgressed.

Ueki certainly towered above most of his fellow liberals in perceiving the central issues of his creed; he even brought the concepts of social democracy into play, emphasizing the natural rights connected with popular livelihood and indicating a very advanced doctrine for his time. Yet, as was only natural, Ueki played heavily upon the national power theme, dwelling repeatedly on the point that a strong people make a strong state. With regard to the Emperor, Ueki attacked monarchical absolutism with bold strokes, but in citing examples, he had to look abroad to the East and West. When it came to Japan, he could cite only the absolutism of officialdom such as the Tokugawa. He said they were overthrown because, in addition to damaging the liberty of the people, they "slighted the Imperial Household, which is honored in our coun-

greatest possible number of people; the latter was written in 1882, in opposition to Kato Hiroyuki's *Jinken shinsetsu* (*New Theories of Popular Rights*). In it, Ueki attacked Kato's idea of gradualism, defending popular rights as a matter of immediate life-or-death concern to the nation. Between the dates of these two works, in 1880, Ueki wrote a strong defense of civil liberties in his "Genron jiyu ron" (Treatise on Freedom of Speech). For a recent appraisal of Ueki and other Meiji intellectuals, see Royama Masamichi, *Nihon ni okeru kindai seijigaku no hattatsu* (*The Development of Modern Political Science in Japan*), Tokyo, 1949.

[74] Ueki Emori, "Minken jiyu ron," in Yoshino (ed.), *op. cit.*, Vol. V, p. 185.
[75] *Ibid.*, p. 186.

try." He did not underscore with clarity the role which the Emperor played in the power structure of the Meiji state, or that which he had played in previous eras.

The task of translating Western ideas and history into the context of Meiji Japan was not easy, but it was the inescapable task for the Japanese intellectuals of that day—both liberal and conservative. It therefore becomes important to note the Western sources to which they turned. The writings of Western philosophers flooded into the minds of Japanese intellectuals in the three decades after the Restoration.[76] In the earlier period, as we have mentioned, this influx was made easier by the remarkable degree of freedom which existed in the society and the eagerness for Western knowledge; nearly every one of the leading figures of the period made at least one trip abroad to study Western institutions and ideas, and few returned unimpressed.

Quite naturally, the new political terminology itself came from foreign sources. The origin of the compound *seito* (political party) is uncertain, but in 1871 Kato Hiroyuki gave some Imperial Court lectures on Bluntschli's *Allgemeines Staatsrecht*, in which he discussed parties. In the next year he published his manuscript under the title, *Kokuho hanron* (*A General Treatise on National Law*). In the first chapter he wrote:

"In countries of civilized culture, the people are divided into many factions [*toha*] and by striving in competition, advocating various things which they believe ought to be done, they finally have the power to cause the course of government laws to be changed. These are called *seirontoha* [political argument factions]." [77]

It is thought that the compound seito came from an abbreviation of these four characters.[78] Even earlier, in his *Rikken seitai*

---

[76] For a very complete list of the most important research works and translations of Western philosophy and politics, see the Appendix in Royama, *op. cit.* By 1877, the major French authors in translation included Rousseau and Montesquieu; the English, John Stuart Mill; and the German, Bluntschli; and there were many secondary works translated. (Actually, Johann Bluntschli was Swiss, but in 1848 he went to Munich as Professor of Constitutional Law, and later he taught at Heidelberg.)

[77] Quoted from *Kokuho hanron* by Osatake Takeshi and Hayashi Shigeru, "Seiji" (Politics), in *Gendai Nihon shi kenkyu* (*Studies of Contemporary Japanese History*), Tokyo, 1938, p. 81.

[78] Osatake, *Nihon kensei shi taiko*, Vol. II, p. 438. The implications of the character *to* (party) continued to carry the feudal opprobrium—a factor of importance, as has been mentioned earlier.

71

ryaku (*Outline of Constitutional Government*), taken from German sources, Kato had introduced the term, "constitutional government," *rikken seitai*. Indeed, Kato was the first to defend liberalism academically, and he did so with considerable force in certain passages of his early works. His exclusive reliance upon German writers, however, together with the close relationship which he held with the Sat-Cho leaders, soon led him in the opposite direction.[79]

It was inevitable that a large proportion of the Meiji leaders would be most influenced by that government of Europe which rendered greatest homage to the Emperor and the military while making its way to a prominent position as a great power. In 1871, when Okubo accompanied Iwakura, Ito, and the others on their trip to Europe, he wrote back to Saigo after visiting the German Reichstag that he was greatly impressed by the way in which the German legislators fortified the strength of the army through their appropriations.[80] Later he remarked that only the German system seemed to be compatible with the character and heritage of Japan. The subsequent influence of such German scholars as Stein and Gneist on Japanese students of politics and Sat-Cho statesmen can be in large measure attributed to such observations as these and to the factors underlying them. The oligarchs wanted something more than a Western pattern for modernization; they wanted a pattern which would conform in the greatest degree to the heritage and the contemporary nature of Japan.

In the early period, however, even among men of the Sat-Cho group, German ideas had to compete with other Western political theories. We have already made reference to the influence of American and French sources evident in the first reforms. Kido,

---

[79] In one of Professor Osatake's last monographs, *Nihon kensei shi no kenkyu* (*A Study of Japanese Constitutional History*), Tokyo, 1943, he lays heavy emphasis on the fact that Kato's early and able espousal of German thought and his position as Imperial Court Lecturer between 1870 and 1875 laid the groundwork for German supremacy. See pp. 3–25. Although this was of importance, it is clear that the central motivating factors lay much deeper.

Professor Royama, in discussing Kato's early liberal theories, states that such a work as *Kokuho hanron* was more influential in fixing in the official mind a *state concept* than in disseminating the liberal theories it expressed. Royama, *op. cit.*, p. 71.

[80] Letter from Okubo to Saigo dated March 12, 1873, quoted in Osatake, *Nihon kensei shi no kenkyu*, p. 5.

in particular, was noteworthy for his support of Montesquieu's theory of the separation of powers. Meanwhile, the early civil rights movement was using the writings of J. S. Mill, Rousseau, and many other French, English, and American writers. Mill, as we have seen, was an early favorite because a translation of *On Liberty* appeared in Japan in 1871; he remained one of the philosophers most popular with the liberals, especially the members of the *Kaishinto* (Progressive Party),[81] since the Jiyuto turned more and more to France for stimulus. The Risshisha Law School and its counterparts drew their main inspiration from Rousseau and the French democratic theorists stemming from the French Revolution. The influence of their concepts in such schools became so great that large numbers of teachers and students found their way into the early liberal associations, provoking government restraints in the form of edicts that prohibited their participation in politics. Words such as *jiyu* (liberty), *byodo* (equality), and *yuai* (fraternity) proved so popular that they served as names for many of the district parties.[82] In 1877 Hattori Naritsugu published *Minyaku ron*, a translation of Rousseau's *Social Contract;* and Nakae Chomin, famed member of the Jiyuto and staff writer for the *Jiyu Shimbun* (*Liberty Newspaper*), published a superb translation of the same work in 1885. From the works of Ueki and Nakae, as well as from the official documents of the Jiyuto, it is clear that

[81] It is clear that the Kaishinto, far more than the Jiyuto, was in touch with the true disciples of nineteenth-century liberalism. Its intellectual circles were students of Mill, Locke, and Spencer. In large measure this was due to the leadership of Fukuzawa Yukichi and the Keio University liberals. Concerning Fukuzawa more remains to be said later in this study, but it is proper here to characterize him as one of the ablest Japanese exponents of individualism and English utilitarianism. His influence and prestige were tremendous in liberal circles, despite the fact that he stayed in the background of party politics; and Keio University, of which he was both founder and president, became a bulwark for the pro-British school of Japanese liberalism represented in the Kaishinto.

Concerning Mill, Osatake and Hayashi say, "From the standpoint of such tendencies [liberalism], the work which had the earliest and also the greatest influence on our people was that of Mill." Osatake and Hayashi, *op. cit.*, p. 103.

The works of Spencer were introduced early, through a summarized translation by Ozaki Yukio (Keio University and Kaishinto man, subsequently one of Japan's greatest liberals), in 1877. In 1880 Matsujima Tsuyoshi published a translation of Spencer's *Social Statics* under the title, *Shakai heiken ron;* see Osatake and Hayashi, *op. cit.*, p. 103.

[82] See Suzuki Yasuzo, *Jiyuminken kempo happu*, p. 188.

Rousseau was the patron saint of this wing of the liberal movement.[83]

To counteract French theories, the government resorted to none other than Edmund Burke and his *Reflections on the Revolution in France*. The publication of Burke's book, translated in part in 1885 by Kaneko Kentaro, a leader among the oligarchy and an aide to Ito on the Constitutional Committee, occasioned a typical debate over Western ideas in Japan.[84] This debate was carried on not only in translations and independent works, but also through the growing Japanese press. After 1874 organs representing the liberals and the government showered polemics at each other over such vital questions as political sovereignty, the proper manner of drafting a constitution, voting requirements, and general questions of political theory.[85] The golden age of press freedom was quickly over, but while it lasted, many provocative issues were raised.

The government and its political supporters made every effort to expose the Jiyuto as the breeder of republicanism and violence. Long before Kaneko's skillful thrust at Rousseauism, there had been bitter attacks against the "desecrators of monarchy." Even within the ranks of the civil rights proponents, certain defections had occurred; in 1880, one faction, headed by Mizuno Torajiro, left the Risshisha, saying:

"Even though they may use thousands of words, in essence, the Risshisha are using Constitutional Monarchy as a pretext, when in fact they are leading the country toward republicanism, and they deceive their fellow compatriots as men who want to stand on a polity of justice." [86]

---

[83] It is true, of course, that other Western works had their influence on the leaders of the Jiyuto. Mill continued to be important in the formulation of their ideas, and Spencer had a sufficient influence on Itagaki to cause him to visit the famous English philosopher while in England.

[84] In the advertisements announcing the book, it was described as a work displaying the "sincere patriotic feelings of an outstanding British parliamentarian" who desired "to protect his national polity" against the poison of Rousseau and the republican ideas of the French Revolution. It continued by explaining that Burke's analysis of the popular sovereignty doctrines of Rousseau proved that they "sow the poison of revolution, kill the monarch, and cause the establishment of an anarchist republican government." Quoted in Osatake, *Nihon kensei shi no kenkyu,* pp. 35–36.

[85] For an extremely interesting selection of newspaper editorials of this period on the question of sovereignty, see the collection entitled "Shuken ronsan" (A Collection of Sovereignty Theories), edited by Nagasoku Sotaro, in Yoshino (ed.), *op. cit.,* Vol. V, pp. 310–352.

[86] Quoted in Osatake, *Nihon kensei shi taiko,* Vol. II, p. 613, from *Kyuka-*

Ito Hirobumi, at the time Premier and greatest single power in the government, wrote Inoue Kaoru in 1885:

"Itagaki's arguments contain the same principles as anarchism and socialism and are completely incompatible with our nation. We have a great moral obligation to recognize harmful ideas to the future of the Imperial Household." [87]

The fact remains that as regards the Jiyuto philosophical foundation its opponents were in some measure correct. Itagaki and his compatriots had based their political principles on such Western concepts as popular sovereignty, human equality, and the right of revolution.[88] The consistency of the party as a whole, however, was tempered both by the practical limitations of the time and the confused aims of the liberal movement. The Imperial Household was the central symbolism of the new era, and to attack it successfully in any form was exceedingly difficult; moreover, to do so required a type of philosophic revolution in the minds of the ex-samurai party leaders which could not, except in the minds of a very few, be produced. The result was that a strident note of confusion ran through the pages of Jiyuto philosophy and characterized Jiyuto action.

In the Jiyuto prospectus and party platform, the emphasis was on the people's rights to self-government (*jishu*) and self-expression. Indeed, departing from the pattern of past pronouncements on civil rights, these documents contained scarcely a reference to the Emperor, and the movement seemed to have veered leftward. The Jiyuto urged not only a constitution, but one decided upon by a national convention.[89] This advanced position alone was enough to cause opponents of the party to decry such insolence to the Throne. It must be remembered, however, that the Jiyuto leaders were under no illusions about the actual seat of

---

kusha jiseki (*Research on Old Associations*). This group later set itself up as the Teiseito, the alter ego of the government.

[87] Letter from Ito to Inoue, quoted in Osatake, *Nihon kensei shi taiko*, Vol. II, pp. 613–614.

[88] Professors Osatake and Hayashi made the following observation: "The Teiseito advocated a theory of monarchical sovereignty, the Jiyuto a theory of popular sovereignty, and the Kaishinto maintained that sovereignty should rest with the Monarch and the Assembly." Osatake and Hayashi, *op. cit.*, p. 120. But, as Professor Suzuki has stated, the historical materials thus far revealed do not indicate a single political society dedicated to republicanism, and the Jiyuto sovereignty doctrine assumed a unique connection between the people and the monarch which obfuscated the entire issue, as will be noted presently. See Suzuki Yasuzo, *Jiyuminken*, p. 16.

[89] Osatake and Hayashi, *op. cit.*, p. 120.

75

authority of that time. They knew that an "Emperor-bestowed" Constitution would in reality be the product of the Sat-Cho leaders' desires. The important thing is that at no time did the Jiyuto leaders analyze the role of the Emperorship as an institution in such a way as to make their position on popular government unmistakably clear. By making the Emperor mystically synonymous with the people, they could and did maintain that to support popular government was to support the Emperor. Thus, in an editorial entitled "The Emperor Veneration Theories of the Jiyuto," appearing in a liberal organ, the writer stated: "No one respects the Emperor like the Jiyuto; through seeking happiness for the people and their satisfaction, we are making the Emperor happy." [90]

In truth, the exponents of civil rights were caught in the meshes of gigantic inconsistencies in trying to effect what amounted to a synthesis of Imperial absolutism and popular sovereignty. As a sort of Rousseauian "general will" concept, the Jiyuto advanced the thesis that under popular government, a united people would speak and act in accord with the Imperial desires. This was inevitable, said they, since the Emperor reflected the wishes of his people and represented the good of his society. Hence there could be no question of popular government conflicting with Imperial interests.

The adoption of this kind of thesis was very natural, in view of the deeply entrenched Confucian doctrines concerning the monarch, the actual role of the Emperor in Japanese society, and the background of the Restoration and its samurai participants. Practically, of course, the Jiyuto professed to see the obstacles to such a course in the intrusion of the oligarchy between the Emperor and his people, a theme which was to have recurrent echoes throughout the history of modern Japan. Thus their political ambitions and jealousies fitted excellently into such a philosophic concept. This theory of Emperor-people relationship was undoubtedly devised in part to meet the savage attack of the government, but that it was sincerely held is shown by many statements of liberal leaders.[91]

---

[90] This editorial appeared in the *Tokai-Gyosho Shimpo* and is quoted by Suzuki Yasuzo in his *Jiyuminken kempo happu*, pp. 176–177. See also an editorial in the *Yubin Hochi Shimbun* of September 12, 1876, quoted in Suzuki Yasuzo, *Jiyuminken*, pp. 55–56.

[91] Itagaki's sincerity on behalf of the Emperor was sufficient to convince Toyama Mitsuru, subsequently one of the most notorious Imperial "patriots" and patron saint of the ultranationalists, that he was attempting merely to perpetuate the Emperor by tearing down a government which was making

A contemporary critic of the Jiyuto pointed up its dilemma in the following passage:

The extremely contradictory thing was that during the ten-odd years from the Kokkai Kisei Domeikai to the period of the Jiyuto, both political crimes and assassination affairs were at their zenith, and the spirit which gave form to their plans was, if we speak simply, that of the Russian Nihilists and the French Revolution. These two were their platform, and studying these, they planned to transform the conditions of the times; but if pressed hard, they ran completely counter to the ideas of the Russian Nihilists and the principles of the French Revolution with a maintenance of *kokutai* [the national polity] and Emperor veneration. It was an extreme contradiction, but that contradiction also became the one fundamental reason for making the Jiyuto great.[92]

One may suggest that the habitual practice of political violence stemmed at least as much from the warrior ethical and political code of the samurai and traditional Japanese agrarian revolt as from the inspiration derived from Nihilism and the French Revolution, but the conflict of principles remains. The philosophy of the so-called left wing was riddled with the inconsistencies of men who were working with the political raw materials of widely separated eras.[93]

As the Jiyuto struggled to reconcile its theories of popular sovereignty with Japanese tradition, the second school of Japanese liberalism, under the name of the *Kaishinto* (Progressive Party), sought to utilize the "King in Parliament" concept of the British. When Okuma Shigenobu broke away from the oligarchy at the time of the Constitution controversy, he gathered about him many personal followers in the bureaucracy, a number of outside intellectuals, and representatives of certain industrial interests who were anxious to find a "middle way" between bureaucratic oppression and the "uncouth extremism" of the Jiyuto.[94] Together

his name odious. Toyama himself was affiliated for a time with the *Aikokusha* (Society of Patriots). See Oi Ittetsu, *Kensei wo hakai suru seito seiji (Political Party Politics—The Destruction of Constitutionalism)*, Tokyo, 1932, p. 14.

[92] Quoted in Suzuki Yasuzo, *Jiyuminken kempo happu*, pp. 175–176, from Ito Jintaro, *Ito Jintaro no danwa*.

[93] It is also true, of course, that there were very diverse elements in the Jiyuto at this time; this problem will be discussed in the next chapter.

[94] The official Jiyuto claim was that Okuma, Iwasaki Yataro (head of Mitsubishi), and Fukuzawa Yukichi together "conspired" to establish an anti-Jiyuto party subsidized with Mitsubishi funds. See Itagaki, *op. cit.*, Vol. I, p. 501.

under Okuma's leadership they founded the *Rikken Kaishinto* (Constitutional Progressive Party).

As we have previously noted, philosophically the source springs of the Kaishinto were much closer to the heart of nineteenth-century liberalism than were those of the Jiyuto. Able young writers like Ono Azusa and Yano Fumio took their cues from such philosophers as Mill, Locke, and Spencer.[95] To these might be added the whole Benthamite school of utilitarians and many American writers whose works were widely read and under whom some of the young Japanese intellectuals studied. No mention of Kaishinto political theory could be made without paying homage to Fukuzawa Yukichi, who had probably divined the meaning of English and American political thought as well as any of his generation. Fukuzawa himself had been an early student of the West, and his enthusiasm for the general economic and political doctrines of Western liberalism remained high. His words, "Heaven did not make men above men or men below men"[96] echoed throughout the Japanese liberal world. And from his school, Keio University, came such men as Ozaki Yukio, Shimada Saburo, and Inukai Tsuyoshi, the most prominent names in the annals of Japanese liberals and all originally Kaishinto members.

Okuma himself was remarkably capable, in some respects, of assimilating the liberal doctrines. The following was contained in his message of 1881 announcing the formation of his party:

"Constitutional government is political party government. Polit-

---

[95] Professor Royama has written a very interesting brief analysis of Ono Azusa in his *Nihon ni okeru kindai seijigaku no hattatsu*, pp. 49–53. Before his death at the early age of thirty-five, Ono had revealed himself as a brilliant spokesman for the empirical method and for the political doctrines of utilitarianism. His *Kokken hanron* (*A General Treatise on National Constitutions*), published in 1882, and *Mimpo no hone* (*The Essence of Civil Law*), published in 1884, showed the strong influence of Bentham, Austin, and Montesquieu. Ono's keynote was "inevitable progress," and in selecting the desiderata for this progress, he leaned heavily upon Benthamite utilitarianism. Of at least equal significance was the fact that Ono emphasized the importance of the Western empirical method in Japanese scholarship, maintaining that Western methodology, even more than Western ideas, should be applied to Japanese problems.

[96] Quoted in Fukuo Takeshiro's *Nihon kazoku seido shi* (*A History of the Japanese Family System*), Tokyo, 1947, p. 19. On Fukuzawa, in English, see E. Kiyooka (trans.), *The Autobiography of Fukuzawa Yukichi*, Tokyo, 1934. Among biographies in Japanese, see Ishikawa Mikiaki, *Fukuzawa Yukichi*, Tokyo, 1935; and Takahashi Seiichiro, *Fukuzawa Yukichi—hito to gakusetsu* (*Fukuzawa Yukichi—The Man and His Doctrines*), Tokyo, 1947.

ical party conflict is a conflict of principles. For this reason, if the majority of the people support their principles, they ought to have that type of government, and if the people oppose, they should lose the reins of government." [97]

He went on to accuse the *shujisha* (political leaders) of rearing a system of absolutism, and stated that the only means of granting political peace to the people was to establish a system of peaceful change.[98]

The Kaishinto, though a less radical party in most respects than the Jiyuto, was neither as chauvinistic nor as provincial, and in many ways it was less contradictory in its principles. This was essentially due to the nature of its support, as is brought out in the next chapter. Nevertheless, its difficulties in thoroughly assimilating the liberal theory were very great. Attempting to approximate the "King in Parliament" idea of sovereignty and institutions, it was confronted with the Japanese shibboleths of loyalty to the Emperor. Okuma himself said of the movement: "At that time [when he left the government] politics were at the wiles of the military force of Sat-Cho-Do [*sic*] and national thoughts had lost their unity. There were plans which would cause a national crisis; I then had a tacit understanding with Ono and we desired to try to establish one great political party [*ichidai seito*] and produce a second Imperial Restoration." [99]

It is to be noted that "unity" and the Imperial institution were of great importance. The same unified Emperor-people concept as that held by the Jiyuto was implicit in much of the Kaishinto program. The party prospectus and platform proclaimed: "If one or two private factions [*shito*] monopolize the country and slight the Throne and people . . . we will become the public enemies of these." [100]

In this prospectus, the Kaishinto mentioned the Throne first, the people second: "The purpose of this party is to promote the

---

[97] Quoted from Okuma's message, as reproduced in Osatake, *Meiji seiji shi tembyo*, p. 65. It should be pointed out, however, that this document was written, not by Okuma, but by Yano Fumio, an able young official who had studied English institutions diligently, and that it was corrected by Ono Azusa. Yano wrote that Ono was considered the best expert on the parliamentary system, and that, although the draft was written without documents, "Okuma did not say anything against my work at that time." Quoted in *ibid.*, p. 66.

[98] *Ibid.*, p. 65.

[99] Quoted from Okuma, *Rikken Kaishinto*, by Suzuki Yasuzo, *Jiyuminken kempo happu*, p. 185.

[100] From "Rikken Kaishinto shuisho" (The Prospectus of the Constitutional Progressive Party), reproduced in Aono, *op. cit.* (pp. 55–57), p. 56.

prosperity of the Throne and the happiness of the people." [101]

As in the case of the Jiyuto, this position was partially dictated by political expediency, but one sees the same tendencies in the writings of Kaishinto intellectuals. Professor Royama notes that Ono Azusa, in common with most other Japanese liberals, was a *kinnoka* (Imperial loyalist) and a nationalist.[102] And Fukuzawa also, as Professor Royama points out, had a special "Throne theory": that the government and the Emperor should be separated, and that if the government broke its pledge to conduct affairs justly, the people should decide, *relying upon the Throne.*[103]

Thus the Kaishinto had philosophic dilemmas almost equal to those of the Jiyuto. If the Japanese Emperor had had a long history of reigning but not ruling, it was also true that the restrictions placed upon his real powers were, for the most part, of a political, not a legal or philosophic, nature. No Japanese Emperor had been subjected to a Bill of Rights or an Act of Settlement, and in this respect as in his religious position, his status differed very greatly from that of the British monarch. The Kaishinto, therefore, could not hope to accomplish any substantial transformation by laying heavy emphasis on complete loyalty to the Throne. This was all the more true because the Emperor and his prerogatives were currently at the beck and call of the powerful Sat-Cho clique. It was not without some reason that the Jiyuto attacked the Kaishinto as a party without spirit or resolution.

There was another factor probably present in the cautious attitude of the Kaishinto toward the Emperor. Even among the exponents of liberalism, the concept of sharing political power was obscured by the bitter personal and han rivalries, and in its absence the cloud of absolutism hung heavily over the goals of each party. Obtaining control of the government, they too could use the Emperor, and this was one reason why some were loath to diminish his authority.[104]

It was also necessary for the Kaishinto to interpret the liberal creed so that it would fit in with the desires of those urban capital-

---

[101] *Ibid.,* p. 55.

[102] Royama, *op. cit.,* p. 53.

[103] *Ibid.,* p. 45.

[104] Professor Osatake remarks that because their pre-Meiji training had been in terms of absolute power, the parties could not grasp the concept of division of power and unity of purpose toward achieving common ends. Each group, therefore, thought of itself as successor to the Sat-Cho clique. See Osatake, *Nihon kensei shi taiko,* Vol. II, pp. 645–647.

ists who formed the financial backbone of the party. The times demanded close coördination between government and industry, and this forced the party to modify substantially the individualistic laissez-faire aspects of economic liberalism. In the end, the Kaishinto could not diverge greatly from the aura of nationalism and the Emperor-centered state which that era begat, nor could it ignore the prevailing paternalistic demands and needs of its urban capitalist supporters.

The third national party, the *Rikken Teiseito* (Constitutional Imperial Party) made use of the Western concept of party to foster ideas that were completely contrary to party government. Formed to support the government against the "civil rights" parties, it represented the philosophy of the oligarchy. The Teiseito manifesto proclaimed the party purpose as being "to cause the mental capacities of the nation-people to return to the one point of *sonno aikoku* [Revere the Emperor; love the country]." [105]

Severely criticizing those who attempted "to mislead" the people by holding up European theories as models, it attacked all the "liberals" for seeking to move too fast. "The Teiseito will revere the Imperial Edict and await the grant by His Majesty of the new Constitution, continuing to protect the Imperial happiness eternally." [106]

Two articles of the party platform defined the Teiseito's position on the question of popular government. The third article read: "The sovereign power of course rests in the Emperor, but its exercise is governed by the Constitution." And the seventh article read: "The final decision on questions decided by the National Legislature is to rest with the Emperor." [107]

It was very significant that a part of the oligarchy had accepted a party to carry on their philosophic battle. Within the oligarchy some of the more "enlightened" men, such as Ito and Inoue, had already voiced the opinion that "civil rights" parties should be opposed by a government party; [108] though they were not openly affiliated with the Teiseito, they were the powers behind it. However, as later events were to indicate, the conclusion that the oligarchy as a whole had given up hope of destroying parties as instruments of political change was premature.

---

[105] "Rikken Teiseito koryo" (General Principles of the Rikken Teiseito), document reproduced in Aono, *op. cit.* (pp. 70–72), p. 71.

[106] *Ibid.*

[107] *Ibid.*

[108] See Oka, *op. cit.*, pp. 242–243, note 1.

While the liberal parties were struggling to reconcile their borrowed philosophy with their own desires and the trends of the time, the oligarchy was methodically planning a course of action which would incorporate its philosophic ideas in permanent governmental institutions. Great care had to be taken in writing the new document; already, as we have noted, several drafts had been discarded. The labors of the Constitution Investigation Committee, established in 1876, had produced a draft in 1878, but this was rejected as not being in accord with the national polity; the revised draft of 1880 had met with the same fate. But now it was essential to put the best minds of the government at work on the problem.

The task was assigned to Ito. In 1881 he left for Europe to study Western constitutions, and he remained there until 1883. During this time he had frequent meetings with two German constitutional law experts, Professor Heinrich Gneist of Berlin and Professor Lorenz von Stein of Vienna. Together with the great German statesman Bismarck, these men created a remarkable impression upon Ito, who became their eager student. Thus his earlier views were reinforced, and he was determined to use the German model as the sole Western source of the Japanese Constitution.[109] Upon his return Ito was appointed Minister of the Imperial Household, in charge of the *Seido Torishirabekyoku* (Department for Institutional Investigation), which was to draw up the Constitution.

Portentous changes in governmental structure began the following year.[110] In 1884, five orders of nobility were created in preparation for a House of Peers, and in 1885 the Council of State was replaced by a *naikaku* (cabinet) consisting of ten ministers, with Ito as the first premier.[111] In the meantime, the opposition parties outside the government had been increasingly throttled by a series of antiparty edicts and laws, and were finally forced to dissolve temporarily in 1884.[112] Step by step, Ito guided the new document along; in 1888 a *Sumitsu-in* (Privy Council) was established, to review the proposed Constitution, and Ito was made its

[109] For an authoritative study of Ito's European trip and of the roles played by Bismarck, Gneist, and Stein, see Osatake, *Nihon kensei shi no kenkyu,* especially pp. 13–20.

[110] Rapid reform was aided by the fact that Iwakura's death in 1883 left only Sanjo as an old superior, and he was very weak; consequently, the Councillors could push ahead with fewer obstacles, to make substantial changes. See Oka, *op. cit.,* pp. 257 ff.

[111] For the documents translated into English, see *JGD,* pp. 88–90, 90–127.

[112] For details, see chapter iii.

head! Finally, on February 11, 1889, the mantle of secrecy was removed and the Constitution was presented to the people in the name of the Emperor.

Behind the scenes there had been some very interesting developments. The government had at this time as legal advisers two Germans, Hermann Roessler and Albert Mosse, both of whom played important roles in the drafting of the Constitution. Roessler, in particular, was of key significance; he actually made a personal draft which was extremely close to the final product.[113] And despite the precautions taken to ensure secrecy, certain liberals got wind of developments and access to important papers. In a secretly published work entitled *Sei-tetsu yume monogatari* (*Dream Stories of Western Philosophy*), Roessler's draft was published under an unrevealing title, and the charge was made that the government was planning a Prussianized, absolutist Constitution.[114] However, the most vocal attacks by liberals against the government during this period were nationalistic criticisms of the government's failure to obtain proper treaty revision, and, indeed, some joined the chorus attacking the general Europeanization program.[115]

Irrespective of minor attacks made upon it, the Meiji Constitution of 1889 was brought forth in splendor with the Imperial imprimatur; and, in the light of the philosophic battles between the liberal parties and the government, it is interesting to note their culmination in this document. In it there were some notable concessions to the Western philosophy of liberalism. Chapter ii, dealing with the "Rights and Duties of Subjects," paid homage to the concept of government by law, equality of rights to office within the limitations of the laws, freedom from arbitrary arrest and imprisonment, right of trial, and limited freedom of religion, speech, and the press.[116] These provisions constituted a notable change,

---

[113] Oka, *op. cit.*, pp. 288–289.

[114] An account of the publication of *Sei-tetsu yume monogatari* and its reception is given in Oka, *op. cit.*, p. 289.

[115] However much the liberals might be undermining their own bases when they encouraged antiforeignism and chauvinism, with such issues as treaty revision they were probably most clearly reflecting popular sentiment and speaking as the voice of the people. Here again, the role of the West stands out; unmindful of its own fundamental interests it was forging popular issues which could do Japanese liberalism no good. The struggle to be free was merged with the struggle to be powerful, and to this merger the liberals— both West and East—contributed in great measure.

[116] Article xxviii read: "Japanese subjects shall, *within limits not prejudicial to peace and order, and not antagonistic to their duties as subjects,* enjoy freedom of religious belief." (Italics mine.—R. A. S.) Article xxix read:

on paper at least, from the old feudal concept of government and the people. It must be noted, however, that few of the rights granted were absolute, and that much of the real meaning of the "civil liberties" clauses would depend upon the administration and the accompanying laws.[117]

The Constitution, moreover, established the first national assembly, for which the political parties had waged their campaign. The legislature, the Imperial Diet, was composed of two bodies with coequal power, the House of Peers and the House of Representatives. The former, with an insignificant exception, was purely appointive and could not be touched by popular vote.[118] The latter was to be elected by the people "according to the Law of Election."[119] It was in this house alone that political parties could have an effective voice, and it is therefore important to note the extent of its powers. In the main, they were of a negative character. Chapter iii, article xxxvii, stated, "Every law requires the consent of the Imperial Diet."[120]

Thus no administrative policy could be carried out without Diet approval, meaning concurrent Peer-House majority approval. Either house could initiate projects of law, but they required the countersignature of a minister of state, if passed.[121] The Diet was

---

"Japanese subjects shall, within the limits of law, enjoy the liberty of speech, writing, publication, public meetings and associations." From translation in *JGD*, p. 138.

[117] Almost without exception, the basic freedoms guaranteed by the Constitution were made contingent upon the "provisions of the law," meaning the administrative laws approved by the cabinet and ratified by the Diet. Note also article xxxi, which stated: "The provisions contained in the present Chapter [chap. ii] shall not affect the exercise of the powers appertaining to the Emperor in times of war, or in cases of national emergency." *Ibid.*

[118] The exception was with reference to the payers of the highest taxes; these representatives in the House of Peers were elected by the entire group of such taxpayers in the country, but formed only an insignificant part of the total number.

[119] The first Law of Election establishing suffrage requirements accompanied the Constitution; it is discussed in chapter vii of the present study.

[120] From translation in *JGD*, p. 139.

[121] In chapter iv, article lv, the Constitution states: "All laws, Imperial Ordinances, and Imperial Rescripts of whatever kind, that relate to the affairs of the State, require the countersignature of a Minister of State." *Ibid.*, p. 141. Moreover, the Privy Council could act as a check on Diet legislation by rejecting it. It should also be noted that when a Diet proposal had been rejected by the government, it could not be brought up a second time in the same session. Chapter iii, article xxxix. *Ibid.*

84

to be convoked once a year, with a regular session of only three months, prolonged if necessary by Imperial order. This and other similar provisions made it clear that the Constitution relegated the Diet to an inferior position vis-à-vis the ministers of state (cabinet) and did not make the latter responsible to the former. Indeed, the responsibility of the cabinet was to the Emperor alone: "The respective Ministers of State shall give their advice to the Emperor and be responsible for it." [122]

Thus the Diet could block administration laws, but its own proposals, to be effective, required acceptance by the cabinet; nor could it oust an unresponsive cabinet, since the executive branch was responsible to the Emperor alone. In case of a stalemate between the Diet and the cabinet, the latter had one strong "ace in the hole"; the traditional legislative control of the purse was carefully circumscribed by the provision that when a budget was not approved, the budget for the previous year automatically came into effect.[123] Thus, if the Diet proved recalcitrant, it could be dissolved even though no funds had been voted for the administration.

In theory, the powers of the Emperor remained well-nigh absolute; after proclaiming that the Emperor "is sacred and inviolable," [124] chapter i, article iv, stated: "The Emperor is the head of the Empire, combining in himself the rights of sovereignty, and exercising them according to the provisions of the present Constitution." [125]

Prince Ito attempted to explain the relationship of the Emperor to the Constitution in various writings and speeches, one of the most interesting of which is recorded from a speech at Otsu in 1889. On this occasion he said:

Under an absolute system of government the Sovereign's will is his command, and the Sovereign's command at once becomes law. In a constitutional country, however, the consent of that assembly which represents the people must be obtained. It will be evident, however, that as the supreme right is one and indivisible, the legislative power remains in the hands of the Sovereign and is not bestowed on the people. While the supreme right extends to everything and its exercise is wide and comprehensive, its legislative and executive functions are undoubtedly most important. These are in the hands of the Sovereign;

---

[122] Chapter iv, article lv. *Ibid.,* p. 141.
[123] Chapter vi, article lxxi. *Ibid.,* p. 143.
[124] Chapter i, article iii. *Ibid.,* p. 136.
[125] Chapter i, article iv. *Ibid.*

therefore cannot be held in common by the Sovereign and his subjects; but the latter are permitted to take part in the legislation according to the provisions of the Constitution.[126]

Ito's words left no doubt concerning the intended locus of power under the new Constitution. In his *Commentaries*, moreover, he struck out not only at the popular sovereignty theory, but at the "King in Parliament" theory as well:

In Europe within the last hundred years, it has happened that the turn of events has tended to favor the prevalence of extreme doctrines, and legislative matters have come to be regarded as specially falling within the powers of Parliament, the tendency being to hold that laws are contracts between the governing and the governed, and that in their enactment, the sovereign and the people have equal share. Such a theory arises out of a misconception of the principle of the unity of sovereignty. From the nature of the original polity of this country, it follows that there ought to be one and only one source of sovereign power of State. . . . The legislative power is ultimately under the control of the Emperor, while the duty of the Diet is to give advice and consent.[127]

One of the most important parts of any constitution is its amending clause, and here also, one may note the strength of the Throne. According to chapter vii, article lxxiii, constitutional amendments could be proposed only by Imperial ordinance, after which they had to be approved by a two-thirds vote of members present in both houses.[128] This provision ensured that the status quo could be changed only by the word of the Emperor and therefore was in strict accordance with the theory that the Constitution was his gift to the people.

One student of Meiji political developments has expressed the view that although the Sat-Cho oligarchy was driven to promulgating the Constitution, the document proved to be their salvation.[129] This observation contains a great deal of validity, for the new fundamental law not only upheld the absolute sovereignty

[126] "Count Ito on the Constitution," a speech at Otsu, 1889, translated in *JGD*, p. 618.

[127] Baron Ito Miyoji (trans.), *Commentaries on the Constitution of the Empire of Japan by Ito Hirobumi*, Tokyo, 1906, pp. 10–11.

[128] The Constitution, as translated in *JGD*, pp. 143–144.

[129] Suzuki Yasuzo, *Jiyuminken kempo happu*, p. 223. Professor Suzuki writes that the Constitution was both a means and an end—both a necessity to which its fathers were driven and a technique which proved to be their salvation. The Imperial Edict announcing the gift quieted for nine years what might otherwise have grown to be a full-scale rebellion, and thus it gave the

of the Throne (behind which worked the oligarchy), but also placed the Privy Council, the cabinet, and the House of Peers effectively out of any popular control. Moreover, the powers of the Diet were sufficiently limited to give popular government (through the House of Representatives) little positive power. At best, it could serve in the nature of an obstructionist force, unless the real rulers in the oligarchy were willing or compelled to accept responsibility before the legislative branch.

The effect of the Meiji Constitution on political party development was very great. Professor Sait, an American scholar, once defined "party" as follows: "Party may be defined as an organized group that seeks to control both the personnel and the policy of the government." [130]

From an institutional standpoint, the Meiji Constitution of 1889 made the attainment of either of these goals most difficult. Direct vote could affect only the House of Representatives, one part of the legislative branch, and a part with extremely limited authority. To control national policy it would be necessary to capture the administrative organ whose power also extended to the prefectures through its right to appoint prefectural governors. Without a system of cabinet responsibility, party control of government depended legally upon appointment by the Emperor, but actually upon the ability of party leaders to persuade the powers behind the Throne, most of whom were Satsuma and Choshu men, to agree to such a move. In 1890, with the oligarchy almost completely opposed to political parties, this seemed to be a dim hope.

The institutional structure of Japanese government and the philosophy on which it was based proved to be powerful deterrents to successful party growth. I have sought in this chapter to analyze the part which the emerging parties and the government played in arriving at "constitutional government," and in so doing, to high-light the major philosophic weaknesses of the Japanese party movement and some of the broad social factors which lay behind them.

On the credit side of the ledger, it must be written that by 1890 the political parties had succeeded in introducing the words of Rousseau, J. S. Mill, Bentham, Locke, Spencer, and a host of other

---

government nine years to mold the interpretations of the document so as to freeze the status quo.

[130] Edward M. Sait, *American Parties and Elections*, New York, 1927, p. 141.

Western liberals into Japanese intellectual currents. They had succeeded in getting government acceptance of political parties as an inevitable, if potentially dangerous, part of modern politics, to be limited as much as possible, but not to be prohibited absolutely.[131] And indeed, the "civil rights" parties must be given a great deal of credit for all the steps taken toward broader participation in government. Although they were not permitted to initiate the reforms themselves, their ideas and activities served to stimulate and coerce a somewhat reluctant oligarchy into instituting a rapid series of local and national reforms.

Despite these successes, the party movement was weak in more than a mere political sense, and its weakness was one that was very clearly evident in the inner philosophy of the parties themselves. Rising out of the political and economic demands of the ex-samurai class, the first political associations represented a militant liberalism which was usually more militant than liberal.[132]

---

[131] Ito, speaking to a meeting of the presidents of the prefectural assemblies on February 15, 1889, four days before the promulgation of the Constitution, stated: "It cannot be helped if, as the people acquire advanced political ideas, political parties grow, and if there are political parties there will be conflicts in the Diet. But it is absolutely necessary for the government to have no connections whatever with any political party. The sovereign power of the State resides in the Emperor; its exercise, therefore, must be absolutely independent of and impartial to all parties; so, to every subject, there will be 'equal recognition and equal benevolence.' If the Ministers of State who assist the Emperor and conduct the government with all its responsibilities have any relation with political parties, it is impossible for them to maintain this impartiality." From Ito's speech, as translated in George E. Uyehara, *The Political Development of Japan, 1867–1909*, London, 1910, p. 218. This is also evidence that Ito, one of the most enlightened of the oligarchy, had—publicly at least—forsaken the concept of a government party which he had earlier expressed in private and to which he would soon return.

[132] As final evidence on this point, note the principles of the *Kamikaze Jiyuto* (Divine Wind Liberty Party—or need it now be translated?), a district party of Mie Prefecture, affiliated with the national Jiyuto:

"When we turn our heads and look at the present conditions of England and France, England oppresses foreign countries with the English spirit and France showers threats upon the world with the French spirit, but in our country, since the Meiji Restoration, there has been an attempt to discard that great gift to the Japanese, the Japanese spirit. For this reason, we, in company with various samurai of like spirit, enter this party, vowing to organize this sentiment, and from now, to cause the Japanese spirit, which is based upon love of country [*aikoku*], to be spread over all the world to all countries, and to plan to withdraw the [foreigners'] extraterritoriality privileges." From the *Choya Shimbun* (*Newspaper of the Whole Nation*), December 16, 1882, quoted by Suzuki Yasuzo, *Jiyuminken kempo happu*, p. 220.

Indeed, it was the failure of the government to achieve a Korean campaign that produced the first political association dedicated to liberalism and began the curious alliance between the goals of internal reform and those of external expansion which existed in some form in Japanese politics throughout the period ending with World War II.

The reasons for this trend in the early parties are not hard to find. The parties were dominated by ex-samurai, and samurai grievances were of two major categories, power rivalry and economic collapse. The solution to the first was dictated by the impossibility of successful revolt; taking liberalism as their weapon and the party as their technique, the dissident samurai refurbished the weapons of what had been mainly an intraclass strife with new political symbolisms and presented them to "the public." A popularly elected national assembly was to be the means whereby Sat-Cho domination would be ended. As a solution to their economic problems, the samurai had first looked hopefully at the prospects of officeholding and military campaigns. Both offered employment consistent with their feudal heritage. The latter offered the additional advantage of placing Japan in her logical position in an imperialistic world and was a natural culmination of the nationalistic trend.

To embark successfully upon expansion, military or commercial, a strong and united nation was necessary; indeed, strength was important purely from a defensive point of view in the light of menacing Western imperialism. It was on this score that the liberals, after intently studying the Western liberal philosophy, acquired an earnest faith. They saw an alert and active people reaching great common decisions and providing the state with a solid foundation on which it could defend itself and expand. In their view, the inner weakness of the nation and the shameful abuses perpetrated upon her by the great Western powers were due to the lethargy of her ignorant people.

Whatever merit these conclusions had, they resulted in two major philosophic weaknesses in Japanese liberalism. The core of Western liberalism was its emphasis on man as an individual and as an end in himself; the liberals of Japan were driven to use man as a means toward the end of a power state. In the process, the most basic concepts of civil liberties, active political opposition, peaceful political change, and power sharing were minimized or distorted, even by the great majority of the "liberals" themselves. In the absence of these ideals, the parties were at once more ab-

89

solutistic in their goals and more factional in their make-up, fighting for exclusive power. Even the Kaishinto, with a less militaristic and chauvinistic aspect than the Jiyuto, was guilty of these imperfections.

As a second major weakness, and one connected with the first, the parties were never able or willing to meet the challenge of Imperial absolutism completely. The Japanese liberals were sufficiently under the sway of the nationalist movement and troubled by current foreign threats to reflect both a worship of unity and a reverence for the Emperor as the symbolism of that unity, and this attitude resulted in a considerable ambiguity in their central theses. It was the misfortune of liberalism to be born at a time when the rising star of Imperial symbolism had the full force of internal and external conditions to assist it. From the same samurai class that led the parties had come the slogan, "Revere the Emperor." Even the Jiyuto, despite its connections with popular sovereignty theories, was never able to do more than seek to join the Emperor and people in a mystic union of common desire that left logic and reality out of account. The Kaishinto, trying to use the end product of a long series of legal and traditional restrictions on the British monarch, was handicapped by the fact that the extralegal limitations on the Japanese Throne could be manipulated more skillfully by an oligarchic clique than by popular government.

Encumbered by these weaknesses, the parties were met by a government which, as we have seen, had ample practical and philosophic reserves at its command. Practically, it resorted to two techniques of ancient vintage, concession and repression. Each weakened the parties considerably. By the former, the government leaders succeeded in periodically drawing party spokesmen back into the fold, thus disrupting the opposition. Itagaki served with the government at a very critical juncture, and Okuma was Minister of Foreign Affairs at the time when the Constitution of 1889 was promulgated, actually signing the document which ensured a major victory to the oligarchy. Goto, as we shall see, was also given political office when he threatened to cause too much trouble. When concessions were not expedient, the government wielded numerous repressive edicts and laws, such as the Press Law and the Public Associations Law, to split up the parties, block their propaganda, and imprison their followers.

Correspondingly, the oligarchy presented strong philosophic arguments against the party movement. Political parties were factions, and thus ran counter to the whole tradition of the nation.

They festered the still unclosed wounds of feudalism by giving vent to the particularism of the districts and outside han, thus threatening to prevent the unity which the government was working so assiduously to bring about. As Ito wrote in condemning the "extremely democratic ideas," "In such a country as ours, it was evident that it would be necessary to compensate for its smallness of size and population by a compact solidity of organization and the efficiency of its administrative activity." [133]

Moreover, the demands of the parties, however worded, were attempts to limit the authority of the Emperor, in direct opposition to the goals of the Restoration and in line with the feudal system of older days. Furthermore, argued the government spokesmen, the liberal parties were led by politically frustrated men who sought to capitalize on the natural upheaval of a transitional period by advocating a system completely impossible in Japan's present stage of development. This was a potent argument.

In the end the oligarchy, not the parties, won the first and very important round of the battle. In the Constitution of 1889, as we have seen, were embedded major safeguards against popular government and correspondingly strong protections against party control. The struggle was far from over, however. Having put their heads in at the doorway to political power, the parties could hope that the course of economic and political trends would aid their advance, preparing the people for the task that representative government would assign them.

---

[133] Ito Hirobumi, "Some Reminiscences of the Grant of the New Constitution," in Okuma Shigenobu (ed.), *Fifty Years of New Japan,* London, 1910, Vol. I, p. 127.

THE POPULAR BASIS OF
EARLY JAPANESE PARTIES

THE HOPE of the Japanese party movement lay in its appeal to the commoners of the nation. They alone could provide the mass foundation which would, in the long run, justify the existence of the parties and make representative government something more than a façade behind which rival cliques struggled. Samurai predominance in the first political associations had tended to breed a quasi-liberal philosophy burdened with the values of an agrarian-warrior class. The addition of commoners, especially those with urban ties, might appreciably strengthen the new parties in philosophy as well as in numbers. The fate of liberalism and political party government depended upon the attainment of some degree of political maturity on the part of the public at a speed commensurate with the modernization of Japan.

This constituted an insuperable challenge. The commoners, who were debased by a social stigma which they themselves had for the most part resignedly accepted, and who for centuries had been denied both arms and education, were notoriously unequipped to take an important part in the political movements of the Meiji era. By the end of the Tokugawa period, however, the commoners of two groups—the commercial merchants and the landowners [1]— could be to some extent excepted from this generalization. Their comparative wealth within the quasi-feudal structure had brought many of them certain cultural and social advantages and a considerable amount of latent political power. The rising merchant

---

[1] The reference here to "landowners" is meant to apply to those outside the bushi class who during the latter stages of the Tokugawa era were accumulating land, receiving tenant income, and reducing the take of the bushi. This development has already been mentioned in the first chapter.

class, in particular, seemed to be the logical successors in political leadership to the bushi aristocracy. And of all the groups of commoners this class loomed as the pivotal one with regard to the party movement. The growth and nature of Japanese capitalism was certain to be the determinant factor in the development of liberalism and of the liberal party movement of the new era. The central question was whether Japanese capitalism could create an economy of sufficiency and a philosophy of individualism indispensable to the development of the liberal creed.

In the light of these necessities it is very important to view early party development and its sources of support in the context of the trends of Meiji capitalism. We shall observe that in the transition from commercial to industrial capitalism, the promising commercial merchant class of the Tokugawa period lost, in the main, its role of leadership. That role was taken largely by a part of the old bushi class working both within and outside of the government. The Meiji oligarchy was forced, as has already been indicated, to build, as rapidly as possible, an industrial capitalist structure largely under state auspices and to train and provide many new industrial leaders. It is important to understand that the overwhelming number of these new captains of industry came not from the old merchant class but from the ex-daimyo-samurai group. The "commercialization" of daimyo-samurai, which had been well under way in later Tokugawa times, developed to much greater proportions in the Meiji period, shunting the old commercial merchant class aside for the most part. And although the members of the bushi class who made a successful transformation were relatively few, they were extremely important in the picture of Japanese industrial capitalism.

Thus there were eminently good reasons for the inability of the new industrial capitalist class of Meiji Japan to act as the true exponents of a Western-style liberal state. Neither in structure nor in personnel was Meiji capitalism prepared to serve the cause of liberalism well. The great majority of Japanese capitalists were most at home in exclusive alliances with the professional politicians, alliances designed to direct the course of a generous paternalism. The Western bourgeois class came to possess a degree of self-reliance and a fear of omnipotent government not realizable by their Japanese counterparts, and it was from these feelings that the drive for a liberal state and its concomitant liberal techniques, such as party government, emerged.

We shall also observe that the party movement developed in

part out of a struggle between Japanese landed and urban capitalist groups. The earliest expressions of liberalism and the party movement came largely as an agrarian protest against urban capitalism and thus differed widely from the declarations of emergent liberalism in the West. The first political associations and the Jiyuto represented almost without exception the agrarian classes. To be sure, the landed entrepreneurs who formed a bulwark of strength within the Jiyuto were capitalist in nature, but for the most part they were opposed to and adversely affected by the development of urban industrial capitalism. To oppose this agrarian protest, a few leading industrialists interested themselves in a rival party, the Kaishinto. Thus each side was partly represented in the liberal movement, but neither group had a very clear understanding of or interest in the most basic aspects of the cause which its party sought to represent, and all but a few industrialists and landed entrepreneurs steered clear of the movement completely. As for the great masses, it was natural that they would make a small dent in the political activities of this period; their emancipation from a serflike status was too recent and too far from completion to permit of more. Some sparks of political consciousness showed in the peasant activities conducted under the banner of the Jiyuto, but when this movement ended in failure, the major lines of liberalism and all the important parties were completely dependent upon a small elite again, and the first suffrage regulations stabilized the situation for the time being. We must now turn to the more essential details of these important trends.

The party movement first emerged as a symbol of samurai unrest, economic as well as political. By 1874 the great majority of the samurai class had been reduced to the status of commoners in all except their inner raiment of education and pride. The abolition of the han system threatened to make the class a vast group of *ronin* (masterless samurai), and almost every samurai faced an ominous future.[2] The institution of conscription and the gradual reduction of class distinctions had destroyed his social

---

[2] Samurai distress was graphically illustrated by the removal of many daimyo to Tokyo and the decay of the old castle towns. Says Dr. Ono of daimyo-samurai decline: "Their mansions and neatly trimmed houses, which once adorned the outskirts of a feudal castle, have now fallen into ruin, the place where they once stood being covered with tea and mulberry trees. The immediate consequence of such a sudden disappearance of the feudal classes was to strike a deathblow to the prosperity of the castle towns." Ono Yeijiro, "The Industrial Transition in Japan," *Publication of the American Economics Association,* Vol. V, No. 1, January, 1890, p. 28.

status as a feudal warrior; the "hothouse cultivation" of capitalism, with its emphasis upon national wealth, had deprived him of his nonproductive special privileges. Except for those few who were to make a successful transition into business, farming, or politics, the samurai were the mournful symbol of a past era, puzzled and angry at the forces which were destroying them.[3]

Hence, in establishing the Risshisha educational program in the fall of 1874, Itagaki and his Tosa comrades were making an effort to rehabilitate a lost class.[4] The aim of the Risshisha educational program was to show the average young samurai how he could act in the face of a deteriorating economic, social, and political situation. If the Risshisha gave him the opportunity to study Western political philosophy and jurisprudence in the law school, it also offered to instruct him in trade and commerce in the business school. Moreover, the Risshisha undertook concrete measures of economic aid such as banding together to secure lower rates of interest.

Similar schools, of course, were operating in other districts, notably the Satsuma school of Saigo Takamori in the vicinity of Kagoshima. But Saigo's school concentrated heavily on the martial arts, and Saigo himself was soon obliged to lead his eager followers

---

[3] I have already briefly alluded to the pension system for the daimyo-samurai classes which was intended to ease the pain of overturning the feudal structure. The abandonment of this system had important political repercussions. In 1871, with the establishment of the prefectures in place of the old han, the central government had assumed payment of the samurai stipends hitherto paid by the han; and even though most of the individual payments were small, the collective burden on the government was prohibitive. The first step toward abolition was taken in 1873, when the government made it possible to obtain a cash settlement for the stipends and at the same time established a high stipend tax; in the ninth month of 1875—by which time about one-third of the stipend holders had settled—the government substituted a money payment for a rice payment, and in 1876 it took the important step of issuing public bonds in lieu of continued payments. By this, the shizoku (second-stratum nobility, below kazoku) became merely the possessors of some bonds representing the face value of several years of their stipend. With very few exceptions, the interest rate on the bonds did not come close to a basic income. Many sold their bonds, and in 1878 the government itself set up a system for buying the bonds. With this money some of the daimyo-samurai went into business; many, however, failed, and these and others took up such vocations as those of primary school teachers and police, or such lowly occupations as jinrikisha pulling and even common thievery. For details, see Oka Yoshitake, Kindai Nihon no keisei (The Foundation of Modern Japan), Tokyo, 1947, especially, pp. 207–209.

[4] Among similar organizations, one of considerable importance was known as the Jijosha (Self-Help Society).

into a hopeless and disastrous struggle. But Itagaki, in coöperation with various Tosa leaders, was trying to drive home one essential point: if the samurai were to be successful in their move to oust the Sat-Cho oligarchy, and if they were to better their economic plight, they had to coöperate with certain groups of the commoners. In the Risshisha literature it was stated that the samurai class could not protect its former position by retreating and falling back into the "vulgar narrow-mindedness" of the other three groups (farmers, artisans, and merchants). We must pool "our knowledge and heritage" with the real resources of these classes, and mutually compensate for each other's deficiencies.[5] "By causing the other groups to study the conditions of distress of the samurai group, we will defeat these causes and be saved . . . and this will strengthen all our people."[6]

Thus, even while retaining a certain superiority complex toward social inferiors, a few discerning samurai saw in these very classes their only salvation. This makes an understanding of the samurai-sponsored representative assembly movement easier. As the proponents of civil rights, the samurai were contributing their knowledge and political skill in the hope that it would attract the attention of those "wealthy farmers and merchants" who Itagaki felt should be immediately enfranchised. Through such an entente, greater pressure for remedial measures might be put upon the political authorities.

The results of this expressed desire to broaden the foundations of the civil rights movement culminated in the Jiyuto. Previously, as we have noted, such associations as the Aikokukoto, Aikokusha, and the Risshisha itself had been confined to the samurai class.[7] Only after the failure of the Satsuma Rebellion in 1877 and the increasing governmental pressure had forced the samurai dissidents into a realization of their political impotence was their inherent reluctance to affiliate with any *heimin* (commoner) group miti-

---

[5] Paraphrased and quoted from the *Risshisha bunken* (*Risshisha Literature*), quoted in full by Suzuki Yasuzo, *Jiyuminken kempo happu* (*Civil Rights and the Promulgation of the Constitution*), in Kindai Nihon rekishi koza (Modern Japanese History Series), Tokyo, 1939, pp. 14–16.

[6] *Ibid.*, p. 16.

[7] The Risshisha prospectus stated that membership was restricted to Tosa samurai and that a prospective member's village registration should be checked prior to his admission. "Risshisha kosetsu shuisho" (Prospectus of the Establishment of the Risshisha), document reproduced in Aono Kondo, *Nihon seito hensen shi* (*A History of Changes in Japanese Parties*), Tokyo, 1935 (pp. 9–12), p. 12.

gated. Thenceforth, the movement for "strength in depth" was intensified. In the second plank of their program, the Jiyuto leaders stated that newspapers must be published so as to expand liberty and cultivate public opinion; books must be printed and lectures given; membership drives and all other necessary undertakings must be started "to advance the principles of our party." [8]

The Jiyuto appeal brought the strongest response from two groups whose roots were in the rural areas, the upper landowner class and the peasantry. An explanation of this curious combination of support and its effect upon the party will contribute to an understanding of later developments in the liberal movement. First, however, the term "landowner" must be interpreted with some care. The important landowning class was composed primarily of three groups: certain wealthy farmers of the Tokugawa period, the ex-daimyo and some ex-samurai, and certain city investors who had acquired agrarian holdings.[9] In addition, there was a very substantial number of small landowners ranging down to various part-tenant, part-owner classifications; many within this larger group could be regarded as belonging in almost the same general category as mere tenants so far as their problems of livelihood were concerned. But despite the fact that landholdings in general tended to be small-scale, there was a considerable economic difference between the top and the bottom of the agrarian hierarchy, a difference that was increasingly magnified by the events of the early Meiji period.[10] Within the landowning class

---

[8] From "Jiyuto kessei sosoku" (General Regulations for the Establishment of the Jiyuto), reproduced in Aono, op. cit., pp. 44–45. The great organ of the Jiyuto was the Kochi Shimbun (shimbun is the Japanese term for newspaper), a Tosa journal with power and influence great enough to frighten even the government. Another Jiyuto paper of considerable importance was the Tosei-Gyosho Shimpo. The Jiyuto, however, was comparatively weak in its press organs, and we shall soon note the relative strength of the Kaishinto.

[9] Many of the district landowners, even of the "wealthy farmer group," were "semisamurai"; that is, many were myoji taito gomen no iegara (of families privileged to wear the sword and have a surname), as a result of the blurring of class lines during the latter stages of the Tokugawa period. These links undoubtedly helped to smooth the path toward alliance. See Osatake Takeshi and Hayashi Shigeru, "Seiji" (Politics), in Gendai Nihon shi kenkyu (Studies of Contemporary Japanese History), Tokyo, 1938, p. 81.

[10] The Meiji Restoration replaced the feudal-type land rules with a Westernized legal protection of individual property rights, drawing clear distinctions between landowners and tenants. In addition, the land-tax reforms of the early Meiji period substantially reduced the burden of the landowners. Professor Ono estimates that their total burdens after the early tax reforms

itself there was another type of division between the "pure" land-owner, whose interests were wholly agrarian, and the landowner-entrepreneur who combined agrarian pursuits with small-scale production or manufacturing. It will be remembered that a sizable part of the commercial development in Tokugawa Japan had rested upon the rise of district enterprises relating to indigenous products and closely connected with the agrarian villages and castle towns. Thus the landowner was also in many cases a district entrepreneur who had investments in *shoyu* (soy sauce), *miso* (bean paste), fertilizer, silk, spinning, or some of the many other district indus-tries.[11] Elements from both the pure landowner and the landed entrepreneurial groups took a special interest in an antigovernment movement, because, notwithstanding certain advantages bestowed upon them, they blamed their economic difficulties primarily upon the policies of the Meiji government, especially the oligarchy's emphasis upon urban industrialization.

In order to understand contemporary and future political de-velopments it is necessary at this point to summarize briefly the economic aspects of early Meiji policy.[12] At the beginning of the Restoration, as we have previously noted, the commercial merchant class was of great value to the Imperial cause. Large merchant houses such as Mitsui, Ono, and Shimada had helped to finance the Imperial armies and tide over a critical period in the early days of the new government. Despite this fact, however, the Restoration was not carried out by the commercial class, nor was it intended originally to be a victory for capitalism. Even before their final success, however, many of the young leaders had become skeptical of the ideal of restoring the ancient agrarian regime, as the con-tinuous pressure of Western imperialism rendered this program

---

amounted to about 10 per cent of the production value, as compared with about 30 per cent or more during the Tokugawa period. See Ono Yeijiro, *op. cit.*, pp. 90–91. The tenants, on the other hand, reaped few, if any, advantages from the Restoration, as we shall later observe. However, as is indicated be-low, the landowners had numerous grievances. Payment of taxes in money increased their dependency upon urban markets, government expenses in connection with urban industrialization necessitated tax increases, and al-though land values showed great rises, the landowner tended to feel that he had been forsaken in favor of urban industry.

[11] See Hirano Yoshitaro, *Nihon shihonshugi shakai no kiko* (*The Mecha-nism of Japanese Capitalist Society*), Tokyo, 1934, pp. 177–178, and espe-cially p. 181.

[12] For a scholarly analysis of this whole topic, see Horie Yasuzo, *Nihon shihonshugi no seiritsu* (*The Establishment of Japanese Capitalism*), Tokyo, 1939. I am much indebted to Professor Horie's painstaking research.

98

unfeasible and uninteresting. Moreover, some of these men were men of experience in the commercialization activities of their han in the later Tokugawa period. Thus it was not difficult for the new Meiji government to accept speedy industrialization along Western lines as the major answer to Japan's problems. Only in this way could the rapid outflow of capital to the West be stopped, the internal economic structure be set in some kind of order, and the nation be made economically, politically, and militarily strong.

It soon became clear, however, that the commercial merchants could not make the rapid transition from commercial to industrial capitalism which the Meiji leaders considered to be so crucial. They lacked the requisite massive capital accumulation, because of the restrictive nature of the feudal markets; and their long conversance with old methods had made them innately conservative and hence, for the most part, quite unwilling to adopt the new ideas, learn the new techniques, and take the great risks that expansion and modernization required.[13] In a period of transition and confusion, moreover, many old and distinguished houses went bankrupt, some of them the pillars of Tokugawa commerce.

It therefore became incumbent upon the government itself to plan and execute the major part of the new industrialization program. As has previously been noted, the precedents for this had been well established in the Tokugawa period. It should be emphasized, however, that the basic motivation was not that of great prejudice against private enterprise; on the contrary, the Western concepts of economic liberalism had a considerable impact and the Meiji oligarchy was most anxious to induce the moneyed classes to invest their funds and their energies in industrial activities. Indeed, a large part of the government's efforts was directed toward the education of capitalists. To this end it set up model factories, hired foreign experts, and granted amazing subsidies and similar inducements.

The old commercial merchant class, however, with a few leading exceptions, was slow to be entranced by these developments. It continued to lack "the progressive spirit"; many failed during the hectic days following the Restoration, others were content to continue in the more cautious ways of the past, and not a few were willing to live off their acquired savings.[14] Under these circumstances, the government, if it wished to carry out the industrialization program in a hurry, had no alternative except to do a

[13] For a detailed analysis, see *ibid.*, pp. 53–59, 237–241.
[14] *Ibid.*, p. 332.

large part of it by means of state industries. Thus, the basic industries in the early period, almost without exception, were owned and operated by the government. Even those industries which were not directly operated by government were subsidized very heavily by public funds.

And since the commercial merchant class manifested a great measure of indifference and ineptitude, the ex-samurai and ex-daimyo groups offered a fruitful field in which to acquire new leaders for capitalist development. Although most of them lacked the necessary capital,[15] they—especially the ex-samurai—had the enterprising spirit born of past leadership and administrative experience. As an added inducement to the government, the oligarchy could not fail to be impressed with the danger of continued economic unrest among this very powerful group.[16] This fact, after all, had been a major reason for the political opposition which took the form of liberalism and the party movement. Moreover, it was only natural that class favoritism and personal connections would play an important part in determining the direction of governmental aid.

Thus the industrial capitalism which emerged under the guiding hand of the government had a structure and personnel quite different from that of Tokugawa commercial capitalism. In every respect it was heavily dependent upon government protection and aid. The government abandoned many of its holdings after 1880, for fiscal and other reasons,[17] but the structure of private industry continued to be marked by close government-business interrelationships, semimonopolism in the basic fields dominated by a few great financial cliques, and an interlocking of financial and industrial power. Equally interesting was the composition of the new

[15] Actually, many of the daimyo had a considerable amount of wealth; the huge debts owed to the merchants were diminished or removed in the confusion of the Restoration, large areas of land and huge homes became their private property, and the lump payment of their pensions provided a sizable amount of capital.

[16] *Ibid.*, p. 267.

[17] The chief reason for the sale of government-owned plants was financial; the fact that they were not paying off was placing a heavy financial strain on the treasury. By this time, moreover, the necessity for model factories was somewhat lessened, and by selling the holdings very cheaply to private parties, government leaders hoped to appease some of the discontented ex-samurai elements and thereby meet the pressure of the liberal movement. Favoritism inevitably accompanied the transactions, however, and only a relatively few well-placed financial groups and individuals benefited. *Ibid.*, pp. 266–267.

industrial capitalist class; there were a few industrialists who had made the transition from the old commercial capitalist group, the largest of whom was the Mitsui family,[18] but there were many new leaders, of whom a large number came from the ex-samurai and ex-daimyo groups. The success of these men, of course, did not alter the fact that the greater number of their bushi compatriots continued to be in sad economic straits, especially ex-samurai reduced to the lower classes and those whose personal connections with the oligarchy were weak. Personal favoritism was important, and this combined with traditional bushi training and a strong economic dependency to make the basis of a liberal philosophy among the business class exceedingly shallow.

It should not be difficult to understand why there was agrarian resentment against the government program. When the government emphasized industrialization, it was concentrating largely upon urban capitalism, not upon the rural entrepreneurial structure. It was logically felt, of course, that such industries as shipbuilding, military supplies, and heavy manufacturing in general were of the greatest importance, and that these, for the most part, had to be urban. It was necessary to support this program through the land taxes and miscellaneous taxes. The whole transition, moreover, involved a trend away from the agrarian-centered economy and an increased agrarian dependency upon urban centers, a trend for which the Tokugawa regime had been roundly castigated.

Thus, the Jiyuto inaugural meeting of October, 1881, was attended by a strong representation of district *sake* (rice wine) manufacturers who were present to protest the taxes listed under the name of increased naval vessel expenditures.[19] In their remonstrance they raised the cry of "freedom of industry" and affiliated themselves with Itagaki's party. This was but one group among other district entrepreneurial interests who, together with some purely landed elements, constituted the backbone of the party.[20]

---

[18] Even Mitsui, as we shall see, was forced to rely heavily on the protection of such leaders as Inoue Kaoru, and to include in its managerial staff ex-bushi like the famous Nakamigawa Hikojiro.

[19] Itagaki himself wrote, "The Sake Confederation, which had already been inaugurated in 1880, became, from the first, one of the most important parts of the Jiyuto." Itagaki Taisuke, *Jiyuto shi* (*History of the Jiyuto*), Tokyo, 1913, Vol. I, p. 616.

[20] It is important to note that the inflationary period following the Satsuma Rebellion gave way to deflation in 1881, and produced a severe depression in agriculture, especially noticeable because of the more rigid monetary taxation system which by that time was in effect.

From these came not only the lion's share of the funds that went into district and national party coffers, but also part of the leadership. Never large in numbers, they were, nevertheless, a substantial element of the party.

Despite its nucleus of landowner groups, however, the Jiyuto became involved with the peasants and tenant farmers. Their relation to the party is one of the most interesting and revealing aspects of the early party movement and requires somewhat detailed treatment. The burden of the tenant farmer had not been lessened by his release from feudalism; it was, indeed, greater in many respects than before. The basis of capital accumulation for industrialization, in the absence of colonies or other means, was agriculture, and this burden fell heavily upon the tenant peasant. He had been emancipated from the land, but this was a detriment rather than an advantage, under conditions which caused him to yearn for security. Whereas he had once shared in the honor of all members of the agrarian class as the chief producer, he and his fellow tenant peasants were now relegated to a special group below that of the private landowners. He continued to pay land rent in kind at extremely high rates, and thus benefited less from the inflationary period than the landowner. Indeed, as the cost of living rose, with manufactured goods pouring into the rural areas and money wages for industrial work rising in comparison with farm income, his plight became worse. Moreover, in 1881 the Matsukata policy of reducing paper money caused a fall in rice prices, inaugurating a period of acute suffering among the lower agrarian classes. These problems were accentuated by the fact that peasant handicrafts, such as cotton spinning and sugar-cane refining, were being destroyed by machine manufacturing. There were other grievances as well: conscription and the enforced public works programs, as we shall note, were tremendously unpopular. These accumulated grievances might have resulted in another series of feudal-type riots with solely economic implications, had it not been for the fact that the civil rights doctrines of the Jiyuto were simultaneously being propagated in the districts. The result was an agrarian reform movement which flew, in some small measure, the banners of Western liberalism.

It must be emphasized that much of the peasant movement between 1881 and 1885 had only an indirect connection with the Jiyuto, and in many cases, none at all; the economic demands bore some relationship to Jiyuto demands; political doctrines of civil rights were often used, and left-wing Jiyuto leaders provided some guidance and support, but the number of peasants who were actually party members was relatively insignificant.[21] It was, however, from the actions of this group that the party drew most of its explosive qualities; these actions divided the samurai leadership and finally produced the results leading to temporary party dissolution. When it reappeared on the political horizon, the Jiyuto had become a more unified party, without peasants and most of the ex-samurai extremists.

The government and the opposition parties naturally concentrated their fire upon the peasant-radical elements in the Jiyuto, a task made easier because in activity they were more conspicuous than the conservative components of the party. Thus one observer was moved to write: "The thing called *Jiyuminken* [civil rights] of that time was a movement in opposition to the government in which the spirit of farmer rebellion and direct redress was coupled with the ronin who were Imperial loyalists and foreign exclusionists." [22]

The question why the leadership was unable to control the activities of their left wing can be answered by two facts. In the first place, the samurai leadership itself was not united on any concrete program of economic or political action, and there were samurai radicals, such as Oi Kentaro, who were not averse to making the peasant movement and radicalism the core of the party. Much more important, it was natural that in any predominantly agrarian political movement, the centrifugal tendencies would be great, and effective coördination almost impossible. This lack of cohesiveness was abetted, moreover, both by the government and the actions of party leaders. In June, 1882, only a few months after Ito had been dispatched to Europe in preparation for the promised Constitution, the government passed a series of stringent amendments to the Public Meetings Law, designed to cripple the growth of political parties. Any centralized control of district party organizations or activities was henceforth made almost impossible.[23] Moreover, in November of the same year, Itagaki and Goto,

---

[21] The parallelisms with the contemporary Communist movement in Asia contained here are striking.

[22] From Uchida Roano, "Shinkyu jidai" (New and Old Eras), in *Jiyuminken no omoide* (*Recollections of Civil Rights*), quoted by Osatake Takeshi, *Nihon kensei shi taiko* (*An Outline of Japanese Constitutional History*), Tokyo, 1939, Vol. II, p. 616.

[23] Article viii, as amended, read: "No political association for the purpose of lecturing or deliberating on politics may advertise a summary of the discourses, excite the public by sending out commissioners or circulars, or cor-

the two Jiyuto leaders, started a tour of Europe, leaving the party bereft of national leadership.

With a new weapon in their hands, the peasants and radical civil rights proponents in the districts could stand only a certain amount of baiting by bureaucratic repression and worsening economic straits. Then they struck back in a series of local riots and mob actions which were uncoördinated enough to be failures, but sufficiently disturbing to confirm the suspicions of the government that the Jiyuto was a dangerous instigator of dissension. One of the first major incidents which alarmed the government was the so-called "Fukushima Affair" of 1883. The Governor of Fukushima Prefecture was a product of the bureaucracy who had once stated that he "would not even put the Jiyuto in as high a category as fire-setting thieves [the worst possible Japanese epithet]." [24] On the occasion of his taking office, he is reported to have said, "I have taken my post with three private orders from the government. The destruction of the Jiyuto is the first, aiding the Teiseito is the second, and building roads is the third." [25]

Whether this report was authentic or not, the Governor set about exactly those tasks. By extremely repressive measures, a public works program was established which included increased taxation and enforced labor.[26] Immediately the Fukushima Prefectural Assembly, which was headed by Kono Hironaka, a Jiyuto stalwart, objected violently and rejected the measure.[27] The Governor pro-

---

respond and join together with other similar societies." Translated in *JGD*, p. 500.

[24] Quoted in Osatake, *op. cit.*, Vol. II, p. 649.

[25] Quoted from Kono Hironaka, *Kono Iwasu den* (Memoirs of Kono Iwasu [Hironaka]), by Suzuki Yasuzo, *op. cit.*, p. 226.

[26] By browbeating village representatives with "wrestlers" and *soshi* (strong-arm men), the authorities had forced them to approve a public works fund of ¥370,000. Men and women from fifteen to sixty years of age were ordered to work one day each month for two years, and taxes in the form of "patriotic money" were to be levied at the rate of 15 sen per day per man, 10 sen per day per woman. See *ibid.*, pp. 469–470.

This system was of course in line with traditional Japanese procedures. It is interesting to note the use of soshi by the authorities, for this came to be one of the great evils of the parties at a later time.

[27] The forty-six prefectural assemblies established in 1878 formed the first focal point for political opposition, even though their powers were extremely limited. Members, to be eligible, had to be males over the age of twenty-five, paying a land tax of ¥10 or more. They were elected by male subjects over the age of twenty (except teachers in public schools, military men, lunatics, and criminals) who paid a land tax of ¥5 or more.

The term was four years, and the assembly was convoked for a period of

ceeded to send more than fifty of the dissenters to Tokyo for prosecution on charges of "riotous sedition."

Scarcely four months later, similar incidents occurred in Gumma Prefecture. In Ibaraki Prefecture, opposition to conscription for labor on public works and to increased taxation took even more violent forms. A group of men styling themselves the "Revolutionary Action Soldiers" issued a manifesto of which the following is a part:

Indeed the necessity of founding a state is in making clear the ideal of each person's equality and in establishing each individual's divinely bestowed happiness and rights. The men who constitute the government should increase the freedom entirely on these aims. Those of our belief will overthrow the arbitrary government of those who recklessly promulgate cruel laws and harsh edicts and carry out oppression, thus making themselves public enemies of freedom, by raising an army of revolution here; and it is our desire to build a completely liberal constitutional polity.[28]

The connection between this philosophy and that of the Jiyuto was too clear to be missed; the seeds of liberalism were sprouting rapidly in the lush fields of popular unrest.

The years 1883 and 1884 saw violence reach an alarming climax. Attempted assassinations and bombings swept over the districts, and many of these acts were traced to the extremist elements of the Jiyuto. In Tochigi Ken, a plot by the nephew of Kono Hironaka and others to massacre the ministerial councillors at a ceremony opening the prefectural office was discovered in time to postpone the opening, but attacks were made upon police stations and wealthy merchants.[29] In the summer of 1884 certain members of the Nagoya Jiyuto, planning to overthrow the government, raised funds by counterfeiting paper money, robbing rich men's houses, and actually attacking government offices.[30]

The zenith was reached with the Chichibu Rebellion of October, 1884.[31] With slogans of "Reduce land taxes," "Cancel debts,"

only one month per year; all decisions were subject to the approval of the governor, and the assemblies had no real legislative power.

[28] Quoted in Itagaki, op. cit., Vol. II, p. 248.

[29] Detailed discussions of these episodes are to be found in Otsu Junichiro, Dai Nihon kensei shi (A Constitutional History of Greater Japan), Tokyo, 1927–1928, Vol. II, p. 308; also Osatake, op. cit., Vol. II, p. 649.

[30] Osatake, op. cit., Vol. II, p. 651.

[31] Hirano states that this rebellion marked the climax of peasant activity in the Jiyuto. Subsequently, heavy government repressions and opposition among Jiyuto leaders over the use of violence reduced their activities. See

"Exempt tenants," "Amend conscription laws," and "Reduce village expenses," a mob of more than one thousand rioters attacked government offices, police stations, courts, and wealthy homes. Peasants, gamblers, and others burned land deed certificates, seized and divided up goods, and attacked landlords. Only after days of rioting was the situation tranquilized, and more than three thousand persons were said to have been punished.[32]

The Jiyuto in the course of its first three years had been connected with a series of district incidents culminating in mass agrarian riots. The reasons are not hard to find. The period between 1881 and 1885 was a period of extreme agrarian distress with widespread starvation in the countryside. Everywhere, the peasantry, often spearheaded by ex-samurai of the lower ranks who were now destitute, were rising up in sporadic waves of violence.

These uprisings were essentially economic in character, but their connection with the Jiyuto political and economic goals was clear. Such objectives as the reduction of high-interest loans and tax relief were cardinal points in the Jiyuto program. Moreover, leadership and the political overtones of the disturbances were frequently provided by the left-wing factions of the Jiyuto. The numerous debtor and tenant parties which were forming in the provinces carried political proposals almost identical to those of the Jiyuto in their platforms.

This markedly violent manifestation of peasant unrest produced two results significant for the Jiyuto. It gave the government an excellent opportunity to strike at the popular movement, and it split the party itself irrevocably. While the Jiyuto left wing was actually raising funds for various "people's armies," government observers were busily detecting these activities. When Itagaki returned from abroad in June, 1883, he found his party hated and feared by officialdom as never before. During Itagaki's political tours, the government went so far as to interfere with his lodging accommodations and speaking schedules. Police surveillance was omnipresent, and bills screaming epithets such as "Fire-setting robber-Jiyuto" were plastered in areas where he was to appear.[33]

Hirano, *op. cit.*, p. 178, also p. 184. Hirano has written a special monograph on "The Chichibu Incident," which appeared in *Rekishi Kagaku*, December, 1933.

[32] This estimate and other details of the affair are quoted from Itagaki, *op. cit.*, Vol. II, p. 302.

[33] The posters bearing the term "Hoka-dorobo Jiyuto" were intended to stir up public sentiment against the destructive violence of the left-wing party members. *Ibid.*, p. 341.

Mass arrests were made, and political prisoners spent months in prison without benefit of trial.

Meanwhile, the cleavage developing within the party itself was becoming serious.[34] The extremist group led by such men as Oi Kentaro urged that everything be risked, even "direct action" if necessary, to force the government's hand.[35] The conservative faction known as the Hoshi (Hoshi Toru) group was opposed to the program of violence; although this group included the majority of leaders and landed donors, it was powerless, in the face of legal restrictions, to control the party branches. As a result, funds for the party became very low, for men of means, frightened by fear of government retaliation and opposed to the waves of violence, refused to contribute any money. On October 29, 1884, just after the Chichibu Rebellion, the Jiyuto in convention voted formally to dissolve, thus temporarily bringing a halt to one very large segment of the party movement.

As an effort to stir up popular support, the Jiyuto had had a measure of success, ending in failure. Of all the groups of commoners, it was the poverty-stricken and uneducated peasants who had formed whatever mass basis the party had. The two greatest weaknesses in this trend were the centrifugal tendencies of an agrarian movement and the inability of the peasantry to play a constructive, long-range role on behalf of the liberal cause. An examination of the *Jiyuto Kaiin Meibo* (*Official Register of the Jiyuto*) clearly reveals the paucity of members. In October, 1881, the registered membership listed by party headquarters was 101;

---

[34] "The knowledge that there were clearly two views which were different [within the Jiyuto] came about the time of the Jiyuto general meeting in the winter of 1883. At this time the divergence was already distinct." Suzuki Yasuzo, *op. cit.*, p. 252.

[35] The most bizarre episode of all was perpetrated by this group after the dissolution of the party in 1885. Oi Kentaro, Kobayashi Kazuo, Arai Shogo, and others decided to produce a "liberal revolution" in Korea. Stating that "just as the French aided American independence, we are arising because of the great principles involved, to aid Korea, bringing about an independent and free country," they proceeded to collect more than ¥3,000 by threatening rich men, store up a quantity of ammunition, and gather a small "army." The scheme was discovered in November, 1885, and by the following year more than one hundred and thirty men had been arrested.

Okubo Kishichi, Oi's great friend, later wrote that the extremists thought that this action would mean war with China, in which case even the han-clique government would see the need for national unity and grant constitutional government. This statement, along with other details, can be found in *ibid.*, pp. 244–245.

in May, 1884, just a few months before the dissolution of the party, the membership totaled only 2,187.[36] Of course these figures are somewhat misleading, for many members were in prison or dead by 1884, and most authorities are agreed that this list is incomplete in various ways.[37] Nevertheless, it is clear that although there was some foundation for the charge that Jiyuto radicals were agitating the peasants, very few of the peasants themselves were enrolled party members.

The centralized leadership remained primarily with a small group of samurai intellectuals, landowners, and district entrepreneurs who did not relish the trend of developments. Owing to the decentralized nature of party development and the restrictions of government decrees, however, they were powerless to control the activities of their more zealous branches. In a few samurai like Oi Kentaro and Kobayashi Kazuo, the revolting peasants found their real leaders, and the words and actions of this group seemed to justify the claim that the Jiyuto had become a revolutionary party. They were men to whom terrorism seemed the only method of producing change. By 1885, however, the peasant riots and radical plots had been smashed, and the Jiyuto lay in scattered fragments until almost the eve of the promulgation of the Constitution. In the revived party, conservative leaders and ideas held undisputed sway; a movement which in its beginning stages had borne some relation to the whole gamut of agrarian social and economic problems became the secure instrument of the propertied agrarian class, with increasing support from industrial groups as well.

If the Jiyuto garnered its support from the rural areas, Okuma's Kaishinto was based on urban recruits. Its nucleus was composed of urban intellectuals and upper bourgeois who desired a party less "radical" than the Jiyuto and less addicted to purely agrarian interests.[38] Okuma, aided by Fukuzawa, gathered around him

[36] Quoted from the *Jiyuto Kaiin Meibo* of October, 1881, and May, 1884, by Suzuki Yasuzo, *Jiyuminken* (*Civil Rights*), Tokyo, 1948, p. 173. All district parties were required to file membership lists with headquarters, based on a biennial tabulation. The October, 1881, records were the first; they were taken from the delegates at the first convention.

[37] Professor Osatake, for instance, points out that the Kyushu Jiyuto and several other district parties did not affiliate themselves formally with the national party. Moreover, the whole period was one of such confusion that party records were never accurate. See Osatake, *op. cit.*, Vol. II, p. 826.

[38] In a letter to Okuma just before the organization of the Kaishinto, Numa Moriichi, editor of the *Tokyo-Yokohama Mainichi*, urged the Hizen politician

several student-intellectual groups whose enthusiasm for Western, and particularly British, ideas made them logical leaders. One of these circles was the *Oto Kai* (Gull Society),[39] an organization of Tokyo University students led by Ono Azusa, Okuma's chief confidant. Another group of equal importance was the Keio University faction, which took the title *Toyo Giseikai* (Oriental Parliamentary Society). These young men were all disciples of Fukuzawa, and included such future leaders as Inukai Tsuyoshi (Ki) and Ozaki Yukio.[40] Many of the students from both groups had been with the government but had left the bureaucracy at the time of Okuma's resignation. A third important faction within the party was the *Tokyo-Yokohama Mainichi* (*Tokyo-Yokohama Daily*) newspaper group led by Numa Moriichi. This major paper and the *Hochi Shimbun* (*News-Dispatch*)—the latter of which had been purchased by Okuma and was being managed by Keio men—became the leading organs of the Kaishinto.[41]

Outside the intellectual and newspaper ranks, the Kaishinto found support among a few of the commercial-industrial figures. The greatest patron of the party was Iwasaki Yataro, head of the Mitsubishi interests. Iwasaki, an ex-samurai of the lower class, was building up a great industrial house and had already made a fortune by obtaining government contracts on shipping; these con-

---

to form a party which could oppose the agrarian interests in the forthcoming Diet. Letter quoted in Osatake Takeshi, *Meiji seiji shi tembyo* (*Sketches in Meiji Political History*), Tokyo, 1938, p. 155.

[39] The name *Oto Kai*, which was formed by adding together the characters *O*, meaning "gull," and *to*, meaning "to cross," was selected because the students crossed the river to discuss politics. For details of this organization, see Hayashida Kametaro, *Nihon seito shi* (*History of Japanese Political Parties*), Tokyo, 1927, Vol. I, p. 169.

[40] Although Fukuzawa was one of the most generous contributors to the Japanese liberal movement, his attitude toward politics was conservative; it was typified by the motto he is said to have coined: "Internal peace, external competition" (*naian gaikyo*). Sugiyama Heisuke, "Shakai" (Society), in *Gendai Nihon shi kenkyu* (*Studies of Contemporary Japanese History*), Tokyo, 1938, p. 19.

[41] In enjoying the benefits of press organs, the Kaishinto had a distinct advantage over the Jiyuto; in addition to having the *Mainichi* and *Hochi*, the party was also supported by the *Choya* and numerous other papers. Although the press was beginning to influence public opinion, circulation was still fairly small. The *Choya* had a circulation of about 12,000; *Hochi*, Okuma's personal paper, about 5,000. These figures and other interesting details are given in Inukai Ki, *Daigaku Hyoron*, August, 1917, pp. 72–83, quoted at length in Kawabe Kisaburo, *The Press and Politics in Japan*, Chicago, 1921, pp. 84–87.

tracts were garnered mainly through a close affiliation with Okuma at the time when he was a part of the oligarchy. Concerning this friendship there were many unsavory rumors, and it was openly alleged that Iwasaki was seeking to ensure a bribed Diet and a return to power of Okuma in order to promote his own economic interests.[42]

Iwasaki himself was not reticent in admitting his heavy contribution to the Kaishinto. He is reported to have said, "If they call me a national robber, it is because they fear that they see me destroying the Jiyuto and the han government by bending all my resources to aid the Kaishinto." [43]

The Mitsubishi-Kaishinto alliance, later to be duplicated by a parallel arrangement between Mitsui and the Jiyuto,[44] marked the beginning of an intimacy between industrial-financial interests and political parties which culminated in serious repercussions for both. Broad public support for the party as expressed in party membership was even more negligible than with the Jiyuto. One tabulation of Kaishinto strength shows it with twenty-nine branches and a little more than 1,000 members.[45] The influence of the Kaishinto, especially with the articulate groups, was obviously much greater than this would indicate, and by means of its press, it had considerable influence among the people who made up the small but growing urban middle class. The mass of urbanites, however, were no better equipped by education or tradition than the agrarian masses to participate in a sustained political movement.

Even the urban merchants and industrialists, for the most part,

---

[42] The government accused Mitsubishi of wishing to ensure a bribed Diet which would overlook the fact that the company owed the government ¥2,000,000 and eleven ships which had been loaned to it. Letter from Kaneko Kentaro to Sasaki Takayoshi, quoted in Osatake, *Meiji seiji shi tembyo*, p. 146. Kaneko also stated that Fukuzawa was given ¥8,000 as expense money for the new movement by Mitsubishi in the fall of 1881. It was currently reported that the same company had contributed ¥12,000 to buy an Osaka newspaper for the party. *Ibid.*

Professor Osatake feels that the evidence clears Fukuzawa completely of any political immorality, whatever relationship existed between Okuma and Iwasaki.

[43] Quoted from Yamamichi Aisan, *Iwasaki Yataro*, p. 246, in Hirano, *op. cit.*, p. 185.

[44] Mitsui had furnished the money for Goto's and Itagaki's trip abroad, unbeknown to the latter.

[45] From the Kaishinto Register, quoted by Suzuki Yasuzo, *Jiyuminken*, p. 182.

remained aloof from the party movement, despite the fact that the bulk of whatever "popular" support the Kaishinto had, came from this group. Considering the conditions of urban capitalism as they have been briefly outlined, this situation should be most understandable. In the first place, the commoners within this group, quite as much as the other commoners, lacked any background suitable for political participation. The most important point, however, was the fact that capitalism during this period, even private industrial capitalism, was so heavily dependent upon government support that few men either wanted or dared to defy the Sat-Cho oligarchy. Iwasaki himself, as we shall see, came perilously close to being put out of business for his frontal assault upon the government. The result was that the party represented a small group of intellectuals, many of them young samurai, and a relatively few middle-class interests, almost wholly from the urban centers. By far the most important among the latter was the powerful Mitsubishi Company. The Kaishinto was temporarily driven into retirement along with the Jiyuto in the latter part of 1884. Although it did not dissolve, Okuma and the vice-president, Kono Toshikama, resigned.

In addition to the two liberal parties, there was, of course, the Teiseito, but it could hardly contain a large element of commoners, dedicated as it was to the support of the government. Its thin ranks were composed mainly of government officials, office seekers, classical scholars, and a number of Shinto priests. It was backed by several newspaper men, notable among whom was Fukuchi Genichiro, editor of the semiofficial newspaper, the *Nichi Nichi Shimbun*.[46] Never important as a popular movement, the Teiseito sought to serve the government as its party representative; the Sat-Cho leaders, however, were considerably embarrassed by the strategic weakness of being supported by one of several factions when they were maintaining the fiction of unity. With the increase of official pressure, which made its position unnecessary, the Teiseito was quietly dissolved in September, 1883.

For a time after 1885, political parties ebbed in strength almost to the point of extinction. Thousands of peasants, party adherents, and assorted radicals were in prison; the heart of the agrarian radi-

---

[46] Suzuki Yasuzo, *Jiyuminken*, pp. 192–193. The three principal men in the party were all editors of conservative newspapers: Fukuchi of the *Nichi Nichi Shimbun*; Maruyama Sakura of the *Meiji Nippo*; and Mizuno Torajiro, former Risshisha member, of the *Toyo Shimpo*. Hayashida, *op. cit.*, Vol. I, p. 175.

cal movement had been broken. To the overwhelming majority of the population, however, this fact was probably of little moment —indeed, of little knowledge. At the time of the Restoration, the "people," to use Ito's words, were "merely a numerical mass of governed units"; [47] that status had not been greatly changed as yet, despite the myriad transformations which had taken place.

And the "economic elite" of early Meiji society offered only the most limited support to party endeavors, as the evidence shows conclusively. In addition to their lack of political experience and their skepticism of a movement in which a power rivalry was bound to be an important element, there was some doubt in their minds whether their interests and desires could really be served by participating in any party movement. Beyond the acute question of becoming the target of governmental repression, there was another factor operative, especially with the commercial-industrial group. Denied even the orthodox protection of high tariffs, because of treaty restrictions, an emerging Japanese capitalism was tremendously indebted to the broad policy of paternalistic support into which the Meiji leaders had thrown their energies. Necessarily, the urban capitalist groups viewed the liberal movement with these factors in mind, and some of its luster was certain, therefore, to be dimmed.

The government, moreover, was not without other advantages. Having committed itself to a Constitution which would provide some representation, it had robbed the parties of a major issue, especially since its periodic political reforms during this period presaged a broad and as yet undisclosed framework of Western-type government. Indeed, the first Ito cabinet of 1885 represented a high tide of enthusiasm for Westernization, competing in a very real sense with the liberal movement for the support of the articulate elements of Japanese society. This period also marked the end of the agrarian depression which had contributed to widespread dissidence. Beginning in 1886, the earlier Matsukata reform measures and other developments began to take effect, with results favorable to Japanese society as a whole.

From this point onward, however, the government's Achilles' heel was its inability to remove the discriminatory treaties placed upon Japan by the Western powers. This afforded its political opponents a new opportunity, and one that produced an interest-

---

[47] Ito Hirobumi, "Some Reminiscences of the Grant of the New Constitution," in Okuma Shigenobu (ed.), *Fifty Years of New Japan*, London, 1910, Vol. I, p. 123.

ing fusion of the goals of liberalism with the goal of "national independence," thus offering the party movement a really popular issue and one with implications which the West, unfortunately, chose to ignore. The government had long been seeking to effect revisions in the unequal treaties, but the new proposals were widely condemned as humiliating to the national prestige.[48] Using this as a major issue, the veteran Tosa politician Goto Shojiro managed to gather together most of the ex-Jiyuto leaders and some Kaishinto men in a political association called the *Daido Danketsu* (Union of Like Thinkers). The Daido Danketsu gave some attention to political and economic reform, but its driving spirit was its attack upon the government's obsequiousness before the Western powers.[49] It was ironic that a strong tide of nationalism should threaten to submerge the very men in the government who had spurred on its development, but it was perhaps not so strange that this tide should carry with it many of the proponents of liberalism, despite its heavily anti-Western connotations.

The Daido Danketsu, however, had no sustaining power and soon collapsed. Out of its disintegration sprang several small factions representing fragments of the two older parties. It was in this form that the parties met the first national election in 1890; seven parties, three of them fragments of the Jiyuto, conducted campaigns. By now, the perimeters of political activity were fixed by the election laws governing suffrage in national elections. The Law of 1890 gave the right of suffrage to all males over twenty-five years of age (certain groups excepted) who paid a ¥15 national land or income tax.[50] The specified groups not granted suffrage were priests, teachers of religion, active servicemen, and insane persons. Of a population of about 40,000,000 Japan had, through this first

---

[48] Some of the ammunition used against the government is reported to have leaked out in a curious manner. M. de Boissonade, a French jurist working for the Japanese government, secretly reported that, in his opinion, the judicial provisions of the new treaties were injurious to the national prestige. This report got into the hands of the opposition, supposedly through a foreign press account; many translated copies were printed and distributed. From Suzuki Yasuzo, *Jiyuminken*, pp. 291–292.

[49] Even some conservatives who were unalterably opposed to the "civil rights" movement, angered by the "Europeanization" of the government, joined Goto's association. The Daido Danketsu did urge land-tax reduction and freedom of speech and assembly, but its motivating spirit was national independence and resistance to the West. See Oka, *op. cit.*, pp. 273–274; Suzuki Yasuzo, *Jiyuminken*, p. 293.

[50] "Elections to the House of Representatives," Imperial Ordinance No. 3, January 9, 1890, translated in *JGD* (pp. 243–247), p. 243.

suffrage law, about 450,000 eligible voters, or about 1½ per cent of the total population.[51] Of these, the landed group was a dominant majority, because of their greater numbers and the proportionately higher land taxes being levied upon them.[52] About one-third of the voters were ex-samurai, that portion of the class who had been able to bridge successfully the reconversion period.[53]

When one surveys the initial impact of the party movement on Meiji society, two significant factors emerge. The first relates to the structure of that society and its developmental processes. The lower economic classes could scarcely play a vital role in a sustained political movement, particularly a liberal movement, occurring in this period. The only group acting as a subsidiary force in some respects was the peasant class, whose activities, as we have seen, took the form of scattered violence under the impetus of economic misery. In the latter part of the nineteenth century, the tactics that characterized the revolutionary mass movements of the twentieth century had scarcely begun to develop; nor were the facilities necessary to them, such as communications, in more than a rudimentary stage. The misfiring of the radical agrarian movement was implicit in the circumstances. And in any case, one must doubt whether under more "advanced" conditions, it would have served the cause of democracy. The rigorous logic of Japanese political evolution dictated that the role of the masses in this period would be one essentially negative in character. As symbols of latent and uncoördinated unrest, they were capable of being agitated sufficiently to worry the government and thus induce occasional concessions—along with reprisals.

The role of landed and capitalist elites, however, was one of greater immediate interest and portent. They had the votes, and party principles, membership, and candidates would for the most

---

[51] Election statistics from Bureau of Elections, quoted by Osatake, *Nihon kensei shi taiko*, Vol. II, p. 832; the exact figure was 450,365 eligible voters.

[52] The law further stipulated that a payer of land taxes was eligible to vote if he had paid a fifteen-yen land tax one full year previous to the making up of the electoral roll, whereas the income-tax payer had to have paid the tax for three full years previously. Article iii, Imperial Ordinance No. 3, translated in *JGD*, p. 243.

[53] Ex-samurai also represented about one-third of the members elected to the first Diet, about 100 of the 300 representatives. In terms of their population (including families) of about 1,976,480 out of a total population of 39,607,234, their representation was extremely high, and the class continued to have a profound influence on party as well as government politics. For the figures quoted and a discussion, see Osatake, *Nihon kensei shi taiko*, Vol. II, pp. 832–833.

part come from their ranks. But neither of these groups could truly represent the cause of liberalism or the principles of a liberal party movement. The landed groups, who were numerically the stronger, were interested primarily in refighting the battle of feudalism and in stemming the tide of urban industrialization. They had an interest in liberalism mainly to the extent that it could be used as a tool in this battle. As a pressure group, they were formidable indeed, despite many diversities in their ranks; as the leaders of a democratic movement, however, they betrayed all the weaknesses inherent in their background and narrow interests.

Most important of all, Japanese capitalism of the early Meiji period, in its dominant aspects, was antiliberal in the Western sense, and hence an evolution toward expanding political liberalism was certain to be made most difficult. The great degree of state capitalism, the heavy dependence of private capitalism upon the state, and the important position which the old feudal artistocracy held in the new capitalist structure were all fundamental reasons why the capitalist class as a whole did not interest itself in the liberal party movement, and why those who did, sought to use the parties not to break down the power of government but to direct it into their own channels. Rather than concentrating upon broadening individual and corporate rights beyond the sphere of government, the rising commercial-industrial groups were quite naturally seeking to exploit the full potentialities of governmental paternalism. In this central drive for an expanded mercantilism the premises of classical liberalism were ill-fitting.

There was one group, however, that offered some encouragement. A Japanese intellectual movement on behalf of democracy had sprung up, and although its participants were few in numbers, they thought of themselves as the democratic vanguard, and worked feverishly in an attempt to probe the roots of Western liberalism and carry their message to the Japanese people. Political groups were rising in the universities and in the numerous mission schools; young liberal authors were pouring out their souls in an increasing series of political novels, newspaper articles, and polemic essays.[54] Yet the formidable obstacles confronting them could not be denied. They lacked a heritage of great political

---

[54] It was during this period that Yano Fumio wrote *Keikoku bidan* (*The Magnificent Story of Administering a Country*), a romanticized version of the history of ancient Thebes. The work played upon the glories of constitutional government and was the first of many political novels by men like Shiba Shiro and Suehiro Tetcho. See Oka, *op. cit.*, pp. 277–278, note 4.

power, the degree of respect accorded the scholar in China, and the requisite amount of freedom. Consequently, they were frequently overtimorous in the open political arena and many of them suffered from a devastating inferiority complex.

The dilemma involved in espousing Westernism, moreover, could be particularly painful to the liberal intellectual, who was forced to be somewhat ambivalent toward a West that combined liberalism with imperialism, and democratic principles with an automatic assumption of superiority. Indeed, this raises a second significant factor relative to the early reception of political parties by the Japanese people. The shifting and always complex Japanese reaction to the West as a whole bore directly upon both the fortunes and the nature of the parties. The exuberance of the Europeanization drive had seemed at one point to be carrying all before it; Western dress, customs, and even food were avidly cultivated in high circles, and in this milieu, Western law and ideology were privileged to enjoy a certain seasonal fashion. When the artificialities of some too hasty and indiscriminate adaptations became obvious, a reaction set in which was powerfully abetted by the nature of Japanese foreign relations after 1885. Thus antiforeignism reëmerged with vigor, both within and outside the liberal movement. If there was a considerable logic in its manifestations from the standpoint of the democratic creed—and even a dynamism implicit in its bold assertion of national independence—it was also a clear sign that the influence of the West could be a source of weakness as well as strength to the cause of democracy. Indeed, there could never be a time when the unfolding processes of the West itself would not play an important role in influencing the position of democracy and the parties with the Japanese people, and Meiji society in the 1880's served as an excellent example of this fact.

IV

THE NATURE OF EARLY
PARTY ORGANIZATION AND
TACTICS

WRITING IN 1917, Ozaki Yukio, one of the staunchest supporters of the Japanese democratic movement, confessed, "Here in the Orient we have had political factions but no political party." [1]

Behind this simple sentence there lies a half-explored world of forces which extend into the whole economic-social background of modern Japan. If previous chapters are to be expanded and some additional aspects of the Japanese democratic problem suggested, the organizational difficulties of the emerging parties must be seen in their true perspective. First, however, by expanding upon Ozaki's observation slightly it is possible to suggest in capsule form the essence of the problem. In many respects, the parties resembled exclusive clubs, yet they were clubs lacking any real unity, torn by violent internal struggles for power which frequently had little or no connection with considerations of public policy. Sectionalism played an important part in producing this scene; han and regional rivalries were often stronger than any other issue. But there was also the complicated network of personal relationships in Japanese society. The party leaders represented daimyo-fathers in the political world, to be followed with that faithful allegiance which had been the model for feudal relationships. Indeed, the smallest element which could ordinarily be isolated

---

[1] Ozaki Yukio, "Japan's Defective Constitutional Government" (from a series of articles first published in a Tokyo newspaper in 1917, subsequently translated by Professor de Becker, and published in book form, 1918), included in *What Japan Thinks*, edited by K. K. Kawakami, New York, 1921, p. 75.

117

within the party was the leader-follower group; this group acted as a unit in seeking to advance its fortunes, with the leader counting upon unwavering support, irrespective of policy changes.

Thus, within the party the premium was upon loyalty to one's group, not upon consistency to one's principles.[2] However, this loyalty was not always easy to maintain, and relations among those aspiring to be leaders themselves were especially unsteady. Nothing is more subject to fluctuation in politics than leadership relations when they are not cushioned by real policy ties—nothing is more delicate than the politics of personal prerogative. Thus Japanese politics was both fluid and highly personalized, with the intricate maze of human relationships constantly shifting, especially among the leaders, and causing many alterations in the balance of power within and among the parties. Under such circumstances, it was difficult for the party organization to maintain any real unity or cohesion, even when it was basically agreed upon policy matters.

It might be assumed from the discussion thus far, however, that at least there was no problem in getting leaders to emerge. But, unfortunately, this was not true. Despite the intense personalization of Japanese politics, few dynamic, individual leaders were produced. Rather, leadership was partially hidden, with only shifting groups in the foreground. Decisions seemed always to issue forth from anonymous sources, and there was no one who would accept responsibility for them. Indeed, the twin problems of leadership and responsibility were as grave as any faced by the political society of modern Japan.

Now it should be readily admitted that some of the above-mentioned weaknesses are not unique to Japanese politics and that, indeed, the nature of organization produces certain universal problems which stem from its innate characteristics. Yet the forces of factionalism, authoritarianism, and irresponsibility have been overwhelming in Japanese society, and they have pervaded every form of public and private organization there. The structural pattern of the parties has had its counterpart in Japanese labor unions, business companies, and universities. The parties, despite certain peculiarities, have represented but one example of a far more general phenomenon, and the weaknesses of all private govern-

---

[2] Ozaki remarked in disgust: "A politician scrupulous enough to join or desert a party for the sake of principle is denounced as a political traitor or renegade. That political faith should be kept not toward its leaders or its officers but toward its principles and views is not understood." *Ibid.*, p. 76.

ment in modern Japan have been pregnant with implications for the fate of Japanese democracy.

The exploration of this complex problem is by no means complete, but by drawing upon the aid of Japanese and Western social scientists, it may be possible to present some hypotheses. In searching out the causal factors, one must begin with certain characteristics of Japanese society deeply embedded in its heritage, several of which have already been introduced in this study. Geography, the traditional family structure, and the pattern of Japanese feudalism were among the forces which interacted in shaping what might be termed the sociological nature of the parties.

It is interesting to conjecture the role that geography itself played in supporting two striking and seemingly paradoxical characteristics of the Japanese—homogeneity and separatism. The peripheral position of the Japanese islands, together with the fact that the Asian mainland held for outsiders more productive fruits of conquest, gave the Japanese people a maximum of isolation during the era of recorded history. Despite the extensive inroads of Asian culture, brought about through a long period of intermittent contact with Korea and China, until well into the modern period Japan was spared large-scale despoliation at the hands of foreign invaders and was not the product of continuous racial mixture.[3] The country contained a well-integrated people among whom the staticism of largely sedentary settlements, traditional birthplace ties, and long-existent political and religious symbolisms played an important part. Although these factors could be used in the long run as powerful instruments for unification, they were by the same token available for various sorts of irrational appeals. In the fashion of a man who had devoted his political career to national unity, Ito Hirobumi once wrote, "We [Japanese] had during the course of our seclusion unconsciously become a vast village community where cold intellect and calculation of public events were always restrained and even often hindered by warm emotions between man and man."[4]

Ito's statement is certainly inadequate and in some respects, in-

---

[3] These remarks, of course, should be applied only to the period of history. The Japanese, like most other peoples, are the product of numerous initial mixtures. The main strain is probably derivative from successive waves of people coming out of northeast Asia, but southern influences are also quite probable.

[4] Ito Hirobumi, "Some Reminiscences of the Grant of the New Constitution," in Okuma Shigenobu (ed.), *Fifty Years of New Japan*, London, 1910, Vol. I, p. 128.

accurate; nevertheless, it recognizes the existence of a major problem. Actually, Japan was far from being one "vast village community," which was, in a sense, the goal of the Meiji leaders; rather, it was a series of communities in which the traits of emotionalism (but traits not fully described by Ito's phrase, "warm emotions between man and man") were coexistent with a deep-seated spirit of provincialism very strong in the early Meiji period. As has been noted, the achievement of internal unification in Japan was a prodigious task, in spite of the comparative lack of foreign complications and the relative homogeneity of the people. Indeed, it was a struggle covering a period of nearly two thousand years, although the area in terms of square miles was relatively small. Here again, geography had some effect. If Japan had been protected, on the whole, from the most violent manifestations of foreign aggression, nature had also assured her a complex series of internal divisions. A country composed of extremely mountainous terrain and isolated coves and valleys was perfectly designed for fostering and preserving provincialism to a rather large degree. Moreover, to this must be added the extraordinary elongation of the Japanese islands in a north-south direction, which assured substantial variations in climate, products, and foreign contracts. Although these geographic features did not seriously detract from the essential homogeneity of the Japanese people, they did help to produce notable differences in the nature and development of internal institutions. This is illustrated significantly, for instance, by the different types of agrarian institutions which predominated in the Northeast and Southwest, and also by the distinctions in the timing and force of commercialism in various localities. The importance of such "backward" areas in Japan as *Tohoku* (the Northeast) to the political scene should not be overlooked.

And naturally geography played its part in shaping the traditional family structure of Japan, a force which was probably of much greater import to the problems here being discussed.[5] Once it emerged from the tribal, nomadic stage, the Japanese family

[5] For information on the general subject of the Japanese family and the agrarian community, I am greatly indebted to the research of two men, Kawashima Takeyoshi and Fukutake Tadashi. Professor Kawashima's valuable work, *Nihon shakai no kazokuteki kosei* (*The Familial Structure of Japanese Society*), Tokyo, 1949, has already been cited. Professor Fukutake's collected essays were first published in 1949 under the title, *Nihon noson no shakaiteki seikaku* (*The Social Character of the Japanese Rural Community*), in Tokyo. The extensive use of both of these works in the succeeding pages requires a grateful acknowledgment here.

was molded mainly by the demands of an intensive, small-scale agrarian economy. Such a system, of course, made the family a central unit of production as well as of consumption, and did much to shape its major characteristics. But these characteristics were also affected by other factors, among which the Japanese feudal system must be accounted very important. For our purposes, there are two interrelated aspects of the Japanese family which require some emphasis: first, the structure of the family organization, and secondly, the nature of power within the familial group. These matters have been touched upon lightly at an earlier point, but must now be more closely examined. At first, this examination may appear to be an unwarranted digression, but ultimately, if successful, it will be seen as completely germane—and indeed, indispensable—to an understanding of Japanese party organization and Japanese political behavior in general.

In any intensive agrarian society in a situation where the amount of arable land is limited, the fear of continuous subdivision of that land is a very great and justifiable worry.[6] The Japanese answer to this problem took the form of a strong emphasis upon primogeniture. As Fukutake points out, this was in sharp contrast to the system prevailing in China and served to distinguish the two societies in a very important manner.[7] China, clinging to the practice of equal inheritance and yet attempting to prevent extensive land division, was forced to uphold as ideal the enlarged family living under one roof. The essence of the Japanese system, however, lay in establishing a social-economic relationship between main and branch families which would preserve the basic continuity of inheritance in the main line of descent. The Japanese familial structure thus placed no great premium upon the continued physical union of the expanding family; married collateral relatives rarely remained within the family fold, and the large-family ideal, characteristic of China, never became a conspicuous factor in Japanese society. Moreover, the importance of blood ties as such was considerably less in the Japanese familial structure. In its drive for continuity and economic sustenance, the Japanese family habitually incorporated nonblood elements into its fold. The custom of

[6] Fukutake, *op. cit.*, p. 9.

[7] *Ibid.*, pp. 49 ff. Fukutake stresses the significance of these differences. First, the Chinese system, based upon an equal division of properties, quite naturally developed a strong sense of the family as a community to which all members would contribute on the basis of their ability, with the certain knowledge of an ultimate division. This differed from the strong sense of unequal obligations derivative from one's given status, so characteristic of

"adopted sons" and the absorption of employees into the family structure were basic to the "main-family" theme which dominated Japanese society.[8]

It should be pointed out immediately, however, that the Japanese family was neither uniform nor static. More recently, certain Japanese economists and sociologists have been developing the thesis that rural organization in Japan stemmed from a mixture of two basic or "ideal" types of union: the *dozoku* (same family, or same clan) type and the *kogumi* (associational) type.[9] In spite of the danger of a certain artificiality in seeking to distinguish types that rarely, if ever, existed in their pure forms, such an analysis does contribute to an understanding of the intricate and varied relationships of economic and social forces in agrarian Japan. The "ideal" dozoku type *buraku* (hamlet) [10] had as its most appropri-

---

the Japanese system. The incipient division produced a general spirit of equality within the Chinese family, with much less of the master-servant concept prevalent in the Japanese family. At the same time, this egalitarianism and the absence of absolute paternal power to the degree present in Japan made the Chinese family much less stable than its Japanese counterpart. It was true, of course, that the family occupied a more exclusive position in the life of the individual in China than in Japan, especially after the emergence of Japanese feudalism. In terms of its own internal structure and "balance of power," however, the Chinese family was far more fluid. Chinese dynastic change was mirrored at the familial level in the recurrent shifts in influence and power which took place both among the groups composing the enlarged family and among the various families themselves in their mutual relations.

[8] Undoubtedly both of these practices were of the greatest importance in preserving the familial productive system, giving it resistance power against new forms. Initially, they were probably substitutes for or adaptations of slavery, growing out of labor demands. Once accepted, however, the adopted son took up the same position as a real son, submitting to that paternal authority sanctioned by the ethical commands of filial piety and the weight of family tradition. And the employee absorbed into the family, while he did not ordinarily command the same status as other elements, was the recipient of the general pattern of benevolence and participant in family rituals, ceremonies, and festivals. Naturally, close ties between paternalism and all economic relations were fostered by such practices. The pattern of modern relations between landowner and tenant or manager and laborer found its precedents here. See Kawashima, *op. cit.*, pp. 27 ff.; Fukutake, *op. cit.*, pp. 25 ff.

[9] For a full discussion of this, see Fukutake's essay entitled "Dozoku ketsugo to kogumi ketsugo" (Same-Family Unions and Associational Unions), which first appeared in the magazine *Shakai* (*Society*), Vol. III, No. 12, December, 1948, and is included in Fukutake's *Nihon noson no shakaiteki seikaku*, pp. 34–48.

[10] It is extremely difficult to translate the term *buraku* in such a way as to convey its full significance. The buraku still represents the basic unit of the

ate economic setting the existence of one or more main houses of cultivator landowners with large holdings, and a number of branch houses—some blood-related and others with no blood ties—operating in a tenant-like relationship to the resident main family. It was thus strongly paternalistic, authoritarian, and hierarchical in structure and pattern of operation. In the ideal kogumi type of rural organization, economic conditions were characterized by the relative absence of major inequities, with the buraku, or hamlet, being composed of households essentially equal in an economic sense, whatever the level of that equality might be. Any trend toward such an economic structure reduced the potency of the superior-inferior relationship and abetted a communal organization of individual and partially equal houses. This union, in its "ideal" form, was comparatively weak when contrasted with the dozoku type, and also one which showed certain innate qualities of competition and egalitarianism.

The relative degree to which these two types entered into the real composite buraku and village structure varied, of course, with the historical development and timing of Japanese agriculture and the social-political forces connected with it, both as these made their impact upon a given era and as they affected differently the diverse regions.[11] At all times, the apparently static buraku and

---

rural community. The overwhelming number of Japanese farmers live together in small settlements adjoining their fields, not in isolated fashion as is usual in America. These settlements or groups of houses constitute the buraku, a term which might be translated as "hamlet" or even "village," although it is often distinct from the administrative village, of which it may form only a part. Provided some explanation is given, it is probably better to avoid translating the term buraku, for any translation is likely to convey a misconception.

[11] Fukutake presents the following historical picture of the development of the two types: The southwest area, peopled and cultivated in ancient times, was organized during the period when the peasantry were becoming separated from the military, with many landowners becoming bushi and divorcing themselves from the actual tilling of the soil. A tendency toward partition of the land was strong and the small peasants who remained on the soil existed in more or less equal status. This was in essence the background for the kogumi type. Another development occurred in late medieval times when the mountain and "backwoods" lands—many of marginal productivity—were developed in the northeast area under the direct supervision of military landlords. In these, of course, the dozoku type achieved its purest forms, under strongly hierarchical controls. Yet feudalism everywhere strengthened the dozoku type, because of its particular economic and political nature, as we shall note later. There was a third phase of alteration in the relatively modern period, consisting of the reclamation and development of new lands. Since

villages were subject in fact to varying fluctuations of an economic or political nature which altered their "chemical" composition. But the general dominance down to the modern period of what has here been termed the dozoku type can never be doubted. First, it had a natural connection with the system of primogeniture that could be offset only under special circumstances, such as emigration or land expansion. But in addition, it was strongly supported by Japanese feudalism, the third interrelated factor mentioned at the outset.

Before the full effect of feudalism upon the family is assessed, however, it might be well to turn briefly to the second aspect of the traditional family which was to bear strongly upon modern political problems, the matter of power. In this regard, the most pronounced Japanese characteristic was that of the absolute power of the family head. His was an authority derived completely from status and all-pervasive in its sway over both blood and nonblood elements connected with the familial circle.[12] In this fashion, it already partook of a master-servant relationship, even within the immediate family, and it therefore had a certain natural capacity to develop into the larger pattern of power operative in the buraku and village.[13]

But the full nature of power in the Japanese family cannot be

---

there were few individual leaders in this and few resident owner-cultivators on a large scale, there was a certain tendency here toward the kogumi type, but actually both types were present.

In essence, the kogumi type showed its greatest strength in the richer and earlier-developed lands of the southwest, while the lands of the northeast which were poor and late in being developed, with the mature feudal influence strong, were heavily dozoku in type. The over-all influence of feudalism was basically on behalf of the dozoku type, and the post-Meiji assault upon feudalism also presented a challenge of sorts to this type. But always, it must be remembered, the true buraku of whatever area was a mixture, and by the Meiji era, the mixture was very thorough in most communities. See Fukutake, op. cit., pp. 37–42.

[12] Ibid., pp. 54 ff. Here again, some comparison with China is interesting. In China, the family head was generally the oldest member; the basis of power, as Fukutake puts it, was "generationism." Because of this, power was shared in some degree by collateral relatives of the same generation living within the family homestead or acting as parts of the family organization. Consequently, the power of the family head was less absolute and also less stable. (See n. 7, above.) There could be no principle of comradeship in the Japanese family, however, because paternal power proceeded from a fixed familial status, was absolute and unquestioned, and was moderated neither by the principle of "generationism" nor that of equal inheritance.

[13] Ibid., pp. 25 ff.

understood without further reference to Confucian ideology, especially with regard to its extraordinary cultivation of psychological power. Despite the over-all strength of eclecticism in Oriental philosophy, there was a certain insistence upon absolute truth in Confucian philosophy. To the true Confucianist, the immutable laws of nature centered around familial relationships; male supremacy and filial piety were their foremost expressions. All ethical and political symbolisms reinforced these central laws, which were also fortified by the continual accretions of centuries of custom and Confucian interpretation of that custom. Recognition and acceptance of these truths marked the dividing line between wisdom and ignorance, civilization and barbarism, social participation and outlawry, virtue and sin. The outer perimeter of respectability lay in reinterpretation of the supreme maxims, a hazardous possibility for scholars alone, but, nevertheless, one of great importance in providing some flexibility. For the ordinary man there remained the constant exhortation to engage in introspection so as to reassess his relationship to truth and to prick his sensitivities and thus cause him to follow the right path. Only if the urge to follow truth came from the inner heart could the individual enjoy tranquillity and happiness. And in this manner, compulsion could be made to appear not compulsion, but freedom.[14]

There was, of course, a supreme paradox inherent in this technique, and in reality the question of the inner heart received scant attention as compared with the value placed upon external forms and ceremony in Confucian literature.[15] In case of necessity, moreover, coercive force was available and used to enforce power: disowning, reproof, and striking were among the familial punishments. Still, the power relationship within the Japanese family was maintained primarily by the voluntary acceptance of certain absolute "truths" on which it was grounded, and hence acceptance of the power itself. If one is to understand the real nature of power in Japanese society, he must first of all understand this. Naturally the act of acceptance was so calculated as not to require any real exercise of discrimination, but at the same time it presented a passable substitute for self-decision. It might be noted that in its method of exerting its psychological power from within the individual, Confucianism bears a striking resemblance in certain respects to Communism, and this has significance in the modern Far East. Our immediate concern here, however, is to emphasize

---

[14] Kawashima, op. cit., p. 125.
[15] See ibid., pp. 7 ff.

the extraordinary weight which this characteristic of Confucianism lent to a system based upon paternal absolutism: it gave to the paternal system a kind of inner strength and resistance to challenge which that system could not possibly have had if it had been forced to rely upon coercion alone. Even in the modern period, this inner strength has been sufficient to break the heart of many a Japanese revolutionary.

One final element in the nature of power at the familial level deserves attention. The power of the family head was not only absolute and unshared; it was not only impersonal, in the sense that it was connected with status rather than with individual ability; it was also a power held "in trust," so to speak, for the perpetuity of the family, especially the main family. And in this connection, it is important to acknowledge the significance of the function of perpetuation, likely to be overlooked if one is completely preoccupied with the purely economic aspects of familial function. Perpetuation demands recognition as a function unto itself. It develops with its own complex psychological and emotional motivations in such a fashion as to defy analysis in sheer economic terms and to create for itself a separate identity. And it has played a far more important role in some of our contemporary institutions, including the modern corporation, than is generally recognized. In no situation, however, has it been more important than in that of the Asian family, in which it has received strong religious-philosophic support. The nature and allocation of power in the traditional Japanese family both bear witness to this fact. The quest for continuity was not only a governing force in determining the concept of power—as a nonpersonal legacy—but it also helped to establish the function of each member within the family. The clear supremacy of the parent-child relationship over the husband-wife relationship, the overwhelming advantages implicit in the position of eldest son, and the ingrained sense of subordination and sacrifice for the family or the main house—all these have their origins in the basic drive to perpetuate the family.

Already it would be possible to draw certain implications concerning Japanese organization and political behavior from the preceding discussion. The significance of these implications might be enhanced, however, if that discussion is first concluded around the question of the continuing feudal influence upon the Japanese family. Japanese feudalism, as has been noted, held sway over a very long period and passed through many stages. It would be inconceivable for it not to have influenced deeply the nature of the

Japanese family; and there can be no doubt that its imprint is to be found everywhere in the family institution as it emerged at the end of the Tokugawa period. Yet it should also be made clear from the beginning that certain elements of what might be called the "prefeudal" traditional family survived, projecting themselves into and beyond the so-called feudal periods. The source or sources of this great resistance power are not entirely clear. Certainly the system of agrarian production itself had an important effect: small-scale agriculture marked by extremely intensive cultivation and low productivity was a system tailor-made for the continuing power of familialism in its traditional forms.[16] Another factor of significance was undoubtedly the degree to which the family system had become the focal point of all philosophic and religious expression. There are two points to be noted in this connection. The first is that such expression in its various forms reached very considerable heights of both intellectual and emotional appeal. In addition, the emphasis upon the familial pattern throughout as a core factor reached a pitch of intensity which went well beyond the requirements of the situation. That is to say, within the latitude afforded by the economic-political requirements of the society, the most expressive ideologies happened to take rather extreme forms in this regard. Aided by these factors, the traditional family system, provided it could maintain any substantial amount of compatibility with the prevailing economic-political demands of the society, not only could survive transition, but could play a formative role in the new era.

Thus, in discussing the full effect of feudalism upon the traditional family system, one must be aware of two factors—influence and resistance. The element of feudal influence can be seen most clearly in two respects: the feudal system greatly strengthened the hierarchical nature of the family, and also facilitated the integration of the family into larger social-economic units. Connected with both of these influences was the concept of loyalty as it operated in feudal relations between superiors and inferiors. Such a concept, of course, was common to feudal systems everywhere, in some form; it was probably innate to any society revolving around land control through military power. It stemmed from a sense of obligation on the part of the inferior for favors granted and on

---

[16] See Fukutake, *op. cit.*, p. 28. Many Japanese sociologists and economists, including Fukutake, are greatly influenced by Weber in the manner in which they make this point. Weber's concept of the "Asian productive system" is frequently used.

the part of the superior for support rendered. Thus under the feudal impact, Japanese social relations were spelled out in much more explicit, detailed form than they would otherwise have been, and with increased reference to man in a broader economic-military system. Indeed, as we have noted earlier, the bushi code even sought to give the warrior's relations with his lord priority over those with his family, a most natural development in any strongly feudal society. Naturally, the inner structure of the Japanese family was influenced by these developments. Within the family, an intricate system of relationships based upon *ko* (filial piety) and *on* (favors, or benefactions) emerged. Each member of the family was distinguished in status through the different obligations he was caused to accept by the actions of other family members. The complexity of family relations was greatly increased, and the hierarchical nature of the family correspondingly emphasized. And through these tendencies, feudalism also gave substantial impetus to the dozoku over the kogumi type buraku, a factor which we noted briefly at an earlier point.

If these were influences of a very important character, still they cannot be assessed accurately without turning first to the factors of resistance involved. Indeed, these are revealed here in formidable manner and one that relates to the whole question of power in the family. The basis of paternal power in the traditional family and that of power in truly feudal relationships was fundamentally different. The former was an unconditional submission to absolute power, whereas the latter, at least in its upper reaches, represented a relation between over-all independent individuals which had some fluidity. In its "pure" feudal form, power rested upon reciprocity of actions, accompanied by a certain possibility for individual decision making and responsibility. Indeed, in the West, feudalism helped to produce the concepts of contingent rights and duties connected to the stream of Western liberalism. In Japan, however, feudalism never implanted these concepts firmly, and the earlier paternalistic forms emerged somewhat altered but still triumphant. The very matter of the ko-on relationship being discussed illustrates this point. Its development in the family marked the true measure of the feudal impact in Japan. Theoretically, to be sure, it injected into the Japanese family the feudal element of reciprocity and the concept of a feudal-type contract based upon an exchange of services. In actuality, however, *ko* (filial piety) continued to hold such a position of supremacy in this relationship that the implications suggested above were largely vitiated. The great emphasis in the family continued to be upon the overwhelming obligations of children innate to their status; the power of absolute paternalism was not basically altered. And such a power was equally apparent in the feudal relationships outside the family, where the father-child image was made a dominant one. As a result, at every level the contractual principle connected with feudalism in the West was barely perceptible in feudal Japan, nor were the rights and concepts derivative from such a principle.

A second influence of feudalism upon the family has been mentioned, that of assisting its integration into the larger economic-social units which made up feudal society. The importance of this can scarcely be overemphasized. At the same time that it served to advance greatly the dozoku-type community, feudalism caused the fusion of the family, the buraku, and the larger rural town into a highly integrated unit, operating in a seemingly organic fashion and governed by the same basic forces. The communal consciousness and the communal operation of Japanese society contrasted in marked fashion with the high degree of family "individualism" and aloofness characteristic of the nonfeudal agrarian society of China. And the whole political-economic structure of Japanese feudalism was brought to play in achieving this result.[17]

---

[17] This subject forms an excellent starting point from which to analyze certain important differences between modern China and Japan, and it could easily become the focal point of a lengthy treatise in itself. The Chinese system was characterized by a drive for exclusiveness and self-sufficiency. The Chinese family showed strong resistance to integration with any larger unit. Blood ties were a necessary factor for entrance into the family; ancestral gods were kept separate from territorial or other nonfamily divinities, with each family giving priorities to its own deities; such communal ties as community-owned lands were few, and the Chinese family or clan acted so as to contain within itself as much of the direction and proceeds of the livelihood activities of its members as possible. Thus the basis of state power was narrow, and the family constantly warred with the village and the larger political units as well. In the nonfeudal society of China, the Confucian dilemma of priorities was revealed in its starkest form. In Japan, on the other hand, the feudal system nurtured the development of the dozoku type into the village system. The leading family's gods became the village gods; the pattern of power and benevolence within the family was transferred to the buraku and village level; and within this pattern, community undertakings, communal ownership of certain resources, and a sense of belonging to the community were all commonplace.

Undoubtedly, as Fukutake suggests, these differences affected the revolutionary potentials of the two societies, in addition to having other effects. Political power in China was not only weak, but essentially was divorced from the deeply ingrained sense of paternal obligation—of benevolence—which

Yet again the factor of resistance must be considered, in an attempt to discover wherein the real balance of influence lay. If the family seemed to merge, in a sense, into the larger units, still it could never be said that the family had been submerged by them. On the contrary, at whatever level, the patterns of organization and relationship established were those based upon the familial pattern, a pattern which, as we have noted, retained much of its traditional form. Indeed, it might almost be said that the significance of the effects of feudalism on the Japanese family lay less in the changes it produced in the familial pattern and more in its enlargement of the scope within which the basically traditional pattern could be operative. Naturally, the general effectiveness of this operation on a larger scale was chiefly due to the fact that under the feudal system, the family could retain much of its compactness and stability, still functioning as a unit in the economic and political scene. Hence, the dilemma implicit in the Confucian emphasis upon both state and family centralism was moderated, and the adaptations accomplished, though they were not perfect or long-range solutions, nevertheless served to distinguish the characteristics and potentialities of Tokugawa Japan from those of China, as well as from those of the West.

It remains now to relate the major problems of Japanese political behavior and organizational weakness to the foregoing discussion. Obviously the pattern of Japanese familial relations set forth above had a pronounced effect upon the individual and his relationship to society.[18] In the first place, two facets of Western individualism,

was, on the whole, well developed in the Japanese ruling class. Thus the Chinese village tended not only to be run exclusively by the landowner classes, but also exclusively for them, and undertakings for the general welfare were few. Consequently, hostility along class lines, abetted by the degree of egalitarianism present in the society, could be developed with some ease in modern China. The Japanese village, on the other hand, was rich in hierarchy and the kind of "welfare state" which stemmed from it; both of these facts served as powerful deterrents to the development of a revolutionary spirit in modern Japan. In the final analysis, hierarchy rests on the side of stability, especially when it is combined with an active sense of feudal-type benevolence on the part of the ruling class. The egalitarian society is essentially unstable, especially when it has no basis in economic fact.

[18] Perhaps one final point ought to be noted briefly. By the Tokugawa period at least, there were substantial differences between the bushi familial system and that of the commoners. In the bushi system, the power of the family head was absolute, but among the commoners, a much greater economic interdependence of all family members tempered this absolutism somewhat. Here influence partook of a more human character with an element of coöperation and collective understanding which led to a somewhat

respect for the individual personality and a sense of individual responsibility, were stunted. The attitude of man toward his fellow men was essentially based upon predetermined conditions of status and relationship; it was not subject to spontaneity or selectivity governed by such considerations as personal attraction or mutuality of respect. Indeed, only those stereotypes of personal behavior that accorded with the orthodox familial rules were acceptable and depicted as proper emotional responses; relationships were matters of duty, not choice. Thus the right to cultivate personal attributes was denied in a system which placed a premium upon conformity, and the concept of respect for the individual personality was correspondingly impossible.[19]

Of equal importance was the absence of a sense of individual responsibility, a trait which has strongly affected every institution of modern Japan. Since the familial system represented a system of fixed unilateral rights and duties, individual responsibility in any real sense was impossible.[20] The submissive did not think of themselves as the possessors of independent values, but rather as the recipients of protection from the "powers"; without self-decisions or self-actions they could have no sense of responsibility. Conversely, those with power had this by virtue of their role, and the determination of its use was governed by an inflexible code over which they had neither in theory nor practice any substantial control. Whatever their actual opportunities for discrimination, the possessors of power conceived of their actions as dictated by their position, hence beyond the realm of personal responsibility.

The only concepts of responsibility which found some roots in Japanese traditionalism were a sense of responsibility on the part

---

easier, more informal relationship than prevailed in the bushi structure. Partially on this basis, the bushi scorned these classes as "changing lower animals." Even when commoner family relations varied somewhat, however, unit rather than individual decisions prevailed and all relationships were fixed essentially by blind custom and tradition, not by personal feelings. Thus the effect upon the individual was basically similar in both familial types. See Kawashima, *op. cit.*, pp. 11–14.

[19] Implicit in this system, however, was a volatile quality in each individual which took the place, in a sense, of accepted personal differences. The struggle to submerge emotional conflicts built up from time to time a dangerous amount of inner tension as a result of the enforced conformity. Occasionally an explosion would occur, especially in the context of a mass situation. Indeed, emotionalism was always very close to the surface in one form or another, and yet it was not the same type as that associated with Western humanism, product of very different forces.

[20] For Kawashima's analysis of this point, see *ibid.*, pp. 10–21.

of the group and responsibility for the group, two interrelated but somewhat different ideas. Upon the group as a whole—family, han, or other—there devolved the collective responsibility for preserving conformity and order in accordance with the accepted rules. Consequently, the individual as a member of a group shared the responsibility for playing his role in maintaining the external forms and atoning by an appropriate symbolistic act for any violation. Yet, this was a particular type of responsibility which did more to obscure than to clarify the relation of the individual to his actions. It made of him a part rather than a whole, and placed upon him burdens which could not necessarily be justified by his own acts, or even by acts over which he had at least nominal control. Moreover, since all actions were viewed with respect to the external forms, the value judgments made upon them paid little homage to the rationale of individual actions—the questions of conscience, motivation, and intent. Responsibility in this framework was often manifested by fatalistic sacrifice—an extraordinary heroism which added to the stigma cast upon those necessitating it, but which did not lay bare the relationship between the individual and his behavior, or indeed, recognize the individual as an entity at all.

If the familial pattern had a tremendous impact upon the individual personality, it had a corresponding effect upon the role of the individual in the larger social group. The use of the cardinal guideposts of filial piety and status was extended to all economic and political organizations. When the political parties developed, relations between leaders and followers naturally bore the earmarks of paternalism. The relationship between landowner and tenant, manager and clerk, capitalist and laborer were all imitative of the family prototype. Before the causes for this can be fully understood, the nature of the Japanese industrial revolution itself must be further examined. Here, however, we can note only certain psychological aspects of the matter, reserving the question of the industrial revolution until later. The great emphasis upon family centralism, in spite of the feudal modifications of that centralism, posed a real barrier to the outward extension of the individual. His lack of individual responsibility made it almost impossible for him to cast himself completely adrift from the familial circle, and the intensity of family relations left him with a certain suspicion and hostility toward all outside groups. The result was an emotional conflict of great proportions, especially after the onset of industrialization. Only as he could continue to transfer the familial pattern of behavior to external organizations did the individual find some inner relief. To take such a course of action amounted almost to a psychological compulsion.

In a certain sense, the society of modern Japan has seemed "associational-minded" in the extreme, especially as compared with the society of China. To the extent that this is true, it represents the reluctance of the individual in Japan to operate outside the protecting confines of a group which can spread over him the cloak of anonymity and obscure individualism and responsibility in their naked forms. It represents also the fact that the transformation of the familial pattern to the external organization has had one form of support from Japanese feudal tradition and contemporary developments that has been lacking in China. But there is another side to the picture. Even in "associational-minded" Japan, there has been a great reluctance to join groups external to the family. It is no exaggeration to state that every other organization has had difficulty in competing with the family, even when it has followed familial patterns. But in any case, the type of fragmentation and factionalism typical of intensely personal relations has been the common fate of Japanese organizations, with particularly devastating results on the political party movement.

Factionalism, to be sure, found bases of support outside the realm of personal relations. As we have noted on several occasions, Japanese feudalism greatly developed a sense of sectionalism and gave it expanded economic and political meaning. The han became a political unit of significance, knitting together the lives of its inhabitants; indeed, the various han were referred to as *kuni,* a term which is now translated as "country" or "nation." Han patriotism and loyalty were assiduously cultivated, especially among the bushi class. If cases of treachery, fickleness, and intrigue were by no means uncommon, our earlier footnote on emotional conflict may afford some explanation. Still, the frequently told story of the forty-seven ronin was probably not untypical of the Tokugawa period, so far as military class relations were concerned. In such "ideal" situations, the paternal rather than the contractual relationship was dominant, thus lending familial-type power to strengthen sectional ties. The network of intense loyalties between retainers and lords was a combined product of filial obligation and sectional patriotism. If this was also to become the "ideal" pattern on a national scale for relations between the people and the Emperor, still, traditional sectional ties were not to be abandoned easily, and it is small wonder that they constitute one important aspect of the factional problem in modern Japanese politics.

But now one final and conclusive factor must be added to this survey of the causes of Japanese organizational weaknesses. The Japanese industrial revolution might have been expected to carry in its sweep the destruction of most of the mores and customs of the preindustrial society, but it fell short of this by a considerable degree. Its impact, of course, should not be underestimated. Capitalism did shake the familial structure, especially in the urban areas; it did foster the creation of economic pressure groups, which operated with some degree of orthodoxy as measured by their Western counterparts; and thereby it did produce the development of issues and ideologies which assumed an increasing importance in the political arena. It would be nonsense, for instance, to maintain that party development had no connection with the economic and political cleavages derivative from the new industrial age. The evidence already presented clearly denies this. Still, these new sources of division supplemented rather than removed the old sources and often occupied a position subordinate to them. Considering the period down to 1940 with which we are to be concerned, some have argued that the space of time was insufficient to permit a different result. But time in this sense is not the key to the problem. It is far more important to emphasize the forms which industrialization took rather than the time during which they were operative, as is shown more fully later in this study. Given a basic framework of neomercantilism from which came the close and permanent ties between government and business, protective paternalism rationalized along traditional lines was most naturally woven into the fabric of industrialization itself. Emerging in this environment, it was possible for the economically privileged groups to retain many of the paternal responses to the lower economic classes, blending them as the occasion demanded with the far sharper "modern management" approach. Thus the advent of the "modern industrial state" in Japan presented far less of a challenge to the traditional patterns of behavior than might have been expected, and this was naturally reflected in the democratic movement.

It remains now to apply these various factors more specifically to the early party movement. Perhaps the most noticeable trait in the initial stages of the parties was the extraordinary amount of sectionalism which characterized their make-up, a sectionalism

134

which reflected the background of han politics in very large measure. Three main areas of political power were existent during the early Meiji period; these were the *Kanto* (Eastern Provinces [Tokyo and vicinity]), the *Kinki* (Inner Provinces [Osaka and Kyoto districts]), and the Kyushu regions. In each area men from the former southwest han occupied important leadership roles.[21] Kanto was the stronghold of the government; the oligarchy, which was controlled by the Satsuma-Choshu, had moved the Imperial Court from Kyoto to the old Tokugawa capital, and Tokyo became the hub of the national administration. The Kinki region became the major center for the early party movement. Although Tosa han had been situated on the island of Shikoku, the Tosa-led associations established their headquarters at Osaka.[22] There were several reasons for this: Osaka was near by, centrally located, and yet far enough away from the government-controlled Tokyo area; moreover, it was in a heavily populated commercial and agrarian district potentially ripe for a political movement. However, a survey of leadership in the early organizations indicates the predominant influence of Tosa men and the relatively slight impact of visitors from other areas. And when the party sought to spread northward into the Kanto and *Tohoku* (northeast) regions, it was handicapped not only by governmental power but also by the coolness shown toward "outsiders." The third region, Kyushu, representing as it did one of the most stubbornly provincial areas of Japan, presented an obstacle to unity both within the government and within the party movement. This was a region which had been characterized by fierce sectional patriotism and a long history of independent power and aloofness. From the two major han of the island, Satsuma and Hizen, came many important leaders of the national government and of the parties, it is true, but by substantial elements of the han these men were regarded as traitors and renegades, bargaining away the sovereign power of the "country."[23] The Saga and Satsuma rebellions were initial expressions of the depths to which this resentment went, and the classical rivalry between Satsuma and Choshu men at the highest

---

[21] For an excellent discussion of political power distribution, see Osatake Takeshi, *Nihon kensei shi taiko* (*An Outline of Japanese Constitutional History*), Tokyo, 1939, Vol. II, pp. 826 ff.

[22] The Risshisha of course was a purely Tosa institution, with its quarters at Kochi on the island of Shikoku, but the Aikokusha, Kisei Domei Kai, and the revived Aikokusha, which led to the Jiyuto, all met in Osaka.

[23] It is significant that in 1869 certain elements within Satsuma proposed a federal system, with han representing the units. See *ibid.*, p. 381.

echelons in the government gave evidence of its force even among those who had partially cast off their han provincialism.

At the same time, Kyushu interests, despite their economic, ideological, and purely sectional grounds for opposing the Meiji government, were by the same token unable to coalesce with other groups, even when their antagonism was based upon similar objections. A bitter rivalry between the two chief opponents to the oligarchy—the Shikoku group and the Kyushu group—developed from the very beginning of political agitation. Its foremost expression finally came in the nature of relations between the Jiyuto and the Kaishinto. To be sure, there were sizable differences between these two parties, as our previous examination of the economic groups attached to them and of their respective philosophies has indicated. In their mutual dislike of the oligarchy and in their common desire for some form of representative government, however, they had logical grounds for working together on certain issues, a procedure which was seemingly made imperative by governmental hostility toward both. But in the face of this need for coöperation, the parties launched attacks at each other which were unparalleled in vituperation and rarely reached the level of political principles. Due allowance must be made for the fact that this is not an unusual trend in the initial stages of party politics, as an examination of early British and American parties would show. Moreover, it was based in part upon the lack of a concept of power sharing, with the result that each political group sought an exclusive prerogative. The part played by the sectional make-up of early Meiji Japan, however, can be illustrated by a closer look at the composition and actions of the two parties.

The Jiyuto, dominated by Tosa men, was never able to retain any substantial support in the Kyushu area in the early period. Even before the establishment of the Kaishinto, various Kyushu separatist organizations existed. One district party, the *Kyushu Doshikai* (Kyushu Fellow Thinkers' Association), had considerable strength. A part of this group did finally join the united Jiyuto in September, 1890, after the first election, but other separatist Kyushu elements emerged. Even within the Jiyuto fold, moreover, there were many clashes between Kyushu and Shikoku representatives. These reached one climax at the general convention called to establish the Jiyuto in 1881; after failing in their effort to "stop Tosa," many Kyushu elements withdrew entirely from the party, some to join the Kaishinto and others to remain aloof from both organizations in local "patriotic" societies. Some of these

136

local societies became the predecessors of the subsequent ultra-nationalist movement, in which Kyushu men played a very important role. If this seems paradoxical, it will be shown later that a substantial part of the Japanese ultranationalist movement was marked by an enlarged provincialism and the type of reactionary thought springing out of strong sectional and agrarian interests.

The formation of the Kaishinto was itself in part connected with the sectional problem. Okuma, it will be recalled, was a Hizen man, and his party ranks were swelled by men of Kyushu and other areas who resented Tosa domination of the civil rights movement. Because of this background, Kaishinto-Jiyuto relations were certain to be marked by great suspicions and hostility. There was often some justification in the mutual recriminations which arose, but they were hardly calculated to raise the prestige of the parties in the eyes of the public. The tactics to which each party resorted in dealing with the other are important enough to merit some exposition.

Okuma launched an early attack when he accused Tosa, along with Satsuma and Choshu, of seeking to rule the country by "military wiles." [24] In an interview with the *Tokyo Nichi Nichi* he also stated that he was worried about the activities of the present political parties (Jiyuto): "They feel that they must attack even *gun* [county, district] officials and policemen without regard to right and wrong." [25]

The Jiyuto was quick to reply with taunts that the Kaishinto lacked any spirit or energy for reform. The attacks grew progressively more personal on both sides. Kaishinto leaders accused the followers of Itagaki of being "illiterate and boorish," of using Rousseau when they did not understand him, and of urging violence.[26] Jiyuto men retorted in kind by attacking Okuma's followers as being elegant gentlemen (many wore European dress) who had everything except spirit and power.[27] Jiyuto members glorified their own humbleness in clothing and appearance. These attacks reached a climax in 1882–1883, beginning with Itagaki's trip to the West. The Kaishinto organs alleged that he had been bribed

[24] From Okuma Shigenobu, *Rikken Kaishinto*, quoted by Suzuki Yasuzo, *Jiyuminken (Civil Rights)*, Tokyo, 1948, p. 185.

[25] Okuma interview, quoted by Osatake, *op. cit.*, Vol. II, p. 625.

[26] From speeches by Ozaki Yukio and Ichijima Kenkichi, in *Nihon kensei shi wo kataru (The Story of Japanese Constitutional History)*, quoted in Osatake, *op. cit.*, Vol. II, pp. 645–647.

[27] Itagaki Taisuke, *Jiyuto shi (History of the Jiyuto)*, Tokyo, 1913, Vol. I, p. 423.

by the government to go abroad.[28] The Jiyuto press came back with a full-scale attack on the relationship between the Mitsubishi interests and Okuma.[29] From October, 1882, the Jiyuto blasted Mitsubishi with all its resources, using the slogan *umi bozu taiji* (Destroy the sea monsters!); against the Kaishinto, their slogan was *gito bokumetsu* (Smash the false parties!).[30] In the meantime, the government had aided in a plan to reduce the Mitsubishi interests by organizing a competitive maritime enterprise with half-official, half-private funds, known as the *Kyodo Unyu Kaisha* (Joint Navigation Company). Thus on one issue the government and the Jiyuto supplemented each other. Mitsubishi survived, however, and in a subsequent amalgamation of the two, it actually increased its power.

The government was naturally overjoyed at the friction between its two leading opponents, often taking the opportunity to widen the breach; and the parties were at times too busy attacking each other to pay much attention to their mutual foe. In their bitter personal feuds they discredited each other in the eyes of neutral onlookers far more effectively than the government could have done alone.[31] The nature of the attacks seemed to be the clearest possible demonstration that both parties were dedicated to personal and exclusive privileges. Moreover, the composition of party

---

[28] This Kaishinto accusation was publicized by Numa Moriichi, leading Kaishinto member, in his *Tokyo-Yokohama Mainichi*. Osatake and Hayashi have written that actually Itagaki was financed, unbeknown to himself, by the Mitsui interests. Goto Shojiro and Inoue Kaoru obtained the money for the trip. "It was Inoue's plan to try to change Itagaki politically by having him see the actual conditions of European and American politics." Osatake Takeshi and Hayashi Shigeru, "Seiji" (Politics), in *Gendai Nihon shi kenkyu* (*Studies of Contemporary Japanese History*), Tokyo, 1938, p. 130. This interesting revelation, upon which Osatake has elaborated in a chapter entitled "Itagaki Taisuke yoko mondai" (The Question of Itagaki Taisuke's Trip), in his *Meiji seiji shi tembyo* (*Sketches in Meiji Political History*), Tokyo, 1938, pp. 157–179, points out the fact that Itagaki, though probably personally faultless, was under heavy pressure, and it is also an indication of Goto's character.

[29] It charged that the Mitsubishi shipping monopoly was the result of Okuma's and Okubo's interventions. See Hirano Yoshitaro, *Nihon shihonshugi shakai no kiko* (*The Mechanism of Japanese Capitalist Society*), Tokyo, 1934, p. 186.

[30] Hayashida Kametaro, *Nihon seito shi* (*History of Japanese Political Parties*), Tokyo, 1927, Vol. I, pp. 194–198.

[31] The governmental promise in 1881 to establish a national assembly by 1890 probably strengthened the factionalism in the party movement by removing the major issue and thus giving full vent to sectional and personal feuds.

leadership, especially in the Jiyuto, revealed in unmistakable terms that the early parties were sectional as well as economic and ideological expressions of discontent. These were certainly among the reasons for the slowness with which support was forthcoming from outside circles.

Toward the end of the nineteenth century, however, sectionalism was already diminishing in influence, and although it never completely disappeared, it was to represent, in the final analysis, a far less stubborn obstacle to the party movement than the traditional pattern of personal relationships and ethics. The abandonment of the Tokugawa political system weakened the sectional ties. The new Meiji government, whatever its temporary divergencies for political purposes, on the whole combatted sectionalism vigorously through a relentless nationalist campaign which extended into political centralization, economic integration, and the expansion of communications and education. By the late Meiji era, sectionalism had come to occupy a more subordinate position in Japanese politics. The problems of personal relationships, however, were as formidable as ever to any organizational structure, and they could operate at least as forcefully on a national as on a sectional basis. Undoubtedly the Meiji government itself could assume some responsibility for this; contrary to the policy it used in dealing with sectionalism, it increasingly cultivated the Confucian ethic, and, aided by modern technology, tried to approach the long-sought Confucian goal of a universally applied paternalism.

When the organizational problems of the early parties are viewed in the light of personal relationships, the full magnitude of the factional problem is revealed. The party organization was set up on a highly centralized basis with the intent of keeping policy control in the hands of the leadership cadre and strengthening party discipline. The Jiyuto provided for a general party convention which elected central officials, together with a standing committee which had the task of deliberating on all important party matters and reviewing policy decisions made at the branch level. It was required that this committee investigate and approve various branch undertakings.[32] Moreover, members were to be

---

[32] The Jiyuto proclaimed that "activities running counter to the main purposes of our party must be avoided." From section 3, "Jiyuto kessei sosoku" (General Rules for the Organization of the Jiyuto), document reproduced in Aono Kondo, *Nihon seito hensen shi* (*A History of Changes in Japanese Parties*), Tokyo, 1935, p. 36. For standing committee powers, see section 6 of "Jiyuto kessei sosoku." *Ibid.*

carefully investigated before being enrolled on the party records.[33] Leaving the party officially was also a formal matter: "If they [members] wish to withdraw from the party, they shall write a letter giving detailed reasons and deliver it to the district division in which they are residing."[34]

The Kaishinto had a similar organizational structure, but neither party was able to produce any basic unity within its own ranks or a concentration upon policy issues, in spite of these institutional measures. The real nature of party organization was revealed in the picture of rival groups within the parties struggling for control, for a favored position vis-à-vis the accepted party leader, or each group striving to obtain the party leadership for its own acknowledged chieftain. The party leaders of this period were in certain respects some of the most remarkable men in the annals of Japanese party history. Itagaki and Okuma were both men of outstanding capacities and deep political convictions. The record seems to cast some shadows upon Goto Shojiro, the third leading figure of this period, and indeed, Okuma himself engaged in certain activities which are not easy to explain from the standpoint of Western ideals of political morality. Nevertheless, these men, as well as others in the party movement, had assimilated enough Westernism to make them fairly unusual, both for their own time and for the future, in party leadership.[35] Personal powers of leadership and persuasion were not enough, however, to explain the extraordinary loyalty shown such men by their respective followers, and the intense jealousy that characterized the relations of men serving under different leaders or vying for the favors of the same one. Nor can it explain the fact that when these men, or leaders who followed them, made abrupt switches in policy, they could depend upon their faithful followers to accompany them. Only when the paternalistic pattern of relationships prevailing in Japanese society is recalled, does this situation become understandable. Thus, in the Jiyuto, the rivalry between the followers of Itagaki and those of Goto threatened on more than one occasion to ruin the party.[36]

[33] Section 11. *Ibid.*

[34] Section 12. *Ibid.*

[35] The popularity of Itagaki and Goto among the commoners has been partially attributed to the fact that, unlike most ex-samurai of the period, they were willing to speak from the same platform as the commoners. See Osatake, *Nihon kensei shi taiko*, Vol. II, p. 618.

[36] Evidences of this can be found in such memoirs as those of Kono Hironaka, and in Itagaki, *op. cit.*, Vol. I. For quotations from the former, see Suzuki Yasuzo, *op. cit.*, especially pp. 171–172.

The problem of personal factionalism within the Kaishinto was even greater. Even though there was little opposition during this period to the leadership of Okuma, rancor and rivalry were strong among the subordinate groups clustering around the Okuma standards. The individuals within the party were identifiable only on the basis of their group affiliation, and this determined their attitudes and attachments. As Ozaki wrote, concerning the situation within the Kaishinto: "For some reason, traditionally the Mita faction [the Keio University group] and the Numa faction [the *Mainichi* newspaper faction] disliked each other and carried on a silent strife . . . But the *Oto Kai* [the Tokyo University faction headed by Ono Azusa] was in the middle; not belonging to either side, it was working first of all for harmony." [37]

Within parties, moreover, there was an element of irresponsibility, both among the leaders and among the rank and file. Possessing personal magnetism and patriarchal authority, men like Itagaki and Okuma still cushioned individual responsibility and dynamic popular leadership with the anonymity of group decisions and a solicitude for the feelings of subordinates, on occasion, which blurred the lines between their own and others' convictions, reflecting the traditional concept of the superior's role.[38] These were, of course, the time-honored safeguards for a paternal absolutism that had no legal limits. Among party subordinates personal responsibility was obfuscated by the fact that, with a very few exceptions, the individual operated within a group, bound by its "collective mind," which in turn was governed by loyalty to the leadership, familial-type ties, and the deep obligations thereby accruing.

In such a situation the government was able to play a decisive role. It had to deal primarily with a handful of leaders about whom were clustered the great majority of proponents of the doctrines of "civil rights." Satisfying these men could do much to cripple the emerging parties. We have noted that the party movement was temporarily halted when Okuma and Ito managed to placate Itagaki during the Osaka Conference of 1875; Itagaki subsequently rejoined the government for a short period, and Goto was appointed to the new Genro-in. After the dissolution of the parties in 1884, the peerage system was established, and this offered a

---

[37] Ozaki Yukio, quoted in Suzuki Yasuzo, *op. cit.*, p. 181.

[38] It is obvious that the spirit of compromise and group decisions are indispensable to the democratic creed. It is equally indispensable, however, to make clear the channels of decisions and the responsibility contingent to them. It was in these respects that the Japanese parties failed.

definite inducement to coöperate with the government. When the *Daido Danketsu* (Union of Like Thinkers) threatened the oligarchy, government leaders executed a brilliant maneuver. First, Okuma was induced to join the cabinet in February, 1888. Then, in March, 1889, Goto himself unexpectedly accepted the portfolio of Communication Minister in the government he had so recently denounced! Goto's action was sufficient to break the back of the antigovernment coalition, and the Daido Danketsu was dissolved. To the cries of some members that he had sold out to the government, Goto merely replied that the objects of the organization had been met. Leaders who held their followers by bonds of personal and han loyalties were left free to execute any number of changes.

The segmentation of the civil rights groups on the eve of the first national election was one of the products of these problems. Deep sectional and personal rivalries had manifested themselves, both among and within the party organizations. The factionalism against which they had striven in philosophy and program was a major obstacle to their progress. And precisely because it was implicit in their whole pattern of culture and yet often conflicted with some of their most basic concepts, the Japanese people had acquired a great hatred and fear of its manifestations, never so strongly felt as at this time when the challenges confronting their society could be met only by remarkable concentration and unity. The Meiji parties, however, could not possibly meet these prerequisites. In addition to the fundamental forces operating, there were, of course, certain contemporary factors acting as deterrents. The development of communications and transportation had still not reached the stage in which it was easy for party leaders to hold mass consultations on political policy or make frequent contacts throughout the nation. Above all, the government had a vested interest in segmenting the parties as much as possible. Such enactments as the Public Meeting Laws of 1880 and 1882 were leaves out of Ieyasu's "Legacy." When, in December, 1887, the Daido Danketsu was threatening to unify political opposition, at least temporarily, the oligarchy produced the Peace Preservation Law, the most repressive measure enacted up to that time. Under its provisions all "secret" meetings and associations were prohibited, books and publications disturbing to the public peace were banned, their authors and printers were made punishable, and any person living within seven miles of the Imperial Palace in Tokyo who was suspected of disturbing the public peace could be banished from the district for three years.[39] On the very day of its promulgation, nearly six hundred persons were exiled from Tokyo, including almost all the prominent opponents of the government.[40] Such laws as these were serious deterrents to party coördination. The timid were frightened, and the parties were forced to organize in isolated segments under the constant scrutiny of a hostile administration.

Some would conclude an analysis of the factional problem in early Meiji parties with the observation that it was derivative in the main from the fact that the Japanese people en masse had as yet no real political consciousness and could not participate in party politics. There can be no denial that this was of vital importance. Only the people can check the excesses of party action; there are few limits in party rivalry without their vigilance and a day of reckoning at the polls. It is a politically minded people who must make the issues and insist that the political parties give voice to their demands; it is the people alone who in the final instance set the ethical standards for party behavior. In early Meiji Japan, the pathway to power for the parties did not lie via the common road of mass support, but wound through the tortuous corridors of the Imperial Court. When fulfillment of the hope of overthrowing the Sat-Cho oligarchy proved to be at least temporarily impossible, private "deals" with the men in control offered the only real chance for political power.

If one asks why the Japanese people were so profoundly incapable of regulating and making meaningful the party system in this period, however, he cannot find the answer merely in their contemporary economic status or a background devoid of representative government. It is at this point that some of their most elemental weaknesses in relation to the task must be remembered: the notions of human relationships, political ethics, individualism, and responsibility derived from the complex of their traditional society. If the parties were weak in numerical support, it was partly because the average Japanese had great difficulty in breaking down his prejudices against organizations outside the family; if the parties displayed all the turmoil of excessive personal factionalism,

---

[39] For a translation of the *Hoan Jorei* (Peace Preservation Law) see *JGD*, pp. 502–504.

[40] Among notable men banished were Ozaki (who took the opportunity to visit England), Hoshi Toru (leading Jiyuto adherent), and Nakashima, Nobuyuki.

the reason lay essentially in the fact that familial-type relations were perforce carried into the party structure as a natural part of the individual and as an unconscious psychological urge to mitigate the stress of a great transitional period. Along with this transference went the classic weaknesses pertaining to individualism and responsibility. Consequently the complicated relations between leaders and followers in the party movement reflected most of the old orthodoxies: loyalty intensified by the sectional nature of the Tokugawa system; paternalism and submission both regulated by a code denying validity to purely individual conduct; a sense of political morality meaningful only in these terms; and personal irresponsibility, premise and product alike of the governing concepts. Obviously, there was an interactive effect between these attributes of party organization and public indifference or hostility.

The period of a few years centering in 1890 may be taken as the end of the early Meiji era, and it is possible to detect within this period some changes which contained mixed implications for the future. The rigid sectional pattern inherited from the Tokugawa system was showing definite signs of submission to the nationalist movement. Moreover, vital economic and political issues were assuming an importance which would make it difficult to contain politics within the confines of personalized conflicts as much as it previously had been. Although these issues had always existed and in some measure provided a source of division, now the impact of an economic revolution was intensifying them and the stimulus of Western thought was making them more clearly understood. But the period around 1890 also coincided with a governmental drive to strengthen the paternal pattern for Japanese society. This movement found its prime expression in the revised educational program, in much new legislation, and in a general reconsideration of many aspects of earlier Europeanization. It was natural to refurbish tested methods of quelling strife and mitigating the "excesses of change." Perhaps the major question was whether the old mold of paternal absolutism, which had survived with only minor modifications the period of feudalism, could fare as well in surviving the vicissitudes of the industrial revolution. The fate of the democratic parties was directly involved, and the initial signs were not very encouraging. There were already strong indications that paternalism could be adapted to the Japanese industrial revolution, in view of the particular circumstances surrounding that economic change.

It would be wrong, however, to leave the impression at this

144

point that these problems—recognized and unrecognized—had cast an impenetrable pall of gloom over the party movement. The most energetic party workers were young men, and although they themselves were enmeshed in party weaknesses, they carried the banners with a spirit of enthusiasm and assuredness which always accompanies a new faith and lofty ambitions. They took hope in certain undeniable developments. Mass education and a rapid development of communications were cutting wide swaths in the intellectual and physical isolation of all parts of the nation. The spreading forces of nationalism and capitalism were injecting a certain egalitarianism into Japanese society. There was every indication that suffrage would be expanded and that increasing numbers of citizens would participate in politics and parties. The parties, moreover, now had a part, albeit a minor part, in the national administration. This participation their enthusiasts hoped to expand by appealing to the public for increased support. Defeatism was far from being the sign of the times; on the contrary, the nineteenth-century beliefs in inevitable progress and in democracy as the wave of the future were the stock-in-trade of party spokesmen. Morale was high, and the parties were eager to do battle.

V

THE EVOLUTION OF
POLITICAL PARTIES IN
JAPANESE INSTITUTIONAL
STRUCTURE AND THEORY

Part I: 1890–1913

ONE OF THE DETERRENTS to Japanese democracy and the party movement was the institutional structure within which these were imprisoned. The term "institutional structure," as used here, refers, first, to that composite set of political institutions fixed by the Meiji Constitution of 1889, its accompanying laws, and subsequent edicts. Together, these fundamental laws not only created the framework of the modern Japanese state, but also specified in a broad sense the power perimeters for each of its parts. The Japanese institutional structure, however, cannot be understood by means of the written law alone, for underlying this was the vast body of unwritten customs which gave form to the Meiji Constitution and shaped the institutions created by it. The Japanese emphasis on "the spirit of the Constitution" and on such mystical terms as *kokutai* (the national polity) are graphic evidence of those basic assumptions and practices implanted in Japanese political relations which were a vital part of the fundamental law.

It is difficult to avoid assigning either too much or too little importance to a written constitution such as the Meiji Constitution in seeking to determine what part it plays in the failure or success of a political theory. Certainly it is desirable for the student of comparative government to correct the mechanically oriented analysis which concentrates upon technical deficiencies and leaves the impression that if a clause had been changed here or there,

146

this by itself would have spelled the difference between defeat and victory for some cause such as democracy. It is an overcorrection, however, to dismiss the written constitution as nothing more than a piece of litmus paper by means of which the dominant socioeconomic forces and traditions of a society are revealed. Although due weight should be given to the fact that the fundamental nature of a society usually determines the form of its basic political code, still it would be erroneous to overlook the potential power that is innate in the act of constitution making and its aftermath. From the moment of its adoption, the written constitution has potentials as a symbol, as a comprehensive and definitive authority, and as a final source of appeal. It plays upon the notions of stability and permanence, which are powerful psychological forces.

Popular impetus toward revolution or defiance of prevailing fundamental law is ordinarily weaker than the present state of the world would seem to indicate. Genuine satisfaction, fear of change, the power of established practice, constant indoctrination on behalf of the basic rules, indifference, passivity, and even opportunism combine, under most circumstances, to provide support for the existing order or gradual change. A written constitution can further stimulate or canalize many of these natural reactions. If consistent with the dominant forces and trends of its society at the time of its adoption, it further strengthens these by giving their concepts of permissible political behavior and institutions additional legitimacy and permanence.

Even when a new constitution is imposed by indigenous groups or foreign sources struggling against the old order, however, as long as it bears some initial relationship to social realities and can be sustained by power it can be expected to influence the political attitudes and actions of both the elite and the common citizenry over a period of time. In this case, to be sure, the initial period may be a critical one, and history is filled with constitutions which were scraps of paper because both the inner validity and the power to sustain them were lacking. But of the two desiderata, power is the more important, for within certain limits, "validity" is likely to accumulate with the passage of time. Hostile traditions can be partially disarmed by the combined use of creative interpretation and frontal assault. Gradually, the aura of tradition and sanctity can be centralized upon the fundamental law itself. At the same time as the constitution induces support by this means, it overcomes some of its firmest opponents by drawing them into the vortex of its operation and sending them scurrying through the

147

corridors of "power." And if it is to develop its potential effectiveness fully, it affiliates the whole of the people with its basic processes and ideals, with the result that even in periods of crisis and upheaval, certain ingrained habits and values connected with it will survive.

Naturally, in this process of adjustment between society and law, the prevailing structure and needs of society will both present demands, and flexibility will be needed to satisfy these demands or fend them off. There is absolutely no reason, however, for assuming, as many people do, that law is merely the passive recipient of social pressures, any more than there is for assuming that it is simply the reflection of them. A fundamental law such as a written constitution creates its own pressures, some exceedingly subtle, but taken together, impressive in the aggregate.

If these general hypotheses be applied to the case of Japan, what relationship can be discerned between the Meiji Constitution and the emerging liberal movement? There can be no doubt that the Meiji Constitution was a fair representation of the contemporary nature of Japanese society and of the balance of forces therein. Liberalism was weak in many senses, and the political domination of a small elite of Imperially countenanced oligarchs mirrored the general social conditions. At the same time, however, the status quo was none too secure, and in spite of deceptive appearances, there was no fundamental agreement on basic principles. To be sure, the Throne and unity were symbolisms to which all paid homage, but the liberals, even though they did not admit or fully comprehend the fact, represented a movement potentially destructive of the connotations which these bore. But in order to develop, Japanese democracy needed many stimuli, including that of favorable political institutions. The Meiji Constitution, however, was scarcely conducive to answering this need. Skillfully timed and cleverly drawn up to give the minimum of concessions to popular government, the Constitution of 1889 put the democratic movement under great political handicaps by placing it within the strictures of an incompatible framework and by robbing it of its major premises.

We have already noted in some detail the unfavorable balance of power which was established against the one popular organ, the House of Representatives. The House, in terms of its powers, possessed the attributes of a gadfly but not those of a leader. It was surrounded by the imposing bureaucratic institutions, including the subordinate administrative bureaucracy, the Privy Council,

148

the war and navy groups, the Peers, and, most important of all, the top Sat-Cho oligarchs, under whose protection the real sources of the Meiji bureaucracy were nurtured.[1] This was a formidable opposition to subordinate to the forces of representative government and would have made the advance of liberalism difficult even if the Constitution had been under the joint auspices of the spokesmen for oligarchic and representative government. In fact, however, the Constitution was legally the property of neither, nor of the Japanese people as a whole—it belonged only to the Emperor.

Liberalism had been robbed of its basic premise by the connection which was fixed between the Throne and constitutionalism. By the simple device of having the Emperor "give" the people their Constitution and of making it virtually his personal property to alter or revise, the ruling oligarchy had taken advantage of the political immaturity and confusion of the liberals by falsifying the true nature of the protest in their society and by projecting this falsification into the future with redoubtable force. The Constitution was made subordinate to the Throne, and thereby to the oligarchs who controlled the Throne. And in this very process, the prestige of the Throne was so greatly enhanced that few men would dare to challenge the political uses to which it had been and could be put—and then, too few and too late.

Indeed, the use to which the Throne was put in the early period is one key to understanding the real effect which the Constitution had on the political party movement. As we shall see, it helps to explain why the "liberal" parties, in their quest for administrative power, were forced to turn inward to the mechanisms of the bureaucracy rather than outward to seek popular understanding and support. We shall best be able to measure the effects of this on party principles, composition, and popular support after we have examined in detail the stages through which the parties passed in their relations with the bureaucracy.

First, however, one exceedingly important factor in connection

[1] An understanding of the term *kanryo* (bureaucracy), as used by the Japanese, is of vital importance. Actually it was used in two senses. In one sense, it referred specifically to the vast, sprawling subordinate officialdom in the various departments and bureaus. But it was also broadly applied to the whole of Meiji officialdom as that class grew out of the oligarchic state; thus it included Peers, members of the Privy Council, war and navy groups, and Genro. It is in the latter sense that I use the term, unless specified to the contrary. For a further explanation in English, see Iwasaki Uichi, *The Working Forces in Japanese Politics,* New York, 1921, p. 17.

with Japanese constitutionalism must be mentioned. The Meiji Constitution was essentially an attempt to unite two concepts which when viewed in the abstract were irreconcilable: Imperial absolutism and popular government. Consequently, if the Meiji Constitution were to be workable in any degree, these abstract concepts had to be compromised in the practical operation of government. As has been suggested, the quota of power assigned each by the Constitution dictated that the popular elements would have to make the major concessions. But in addition to the disadvantage of their weak bargaining position in terms of legal power, those representing democracy faced the full adverse weight of the unwritten elements of Japanese constitutionalism. These elements consisted mostly of extralegal institutions and procedures which facilitated compromise away from democratic ideals in a great variety of ways. One of their most potent effects was the complete obscuring of responsibility.

Indeed, it is through this element of irresponsibility that one can reach into the very essence of the unwritten constitution and modern Japanese government. It was evident, first of all, in the unwritten rules governing superior-subordinate relations. The collective power of subordinates—whether in the bureaucracy or in the parties—tended to dominate the individual chief in the person of a minister, bureau head, or party leader, removing his sense of personal decision or responsibility and blurring all principles other than compromise and unity. Irresponsibility was also the genesis of procedural methods within and between all branches of government. Go-betweens, informal meetings, and group discussions were consistently used to reach decisions for which no individual or group was ordinarily responsible. This also encouraged the subordination of principle to the interests of an elitist harmony. Finally, irresponsibility was cultivated by the use of extralegal institutions, one of which, the council called the *Genro* (Elder Statesmen), occupied a supreme position in Japanese politics up to the 1920's. No political institution was as powerful as the Genro in the early constitutional period, although it operated without a vestige of legal power and hence was not legally accountable for its actions.[2] But, although it had no legal position guaranteed by

---

[2] The Genro Council did not come into formal operation until after 1900, when the early leaders of the Meiji Sat-Cho oligarchy retired, to carry on their activities behind the scenes. It was at that time that the inner circle of court power was formalized by the establishment of the principle that the Emperor would consider a man as one of his chief advisers if that man had

the written constitution, it served to shield the Emperor from responsibility for his theoretically absolute powers by making all important political decisions in his name and serving as the real centralized power of the Japanese state.

These unwritten institutional and procedural elements of Japanese constitutionalism were deeply implanted in political tradition, as we have seen. Under any conditions they would have been difficult to eradicate, but the structure of the written constitution was such as to make them indispensable. Only in diversity is there real responsibility, and this is the essence of democracy and parliamentary government. But the premise of the Meiji Constitution was a type of unity which, if it were to be complete, called for the totally fulfilled sacrifice of individual opinion. Thus all the elements of the unwritten constitution available in the background of Japanese society and necessary to the functioning of the new fundamental law, operated to subvert the democratic forces.

Turning now to the picture of the party struggle, perhaps we can best analyze trends and problems by dividing relationships between the parties and the bureaucracy into four phases developing in the years between 1890 and 1932.[3] These phases cannot always be separated on a purely chronological basis, because the parties and the bureaucracy each came to be divided into two major groups, and the relationship between the Jiyuto element and the one bureaucratic faction moved at a different speed from that of the Kaishinto element and another bureaucratic faction. Ultimately, however, both groups passed through approximately the same evolutionary cycle, and to both the results were the same.

The opening phase of this cycle may be called the phase of

---

rendered "exceptionally meritorious service," which came to be interpreted as having served as premier twice. The original Genro Council included such Sat-Cho leaders as Ito, Yamagata, and Matsukata.

The functions of the Genro centered in the selection of premiers and extended outward from this to all important political matters, and thus it came to represent the supreme coördinating organ of the national government.

In spite of the relatively late date of its formalization, the Genro was actually an institutional force at the time of the promulgation of the Constitution, since it was no more than the inner circle of the Sat-Cho oligarchy. Consequently, Japanese scholars frequently use the term Genro with reference to the earlier period and I have followed that custom in the present study, having given the above explanation.

[3] I am greatly indebted to the research and writings of Royama Masamichi in the field of modern Japanese politics, as numerous citations in this section from his works will attest.

complete separation between the "liberal" parties and the ruling bureaucracy. The duration of this phase was, roughly, from 1890 until the Sino-Japanese War of 1894–1895. The second phase was that of the development of party-bureaucratic ententes, which dominated at least certain parts of the political scene from 1895 until 1918 and continued to be manifested throughout the entire life of the parties. The third phase, which was a refinement of the second and ran concurrently with it, was the phase of the Sat-Cho oligarchs' affiliation with and leadership of the party movement. This phase started when Prince Ito took over the Jiyuto and made it into the *Rikken Seiyukai* (Friends of Constitutional Government Association) in 1900, and reached its zenith in 1913 with Prince Katsura's (Katsura Taro) formation of the *Rikken Doshikai* (Constitutional Fellow Thinkers' Association), a party which eventually contained the majority of the old Kaishinto members. The fourth and final phase was marked by mixed bureaucratic and "pure party" leadership, membership, and principles in the major parties and heralded the arrival of party cabinets and the quasi-supremacy of the party movement. This phase was in effect the culmination and end product of the other three and established the characteristics by which the parties were known in the period of their greatest power. We must now turn to a detailed examination of these phases.

The first phase, that of more or less complete separation between the liberal parties and the bureaucracy, was of tremendous importance, despite its relative brevity. It was during this phase that the overwhelming necessity for compromise under the Japanese constitutional framework was demonstrated, the uncompromising unity of both sides was dented, and certain ways of compromise were suggested. These were the crucial, exploratory years during which the methods and relative powers of each side were sounded out.

The dimensions of the opening conflict between the parties and the bureaucracy were clearly outlined in the rival interpretations of constitutionalism which they put forth. The top statesmen, in addition to making certain formal preparations for the Diet,[4] had

---

[4] Under the Kuroda ministry, in June, 1889, Privy Councillor Kaneko Kentaro and four Justice Department officials were sent overseas to observe parliamentary institutions. In October, the *Rinji Teikoku Gikai Jimukyoku* (Temporary Imperial Diet Affairs Bureau) was established, with Inoue Kaoru (subsequently a Genro) as its head. For Inoue's report to Premier Yamagata dated August, 1890, see *Hisho ruisan Teikoku Gikai shiryo* (*Collection of*

taken particular care to state the proper position of officialdom in its relations with the House of Representatives and the parties therein. On February 12, 1889, one day after the Constitution had been promulgated, Premier Kuroda (Kuroda Kiyotaka)[5] made the following remarks at a meeting of the district governors:

The existence of so-called political parties in political society formed by people who have joined together for mutual purposes and who have formed alliances is inevitable under present conditions. However, the government must always take a fixed attitude and stand outside the political parties as a transcendental [*chozen to shita*] body . . . Each official . . . must come near to the people with an unprejudiced, nonparty mind and rule tranquilly and well.[6]

Ito, at the time president of the Privy Council, said much the same thing in addressing a meeting of *fu* (metropolitan) and *ken* (prefectural) assembly members on February 15, and added these remarks:

We cannot avoid the extremely risky matter of having the Diet political groups, that is to say the political parties, desire to form a Cabinet. Although there are probably not a few who would speak of the advantages of party factions, such a course demands the cultivation of sufficient power already established as the axis of a country so that it can be dependent upon the processes of public discussion for administration, and if it lacks this necessity, if it shakes the basis of the nation, how much future disadvantage this will result in, is the thing which alarms me.[7]

The oligarchy had thus already established a policy which came to be known as *chozen naikaku shugi* (the principle of transcendental cabinet)—a principle based fundamentally on the premise that the administration derived all its power from the Throne and hence could not presume to represent any less than all the Emperor's subjects.[8] Despite its transparencies, such an argument

Private Papers—Imperial Diet Materials), edited by Ito Hirobumi, revised by Kaneko Kentaro and Hiratsuka Atsushi, Tokyo, 1934, Vol. I, pp. 109–112.

[5] The Kuroda cabinet had replaced Ito's first cabinet on April 30, 1888. This change had been induced primarily because of the controversy over treaty revision, and the agitations of the Daido Danketsu had given the oligarchs a fair indication of the potential power of the parties.

[6] Speech of Kuroda, February 12, 1889, quoted in Royama Masamichi, *Seiji shi (Political History)*, in Gendai Nihon bummei shi (History of Contemporary Japanese Civilization Series), Tokyo, 1940, p. 269.

[7] Speech of Ito, February 15, 1889, quoted in *ibid.*, pp. 269–270.

[8] This basis was never more clearly revealed than in a speech of Premier Yamagata to the prefectural governors on December 25, 1890: "Neces-

was quite in keeping with the written word of the Constitution.

The liberal parties, on the other hand, had their own interpretations of constitutional government, and perhaps these were best expressed by the third plank of the 1890 Jiyuto platform: "We pledge ourselves to raising the practice of the representative [parliamentary] system and establishing political party cabinets." [9]

These sentiments, reflected in the Kaishinto platform as well, made it clear that the liberal parties intended to use the Constitution as a means of subordinating the bureaucracy and extending the party movement in scope and power.

With the opening of the First Diet, on November 25, 1890, the two opposing forces confronted each other for the first time in the arena of practical politics. The chance had at last arrived to put into action the principles and powers which each side possessed and in so doing to determine the nature of those principles and the extent of that power. The Sat-Cho oligarchs, for their part, were ready to meet the Diet with a new cabinet headed by the staunch Choshu militarist, Yamagata Aritomo.[10] In picking Yamagata, who was to become the great leader of the militarist faction and the symbol of conservatism in Meiji and Taisho Japan, the oligarchs could not have shown a more hostile front to the party movement. The liberal parties, however, were in a relatively strong position. The so-called *minto* (popular parties—the Jiyuto, the Kaishinto, and their affiliates) held a combined strength exceeding 170 seats in the 300-member Diet.[11] Indeed, this display of strength symbolized an important weakness in the government's "transcendental" position. Having insisted upon separating itself from party politics, the administration now faced a lower house in which its political support was negligible. Its efforts to keep the parties disunited had suffered a serious setback by the time

---

sarily, because administrative rights are the sovereign prerogatives of the Emperor, those who are given the responsibility of their exercise shall stand outside the various political parties." Speech quoted in *ibid.*, p. 265.

[9] Quoted from Hayashida Kametaro, *Nihon seito shi (History of Japanese Political Parties)*, Tokyo, 1927, Vol. I, p. 289.

[10] The Kuroda ministry had been forced to resign on December 23, 1889, when it proved unable to revise the foreign treaties to suit nationalistic tastes. Its resignation was precipitated by a bomb attack on Foreign Minister Okuma which cost him his leg.

[11] The actual figures were: Jiyuto, 130; Kaishinto, 41. In addition, there were 45 independents, some of whose votes were certain to be antigovernment. Figures from Otsu Junichiro, *Dai Nihon kensei shi (A Constitutional History of Greater Japan)*, Tokyo, 1927–1928, Vol. III, p. 542.

of the First Diet. The parties, badly split since the collapse of Goto's Daido Danketsu had succeeded in reëstablishing themselves in the old Jiyuto and Kaishinto groups. In fact, a complete union of these two failed only by a narrow margin.[12] Worst of all, from the government's point of view, there were no real administration parties to oppose the reorganized minto.[13]

The Diet thus opened in a spirit of tension and hostility. One cannot read Yamagata's introductory speech to the House of Representatives without sensing all the arrogance and contempt with which this prince of han bureaucrats treated the elected representatives.[14] The entire speech typified the bureaucratic approach which one authority had called *yorashimubeshi,* meaning, "You should depend upon us (and ask no questions)." [15] The Premier constantly referred to the need for complete unity and implicit trust in officialdom.[16] Concerning government policy, the speech was extremely vague; absolutely nothing was said about pending legislative bills.

The popular parties were quick to take up the challenge. They utilized the only weapon which the Constitution had granted them by striking at the administration budget. The Budget Committee of the House, dominated by minto men, cut the total budget by

---

[12] After the first election, held in February, 1890, the three factions of the old Jiyuto were reunited, calling themselves the *Yayoi Club.* Beginning on August 13, a series of meetings was held to unite all the popular forces into one party. It was finally decided to call the party *Daigi Seito* (Representative Party) and to make its central principle "the principle of liberty." However, on September 1, at a general meeting of the Kaishinto, a resolution to accept entrance into the new party was defeated. During this entire period, the government applied its Public Meeting and Political Association Law, strictly prohibiting the circulation of correspondence on questions of political amalgamation. For details, see Fukaya Hiroji, *Shoki Gikai joyaku kaisei* (*The First Diets: Treaty Revision*), in Kindai Nihon rekishi koza (Modern Japanese History Series), Tokyo, 1940, pp. 191–195.

[13] The Taiseikai, composed of seventy-nine former bureaucrats and progovernment men, and the Kokumin Jiyuto, a small group of ultranationalists, were considered as on the government side, but neither of these groups was officially connected with the government, nor were they pledged to continuous government support.

[14] Yamagata's speech to the First Diet, December 6, 1890, is printed in Ito Hirobumi (ed.), *op. cit.,* Vol. I, pp. 482–485.

[15] Fukaya, *op. cit.,* p. 207.

[16] As might have been expected, Yamagata's defense of Imperial sovereignty was extreme. The protection of *shuken sen* (the sovereign line), he stated, may be called the purpose of the nation. From Yamagata's speech, in Ito Hirobumi (ed.), *op. cit.,* Vol. I, p. 484.

about 10 per cent. It is important to realize that this action manifested far more than a desire for monetary saving; by revising the budget, the parties hoped not only to reduce taxation, but also to strike at the opponents of party government by clipping the wings of the civil and military bureaucracy. The most important budgetary reductions were those on official salaries, retirement pensions, social allowances, and such privileges as official residences and traveling expenses.[17]

The parties had eminently good reasons for starting their campaign for representative control of the government by an attack on the subordinate civil and military bureaucracy. The position of this group was then and gave signs of continuing to be the broad foundation of administrative power.[18] In a state in which numerous controls on every political and economic front were the rule, the departmental bureaucracy—and oftentimes even the minor officials—were the real drafters and administrators of this legislation.

This bureaucracy, moreover, was completely hostile to the liberal parties, and in full alliance with the Sat-Cho administrators. The oligarchy had established the structure and hand-picked its entire personnel, and its machinery was already twenty years old when the Constitution was promulgated. During these years, the oligarchs had controlled the appointment system, using it as a means of meting out rewards to deserving compatriots and followers from their han. It is true that certain excesses had forced some revision. In July, 1887, a Civil Service examination system was set up, similar to the German system, allowing certain appointments to be made without examination to graduates of the Imperial University Law School. The net effect of these changes, as Professor Royama has pointed out, was to change the Meiji bureaucracy slowly from a *hambatsu* (han clique) to a *gakubatsu* (University clique),[19] but the important point which should be made is that both elements were, with few exceptions, hostile to the parties and the lower house. Socially, in knowledge, and even economically, the officials considered themselves above the commoners, and the old feeling of "officials honored, people despised" was still prevalent.

Thus the liberal parties were well justified in their attack on

---

[17] The Budget Committee Report is reproduced in Fukaya, *op. cit.*, p. 207.

[18] For an important analysis of the early Meiji bureaucracy, from which much of this material is taken, see Royama, *op. cit.*, pp. 287–295.

[19] *Ibid.*, p. 290.

the subordinate bureaucracy, but such an attack provoked immediate government action and revealed in a preliminary way the obstacles to party power. In the first place, the parties could not cut through to the subordinate bureaucracy without first coping with its sponsors, the Sat-Cho oligarchs. As the revised budgetary report itself stated, "Although we should investigate and revise the expenditure budget with the object of rectifying the bureaucratic system and salary regulations, since these originally belong to the sovereign powers of His Majesty, we entrust the execution of this to the action of those specifically concerned." [20]

There could not be much hope for drastic reform from "those specifically concerned," even if certain budget cuts were allowed to pass. Moreover, the government had no intention of giving way without a struggle. Immediately, it utilized a little-discussed provision of the Constitution which prohibited the reduction of already fixed expenditures without administrative provision, and thereby demonstrated that the report exceeded the privileges of the House.[21] As further persuasion, government forces hired *soshi* (strong-arm men) to intimidate the members of the opposition and prevent them from entering the Diet chambers. Dissolution was threatened,[22] but to no avail; despite its repressive measures, the government could not prevent the revised budget from being passed by the House.

When repression failed to work, the administration seems to have turned to a somewhat more delicate maneuver—corruption. After prolonged negotiations between certain cabinet ministers and the Tosa branch of the Jiyuto, a compromise of suspicious nature was reached, and enough Tosa votes were obtained to pass a more suitable budget.[23] The result was still no great victory for

[20] Quoted in Fukaya, *op. cit.*, p. 207.

[21] The article in question, article lxvii, read: "Those already fixed expenditures based by the Constitution upon the powers appertaining to the Emperor, and such expenditures as may have arisen by the effect of law, or that appertain to the legal obligations of the Government, shall be neither rejected nor refused by the Imperial Diet without the concurrence of the Government." From Imperial Constitution as translated in *JGD*, pp. 142–143.

[22] It is stated that certain members of the oligarchy, especially Ito, were opposed to a dissolution of the First Diet on the score that it would create a bad impression on foreign countries. See Fukaya, *op. cit.*, p. 209. There was a certain logic in this, since Japan was desirous of immediate treaty revisions.

[23] There seems little doubt that the ministry employed open bribery. Hayashida writes that twenty-eight Tosa faction men switched sides temporarily *after* a visit to the finance minister's official residence. For his "eye-witness" account of the shady events, see Hayashida, *op. cit.*, Vol. I, pp. 309–312. The

the government, for the terms of the compromise were harsh, but even this would not have been attained had not the Yamagata cabinet resorted to questionable tactics and thus brought the Diet to a close without complete chaos.

A study of the First Diet is productive of some highly important conclusions. Already the Constitution had been revealed as a founder of an institutional structure of precarious instability. If it were to prove workable, certain very basic compromises would have to be made, and the nature of those compromises would determine who would "work" it. On the surface, there seemed to be little indication that either side was preparing to surrender any basic principles, but there were several signs that this might not be the case.

In the first place, minto unity against the oligarchy had been injured by a type of political immorality made easy by political traditions, a lackadaisical public attitude, and, not least of all, the insuperable difficulties of the party position. There was no indication as yet, however, how deeply the streams of corruption and discouragement would run. The great majority of liberal party men remained untainted and unreconciled to the government, though their first hopes of a quick and easy victory over the "han clique" were considerably diminished.

There was another trend, however, of equal or greater importance although it was to remain for some time hidden from the contemporary eye. Discord was brewing within the oligarchy itself concerning the best manner of dealing with the insurgent parties. The best proof of this cleavage is shown by the attitude of Ito toward the Yamagata ministry. In a letter to his friend, Ito Miyoji, written near the end of the Diet session, Prince Ito expressed his reservations concerning both the constitutionality and the wisdom of the ministry's policy toward the Diet, and about administrative policy in general.[24] Ito's words were carried to Yamagata by the recipient of the letter, and they constituted one of the chief reasons for resignation of the cabinet soon after the close of the Diet.[25]

---

final compromise was a cut of ¥6,510,000, with the promise of the cabinet to make suitable administrative reforms.

[24] See the very important "Ito Miyoji yori Gikai oyobi naikaku keisei wo hozuru shoshin" (Correspondence from Ito Miyoji Reporting the Diet and Cabinet Situation), in Ito Hirobumi (ed.), *op. cit.*, Vol. I, pp. 178–188.

[25] Yamagata resigned on May 5, 1891. Certainly one of the reasons for his resignation was the well-justified fear that the parties would not be satisfied with the few administrative reforms which the ministry had ordered, but

The real significance of this lies in the fact that a split was deepening between what came later to be known, somewhat inaccurately, as the "civil" and "military" factions of the oligarchy—a split which was hidden and, on occasion, temporarily patched up in the face of the minto menace, but one which colored this whole period and was to grow to ungovernable proportions. The lines were already etched in. The "civil" faction was represented by Ito and his friend and protégé, Inoue Kaoru. The "militarist" faction included several members of the Genro—Kuroda, Saigo Tsugumichi, Oyama Iwao, Matsukata Masayoshi, and Yamagata, who was the leader and real power of the faction. The over-all issues comprised both personal and policy matters, and they found a convenient focal point in the question of administration-Diet (i.e., administration-party) relations. Ito, though a thorough-going conservative, was anxiously concerned about the alternate haughtiness and corruption which characterized the "militarist" approach. He was beginning to realize that truly constitutional government demanded a more permanent solution to the problem of parties.

Despite these signs of impending change, however, the period up to the Sino-Japanese War of 1894 continued in the main to be one during which both the liberal parties and the bureaucracy preserved the outward appearances of internal unity and of opposition to each other—a period of extreme bitterness and hostility, and one in which each side used every weapon at its command.

The great question which faced the Sat-Cho oligarchs, as we have seen, was how to control the liberal parties. After Yamagata's experiences, the government leaders were all genuinely alarmed by the conduct of the House. Indeed, none of the leading statesmen, including the critical Ito, wanted the responsibility of the premiership. Finally, Matsukata, a man who lacked strong leadership qualities, was given the post. In reality, however, all the experienced statesmen sat behind "the black curtain," seeking to counsel each cabinet move and causing one careful historian of this period to remark, "The starting point of the rise of Genro politics which continued to hold special significance in Meiji and Taisho political history can be sought in the era of this Cabinet." [26]

If this joint Genro supervision was reflective of the desire to overcome friction between the administration and the Diet and to present a united front, it had not been founded upon any

Professor Royama concludes that the chief reason was Ito's critical attitude toward the cabinet's policy vis-à-vis the Diet. See Royama, op. cit., p. 275.

[26] Fukaya, op. cit., p. 241.

basic agreement concerning means.[27] As the Second and Third Diets produced progressive crises under the Matsukata ministry, two radically different solutions to the problem were advanced by the inner circle, one by Ito and his faction, the other by the Yamagata faction, whose temporary spokesman in the cabinet was Home Minister Shinagawa Yajiro.[28] Both of the proposed solutions were of the greatest importance in the evolution of Japanese politics; both were eventually to have the greatest repercussions on the party movement.

In the beginning, Shinagawa's plan of attack was put into practice, for the simple reason that the Yamagata faction controlled a majority of the Matsukata cabinet members.[29] His plan, as befitting that of a fanatic, was simple and ruthless: give the popular parties no quarter, refuse compromise, smash party connections with the people.

The execution of this general plan led to the immediate dissolution of the Second Diet when the popular parties cut the budget by nearly ¥8,000,000,[30] and this dissolution was followed, on February 15, 1892, by the most brutal election in Japanese history.[31]

[27] The best proof of Sat-Cho disunity is the fact that almost immediately, the Matsukata cabinet had the Emperor issue, in the form of an Imperial rescript, a document known as the *Naikaku Gigetsusho* (Cabinet Resolution Document), the gist of which was that there must be cabinet unity on policy, ministerial answers in the Diet must agree, and all should agree when presenting their views to the press. See Royama, *op. cit.*, p. 278. Says Professor Royama, "In truth, it was nothing other than fear, but the Matsukata cabinet expected to preserve the unity of the cabinet in obedience to something which had the sincere wish of the Emperor." *Ibid.*, p. 276.

[28] Shinagawa was a driving Choshu nationalist, briefly a pupil of Yoshida Shoin, and a bitter opponent of the party movement. He had been heavily imbued with German ideas and took a leading position formulating agrarian policy.

[29] Only two of the ten cabinet members could be accounted followers of Ito. These two, Goto Shojiro and Mutsu Munemitsu, opposed Shinagawa's tactics.

[30] The new budget included provisions for a scheme to buy the railroads not in government hands and represented a ¥6,490,000 increase over the previous budget. Diet procedure was similar to that of the first session; a revised bill with cuts totaling ¥7,940,347 was introduced. See Fukaya, *op. cit.*, pp. 254–255, for details.

[31] For detailed accounts of this election, see Hayashida, *op. cit.*, Vol. I, pp. 336–344, and Otsu, *op. cit.*, Vol. III, pp. 679–683. Government tactics included molestation of voters by soshi, arrest of liberal candidates, and burning of the liberals' property. Both Okuma and Itagaki were prosecuted under the Assemblage and Political Association Law when they printed their announcements of endorsement in the press. These facts and many more were

The government, under Shinagawa's supervision, used every possible repressive measure against the popular parties. The figures of casualties speak for themselves: officially, reports listed 25 killed and 388 wounded; and the actual numbers were probably much higher.

Despite these drastic steps, however, the Shinagawa approach was hopelessly inadequate, for the reason that although the government could savagely maul the popular parties, it had no coördinated plan of raising up successors to them. Standing officially loyal to its principles of aloofness from parties, it was forced to back various small and disorganized conservative and bureaucratic groups from behind the scenes. The result was that in spite of all the violence used against them, the minto emerged from the election with a clear majority of 163 seats in the new Diet.[32]

Not only did the Shinagawa policy fail to oust the liberal parties; it gave them the strength that comes from martyrdom. Indeed, the minto achieved during this period a unity of purpose and an enmity toward the "han clique" which was to make compromise increasingly difficult. On November 8, 1891, even before the opening of the Second Diet, Itagaki and Okuma had met and had pledged their respective parties to a coalition in the forthcoming session. The Second Diet had opened with a rousing attack on the ministry for failing to keep its pledges of administrative reform given in the Yamagata compromise, and after dissolution, the two popular parties coöperated in defending themselves as best they could against government election interference.

Minto hostility had reached a new height by the opening of the special Diet session after the election, on May 2, 1892. An immediate drive was launched to impeach the government. The more ardent party men demanded impeachment in the form of a *josoan* (resolution memorializing the Emperor), but this was defeated by three votes, "because of the gravity of troubling the Emperor's mind" over such an issue.[33] A simple resolution of condemnation was easily passed, however, and the liberal parties awaited its results. This move gave the administration a chance

recited by Shimada Saburo in his brilliant and lengthy speech before the Diet, May 12, 1893, reproduced in full in Otsu, *op. cit.*, Vol. III, pp. 696–720.

[32] The Jiyuto obtained 94 seats, the Kaishinto 38, and an antigovernment group called the *Dokuritsu Club* (Independent Club), 31; the government groups totaled 137 seats, although some of these votes were in doubt. Otsu, *op. cit.*, Vol. III, p. 693.

[33] Fukaya, *op. cit.*, p. 255. For a defense of the memorial, see Shimada's speech, already cited, in Otsu, *op. cit.*, Vol. III, pp. 696–720.

to demonstrate its constitutional immunities and its long-standing position on responsibility. Not only did it completely ignore the nonconfidence vote (and a similar one passed by the Peers),[34] but it adjourned the House for seven days as a disciplinary measure! The parties were then forced to turn again to the budget as their sole weapon of attack, and they succeeded in forcing a serious reduction on the unwilling ministry.[35] The Matsukata cabinet, however, weathered the storm and proved conclusively that the institutional procedures granted to the Diet were completely insufficient to enable the liberal parties to topple even a most arrogant foe.

The "militarist" solution to the problem of the liberal parties, however, had been a conspicuous failure, notwithstanding minto impotence. And Ito, who had recognized this and had constantly opposed the policy, was working out a different solution. Soon after the dissolution of the Second Diet, in a secret memorandum dated December 10, 1891, he had severely criticized the Matsukata cabinet for having "no fixed policy, internal disagreements, and no control or management over the Diet," as well as for numerous other shortcomings, among which were the misuse of secret funds and the use of unethical practices, including spying.[36] In this long document, he revealed his contemporary opinion on the need for a Diet policy and concluded with a plan which, although vaguely expressed, seemed to call for the issue, simultaneously with Diet dissolution, of a *taisho* (Imperial rescript) in which the Emperor

---

[34] This resolution demonstrated the true measure of the cabinet's unpopularity, for the Peers were certainly not seeking to support the popular parties, as their subsequent actions clearly showed.

[35] This was, of course, a supplementary budget, since the session of the Third Diet was a special postelection session, and the Yamagata budget had gone into effect automatically upon the dissolution of the Second Diet. The cuts made were primarily in strict revisions of military expenses and government enterprises. An interesting constitutional problem arose when the Peers refused to agree to all the House cuts; the Peers passed a message to the Throne asking advice, and the Emperor turned the matter over to the Privy Council (controlled, of course, by the Sat-Cho group). The Privy Council handed down a ruling that a compromise should be effected in joint committee, thereby negating House hopes that on budgetary matters its decisions would be final.

[36] Taken from *Ito Hirobumi hiroku* (*Secret Records of Ito Hirobumi*), reproduced in Fukaya, *op. cit.*, pp. 257–258. Chapter xi of Professor Fukaya's work, entitled "Ito Hirobumi no seito soshiki mondai" (The Question of Ito Hirobumi's Organization of a Political Party), is a detailed and excellently documented revelation of Ito's early interest in the party idea.

would "admonish the people." [37] This, Ito seemed to feel, would control the situation by limiting the excesses of the popular parties and causing the people to join with the officially inclined candidates, in obedience to an Imperial request. Such an amazing proposal he defended in a letter to his friend, Inoue Kowashi, stating that since the Emperor was the mother and father of the people, it was his duty to advise and counsel them. [38]

Inoue disagreed, stating that it was impossible to involve the Imperial House in political matters, [39] but Ito was already pushing ahead to a further phase of his plan. On January 22, 1892, in an audience with the Emperor, he stated that the only way to save the situation was to establish a government party, and that if His Majesty objected to this, he, Ito, would request to be dispatched overseas in connection with treaty revision, or to be retired in peace. [40] Somewhat later, on March 9, Privy Councillor Sasaki Takayuki wrote that Ito had proposed resigning his official duties, assembling the men of the Taiseikai, and organizing an administration party. [41]

These interesting details are of vital importance to an understanding of all later events, even though Ito's ideas were temporarily shelved because of the united opposition of the other Genro. What is clear is that Ito, who was politically the most perceptive of the government leaders, was beginning to recognize the illogical position of the *chozen naikaku shugi* (principle of transcendental cabinet) and was even prepared to unite the Throne and an administrative party in order to produce internal stability. [42] Here

---

[37] *Ibid.*, p. 258.

[38] Letter from Ito Hirobumi to Inoue Kowashi, from *Ito Hirobumi Ko den hensan shiryo (Compiled Records of the Biography of Prince Ito Hirobumi)*, reproduced in Fukaya, *op. cit.*, p. 262.

[39] *Ibid.*, pp. 262–263.

[40] *Ibid.*, p. 263.

[41] From Sasaki Takayuki, *Meiji Seijo to shin Takayuki (His Majesty Meiji and His Servant Takayuki)*, quoted in Fukaya, *op. cit.*, pp. 265–266.

[42] Ito's position as a conservative was honest, and his logic demands some recognition. His greatest desire, like that of most Japanese politicians of whatever faction, was always for an internal political unity which would enable the nation to progress rapidly and to meet the foreign situation. He was rightly afraid that "the public" lacked as yet the political education to govern indirectly through representative institutions. As he stated in his secret memorial of December 10, 1891, "Our people are still childish and simple; childish, simple people, like white silk, are easy to dye various colors." Ito's greatest shortcoming, however, was that as an official trained in the classical approach, he lacked the capacity to formulate institutions and techniques

was a solution to the minto menace which offered a real chance of success.

Ito's party proposal, however, was still premature, not only because of the Yamagata faction's opposition, but also because of the liberals' enthusiasm for their cause and the optimism with which the popular parties viewed their chances for victory. First, the uncompromising spirit of the minto would have to be broken on the rack of their own charter. The Constitution would have to be revealed to them in its true light—in the awe-inspiring light of the Throne. The events leading up to this action are well worth recording.

The Matsukata cabinet resigned on August 7, 1892, and Ito, whose violent opposition had really caused its downfall, finally accepted the premiership. His conditions for acceptance were Sat-Cho unity, and to this end he constructed what was known as the *genkun naikaku* (elder statesmen cabinet), including in the ministry the Genro Yamagata, Kuroda, Oyama, and Inoue. Previous internal disagreements did not prevent the older statesmen from now stepping unitedly to the front in an effort to protect the fate of their political program. Ito, moreover, soon made it clear that whatever his secret plans, he was still prepared to go on public record in resolute opposition to automatic party government. In his instructions to the prefectural governors' conference, he stated:

> As for the spirit of our Constitution, the Ministers of State by serving the sacred desires of His Majesty and taking all political responsibilities, are not men who should be controlled by the power of others. If in future events, there is a general trend that party cabinets should be established—although the Constitution does not protect against changes to the present spirit—the spirit of our Imperially ordered Constitution never anticipated the establishment of this type of cabinet.[43]

The Fourth Diet, which was convened on November 25, 1892, marked a testing of the extremities permitted under the Constitution, and was in many ways the most significant Diet session ever held under that fundamental law. The test was brought on by the liberal parties themselves. After their attempt to reduce the budget by cutting bureaucratic expenses and the appropriations for a large naval building program had failed because of cabinet op-

---

which would train the public mind for participation in representative government. He was too much a part of the old order to drop his idea that government should be obeyed rather than understood.

[43] Quoted from *Meiji kensei shi* (*History of Meiji Constitutionalism*), Vol. I, by Fukaya, *op. cit.*, p. 298.

position,[44] the liberal parties produced 146 signatures on a memorial to the Emperor impeaching the ministry. The government ordered a fifteen-day Diet suspension, but following this, on February 7, 1893, the memorial was passed by the House, and Hoshi Toru, president of the House, took the petition to the Emperor on February 8. Party criticism of the oligarchy, as voiced in the memorial, ran the whole gamut of past abuses, but particularly heavy fire was concentrated on the Ito cabinet's refusal to allow budget reductions in the sums requested for the bureaucracy and the navy.

The Emperor's response was a masterpiece of strategy and an unprecedented blow to the minto. After consulting with the cabinet ministers, Privy Councillors, and certain leading members of both houses, the Emperor issued his reply (drafted undoubtedly by members of the inner circle) on February 10. First, he took care to restate the Imperial interpretation of the Diet, "By opening the Diet and extending public discussion, I established the fact of their being permitted *to aid* [*yokusan*] in the great task [of administration]." [45] When it came to the vital question of naval appropriations, the Emperor wrote:

Arriving at the matter of national defense, when we let slip even one day, we leave behind us one hundred years regret. I hereby will save expenses of the Imperial Household and for six years, every year, I will give ¥300,000, and I order the civil and military officials, omitting persons who are in special circumstances, for the same period, to pay one-tenth of their salary, and by this, the naval construction expenses will be sufficiently made up.[46]

The injection of the Throne into politics was a great victory for the ideas of Ito and spelled a major defeat for the liberal parties. Its immediate effect was to force the parties to compromise with the government despite their realization of the true nature of events.[47] Its long-run effect was even more serious. Professor

[44] The Budget Committee made cuts in the original budget amounting to about 11 per cent. The government threatened and cajoled, but the Diet sent the revised budget back three times over ministry objections. For Kono Hironaka's devastating speech against Sat-Cho monopolism, extravagance and waste of public funds, and bureaucratic corruption, see Otsu, *op. cit.*, Vol. III; the main part of the speech is reproduced on pp. 797–806. This speech is an excellent summary of the party position vis-à-vis the administration.

[45] Imperial Rescript, February 10, 1893; reproduced in *ibid.* (pp. 831–832), p. 831. (Italics mine.—R. A. S.)

[46] *Ibid.*, p. 832.

[47] In the party-administration conferences on the budget, the party leaders

Fukaya, a specialist on this period, has remarked that from the end of this Diet session, the Jiyuto tended to lose its pure minto character.[48] The major reason for this was the discouraging fact that although a popular party might oppose the Peers, the Privy Council, and even the Genro in cabinet or out, it could not oppose the Emperor, and a spirit of defeatism was certain to arise among the party men which would hasten the way toward compromise and corruption.

It is as yet, however, very premature to speak of party capitulation. The next few Diet sessions were in reality a transitional period, and in terms of events, they proved to be quite as hectic as the preceding sessions. The most significant factor, however, was that minto unity, which had been exceptionally strong up to this point, began to crack under the terrific pressure of these first years. This split was considerably aided by a major shift in the nature of the issues; foreign policy and questions of national power again became the primary topics of the day.

A split between the Jiyuto and the Kaishinto was clearly apparent by late 1893, for by the time of the Fifth Diet, which opened on November 25, the Ito cabinet faced a disorganized opposition. Hoshi, by now the real leader of the Jiyuto, had been publicly attacking the Kaishinto for many months, and more important, he was secretly conferring with Foreign Minister Mutsu on matters of foreign policy.[49] The Kaishinto, in the meantime, had shifted the major basis of its attack to the question of Ito's foreign policy, and, together with a group known as the *Dai Nihon Kyokai* (Greater Japan Society),[50] it was actually spearheading a nation-

tried to salvage some of their prestige by writing in some stipulations concerning administrative reform. Anger was openly expressed over Ito's tactics, but under the conditions, the minto elements were helpless.

[48] Fukaya, *op. cit.*, p. 316.

[49] Mutsu and Goto Shojiro had both been friendly with Hoshi and certain other Jiyuto leaders for many years. Goto, of course, was at one time a leader of many of these men as Daido Danketsu president. Both ministers had participated in the negotiations over the budget in the first Yamagata cabinet. Hoshi himself was one of the most brilliant and unscrupulous leaders that the liberal movement ever had. He has often been referred to as the Tammany Hall leader of Japanese politics, and his tactics were remarkably similar to those of Tammany Hall. His personal sentiments on the question of foreign policy were less important than the fact that he had come to recognize compromise as a *sine qua non* of political power.

[50] The Dai Nihon Kyokai had started out as a group opposed to the mixed residence of foreigners in Japan, and was led by the veteran "radical," Oi Kentaro. It was subsequently dissolved by the government. See *ibid.*, pp. 318–321.

alist movement in opposition to the general "Europeanization" program of the government. The parties representing liberalism were now divided into two groups, the *Taigaiko ha* (strong foreign policy group), led by the Kaishinto and its associates, and the *Shimpo ha* (progressive group), led by the Jiyuto.

Thus the first attack in the Fifth Diet was leveled against Hoshi, who was president of the House.[51] The Kaishinto, allied with the ultranationalist groups, succeeded in impeaching him on charges of corruption and ousting him from the Diet.[52] The charges spread to Agriculture and Commerce Minister Goto and his assistant, and these accusations were coupled with a strong attack on the cabinet treaty revision policy in a memorial to the Throne which passed the House.[53] Thus, in two consecutive sessions, the Emperor was called upon to make a major political decision, and again his reply was decidedly against the petitioners. His message of December 24, 1893, which was the result of consultations with the Genro, particularly Ito and Yamagata, and the Privy Council, minced no words in telling the Diet that with regard to matters of appointment or dismissal of cabinet ministers, the Imperial sovereignty would brook no outside interference.[54]

If the parties could not control the administration, however, they had the power to stalemate it completely. Despite Imperial criticism and the lukewarm attitude of the Jiyuto, the group favoring a strong foreign policy hammered away at government proposals for treaty rectification, and Ito was finally compelled to dissolve the Diet. He fared no better in the Sixth Diet, which opened on May 12, 1894, even though the opposition had lost some ground in the election of March 1. Another message to the Throne was introduced, criticizing the cabinet for its weak attitude toward treaty revision and for numerous other shortcomings. The government squeaked through with a five-vote margin because the Jiyuto refused to approve the foreign policy section, but a similar message omitting this part was passed and presented to the Emperor on June 1, 1894. Ito, after some consultation with Yamagata, again

---

[51] See further references to Hoshi in chapter vii.

[52] The charge against Hoshi was that he had used his position as president of the House to engage in corrupt practices (accepting money and gifts) in connection with the establishment of the stock exchange. The charges against Goto and his vice-minister were similar. It was the Dai Nihon Kyokai group that introduced the resolution of nonconfidence in Hoshi. See Hayashida, *op. cit.*, Vol. I, pp. 402–414.

[53] The Memorial to the Throne is reproduced in Fukaya, *op. cit.*, p. 323.

[54] The Imperial Rescript, December 24, 1893, reproduced in *ibid.*, p. 325.

dissolved the Diet. Two months later, the Sino-Japanese War broke out, ending one of the most turbulent periods in Japanese domestic politics down to 1932.

In the short space of less than five years, constitutional government had had tremendous repercussions on the liberal parties and their opponents as well. In the first place, both sides had attempted to maintain irreconcilable interpretations of Japanese constitutionalism. The Sat-Cho oligarchy's position was adequately expressed in the phrase chozen naikaku shugi, and in the positive steps which they had taken to ensure that Diet (party) functions be restricted to acquiescence in administrative policy. It was a position that was based upon the sanctity and absolutism of the Throne. The popular parties, on the other hand, viewed the Constitution as a means toward establishing the principles of party cabinets and the supremacy of the representative branch, and they had governed themselves accordingly.

Certain elements of both sides, however, had come to recognize the dire necessity of compromise, in the process of working within the framework of their fundamental law. Among the elder statesmen, Ito, as we have seen, early came to the private conviction that nothing less than an out-and-out official party led by himself could bring any order to internal politics. Even the "militarist" faction, though in theory it persisted in maintaining that the government should have nothing to do with the party movement, resorted in practice to the most drastic means of participation—corruption and sheer force—and in so doing, it was compelled to aid those popularly elected elements who would support its position. And beyond this, both factions of the bureaucracy, for all their theories of responsibility to the Emperor, were in fact forced to make him responsible to them and to use his prestige in order to save themselves from disaster. How long this use of Imperial prestige would continue to be potent was a question which worried the bureaucracy greatly, especially in the light of repeated memorials to the Throne. A new solution was imperative.

To the liberal parties, also, compromise was a beckoning siren, for in many ways, this period seemed to reflect the futility of continued resistance. As against the powerful weapons of the oligarchs, which included dissolution, interference in elections, and finally the intervention of the Emperor himself, the parties had only the budget and their memorials to the Throne. Neither—and certainly not the written appeals—had proved very effective. Indeed, against the oligarchic use of the Emperor, the parties had little recourse, either in law or in spirit. In such a situation, it was not unnatural that the avenues of compromise would be explored.

To the less scrupulous of either side, outright corruption was an easy and too convenient method. Already the name of an eminent Jiyuto leader, Hoshi Toru, had come under a cloud, and it would soon enough become the very symbol of party evils. Within this pattern of compromise, the "militarist" faction of the oligarchy, having no constructive program of *rapprochement,* fitted best. There were other possible methods, however, such as the one suggested by Ito. By the end of the period, one can see the faint beginnings of the compromise era, with the Jiyuto, once the most resolute foe of the Sat-Cho, cautiously siding with the government on matters of foreign policy, and breaking up the once harmonious unity of the minto. To greet this inclination and put it on a permanent basis, Ito was prepared to make certain concessions now which the parties had discovered, to their sorrow, could not be obtained from the paltry powers he had given them in the drafting of the Constitution.

However, it was the victorious conclusion of modern Japan's first major war which really ushered in the second phase of party-oligarchic relations—the phase of ententes. The war itself brought internal peace to Japanese politics for the first time since the Restoration. The Seventh Diet, which met in special session at Hiroshima in October, 1894, was a model of unanimity and perfect subordination to administrative requests. The Eighth Diet was equally peaceful.[55] Internal friction was revived, however, when the aftermath of the war produced an issue that had already loomed up as Ito's great problem—foreign policy. Even as the Japanese people were celebrating their easily won victory, word came that the three great powers, France, Russia, and Germany, had demanded Japanese recession of the Liaotung peninsula to China. The "strong foreign policy group" shouted their denunciations of "diplomatic defeat" at the government.[56]

Out of this crisis arose the first semiofficial alliance between the government and a "liberal" party, for on November 16, 1895, the

---

[55] For a detailed and well-documented study of this entire period, see Matsushita Yoshio, *Ni-Shin senso zengo* (*The Period Around the Sino-Japanese War*), in Kindai Nihon rekishi koza (Modern Japanese History Series), Tokyo, 1939, especially pp. 274–306.

[56] *Ibid.,* pp. 274–275.

president of the Jiyuto, Itagaki, and one of its leading members, Kono Hironaka, called on Ito and pledged a coalition.[57] The maneuverings of the Premier, Mutsu, and other proalliance Sat-Cho statesmen had finally borne fruit. The Jiyuto, disillusioned by its experiences in fighting the oligarchy, desirous of gaining some administrative power, and now alienated from the Kaishinto, had cautiously joined hands with its erstwhile foes.[58] By means of this alliance, the Ito cabinet escaped impeachment in the ninth session, despite the earnest endeavors of the Kaishinto and allied groups. In return for its support, the Jiyuto received a valuable remuneration after the close of the session. Itagaki was made Home Minister in the Ito cabinet. The entente seemed to have bestowed the twin benefits of administrative stability and some party access to power.

With the major "liberal" party now in the Ito camp, the Kaishinto was obliged to counteract this new alignment. The course which it followed led it along a similar path. First, the Kaishinto effected a merger with certain other antigovernment groups in the Diet to form a new party, the *Shimpoto* (Progressive Party), electing Okuma as president. An understanding was then reached with the Satsuma faction of the bureaucrats, namely Matsukata and Admiral Kabayama Sukenori, one of the most influential Satsuma leaders.[59]

These alliances, as we have seen, were reflective in part of the troubled, chaotic early period during which the minto had strug-

---

[57] For details, see Otsu, *op. cit.*, Vol. V, pp. 610–636. Concerning this move, Matsushita writes: "The political warfare, which had hitherto been between the minto and the government, now changed, and became warfare between the government and antigovernment parties, and at this point, Diet politics took on a new aspect." Matsushita Yoshio, *op. cit.*, p. 276.

[58] Kono's words throw a great deal of light on the Jiyuto attitude. Otsu has quoted a large section from Kono's works. The Jiyuto leader remarked on the overwhelming need of unity for postwar advances. "If we enter into the struggle to impeach the government, the government in turn will advance oppression after oppression, and pile dissolution upon dissolution, and it can hardly be foretold where such a collision between the officials and the people will end." From *Kono Hironaka den* (*Works of Kono Hironaka*), quoted in Otsu, *op. cit.*, Vol. IV (pp. 611–616), p. 612.

[59] For interesting details, see Otsu, *op. cit.*, Vol. IV, pp. 675–678. In many respects, this alliance, like many other "party-oligarchy alliances," was primarily a tentative agreement between the respective leaders. Okuma and Matsukata had much in common in their views on financial and foreign policy. (Not the least significant factor was that the alliance was concluded at the home of Iwasaki [Mitsubishi]. *Ibid.*, p. 677.)

gled so unsuccessfully against great odds. But by the very nature of their motives and their origins, the party-bureaucratic ententes were extremely precarious. In each case, they had been cautiously concluded, with grave reservations on both sides. Stripped to its barest political essentials, the party motivation was a greater share in administrative power. Neither party had given up its major principles; both continued to press for party cabinets and responsible government. This was no surrender. Continued support was contingent upon having certain political demands met.[60] The Sat-Cho oligarchs, on the other hand, had made and even welcomed the alliances, to extricate themselves from impossible difficulties, but they had certainly not changed their attitude toward party premises or the parties themselves. In such an atmosphere, the alliances were likely to continue the instability which they had been created to overcome.

One certain result of the alliances was to drive the "liberal" factions further apart by abetting the han, factional, and personal jealousies which had always marred any unity of the liberal cause. No better illustration of this can be shown than to note the fate of the second Ito cabinet. Since the cabinet had achieved a *rapprochement* with the Jiyuto, its future looked bright, despite the grave diplomatic and financial problems which plagued it at the end of the war. However, when Ito, under heavy outside pressure, sought to have Okuma and Matsukata admitted into the cabinet and thus give it that air of complete unity which was always a goal, the jealousies of Itagaki and the Jiyuto prevented it. Itagaki threatened to resign if Okuma were admitted, and at last the entire cabinet resigned.

The next two cabinets, moreover, revealed the precarious nature of the new alliances. The second Matsukata cabinet, which followed Ito on September 18, 1896, was completely dependent on Okuma and the Shimpoto for Diet support. Okuma had been given a cabinet post, but party demands were much greater than this. The Shimpoto had included in its platform three major planks:

---

[60] Again Kono's words are extremely interesting in revealing the hope and intent of at least some Jiyuto leaders: "There was never such a good opportunity as at present to get the elder statesmen into political parties, to assimilate the *hambatsu* into political parties, and to lay the basis for the establishment of two great parties." From *Kono Hironaka den*, in Otsu, *op. cit.*, Vol. IV, p. 612. The Jiyuto was thus hopeful of swallowing up an enemy it had been unable to defeat.

"1. To pledge a correction of political evils and the perfection of responsible cabinets.

"2. To pledge a reform of foreign policy and the expansion of national rights [*kokken*].

"3. To pledge a rectification of financial policy and the development of private enterprise." [61]

Before joining the cabinet, Okuma had insisted that these planks be incorporated into the ministry program, and that, moreover, "capable men" (party men) be given a large number of the official appointments.[62] This was the *quid pro quo* for party support. Although there was some measure of agreement on the second and third planks, the first was hardly conducive to similar interpretations by the party and bureaucratic groups. Matsukata gave his pledge and then proceeded to disregard it in the eyes of the party men. Okuma finally resigned in disgust in November, 1897. The government tried to weather the storm by revising its cabinet and seeking the support of the Jiyuto, but its overtures were rejected and a vote of nonconfidence would certainly have carried, had not the government first dissolved the Diet. Lacking party support and thus having no hopes for victory in the general election, Matsukata resigned, to be replaced by Ito.[63]

Now it was the turn of the Ito-Jiyuto alliance to break down. The general election of March 15, 1898, was very quiet, and the two major parties retained their near equality. Ito had made certain preëlection promises to the Jiyuto, but after the election, he was unable to fulfill them, because of cabinet opposition.[64] The Jiyuto, having hoped for a major share of influence in the new administration, angrily announced that it was severing all connections with the Ito administration. When all party connections failed, Ito had to face a withering barrage of criticism in the

---

[61] Shimpoto platform, quoted from Royama, *op. cit.*, pp. 334–335.

[62] This marked the first time that party men were admitted into the subordinate bureaucracy in any numbers.

[63] Matsushita reckons this as marking the decline of Satsuma power in over-all Japanese politics; Satsuma men continued, however, to control the navy, many important subordinate bureaucratic posts, and to have great influence in court circles. See Matsushita Yoshio, *op. cit.*, p. 290.

[64] Ito had promised Itagaki admission into his heavily Choshu cabinet after the general elections, thus hoping to keep Jiyuto campaign opposition down. Afterward, however, the cabinet split, with Inoue leading the opposition to this move. See Otsu, *op. cit.*, Vol. IV, p. 796; and Matsushita Yoshio, *op. cit.*, pp. 290–291.

Twelfth Diet, convened on May 14.[65] The heaviest attack was launched against the administration's foreign policy, for in the face of Western imperialistic advances on China, Japan seemed impotent either to control or take part in them.[66] When a government proposal for increased land, sake manufacturing, and income taxes was defeated by the landlord-conscious parties, another deadlock had been reached and the Diet was dissolved.

Both the Jiyuto and the Shimpoto had now had the bitter experience of seeing their alliances with the elder statesmen dissolved through what seemed to them the callous and indifferent attitude of the oligarchy toward party programs and welfare. Itagaki expressed the party attitude when he said, "Each party has tried the experiment of coöperation with the clan statesmen, and each has found it a failure, because the Government attaches no real importance to political parties, but merely consults its own convenience in taking them up and casting them off." [67]

Out of this disillusionment came a short-lived attempt to reunite the "liberal" parties and substitute party government for the Meiji oligarchy. Disappointed in their flirtations with the Sat-Cho powers, the Jiyuto and Shimpoto momentarily gave up their past differences and joined together in a new party, the *Kenseito* (Constitutional Party). The Kenseito held its preliminary meeting on June 28, 1898, and proclaimed as its platform the long-standing principles of party cabinets, cabinet responsibility to the Diet, and the advancement of self-government.[68]

An astonishingly rapid success seemed to greet Kenseito efforts, for when the party was less than a week old, Ito resigned and recommended Okuma and Itagaki as his successors. The first "party cabinet" was formed on June 30, 1898. Behind this change, how-

---

[65] Otsu writes that Goto sought for an alliance between Ito and Okuma, but that the Premier hesitated when Okuma asked for three cabinet seats. Otsu, *op. cit.*, Vol. IV, p. 744.

[66] It was during this period that Germany got a lease on Kiaochou, England leased Weihaiwei, Russia received Port Arthur and Dairen, and France was active in Kwangsi Province. Even the Jiyuto demanded that Japan either take part in this imperialistic plunder or take steps to curtail it. The Shimpoto Impeachment Memorial, however, was defeated because of lack of Jiyuto support. For this memorial, see Royama, *op. cit.*, pp. 337–338.

[67] Itagaki's statement, quoted in W. W. McLaren, *A Political History of Japan During the Meiji Era, 1867–1912*, London, 1916, p. 252.

[68] For the Kenseito platform, see Aono Kondo, *Nihon seito hensen shi* (*A History of Changes in Japanese Parties*), Tokyo, 1935, p. 84.

ever, lay a now-familiar pattern of Genro disunity, rather than any acceptance of new conditions. Ito, anxious over the growing strength of the "militarist" faction and prevented, by this very group, from establishing his own party, at last turned to the new party as a bulwark against Yamagata's power.[69]

The Okuma-Itagaki cabinet, however, was a complete failure, and although it was in itself the result of the inadequacy of party-bureaucratic alliances, it demonstrated further the insuperable difficulties which the parties faced in conducting the Japanese administration alone. It also high-lighted the inner ills of the parties themselves.

Itagaki, in an interview with the *Jiji* newspaper on June 26, 1898, outlined the administrative problem briefly, but in its entirety, in these words: "The organization of a Cabinet is a very hard task. The present Government officials are in their nature a political party supported by the strong clans, and they are a very powerful body. The subordinates are in a position to rule their heads." [70]

He went on to relate that bureau heads had been selected because they were Sat-Cho men and told how completely they controlled the real heart of the administration. Moreover, "the military and naval men are still more powerful, and are difficult to deal with." [71]

That they would have to be dealt with, however, had been ensured by Yamagata, when in 1895 he had sponsored a principle that the ministers of war and of the navy in the cabinet should

---

[69] For a detailed discussion of the inside events of this move, see Hayashida, *op. cit.*, Vol. II, pp. 5–13. Ito actually wanted to start a party of his own, and he drew up some rather detailed plans on this basis, but at a Genro conference begun on June 24, Yamagata registered his violent opposition. The conference became one of the most bitter ever held. Ito submitted his resignation, recommended Okuma and Itagaki, and then persuaded these two party leaders to accept. The "militarists" responded to Ito's move with anger and disgust.

One group went so far as to urge a "constitutional suspension" cabinet headed by Yamagata, which should dissolve the Diet endlessly if necessary. From *Nichi Nichi Shimbun*, pro-Ito newspaper, quoted in the *Kobe Chronicle*, weekly edition (hereinafter referred to in the notes as *KC*), July 9, 1898, p. 10. The *Keika Nippo*, commonly regarded as Yamagata's organ, interpreted the change to be "the ruin of the Meiji Government" and blamed Ito, whom it described as a "worshipper of European methods." Quoted in *KC*, July 2, 1898, p. 584. Most Japanese historians date the final cleavage between Ito and Yamagata from this time.

[70] Itagaki interview with *Jiji*, June 26, 1898, quoted in *KC*, July 2, 1898, p. 584.

[71] *KC*, July 2, 1898, p. 584.

be selected from the top two ranks of officers on active duty in the respective services.[72] This procedure could completely throttle the real independence of any popular party from the demands of the military clique by enabling the military and naval men to block the completion of any cabinet until their terms were met. In the Okuma-Itagaki cabinet, the war and navy portfolios remained unchanged. Yamagata's disciple, Katsura Taro, continued to sit as Minister of War, while the Satsuma reactionary, Saigo Tsugumichi, clung to the post of Minister of the Navy.[73]

The seriousness of dealing with the bureaucracy, however, was best illustrated by the complete failure of the Kenseito's attempts to carry out its long-standing pledges of administrative reform. A *Rinji Seimu Chosakyoku* (Temporary Administrative Affairs Investigation Bureau) was established, with Itagaki as its chairman, but the results were negligible. The Bureau was able to reduce the bureaucracy by merely 4,522, and savings amounted to only ¥742,500.[74] What was more important, the party men who were put into bureaucratic posts found themselves frozen out and unable to execute even the most minor changes.[75]

These administrative problems were grave enough to have weakened any cabinet, and had the Kenseito cabinet faced a Diet session, the resolute opposition of another bureaucratic stronghold, the Peers, would have made their fate even more precarious. Before this could occur, however, the old weaknesses of the Japanese party movement arose, to destroy party harmony and the cabinet itself. Even here, the constrictive nature of the institutional framework played an important part. The parties, never having an opportunity for administrative leadership or legislative initiative, had rested content with a series of platforms which were extremely

---

[72] Articles in the army and navy regulations of May 19, 1900, officially provided that the ministries should be held by active-service officers of the top two ranks.

[73] Katsura seems to have made serious demands upon the new cabinet, and it was reported that he was secretly conferring with Yamagata. See *Yomiuri* report, quoted in *KC*, July 9, 1898, p. 9.

[74] Royama, *op. cit.*, p. 341. For evidence of the effective Genro opposition, see Hayashida, *op. cit.*, Vol. II, p. 20.

[75] One example of bureaucratic power can be shown in the so-called "Sonoda Incident." From early days, the Tokyo Metropolitan Police had been controlled by Satsuma men. The contemporary chief, Baron Sonoda, a Satsuma man, took such a strong stand against the cabinet that he threatened to produce mass resignations, which would have left Tokyo unprotected. Sonoda was finally dismissed, after causing much anxiety. See *KC*, July 23, 1898, pp. 45–46.

general and vague with regard to legislative programs. The Kenseito platform was no exception. It lacked positiveness, and the result was that an immediate difference of opinion arose, once concrete measures had to be taken. This was particularly evident in the question of tax legislation.[76]

Beyond this problem, however, there remained the festering personal and factional rivalries of the past.[77] These quarrels reached their zenith over the question of the proportions of patronage to be allotted. Originally, the Okuma faction held five seats to the Itagaki faction's three; when Ozaki Yukio was forced to resign because of a speech in which he used the term republicanism in an allusion to Japan,[78] the cabinet broke up over the appointment of his successor. Largely at the instigation of Hoshi, the old Jiyuto members Itagaki, Matsuda Masahisa, and Hayashi Yuso resigned, and two days later, on October 31, 1898, Okuma was forced to turn in the cabinet's collective resignation. The first party cabinet had lasted just four months and had not met a single session of the Diet.

The Kenseito collapse marked a return to the entente phase in its most obnoxious form. The fall of Okuma and Itagaki was in reality a great triumph for the Yamagata clique, a triumph sealed by the return to office of Yamagata himself. During the next two years, the parties were dealt a serious blow, both internally and externally. The problem of administration-party relations was handled by Yamagata in the militarist faction's traditional method. Conflicts in principle were short-circuited by unprecedented Diet bribery and corruption.[79] By this means, Yamagata was able to

---

[76] The cabinet had decided not to raise the land tax, but its members could not agree on other means of increasing revenue, such as increased sake-manufacturing taxes or establishing a tax on sugar, or a tobacco monopoly. Actually these differences reflected the cleavages between the commercial and agricultural groups, the former being represented largely by former Kaishinto men.

[77] The new party was, after all, less than a week old when it took office.

[78] Ozaki's much-quoted remarks were to the effect that if Japan were a republic, the president would most certainly be from Mitsui or Mitsubishi. This was considered *lèse majesté*. For the implications concerning growing business power, see chapter vii.

[79] In the beginning, Yamagata, despite his official stand of aloofness from parties, tried desperately to reach a permanent agreement with the old Jiyuto faction. For this purpose, several spokesmen for the government and later Yamagata himself met with Itagaki, Hoshi, and Kataoka. When it came to the question of admitting party men into the cabinet, however, Yamagata refused. The old Jiyuto leaders then drew up their demands in return for cabinet sup-

build up the bureaucracy to a new pinnacle of power and invulnerability. Such events, as we have seen, were in large measure the price paid for the institutional inadequacies of representative government.

In his program of action, Yamagata was aided by the complete disruption of the Kenseito. Instead of a united minto, there were now two violently opposed groups, the one led nominally by Itagaki (actually by Hoshi) and the other by Okuma. Hoshi's faction (the old Jiyuto) retained the name Kenseito, and Okuma's faction took the name *Kenseihonto* (Orthodox Kenseito). Because of the defeatism that permeated the parties after the collapse of the united Kenseito, it was easy for the Yamagata ministry to conduct negotiations with Hoshi and his followers, and the ministry stooped so low as to guarantee a certain amount of money for every government bill passed. Even so, because the new Kenseito was a minority party, bribery had to be carried out on a more extended scale and reached almost every faction in the Diet.[80]

Yamagata was enabled by this slush fund to by-pass earlier agreements and to disregard violations of party principles. He succeeded in raising the land and residential taxes on the basis

port, which included the ministry's dropping of *chozen naikaku shugi* (the principle of transcendental cabinet), acceptance of the general principles of the party including railroad nationalization, and suffrage extension. On November 30, the Premier invited the party members to his residence and accepted the party proposals in general terms. As his subsequent actions showed, however, he had little intention of complying with party requests, and he had already started to make use of other means to retain party support. For a detailed and documented account, see the section entitled "Yamagata Naikaku to Kenseito to no teikei" (The Coalition Between the Yamagata Cabinet and the Kenseito), in Otsu, *op. cit.*, Vol. V, pp. 20–32.

[80] The *Osaka Asahi* quoted rumors to the effect that the government was buying votes for the land-tax bill, at a price of ¥500 to ¥1,500 per head. Quoted in *KC*, December 17, 1898, p. 503. These reports were lifted out of the rumor stage when one Koyama, a Kenseihonto Diet member, openly declared that he had received ¥2,000 from the government to vote for the land-tax bill, but that he had then voted against the bill. This type of action, he declared, would stop bribery, for the government would not be able to make sure of its votes. When the Kenseito proposed expulsion, Koyama said that if this were attempted, *he would expose all the details of Katsura's action and that of one or two other ministers*, as well as the actions of the "government merchants" and agents in purchasing votes, and thereby reveal the real state of corruption in the Diet. Koyama was not expelled! Detailed report from *Yorozu Choho*, printed in *KC*, January 11, 1899, p. 20. Hoshi now had, in addition to his power in the Diet, complete control of the Tokyo municipal government, which was mired in scandal.

of a five-year time limit, in passing a budget which included heavy sums for military expansion, and in reforming the Civil Service regulations in such a way as to tighten the bureaucratic defenses. This last move was particularly significant. The revised Civil Service appointment code placed even the great majority of *Chokuninkan* (Imperially appointed officials) under an examination system, thus preventing party infiltration under any patronage program. Moreover, after this time, all revisions of the regulations were to be made the subjects of Privy Council inquiry—a stipulation sufficient to stabilize Yamagata's reform without any major change throughout the whole remaining period before World War II.[81]

Gradually, however, the Kenseito began to increase pressure on the cabinet, especially after the unsatisfactory Civil Service "reforms," and to demand that all ministers join the party or that some Kenseito men be admitted into the cabinet. These demands, of course, Yamagata was unwilling to meet, and another entente began to dissolve.

By now, it was overwhelmingly clear that neither the alliance system nor "pure" cabinets, be they oligarchic or party, could work very satisfactorily within the Japanese institutional framework. The alliances, one after another, had broken down, either over a separation of principles, dissatisfaction with the allotment of power, or the inadequacy of bribery. They had left chaos and corruption in their wake. The Diet had been dissolved five times in eight years; this problem was a greater worry when continuous internal confusion was taking place at the very time of Europe's greatest imperialistic drive on the Asiatic continent. The corruption involved in these bargains was never more adequately expressed than in the following words of Okuma:

It is now more than ten years since representative institutions were put on their trial in Japan, and yet within these ten years there is scarcely any one form of political corruption known in the whole history of parliamentary institutions in the west that has not shown its head here. I do not mean to say that all, or even a majority, of our legislators and electors are corrupt, but the minority prone to being corrupted is large enough to make things look very ugly and very disquieting.[82]

[81] The Yamagata revision was encompassed in Imperial Ordinance No. 61, March, 1899. See Royama, *op. cit.,* p. 295.

[82] Count Okuma, in an interview with a representative of the *Kobe Chronicle,* printed in that paper on July 18, 1900, p. 53. Okuma, however, did go

The independent cabinets were even more productive of instability and tension. Oligarchs could not get along without the support of the lower house, and the party cabinet of Okuma and Itagaki had demonstrated clearly that the popular parties were hopelessly entrapped by the bureaucratic-military mesh that surrounded them.

Out of these realizations, the third phase of party-bureaucratic relations was produced—the oligarchic leadership of the "liberal" parties. It was inaugurated by Ito, whose long-expressed hopes and plans finally bore fruit. The Kenseito, disgusted at the faithlessness of the Yamagata ministry and alarmed by the prospects of a bleak future, went hat in hand to Prince Ito and requested that he lead them.[83] Ito had his terms: the old party must be dissolved, and in the new party, which he hoped would include all groups within the state, every member must accept his mandates. The Kenseito agreed, and on September 16, 1900, a new party called the *Rikken Seiyukai* (Friends of Constitutional Government Association) was inaugurated, with Ito as its head.

The old Jiyuto, self-proclaimed as the greatest enemy of Sat-Cho power and oligarchy, had thus submitted to being ruled by one of the foremost Sat-Cho oligarchs. And why? Partly because it had become apparent to the party leaders, from bitter experience, that under the Japanese Constitution, the only access to administrative authority was to come under the auspices of the elder statesmen whose keys opened the doors to political power. The Seiyukai represented a marriage between that power and political parties. To gain power, the Kenseito men had committed themselves to follow a program and policy which remained as yet unannounced. And because most of the Kenseihonto lacked the willingness to follow in the footsteps of their more realistic brethren, they were to remain entirely without power or prestige for more than a decade—until they, too, acquired new sponsorship.

The extent of party submission, in terms of principles, became apparent when Ito spoke at the founding meeting.[84] After openly

---

on to say that conditions were "not perhaps worse than [in] America or France," certainly not on the "colossal scale of Tammany Hall."

[83] For details, see Otsu, *op. cit.*, Vol. V, pp. 116–124.

[84] At the time of the inaugural ceremony, September 16, 1900, Viscount Watanabe (Watanabe Kunitake), chairman of the organizing committee, announced to the press that the new party had 152 Diet members and numbered close to 500,000. From *KC*, September 19, 1900, p. 257.

It is true that many of the old-line "liberals" had no intention of agreeing with Ito, even though they would silently follow him. Ito's leadership, how-

stating that parties in the past had betrayed the Constitution in words and deeds, he set up the position which should govern his party:

The appointment and dismissal of Cabinet Ministers appertain, under the Constitution, to the prerogatives of the Sovereign, who consequently retains absolute freedom to select His advisers from whatever quarters He deems proper, be it from among the members of political parties or from circles outside those parties. When once Ministers have been appointed and invested with their respective official functions, it is not under any circumstances whatever, permissible for their fellow party men or their other political friends to interfere in any manner with the discharge of their political duties.[85]

The Imperial interpretation of the Constitution had implanted itself squarely in the heart of the liberal party movement. To be sure, Ito had made some minor deviations from the original bureaucratic positions. It was clear that he had given up the chozen naikaku shugi theory to the extent of recognizing party cabinets and, of course, desiring them, provided the party was the Seiyukai. This must be understood, however, in the context of Ito's hopes and expectations. As he stated to the new party, he had established the Seiyukai to expound the "true" meaning of the Constitution, and he "expected" all groups to join its ranks.[86]

In this hope, Ito was disappointed—or perhaps one should say forty years premature—for two important groups held aloof. The Kenseihonto, as we have mentioned, castigated the action of the Kenseito as servile submission to bureaucracy, and with a few individual exceptions, refused to align itself with the new party. Of equal importance was the fact that the Yamagata "militarist" faction and the major part of the Meiji bureaucracy which it controlled, viewed Ito's move with great alarm and hostility. And this reaction continued to play an extremely important part in subsequent Japanese politics. The contestants in the struggle for power were somewhat realigned, but the struggle continued. In the next thirteen years there was a crescendo of conflict between the "civil" and "military" factions of the bureaucracy. At times, however, especially during the Russo-Japanese War, a note of unexpected harmony was struck, and in truth, the quarrel was not

---

ever, affected not only party principles but, as we shall see, party membership as well. The latter factor was of the greater importance.

[85] Ito's speech to the Seiyukai, September 16, 1900, translated in *KC*, April 12, 1902, p. 392.

[86] Otsu, *op. cit.*, Vol. V, pp. 125–126.

so much over ends as over means and over the plain question of which side should wield the most power, but this made the struggle none the less bitter.

It was within the context of this conflict that the major part of the party movement was confined. The issue could no longer be called one of representative or popular government versus oligarchy, for the Seiyukai, which dominated the party scene, was now under the rule of Ito and was infiltrated by a growing number of his "civil" bureaucratic followers.[87] The Kenseihonto, now the purer exponent of the liberal cause, hardly had enough power to make its principles real issues. In these circumstances, "the party movement" might flourish, but its foundations were slowly disintegrating.

A major battle between the Ito and Yamagata forces was not long in getting under way. Yamagata purposefully resigned with embarrassing haste following the establishment of the Seiyukai, and Ito, on October 18, 1900, was forced to assume a premiership for which he was not prepared. Almost immediately, he ran into trouble with the House of Peers, since a majority of its members were supporters of the Yamagata faction. When the Peers refused to accept an administration bill to increase taxation, there seemed no way to control the situation.[88] Ito, however, had a personal weapon which the party movement had hitherto not possessed— the Throne. When consultations over the tax bill with the president of the Peers and among the Genro proved insufficient, Ito persuaded the Emperor to order the Peers to come to terms, and the bill was immediately passed without a single negative vote being cast.

Actually, however, Ito's victory was of passing moment, for he faced the same over-all obstacles—though in lesser degree—which

---

[87] One need only look at the list of Seiyukai members of the fourth Ito cabinet (see below) to note some strange names enrolled on the party registers. Both Watanabe (Minister of Finance) and Kaneko (Minister of Justice) were personal friends of Ito who had joined their first party. Watanabe had previously been known as a violent opponent of liberalism and the liberal party principles, despite the fact that he took a leading part in the Seiyukai organization. His presence caused much opposition from the old-line party men, and he finally resigned from the cabinet.

[88] The antagonism of the Peers concentrated upon Hoshi, Minister of Communications. Unfortunately for Ito, Hoshi was involved in another scandal, but this issue was in reality little more than a pretext for discrediting Ito and his party movement. See *ibid.*, pp. 144–171, for this whole controversy. From this time on, the Peers loomed as one of the more important obstacles confronting the parties in their struggle for power.

had always faced the parties and representative government under the Meiji Constitution. To be sure, his own followers in the bureaucracy had been willing to cast their lot with a party carefully controlled by him, but the vast majority of bureaucrats, including the subordinate officialdom and most of the higher bureaucrats of the Privy Council, Peers, and Genro Council as well, were as hostile as ever to the party movement, and under Yamagata's direction they had transferred this hostility to Ito. Thus, even under the powerful Ito, the Seiyukai was compelled to give way under the bureaucratic pressure. Although the Throne was of great utility in a crisis, it might not serve so well under steady use, particularly when the Genro were disunited. Ito, who undoubtedly recognized this, quit office on June 1, 1901, and this date marked the final retirement of the older oligarchs into behind-the-scenes activities in favor of "second-row" men. Yamagata, instead of assuming the premiership himself, placed in office his Choshu protégé, General Katsura.

The new administration was the beginning of a twelve-year period during which the premiership and the reins of administrative authority were to be passed back and forth between two men —Katsura, representing the Yamagata faction, and Saionji Kimmochi,[89] representing the Ito faction. Of particular interest is the position of the major parties during the first part of this era. The Kenseihonto continued on its lonely way, impotent and feeble.

---

[89] Saionji's tremendous influence in subsequent Japanese politics calls for a sketchy biographical summary of his life up to this point in his career. It was a life that would have been amazing anywhere except in Meiji Japan. Born in 1844, the younger son of the court noble Tokudaiji, he was adopted by the Saionji family, which possessed one of the most distinguished lineages of the country. At the time of the Restoration, though just over twenty years of age, he had charge of one of the Imperial forces, and earlier, had held an official post at the age of nineteen. In 1871 he went to Paris, where he became so enthusiastic over the theories of liberalism that he returned to Japan to start a liberal newspaper, the *Jiyu Shimbun*, in Tokyo (publication was begun in March, 1881). In November of 1881, however, he was half persuaded, half forced by officialdom to drop his connections with the liberal movement and enter the ranks of the bureaucracy. Abetted by a close personal friendship with Ito and several other high officials, his rise was meteoric, and by 1894 he was a Privy Councillor, which post he left in 1903 at Ito's request to head the Seiyukai.

From this point on, Saionji's political career will play an important part in our study, but it is apropos to note here how well his background fitted him for the dual role of party leader and compromiser with the bureaucracy, and how, as the last Genro, he could be unique in generally bolstering the party movement.

The Seiyukai, which had found itself tied to Ito's apron strings during his cabinet's tenure, became even more constricted by his maneuvers in the role of an opposition party head, for so long as it accepted his leadership it was compelled to follow his decisions, however inconsistent with the popular party cause they might be. At no time was this more apparent than during the sixteenth, seventeenth, and eighteenth sessions of the Diet, the first three sessions held under the new administration.

When the Sixteenth Diet was convened on December 7, 1901, the Seiyukai had been weakened internally by two important events. In the first place, Hoshi, the important if unscrupulous leader of the party men, had been assassinated by a fanatic disgusted with his corruption.[90] In the second place, Ito, the party's iron hand, was abroad. Deprived momentarily of leadership, the party was threatened with revolt. A group of "rebels" within the ranks were trying to force the repudiation of the "conciliatory" policy toward the Katsura ministry decreed by Ito before his departure. This group had gained enough power in the early period of the Diet to make the government consider dissolution.

The "militarist" faction, however, knew the proper solution. Immediately, they communicated with Ito and requested that he unify the nation by rectifying his party's erring ways. Ito promptly sent a message to the Seiyukai via Inoue, demanding that the party support the ministry, and his request was obeyed.[91] However difficult it was for the old-time "liberals" to reconcile themselves to their new position, the rewards of political power under the sponsorship of such an influential figure as Ito were heady wine to their hitherto battered ranks. This had been the reason for their acceptance of his rule; to many, it was to be the reason for continued sufferance of his leadership.

The seventeenth and eighteenth sessions of the Diet pointed up with even greater clarity the subservience of the Seiyukai to Ito's will and the incapacity of the popular party movement as a whole. The major issue in the seventeenth session, as in past and future sessions, was the question of striking a balance between military expenditures and the ability of the taxpayers to meet the bills that would satisfy both the military and the landowner-capitalist groups. The Katsura ministry, as might have been expected, sought to launch a program of armament expansion, and to accomplish this, it desired to retain permanently the law increasing the land

---

[90] For some details on Hoshi's assassination see chapter vii, pp. 264–265.
[91] Hayashida, *op. cit.*, Vol. II, p. 133.

tax that had been passed under the last Yamagata ministry with a five-year time limit.

The position of the major parties in regard to this problem was in many respects guided by ambivalent desires. They had long been committed to "strengthening national defense," and the Kenseihonto, under Okuma's leadership, had more than once displayed a brand of chauvinism scarcely distinguishable from that of the militarists themselves.[92] On the other hand, as representatives of groups subject to large taxes, particularly the landowning classes, they found it politically unwise and personally undesirable to sanction land-tax increases. Both parties, therefore, took a definite stand against the continuation of the Yamagata measure.[93]

Katsura and the militarists knew, however, that they need only win over Ito, whose control over his party was sufficient to ensure its obedience. The Diet was dissolved; new elections were held; and, in the interim, heavy pressure was put upon Ito to compromise. Finally, an agreement was reached whereby the administration would accept loans in place of the higher land taxes. Thus, in the new Diet, despite the fact that the two major parties had both waged a vigorously hostile election campaign against the ministry, Katsura carried the day with relative ease. The Seiyukai, not without some grumbling, to be sure, voted with a government they had so recently denounced, not only on the budget, but on the other important matters as well.[94] Here was a good case study demonstrating one reason why elections and "representative government" were ridiculed or regarded with indifference by the informed public at large.

The events of this period make possible another significant ob-

---

[92] We have already observed the seeds of militarism in early Japanese liberalism; we shall deal with the culmination of this problem in chapter ix.

[93] Katsura was misled until the last moment into thinking that Ito would "go along" with the administration. However, although both Okuma and Ito took a stand in favor of naval expansion (the immediate goal), Okuma urged a tax on articles of consumption, and Ito, goaded by his party, merely opposed the land tax without offering anything concrete in its place. See Otsu, *op. cit.*, Vol. V, p. 452.

[94] When Inukai (Kenseihonto) introduced a Memorial to the Throne seeking to challenge the Katsura cabinet for not resigning after the election, it was defeated 228 to 123, with the Seiyukai voting on the side of the government. Thus, by means of its alliance with Katsura, the Seiyukai actually defeated an appeal to the party cabinet principle. For the text of Inukai's Memorial translated, see the *Japan Mail*, weekly edition (hereinafter referred to in the notes as *JM*), May 30, 1903, pp. 592–593.

servation on the effect of the institutional structure on liberalism and the party movement. Ito's Seiyukai and Okuma's Kenseihonto had conducted a joint campaign against the Katsura cabinet, and on the issues of the day they stood together. Why did they not pool their resources and unite in a common cause, as the contemporary press was urging them to do? The factors behind their abstaining from joint action were numerous, but one basic reason was that such a union would not have combined the *nonparty* ingredients essential to a successful Japanese administration. If this crucial point is understood, the inability of the proponents of representative supremacy to unite, or at best to stay united for longer than a fleeting moment, will be partially explained.

Despite the neutralizing effect which Ito had on the party "menace," however, the militarist faction had never reconciled itself to the added strength he had given to the party movement in a political sense. At last, they were able to catch him in his own inconsistencies and, by using his own weapon, remove him from the party scene. Ito's position, after all, was an anomaly, for he was both a Genro and a party leader. In the former role, he was supposedly the impartial confidant of the Emperor in concert with his Genro colleagues, theoretically dedicated to the whole nation. As a party leader, however, his position was entirely different, however much he tried to rationalize it by seeking to use "unity" as his keynote. His theories of unqualified support to whatever ministry the Emperor [actually, the Genro] might choose, broke down under the impetuosity of his party and the inner antagonism which he himself felt toward the militarist faction. Thus Ito was driven to support and attack the principle of unity at the same time.[95]

The issue came to a head when Katsura submitted his resignation and urged that another Genro cabinet be installed to restore unity.[96] Katsura, however, was commanded by the Emperor to remain, and it was Ito instead who received a change of post. 'An Imperial message was written requesting Ito, in effect, to give his

[95] This political dualism, as we have noted, made for a growing discontent in Seiyukai circles as well. The old Jiyuto men who had taken Ito in the hopes of obtaining power, found themselves still usually ignored and powerless, because Ito's "poor party strategy," in dictating continuous compromise and refusing to expose his policy, subjected the party members to ridicule.

[96] For a detailed analysis of this episode, in English, see Takekoshi Yosaburo, *Prince Saionji*, Kyoto, 1933, chapter lvi, entitled "Ito 'Enshrined Alive' in the Privy Council," pp. 200–205. •

undivided attention to the Throne and to accept the presidency of the Privy Council.[97] Previously Ito had generally managed to circumvent the conspiracies of the Yamagata faction directed against him. He had been very adept at parrying their thrusts. Now, however, he had no alternative except to obey the Emperor and resign as president of the Seiyukai, returning completely to the rarefied atmosphere of the Genro sanctums.[98]

Ito's resignation, however, did not return the Seiyukai to its original Jiyuto members, the men who had fought the Sat-Cho oligarchy and flown the banners of popular government. In his last official act, Ito placed Saionji, his friend and bureaucratic protégé, in office as Seiyukai president. This maneuver dismayed the militarists, who rightly saw Saionji acting as a bridge between Ito and the party, but it offered little consolation to those who hoped the party might find a way to free itself from all bureaucratic ties. Even more important, if one looks at party membership he will discover a rather large number of former officials, and one of these, Hara Takashi (Kei), was already a leading lieutenant of the party and was destined soon to become president himself.[99]

The last ten years of the so-called Katsura-Saionji era therefore constituted a period during which politics was dependent upon an uneasy compromise between these two men and between the forces which they respectively represented, and a period in which the Seiyukai bureaucratic affiliation played an important part. When Katsura was in power, Saionji's Seiyukai pulled him through. When Saionji was in office, the groups dominated by the Yamagata faction gave him a certain amount of support. But when the ever simmer-

---

[97] The *Jiji* ran a cartoon showing three genii, Yamagata, Matsukata, and Katsura, endeavoring to hoist Ito into their place above the clouds, while Ito dangled midway, waving good-bye to his followers. From *JM*, July 11, 1903, p. 31. For Yamagata's advice to the Emperor, see Takekoshi, *op. cit.*, p. 204.

[98] How much the growing Seiyukai unrest had to do with Ito's decision is not clear.

[99] Hara, like Saionji, had taken an early interest in the liberal movement only to leave it later in favor of officialdom. He had been at one time a staff member of the *Hochi Shimbun*, Okuma's paper, and thereby a colleague of Osaki and Inukai. He resigned this position, however, and came under the wing of Mutsu, working in the Foreign Office, on overseas assignments, and in various other official capacities. In 1896, he left government service to become editor of the *Osaka Mainichi*, but was drawn into political prominence at the time of the formation of the Seiyukai, when he acted as one of Ito's right-hand men. After Ito's resignation, Hara and Matsuda, an old-line party man, became the two real leaders of the party.

ing rivalry between the civil and military factions boiled up in open warfare, the thin bonds of compromise dissolved, and their dissolution finally produced the so-called "Taisho change," which we shall presently discuss.

The Katsura-Seiyukai alliance, however, had not yet been stabilized by late 1903. The latter stages of Ito's rule had been marked by a rather serious disaffection within the Seiyukai ranks, and Saionji inherited a party weakened in number and uncertain in course.[100] A majority of the party was inclined to attack the arrogant ministry, and to that end an agreement was reached with a somewhat dubious Kenseihonto. Before this alliance could become firm, however, the 1903–1904 Diet was unexpectedly dissolved,[101] and some two months later, Japan was at war with Russia.

The years of the Russo-Japanese War were a period of submission and unanimity within the Diet, similar to the wartime period of 1894–1895. Curiously enough, the sequels to the two wars in an internal political sense were also identical. During the war, the parties—and particularly, the Kenseihonto—had vied in portraying a picture of what Japan's Asiatic position should be and what price the Russians should pay for their crimes.[102] The Portsmouth Treaty, however, reflected the financial and military exhaustion of the victors, and Japan was forced to accept a compromise peace which gave her no indemnities and only about one-half of the island of Karafuto (Saghalien). The reaction of the Japanese parties, press, and public was a flood of scathing denunciation.

---

[100] By the time that Saionji took over, the Seiyukai Diet members were reduced in number to 128, having lost 47 members. Two important factions had resigned from the party. The "Tosa group," led by Kataoka, Hayashi, and Takeuchi (the core of Hoshi's old faction), left the party. Another group, headed by Ozaki Yukio, also had resigned. The "Tosa group" was anxious to have the party collaborate more closely with Katsura than had been Ito's will, whereas the Ozaki faction was disgusted with the extent of such collaboration. See Hayashida, *op. cit.*, Vol. II, pp. 148–149; and Takekoshi, *op. cit.*, p. 207.

[101] This dissolution resulted from one of the most amusing incidents in Japanese parliamentary history. Soon after the Diet opened in December, 1903, the House passed unanimously (and without listening to it) a Reply to the Opening Address of the Throne, a resolution always formal in nature. It was then discovered that Kono Hironaka, president of the House, had inserted a clause which amounted to an impeachment of the government. (For English translation, see *JM*, December 12, 1903, p. 644.) The government reacted by dissolving the Diet the very same day, December 10.

[102] See reviews in *ibid.*, April 29, 1905, of several articles in the April and May, 1905, *Taiyo*, by party men, including Okuma, on proper policy toward Russia.

The Seiyukai, which had been slowly led by Saionji into a conciliatory position vis-à-vis the administration, was constrained to adopt officially a more temporizing attitude,[103] but the sections of the party outside the Diet unanimously condemned the Katsura regime. The Kenseihonto passed the following resolution, which made its position clear: "The peace concluded by this Empire's Plenipotentiaries loses sight of the objects of the war and is contrary to the views of the nation. Therefore we consider it an unprecedented disgrace to the country." [104] Despite the efforts of the Genro to support the cabinet [105] and Katsura's own efforts to subsidize his Diet supporters,[106] the press and parties produced an inflamed public opinion resulting in riots and ultimate martial law in Tokyo. Because of this unprecedented reaction, the Katsura ministry resigned during the Diet vacation recess, and Saionji was selected by the Genro as the most likely man to control the situation. His cabinet was completed on January 7, 1906.

In spite of the great sacrifices which the Seiyukai had made during the past few years, in terms of its original principles, party government was still a distant goal. This was apparent in the construction of the first Saionji cabinet. Though Saionji was president of the Seiyukai he could not freely select Seiyukai members to fill the cabinet posts. Only Hara and Matsuda were included. To have entrusted the party with more power would have immediately called forth the antagonism of major blocs within the Genro,

---

[103] For Saionji's cautionary speech to Seiyukai Diet members, see *JM*, September 16, 1905, p. 276.

[104] English translation from *ibid.*

[105] Yamagata went so far as to give an interview to the *Nichi Nichi Shimbun* in which he said: "We shrank . . . from wasting the resources which the country would need for its future enterprise in Korea and the leased regions of Manchuria. From this decision there was not one dissentient person, nor was there any division into 'weak' and 'strong.' If to make peace was wrong, then we are content to be called 'weak,' all of us together, the Elder Statesmen, the Cabinet Ministers, and I who speak." As translated in *ibid.*, p. 303.

[106] It was at this time that a group calling itself the *Daido Club* (Club of Like Thinkers, 78 members) was formed in the Diet and actually held the balance of power between the Seiyukai (147) and the Kenseihonto (98). In its manifesto, the new group disavowed any consciousness of "party factions" or "han government," recognizing only Sovereign and country. Actually, however, it had close connections with Katsura, who controlled it through certain of his supporters and aided it in acquiring funds, some of which seem to have come from Mitsubishi.

the bureaucracy, and the Peers, opponents whose powers could spell the doom of any ministry.[107]

And even though this period was one of conciliation between the Seiyukai and the bureaucracy (known to Japanese historians as a period of *joi togo* (mutual understanding),[108] such conciliation had its limits, as the first Saionji ministry was to show. At first, the new cabinet followed the lines of its predecessor, adopting the Katsura budget, continuing emergency taxation, and pushing through the railroad nationalization bill, which had long been a goal of certain militarist and nationalist groups. However, in the Twenty-third Diet, which convened in December, 1906, the Saionji ministry tried to launch an independent program incorporating some of the Seiyukai desires, and this was overwhelmingly defeated by the Peers, with Katsura's support and encouragement.[109] The cabinet, moreover, had fallen into disrepute with the business interests for its postwar fiscal policy and for the financial depression then troubling Japan.[110] Thus, even though the Seiyukai won an easy victory in the regularly scheduled general elections of May, 1908, the Saionji ministry submitted its resignation only two months later—a surprise only to those who thought that a ministry with representative but not bureaucratic support could continue.[111]

---

[107] Said the *Yomiuri* at the time of the Saionji cabinet formation: "The shadow of the Elder Statesmen broods over the whole political arena in Japan. They control everything and accept no responsibility for anything." As quoted in *JM*, January 13, 1906, p. 26. There was some indication, however, that Katsura, at least, dared on occasion to act independently, and later he incurred the wrath of his mentor, Yamagata, because of this. The subordinate bureaucracy was constantly growing in numbers and in power. As for the Peers, the *Jiji Shimpo* in April, 1906, provided an analysis showing their great power in the legislative process. The number of bills that were passed in exact form after House passage was less than the number either rejected or amended by the Peers in the recent sessions of the Diet. Article quoted in *JM*, April 21, 1906, p. 403.

[108] See Royama, *op. cit.*, p. 379.

[109] The Peers defeated Hara's bill to abolish the *gun* (district office) system, a project of the Seiyukai, by a large majority. This system, relating to local government offices, had been established by Yamagata.

[110] For further details, see chapter vii.

[111] It is interesting to note the nature of the administrative bureaucracy as it affected the parties at this time. A most significant article by Yamaji Aizan entitled "Academic Cliquism and Exclusiveness in Japanese Officialdom," from the July, 1909, *Taiyo*, is reported in *JM*, July 10, 1909, pp. 46–47. Yamaji's major point was that some departments, e.g., Home Affairs,

Katsura's return to power on July 14, 1908, marked the reëstablishment of his alliance with the Seiyukai as the dominant party, but it was also the signal for important repercussions within the Kenseihonto. That party, representing the most intransigent bastion of opposition to controls by nonelective officials, had suffered much for its aloof position. As a result, there was now a sizable number of party members and affiliates who, starved for power and prestige, were urging a compromise with the Katsura forces that might enable them to supplant the Seiyukai as the dominant party.[112] This problem became the root of great dissension within the party, especially after the temporary retirement of Okuma from active politics in 1907. From that time, the party was governed by a committee of fifteen, divided actually into three factions. The Oishi faction, led by Oishi Masami, urged coming to terms with the bureaucrats as the only means of attaining political power. The Inukai faction, led by Inukai Ki, demanded that the party be true to its principles as a people's party and reject all overtures of the bureaucrats. The Hatoyama faction, led by Hatoyama Kazuo, occupied a neutral position and sought party harmony.

Oishi's desires were temporarily destined for defeat, both because of inner party opposition and because the Kenseihonto was too much of a minority in the Diet to bring about the fulfillment of Katsura's aims. By 1910, however, the entire party was determined to create some sort of anti-Seiyukai bloc which could successfully challenge the long-time supremacy of that party. Consequently, the old Kenseihonto was dissolved, and its members joined with minor Diet factions to establish a new party, the *Rikken Kokuminto* (Constitutional Nationalist Party), on March 13,

---

Foreign Affairs, and Education, were completely or almost completely controlled by Imperial University graduates. In the Department of Finance, University influence was growing, and only the Department of Agriculture and Commerce, he reported, was a fairly free area for non-University men. Party men had little chance to accomplish anything, even when certain patronage appointments were made, because of the hostility of this University clique. Somewhat later, Hatano Shogoro complained about the training of civil servants and the examination system, which included "only law, rote memorization and such things." He stated, "Because the most mechanistic men pass the examinations and become the administrative officials, it is unavoidable that the administration of our country is a mechanistic rather than a common sense one." Hatano Shogoro in "Gyosei seiri iken" (Opinions on Administrative Reform), *Taiyo*, March, 1912 (pp. 92–102), p. 93.

[112] For details, see Royama, *op. cit.*, pp. 383–386.

1910.[113] The political principles calling for party cabinets and the "consummation of the constitutional system" were again set forth in the platform of this new organization, but the divergence between the Oishi and Inukai groups on political strategy was even more pronounced than before. Oishi was intent upon using the new party as a means of weaning the Katsura administration away from the Seiyukai by putting his own party in its place.

Before such an alignment could materialize, however, Katsura gave way to Saionji, in August of 1911. Behind this shift lay the ticklish problems of conciliating the differences among han rivals and the militarists themselves. In general politics, the Satsuma men had given way to Choshu men, but the navy was still controlled mostly by Satsuma forces, headed by Admiral Yamamoto Gombei. In policies, the natural rivalry between Satsuma and Choshu personalities and between the army and the navy had combined to make Yamamoto a follower of the Ito rather than of the Yamagata forces. It is also significant that the Satsuma clansmen had long held an alliance with the Seiyukai, and that all the Satsuma men in the Diet in 1910 were Seiyukai members. These facts pertained very directly to Katsura's problems, for he was confronted with the practical necessity of dealing with military and financial problems in such a way as not to antagonize either the armed forces or the payers of large sums in taxes. The armed services both made extraordinary demands on the 1911–1912 budget which Katsura with difficulty induced them to postpone. Having survived a crisis by delaying it, Katsura turned the problem over to Saionji and the Seiyukai by yielding his office on August 30, 1911.

The next few years, which formed one of the most revealing periods in Japanese political history, really tested the power and the political creeds of the party movement. The Saionji cabinet was soon confronted with the full power of the militarist faction. In the Twenty-eighth Diet, which met from December, 1911, to March, 1912, the ministry depended upon its Seiyukai majority in the lower house to push through a program of retrenchment which included administrative and taxation reforms and was hindered only by the traditionally obstinate policy of the Peers toward a proparty ministry. After the Twenty-eighth Diet had been terminated, another general election was due and the Seiyukai gained a clear majority, some 214 seats.

---

[113] For details and for party documents, see Hayashida, *op. cit.*, Vol. II, pp. 168–173.

The army was now determined, however, to press its long-standing demands for two new divisions. When War Minister Ishimoto Shinroku died, in April, 1912, his post was taken by Uehara Yusaku. Uehara, at the instigation of the Yamagata faction, demanded that the cabinet agree to including the two-division increase in the next budget, and when cabinet assent was not forthcoming he presented his resignation directly to the Emperor without prior consultation with the Premier.[114] The real power of the militarists manifested itself when Saionji was unable to obtain a successor to his minister of war. By previous agreement, and pressure, no active-service general or lieutenant general would accept the portfolio. Instead of resorting to Ito's dubious tactic of appealing to the Emperor (the Emperor Meiji had just died, and the new Emperor Taisho was securely in the hands of the hostile forces), Saionji resigned. All the power of the Seiyukai majority in the House was of no avail.

The militarists had won a great victory, but their position was precarious. The task of picking a successor to Saionji proved so difficult that finally Katsura, though he had recently lost favor with Yamagata,[115] was removed from his new post as Lord Chamberlain and was returned for a third time as Premier. A veritable wall of opposition confronted him. The navy, piqued by army insolence, tried to use identical tactics by refusing to furnish a minister of the navy, but Katsura, unlike Saionji, was quite willing to use the new Emperor Taisho by having him issue an Imperial rescript forcing the navy faction's hand. But the parties, including even the long-suffering Seiyukai, were at last prodded into united opposition; and, aided by the press and public opinion, they joined to form a *Kensei Yogo Kai* (Protect the Constitution Association), led by those two outstanding parliamentarians, Ozaki and Inukai. In its first meeting, held on December 19, 1912, the Association passed the following resolution: "The tyranny and arrogance of the han factions have now reached their extreme, and the crisis

---

[114] This feat could be legally accomplished, because, as we have noted, under the Constitution, the armed services had direct access to the Emperor in his capacity as Commander-in-Chief and did not need to proceed via civil channels.

[115] Katsura had ignored Yamagata's "position" on occasion, had flirted too much with the parties to suit the old Genro, and had developed an air of superiority and independence which antagonized his one-time master. Yamagata seems to have deliberately placed Katsura in his court position to remove him from the political scene. See Royama, *op. cit.*, p. 391; and Takekoshi, *op. cit.*, p. 259.

of constitutional government is pressed before our eyes. We intend to preserve constitutional government by decisively rejecting compromise and by eradicating han factions." [116]

Hope was thus raised that, by some means, the parties—and especially the Seiyukai—were going to break with the past and raise the issues of responsibility and representative government in their entirety. Unfortunately for Japanese democracy and for the party movement, this proved to be an impossible maneuver, and, ironically enough, the aftermath of the attempt marked the entry of almost all the holdout bureaucratic forces into the party fold.

Katsura was experienced enough as a political strategist to realize the need for a change of tactics.[117] He could no longer depend on shaky political alliances with parties which he could not completely control. Thirteen years after Ito had crossed the Rubicon to found the Seiyukai, Katsura also reached the decision that parties led by the bureaucracy were indispensable. Using Goto Shimpei as his staff officer, and the Oishi faction of the Kokuminto together with the *Chuo Club* (Central Club) as a foundation, Katsura formed his new party and started to unfurl its banners. In a notice which he read to the press on January 20, 1913, he stated, "I propose in conjunction with men with similar views all over the country to organize a new political party in order to meet the requirements of the ever changing situation, following the advent of the Taisho era, and thus to aid in the consummation of Constitutional Government." [118] On February 7, the manifesto of the new party, called *Rikken Doshikai* (Constitutional Fellow Thinkers' Association), was proclaimed at a Tokyo meeting attended by Katsura and eighty-one Diet members headed by

---

[116] Quoted in Royama, *op. cit.*, p. 392.

[117] Actually, of course, Katsura had long had more or less direct control of the Daido Club, which group was now known as the Chuo Club. One evidently well-informed writer using the pen name "Jubanba" wrote a series of articles entitled "Choya no seijika" (Statesmen In and Out of Power) for the *Tokyo Asahi Shimbun*, in which he charged that Katsura, through Baron Oura (Oura Kanetake), had spent ¥100,000 on the Chuo Club, and remarked that the positions of the Chuo Club and the Seiyukai in the Katsura administration were like that of wife and concubine respectively. Articles paraphrased in *JM*, July 1, 1911, pp. 24–25.

[118] English translation of Katsura paper read to press, in *JM*, January 25, 1913, p. 86. Dr. Egi, one of Japan's most astute political observers, remarked cynically that the size of Katsura's party would be in direct relation to the corruptness of the Diet.

Oishi.[119] Despite the outright corruption that was used to obtain some adherents, however, the Doshikai was far from controlling the Diet, and Katsura was forced to face an embittered Seiyukai-Kokuminto majority.

February 5, 1913, marked one of the truly great days in Japanese parliamentary history, for it was on this day that Ozaki Yukio delivered a most remarkable speech on behalf of the "popular" parties. Having begun by challenging Katsura's abuse of Imperial rescripts, he ended by an all-out attack on the Sat-Cho oligarchy's use of the Throne:

> The principle of the Emperor being sacred and inviolable emanated from the fact of Ministers of State holding themselves responsible in his stead. [*Applause.*] Prince Katsura explains away his appointment to the Palace and from thence again to the Government as being the result of Imperial wishes, which must be obeyed by all means. From this, the Prince appears free of all responsibility, but then he must know that responsibility is ultimately ascribed to the Emperor. [*Applause.*] I firmly believe it is not the part of a loyal subject to shirk his responsibility and attribute it to another. . . .
>
> Prince Katsura must have known what mood swayed society when he first entered the Palace. He received no doubt, scores of letters of threatening import, some written with blood, when he made it appear, by not taking the proper path for entry to the Palace, as though he were going to hold the new Emperor in his grasp and lord it over the world. . . . They always mouth "loyalty" and "patriotism" but what they are actually doing is to hide themselves behind the Throne, and shoot at their political enemies from their secure ambush. [*Applause.*] The Throne is their rampart. Rescripts are their missiles.[120]

Ozaki was seeking to wrest the oligarchs' greatest weapon from their hands. Fortified by press and public opinion and by temporary party unity,[121] he had had the audacity to lay bare before

---

[119] For party manifesto and other party documents, see Hayashida, *op. cit.*, Vol. II, pp. 194–204.

[120] Speech by Ozaki Yukio, House of Representatives, February 5, 1913, as published in *JM*, February 15, 1913, pp. 197–198.

[121] Like most momentous events in a nation's history, the events of this period were the results of a great variety of factors. Economic and social conditions were changing rapidly. Press and public opinion were growing in importance; intellectuals were beginning to wrestle with the fundamental problems of the Japanese state; the power of the Genro was weakening; Katsura was arrogant, overbearing, and most unpopular, and he had misused the Throne with more ill-concealed flagrancy than had his predecessors; and the young Emperor Taisho's inexperience and mental weakness high-lighted

the nation one of the chief means whereby the Sat-Cho oligarchs had used the Constitution for their own purposes, and with it, the popular parties and representative government.

An equally revolutionary step was taken a few days after Ozaki's speech. The Seiyukai actually refused to accept an Emperor's request—an action unprecedented in parliamentary history. The details of this event reveal with clarity the tenor of the times. Katsura, during this period, was trying desperately to reach some compromise with the Seiyukai, since his new party proved insufficient in numbers to save him. As a last resort, he acted through the Emperor himself. In accordance with Katsura's plan, Saionji was called to the Palace. There he was ordered to bend every effort to avoid a political disturbance and was notified that he was being treated as a "chief retainer of the nation." [122] This occurred on February 9, and on the following day, Saionji dutifully visited the party leaders and members, reporting to them the Emperor's request that they withdraw their nonconfidence bill. The Seiyukai, with some hesitation, finally refused, thus, in effect, defying an order from the Throne.[123]

In many respects the political upheaval of 1913 was a signal victory for the party movement, and it demonstrated the power the parties could have when they were strengthened by their own unity and by the support of the public and the press. They had challenged the political misuse of the Throne so vigorously that personal intervention by the Throne in political controversies practically ceased.[124] Moreover, Katsura was forced to resign, a broken

---

this misuse. I shall allude to these factors more fully in their respective categories.

[122] See Royama, op. cit., p. 394.

[123] This event, however, related to a very important development, for between the time when Saionji urged the party leaders to withdraw the bill and the time of the Seiyukai meeting, Admiral Yamamoto visited party headquarters and consulted with the party men. Up to that time, says Takekoshi, the leadership of both parties, with the exceptions of Inukai and Ozaki, had been prepared to obey; Yamamoto's stand changed their minds. See Takekoshi, op. cit., pp. 276–278.

[124] The Throne continued to be of great symbolic importance, of course, and in a very real political sense. Many a future ministry was attacked on the score that it had betrayed the trust placed in it by the Emperor, or that it had caused the Emperor worry and anxiety. Moreover, the Emperor continued to ask questions and express regrets, and his status again became controversial in the 1930's, as we shall note. However, he did not again exercise the personal power of the Emperor Meiji, nor was he used by the Inner Court aides

and discredited man. But, despite these results, the culmination of the struggle was another defeat for representative government. The successors in power were not the united popular parties, but another faction of the old bureaucracy, aided and abetted by the Seiyukai.

The Satsuma navy faction had long been jealous of the power of Choshu and the army, as has previously been noted. Katsura's actions—and especially his use of the Throne—antagonized Yamamoto and the Satsuma clique so greatly that it was comparatively easy for Hara and the Seiyukai leaders to arrange an understanding with the clique by which they would jointly take over Katsura's place. And it was this understanding, far more than Ozaki's heroic speech, which felled the Katsura ministry. The matrix of a new administration had been formed, but the process of parliamentarism and representative government had again been blocked by the pragmatic political tactics of the leading "people's party." And these tactics, as we have seen, were necessitated, fundamentally, by the institutional requirements of the Meiji Constitution. Once more the Seiyukai found power and prestige through alliance with a bureaucratic faction.

Moreover, the Kokuminto, long a holdout against bureaucratic advances, had not escaped unscathed. Oishi had led a large number of its members into Katsura's Doshikai, and although the ex-Premier died soon after his resignation, the work of party organization continued, and a number of the most influential and powerful bureaucrats joined the new party. To recite some of their names— Kato Takaakira, Wakatsuki Reijiro, and Hamaguchi Yuko—is in reality to read off the roster of future party leaders. It was not long before the Doshikai swallowed up most of the remaining Kokuminto group. As Professor Royama has so excellently pointed out, the power of the "militarist" and "civil" bureaucratic factions was not disappearing, but, regardless of the leanings of their respective cliques, the leading bureaucratic aspirants to political power were almost forced to join political parties.

If this was a victory for the party movement, it was also a sign that the parties had lost much of their meaning as spokesmen for representative government and popular movements. The new bureaucratic party leaders were by no means completely involved

so extensively in the open political arena. The fact that Emperor Taisho was mentally incompetent was important, of course, in effecting a change, although the exact role which the Emperor could play personally was never completely clarified in the prewar Showa era.

196

with the militarist elements, as was later to be shown very clearly. Many were representative of the high-class career official who had had both administrative and legislative experience. Nor were they all opposed to strengthening the parties and the Diet; some of them worked mightily for party government, as they understood it. On the whole, however, they were not the ideal leaders of democracy or of a popular movement. Whether their contacts were with the army, the navy, the civil bureaucracy, or the business world, as a group they lacked an understanding of truly popular government and sympathy for its aims. Many of them feared democracy—a fear born of their own training and background— and the basic principles of democracy remained very foreign to them, even when they rendered support to some of its procedures.

With the retirement of Saionji to the Genro Council and the death of Katsura, the phase of leadership of the party movement by elder statesmen ended. Kato Takaakira eventually became the leader of the Doshikai, and Hara was the new president of the Seiyukai. Thus the year 1913 marked an interesting break in Japanese political history and, incidentally, proved to be the halfway point in the existence of the old parties under the Meiji Constitution. It might be well, therefore, to draw some basic conclusions about party development during the first twenty-three years of constitutional government in Japan.

Basically, the institutional structure of Japan during these years had three deleterious effects on the party movement: it rendered "liberal" party unity useless and therefore largely unsought; it helped to corrupt party principles and integrity; and it shifted party leadership, and even membership, more and more into the hands of a basically antidemocratic Meiji bureaucracy. To be sure, there were major factors other than the framework of government that played a vitally important part in bringing about each of these results, factors that merit discussion in other sections of this work, but the evidence shows that Japanese constitutionalism is an excellent beginning point from which to discern the weaknesses of Japan's prewar attempts to achieve democracy.

Unity of the "liberals" was meaningless, because, even acting in unison, they could not include the forces necessary to control the Japanese administrative machinery. The tendency, therefore, was for parties supposedly representing the same cause to struggle against each other and to vie for the favor and support of the Genro and its bureaucratic adjuncts, whence power came. Men being human, it is inevitable that in any society the seekers of

197

political power will sooner or later trim their policies and alter their course to fit the arbitrators of their fate—whether these be the people or, as in Meiji Japan, the oligarchs behind an omnipotent Throne.

Inevitably, this process contributed to the corruption of the original premises and integrity of the liberal parties. This loss of idealism was certainly hastened by a Constitution which demanded a workable union of forces whose ideas were incompatible and in circumstances that forced the liberal parties to be no more than junior partners, because of the paucity of their bargaining weapons. Thus, when they compromised with Ito and his faction, as in the formation of the Seiyukai, they forsook, temporarily at least, the major premises on which ultimate party success would depend. When they compromised with the Yamagata faction, they gave up both principles and integrity, and especially the latter, for it was easier for the militarists to buy votes than to adjust policy. By the end of this period, Ozaki, a man remarkable for his political integrity, could cry out:

"Our politicians one and all strive for political power and contend for their own pecuniary interests, but beyond this they do not go. They have no principles of any kind and no decided views. . . . They are attached to nothing and follow nobody in particular. A man who has been visiting Marquis Ito today will be seen creeping through Count Okuma's portals tomorrow, and knocking at Marquis Yamagata's door the day following." [125]

It is rather profitless to proclaim principles, however, when there is no possible means of carrying them out independently, and when programs have to be hacked out in the secret bargaining meetings between party leaders and the various han statesmen. And it leads not only to obscuring principles but to obscuring responsibility as well.

And the same conditions which helped produce a lack of party unity and integrity bequeathed to the old "liberal" parties a new type of member and leader—the bureaucratic politician. It is perfectly true that the liberal parties had always been led by and composed of ex-samurai and ex-officials for the most part. The commoner had never played a significant role in the party movement. However, the early leaders, as we have seen, had championed the supremacy of representative institutions as a weapon against the Sat-Cho oligarchy, and in so doing had placed them-

---

[125] Translated in *KC*, June 18, 1908.

selves at the head of a democratic movement that centered on the concept of unfettered popular government. Some of the older party men had been weaned from their more altruistic principles either by power or by graft, but the newcomers, for the most part, needed no such inducements. They entered the party ranks under pressure and with a preconceived prejudice against democracy in the sense of strong popular controls.

These were some of the ills which beset the party movement on the eve of the First World War. There was, however, one important administrative change taking place (not to mention powerful social changes) which offered some hope for the future. The Genro, under whose aegis all power had lain and by whose central decisions a type of unity of all elements had been enforced, were gradually losing their controlling positions through death, old age, and a rise of new factors. As Professor Royama says:

The influence and popularity of the han Genro, who had the power of leadership of the Meiji political world, was gradually waning, and at the same time the political parties, which had been existing for many years more or less as an opposition power outside the government, had gradually begun to have self-confidence in their own power, and transitional politics according to unions and compromises of both sides no longer played a sufficient function. Thus, among the military group, the bureaucrats, and the political parties, each of whom had been educated in their respective elements under han Genro supervision, a kind of independent, equal attitude was brought forth. We may say that the "Political Change of Taisho" was truly the result of that spirit.[126]

The effect which this gradual relaxation of Genro absolutism was to have on the position of political parties and their relationships with the other groups vying for power forms an important part of the next chapter.

---

[126] Royama, *op. cit.*, p. 389.

VI

THE EVOLUTION OF
POLITICAL PARTIES IN
JAPANESE INSTITUTIONAL
STRUCTURE AND THEORY

Part II: 1913–1932

THE AFTERMATH of the "Taisho Change" of 1913 found the major parties with more strength and less validity in terms of their *raison d'être* than at any time in the past. We have traced in some detail the part which Japanese constitutionalism had played in creating this anomaly—the ways in which the original weaknesses of the democratic movement had been exploited and its potentialities constricted by a permanent and essentially hostile fundamental law. The period 1913–1932, now under study, represented the logical culmination of earlier trends within the institutional framework of modern Japan.

No party victory under the Meiji Constitution could permanently undermine those residual powers of the bureaucratic and militaristic forces fixed by Imperial law. Hence, "party victory," as in the past, tended to be the result of carefully predetermined alignments with these forces far more than the effect of a' frontal assault upon them. And the hand of the past had also affected the crucial matters of inner strength and will. The parties were increasingly bolstered by a growing antagonism toward the bureaucracy on the part of the press, the intellectuals, and the general public. If the major parties had been equipped with dynamic leaders willing to serve as tutors for democracy, substantial changes might have been effected. Even a modification of the Constitution might have been secured from "a benevolent Emperor anxious to meet the needs of his people." However, given the major Japanese parties as they actually were, any design to achieve these ends through their instrumentality would be little more than a dream, as later events were to show very clearly. It is true that the central determinants lay in the nature of modern Japan's economic development, as we shall note in the next section; nevertheless, the constitutional mold was also important. In conformity with the dictates of Japanese constitutionalism, the major parties were now led and peopled more than ever before by a congeries of state officials, militarists, and titled peers. Such amalgamations under the party label had opened new doors of power and influence. To be sure, even this did not mean that the struggle for party supremacy had been won. The greater part of nonparty officialdom, civil and military, remained hostile to party encroachment and bitterly critical of party government. Major battles lay ahead—and bitter defeats. In an attempt to meet the hostility, however, it was in the nature of Japanese institutions and party direction that temporizing measures, unequal compromises, and even abject surrender would be used to an extent that differentiated the major parties very little from their "opponents" in the public eye. There were a few leaders in the party movement who openly challenged the bureaucratic forces, but they were very few and usually not the most successful, as the following study of the post-1913 politics of Japan may serve to indicate.

If proof of increasing party power were needed, the events of the Yamamoto ministry that followed the Katsura regime gave abundant evidence. When Yamamoto took office on February 10, 1913, the Seiyukai possessed more actual power than it had ever held previously, not excluding the times of the Ito and Saionji cabinets. The party had almost dictated cabinet composition. The early demand of the Seiyukai that the entire cabinet be composed of party members, or men who would join the party, was finally modified to a demand for the control of all portfolios except those of premier, foreign minister, and army and navy ministers. Since there were only two in the cabinet who were already Seiyukai members, Hara and Matsuda, four leading officials—Takahashi Korekiyo, Yamamoto Tatsuo, Motoda Hajime, and Okuda Yoshito —had their names duly enrolled in the party register and thereby automatically became influential party leaders.[1]

---

[1] The contemporary press was quick to question the value of such tactics on the part of Seiyukai leaders. The *Chuo Koron*, however, defended Seiyukai actions to a certain extent by saying: "Probably politics is power, not utopian-

Moreover, the Seiyukai had not stopped with merely forcing prominent officials into its ranks. It had also demanded the execution of party policies, including the removal of certain obstacles to party power. Among the requests were those for a relaxation of the Civil Service regulations, revisions of the qualifications for war and navy ministers, administrative reforms, and tax reduction.[2] The degree of Yamamoto's acquiescence was indicated in an exchange which took place in the Thirtieth Diet (1913–1914) between the administration and the *Seiyu Club* (Political Friends' Club), a group headed by Ozaki Yukio.[3] The Seiyu Club presented the following questionnaire to the government:

1. We believe that political party Cabinets are necessary from the standpoint of carrying out constitutional government. What is the viewpoint of the government concerning this?

2. According to the present administrative system, the Ministers of War and Navy are limited to men in the active ranks, lieutenant general or general (vice-admiral or admiral). Does not the present Cabinet recognize that this is an obstruction to the application of constitutional government?

3. We believe that the present Civil Service appointment regulations should be quickly revised and that there is a necessity to open the gates to promote men of talent. What is the viewpoint of the present Cabinet concerning this? And if the present Cabinet has any idea of correcting this, what are its plans?

4. The problem of the increase of the Army by two divisions was the thing which actuated the overthrow of the Saionji Cabinet. Does the present Cabinet contemplate the execution of this increase?[4]

Yamamoto's answer, presented to the House on March 11, 1914, was as follows:

---

ism. For example, even if there are heaven-born heroes, if they cannot yet control the various forces of the political world, then they are not sufficient to cause a premier to be set up. They can only wait for a ripe opportunity and for the increase in actual power of their men." From the editorial, "Seihen ichinen go no chobo" (Views One Year After the Political Change), *Chuo Koron*, February, 1914 (pp. 1–11), p. 5.

[2] *Ibid.*, p. 2.

[3] The Seiyu Club represented a small group of "down-the-line democrats," most of whom had left the Seiyukai in disgust over its alliance with the Satsuma men.

[4] Seiyu Club questionnaire, presented in the Thirtieth Diet, reproduced in Royama Masamichi, *Seiji shi* (*Political History*), in Gendai Nihon bummei shi (History of Contemporary Japanese Civilization Series), Tokyo, 1940, p. 397. A fifth and final question concerned taxation revision. It must be recog-

1. As for the organization of the Cabinet, although it was based on the authority of Imperial Sovereignty, those who were in charge of the administrative branch recognized that placing importance on political parties and having respect for public opinion of the people were essential from the standpoint of constitutional government.

2. As for the present system of limiting Ministers of War and Navy to the first two grades of the active list, because it was difficult to maintain that it was not a barrier from the standpoint of the administration of constitutional government, the government was pressing serious consultations and expected to grant suitable revisions.

3. Together with the progress of conditions, Civil Service appointment regulation revisions are recognized as necessary. However, we cannot at this time make clear the limits of those revisions.

4. We believe that the question of an increase of two divisions should be decided with regard to fiscal and all other related conditions.[5]

Yamamoto's reply was definitely conciliatory. It appeared that the government might make some inroads on bureaucratic power. On no score, however, did the Premier commit himself to specific details. Moreover, special care was taken to avoid any statement that might be construed as an advocacy of automatic party cabinets based upon Diet majority. Indeed, special homage was paid to the doctrine of Imperial sovereignty, and the best that supporters of party cabinets could hope for was that "importance" would be placed upon the views of the parties and public opinion.

When Yamamoto's words were translated into action, the strongest exponents of representative government had even more reason to doubt the capacity of the Seiyukai-Satsuma coalition to open wide the gateway toward popular government. Civil Service regulations were broadened to give party patronage somewhat greater opportunity to operate, and there was a rather sizable reduction in the bureaucracy.[6] But the service groups were handled gingerly indeed. Qualifications for the war and navy cabinet posts were changed only to the extent of admitting retired as well as active servicemen of the two top ranks. And in terms of the over-all balance of power between party and bureaucratic forces, all the "reforms" put together were trifling. However, the Seiyukai readily

---

nized, of course, that the Seiyu men were, generally speaking, more progressive than Seiyukai and Doshikai men, and constituted a very small fragment.

[5] Yamamoto's Reply to the Seiyu Questionnaire, presented to the Diet March 11, 1914; reproduced in Royama, *op. cit.*, p. 397.

[6] Bureaucratic personnel was reduced by 6,428, and expenditures in this category by more than ¥4,000,000. Figures from *ibid.*, p. 400.

accepted these modest revisions, satisfied on most scores that it had done so well.

Indeed, it seemed to the uninitiated a parodox that as the party movement grew stronger the major parties themselves grew more timid and hesitant to push for basic reform. If Seiyukai action in the Yamamoto ministry tended in this direction, the Okuma ministry which followed presented an even clearer example.

The occasion that led to the downfall of Okuma's predecessor was the so-called "Siemens Affair," one of the greatest scandals that ever shook Japan. Involved in it were several high naval officers, who had accepted bribes from foreign companies for construction contracts.[7] As an aftermath of shocking disclosures made in the press and Diet, the antigovernment forces toppled the ministry: Yamamoto turned in his resignation on April 15, 1914. It was not the parties, however, that produced the change, but the House of Peers, and the method used was that of slaughtering the ministry's budget.

Succeeding events demonstrated how little the basic situation had been altered by the so-called "Taisho Change." The Genro, whose power of selecting the premier neither major party had seriously challenged, again played the dominant role in choosing Yamamoto's successor. Their ranks now included Yamagata, Matsukata, Oyama, and Inoue; Saionji was not yet a member. Death, old age, and public antagonism had considerably dimmed their earlier luster, and they were gradually losing their constant directive power; but by controlling the premiership, they retained a firm hold on groups competing for administrative control. And Yamagata, who had never given up his antiparty attitude, dominated the Genro Councils. Neither Hara nor Kato, the leaders of the two major parties, was given serious consideration for the post.

---

[7] For a detailed report of this whole affair, including lengthy quotations from the Diet speeches of Shimada Saburo, Admiral Saito, Inukai, and others, see "Dai sanju ichi Teikoku Gikai o ronzu" (Discussing the Thirty-first Imperial Diet), in the Spring Edition, 1914, *Chuo Koron*, pp. 1–20. The exposé of the scandal occurred during the discussion of a new budget which included large sums for naval expansion. The reports of the bribery of Admiral Fujii and Captain Sawasaki by Siemens, Schuckert, and Company, a German firm, reached Japan via Germany in the course of the trial of a German employee on charges of blackmail. Vickers and Company, the English firm, was also involved. Immediately, the naval appropriations were attacked, and though the Seiyukai exercised a moderating influence in the lower house, the Peers cut the budget by ¥70 million, after which Yamamoto resigned.

Instead, after three false starts, the Genro turned to Okuma, now retired from active politics for some years.[8]

Okuma's return to political power was hailed as a major victory for democracy, despite the fact that it had come via the Genro Council. Few men had championed the causes of representative government and political honesty with more vigor than the "Sage of Waseda." [9] He had been in the vanguard of the popular party movement almost from its beginnings, and during that long period when the Seiyukai leaders were cavorting with the bureaucratic forces he had denounced their corruption and their treachery to the popular cause.

If there was rejoicing in the independent progressive circles at first, however, doubts soon grew as the Okuma ministry betrayed the same tendencies as its predecessors. From the very beginning, Okuma had had to make adjustments with various important groups. In this difficult process, many "understandings" were

---

[8] Among sources containing details, see Imamura Takeo, *Hyoden Takahashi Korekiyo (A Critical Biography of Takahashi Korekiyo)*, Tokyo, 1948, pp. 72–82.

Yamagata's first choice was Saionji, who immediately declined. Then he turned to the ex-shogun, Tokugawa, long an honored peer and president of the Peers. Tokugawa also declined, stating afterward that he would never accept a premiership unless he had first formed his own party. The third choice was Kiyoura Keigo, an older official, who lacked not the will but the means, for neither the navy clique nor a major party would support him. Finally, upon Inoue's advice, Okuma's possibilities were canvassed, and after discussions between the Genro and him, he was given the post. Inoue was now bitterly anti-Seiyukai, because of that party's alliances with Satsuma groups—a fact that shows how strong embers of han factionalism still were in Japanese politics. Certain of the Genro, however, particularly Yamagata, remained extremely skeptical of the Okuma administration and applied very heavy pressure upon it from time to time. Behind-the-scenes communications were sometimes bitter, and friction between the Genro and Foreign Minister Kato was great. For this period, see Ito Masanori, *Kato Takaakira*, Tokyo, 1929, Vol. II, pp. 1 ff.; Wakatsuki Reijiro, *Kofuan kaiko roku—Wakatsuki Reijiro jiden (Recorded Memoirs of Kofuan—The Autobiography of Wakatsuki Reijiro)*, Tokyo, 1950, pp. 206–243; Watanabe Ikujiro, *Okuma Shigenobu*, Tokyo, 1943, pp. 175–190; and Hayashida Kametaro, *Nihon seito shi (History of Japanese Political Parties)*, Tokyo, 1927, Vol. II, pp. 221–225.

[9] Okuma had founded Waseda University in 1882, and always retained the greatest interest in its development, serving as chancellor from the time of his political retirement in 1907 until his acceptance of the premiership in 1914. From this vantage point, he had delivered some of his trenchant criticisms of Japanese politics, thereby advancing his reputation as a popular leader.

reached with the Genro, and through them, with such groups as the military elements and the Peers. Support was pledged for the two new divisions which the army had long been demanding. Okuma was, of course, dependent upon the Doshikai, his old party, for support; and its president, Kato, together with some prominent Doshikai members, acted as a counterforce to Genro pressure. The cabinet represented a balance, of sorts, between Yamagata and Kato.[10] In truth, Okuma had followed much the same technique that had always marked Seiyukai policy, entering into the very bureaucratic alliances he had previously decried. He and even the Doshikai were in some measure prisoners of the opposition. Under the Japanese institutional structure there seemed, indeed, no alternative. The Genro were entrusted automatically by the Emperor with the selection of each new premier, a selection which need bear no relationship whatsoever to the prevailing majority party in the House of Representatives. The only real necessity which a premier faced was that of placating the various groups that controlled the vital parts of the administration. A compromise had to be reached with the Genro in the first place, and then with the army and navy, which controlled two cabinet posts, and also with the House of Peers, which could not be dissolved. As for the House of Representatives, any cabinet, as the Okuma ministry was to show, could enter a hostile Diet, dissolve it, and manipulate the elections in such a manner as to come out with a controlling majority.

It was at this point, indeed, that some of those party men who had newly come from the ranks of officialdom could provide experience and guidance. Okuma's minister of agriculture and commerce, Oura Kanetake, was, it will be remembered, a long-time official who had helped Katsura form the Doshikai and was now one of its leaders. When the cabinet faced the Thirty-fifth Diet (December, 1914) with minority support and the necessity of passing the "two divisions" bill, Oura attempted to help "persuade" part of the opposition.[11] Through the medium of Hayashida Kametaro, chief secretary of the House, a campaign to split the Seiyukai

---

[10] See Royama, *op. cit.*, p. 401; Wakatsuki, *op. cit.*, pp. 208–210.

[11] See Royama, *op. cit.*, pp. 407–409. Most contemporary accounts lacked inside details, but they gave many interesting points. See anonymous article, "Okuma no naikaku hyoban ki" (The Story of the Okuma Cabinet's Reputation), in *Chuo Koron*, January, 1915, pp. 16–25; also Asada Koson, "Ni dai shito tairitsu no susei" (Trends in the Rivalry of Two Great Private Parties), in *Taiyo*, February, 1915, pp. 16–25.

was undertaken, and in this endeavor much bribery was used.[12] One faction within the party agreed to secede and form a new party if sufficient funds were provided for "party organizational expenses." Some money was given, but too few members responded, and some of those were not faithful in terms of their votes; therefore the Diet had to be dissolved.[13]

The next election, on March 25, 1915, was marked by an amount of government interference which was at least as great as that in any election since 1892. Oura, who had been transferred to the post of Home Minister for the purpose of supervising the election, used all the techniques he had learned at the knee of Katsura.[14] The results were twofold: a resounding Doshikai majority was produced in the new Diet; and the antagonism of the press, the public, and the Seiyukai toward the victorious party was unmistakable. The Doshikai majority was attacked on all sides as being "unrepresentative" and the result of corrupt practices.

Even within the Okuma cabinet, there were repercussions. Ozaki, though he was Minister of Justice at the time, could not stomach Oura's tactics and openly denounced his colleague. Finally Oura resigned, as did the entire cabinet, on July 30, 1915. Three ministers, Kato, Wakatsuki, and Yashiro Rokuro, did not reënter the new Okuma cabinet, partly as a result of the widespread censure of Oura's methods. The Genro, however, were willing to see Okuma continue in power. His assurances on the "two divisions" question and his "strong" foreign policy were important factors in his favor, and he was quickly reinstated in office.[15] The rest of Okuma's ministry was fairly calm, and he finally submitted his resignation on October 8, 1916, after pushing the military expansion program through the new Diet.

Okuma's ministry was more than a personal failure. This and the preceding ministry demonstrated that neither the Seiyukai

---

[12] Hayashida's own account glosses over the question of bribery and gives few details except that the two divisions were very necessary and that patriotism demanded that all work for their passage. See Hayashida, op. cit., Vol. II, pp. 229–231.

[13] Only nineteen members of the Seiyukai left the party. Ibid., p. 231.

[14] See the article by Professor Ukita Kazutami, "Sosenkyo no koto hihyo" (Advanced Criticism of the General Election), in Taiyo, April, 1915, pp. 2–10. Oura's chief method was to hold the prefectural governors responsible for government victory in their districts—with few questions asked concerning the means. This was, of course, a technique which had been used widely in the past.

[15] See Royama, op. cit., p. 413.

nor the Doshikai (now the *Kenseikai*) [16] had the capacity to assert the supremacy of representative government. It was almost as if there had been no "Defend the Constitution" movement in 1913.[17] It is true that there were some evidences of a transitional period with future promise for the parties. Party power had obviously increased, and party demands—when backed by unity and strength—weighed more heavily than before in the adjustments between conflicting groups. In a man like Kato Takaakira, moreover, the Genro found a conservative but stubborn opponent. Kato flung down the challenge to the Genro on more than one occasion. However, the composite power of the antiparty, nonrepresentative groups still lay athwart the pathway to party supremacy, and there were many indications that this situation would outlast the period of Genro decline. As party men tasted the fruits of partial victory, moreover, temptations mounted. Even earlier, however, as we have noted, the major parties have found it indispensable to assimilate more and more bureaucratic personnel and techniques in order to meet the institutional demands.

The result was that when either major party held the reins of administration, its actions were little different from those of the old oligarchy. It was only in the role of a minority opposition party that it could afford to pay homage to the basic principles of representative government. In this general situation, the antiparty forces had an excellent political opportunity, and even a moral argument,

---

[16] During the months of September and October, 1916, the Doshikai, working with several minor factions within the Diet, built a new party, the *Kenseikai* (Constitutional Association). The first proclamation of this party was issued on October 8, 1916, the same day that Okuma resigned. The timing was, of course, designed to create a feeling that the new party and its president, Kato Takaakira, should have the right to succeed the Okuma ministry. When the relations between the Genro and Kato are considered, the failure of this tactic should be no surprise.

[17] Hopes for more democratic procedures had been very high after the events of 1913, and it is interesting to note one interpretation of what those events should have meant to the party movement: "What is the rise of the *Taisho Ishin* [Taisho Restoration]? . . . Even though it was strongly championed scarcely little more than a year ago, now it has almost been forgotten by the political world, but if we describe it in a sentence, it is merely saying that we should utilize the *rikken no jodo* [true constitutional road], rejecting temporizing, compromise politics, the transcendental principle, and *Genro* politics, organizing cabinets on the basis of the majority party." From anonymous article "Okuma no naikaku hyoban ki" (cited in note 11, above), pp. 10–11.

for retarding the introduction of automatic majority party cabinets. In the state of affairs created by Okuma's resignation, the Seiyukai was a minority party and thus without claim to power, whereas the Kenseikai was a majority party representing a discredited administration and owing its majority, in part, at least, to the unscrupulous tactics of that government. Thus it was comparatively easy for the leading Genro to ignore Kato, whom they disliked, and to put in Okuma's place General Terauchi, a Choshu militarist and a favorite of the Yamagata faction. This was done, moreover, with the covert support of the Seiyukai, anxious to utilize the new cabinet in recouping its Diet majority.

Officially, Terauchi proclaimed the basic "military" principles of national unity and aloofness from party conflict. In the prefectural governors' meeting held soon after his assumption of office, he announced: "The expansion of our national destiny must await a nationally unified power. However, with regard to the differences of political views in the various political party factions, a strict impartiality will be maintained." [18]

This was traditional Yamagata doctrine, long since outmoded and proven impossible. And in reality, Terauchi soon jettisoned such a doctrine—if he had ever sincerely held it—in the words which he used to justify the dissolution of the Thirty-eighth Diet in January, 1917: "There existed a minority party which was diminished unnaturally and a majority party which was established unnaturally." [19]

Pursuing this logic, the government issued instructions to the prefectural governors to aid in the defeat of the Kenseikai, and the result was a tremendous victory for the Seiyukai.

The Terauchi ministry was thereafter enabled to retain its position by depending upon the support of the Seiyukai to counteract the attacks of the opposition elements in the Diet. To be sure, Seiyukai support was not enthusiastic, and the price to be paid for that party's approval was very high. Thus, when the cabinet tax program was vetoed by the Seiyukai, the *Osaka Mainichi* (*Osaka Daily*) remarked: "The incident [defeat of cabinet tax revision proposals] has, however, demonstrated beyond all doubt that a bureaucratic cabinet, which enjoys no genuine support of

---

[18] Terauchi's speech to prefectural governors' meeting, Tokyo, 1916, quoted in Royama, *op. cit.*, p. 415. Terauchi's formula was contained in the words *heiko jibyo* (strict impartiality).

[19] Quoted in *ibid.*, p. 420.

any political party, stands on very unsafe ground and is liable to fall, like the walls of Jericho, at the first sound of the trumpet of a majority party like the Seiyukai." [20]

In an attempt to remedy some uncertainties and develop greater unity, at least in foreign affairs, Terauchi established the *Gaiko Chosa Kai* (Foreign Policy Deliberation Committee), in which he hoped representatives of all the major parties would join, along with key nonparty figures. Some results were produced, but the Gaiko Chosa Kai experiment reflected, more than anything else, the need to coördinate the ill-defined Japanese political institutions. As Kato Takaakira pointed out in refusing to join this committee, however, it was an effort which did not answer the real questions of power and responsibility.[21]

The Terauchi cabinet finally succumbed to the serious inflationary problem produced by the war. Extraordinarily high rice prices produced a series of riots all over Japan in August, 1918, with property damage and casualties running very high.[22] This climaxed the ministry's unpopularity, which had been growing because of its general fiscal policies and its severe suppression of the popular movement. On September 28, 1918, the cabinet resigned.

With the resignation of the Terauchi ministry the era of party cabinets began. Hara Takashi, Seiyukai president and the first commoner to hold the premiership, took office on September 29,

---

[20] From the *Osaka Mainichi*, quoted in the *Japan Chronicle* (formerly the *Kobe Chronicle*), weekly edition (hereinafter referred to in the notes as *JC*), February 14, 1918, p. 253.

[21] For Kato's views on the Gaiko Chosa Kai, see Ito Masanori, *op. cit.*, Vol. I, pp. 260–275. One of Kato's major points was that this was the old theory of "transcendental government" working in a new form, with party leaders being brought in to provide the appearance of unity, whereas, actually, control was still denied them and responsibility for actions taken was left more obscure. Kato vigorously denied that foreign policy could or should be wholly nonpartisan.

Both Inukai Tsuyoshi and Hara, presidents of the Kokuminto and Seiyukai, joined the new organization. Naturally, the respective attitudes of Inukai, Hara, and Kato were governed to some extent by political considerations. The attitude of Inukai is particularly interesting, for he had hitherto been most adamant in his support for the principles expressed by Kato on this matter. At the same time, however, he had also been close to the exponents of a "strong" foreign policy.

[22] For one contemporary discussion of the rice riots and their social and political significance, see the symposium entitled "Bodo jiken no hihan" (Criticism of the Riot Incidents) in *Chuo Koron*, September, 1918, pp. 69–98.

1918.[23] His cabinet was composed entirely of Seiyukai leaders, except for the service posts and the post of foreign minister, held by Uchida Yasuya, a diplomat and formerly Minister of Foreign Affairs in the second Saionji cabinet.

We have noted three political factors which contributed to this fulfillment of party aspirations. In the first place, there had been a decline in Genro politics, long the focal point of the bureaucracy and the real mechanism whereby the oligarchic intentions of the Japanese Constitution were translated into action. The Genro now consisted of three old men—Yamagata, aged 81, Matsukata, aged 84, and Saionji, aged 70. Okuma, who was officially a Genro despite his disregard for that position, was 81. Although these old men still wielded great influence, they could no longer control the day-by-day activities in all the complicated channels of Japanese politics, and they had not raised up successors to their power. Moreover, their prestige and popularity had been seriously affected by developments within Japanese society.

Indeed, the rise of what may loosely be described as "the popular movement" was a second factor of great importance in increasing party power. The tides of democratic thought and theories of representative government, set in motion by great social and economic changes, were cutting somewhat more deeply into the "substrata" of Japanese society. The concept of the "common man," with new and expanded implications, was beginning to be felt in Japanese politics. I shall deal with this development later, but its importance must be noted here. The parties, despite their aberrations, were still the chief symbols of popularism in Japanese administration, and consequently could ride these tides with a fair degree of success.

Finally, there was the harmonization of the major parties and the general bureaucratic forces. It was only by this means that the parties had rendered themselves partially acceptable to the elements of the institutional structure that were still in a position to control vital aspects of political affairs. The quasi-supremacy of the parties under the Meiji Constitution was possible only because

---

[23] In the thirty-five years since the inauguration of the cabinet system in 1885, there had been eighteen cabinets; thus the average age of each ministry was slightly less than two years. However, the premiership had rotated among nine men, only two of whom—Saionji and Okuma—had been outside the Satsuma and Choshu ranks, and five of the nine (Kuroda, Yamagata, Katsura, Yamamoto, and Terauchi) had been military men. Yamamoto was a navy officer, the others army men.

the parties had gone through a process of alliances, ententes, "mutual understandings," and actual amalgamations with the bureaucratic forces.

The membership of the Hara cabinet itself was reflective of this evolutionary development.[24] Hara, as has been noted, had reëntered political life in 1900 as a protégé of Ito and an organizer of the Seiyukai, having formerly served in several capacities, including that of a head official in the Foreign Office. Tokonami (Home Minister), Takahashi (Finance Minister), and Yamamoto Tatsuo (Minister of Agriculture and Commerce) were all former administrative officials who had joined the Seiyukai at the time of the Yamamoto cabinet in response to the party's insistence. Also, Hara was on good terms with certain military men. Tanaka Giichi, Minister of War, was both a friend of Hara and a protégé of Yamagata and Terauchi. Kato Tomosaburo, Minister of the Navy, was a holdover from the previous administration. Taken as a whole, such a cabinet was hardly likely to echo the reverberating press cries for truly "popular" government.

Hara retained his premiership for more than three years, until November 12, 1921, when he was assassinated by a young fanatic. From the standpoint of administrative harmony, the Hara ministry was possibly the most successful cabinet since the founding of the Constitution. But the secret of Hara's and the Seiyukai's nominal success lay almost wholly in the way in which they conciliated the conflicting institutional forces, and not by any process of building up either the theory or the prestige of representative government. Stated briefly, Hara's policy toward the Genro was deferential; toward the militarists, ambivalent; toward the Privy Council and Peers, conciliatory; toward the Seiyukai rank and file, arbitrary; and toward the opposition parties and the general public (except certain industrial and landed elements), unconcerned. As one proceeds to examine each part of this picture, one sees the panorama of the past and the portent of the future. One sees that in the midst of what seemed to be their greatest triumph, the major political parties were mired so deeply in the rut of oligarchic and autocratic institutions that most of the appealing democratic symbolisms became grossly distorted in the minds of the Japanese people.

[24] For interesting views on cabinet personalities and issues confronting them, see the symposium "Hara naikaku ni taisuru yobo" (Demands upon the Hara Cabinet), in the *Chuo Koron*, October, 1918, pp. 71–107, especially the articles by Professors Fukuda and Yoshino.

Before discussing the nature of the ministry's relationships with these various groups, however, it might be well to put these relationships in context by briefly describing Hara's personal attributes and sketching the broad lines of policy which his cabinet followed.[25]

Hara was in many respects one of the most capable politicians Japan ever produced. Certainly he was the greatest party leader, if measured by party success, and after his death, no party was able to raise a man who could compare with him in shrewdness, political acumen, and a capacity to hold together the divergent forces in the Japanese political world. But as for personal characteristics, Hara lacked many of the traits which would have been desirable in forwarding the Japanese democratic cause. He was a master of compromise and conciliation, but he showed a certain carelessness when it came to abiding by fundamental principles essential to the future of liberal parties. He was a canny bargainer, but he never let previous commitments of policy stand in his way. He may have been honest personally, but he was able to wink at the corruption that surrounded his associates and his party. And though he was known as "The Great Commoner Premier," he was extremely conservative, if not reactionary, opposing the labor movement, almost all social legislation, and even the immediate granting of universal manhood suffrage. He built the Seiyukai into the most powerful political party yet seen in Japan, but he treated most of its rank and file with an officiousness which they accepted only because he had brought them the spoils of victory. All in all, his greatest qualification as Premier was the fact that his personality fitted so well into the pattern of contemporary Japanese politics, but, by the same token, he was poorly qualified to lead his party or his people toward representative government or a rectification of past abuses.

The Seiyukai program for the three crucial years during which Hara was Premier was a reflection of the party's leadership, built largely around four major policies. These were the "fulfillment of national defense," the extension of education, the encouragement of industry, and the expansion of communications. There were certain subsidiaries to this major program, such as the moderate extension of suffrage rights and rather minor changes in the bureaucratic structure. Taken as a unit, the program represents the so-called "positive policy" of the Seiyukai; when closely analyzed, it

---

[25] One valuable addition to materials on Hara is the Hara diary, just published. See Hara Keiichiro (ed.), *Hara Takashi nikki* (*The Diary of Hara Takashi*), Tokyo, 1950–1951, 9 vols.

reveals major concessions to the strongest Japanese pressure groups. Its significance can be partly explained in terms of the Hara cabinet's dealings with the various institutional elements.

The Genro, and particularly Yamagata, demanded special handling if they were not to cause the ministry serious trouble. Hara had not been Yamagata's first choice to succeed Terauchi; and when Saionji refused the post, it was only with some reluctance that Yamagata agreed to Hara's nomination. However, Inukai made the following remarks in an interview with the *Jiji Shimpo* (*Current News*): "It is a great mistake to think that the Genro have at last recognized the principle of party politics. They desire in their innermost hearts to give the reins of State to bureaucratic statesmen, but a scarcity of suitable men among the bureaucrats who came forward to assume power has compelled them to turn to Mr. Hara." [26]

Applied to Yamagata and Matsukata, Inukai's remarks were undoubtedly true, and no one was more aware of this than Hara. He had, however, done much to better his relations with Yamagata, through his working arrangement with Terauchi during the latter's tenure of office as Premier. Moreover, the choice of Tanaka Giichi as War Minister in the Hara cabinet provided a strong connection with the old Choshu statesman, for Tanaka was fairly close to Yamagata and served as one of the important channels of information between the Premier and the Genro. It was, of course, Hara's good fortune that the antagonism between Yamagata and Kato Takaakira, president of the Kenseikai, was great. The chances of Kato's becoming Premier as long as Yamagata was active seemed very slight.

Once the cabinet was established, Hara and several other ministers made frequent pilgrimages to Yamagata's villa, "keeping him informed" and "seeking his advice." Hara was a very shrewd man and obviously regarded this partly as a game; nonetheless, he went to great lengths to avoid giving any offense, and he modified his policies on occasion to fit pressures exerted from Genro quarters.[27]

---

[26] Inukai, in an interview with the *Jiji Shimpo*, quoted by *JC*, October 10, 1918, p. 512.

[27] Some very interesting discussions between Hara and Yamagata are reported by the former in his diary. In general, these meetings revealed both men sounding each other out, with Yamagata making various suggestions in a manner which was often deliberately vague or indirect. In the September 13, 1920, conversations, for instance, Yamagata warned Hara against making an excessive number of visits to the Imperial Palace, questioned the worth of Minister Takahashi, and expressed himself as opposed to any change of

The Hara ministry showed no inclination to seek the destruction of the Genro as an institution, nor to overlook its potential powers.

With the Peers, Hara scored a notable advance by effecting an alliance with the *Kenkyukai* (Study Association), the dominant faction in the upper house.[28] This temporarily removed one of the greatest obstacles to party administration, for the Peers had long been a stronghold of antiparty sentiment and had the power to make their opposition effective.[29] But the alliance was naturally reflected in cabinet policy, for care had to be taken to sidetrack or oppose those measures which met with Kenkyukai disapproval. One of the reasons for Seiyukai opposition to immediate universal manhood suffrage was the antagonism within the House of Peers, the Privy Council, and the Genro Council to such a policy. On a

cabinet. Yamagata also spoke about Okuma's desires for a Kenseikai government, conveying his own strong opposition to Kato and to immediate universal suffrage, although he conceded that the latter would eventually come. Hara played up to the aged Genro in many ways, questioning him about his past experiences, expressing concern over leftism, and pledging that the government would be responsible for general politics but hoping that the Genro would handle Imperial Household matters, in connection with the issue of the Crown Prince's overseas visit which was presently a matter of controversy. See Hara Keiichiro (ed.), *op. cit.*, Vol. IX, pp. 62–66.

[28] The greater number of Peers were not officially affiliated with any national party, but were united in various "Peer parties" representing personal-political factions. The orthodox "code" of the Peers, as set by the oligarchy, had called for the Peers to transcend partisan politics and to exercise "impartial judgment on behalf of the nation." This was, of course, in line with the *chozen naikaku shugi* (principle of transcendental cabinet) thesis.

Hara had assiduously wooed the Peers over a period of years, especially the Kenkyukai, which contained far more members than any other group. The agreement was worked out by certain close personal friends in the group. However, announcement of the move met with vigorous opposition within the House of Peers, especially from anti-Hara forces. One critic said, "Even though the Kenkyukai, which has maintained its credit as the main body of power in the upper house by upholding an attitude of fairness and integrity for many years, probably thinks its action is calm and impartial, from the viewpoint of outsiders, its action can be criticized as unreasonable. . . ." Nagashima Ryuji, "Nampa seru Kenkyukai" (The Kenkyukai in Peril), in *Taiyo*, April, 1921, p. 50.

[29] The parties were making some inroads into the House of Peers at this time, for several reasons: the Genro influence, especially that of Yamagata, had been very strong in the Peers, but with his death (February, 1922) this hold was relaxed; furthermore, the party ministries were enabled to make some appointments (in the name of Imperial appointees) to this once heavily bureaucratic body. Hara, in particular, made effective use of this power. Nevertheless, the Peers continued to be predominantly antiparty, except when the Kenkyukai, their major faction, chose to make an alliance.

great range of issues, the Kenkyukai periodically presented formal or informal warnings to the government that continued support was dependent upon the execution or abandonment of various policies.

In many respects, however, the problems and complexities of "party government" were revealed best during the Hara era by civilian-military relations and the points of view taken on certain acute questions of foreign policy. A detailed study of these problems would reveal many omens of things to come. The Hara administration had inherited the Siberian expedition from Terauchi, and troublesome developments in China and Korea further complicated the situation. On the surface, there were many reasons to suggest that the military could be set back severely in power and influence. Army prestige and popularity was reaching an all-time low because of the fiasco in Siberia, resentment over heavy military expenditures, especially after the 1920 depression, and the rise of democratic ideas in the postwar period. Yet after nearly five years of a Seiyukai cabinet, military power—legal and extra-legal—remained relatively unimpaired, still an omnipresent threat to the parties and civilian control of government. Why? The answer involves first of all Hara's position on foreign policy. Hara had a "positive" foreign policy as well as a "positive" domestic policy, particularly discernible with regard to northeast Asia. It was basically an expansionist policy which required substantial military support. Hara's desire for troop withdrawal from Siberia has been well known, but the record would also indicate that his interest in a "strong" China policy figured even in this stand.[30] And the decision to withdraw from northern Saghalien was almost too painful for the Hara cabinet to contemplate.[31] Regarding China, Hara's great hope was that Japan could use Chang Tso-lin, the Manchurian war lord, so as to expand Japanese influence in Manchuria

---

[30] For example, Hara reported, on August 18, 1920, that in a private conversation, Tanaka had stated that the removal of troops from Siberia would permit Japan to concentrate attention upon China, a matter of some urgency. And Hara indicated complete agreement with this concept. Hara Keiichiro (ed.), *op. cit.*, Vol. IX, p. 45.

[31] In a cabinet meeting which Hara reported on September 10, 1920, the question of the occupation of northern Saghalien arose. The Minister of Agriculture and Commerce stated that from a fisheries point of view, this occupation was very desirable. There was general agreement, however, that both internal and external circumstances would make long-continued Japanese control very difficult. *Ibid.*, p. 59. The final withdrawal from northern Saghalien was not completed until May, 1925.

and Mongolia.[32] The Premier worked closely on many of these matters with Tanaka Giichi, his friend and War Minister.

To be sure, the Hara-Tanaka foreign policy was too moderate for many Japanese chauvinists and military elements, both within the General Staff and overseas. Indeed, Hara and Tanaka were much concerned with control of their opponents and discussed various personnel and organizational changes.[33] As had been true of other premiers, Hara was particularly troubled by a lack of coordination between the various branches of government, by intradepartmental friction, the collective power of subordinates, independent action on the part of the overseas branch of the army, and irresponsibility in general. He not only continued the Foreign Policy Deliberation Committee established by Terauchi, but, since this was not too effective, scheduled various *ad hoc* conferences. In May, 1921, for instance, a joint meeting of military commanders, consular officials, and civil governors from Siberia, Manchuria, and Korea was convened in an effort to obtain a coördinated policy on relations with northeast Asia.[34]

In the eyes of certain army and civilian extremists, as we have noted, the Hara-Tanaka foreign policy was too moderate, and its formulators were bitterly opposed. However, Hara was much too deeply involved in developing his "positive" program and much too closely affiliated with certain military elements to launch any campaign for a sweeping reduction of military powers or expenditures. Indeed, the Hara administration bequeathed to succeeding party governments a military problem that had been made even more explosive by Seiyukai policies.

The Seiyukai did make some inroads into the subordinate bureaucracy, which had hitherto played a major part in subverting

---

[32] For this particular statement, see the entry for May 18, 1921, in *ibid.*, p. 311. See also May 17, 1921, entry, p. 310. Chang Tso-lin was given financial assistance and political backing, but it was determined not to equip him for a southern expedition, although this was his desire, partly because the Japanese government felt he had no hope of success.

[33] Opposition to any withdrawals seems to have been strong in elements of the General Staff and among certain overseas commanders. General Tanaka and Hara agreed that if the Chief of Staff persisted in his opposition, he should be removed. It is interesting to note that Yamagata supported the Tanaka view on withdrawal, and, according to Hara, Yamagata informed him that, under the circumstances, withdrawal of troops in Siberia and Shantung was necessary, and added that he wouldn't get anywhere by consulting with army people on this score! *Ibid.*, entry dated September 7, 1920, p. 57, and entry of May 31, 1921, pp. 323–324.

[34] See the entries for May 16, 17, and 18, 1921, *ibid.*, pp. 308–311.

party power. The prefectural governorships were the first major prize. On April 18, 1919, changes in twenty-seven prefectures were announced, and ten governors were relieved of their posts or retired. Many of these positions were, of course, filled with Seiyukai men who, in addition to following central administrative policy, could be counted on to help in the future elections.[35]

After the ministry was well established, it penetrated another area of the bureaucracy, colonial administration, by amending the system of colonial appointments so as to make party participation in this field possible. Korea became the first area to have a civilian and a party man nominated as colonial administrator.[36] Some party appointments were made in the centralized bureaucracy, also, but, on the whole, officialdom retained its strong resilience in the face of party thrusts.

And if the Hara ministry could not or would not lessen the power of the nonelective forces in Japanese government, it did as little to build up the power and prestige of the House of Representatives.[37] The House now stood at a crossroads, weighted down by evils of procedure and practice which had accumulated in part through the nature of its position in the administrative framework, yet it remained the chief hope of Japanese democracy. Many of the weaknesses of the Diet were due directly or indirectly to the subordinate part which it had previously played in terms of actual power. Diet sessions, which ran for only three months legally and

---

[35] For the official notice, see *JC*, April 24, 1919, p. 619. Somewhat later, the *Osaka Asahi* stated: "It is largely through the instrumentality of these partisan Governors that political parties are arbitrarily setting up in the provinces what they call their strongholds or bases for the purchase of votes. . . . If a Governor of pro-Seiyukai tendencies acts in collusion with the local Seiyukai members of the Diet or leaders of a local branch of the Seiyukai, local administration can be conducted absolutely as the Seiyukai wishes. Partisan Governors are faithful agents of the party headquarters. The task of enforcing official discipline, or of purging local politics of baneful elements, must therefore begin with the removal of such Governors." Translated from *Osaka Asahi*, October 25, 1923, in *JC*, November 1, 1923, p. 613.

[36] Diplomatic appointments were in general controlled by the *Kasumigaseki* (Foreign Office) clique, concerning which the *Osaka Asahi* stated: "This might be borne if that clique were particularly rich in men of capacity, but exactly the reverse is the case. For the past twenty years and more, this bad practice has been strictly adhered to and ability has seldom been sought outside that narrow clique which is apt to regard diplomacy in too technical a light." Quoted in *JC*, October 30, 1919, p. 671.

[37] See the scathing article on the Diet and parties by Uehara Etsujiro (Kokuminto), entitled "Sensei ni hitoshiki rikken seiji" (Constitutional Government Which Is Equal to Absolutism), in *Taiyo*, May, 1921, pp. 77–83.

about two months actually, owing to the New Year vacation, were far too short to permit full debate on government bills.[38] This was especially true since the administration invariably thrust scores of major bills into the hoppers at the last minute, and then pushed them through with unseemly speed. Voting was preordained by the prior commitments of party leaders, from which no rank-and-file member would ordinarily dissent.[39] This meant that debate in the House, or even intelligent questions, were more or less useless, particularly since the real discussions ordinarily took place secretly between party leaders and administration representatives.

The result had been a growing tendency for the Diet sessions to be filled either with trivia or with unruly and openly violent demonstrations. The minority groups, unable to do anything constructive, often resorted to the wildest possible scenes in order to distract the steam-roller majority and to get publicity for their cause in the press. So-called *yaji* (jeerers) held attention by hooting down administration spokesmen, creating a din in the chamber by thumping their wooden name plates on the desks, or actually engaging in free-for-alls. The major parties had copied the old bureaucratic technique of employing *soshi* (strong-arm men) whose chief task was to act as bodyguards for their employers and as "rough men" toward the opposition.

It was clear that these deplorable conditions were not being rectified, and probably could not be rectified until the Diet had a more important role to play in exercising the actual powers of administration.[40] Otherwise, it would continue in the nature of an artificiality behind which the real political decisions and compromises were made. Once made, they would be revealed only to the extent necessary, except on those occasions when the opposition party could proclaim them to the nation by making some sensational charge.

---

[38] The Diets had originally been convened in late November, but at the time of the Sino-Japanese War the opening date was changed to December. Also, the New Year vacation had been lengthened by an additional eleven days. Recess usually came about the middle or end of March.

[39] See a revealing article by Matsuyama Chujiro, "Seito dotoku ron" (Discussion of Political Party Morality), in *Chuo Koron*, February, 1914, pp. 45–50. Although this article was concerned with an earlier period, Matsuyama's criticisms were equally valid during the 1920's.

[40] Naturally, one must relate to this state of affairs in the Diet the political immaturity of the people as it was reflected in consciousness of issues, elections, and general political interest. This question is dealt with in chapter viii, but it may be noted here that the impotence of the Diet and public indifference or hostility each had an effect upon the other.

Although the Seiyukai had always been dedicated to the idea of party cabinets, the Hara ministry gave every indication of following time-honored procedures with regard to the Diet and thus revealed once again the prevalence of the "official" mind in Seiyukai leadership. The Forty-first Diet, which opened in December, 1918, was comparatively peaceful, and the Seiyukai was able to put through its own suffrage amendment bill as well as the small-district electoral bill which it had long desired. The 1919–1920 session of the Diet, however, was abruptly dissolved, not over the issue of tax increases, as the ministry had expected, but, rather, because the Kenseikai and Kokuminto joined together in proposing immediate universal manhood suffrage. The first dissolution of a "popular" party cabinet thus came because the ministry objected to universal suffrage! [41]

The Seiyukai won a spectacular victory in the election of May 10, 1920, amid many charges of corruption and official interference.[42] The next two Diets were handled with typical steam-roller tactics. The ministry was intimidated on occasion by frowns from the Peers and from other sectors of officialdom, but it treated the House with a callous disregard of opponents' questions and freedom of debate. The Kenseikai brought charges of unprecedented graft and corruption against the major party, and the Seiyukai answered in kind.[43] When Hara was gone, he had left behind him no real improvement in the Japanese ministry's attitude toward the lower house, and a definite deterioration of conduct and procedure in the House. Even the Diet members of his own party were ignored in policy making and then were required to hold fast to cabinet decisions.[44] These were signs that past institutional prac-

---

[41] The Seiyukai held a greater number of seats than any other party (165), as a result of Terauchi's support in the 1917 election, but did not control a majority of the Diet (total, 379 seats at this time).

[42] The new Diet numbered 464 members, owing to the electoral changes. Of this total, the Seiyukai captured 281 seats, a clear majority, the Kenseikai got 108 seats, and the Kokuminto only 29; the remaining members were classified as independent. Figures from Hayashida, *op. cit.*, Vol. II, p. 274.

[43] For some details, see chapter vii of the present study.

[44] Party members, especially those of the younger group, were very bitter about the officious way in which the cabinet treated them. On one occasion, when four younger Seiyukai Diet members called on Takahashi, Finance Minister, to inquire about increased taxation, they were told that this was "the exclusive concern of the government." In consequence of this type of treatment, the party adopted a resolution in November, 1919, that closer relations between the government and the party for policy execution must be established. For translated text, see *JC*, Novmber 13, 1919, p. 740.

tices and the theories which supported them were not to be changed easily in the era of so-called "party government."

Thus, with Hara's death, the Seiyukai—and one might say the party movement in general—inherited a situation in which it was quite possible for the parties to be forced back into their old subordinate position. Public opinion, the one instrument that might have been decisive, they had done little to cultivate or solicit. Indeed, both in omissions and commissions, the major parties had disappointed the intellectuals and other enlightened persons who had held such high hopes for the new era.

It is true that the Seiyukai had grown powerful and arrogant under Hara, but this was not the result of any major institutional change. On the contrary, it was due in part, at least, to the consummate skill with which the ministry had avoided such changes. The Genro were growing progressively weaker in over-all power, but still controlled completely the nomination of premiers. The Peers and Privy Council had softened under Hara's magic touch, but this attitude could well be ephemeral, and every sign toward the end of the Hara regime seemed to indicate that it was. With the important exception of the prefectural governorships, the subordinate bureaucracy had barely been scratched. The military were somewhat subdued by failure, scandal, dissension in the ranks, and the aura of world peace, but the administration itself had certainly not damaged them by any reduction of their institutional powers. The Seiyukai leadership had shown, on the whole, that it possessed neither the strength nor the will to advance the cause of representative government.

Some of the rewards of this failure were reaped by Hara's successor, Takahashi.[45] Even his succession to office was by no means assured. If the ailing Yamagata and Matsukata had had their way Hara would have been followed by Saionji, but when Saionji refused, Takahashi was accepted and simultaneously became president of the Seiyukai. But whereas Hara had been able to hold together a party which had few fundamental political principles, Takahashi lacked that capacity. The new premier was known as a financial wizard, a friend of the industrial-commercial circles, an antimilitarist, and a mediocre politician. The two characteristics last mentioned were certainly no assets to a Japanese premier.

Almost immediately, the new cabinet was placed under attack from two quarters, the opposition parties and the Peers. In the

---

[45] For one account of the Takahashi ministry, see Imamura, *op. cit.*, pp. 103–109.

Forty-fifth Diet, which opened in December, 1921, the Kenseikai and the Kokuminto skillfully used their universal manhood suffrage bill as an instrument to arouse public opinion against the Seiyukai cabinet. The small but hardy Kokuminto went further to demand that Takahashi effectuate earlier views he had expressed about militarism and establish civilian appointments to the service portfolios.[46] If any indication of party reluctance to tackle this problem were needed, Takahashi's answer that as Premier he preferred not to express an opinion gave striking evidence.[47]

The Peers, who had been growing restive under the long Seiyukai reign, raised innumerable trivial obstacles and bitterly opposed the government's railroad construction bill and jury service bill. In the end, the Kenkyukai supported the cabinet in all except the jury bill, but they made it clear that the cabinet contained certain persons who were *persona non grata*. When Takahashi tried to "purify" his cabinet in response to such pressure, however, he found that men who were tied to a party because of its power were not easily purged. Neither Nakahashi Tokugoro, Minister of Education, nor Motoda Hajime, Minister of Railways, would accede to Takahashi's request that they resign. Both were Seiyukai leaders who controlled strong factions of the party, and political factionalism, which had its roots in the distant past, was now abetted by the mixed bureaucratic and "pure party" nature of the parties and by weak leadership. As a leader, Takahashi differed markedly from his predecessor, for he lacked Hara's firmness, dominating personality, and political astuteness. From the beginning, he had been disliked by the rising generation within the party, which favored having a younger leader. Moreover, he was not popular with the promilitarist element within the party, which now constituted a sizable group.

The purge attempt was temporarily dropped, only to be taken up

[46] One of Takahashi's greatest embarrassments was his having distributed a pamphlet, in 1920, which urged the abolition of the General Staff. When questioned about this in the Diet, the Premier confusedly stated it was written in his private capacity and that his views might have undergone some change. See transcript of Budget Committee Meeting, House of Representatives, January 28, 1922, as reported in *JC*, February 9, 1922, p. 197.

[47] The Kokuminto submitted a representation in February, 1922, to the effect that a change should be made in the rule requiring war and navy ministerial appointments from service ranks only. Questioned on January 31 in the Peers, however, Takahashi had already declared that he preferred not to express any opinion on the matter, thus giving clear indication that no action was contemplated. See *JC*, February 16, 1922, pp. 232–233.

again at the insistence of one section of the party. Finally, unable to solve the problem, Takahashi submitted the cabinet's resignation on June 11, 1922, although the Seiyukai still held 280 seats in the lower house. Nearly five years of Seiyukai rule had been brought to an end by a combination of external pressure and internal conflict.

The three short-term ministries which followed the Takahashi cabinet were excellent illustrations of party weaknesses and of the fact that the party drive to control Japanese political institutions lacked real force. Indeed, some Japanese authorities on political history feel that the true "era of party cabinets" was the period between the formation of the Kato Takaakira cabinet of June, 1924, and the fall of the Inukai cabinet on May 25, 1932, for the three cabinets which followed Takahashi were all of a "nonparty" variety.

The immediate reasons for this shift away from "party government" lay not so much in the power of the Genro or of the antiparty bureaucracy as in party policy. The parties were by no means united, in practice, around the goal of automatic party cabinets. Indeed, the Seiyukai agreed to, and even aided in, the establishment of the next ministry, that of Admiral Kato Tomosaburo. One analysis of the reasons was advanced by *Yomiuri*, a leading newspaper:

"What the *Seiyukai* wants is not the establishment of party government, but the perpetuation of the *Seiyukai* government. For this purpose it is more expedient for it to leave power in the hands of the *Genro* and thereby facilitate the alternate transfer of government between the *Seiyukai* and the bureaucrats rather than to wrest power entirely from the *Genro*." [48]

This stand was most logical, in view of the fact that the Seiyukai by this time lacked any strong democratic principles. Finding itself ineligible because of party and cabinet disunity and fearing that a Kenseikai cabinet would perpetuate itself in office by controlling elections, it backed Admiral Kato, Minister of the Navy in the Takahashi cabinet. The two remaining Genro, Matsukata and Saionji,[49] were besieged with advice and entreaties from Kenseikai

---

[48] From *Yomiuri,* quoted in *JC*, June 22, 1922, p. 894.

[49] Two of the most important figures of Meiji and Taisho Japan, Okuma and Yamagata, died within a month of each other, in January and February, 1922.

Yamagata's death removed the most powerful figure in Japan and a man who had never reconciled himself to the parties or party government. Although he himself felt in his closing years that his work had been in vain, he had helped to shape the major parties better than he knew.

adherents.[50] Admiral Kato, however, had not only the support of the major party in the lower house, but also that of the *Kenkyukai* (Study Association) in the Peers as well, and he was therefore the only logical choice.[51] The personnel of his cabinet was a clear indication of this coalition, for the portfolios were assigned almost entirely to two factions of the Peers, the Kenkyukai and the *Koyu Club* (Fraternal Club), a pro-Seiyukai group, many of whom were actually Seiyukai members.

Inukai, who was still president of the Kokuminto, presented his interpretation of these events in an interview on June 15, 1922, when he bitterly denounced both major parties.[52] The Kenseikai, he alleged, was no better than the Seiyukai, for it had dropped its antimilitarism when the Takahashi cabinet fell and was fawning on Matsukata and the militarists, "willing to eat words for power." [53] Neither of the two parties, he stated, was a true party; they were only rival combinations of bureaucrats seeking power.[54] Only the Kokuminto, he asserted, had abided by its platform and preserved its honesty.

A short time later, on September 1, 1922, the Kokuminto dissolved to form a new group, the *Kakushin Club* (Reform Club), and part of the dissolution declaration read: "Political parties make the struggle for power their only aim, and their original object is submerged. Of course, it is partly due to the motive and history of the development of our political parties, but still the fact that they are behind the spirit of the age is their conspicuous defect." [55] In harmony with this statement, the Kakushin Club announced that one of its objectives would be the overthrow of existing parties. Uehara Etsujiro, one of the group's spokesmen, stated: "The or-

---

[50] The press vehemently supported the Kenseikai and denounced the Satsuma-Seiyukai-Kenkyukai alliance.

[51] The Peers constituted a very important block against the Kenseikai, because the rank-and-file members of the party had greatly antagonized the upper house, and particularly the Kenkyukai, through their attacks on the floor of the Diet. See Royama, *op. cit.*, p. 451.

[52] Press interview with Inukai, June 15, 1922, quoted in *JC*, June 24, 1922, p. 938.

[53] *Ibid.*

[54] Inukai went on to say that Ito had made the Seiyukai in a night and Katsura had made the Doshikai in another night. Only Noda of the Seiyukai was a true party man; the others were ambitious bureaucrats. *Ibid.*

[55] Kokuminto Dissolution Resolution, September 1, 1922, as reported in *JC*, September 7, 1922, p. 327. See excerpts from Inukai's speech in Uzaki Kumakichi, *Inukai Tsuyoshi den* (*Biography of Inukai Tsuyoshi*), Tokyo, 1932, pp. 335–336.

ganization must be based on the life of the nation. With a view to realizing such a new political party, we are fighting against existing political parties, which might be called joint-stock companies for the acquisition of power and benefits." [56] No stronger denunciation of the party movement as it then existed could have come from the most violent antiparty sources. The fact that it had come from the more progressive elements of the old parties was doubly significant. In view of the contemporary political situation, however, the Kakushin Club faced grave obstacles in effecting its program, which was amazingly democratic.[57] In the first place, the new party had only forty-five Diet members and was equally weak in financial support. Moreover, its program would automatically alienate the nonparty elements in the government. Yet this small group was now the only coherent faction, aside from a part of the left, that represented certain basic democratic principles.

In the meantime, however, the two major parties struggled with each other and with their other rivals, paying scant regard to popular trends except when these could be used as an impetus toward party power. The Kato Tomosaburo cabinet, always weak, was finally dispatched by the death of the Premier in July, 1923. Saionji, who was now the only active Genro, chose Yamamoto Gombei, taking the political world by surprise.[58] Yamamoto had been thought to have been permanently retired from active politics as a result of the navy scandal in his first ministry. Press, public, and party reaction was generally unfavorable.

Saionji, however, had one very cogent reason for desiring another "transcendental" cabinet, and a reason which did not speak well for the status of the major parties. He seems to have desired quite sincerely to make sure that the next election would be conducted as fairly as possible.[59] Moreover, neither major party was in a good position to demand the premiership. The Seiyukai was still

---

[56] Uzaki, op. cit., p. 327. For details of the organization, see Hayashida, op. cit., Vol. II, pp. 286–290.

[57] For all the Kakushin Club documents, see Hayashida, op. cit., Vol. II, pp. 286–289. The party platform included demands that civilians be allowed to hold the war and navy posts in the cabinet and that prefectural governors be elected.

[58] Matsukata was now ill. It should be pointed out that although the Genro continued to be final authorities on the selection of a premier, beginning with Kato's appointment, the Inner Court officials started to take an active part in the negotiations.

[59] See Ando Tokuki, Saionji Kimmochi, Tokyo, 1938, p. 164.

plagued with internal friction, and the Kenseikai lacked influence both in the Diet and in the bureaucracy.

Nevertheless, the second Yamamoto cabinet, together with its successor, the Kiyoura cabinet, demonstrated beyond question that the parties, with all their weaknesses, now possessed a political power that could not be ignored. Yamamoto stayed in office only four months, harassed by a lack of party support, the chaos of the Tokyo earthquake, and cabinet disunity. Only one development significant to the party movement took place during his tenure, and that was Inukai's agreement to join the cabinet. Yamamoto had tried to form a "whole nation united" ministry by inviting the three party presidents, Takahashi, Baron Kato, and Inukai, to accept portfolios. The former two, in accordance with the demands of political strategy, refused, but Inukai astonished everyone by accepting the post of Minister of Education. In the light of his past denunciations of nonparty cabinets and his censure of party affiliation with the bureaucracy, this move seemed to be an anomaly. To be sure, his defense was ardent.[60] He stated that the Kakushin Club had denounced existing parties and that there was nothing to prevent him, as a member of a nonparty ministry, from seeking their overthrow. Nor was he giving up any of his principles, he asserted. By entering the cabinet, he hoped to effectuate his dream, universal manhood suffrage. But despite these rationalizations, Inukai had fallen under his own definition of iniquity, and in doing so had again demonstrated the corrupting influence of Japanese institutions on the democratic movement.

When Yamamoto resigned and Saionji turned to Kiyoura, an ancient bureaucrat, party anger rose to new heights. Kiyoura was forced to rely almost entirely upon the Peers in cabinet formation, and it soon became evident that a dissolution of the Diet could not be avoided. However, there were some party spokesmen, especially within the Seiyukai, who were prepared both by sentiment and political considerations to support any bureaucratic cabinet which might share power with them. The factional feud within the Seiyukai had never been healed, and this marked a formal break, for the elements favoring compromise left the party.

---

[60] Various analysts have pointed out that Inukai had many friends among the Satsuma-navy group, in opposition to the Choshu-army elements. Undoubtedly, rivalries derivative from the early Meiji period were involved. See Watanabe Ikujiro, "Inukai to Okuma" (Inukai and Okuma), in *Chuo Koron*, October, 1932. For Inukai's explanations, see press reports as recorded in *JC*, September 13, 1923, p. 364.

The powerful Seiyukai then split into two almost equal groups. The newly organized group, which called itself the *Seiyuhonto* (True Seiyu Party) and included such leaders as Tokonami, Naka-hashi, Motoda, and Yamamoto Tatsuo, numbered in all 149 Diet members, leaving the old Seiyukai with only 129 Diet members.[61]

Despite the defection of the Seiyuhonto to the Kiyoura cabinet, the lower house was still in the hands of antigovernment forces. The two major opposition parties, together with the Kakushin Club, now sought to end the succession of "transcendental" minis-tries by forming an "antibureaucratic alliance" and organizing a second "safeguard the Constitution" movement. Three party lead-ers, Kato, Takahashi, and Inukai, issued a joint declaration stating, "We pledge the establishment of a political party cabinet system in accordance with the basic principles of constitutional govern-ment." [62] The result of this union was a notable victory for the party coalition and an impressive demonstration of the power a party could wield when united with other parties and backed by public sentiment. Kiyoura was forced to dissolve the Forty-eighth Diet, and, despite government assistance to the Seiyuhonto, the "Con-stitution protectors" won a joint victory in the elections of May 10, 1924.[63] Faced with a hopeless situation, the ministry resigned exactly one month later.

In many respects, political conditions now seemed ripe for the institution of automatic party cabinets as a permanent factor in Japanese government. Some of the conditions which had favored this in 1918 were much stronger in 1924. The political prestige of the nonparty groups was at its lowest ebb. Three successive failures seemed to indicate that the oligarchic bureaucracy could no longer control the state. Perhaps most important of all, there was now only one Genro left,[64] Saionji, and he was admirably suited by tem-perament and inclination to relinquish his weighty powers. He had none of the aggressive hatred of parties or love of clanism that

---

[61] Figures from Hayashida, *op. cit.*, Vol. II, p. 302; see pp. 299–302 for party documents.

[62] Ito Masanori, *op. cit.*, Vol. II, p. 460. For this whole development see the section entitled "Goken Undo" (The Protect the Constitution Movement), in *ibid.*, pp. 458–462.

[63] Election figures gave the Kenseikai 153 seats, the Seiyukai 101, the Kakushin Club 30—a total of 284 seats to the coalition, with Kenseikai gains making up for the losses which both the Seiyukai and Kakushin Club suffered. The Seiyuhonto lost some strength, receiving 114 seats, while the various independent groups held 66. Figures from *ibid.*, p. 469.

[64] Matsukata died in March, 1924.

had characterized Yamagata and Matsukata. Indeed, Saionji fell in with what seemed to be the spirit of the times to such an extent that he was soon to suggest the abandonment of the Genro system in favor of Western-style procedures at the time of changes of ministry.

With the "fathers of the Constitution"—who had so zealously guarded their document—out of the scene, and with the high tide of public sentiment running against the old bureaucracy, the party position seemed assured to many. From the standpoint of party supremacy, however, there were more than enough weaknesses in the fabric of Japanese political institutions and society to off-set these advantages. The Genro had been an extralegal, even though supremely important, part of the Japanese governmental structure. The groups within legalized institutions in the administrative framework who opposed the ideas of political parties and representative supremacy remained, with their prestige lowered but their real powers almost as great as before.

It was, therefore, a dramatic period in Japanese politics when the Kato coalition cabinet came into power on June 11, 1924. The new ministry was composed of representatives of the three parties which had fought side by side against the Kiyoura administration. The new premier was Kato Takaakira, president of the Kenseikai and, with the exception of Hara, the most important party figure during the postwar era. Also, of all political leaders, Kato was the one who had been, in many respects, the most faithful to the cause of democratic institutions in prewar Japan. As a great admirer of English institutions he had long championed the concepts of "pure party" cabinets, subordination of bureaucratic forces, and the importance of political opposition and debate. Perhaps more than any other leader, Kato had repeatedly challenged the Genro and other elements of the bureaucracy, asserting these principles and generally acting in accordance with them in the midst of great temptations. In contrast to Hara, Kato was an aristocrat in personality as well as in wealth. He exhibited few signs of subserviency or of an inferiority complex before the Sat-Cho titans. He combined the trait of stubbornness with the qualities of a dignified, somewhat reserved personality in such a manner as to win strong respect but also many enemies.

Perhaps Kato exemplified the "enlightened conservative" of Japan at his greatest strength in terms of service to the democratic cause. Certainly there were few others of his own group who could reach his degree of understanding and acceptance of democratic principles. Yet in some respects, as we shall note, the Kato ministry was a great disappointment to those who had hoped for a new dawn in Japanese politics. Once again, weaknesses of leadership and program quickly made themselves manifest. To begin with, Kato himself was no popular leader, and even within his own party there had been periodic grumbling over his personal characteristics and actions. In considerable part, this criticism was incurred by his lack of opportunism, but it was also a dubious tribute to his lack of warmth and informality. In personality, Kato retained much of the old-type Japanese official about him, a natural reflection of the background from which he had come. Of at least equal importance, however, was the fact that the policies of the Kato cabinet did not measure up to the causes which Kato and his colleagues sought to represent, or at least purported to represent. Not only did his ministers pay scant attention to the vital economic and social problems that were affecting the public mind and were crying out for solution; these men proved very inadequate to the task of reforming national institutions, a task which the new ministry had pledged itself to perform. The psychological and legal obstacles posed in front of basic reform had grown ever more formidable.

It is true that the Kato coalition government represented a high point of attack upon the antirepresentative forces. The universal manhood suffrage bill was finally enacted into law, receiving the grudging assent of the Peers. Also, substantial economies were effected, over the opposition of major parts of the bureaucracy. Fairly sharp reductions were made in the army and navy budgets, despite bitter protests from the military.[65] The personnel of the bureaucracy was reduced by some twenty thousand.[66]

But in the matter of Peerage reform the ministry failed miserably, and this was the critical test. The Peers, as we have often noted, stood as one of the greatest obstacles to party supremacy,

---

[65] Professor Imanaka uses the following chart to indicate the percentage of the total national budget, including special funds, which was allocated to the military:

1877: 19%	1913: 33%	1922: 42%
1887: 28%	1919: 46%	1923: 33%
1897: 49%	1920: 48%	1925: 29%
1907: 33%	1921: 49%	1927: 28%

Imanaka Tsugimaro, *Nihon seiji shi shinko* (*New Materials on Japanese Political History*), Tokyo, 1948, Vol. II, p. 441.

[66] Royama, *op. cit.*, p. 440. See also Ito Masanori, *op. cit.*, Vol. II, pp. 493–494.

and time and again they had successfully blocked legislation passed by the lower house. Their part in the Kiyoura ministry had been so prominent that the coalition parties had made reform of the House of Peers an immediate issue. The press and the informed public had never backed any party proposal with so many open signs of approval.[67] Any real reform of the Peers, however, depended upon amending the Constitution. Would the cabinet tackle this thorny and unprecedented problem? Kato gave his first answer in his maiden speech before the Diet on July 1, 1925. "Concerning the improvement [*kaizen*] of the House of Peers," he said, "there are already discussions on the outside and proposals from within the House on this. The government pledges that it will meet this central problem properly, adjusting to the intentions of constitutional enactments, taking into consideration the demands of the times, and proceeding with weighty deliberations." [68]

In spite of the rather vague wording, Kato's remarks carried the clear implication that the Constitution would be left untouched. There had already been great pressure upon him from various elements of the bureaucracy, some of his fellow Peers included, voicing confidence that a *modus vivendi* might be worked out and that a major battle might thereby be avoided.[69] Kato was also faced with the necessity of obtaining the adoption of major legislation, including a special appropriation bill, and almost immediately he fell into the contradictory position of both wooing and attacking the upper house. The Diet stayed in special session only a short time, and although the reform threat may have aided the government in keeping the Peers under temporary control, such legislation remained no more than a threat.[70]

The issue carried over into the regular session, and many public organs began to attack Kato and the ministry for failure to effect some major change. But Kato seemed even less inclined than before to act vigorously.[71] The leaders of both the Seiyukai and the Koku-

---

[67] The Japanese press poured out an unending stream of criticism against the actions of the Peers, and an organization known as the *Kizokuin Kaikaku Kisei Kai* (Association Pledged to Peerage Reform) was formed by rank-and-file Diet members and journalists.

[68] Ito Masanori, *op. cit.*, Vol. II, p. 498.

[69] See *ibid.*, pp. 490 ff., for a lengthy discussion of various phases of the question of the Peers.

[70] In the closing session, the House of Representatives passed a resolution to the effect that the government should carry out reform of the House of Peers "within the limits allowed by the Constitution."

[71] See, for instance, Kato's very equivocal speech before the Peers on

minto seemed prepared to go much further; and many within the Kenseikai, Kato's own party, complained about his timidity. Ultimately a bill was passed, and it was accepted by the Peers without much outcry, for it did not make a single change of major importance.[72] Kato's success in this matter did aid him in passing the measures mentioned earlier, and even won for him the vigorous support of a certain segment of the House of Peers. It did not advance the cause of representative government, however; another crusade had gone awry.

The Kato cabinet was even less inclined to attempt any reduction in the powers of the inner bureaucracy or of the military elements. When Ozaki questioned the ministry on these matters, he received a written reply dated March 22, 1925, and signed by the Premier and the ministers of war, the navy, and justice. The gist of the reply was that no interference with the officials of the Imperial Court could be contemplated, and that the question of the service portfolios was one which "calls for thorough study." [73]

There was, however, a second event of equal importance in laying bare the real nature of the contemporary major parties. The Seiyukai, despite its participation in the coalition ministry, was longing for a restoration of its complete supremacy and was looking for a new leader who had the finances, aggressiveness, and influence to reëstablish this condition. When such a man could not be found within the party, it turned to none other than General Tanaka Giichi.[74]

Takahashi had had many weaknesses as the president of a "popular" party, but he had at least been a symbol of civilian supremacy over the military, he had supported political honesty and administrative efficiency, and in the end he had resigned his peerage so that he might become a "commoner" representative in the House. Tanaka, on the other hand, had practically no qualifications as a democrat or as a leader of a truly popular party. The General, to be sure, had worked closely with the Seiyukai under Hara's regime, and had won the undying enmity of many of his fellow army men

---

March 10, 1925, in *ibid.*, p. 570. Kato had argued earlier that if a strong reform bill were put up, universal manhood suffrage would be stopped by the Peers, but Kato never favored "reform"—only "improvement"—and the distinction was significant.

[72] For a brief enumeration of the changes see Royama, *op. cit.*, pp. 445–446.

[73] For translation of the cabinet's reply, see *JC*, April 9, 1925, p. 468.

[74] See Baba Tsunego's very revealing article, "Tanaka Giichi," in *Chuo Koron*, August, 1928, pp. 43–58.

for this collaboration. Indeed, in his speech of resignation, Takahashi defended the General stoutly against charges of militarism
and of having antiparliamentary views.[75] Actually, Tanaka represented a fairly orthodox product of Japanese military training
who had been somewhat "corrupted" by his political associations
and ambitions. He was not in sympathy with the military extremists, especially those of the branch that threatened an internal revolution. Yet the "positive" foreign policy and the economic nationalism which he had helped to establish, and was soon to amplify,
played directly into their hands. It gave them new opportunities
for initiating action both at home and abroad from which the cabinet could not effectively retreat. It greatly increased the potency
of their pressure upon government and people. And the Seiyukai
could accept Tanaka because a fairly large number of those within
the party held policy views that were identical to his. In addition,
of course, Tanaka's assets to the party were by no means negligible:
he had access to financial resources, and he had prestige with many
of the bureaucratic elements whose support was crucial to party
success.[76]

The shift in Seiyukai leadership, along with certain other developments, contributed to the eventual breakdown of the coalition
ministry. Tanaka refused to take a place in the Kato cabinet,
though he promised to supply a Seiyukai man. It was clear, however, that the Seiyukai intended to support Kato only until it could
reorganize and strengthen its forces. It had been hoped that the
shift in the party presidency might induce the Seiyuhonto to return
to the fold, by giving the party a right to demand a new ministry.
This expectation was premature, but a more startling event occurred: Inukai Tsuyushi decided to dissolve the Kakushin Club
and join the Seiyukai. Inukai, who had long symbolized the fight
against the corruption and intrigue within the major parties,
seemed almost to repudiate his past life by this action. His justifi-
cations were most interesting. Perhaps the most revelatory one
was that he could not leave his faithful followers as a minor fragment divorced from hope of power, and that this was his method

---

[75] The following is a section of Takahashi's resignation speech of April 4,
1925, as reported in *JC*, April 16, 1925, p. 492: "Although General Tanaka
is a soldier, he is very much of a statesman. He is called a militarist, but as
a matter of fact, he abhors militarism. He is a perfect constitutional statesman.
I served in the Hara cabinet with him, and as his colleague, I am fully acquainted with his political views and acumen."

[76] Okazaki, party adviser, said with reference to this, that there were only
two or three men who could be premier, and that Tanaka was one of these.

232

of repaying their loyalty to him.[77] Thus, the last organized element among the old parties to hold out for basic reforms fell by the wayside, and there were only isolated individuals left. Inukai was himself to get full repayment for this act, beginning with his presidency of the Seiyukai, continuing with his premiership, and ending with his assassination.

The coalition cabinet, under these circumstances, was doomed, and the Seiyukai participants resigned in July, 1925, enabling Kato to establish an all-Kenseikai ministry. The omnipresent problem of bureaucratic support, however, now became even more important in the presence of a hostile party with formidable strength. The Kenseikai therefore abandoned still further its previous hostility to the Peers and formed an open alliance with the Kenkyukai. The press and public criticism which followed could not negate the fact that this was a political necessity if the cabinet were to survive. Another alliance was effected, this one with the most pro-bureaucratic party, Tokonami's Seiyuhonto. Once again the major political forces in Japan were almost indistinguishable.

Even as these events were taking place, Japan was half unconsciously moving into a period of conflict and confusion among the political elements unequaled in her modern history, a period of chaos that reached its first climax in the years 1931 and 1932. The backdrop for these events was larger than the Japanese political scene, for it included the whole panorama of world trends. What should interest us at this point, however, is the adequacy with which "party government," as it existed during this period, could control or regulate domestic trends, and the strength which the party movement was able to gather to meet successive crises. In seeking the answers to these questions we will have explored the culmination and true significance of the evolutionary developments through which the parties passed in their struggle for power under the Meiji Constitution.

---

[77] Inukai's position has been well explored in the biography written by Uzaki Kumakichi (*op. cit.*, pp. 369–378). Among the reasons which Inukai gave to his supporters and the public, the following are of interest: (1) His previous attacks on the Seiyukai had been against the leaders, not the members, many of whom were first-rate men. Moreover, the Seiyukai "positive" policy was one in which he had always believed. (2) The Kakushin Club had no financial support and no hopes of political success. The hope for an expanded party after the dissolution of the Kokuminto had failed, and this amalgamation was a natural development. (3) International conditions and the threat of "leftism" placed a premium upon unity and coalition to support the Emperor and the structure of the Japanese state.

At no time before had the institutional framework of Japan seemed so inadequate. The conflicting agencies of authority were like wild horses, each tied to the body politic, heading in different directions and threatening to tear it apart. Both major parties found themselves attacked first by one and then by another of such rivals as the Peers, the Privy Council, and the militarists, but the problem of fighting back was complicated. The institutional devices were still weighted heavily against the parties, and now the parties lacked any semblance of inner cohesion. With their ranks full of professional officials, militarists, and opportunists, they were split more basically than ever before in struggles over either principles or power. And the result of their serious handicaps and their jockeying for power was a minimal amount of public support.

The growing political tension became very evident during the regime of the Wakatsuki cabinet. Kato died on January 28, 1926, and his place as Premier and Kenseikai president was taken by Wakatsuki Reijiro, an old follower of Kato's and a politician who, in the main, had been shaped in Kato's image. Wakatsuki had first entered the party movement from official life at the time of the formation of Katsura's *Rikken Doshikai* (Constitutional Fellow Thinkers' Association).

The new premier continued his party's alliances with the Kenkyukai and the Seiyuhonto.[78] In spite of these concessions to successful control, however, the Wakatsuki ministry was unable to cope with certain important parts of the bureaucracy. The military were increasingly antagonistic to Foreign Minister Shidehara's conciliatory policy toward China. It was the Privy Council, however, which finally toppled the Wakatsuki government. It took advantage of the cabinet's weakening position and declared unconstitutional a proposed emergency ordinance, desired by the government, that would have granted funds in the bank crisis of 1927.[79] Rather than challenge the Privy Council, Wakatsuki and his cabinet resigned.

---

[78] Wakatsuki points out in his memoirs the absolute necessity of continuing these alliances and comments upon the close relations established between Tokonami, president of the Seiyuhonto, and himself, foreshadowing the later establishment of the Minseito. See Wakatsuki, *op. cit.*, pp. 309 ff.

[79] For an interesting account, see *ibid.*, pp. 323–329. The Wakatsuki ministry was already under heavy attack from various quarters when the banking crisis broke. The Minister of Finance helped set off the panic by some ill-advised remarks in the Diet, and Mitsui subsequently aided it by suddenly withdrawing a large sum of money from the Bank of Taiwan. For other de-

It was now the turn of the Seiyukai to meet successive crises. Tanaka and his party reaped the fruit of their union and of the failure of the Kenseikai by coming into power on April 19, 1927. Their first and potentially easiest problem was to deal with the House of Representatives. Tanaka had been given the premiership even though the Seiyukai was a minority party. Soon after he took office, moreover, the Kenseikai and Seiyuhonto amalgamated to form a new party, the *Rikken Minseito* (Constitutional Democratic Party), which held a clear majority of seats. Tanaka moved quickly to dissolve the House of Representatives and the first election to be held under the Universal Manhood Suffrage Law took place on February 20, 1928. The government exerted substantial pressure; still, the results were extremely close. The Seiyukai garnered 219 seats, whereas the Minseito collected 217; the remainder (the House of Representatives now totaled 466) was divided among independents and the newly emerged labor parties.[80] The new session of the Diet was a bedlam. There were strong indications that the government was attempting to buy votes in a variety of ways in order to bolster its slim plurality. Nevertheless, an impeachment resolution was passed, charging Suzuki Kisaburo, Home Minister and later Seiyukai president, with interference in the election. A Minseito motion of nonconfidence was narrowly defeated, and the session ended in chaos.

As usual, the Peers and Privy Council began to put in their thrusts with increasing effectiveness, especially in the Fifty-sixth Diet, which met between December, 1928, and March, 1929. No issue was more fantastic than the attack upon the ministry for signing the Kellogg antiwar pact, because it contained the words "in the names of their respective peoples." The opposition castigated this act as derogatory to Imperial sovereignty and demanded the resignation of the cabinet. The Privy Council did its best to block passage of the treaty, and finally the government was forced to state formally that this section did not apply to Japan, "in view of the provisions of the Japanese Constitution." [81] During this session, the Peers killed seven important administration bills.

---

tails, see chapter vii of the present study. The Privy Council, with the majority bitterly hostile to the Wakatsuki government, vetoed the emergency ordinance which would have established a fund of ¥200,000,000 for bank relief purposes.

[80] Figures from Royama, *op. cit.*, p. 458.

[81] For the English text of the government note, see *JC*, June 27, 1929, p. 729. That even the Minseito would throw its strength into an attack of this type reveals the depth to which the "democratic" parties had sunk.

Ironically, however, it was really the military that brought the Tanaka government down. Tanaka had overturned the Shidehara policy, which was generally conciliatory toward China, and had revived the "expansion" policy which had been followed in the Hara era. The plan was still to use Chang Tso-lin and other Manchurian authorities in order to develop Japanese interests in northeast Asia to the utmost.[82] The Tanaka policy paralleled Hara's even to the extent of pushing joint conferences with military and civilian leaders in order to develop a unified program.[83] However, Tanaka was burned by his own fires. In the first place, Chinese resentment against the Japanese mounted as the "strong" policy was applied, and this led to boycotts, incidents, and a new low for Japanese prestige on the continent. Moreover, Chang Tso-lin was defeated in his efforts to expand southward, and had to be advised by Tanaka to concern himself solely with Manchurian affairs.[84] Chang had always seemed somewhat undependable as an ally, and never more so than now. Then came the really dramatic development. Chang Tso-lin was murdered by a group of conspirators within the Kwantung Army who were dissatisfied with the Tanaka policy and anxious to move into Manchuria quickly.[85] Immediately Tanaka, with the support of the cabinet, including the service ministers, went to the War Office in an effort to get punishment for the responsible parties and "reëstablish control over the army." But the government got nowhere. Powerful generals at military headquarters, including Sugiyama Hajime, Chief of the Military Affairs Bureau, and Kanaya Hanzo, Chief of the General Staff, insisted that the army would take care of its own problems and discipline. The plotters remained unpunished, and the Tanaka cabinet re-

[82] For this whole episode, see the Affidavit of Okada Keisuke, Navy Minister in the Tanaka cabinet, Document No. 1749, Exhibit No. 175; Document No. 11525, Exhibit No. 176, in the manuscript document collections of the International Military Tribunal for the Far East, "Proceedings" and "Exhibits" (hereinafter cited in the notes as IMTFE).

[83] It was during this period that the widely known "Tanaka Memorial" made its appearance. This "Memorial" was a forgery, although the "program" outlined therein did reflect the ambitions of some of the Japanese expansionists.

[84] See the Okada Affidavit in IMTFE, cited in note 82.

[85] See documents cited, in IMTFE. Okada stated at the war trials: "This incident, plotted and instituted by the clique in the Kwantung Army, represented the first overt army move during the Tanaka regime to project itself into the formulation of the policies of the government. The occurrence greatly embarrassed and prejudiced the program of the Tanaka cabinet with respect to Manchuria and created a crisis which ultimately resulted in its resignation."

signed.[86] It did not dare challenge certain top army leaders who, in turn, were often being driven, led, and pulled by subordinate groups. The independent power of the military was now a real threat to civilian government, and all the more so because the personnel and expansionist policies of governments like that of Tanaka made it inconceivable to conduct any frontal assault.

The Minseito, under its new president, Hamaguchi Yuko, now stepped into office, recommended by a worried Saionji, the last remaining Genro. A largely Minseito cabinet was established on July 2, 1929, with Hamaguchi as Premier and Shidehara (non-party) returning to be Minister of Foreign Affairs. In its two and one-half years of office, this cabinet was to be confronted with a series of challenges from every rival branch of the heterogeneous administrative structure. The weakness of popular support, the confusion of basic principles, and the unwillingness of the major parties to seek administrative and constitutional reforms when these might have been possible, were now plaguing the parties with telling effect.

The ministry cleared the decks for action by dissolving the Seiyu-kai majority Diet and winning the election of 1930 on a campaign of economy, disarmament, purification of politics, reform of the China policy, and removal of the gold embargo.[87] When it came to effectuating this program, however, the government met with the greatest obstacles. The subordinate bureaucracy was the first to reveal its hostility and its power. When the cabinet decided to cut by 10 per cent the salaries of all government employees earning over ¥100 a month (including military and naval officers), opposition naturally was vigorous. Railroad employees, many department officials, and even judges threatened mass resignations.[88]

---

[86] Okada testified that during a conference which Tanaka had with the Emperor, the latter stated that the time had come "to take strong disciplinary action with respect to the army." When this proved impossible, Tanaka had to resign. See documents cited, in IMTFE.

[87] For an analysis of the election, see Royama, *op. cit.*, p. 465. The Minseito group, which was usually more scrupulous about elections than the Seiyukai, had made drastic changes in the prefectural governorships, but, on the whole, the election was fairly free from central governmental interference, although little different from past elections in terms of monetary expenditures, voter bribery, etc. See chapter viii of the present study.

[88] Professor Minobe, writing in the *Chuo Koron* for August, 1931, gave an excellent short analysis of the contemporary administrative bureaucracy in its relation to the political parties. Minobe pointed out that the "supremacy of party government" had had two seemingly contradictory effects on the subordinate bureaucracy. In the first place, part of their officialdom had been

Although the resentment may have had some justification in this particular issue, the significant thing was the demonstration of power.

The subordinate bureaucracy was not the only force to assert itself against the new government. Hamaguchi had not been in office a year before his cabinet was involved in a bitter struggle with the military and the Privy Council over the London Naval Reduction Treaty of 1930.[89] The Hamaguchi cabinet had sent Wakatsuki as its chief delegate to London, and it was under his sanction that the Japanese representatives agreed to the continuation of the famous 5:5:3 naval ratio among the United States,

---

drawn into the parties. This we have seen to be true of both the party leadership and the rank and file. The Minseito of 1930 was led by Hamaguchi, Wakatsuki, and Adachi Kenzo. The first two were ex-officials, and Adachi had constantly affiliated himself with that group. Under the aegis of these men and their famous predecessor, Kato (himself a former official), the party had accumulated many bureaucrats, especially those whose appointments depended upon political affiliations, such as the prefectural governors.

The Seiyukai was in the same position. Tanaka died in October, 1929, and the party presidency was filled by Inukai when the major factions within the party were unable to agree on a leader. However, the real leaders of the party were now Tokonami (who had returned to the fold), Suzuki (Kisaburo), Nakahashi, and Kuhara Fusanosuke. The first three were old-time officials, and Kuhara was a businessman with political ambitions and funds to match.

Minobe noted, however, a second effect of party government on the administrative bureaucracy, namely, the growth of the bureaucracy away from the government. This fact, of course, was obvious in the general hostility and contempt with which civil servants viewed party government. In the old days, the oligarchs had maintained a continuity in office and a personal and clan control which made their authority sure and ineradicable. They had bound their subordinates to them as servants to masters, inculcating in them a hatred of the parties. With the advent of the parties to power, instability had increased at the ministerial level, augmenting the real power of the lower echelons of the bureaucracy. Contempt for the parties, fostered by oligarchic tutelage, increased as party corruption and general inadequacies were revealed. In terms of an over-all percentage, the number of officials who entered the party movement was relatively small, even though these few had a tremendous effect on the parties themselves.

In short, with the disappearance of Sat-Cho domination and the new instability of political tenure, any administration was exceedingly handicapped in controlling the subordinate bureaucrats, whose permanence and antiparty predilections combined to make them effective opponents. Minobe Tatsukichi, "Seito seiji ni okeru kanryo" (The Bureaucracy in Party Politics), *Chuo Koron*, August, 1931, pp. 2–15.

[89] For one detailed discussion of the events surrounding the London Naval Reduction Treaty, see Wakatsuki, *op. cit.*, pp. 338–366.

England, and Japan. The moment the treaty was received in Japan, there was great indignation in service circles. The chief of staff of the navy and his subordinates strenuously opposed ratification, and in the negotiations between the cabinet and the Supreme Command, no compromise could be reached. The Premier bravely insisted on the right to determine national armed strength, rejecting navy proposals. Finally, on April 21, 1930, the government affixed its seal to the London Naval Reduction Treaty. Drastic changes were made in the naval staff, and the administration stood fast.

This conflict with the naval authorities had two immediate repercussions. First, the Privy Council took its turn in attacking the treaty. The treaty was submitted to that body for approval on July 24, the day after the administration had received new national defense plans from the Supreme War Council. The Privy Council immediately demanded to see a message which the cabinet had sent the Emperor concerning these plans, but the government refused, saying that such an action was beyond its powers.[90] The courage and forcefulness with which Hamaguchi handled the Privy Council resulted in an administration victory, for the Council approved the treaty, albeit with great reluctance.

But in its fight with the military [91] and Privy Council, the government was hindered both by the Seiyukai and by a growing number in the Peers. The Seiyukai saw in the disarmament issue an excellent opportunity to overthrow Minseito power. The fifty-eighth session of the Diet found Inukai Tsuyoshi, now president of the Seiyukai, attacking the government for its refusal to heed the advice of "military specialists" and actually questioning the cabinet's "patriotism." [92] Also, the Peers were threatening to block major government proposals, and the government was in a weak position to resist any of these attacks, because the cabinet's "negative" economic policy of administrative retrenchment, removal of the gold embargo, and restrictive loans, was lending itself to growing depression and unemployment.[93]

---

[90] Royama, *op. cit.*, p. 464.

[91] The Hamaguchi cabinet had increased its trouble with the militarists by appointing Abe Nobuyuki, Vice-Minister of War, to the post of Minister pro tem during the illness of War Minister Ugaki without the consent of the Supreme Command.

[92] One of Inukai's questions to Hamaguchi was, Why did you overlook the fact that 70 per cent was the figure established by the military specialists as the limit of conciliation to which Japan should go? Quoted in *ibid.*, p. 462.

[93] The economic aspects of this period will be discussed in the next chap-

In the midst of these troubled times, Premier Hamaguchi was shot and seriously wounded while standing in the Tokyo Railroad Station, and Foreign Minister Shidehara became Premier pro tem. Shidehara was not a party man and not at all popular with the Minseito rank and file, but he carried on until Hamaguchi's return, in March, 1931. Soon after the end of the Diet session, Hamaguchi resigned because of his health, and Wakatsuki replaced him both as Premier and as Minseito president. Wakatsuki retained Hamaguchi's cabinet in its entirety and retained as well the bitter opposition which that cabinet had aroused.

The new premier had been in office only a few months when the fateful *Manshu jihen* (Manchurian Incident) broke out, plunging Japan into an undeclared war with China—and, in a sense, with the League of Nations and the United States.[94] No single event could have demonstrated more dramatically the schismatic character of Japanese government. Fear, uncertainty, and paralysis gripped the top branches of the government. The cabinet seemed helpless to prevent the initiation of an independent foreign policy by a small overseas clique aided by various forces at home. Exhorted and counseled by the high officials surrounding the Throne, and given moral support by the Emperor himself, the cabinet still could find no solution. One painful dilemma was that if the most strenuous measures were not taken, the government could not possibly gain control, but if such measures were attempted, the world prestige of Japan would be gravely jeopardized by the resultant disclosures. In any case, it was exceedingly difficult to devise a policy that could promise success under the circumstances. The parties were at low ebb of popularity and prestige, and deeply divided, with many internal elements willing to encourage the "direct actionists." Somewhat offsetting the difficulties of the government was the fact that the military itself was split by a variety of factors and that some of the high service officials were therefore willing to work with the cabinet in an effort to contain the situation. Given the lack of unity among these elements, however, and

---

ter. As for the nature of the Peers' attacks, one illustration may indicate the ridiculous extremes to which they could go. On May 5, 1930, one peer asked the minister of justice why he had permitted the report of the preliminary examination of certain Communists to be made public on the Emperor's birthday. Significantly, the minister took care to explain that the papers had been forwarded the day before, but that the newspapers had borrowed the documents the next day. From House of Peers Proceedings, May 5, 1930, transcript in *JC*, May 15, 1930, p. 510.

[94] See chapter ix for some details on the Manchurian Incident.

the nature of Japanese institutions, especially the system of ill-defined control and responsibility, the effectiveness of those who might attempt to coöperate could only be limited. The subordinate bureaucracy presented another complex aspect of the picture. In the Foreign Office and in many other departments there were bitter divisions. Increasingly, certain groups within the Civil Service were being influenced by the growing nationalist tide, by economic conditions, and by party impotence, as well as by their disgust with the entire status quo, in such a way as to move in the direction of the exuberant plotters. Especially was this noticeable at the lower levels of officialdom. And these elements, exercising the traditional powers of a Japanese subordinate group, applied effective pressures and forms of sabotage.

An institutional structure created on the premise of organic unity never showed its inadequacies more clearly. The unifying force of the Genro had now nearly ceased to exist, despite the attempt to strengthen it by the increasing use of the officials of the Inner Court. These officials might influence, but they could not control, the conflicts that raged within and among the parties, the military groups, and the civil bureaucracy. Certainly the party system had not taken the place of the Genro. The Manchurian Incident clearly demonstrated that party supremacy was a mere fiction—a fiction long transparent to the astute observer of Japanese politics.

The Wakatsuki cabinet finally went down on December 12, 1931, after drifting hopelessly for several months. The immediate cause was a quarrel within the cabinet itself over the issue of a coalition government. Initially, Wakatsuki had suggested the possibility of strengthening the cabinet by winning the aid of the Seiyukai. This proposal, however, met with the vigorous opposition of Inoue and Shidehara, two of the most important cabinet members, on the score that the policies of the two parties were not compatible. Consequently, Wakatsuki desired to abandon the plan, but Adachi Kenzo, now Home Minister, insisted upon making it a major issue.[95] Adachi had long nurtured ambitions for party leadership and the premiership. To advance these causes, he was engaging in negotiations with diverse factions, including certain military and Seiyukai elements. Aided by Kuhara Fusanosuke of the Seiyukai, he defied the Premier by launching an independent movement to unite the two major parties. The cry of "One party— one power," which had played such an important part in the early

---

[95] Wakatsuki provides some details concerning party factionalism during this period. See Wakatsuki, *op. cit.,* pp. 383–387.

Meiji politics, was raised again. On December 9, 1931, a public demand for a coalition government was made by the Kuhara and Adachi forces. Adachi refused to resign from the cabinet, and hence, three days later, Wakatsuki submitted the joint resignations of all members.

"Party government" continued for six months longer. Saionji, taking counsel with certain court officials, now turned to Inukai and the Seiyukai. Inukai was opposed to the coalition idea and assigned all portfolios except the service posts to Seiyukai men. It was necessary to dissolve the hostile Sixtieth Diet, and in the ensuing election the Seiyukai won a crushing victory, securing 304 Diet seats. In view of the conditions with which the parties now had to deal, however, this victory meant relatively little. Within the party, the Seiyukai faced a rampant factionalism. Tokonami, Suzuki, and Kuhara were all contenders for supreme power, with hopes of succeeding Inukai as president and with sizable blocs of followers behind them.[96] As a party, moreover, the Seiyukai was far less likely to pose an effective barrier to militarism or the forces seeking to overturn parliamentary government. Its "positive" foreign program had always been conducive to the growth of military power. Now, from within the party, there were many feelers into militarist circles, and chauvinism was a keynote of almost every party declaration. Inukai himself, while struggling rather vigorously behind the scenes to control runaway elements of the army, compromised his cause more than once in public. Even when he sought to uphold the doctrine of parliamentary politics, his words were defensive and a little forlorn. Just one week before his assassination, he uttered these words in the course of his last major address: "Recently among a certain class, there has been a tendency to conduct discussions negating the Diet, but this is unrealistic under the actual political conditions, and it is an opinion which concludes that thorough reform is impossible. Opposed to this, we believe in the wise use of parliamentary politics to the greatest degree, and we believe that sufficient reform is possible." [97] Inukai continued by discussing various means of reform, but he concluded

---

[96] For the political intrigue of the period, the Harada-Saionji and Kido diaries are two of the best sources of information. Both have been translated into English, and a Japanese edition of the Harada-Saionji diary in nine volumes is now (1951) being published. See Harada Kumao, *Saionji-Ko to seikyoku* (*Prince Saionji and the Political Situation*), Tokyo, 1950—.

[97] Quoted from *Inukai Tsuyoshi* [*Ki*] *den* (*Biography of Inukai Tsuyoshi* [*Ki*]), Vol. II, pp. 456–457, in Royama, *op. cit.*, pp. 475–476.

this part of his address by admitting that electoral reforms alone were not sufficient. "However, in the final analysis," he said, "such a reform of the system [of elections] depends upon the attitude and actions of the politicians who apply it." [98]

It was too late to talk about a "wise use" of the Diet and about party reform. A week later, on May 15, 1932, Inukai was dead—murdered by a group of young army and navy officers who terrorized all Tokyo. The cabinet resigned ten days later and the era of party government was over, for this was the last party cabinet to hold office in Japan until after World War II.

The new era, which is discussed in a concluding section, may well be called the era of militarism, although this designation possibly connotes too abrupt a change. Actually, the demise of civilian government was not immediate, nor was military control ever complete or wholly unified. The whole era, moreover, was exceedingly complex and should not be oversimplified. The old parties, however, grew steadily weaker until their final dissolution in 1940. The struggle for democracy and party government in prewar Japan had ended in failure.

The Japanese institutional structure played a part in this failure that should not be overlooked. The great weaknesses of the party movement before 1890 can be grouped in three interrelated categories: the early parties interpreted democracy in certain ways not calculated to facilitate its growth; they lacked any broad basis of support; and they were frustrated by a deeply entrenched factionalism which had significant implications for party organization and principles. In each case, these party weaknesses were aggravated and given additional opportunities to grow after 1889 by Japanese constitutionalism.

Prewar Japanese political institutions rested upon the dual concepts of Imperial absolutism and popular government, with the former taking precedence in every respect. The power of constitutionalism to serve as a symbol for popular rights was greatly reduced in Japan by the way in which Imperial prerogatives were allowed to dominate in both the drafting and the provisions of the Meiji Constitution. Thus, despite certain democratic overtones, this constitution stood as a monument to the Throne—its benevolence and omnipotence. In all of these respects, the new law fitted well into the traditional Japanese pattern of eclecticism, seeking broad compromises—one might almost say total integration—of the diverse forces operative in the Meiji political scene. Indeed,

---

[98] *Ibid.*, p. 476.

because these forces were so diverse now, the Constitution actually carried eclecticism to new extremes, extremes untenable in logic and devastating to Japanese democracy. For in seeking to sustain the eclectic approach, the Meiji Constitution placed a premium upon certain procedures and techniques which continued to retard the development of doctrinal consistency, intellectual independence, and individual responsibility. And always, constitutional symbolism and power in Japan forced the heavier concessions from the elements closest to the democratic cause. Thus, in the final analysis, the ideological corruption of the liberal party movement was rendered easier in a great variety of ways by the spirit and provisions of the Japanese Constitution.

These same factors had an impressive effect upon the sources of party support. As the parties turned inward to the bureaucracy rather than outward to the people for their sources of power, a continuous process of party "bureaucratization" took place. Some of the ex-officials served the party cause reasonably well, but few avoided the time-honored techniques and attitudes of the old Japanese ruling class. And because of these trends, exclusivism, officiousness, and disdain for the common people became salient features of the major parties. All the weaknesses of the early period were nurtured, and a deep wedge was driven between the parties and the "man in the street." Thus the major parties did not concern themselves with the need for a strong popular appeal—for a mass movement on behalf of democracy which would carry with it the dynamism of a new faith.

The initial problems of factionalism were also augmented by the institutional position of the parties. With principles and responsibility obscured, factionalism based upon personalities and mutual power interests was given full rein. Japanese politics was above all else a process of coalition for power and collaboration in power. Union of the liberals based upon a mutuality of principles was meaningless, for it did not combine the forces necessary to control the administrative structure. Alliances had to be consummated between elements with alien principles, splitting the ranks of party men and bureaucrats alike.

The founding of the Meiji Constitution was an effort to stem the tide of ideas which jeopardized oligarchic control. If it was not perfectly adapted to that purpose, that was because in its very definition it had to contain certain paraphernalia of limited and legal government; and also because even within the oligarchy, there was an ambivalence toward Westernism which inevitably crept into the question how best to create power. Government within the Constitution's framework had some flexibility, as a necessary corollary to the movement of the society for which it was designed; fundamentally, however, the Constitution froze the ideas of absolutism in new and more impervious forms by making the apparatus of representative government, in theory a potential instrument of their destruction, into their appendage and reinforcement.

The institutional structure of modern Japan, however, was not the sole determinant of Japanese democracy, nor, indeed, its most important one. Capitalism could conceivably have removed the central obstacles which blocked the democratic movement, as it had done in the West. We must now seek the causes of its inability to accomplish this result, first in the characteristics of Japanese capitalism itself, and then in the leftist movement which was one of its consequences.

VII

THE DEVELOPMENT OF
JAPANESE CAPITALISM AND
ITS IMPACT ON THE PARTY
MOVEMENT

WHEN THE EPITAPH was being written on the Japanese parties of
the period before World War II, the inscriptions offered were
rarely eulogistic, even those from friends of Japanese democracy.
Yoshino Sakuzo, leading intellectual and spokesman for the Social
Democrats, savagely attacked the major parties in the following
words: "The party politicians work under the orders of their pay-
masters, the plutocrats, and these orders are obviously to serve
the interests of big business, while the little man, and particularly
the farmer, is progressively impoverished." [1]

Stronger than this were the words of the antidemocratic left
and right. The newspaper *Yorozu*, echoing the line of the radical
militarists, published many editorials showing at least one bond
of kinship with the Communists, as this excerpt will indicate:

The masses in this country are suffering because of the exploitation
of a small capitalist class whose power has been greatly expanding. The
people are given the honorable title of "nation" but they are placed
under unspeakable miseries. Our people now clearly understand the
deception to which they have been placed these years. Politics has become the chief instrument of the ruling class to exploit the masses. [2]

But even in the minds of conservatives holding close ties with
the major parties, there ran certain undercurrents of disgust and

---

[1] Yoshino Sakuzo, "Fascism in Japan," *Contemporary Japan*, September,
1932, p. 194.

[2] Quoted and translated from the *Yorozu* in *JC*, June 17, 1930, p. 110.

despair. One of the most remarkable early Japanese industrialists, Shibuzawa Eiichi, managed to live to the period of party decline, and at its outset he gave this admonition, couched in phrases with Confucian overtones:

Recently voices have flourished mourning the deterioration of political morality and violently abhorring the scandalous disintegration of the political parties. In this matter, however, even more than in the case of most strengths and weaknesses of a nation, the problem arises from the matter of personal strengths and weaknesses, springing from the initial forgetfulness of the people toward the various duties which they should advance in a national society.[3]

Obviously these accusations were not confined to one element within Japanese society. That they reached into the grass roots with great potency, moreover, is illustrated by the general cynicism with which party politics was viewed and the impervious attitude taken by the average man toward parliamentary decline. There were, of course, honest and honorable men within the major parties, but their virtues could not counterbalance the corruption rampant in party politics; nor, except in rare instances, could even these men take the part of an enlightened elite seeking to meet the problems of the lower economic classes. In such a situation, democracy and the party system came to be equated in many minds with the most sordid combination of exclusive privilege and personal immorality.

To explore the most vital aspect of party failure in its unfolding, and also to cast light upon the remarkable strength of antidemocratic institutions in Japan, special attention must be given to the political role of modern Japanese capitalism. Out of the Meiji Restoration emerged two formidable pressure groups, the landowners and the urban business classes. Much of the chronicle of the leading parties must be written in terms of their political propensities, and since these were connected with the socioeconomic forces developing within and outside Japanese society, some brief examination of these forces must be undertaken, with particular emphasis upon the rise of Japanese industrialism.

The initial structure of Meiji capitalism has already been outlined, and some of its early political effects noted. At the outset of constitutional government, however, the industrial revolution had only begun to unfold. In the recent background was a record

---

[3] Quoted in Tsuchiya Takao, *Nihon shihonshugi shijo no shidoshatachi* (*Leaders in the History of Japanese Capitalism*), Tokyo, 1941 ed., p. 121.

of feverish governmental activities, the overcoming of certain political and economic obstacles, and the beginnings of an expansion of private enterprise. In the future there was to be an incredibly rapid development in all these directions.[4] Its first phases unfolded in the decade between 1885 and 1895, a period in which further progress in meeting fiscal, technical, and supply problems resulted in significant advances in capital investment and industrial production. Progress in the spinning industry, in particular, presaged gains in other fields. Developments in spinning were largely attributable to the importation of Indian cotton and to increased mechanization. The former served to solve the question of supply, gradually eliminating the meager domestic cotton production. The latter caused the rapid collapse, after 1887, of the cotton-spinning handicraft industry, now unable to compete successfully with mechanized industry.[5] Inexpensive labor was available to the new industry in ever increasing quantities, and business administration experience, reaching back into the Tokugawa period, was being enriched by Western techniques. Low prices and standardization, products of this experience and the plentiful supply of cheap labor, augmented market possibilities at home and abroad.

Advances were not limited to the spinning industry, however. In transportation, the railroads and the shipping business expanded; beginnings were made in the chemical industry. These developments, in turn, stimulated subsidiary fields.[6] The foreign trade figures reflected the emergence of industry by showing a

---

[4] For sources from which to draw this brief account of Japanese industrial growth, the author has relied mainly upon Horie Yasuzo, *Nihon keizai shi* (*An Economic History of Japan*), Tokyo, 1949; Tsuchiya Takao and Okazaki Saburo, *Nihon shihonshugi hattatsu shi gaisetsu* (*A General Outline of the Development of Japanese Capitalism*), Tokyo, 1937; Honjo Eijiro, *Nihon keizai shiso shi gaisetsu* (*A General Summary of the History of Japanese Economic Thought*), Tokyo, 1948 ed.; Takahashi Kamekichi, *Nihon kogyo hatten ron* (*A Treatise on Japanese Industrial Development*), Tokyo, 1936; and Takahashi Kamekichi and Aoyama Jiro, *Nihon zaibatsu ron* (*A Treatise on the Japanese Financial Cliques*), Tokyo, 1938.

[5] Horie, *op. cit.*, pp. 237–238. Note the following figures on the spinning industry (from table in *ibid.*, p. 237):

Year	No. of Factories	Spindles	Bales of Raw Cotton Used
1886	20	71,604	16,757
1890	30	277,895	112,500
1894	45	530,074	322,250

[6] As compared to other companies (excluding financial companies) industrial concerns had, in 1886, 29.2 per cent of the capital; by 1893, this had increased to 37.3 per cent. *Ibid.*, p. 240.

percentage decline of imports and increase of exports.[7] In an overall sense, to be sure, only the first steps toward industrialization had been taken, development in heavy industry on the whole was negligible, and in many important fields, such as those of *sake* (rice wine) production and match manufacturing, the old techniques prevailed. Still, the Japanese industrial revolution was passing beyond the cradle stage.

Old trends continued and new ones were initiated in the next decade, from 1895 to 1905. This period, sandwiched between two successful wars, was marked by substantial increases in industrial capitalization and in foreign trade, the strengthening of policies of aid by the government, and the mechanization of new fields.[8] The Sino-Japanese War of 1894–1895 caused large capital expenditures to be funneled into industries essential to the war effort. It also produced a sizable indebtedness, accompanied by wartime and postwar inflation. These occurrences promoted general expansion, and the closer relation between domestic and international financial markets due to foreign loans brought a certain stability conducive to industrial growth. In 1897 Japan went on the gold standard. After the war, moreover, external markets in Asia greatly expanded, with the reopening of Chinese and Korean markets and the acquisition of Formosa. During this period, also, the Japanese government was particularly active on behalf of industrial efforts, creating special credit facilities to augment the rather scanty capital resources, passing much protective legislation, and engaging in a great variety of aid and subsidization tactics. In these projects its hand was strengthened by treaty renegotiations which essentially restored tariff autonomy to Japan in 1899.

The results were omnipresent in the Japanese economic scene. In 1894, industrial companies had numbered 778 and had had a capitalization of ¥44,590,000; in 1897 there were 1,881 such companies, capitalized at ¥105,380,000; by 1903 the total number was 2,441, and the total capital more than ¥170,000,000.[9] Accumulated capital was increasingly being placed in the industrial field. Steady development was going on in the fields previously favored, and in such additional industries as those of silk and paper. The shipbuilding and railroad industries scored phenomenal gains, as did

---

[7] From 1883 to 1893, the percentage of all manufactured imports, in money, dropped from 45.2 to 33.1; the percentage of exports in money rose from 6.5 to 24.5. *Ibid.*

[8] See Honjo, *op. cit.*, pp. 187–188.

[9] Horie, *op. cit.*, pp. 241–242.

the cotton-spinning industry.[10] There were also sizable increases in iron and steel production, but as yet the general field of heavy industry was subordinate to that of light industry, and such branches as machine manufacturing were still relatively undeveloped.[11] However, mechanization of existing industries was gaining rapidly, serving as one index of productive potentialities and progressively eliminating handicraft factories. By 1899, 42.2 per cent of the 6,551 factories employing more than 10 persons used power-driven machines, and the workers in these power-equipped plants constituted 71.3 per cent of the 392,000 factory-employed workers at this level.[12] Techniques of financing and industrial skills were also being greatly improved. By the time of the Russo-Japanese War, the industrial revolution was sweeping over Japan.

Before proceeding, it is important to review the political developments that had accompanied the growth of industry and commerce in this earlier phase, particularly as they related to the role of business in politics. Perhaps the most significant generalization which can be made concerning the period before the Russo-Japanese War is that the industrial-commercial groups, despite their growth in power and importance, participated only to a very limited extent in public politics in general or in the party movement specifically. There were two interrelated reasons for this, both of which have been previously suggested but which must now be studied for their importance in this period. The first lies in the nature of the Japanese industrial-commercial revolution and that of the society from which it emerged; the second lies in the numerical superiority and political power of the agrarian landowners.

In order to place the political limitations of late Meiji capitalism in perspective, some recapitulation of its antecedents is necessary. It had emerged hastily and at a comparatively late date in the midst of an unprepared society, and therefore its development was initially dependent upon intensive government planning, supervision, and subsidization. Subsequently, beginning with the 1880's, outright state capitalism receded in favor of private enterprise sustained against domestic weaknesses and foreign threats by a

---

[10] Professor Honjo says of this period that enterprise development as a whole was sparked by the three great enterprises: railroads, banking, and cotton spinning. Honjo, *op. cit.*, p. 188.

[11] Horie, *op. cit.*, p. 244.

[12] *Ibid.*

neomercantilist policy. Such a transition was in accordance with the desires of the early Meiji political leaders, whose chief energies had been directed toward utilizing all methods of rapid industrial expansion.

This pattern of development, together with the prior traditions which supported and were supported by it, was vitally important in shaping the personnel, structure, and philosophy of modern Japanese capitalism. We have already noted that one product was the large number of new industrial leaders who were men of the old bushi class and consequently men whose political predilections and personal friendships—not to mention economic security— lay with the government. With Meiji political and economic elites extremely small in numbers, with the latter frequently selected by the former and having a similar background, close personalized contacts were most natural. At the same time, however, these were ordinarily not contacts between "equals," despite changes in the official attitude toward business. The social stigma attached to commercialism was not to be cast off lightly, and this, supplemented by the very great obligations of commerce and industry to government, tended to produce strong notes of apology and deference in the attitude of the business class toward public officials. Even ex-bushi members, frequently affected by inner pangs of remorse or chagrin at a status which conflicted with the tenets of their own past philosophy, and heavily dependent upon political support, tended to find simultaneous release from psychological and economic insecurity by assuming the subservient role. These inclinations were of course much stronger among the ex-commoner elements of the new business world and were slow to diminish, especially in the first generation.

In structure, as well, industrial capitalism reflected in graphic form the nature of its development and certain characteristics of its political impact. The keynote of Japanese industry was centralization, with the ultimate financial-economic controls held by the government and a few powerful groups known popularly as *zaibatsu* (financial cliques). Although small and medium businesses occupied a far more important position in over-all production than has generally been recognized, as we shall have occasion to note later, still, in the final analysis, their position was one of great dependency upon zaibatsu and government. And in many basic fields, moreover, the tendencies toward oligopoly were pronounced, only rarely challenged, and usually progressive, with

251

cartelization developing toward the end of the Meiji period.[13] There are undoubtedly many factors which enter into an explanation for these characteristics; the paucity of capital, the lack of adequate resources, and the shortage of trained personnel constituted barriers to internal competition or a broad productive base. Selectivity and an avoidance of duplication or waste were doubly important as considerations of governmental aid, given the premium on speed and the pressures of foreign competition. But perhaps it is most significant that the governmental policy of neo-mercantilism was applied at a time when industrial techniques were sufficiently advanced in the world to permit the structure based on this policy to be quickly established throughout the entire economy, and with a scope and tenacity which defied fundamental alteration.

Thus the zaibatsu were leading actors in the industrial-financial scene, symbols of Japanese capitalism, and ultimate recipients of tremendous economic and political power. The term zaibatsu, like most epithets, has been applied without too much regard for discrimination. Takahashi and Aoyama would divide the zaibatsu into three general groups: those whose activities centered in the finance and banking field, including Yasuda, Kawasaki, and Shibuzawa; those whose activities were industry-centered, such as Asano and Okura; and those whose activities spread into all fields—finance, commerce, and light and heavy industry—of which group Mitsui, Mitsubishi, and Sumitomo were the outstanding examples.[14] Generally, these last three and Yasuda were considered the big four zaibatsu. Among the so-called zaibatsu, large or small, however, there were many variations and changes of organization, operational plans, and political activities. The term zaibatsu was even applied on occasion to district capitalists, with reference to their local control. Moreover, the emergence of new groups after World War I, and particularly after the rise of the military about 1932, constituted a further complication.

In spite of the intricacies of the situation, however, the increasing influence of a few great industrial and financial concerns in collaboration with the government became a vital part of the unfolding Japanese economy. Time served to separate the zaibatsu prototypes further from small and medium business, both in size and in power, and to increase the dependence of the latter

---

[13] Horie mentions the fact that a cartel had been established in the paper industry by 1901. *Ibid.*, p. 243.

[14] Takahashi Kamekichi and Aoyama, *op. cit.*, p. 2.

upon the former. Almost down to the Russo-Japanese War, however, the economic position of the zaibatsu was quite uncertain, and their political role was generally marked by great caution;[15] quite as much as the elements representing smaller business, they were supplicants at the government door, seeking protection, cultivating political friends, carefully repaying obligations, and accepting subordination. In these regards, Meiji zaibatsu set a tone of behavior for lesser lights in the business world and exemplified the general position of the industrial-commercial class.

Out of the general circumstances affecting business came a philosophy which carried important political implications. There is much justice in portraying the newly emerging businessmen as among the most Westernized and "enlightened" elements of Japanese society. Many businessmen had been abroad, and some had been educated in the Occident. Admiration for Western industrial techniques, Western education, and Western friends represented a new stimulus, challenging to the old order. Still, there were powerful factors operating within Japanese society to alter or confine these influences. The conjunction of nationalism and the industrialization drive, together with the world circumstances which a weak Japan faced, imposed upon the business groups a unique sense of their functional purpose as defined by the political leaders. In a period of succeeding crises, and with the voice of government constantly imploring unity and the creation of state power, the Meiji business class was ever mindful of the national goals; business enterprises even became a patriotic venture calling for unremitting zeal and wholehearted conformity to the purposes of the time.[16] In this atmosphere there was a natural tendency to accept the supremacy of political and military leadership.

Abetting this, moreover, was the inescapable stigma of social inferiority; industrialization might be vitally necessary and call forth the most resolute efforts of the government; yet there remained a sense of disdain for the commercial occupation among officialdom and also, deeply entrenched and even stronger, among landed elements and intellectuals. The predilection was against

---

[15] It will be recalled that Iwasaki had been threatened with ruin as a result of his open support of the Kaishinto against the government. This was a lesson not to be forgotten easily.

[16] According to Takahashi, such big companies as the Japan Railway Company and the Fifteenth Bank were organized mainly by peers, more as an expression of patriotism than as a business venture. See Takahashi Kamekichi, *Kabushiki kaisha—bokoku ron* (*A Treatise on Share Companies—the Ruin of the Country*), Tokyo, 1930, p. 74.

"materialism" among these circles in modern Japan, reflective of the Tokugawa background and further supported by the increasing signs of personal and mass corruption accompanying the modernization period. There were many other charges made against the insurgent business class, and their general position was a defensive one, since antagonism on the part of other classes was always present or close to the surface.

Probably of greatest significance in molding the philosophy of the early modern business class, however, was the extraordinary dependency upon governmental support and the consequent reluctance to attack the power or purposes of the state. Thus, out of an inferiority complex, an ingrained nationalism, a lack of modern political experience, and a rational appraisal of their own economic interests came a philosophy which supported neomercantilism, abjured open political action, and sought to confine political activities to behind-the-scenes operations which would involve the least risks and promise the greatest rewards.

The second major factor to be discussed in analyzing the political nature of the Meiji industrial-commercial elements was the collective power of the agrarian propertied groups. What the landowners lacked in concentrated wealth or state priorities they made up in votes. The rural-urban cleavage has run very deep in modern Japan and a complete analysis of its many aspects remains to be made. Clearly, the struggle in Japan, as elsewhere, has encompassed a range of issues broad enough to justify the phrase "cultural conflict," although admittedly the lines and forces have not been completely coterminous with rural-urban boundaries. Despite the breadth of the conflict, however, in the Meiji era, the open political struggle was primarily confined to the rural landowner and urban business groups. Within their respective categories, these were naturally the more articulate elements. They had the power and the vote. And the burning economic issues such as taxation, subsidization, and price policy were ones in which they had a great stake. Although the administration often sought to harmonize the interests of these two important segments of Japanese society, neither it nor the parties could fully reconcile all the divergencies nor maintain perfectly balanced policies.

With the advent of constitutional government, the potency of the landed elements in the parties and in the representative branch of government was assured; in numbers and voting strength, they were far ahead of the urban industrial-commercial groups. The landowners, indeed, were the backbone of the Jiyuto, and without some agrarian support, no party could be more than a minor fragment. A sampling of properly spaced early elections can easily illustrate this point. In the first election of 1890, of the 300 elected members of the Diet, 129 represented the agrarian landed class directly, whereas only 19 came from the commercial and industrial classes.[17] Occupational groupings of Diet members after the elections of 1898 gave agriculture 168 members, whereas commerce and industry had only 42.[18] In 1902, a 369-member Diet was elected, of which 127 members were classified as farmers and the next closest occupational category was "law," with 58 Diet members.[19] The election of 1908 showed approximately the same proportions. The Jiyuto (Seiyukai) was of course heavily favored by the fact that its origins and early emphasis lay in the rural dis-

---

[17] Actually, before the election law revision of 1900, all except 17 of the 300 electoral districts were rural districts. Somewhat before the 1900 revision, Ito, who was greatly troubled by the overwhelming agrarian representation, proposed a change which would have increased the Diet from 300 to 473, raising the number of urban seats to 103.

[18] These figures are from the *Yushin Nippon,* quoted in *JC,* August 20, 1898, p. 141. The occupation categories of forty-three Diet members was listed as unknown.

[19] A government report on the occupations of the 1902 election winners gave the following results: farmers (landowners), 127; lawyers, 58; bankers, 33; journalists, 26; commercial interests, 16; ex-officials of the government, 14; sake brewers, 12; physicians, 9; ex-officials of the municipal governments, 9; mine owners, 5; railroad people, 3; government officials, 3; money lenders, 3; and contractors, 3 (others were miscellaneous or unknown). Report translated and published in *JC,* August 27, 1902, p. 198.

Obviously, this breakdown cannot be used for obtaining definite representation percentages of rural versus urban groups or of agrarian versus commercial interests. Nevertheless, it illustrates the heavy proportion of rural agrarian or semiagrarian members; even such categories as "bankers" included provincial bankers with rural ties, and the sake brewers, it will be recalled, came wholly from the district entrepreneurial class, being landowners as well.

Considering the relative ratios of voters and districts, however, representation of the urban or commercially inclined groups may actually have been high. Of the total of 376 electoral districts, only 75 were classified as "urban districts." See Foreign Affairs Association of Japan, *Japan Year Book for 1905,* Tokyo, 1906, p. 38. Figures published in *JC,* May 17, 1902, p. 532, gave the total number of voters as 967,227, of whom 896,646 were classified as "rural," with only 67,970 called "urban," and the remainder classified as "insular" (the small islands).

tricts, and this was one important reason for its usual majorities.[20]

Thus in commenting upon the 1908–1909 Diet, the *Keizai Zasshi* (*Economics Magazine*) remarked:

The Lower House must still be said to represent mainly the agricultural classes just as it did in the first session twenty years ago, when its proceedings were almost entirely swayed by the question of the Land Tax. The *Seiyukai* are conscious that they receive their mandate from agricultural constituencies and their policy is governed by the necessity of placating the farming [landowning] classes.[21]

The *Keizai Zasshi* was mostly correct in its analysis, both of the Diet and of party policy. It will be remembered that the great cry of the parties was for lower taxes, meaning lower land taxes, and that frequently government budgets, including funds for industrial subsidization, were slashed by party men, especially Jiyuto members. Even the Okuma party could not afford to ignore the registration figures; though the Shimpoto platform of 1896 was hailed as

---

[20] The following Department of Home Affairs chart on the 1908 election (as translated in *JC*, May 23, 1908, pp. 570–571) presents an urban-rural breakdown of election results:

	Urban Representation	Rural Representation	Total
Seiyukai	24	162	186
Kenseihonto	3	72	75
Daido Club	9	23	32
Yukokai	9	16	25
Unattached	31	29	60
	76	302	378

(1 vacancy)

These figures reveal two very interesting points. The first is the proportionately heavy urban strength shown by the "agrarian" Seiyukai and the weak showing of the Kenseihonto, which was always hailed as the spokesman for the business groups. There were both general and specific reasons for this situation. This particular election was held under the first Saionji cabinet, with the Seiyukai having the support of the government in power and spending a great deal of money. Moreover, from the time of the Sino-Japanese War on, and especially after the formation of the Seiyukai, the ex-Jiyuto group, in addition to holding its agrarian support, developed an urban wing, garnering support especially from businessmen who had personal connections with Seiyukai leaders or who merely desired to be on the side of a strong party.

The other significant factor is the large number of unaffiliated representatives sent by the urban districts. This was a tendency which, with few exceptions, remained very strong. Many urban voters looked with disfavor on both major parties.

[21] Quoted from *Keizai Zasshi*, in translation, in *JC*, February 6, 1909, p. 397.

a probusiness platform, Okuma was forced for political reasons to oppose publicly an increased land tax. His party was also heavily dependent upon rural votes if it hoped for control of the House of Representatives.

The above-mentioned facts simply reëmphasize the central point that Japan was still a strongly agrarian nation. Moreover, landowner voting strength had been made additionally effective by suffrage laws which established the electorate on the basis of national tax, for rural landowners paid proportionately heavier taxes than did the urban interests. Hence representative government meant, at least initially, majorities for the landowning agrarian and semiagrarian classes; and the popular parties, even the Okuma party, reflected this fact. This naturally affected the type of urban commercial participation in politics, for without a sufficiently large electorate to promise success at the polls, the urban business groups were called upon to safeguard their political position through more traditional means.

Keeping in mind these conditions implicit in the initial stages of the Japanese industrial revolution, we may now focus attention upon the precise role which business played in Japanese politics and parties in the period that ended with the Russo-Japanese War. During this period a great majority of the businessmen displayed a considerable degree of indifference to politics, except in matters directly affecting their immediate economic interests; the number of active participants in the open political arena from the industrial-commercial groups was negligible. Interestingly enough, this attitude provoked dismay and resentment from the government and parties alike, both sides coveting more active support. Ito, greatly disappointed by the election of 1892, wrote:

> Business men and men of moderate disposition such as the so-called "shisanka" [men of means] are indifferent to ordinary politics. The normal condition of men of means is to avoid things which are not connected with their own business and because of this, they dislike even participating in election competitions. To the extent that business men are disinterested in politics, the run of politicians is poor in character, but getting them to be candidates is a great difficulty.[22]

---

[22] Quoted from *Ito Hirobumi mitsuroku* in Fukaya Hiroji, *Shoki Gikai joyaku kaisei* (*The First Diets: Treaty Revision*), in Kindai Nihon rekishi koza (Modern Japanese History Series), Tokyo, 1940, p. 263. Ito was, of course, strongly probusiness, and these remarks were made in 1892 after the failure of Shinagawa to get businessmen to run for office representing the government in the 1892 elections.

The more articulate members of the business group attempted to answer complaints such as this by pointing out that enormous developments in the economic world required complete attention, since many persons in their group were, relatively, novices in this field, quite as much as in the field of constitutional government. Furthermore, they charged, entering open politics produced violent personal attacks upon them, jeopardized their business interests, and subjected them to an intolerable officiousness on the part of the career civil servants and political leaders.

But if the members of the business community showed a reluctance to become active political participants on behalf of the government, they were usually even more hesitant to give open and active support to an antigovernment party. In most cases, adequate motivations for the latter course were lacking; but even when these existed, they were usually offset by the risks involved. After twenty years of constitutional government, Inukai chided the Japanese business elements for their "indifference" to liberalism and the party movement, writing: "Their chief concern is to assist the Government and go in for enterprise out of which profit is to be made." [23]

He was willing to add one of the many reasons for this: "If a business man speaks out against the Government, officials carry their custom elsewhere." [24]

The words of Ito and Inukai present one important part of the picture, but by no means the whole of it. It is true that the political activity of the business groups was limited; most of it was conducted in private, usually in the hands of a small group, and generally it was confined to furthering personal interests. Precisely because this activity was quiet and confidential, however, it was having a great effect upon politics and the parties, and this effect can be summarized under two main categories: first, the business elements were facilitating the amalgamation of the parties and a part of the bureaucracy, the significance of which has already been discussed; secondly, the activities of the "political merchants" were contributing freely to the corruption of political leadership and of the rank and file. In these two important effects is revealed some measure of the inadequacy of Japanese capitalism to support liberalism and the party movement, and of its role in the failure of democracy.

One of the most significant contributions to Japanese politics

---

[23] Quoted from Inukai Ki, "The Government and the Corrupt Political World," *Taiyo*, April, 1911, translated in *JM*, April 29, 1911, p. 475.
[24] *Ibid.*

made by members of the Meiji business world, and particularly those elements later classified as zaibatsu, was to allow their threshold to become a common meeting ground for the oligarchy and party leaders. Although the initiative in this matter was not always theirs, the function was nevertheless in line with their personal friendships and their occupational necessities. Indeed, the paramount need of the rising industrialists was to obtain the support of a unified government which would look favorably upon their requests. The first step in achieving this goal was to cultivate friendships and win supporters at the top government and party levels; the final step was to unite these friends into a workable coalition on their behalf.

As has been suggested, substantial pressure was often put upon individual business leaders by political mentors, from one side or another, to perform this task, and given the general status and dependency of business, this pressure could not be easily resisted. Moreover, before seeking to detail either of the two central aspects of business-political relations suggested above, it is only proper to admit that in the absence of sufficient trustworthy documentation on many individual cases, it is not easy to separate fact from fiction, or to avoid applying generalizations that may be accurate, to particular instances in which they are not warranted.[25] Finally, it should be said at the outset that it is very difficult to avoid also a type of distortion which passes under the general label of the "plot" or "devil" theory of history. There is a temptation to sum up the entire story as the result of the iniquities and calculated plots of certain business and political leaders. Of course it should not be denied that Japan, like all societies, had its "devils," and that there is some truth in an analysis based upon such premises;

[25] For some additional sources on this, see Ikeda Seihin, *Zaikai kaiko* (*Reminiscences on the Financial World*), Tokyo, 1949, and *Kojin konjin* (*The Living and the Dead*), Tokyo, 1949; Suzuki Mosaburo, *Nihon zaibatsu ron* (*A Treatise on the Japanese Financial Cliques*), Tokyo, 1934; Ono Takeo, *Nihon sangyo hattatsu shi no kenkyu* (*Studies in the History of the Development of Japanese Industry*), Tokyo, 1941; Tsuchiya Takao, *Nihon no zaibatsu* (*The Japanese Financial Cliques*), Tokyo, 1949.

For sources in English, see H. C. Huggins, *The Great Fortunes of Japan*, Hayama, Japan, 1930, 11 vols.; Oland D. Russell, *The House of Mitsui*, Boston, 1939. Several articles of interest are "Rich Men Connected with Politics Today," a symposium by Dr. Miyake Setsurei, Matsui Hakken, Tagawa Daikichiro (Diet member), "A Certain Doctor," and Professor Matsuyama Chujiro, in *Chuo Koron* in July, 1910 (these articles have been partly translated and partly paraphrased in *JC*, July 16, 1910, pp. 90–91); Muto Sanji, "Seiji to kane" (Politics and Money), *Taiyo*, May, 1926; Takahashi Kamekichi, "Mitsui, Mitsubishi, Sumitomo," in *Chuo Koron*, February, 1930.

still, if this oversimplified interpretation is offered alone, or even as the basic explanation, it must be considered superficial and warped when measured against more fundamental causal factors.

In opening any discussion of individual business-political relations, it is logical to start with the House of Mitsui, which, as the largest industrial-financial combine, played an extremely important part in building up the industrial and monetary structure of modern Japan.[26] Behind Mitsui's success, especially in the initial period, lay a number of close contacts with important political leaders, chief of whom was Inoue Kaoru, friend of Ito and one of the most important Meiji statesmen in his own right.[27] Inoue actually became an adviser and confidant of the Mitsui family, and it was he who encouraged the Mitsui to aid the government and themselves by expanding their activities; through the active support of Inoue the company was given permission to establish a modern banking system. In 1890, when Mitsui was temporarily in difficulties because of a banking and business panic, Inoue helped to reorganize the company, placing several of his able acquaintances in positions of great importance.[28] Besides Inoue, Mitsui had important contacts with such figures as the Jiyuto leader Goto Shojiro, and with Ito himself.[29] Mitsui, it will be recalled, had put

[26] See Takahashi Kamekichi (ed.), *Nihon concern zenshu* (*Collected Works on Japanese Concerns*), Vol. II: *Mitsui*, Tokyo, 1937.

[27] Evidence indicates that it was Inoue's warning to Mitsui ahead of time that the government was going to demand security on its banking deposits which enabled the firm to save itself from bankruptcy during the panic of 1874; this fate befell its colleagues, Ono and Shimada, which concerns had no advance notice and had expanded their enterprises too greatly. See Takahashi Kamekichi and Aoyoma, *op. cit.*, p. 50.

[28] Inoue played an important part in persuading the House of Mitsui to make changes in its organization; the traditional tight control of the family was relaxed, and a system of "*banto* administration" vesting considerable power in the hands of *banto* (managers) was inaugurated. In its initial stages, the system enabled government leaders to sponsor bright young men for key posts.

[29] In the early Meiji period Goto had sold his mining interests to Mitsui for a sum great enough to make him very wealthy. Also, Mitsui had lent certain Sat-Cho leaders substantial sums of money and then had written many of these loans off as "gifts." When a new general manager, Nakamigawa Hikojiro (who had been recommended by Inoue), tried to stop this practice in the early 1890's, he ran into great difficulties. He actually went as far as to threaten to attach the property of Katsura, and he refused to make a loan to Ito, thereby incurring official wrath. Nakamigawa's early death brought to a close the career of one of the most able and liberal early industrialists; undoubtedly the fact that he was the nephew of Fukuzawa Yukichi had much to do with his philosophy and administrative tactics.

up the money for the European trip of Itagaki and Goto in 1882, at the request of Inoue and Goto. The Jiyuto attack upon Mitsubishi did not include a similar assault upon Mitsui. In view of such prior connections, upon the formation of the Seiyukai, which united Ito and the civil faction of the bureaucracy with the Jiyuto, it was natural for Mitsui to become closely associated with the new party. Through such men as Yamamoto Teijiro, originally president of the Taiwan Sugar Company (a Mitsui subsidiary) and subsequently a Seiyukai leader, the Seiyukai-Mitsui relationship became very strong.

Mitsui, however, was but one of a number of industrial companies that had contacts with government and party leaders which helped to bring various elements of the two groups together. The friendships of the Furukawa family, whose chief interests were in mining, were another excellent illustration. Contacts centered at first in and about Mutsu Munemitsu, later Foreign Minister in the Ito cabinet of 1892–1896, and, to a somewhat lesser extent, were made through Inoue and Ito. The growing intimacy between Mutsu and Hoshi Toru, Jiyuto leader, seems to have been connected with the Furukawa relationship, and through Mutsu, Hara Takashi, then a Foreign Office official, attained a close affiliation with the Furukawa interests. In 1905 Hara became one of the four top directors of the Furukawa Mining Company, acting simultaneously as a chief aide to Ito in the Seiyukai.[30]

If Mitsui and Furukawa, among others, helped to bridge the gap between the Ito group and certain Jiyuto leaders,[31] Mitsubishi had a similar connection, in the relationships between Okuma's party and the Satsuma faction, especially Matsukata. The personal ties between Okuma and Iwasaki Yataro, founder of the House of Mitsubishi, have already been noted. When Iwasaki Yataro died, in 1885, his younger brother, Yanosuke, took over the Mitsubishi interests. Under his aegis the alliance between Okuma and Matsukata was facilitated, the two men actually meeting at his home. When this alliance collapsed, Mitsubishi was constantly available to support a political group which would counterbálance the Seiyu-

[30] For a picture of the Furukawa political connections, see Takahashi Kamekichi (ed.), op. cit., Vol. IX: Furukawa; also Huggins, op. cit., Vol. X: The Furukawa Interests.

[31] There is no evidence to suggest that Itagaki had any personal attachments to Mitsui or Furukawa, but he had resigned from his party before the formation of the Seiyukai. Hoshi became the chief party leader not long after the beginning of the parliamentary era, and Goto still had many followers within the party.

kai-Mitsui group. Mitsubishi, through its remarkable "foreign minister," Toyokawa Ryohei, was probably the most active politically of any of the industrial elements. It has been commonly alleged, though usually without any evidence being offered, that Mitsubishi money was behind both the Boshin Club and the Kokuminto, and that sizable funds were given to such individuals as Okuma, Inukai, and Oishi.[32] It is clear that later Mitsubishi figured in the Rikken Doshikai, the party formed by Katsura which included strong bureaucratic as well as "pure party" elements; it will be recalled that Kato Takaakira, the younger Iwasaki's son-in-law, became president of the new party after Katsura's early death.

Thus by the time of forming the Doshikai, which event occurred somewhat later than the period under present discussion, lines were clearly drawn between the Seiyukai-Mitsui-Furukawa-Sumitomo [33] "alliance" and that of the Doshikai and Mitsubishi. Although our description has dealt only with the large industrial interests and the most important political leaders, there are indications that the same process was operating equally well at lower levels. The general harmonization of the parties and the bureaucracy had been greatly facilitated by a large proportion of the business community. In performing this function, the industrial-commercial elements were cognizant of the need to strengthen their position against the "antibusiness" forces still present in government and in the country. Considering the status of Japanese capitalism at that time—its personnel, structure, dependency upon governmental support, and inextricable connections with administrative fiscal and economic plans—their policy was eminently logical. The business stake in democracy was quite insufficient to motivate any strong efforts on the part of business to clarify democratic lines and forces. For the most part, business was in a weak position during this period, still fighting the battle against traditional "anticommercialism" and struggling to survive in a world containing industrial giants, and in such a situation it was important to avoid making enemies and to cultivate coalitions with power.

Implicit in these circumstances, moreover, was something more than the philosophic deviation of the parties; there was also the

---

[32] See, for instance, Tagawa Daikichiro, in the symposium, "Rich Men Connected with Politics Today," as summarized in JC, July 16, 1910, p. 90.

[33] Sumitomo was connected with the Seiyukai through the fact that its president, Baron Sumitomo Kizaemon, was the brother of Saionji; Yasuda also, though less connected with politics, was counted in the Seiyukai camp.

personal corruption engendered in this type of business-political relations. Such big *"seisho"* (political merchants) as the so-called "zaibatsu" were constantly making personal gifts to party leaders and high government officials, wholly apart from the large campaign donations which were given before each election. One reason why well-placed gifts were more effective than they might otherwise have been was that the leaders held strong controls over their followers. However, corruption was not confined to the zaibatsu and political leaders by any means; it ran the whole gamut of business and politics.[34] Nor, again, did the initiative in cases of corruption always rest with the business community; on the contrary, there were many instances in which politicians—both government officials and party members—collected a forced draft from businessmen and used it for personal purposes or to bribe legislative representatives. Still, far too few elements of the business world —large or small—were immune from following a course that was in conformity with past tradition and present circumstances.

Certain of the major scandals involving business and the parties are worth investigating, to note the pattern which they took and the scope of their operation. One of the first big scandals to be made fully known was the Greater Japan Sugar Refining Company Scandal of 1907–1908.[35] In brief, the story behind this case was that in order to cover up frauds, the directorship of the company bribed a number of Diet members so as to secure the passage of a bill making sugar a state monopoly. It was hoped that the government would buy the companies at an exorbitant price. The bill did not pass, and in the disclosures which followed, sixteen members of the Diet and three ex-members were indicted, along with six directors of the company. Of the Diet members and ex-members, twelve belonged to the Seiyukai, five to the Kenseihonto, and two were members of the Daido Club; thus every major party was represented, and in fair proportion to its voting strength. A total of ¥79,300 was dispersed, some of it presumably destined to go to other Diet members.[36]

This particular scandal happened to be revealed rather fully

---

[34] The problem of personal corruption in business-political relations is of course not peculiar to the Far East. Recent research on the nineteenth-century United States, for instance, would indicate far closer parallels with the Japanese situation than has generally been assumed; nor can contemporary evidence be ignored.

[35] For details of this case, see *JM*, April 24, 1909, pp. 530–531; May 1, 1909, p. 562; and May 15, 1909, p. 636.

[36] *Ibid.*, May 15, 1909, p. 637.

because of the failure of the bribery attempts and the revelation of company books. There is no reason to suppose, however, that corruption on such a scale was uncommon. The press was full of accounts of shady dealings year after year.[37] Undoubtedly some of these reports were unfounded or were grossly exaggerated to serve political purposes, but so great was the cumulative evidence that all reports gained some credence. And this was already having a devastating effect upon the attitude of the public toward the parties and party leaders. Hoshi Toru, for instance, had long been accused publicly of the most corrupt practices on behalf of the Seiyukai and himself. When he was assassinated, on June 21, 1901, his slayer wrote a letter of explanation of which the following is a part:

I have up to recently had no personal acquaintance with Mr. Hoshi Toru, neither do I bear any personal enmity or ill-feeling towards him. . . . I came to know Mr. Hoshi Toru for the first time when he was appointed Chairman of the Society [Tokyo City Educational Society]. His arbitrary and dishonest dealing and behavior as Chairman of the Society disgusted me so much that I deemed it dishonourable even to discuss with him the sacred educational affairs, and I shortly afterwards resigned from the Society . . .
This old rogue, Hoshi Toru, has, as was expected, disorganized and corrupted the municipal administration of the city of Tokyo and has caused a degeneration in the moral character of the people of the city. While holding the honourable office [Chairman of the Tokyo Municipal Assembly] which requires him to protect the city against the misconduct or dishonesty of its servants, he has dared to commit the most ignoble

---

[37] One purported scandal given wide publicity was in connection with railroad nationalization. In 1900, when the nationalization of the railroads was being considered, Okuma's paper, the *Hochi Shimbun*, charged that the Jiyuto leaders demanded ¥1 per share of stock for having urged the government to introduce the bill, on the grounds that the stock would rise ¥3 per share on the average and that they were entitled to one-third of the profits. According to *Hochi*, the businessmen refused to meet these terms. At any rate, the bill did not pass. *Hochi Shimbun* reports, quoted in *KC*, February 21, 1900, p. 158.
Whether this report is true is uncertain, but it is very much in line with similar incidents reported from a variety of sources. Actually, of course, Okuma's party was very much opposed to railroad nationalization, in accord with the opposition of Mitsubishi, which owned important lines and did not want to sell them. When the railroads were finally nationalized under the Saionji administration in 1908, for military and economic reasons, Kato, Iwasaki's son-in-law, resigned his post as Foreign Minister in protest. The railroads were purchased at a handsome price, however, and were paid for in 5 per cent bonds; therefore many of the small companies were not unhappy.

crime of receiving bribes, and thus has caused disgrace to the nation, from His Majesty the Emperor down to the mass of the people.[38]

In this case, as in others which were to follow, much of the press and public sentiment was more generous to the assassin than to his victim. A frequent reaction was that a degenerate political leader had met with his proper fate.

Just one year before the Sugar Case, another incident occurred which illustrated the general acceptance of bribery by small businessmen as well as large. A law on the statute books at the time provided that if an urban or rural community desired to have a public slaughterhouse it could order the closing of any private slaughterhouse with reasonable notice. The owners of four private slaughterhouses, worried by this prospect, prepared a petition to the chairman of the Petitions Committee of the Diet (a Seiyukai man) and accompanied it with ¥2,000, promising an additional ¥2,000 if the bill were changed. When the facts were revealed, the chairman was committed to trial and convicted.[39]

It would be quite unfair to leave the impression that corruption was largely confined to the party men in politics. We have already noted the multifarious ways in which oligarchic leaders obtained personal funds from the capitalist class; whether it was by outright monetary bribery, shares in the company, or loans written off, they received sizable benefits. Moreover, this procedure on a lesser scale was prevalent in the subordinate bureaucracy as well. Such exposés as the Textbook Scandal,[40] which brought the arrest of some one hundred and fifty persons, ranging from lowly examiners of texts to prefectural governors, served to illustrate how widespread corruption was in the bureaucracy. Later, when the Navy Scandal of the Yamamoto ministry was revealed in 1914—a case

---

[38] Quoted from letter of Iba Sotaro to *Nippon,* translated in *KC,* June 26, 1901, pp. 581–582. Iba Sotaro, Hoshi's assassin, was not a complete unknown; he had formerly been president of a small college, Tokyo Agricultural College, adviser to a bank, and holder of several honorary posts, and was a member—to use his own words—of a house "engaged in' teaching military arts."

This case is interesting because Iba, as a man with an agrarian and military background, emerges as a type revealing in some measure the "rural-urban" conflict; and this event, even in terms of the personalities involved, shows a striking similarity to the climactic events of the 1930's.

[39] For reports on the Slaughterhouse Case, see *JM,* June 20, 1906, p. 95.

[40] For a report on this case, which occurred in 1903, see *JC,* March 18, 1903, p. 233. A number of officials in the Department of Agriculture and Commerce were arrested at the same time.

involving some of the highest naval officers in the country [41]—it became clear that almost no segment of the Japanese bureaucracy was free from guilt. Other involvements, however, did not serve to lessen the onus of party corruption; indeed, they seem to have heightened the growing demands that all the current political groups be cleansed or swept away.

Thus, in the period ending about the time of the Russo-Japanese War, three tendencies in the early capitalist impact upon Japanese politics and parties can be noted. Clearly, the new business community was serving as a unifying force for party-bureaucratic alliances. If these were generally alliances which combined the more "enlightened" or "probusiness" officials with similar elements in the parties, still, they produced basic perversions of liberal philosophy and action, as has been noted in preceding chapters; the resulting damage to the party movement is difficult to exaggerate. Also, it was the fate of the business elements—large and small—to be cast in the role of great corruptive influences in the political scene. Although the worst in this respect was probably yet to come, even at this point, political corruption touched every major party and many party leaders, as well as many groups within the bureaucracy. Finally, the influence which business was having on the general tenor of Japanese politics was as much the product of its weakness as of its strength. During this period the Japanese business world took a relatively limited part in political activities as a whole, and one characterized chiefly by indifference and inaction, together with a general attitude of subserviency. Concentrating upon other tasks, operating under traditional handicaps, and greatly dependent upon the government, business was, as a rule, exceedingly careful to shun the political limelight. By the end of the period, however, there were signs that some changes were occurring in the political status and activities of the business elements. A somewhat greater degree of self-confidence was creeping into the psychology of the industrial-commercial class. It was being stimulated by the writings of such men as Fukuzawa, Shibuzawa, and other progressive spokesmen for commercialism. Fukuzawa, in decrying the prevalent attitude toward business, proclaimed that although wealth had connoted no advantage to the country in the period of isolation, now combined capital was like an army of

---

[41] This affair was reported to have involved Mitsui also—Mitsui was alleged to have obtained £75,000 in English currency illegally. This amount was given to charity by the firm to appease public sentiment. See *ibid.*, March 27, 1918, p. 482.

soldiers, fighting the nation's commercial battles and benefiting all.[42] Shibuzawa echoed this theme, demanding that the business class abandon its servile attitude and fight for its just rights.[43] Nor was he content with words; as a leading financier-industrialist, he helped to lead the newly organized Japanese Chamber of Commerce in its battles to abolish the export tax on cotton thread, the import tax on raw cotton, and, after the Russo-Japanese War, to reduce military expenditures.[44] The rising influence of business was exemplified by an increasing number of incidents between 1896 and 1908; the fall of the Saionji cabinet in 1908 was due in large part to business opposition to government fiscal and administrative policies. Perhaps an article appearing in the September, 1896, issue of *Taiyo*, a leading Japanese magazine, best reveals certain aspects of the transition then getting under way. The following is a rather lengthy excerpt:

Up to the present in our country, the customs bequeathed from feudalism have not yet been completely driven out of the heads of the people. The officials of the government are considered men of high esteem; the private entrepreneurs are men looked down upon. Even in private banquets where there should be an equality of relations, the officials sit at the head and act arrogantly and the people use humble speech and bow their heads before them, even the powerful entrepreneurs. If this after all is only caused by frequent situations where they rush with a servile heart to do things, depending upon the government, engaged in profits, and seeking out the pleasure of everyday officials, still, compared with conditions in the countries of Europe and America where government policy is first of all determined in accordance with the advantage of commerce and industry, and officials seek the pleasure of business men, there is the difference between clouds and mud.

But recently even the business men of our country have by degrees

---

[42] From *Fukuzawa Yukichi zenshu* (*The Collected Works of Fukuzawa Yukichi*), Vol. IX, pp. 193–194; I am indebted for this citation to Takahashi Kamekichi and Aoyama, *op. cit.*

[43] Fukuzawa and Shibuzawa were both uncommon examples of men whose creed closely approximated the creed of the Western business class. As early as 1871, Shibuzawa wrote: "The path of commerce must not be blocked by the authority of government or bound by legislation. . . . If the position and influence of the industrialist cannot easily produce a change on the part of the politician, true development cannot be expected." Quoted in Tsuchiya, *Nihon shihonshugi shijo no shidoshatachi*, p. 117.

Irritated by the indifference and subserviency of businessmen, Shibuzawa was constantly exhorting his colleagues to throw off their shackles and be heard. For other examples, see Koda Rohan, *Shibuzawa Eiichi den* (*Biography of Shibuzawa Eiichi*), Tokyo, 1939.

[44] Tsuchiya, *Nihon shihonshugi shijo no shidoshatachi*, p. 120.

advanced their position and have sought to influence by their attitude the position of the politicians. Actually in the present Cabinet change [the resignation of the Ito Cabinet and the establishment of the Matsu-kata Cabinet] the strength of the business men contributed greatly. One should note that the main reason for the resignation of Finance Minister Watanabe was that in attempting to raise a loan of ten million yen, scarcely three million could be obtained, and this failure was a central factor. The business world of that time certainly had the power to negotiate a ten million yen loan, but unlike men of reputation such as Count Matsukata who had hitherto consulted with business men secretly respecting [the possibility of] resignation before the announce-ment of a loan flotation and depended upon subscription, Watanabe with his sudden independent announcement attempting to collect this, caused many to be ill disposed, and the fact that he lost popular support and consequently exposed a lack of confidence in the government in such a manner as this approached a display of mismanagement. How-ever, the canvassing of Matsukata for entry into the Cabinet was made necessary not only by the particular matter of Mr. Watanabe's resigna-tion but in the general fact that large industry of the post-war adminis-tration required men of reputation in the Finance Ministry and if there were not to be men sincerely trusted by the business group, it has been realized that governmental affairs cannot be conducted.[45]

The trend which *Taiyo* discerned even at this early date was greatly advanced by the events following the Russo-Japanese War. Again, a brief survey of general economic developments will pro-vide a partial setting for a discussion of the growing political in-fluence of Japanese capitalism. It is probably no exaggeration to say that the period from 1905 to 1920 marked the real transition in Japan from an agrarian to an industry-centered economy.[46] Con-tributions to this development were many. The Russo-Japanese War aided the general expansion of the Japanese economy and the creation of great amounts of new enterprise capital directly and indirectly. Large domestic and foreign loans were contracted by the government, and foreign investments in Japanese industry were encouraged. Supported by additional capital, industry rap-idly improved its techniques. Especially important were the ad-vances made in the development and use of hydroelectric power as a substitute for steam. The postwar period witnessed a continued expansion of commercial markets, particularly Asian markets. The year 1911 marked an end to the unequal treaties, and industry ob-

---

[45] From *Taiyo,* as quoted in Takahashi Kamekichi and Aoyama, *op. cit.,* pp. 122–123.

[46] See Horie, *op. cit.,* pp. 245–251.

tained additional protection and support from legislation passed before and during this time, laws designed to strengthen and expand the industrial base. It was the First World War, however, that produced the phenomenal increases in light and heavy industry. While Europe was spending her man power and her productive facilities, Japanese industry was expanding with a rapidity that enabled it to keep up with the lucrative foreign trade and make the most of its opportunity to meet domestic consumption demands now cut off from important foreign sources. Unprecedented business prosperity produced a surplus of investment capital, which flowed not only into channels of expansion and modernization, but also into landed investments.

There are many indices to the economic power that was being developed by industry during the period. The following chart high-lights some of the important facts:

CHART ON JAPANESE INDUSTRIAL DEVELOPMENT
1905 TO 1920 [47]

Year	No. of industrial companies	Capital assets in 100,000 yen	Proportion of assets, in per cent of total Japanese company assets *	No. of factories **	Per cent using power	No. of workers **
1905	2,449	189	19.4	9,776	44.3	587,851
1908	3,065	441	36.3	11,390	49.3	649,676
1911	3,921	629	40.6	14,228	54.5	793,885
1914	5,266	833	40.3	17,062	60.6	853,964
1917	6,677	1,156	36.4	20,966	68.2	1,280,964
1920	11,829	3,057	37.5	45,806	65.2	1,486,442

* Does not include banks, other financial institutions.
** Factories employing more than ten workers.

This chart, of course, does not present a complete picture, and certain factors not revealed here should be mentioned. The most spectacular rises were occurring in the field of heavy industry: the shipbuilding, iron-and-steel, chemical, and machine-tool industries, as well as others in this category, were challenging light industry for supremacy. Naturally, banks, insurance companies, and financial institutions in general were enjoying great expansion. As for structure, although the industrial-commercial base was being broadened in many respects, with a new generation of *narikin* (newly rich) arising and with many small businesses being established, still, the scale of big industry was being enlarged, and concentrated controls in many fields were developing.[48] In comparison

---

[47] Table taken from *ibid.*, p. 250.
[48] The proportion of workers in factories employing fifty or more increased

269

with agrarian productivity, industrial productivity was now clearly superior,[49] and, as has been mentioned, urban capital was making itself increasingly felt in land and land-enterprise investments.

Under these circumstances it was natural that the political power and influence of the business community would spurt forward. Connected with the growth of the economic position of business was an increasing awareness of importance and authority; higher education, especially when obtained abroad, was nurturing these feelings. Moreover, the walls of agrarian supremacy were cracking wide open, and the political pressure of even its strongest representatives was showing less potency. In addition, Western science and technology were now making profound impressions upon nearly the whole of Japanese society. That this was the age of technology had never been clearer than in the crucial years of World War I; a greater acceptance of industrialization and a glorification of its accomplishments in Japan strengthened the prestige and influence of its leaders.

The future of Japanese democracy and of the party movement, however, was connected with the degree to which increased business power would be used on behalf of democratic theory and practice, as well as with the capacity which Japanese capitalism could show for coping with the problems of its society. It has been a favorite thesis among some Japanese and Western writers that the Japanese business class in this new period took up the cudgels vigorously for liberalism and led the struggle for Western-style democracy until overwhelmed by other forces. The evidence already presented should cast some doubt upon this concept; at the same time, however, one must recognize the substantial transition taking place in the position, prestige, and power of the business elements, portending possible changes in their political role.

---

from 56 per cent in 1909 to 64 per cent in 1920; the capacity of small and medium business to remain important in production, according to Takahashi, was based on the relative scarcity of capital in Japan, advantages in certain fields due to production techniques, markets, and raw materials, cheap hydroelectric power, and cheap labor. See Takahashi Kamekichi, *Nihon kogyo hatten ron*, pp. 58–59. In the vital field of domestic necessities, however, large-scale industry predominated and competition narrowed; moreover, the financial institutions that governed much of the small and medium business potentialities were also becoming increasingly concentrated.

[49] Whereas agrarian production value rose from ¥1,401,210,000 in 1914 to ¥3,420,400,000 in 1921, industrial production values spurted up from ¥1,371,600,000 to ¥5,978,400,000 in the same period. Horie, *op. cit.*, p. 251.

Actually, the thesis mentioned above, like most powerful myths, has within it certain elements of truth. With the possible exception of the "intellectuals," business as a class was of all Japanese groups the one that knew most about Western democracy and was most sympathetic toward it. Education and, in many cases, international contacts and interests, developed in business circles a strong cosmopolitan sense and an awareness of the philosophic proclivities of the West. The period around the First World War was one characterized by the rise of democratic sentiment everywhere. And the restraints inherent in Japanese paternalism became somewhat more irritating to men of the business world as their sense of power increased. Especially when government threatened to engage in activities which they considered injurious to their interests did the industrial-commercial groups protest with increasing vigor. Incipient in this resistance was an element of laissez faire, which in similar forms had gone hand in hand with nineteenth-century democracy. Indeed, concomitant with this protest in Japan was a drive for greater recognition and representation, reflective in some degree of Western democratic trends, and one of its most logical means of expression was through the parties; there can be no doubt that the party movement found growing support during this period from important segments of business.[50]

When all this has been said, however, it must be emphasized that the forces counteracting this tendency were even more compelling. Not even in the "new era" did the nearest Japanese equivalents to the Western middle class find it possible, as a group, to accept the basic tenets of democracy without major equivocation. The growth of the democratic creed among members of this class was stifled, not merely because of a background of hostile traditions, but also because of the contemporary forces which sustained that background, in logical conformity with current needs. Thus the dominant political philosophy of the modern Japanese business class was an organic theory of state. It was this concept which showed through in its theory of representation, one that continued to center in the idea of the integration of parties, bureaucracy, and Emperor. Here was not only a theory which encouraged irresponsibility, but one which could never remove Japanese politics far from the shadow of authoritarianism. The organic premise also colored any appreciation of individual dignity and rights, es-

---

[50] The structure of the major parties by this period must be kept in mind, however.

tablishing as it did a primacy of state power and authority. At the same time, it contributed to the expression of personal interests through subterranean channels, symbolizing the lack of a philosophy which would give adequate ethical support to the open expression of individual or group interests. In the absence of a theory which would recognize the legitimacy of private interests, there was a compulsion on the part of the business class to protect and advance its interests secretly, with minimal resort to open political action or democratic procedures. This in turn tended to produce in the class as a whole a schizophrenic approach to the very concept of democracy, and on occasion a personal guilt complex which later helped to create many cases of recantation of Westernism. In some individuals the conflict was very intense, with all the overtones of tragedy and pathos.

A more detailed explanation of the forces that caused this philosophic dilemma, with particular emphasis on their mature forms, is necessary. Of greatest importance was the evolution of Japanese capitalism. Even when capitalism in Japan reached the stage of its greatest power before World War II and seemed to have captured the commanding heights of Japanese society, it continued to suffer from a sense of great insecurity, and one derivative in part from logical economic grounds. With the extraordinary expansion of industry there loomed up the haunting specter of an artificiality incapable of being sustained by the nature of the domestic market or "normal" foreign trade conditions. In considerable measure Japanese production had been the creature of state necessities or state-projected goals, and in the very rapidity and nature of its growth it tended to be divorced from the assimilative capacities of its society.

The wedding of state power and Western technology had not only drastically affected the structural forms of Japanese capitalism, but had also fashioned a productive machine that could easily run rampant in a society in which conditions suitable for bringing the domestic consumption market into line with productive capacities did not exist. Given the extreme political unbalance in Japanese society itself, there was no forceful pressure to readjust serious economic inequities and broaden the internal market. Moreover, the rising standards, which might in any case have been expected in some degree, were severely restricted by the host of problems connected with population rises out of all proportion to land area. Hence, even in the era of its greatest glory, Japanese business was acutely aware of its fundamental weaknesses, and consequently of its continued dependency, in the broadest sense, on governmental power and policy. That by now it was a vital part of government itself did not change this psychology. To be sure, there were differences in attitude, as between the *nouveaux riches* and the established zaibatsu, for instance. The former were more dependent upon government, and the latter more interdependent with it, and this created some difference in their respective political attitudes and actions. In the final analysis, however, this fact could not be significant, for, given the nature of the threats and pressures, the emphasis had to be on the supremacy and unity of the state.

Thus, in terms of democratic theory, the Japanese business groups could neither follow the historic Western route of laissez faire nor hew out a different pathway suitable to the circumstances of twentieth-century Japanese society. The latter procedure would have required a more delicate balance of competing forces than was existent in modern Japan; in the very ingredients of overwhelming success lay the materials which precluded the business community from groping its way to the "open society.".

There was also the omnipresent force of nationalism, which rushed like an angry torrent throughout the whole of Japanese society, checked on occasion but never stilled. The fierce determination to create unity out of conflict, stability out of tension, and build a state which would secure recognition and respect was firmly implanted and encouraged by every resource at the command of the state. In greater or lesser degree, the business elements, like all other groups within Japan, were motivated by this basic drive; in it they found a measure of security not obtainable elsewhere, some refuge from attacks, and, in certain of its forms, a useful handy maid to economic-political interests. Although never unmindful of the traditional anticommercial biases implicit in Japanese nationalist doctrines, the business groups assimilated nationalism in ways which helped to sustain their organic theory and remove them further from the democratic philosophy.

These were the central forces which produced the philosophy and actions of the Japanese business community. By 1920, industrial-commercial interests occupied an important political position in the ranks of the major parties and in the bureaucracy. And, of course, they could not avoid coming into conflict with hostile forces, in spite of the organic theories to which they were basically dedicated. The paradox between the ideals of absolute unity in Japan and the realities of vital differences within the nation could become less critical only by the application of over-whelming power or the revitalization of Japanese institutions. Neither of these remedies was used effectively during the 1920's, and this fact is, in a sense, the keynote of the era. Certain of the prerequisites of a democratic society, such as freedom of speech and freedom of the press, were advanced to some degree, and indeed there was in many different facets of Japanese society a reflection of Western democratic trends. Yet these forces could only move erratically and with dubious symbolism, for they had neither sufficient law nor adequate philosophy on their side. Without legal safeguards, who could draw distinctions between anarchy and freedom, subversion and rights? If nine hundred examples of free expression were allowed to pass, but the nine-hundred-and-first was adjudged dangerous under the statute books, who could measure with certainty the progress being made? Freedom was not to be secured by laxity, however much that laxity might be due to indecision and doubt. And the failure to institutionalize freedom more fully, although it could be blamed in part on the rise of Japanese Communism, was traceable chiefly to the very great philosophic barriers erected in the minds of the Japanese elites, economic and political barriers that were motivated and made effective by the general status of these groups and that of their society.

Thus the specific emphases of the political activity of businessmen during this period were placed on promoting "probusiness" policies, on resisting agrarian and military elements when their own position seemed threatened, and on opposing any broad social change or reform. In connection with the second emphasis, however, it should be noted that compromise or actual union was not uncommon, the product variously of fear, indecision, or choice. In no case did these policies, however natural, necessarily advance the frontiers of Japanese democracy; many retarded it. And in addition to this expanded role in the active political theater, all the backstage maneuvering characteristic of Japanese political behavior continued, and the flow of money to parties, individual politicians, and public officials became staggering in its volume and scope. Thus the years of "party government" produced in the public mind a picture of callous disregard for the needs of the lower classes and of a continuous series of scandals dwarfing the prior disclosures of corruption, without successfully establishing the major philosophic premises of democracy.

Before detailing some of these developments, it is proper to set forth briefly a final interrelated aspect of the period. That there was good reason for the insecurity felt by Japanese business was shown by the trends after 1920. The prolonged depression which followed reflected all the weaknesses of the prewar capitalist structure in Japan and produced one crisis after another. Large segments of the Japanese populace were made destitute, especially among the urban labor and small farmer groups. Almost the whole of Japanese agriculture faced bankruptcy. Attempted corrective measures followed a zigzag pattern and were hopelessly inadequate; ameliorative action for the desperate was pitifully weak. The result was the great social unrest which, without being completely galvanized, made possible the overthrow of the old parties with relative ease. That this deterioration was connected with world developments impossible to control made it none the less disastrous to the prestige of the status quo ·in Japan, and indeed parallel Western experiences provided new stimuli in ideas and actions. These facts must also be accorded an important place in an estimate of the total impact of Japanese capitalism upon the party movement.

Many of the factors mentioned above can be noted in the first party cabinet, that of the "Great Commoner," Hara Takashi. When the Hara Seiyukai ministry took power in September, 1918, the wartime boom was in full swing, and despite the unrest produced in some circles by inflation, Japan was to enjoy a period of unprecedented prosperity for nearly two years. The end of the war, however, signaled the dangers ahead; the vast program of expansion initiated by wartime opportunities was far from completed when peace suddenly struck. Under the leadership of Finance Minister Takahashi, the Hara ministry pledged itself to support the continued expansion of capital investment and production.[51] Takahashi showed no great fear of inflation, believing it to be a natural sign of an expanding economy. The extent to which it developed in the period immediately after the war, however, affected foreign markets even more quickly than might otherwise have been the case and also further diminished the consumer market at home. With production growth continuing despite shrinking markets, a crisis was at hand, and in March, 1920, the bubble

---

[51] For a background of Takahashi's economic theories and a sympathetic discussion of his general leadership during this period, see the section entitled "Takahashi Korekiyo" in Tsuchiya, *Nihon shihonshugi shijo no shido-shatachi*, pp. 75–104.

burst.[52] Prices and stocks fell as much as one-half, and thousands of business concerns faced bankruptcy. The Hara administration quickly plunged into large relief measures directed toward salvaging urban and provincial enterprise. This so-called "positive" policy had as its objectives maintaining the expanded economy to the fullest extent possible, by temporary artificial stimulation, and the simultaneous encouragement of a "rationalization" of industry so as to increase its efficiency and coördination. Even before the crisis, Seiyukai economic spokesmen had urged greater amalgamations in the interests of efficiency. The substantial position of small and medium industry in the productive picture was a cause of great concern. Note the following remarks of Yamamoto, Minister of Commerce and Agriculture, on May 6, 1919:

Hitherto the industrial system of our country has not been upon a large scale, but many small factories have been scattered here and there, and the lack of uniformity of their output has been the object of constant complaint. In such circumstances it is very difficult for us to succeed in economic competition with those States in Europe and America which are equipped with factories on a large scale. The Government, therefore, thinks it to be an urgent necessity to accelerate the tendency towards amalgamation of enterprises on the present occasion.[53]

The concentration of financial and industrial controls was greatly speeded up after 1920, spurred on by general economic conditions and government policy.[54] The political repercussions of this development were naturally far-reaching. Meanwhile, however, business relief measures were operating on an increasing scale, and to some extent at cross-purposes with the "rationalization" efforts.[55] The formation of the Imperial Silk Company was a good example of one type of government aid devised for the purpose of tying agrarian and business relief together. This joint-stock company was set up in 1921 to hold the market price of silk yarn at the 1920 level by purchasing and storing silk as might be deemed necessary. The government agreed to make good any deficit when loans ob-

---

[52] Among other accounts of this period, see Takahashi Kamekichi, *Nihon kogyo hatten ron,* pp. 46 ff.

[53] Speech of Yamamoto Tatsuo to prefectural governors' council, Tokyo, May 6, 1919, as reported in *JC,* May 22, 1919, p. 776. See pages 269–270, note 48.

[54] For examples, see Horie, *op. cit.,* pp. 258–262.

[55] Takahashi blames the government relief projects of the early 1920's for delaying the removal of inefficient and "surplus" companies and assets, consequently helping to produce the 1927 crisis noted below. Company managers thought less about efficiency and cost curtailment than about subsidization, he states. See Takahashi Kamekichi, *Nihon kogyo hatten ron,* pp. 52–53.

tained by the company from the banks were due. One problem with this type of support was that by such means commodity prices were kept abnormally high after unemployment, a decreased demand for funds, and a general tightening of the money market had already begun, thus increasing the hardships of the lower classes at home and further inhibiting foreign trade.[56] The "positive" policy of the Hara ministry, however, did not extend to any basic social, labor, or farm-tenant legislation. The growing trade unions, still under the heavy restrictions of the old Peace Preservation Law, were requesting sympathetic legislation. Although a very conservative law legalizing moderate union activities was proposed by a special investigating committee, the measure was not brought up for a vote.[57] The only positive actions of the ministry centered around a government-sponsored organization known as the *Kyochokai* (Conciliation Society). Home Minister Tokonami explained its purpose as follows:

The *Kyochokai* aims at the study and consummation of social policy, and at the harmonious coöperation between capital and labour. . . . The Government has entrusted to it the important task of acting as the central organ for the public employment agencies throughout the country, in order to effect their unity and coöperation. The *Kyochokai* will make a thorough and extensive study of all social enterprises at home and abroad. In view of the worthy objects it has in mind, the Government has decided to give a subsidy to the organization in order to assist the attainment of its objects. It is my desire that you will afford every facility to the work of the organization so that it may reap the desired fruit.[58]

Toward the agrarian groups the Seiyukai administration was naturally more solicitous, but this concern did not produce any legislation at the tenant level worthy of consideration. And from all agrarian groups the Hara administration received a considerable amount of criticism. Bitterness ran particularly high, for instance,

---

[56] For a trenchant contemporary criticism of this type of policy, see the article by Horie Kiichi which appeared in the October, 1920, *Taiyo*, translated and paraphrased in *JC*, October 28, 1920, p. 600.

[57] See Azuma Mitsutoshi, *Rodo ho* (*Labor Law*), Tokyo, 1950, p. 17.

[58] Speech of Home Minister Tokonami Takejiro at the prefectural governors' conference, Tokyo, July 22, 1920, reported in *JC*, September 30, 1920, p. 456. It should be noted, moreover, that the attitude of the Home Ministry was considerably more liberal than that of the Ministry of Agriculture and Commerce toward improvements in labor legislation. The 1920 bill which was shelved was a compromise, of sorts, between the two departments. See Azuma, *op. cit.*, p. 17.

over the continued importation of rice and cereals from Korea and Formosa in the face of falling agrarian prices and heavy surpluses at home. The *Teikoku Nokai* (Imperial Agricultural Society), reflective mainly of the interests of upper-class landowners, organized a nation-wide protest despite its general affiliation with the Seiyukai.[59] As for the tenant farmer, he continued to face a deteriorating situation with absolutely no protective legislation. Numerous studies of agrarian problems were undertaken, but not until 1924 was one piece of legislation pertaining to the tenant problem passed, and this only a law establishing machinery for the mediation of disputes.[60]

In the midst of grave economic problems which were already affecting political stability, charges of corruption implicating the highest political leaders were being broadcast through the Diet and the press. Postwar expansion had resulted in the mushrooming of thousands of new companies, many of which were seeking access to government funds and privileges. Charges were published openly that a large number of Diet members had been "bought up" by these new companies via high positions, shares of stock, and special privileges.[61] Hardly had these received wide circulation when Shimada Saburo (Kenseikai) leveled a double-barreled charge on the floor of the lower house. In a written interpellation, he accused three cabinet members—Takahashi, Yamamoto, and Nakahashi—of taking advantage of administration secrets to profit on the stock market.[62] He went on to remark: "It is also stated that of a total of over 5,500 companies with a capital of over a million yen established from September last year up to February last, *Seiyukai* members are closely connected with no less than 4,500." [63]

The ministers of course denied all charges, and little proof was offered except in the case of Nakahashi.[64] Nakahashi's retort

---

[59] Ono Takeo, *Kindai Nihon noson hattatsu shiron* (*An Historical Treatise on Modern Japanese Rural Development*), Tokyo, 1950, pp. 160–161.

[60] *Ibid.*, p. 161. The overwhelming representation, in the Diet, of landowners from the rural districts made tenant legislation extremely difficult.

[61] For a general discussion of this development, see Takahashi Kamekichi, *Nihon kogyo hatten ron*, pp. 52–53.

[62] Written interpellation of Shimada Saburo, House of Representatives, July 26, 1920. From the House Proceedings, as reported in *JC*, July 29, 1920, p. 155.

[63] *Ibid.*, p. 159.

[64] For a brief comment on this episode, see Hara Keiichiro (ed.), *Hara Takashi nikki* (*The Diary of Hara Takashi*), Tokyo, 1950–1951, Vol. IX, pp. 17–18.

seemed rather weak; he claimed that he had purchased 770 shares of Japan Nitric Fertilizer Company stock to give to his old maid-servant; the maid was then kept incommunicado from inquiring reporters.

The South Manchurian Railway Scandal of 1921, however, was of an even more serious nature, for it threw suspicion upon the entire Seiyukai leadership. The company, the chief officials of which were appointed by the government as political patronage, was charged with purchasing the Talien colliery and a ship from the Uchida Ship Company, both at extraordinarily high prices; and it was charged that much of the money, in return, went into Seiyukai coffers as election funds.

When this scandal was at its height, the Seiyukai countered by stating that Uchida himself had given Kato, head of the Kenseikai, ¥50,000 for election expenses, on the promise that, if in power, he would oppose universal suffrage. This was the so-called *"chimpin itsutsu"* (five rare articles) affair, for Kato's letter to Uchida acknowledging receipt of the money closed by saying: "From him [Uchida's elder brother] I have accepted five rare articles [five ten-thousand-yen notes] for which I thank you most profoundly." [65]

Kato denied that he had made any pledge, and he produced a letter from Uchida which urged only that the money not be used to support "extremists." In the aura of general scandal and unrest, however, even political contributions that might have otherwise been considered legitimate were subject to serious questioning.

The combined effect of these charges [66] and of the consequences of the Seiyukai economic policy was, as might be expected, very damaging to party prestige in general and to the reputation of the Seiyukai in particular. Criticism poured in from the press, the intellectual class, the opposition parties, and the common people themselves. The refusal of the government to control prices in the early period provoked a typical comment from the *Kokumin*:

By acting as faithful servants to the rich and mushroom millionaires, as they have done so far, the Hara Ministry is really doing these classes

[65] Letter from Kato to Uchida, translated in *JC*, March 24, 1921, p. 404. This case serves to illustrate the fact that many political merchants kept their fences mended with both major parties.

[66] Speaking of party guilt, Shimada wrote, "If A has committed ten crimes and B has committed five, one can say that B's crimes are fewer than A's, but one cannot say he is not a criminal." Shimada Saburo, "Shizai o kasume kokin o oryo shi seisho to shitashimu" (Taking Private Capital, Usurping Public Money, Being Friendly with Political Merchants), *Taiyo*, May, 1921, p. 91.

a disservice and making the latter the object of enmity to the middle and propertyless classes. Forgetful of this fundamental cause of trouble, however, they are now trying little palliatives against the outward symptoms and throwing a few drops of oil into the turbulent sea of high prices. Their folly is truly pitiable.[67]

Partisan attacks were of course vehement, with the Kenseikai ripping into the administration at every level and getting wide publicity. Even though Kato's party as a whole represented the same basic philosophy, it was not averse to using the charge of Seiyukai collaboration with "the few" to win public support for itself. It is interesting to note a speech made by Professor Nagai Ryutaro, also a Kenseikai Diet member, on July 8, 1920, on the floor of the House. After discussing the necessity of harmonizing the various economic classes of the state, Nagai remarked:

If he [the Premier] fails to do this, he throws himself open to the charge that he indirectly encourages dangerous thoughts. From this point of view, Mr. Hara, the Japanese Premier, may be ranked with Mr. Lenin of Russia, as the holder of dangerous thought. It is patent that the Hara Cabinet is bent upon furthering the interests of the minority at the sacrifice of the interests of the masses of the people. The fact that a few Ministers gained illegal profits in collusion with merchants under the Government's patronage is most reprehensible and such conduct on the part of the Ministers will have a most serious effect on national ideas.[68]

As if to prove Nagai's words, a youthful radical murdered Yasuda Zenjiro, president of the Yasuda Bank, on September 28, 1921.[69] Shortly afterward, threatening letters were sent to Baron Sumitomo, head of the giant Sumitomo interests, and a bomb exploded in front of his home. Only a few months later, Hara himself was murdered. These were all signs of a greater danger which could not be met by suppression alone, as was evident from a growing public indifference or outright hostility to the major parties, caused

---

[67] *Kokumin* editorial, translated in *JC*, November 6, 1919, p. 707.

[68] Speech of Nagai Ryutaro, House of Representatives, July 8, 1920. Reported from the House Proceedings in *JC*, July 15, 1920, p. 187.

[69] The assassin of Yasuda was motivated, according to his own account, by the reading of the famous *Nihon kaizo hoan taiko* (*A General Outline of Measures for the Reconstruction of Japan*), Tokyo, 1919, by Kita Ikki, father of Japanese Fascism. (See chapter ix of the present study.) Press comment on Yasuda's murder was typified by the *Asahi* comment that it was to be hoped that this would be a warning to the wealthy. See press comments reported in *JC*, October 6, 1921, p. 520.

especially by disgust for their relations with segments of the business world.

The new premier, Takahashi, however, made no major changes in Seiyukai policy, as was to be expected since he had been Finance Minister in the Hara cabinet. He refused to consider deflating the currency by removal of the gold embargo. Meanwhile, Japan's unfavorable balance of trade was steadily draining the enormous reserves built up during the war, making ever more precarious the entire financial structure. Moreover, government expenditures continued high, the military appropriations taking a substantial part of the budget and almost none of the money going for the direct relief of the lower classes. The same general policy was followed by Takahashi's successor, Admiral Kato, whose cabinet, as we have noted, was dominated by the Seiyukai.

Because of continuous depression and because no remedies were afforded by the Seiyukai's "positive" policy, the popularity of the party ebbed further. Even the business class grew increasingly restless. One of the most interesting developments was the union of a small group of industrial capitalists into a political organization sponsored by Muto Sanji, managing director of the Kanegafuchi Spinning Mills.[70] The group, calling itself the *Jitsugyo Doshikai* (Business Fellow Thinkers' Association), organized officially in April, 1923, and dedicated itself to supporting businessmen for the Diet who would espouse its laissez-faire program. This program

---

[70] Muto himself was a tremendously dynamic person. He had many of the characteristics of the small group of Japanese who had gone the farthest down the path of Western liberalism. He had studied in America; he was a Christian (Shimada, Itagaki, Kataoka, and many other liberals either were Christians or belonged to families that had some Christian members). Equally interesting, however, was the fact that Muto had been a Mitsui man and that Mitsui stock controlled the Kanegafuchi Mills. This may seem quite remarkable, in view of Muto's words and actions.

Actually, there were elements within Mitsui and others of the well-established zaibatsu desirous of reducing or bringing to a halt the heavy contributions being made to the parties. In a sense, this was due to the fact that they now occupied a very prominent position in respect to policy formation and in the whole financial-economic structure of the nation. Having advanced from a position in which they had been obliged to supplicate authorities for favors to a far more dominant status, it was natural that they should, on occasion, grumble at the fact that they not only had assumed vast responsibilities which made the state partially dependent upon them, but were then dunned continuously for heavy contributions after some of the necessity for this, in their eyes, had disappeared. See Takahashi Kamekichi and Aoyama, *op. cit.*, pp. 22–23.

was symbolized by a letter which Muto sent to Inoue Junnosuke, Minister of Finance in the Yamamoto cabinet of 1923; the following is a section:

"Fifty years have already elapsed since the Restoration and it is now time for our business world to be emancipated from those businessmen who have constantly conspired with the Government and the Bank of Japan, and it is time for businessmen independent and self-supporting to exert themselves for the harmonization of all classes of the nation." [71]

Some 610 representatives of 124 business organizations met at the inaugural meeting, and under Muto's call to save themselves from professional politicians, they passed a program which sounded like the platform of Western business.[72] The new party, however, caused scarcely a ripple in the political tides. Though it dragged on for some years, it was never more than a minute fragment. This movement marked the only organized political attempt on the part of the commercial class to bring about a fundamental reform in the relationship of the economic and political structures of Japan, and the result revealed the formidable nature of the obstacles to be overcome.[73]

In the meantime the "transcendental" cabinets had fallen rapidly, and on June 11, 1924, Kato Takaakira became Premier, first as the leader of a coalition ministry, then as head of an all-Kenseikai cabinet. And it was this cabinet which was popularly referred to as the "Mitsubishi cabinet," for three of its members, the Premier, Foreign Minister Shidehara, and Minister of Railways Sengoku Mitsugu, were all closely affiliated with Mitsubishi.[74] The first two, as has been noted earlier, were sons-in-law of Iwasaki, and Sengoku was a former banto. Moreover, it was widely publicized

---

[71] From the second "Open Letter" sent by Muto Sanji to Finance Minister Inoue via the *Osaka Asahi*, translated in *JC*, September 21, 1922, p. 388. In his first "Open Letter," Muto wrote: "Businessmen in Japan, unlike those in America, take every opportunity to secure the protection and support of the Government. Some even boast of it as though it were a merit." *Ibid.*, p. 387.

[72] See Jitsugyo Doshikai platform in Aono Kondo, *Nihon seito hensen shi* (*A History of Changes in Japanese Parties*), Tokyo, 1935.

[73] Capitalists most interested in Muto's party were generally those whose businesses were least connected with "political merchandizing" and included some provincial entrepreneurs.

[74] For such a contemporary charge see Tagawa Daikichiro, "Mitsubishi naikaku" (The Mitsubishi Cabinet), *Taiyo*, August, 1924, pp. 48–56.

that in the elections of 1924, Mitsubishi had contributed, directly or indirectly, a tremendous sum for Kenseikai expenses.[75] Similarly, of course, the Hara and Takahashi ministries had been dubbed "Mitsui cabinets" by their critics, on much the same basis.

Though these charges had an undeniable core of truth, there was also an element of distortion and oversimplification in them. The major parties were not tied to any one industrial concern, and in the various political and economic associations representative of business pressure, the old zaibatsu actually played a less dominant role than at an earlier period.[76] The newly emerging "political merchants" often had greater need to make the proper contributions and establish the correct connections.[77] In addition, although the influence of the rural landowning class was not as great as previously, until the universal manhood suffrage election of 1928 they controlled a preponderant majority of the votes—a fact which party leaders never forgot. The Seiyukai in particular, though it had changed considerably, was still considered a heavily agrarian party; its policy was constructed around concessions to both landowner and urban business groups whenever possible.[78] Conflicts within such a policy were inevitable. Indeed, one of the reasons for the split in the Seiyukai and the emergence of the Seiyuhonto seems to have been this factor. Tokonami and the Seiyuhonto, according to one writer, represented the "rural" branch

[75] Concerning the election of 1924, the Kokumin published the following undocumented list of party election-fund contributions. The Seiyukai: Tokyo Electric Light Company—¥550,000; Godo Electric Power Company—¥350,000; Mitsui Bussan Kaisha—¥300,000; Yamamoto Jotaro (Mitsui)—¥300,000; Yamamoto Teijiro (Mitsui)—¥50,000; Takahashi—¥200,000; Uchida Shinya (Uchida Ship Company)—¥100,000; and Koizumi Sakatano—¥100,000. The Seiyuhonto: Baron Yamamoto (connected with Mitsui)—¥600,000; Nakahashi Tokugoro—¥500,000; Tokonami—¥500,000; and Uhachi—¥300,000. The Kenseikai: Kato—¥600,000; Kataoka—¥100,000; and Wakatsuki—¥100,000. Reported in JC, March 27, 1924, p. 447.

This list, even if accurate, would naturally be incomplete. Moreover, it of course does not indicate the real sources of some of the funds, because few of the individual party leaders' donations came from their own funds; Tokonami, for instance, was not a rich man, but he collected heavily from Satsuma businessmen. Kato's contributions came either directly or indirectly from Mitsubishi.

[76] See Takahashi Kamekichi and Aoyama, op. cit., pp. 31–32.

[77] See page 281, note 70.

[78] The Rice Control Law, which sought to stabilize rice prices by government purchases, and similar laws in the field of sericulture attest to this fact.

of the party, whereas Takahashi and his following were more strongly urban.[79] Urban capitalism still had to share its political influence with the agrarian propertied group.

There remained one further factor. One must not minimize the power of the civil and military bureaucracy, a power exercised both independently and through the parties; despite the inroads made by the business class into this bureaucracy, there were also "nonbusiness" and "antibusiness" elements in abundance. The spirit of "officials honored, people despised" was not dead; the low pay of the civil servants often nourished the seeds of jealousy; agrarian rather than commercial backgrounds were sometimes a basis for resentment; hatred for the supporters of the parties was prevalent; and the conflict of interests, especially as between business and the military bureaucracy, was by no means uncommon. That part of the bureaucracy which was outside the party movement, at least the groups to which these remarks best apply, formed a fairly potent source of external opposition; that part of it inside the parties acted as competitors in policy formulation.

These are only qualifying remarks, however; there can be no doubt that business exerted great influence on party policy and that the ties between the parties and certain industrial groups were exceedingly close. Public knowledge of this did not contribute to the prestige of an administration like that of the Kato Kenseikai cabinet. It was the inability of the Kenseikai to relieve prevailing economic conditions, however, which struck the most severe blow at the popularity of the party. Even under the coalition cabinet, the Kenseikai "negative" economic policy had been proclaimed as the only hope for Japan's economic ills. Finance Minister Hamaguchi, in a speech of August 14, 1924, broadly outlined his view of the problem and its solution. He said:

Japan is confronted by a grave crisis at present, financially and economically. Although more than four years have already passed since the post-war business depression set in, there is still insecurity in the financial and economic world. Industry is stagnant and trade is inactive. Furthermore, the great earthquake has considerably increased the burdens on the Government and local finances. In the meantime, the trade balance has become more and more unfavorable.[80]

---

[79] See the section written by Shiroyanagi Shuko in *Gendai Nihon shi kenkyu* (*Studies of Contemporary Japanese History*), Tokyo, 1938, p. 185.

[80] Speech of Finance Minister Hamaguchi, prefectural governors' conference, Tokyo, August 5, 1924, translated in *JC*, August 14, 1924, p. 230. Hamaguchi gave the following figures to illustrate his statements: The na-

The only solution, Hamaguchi stated, was a policy of strict governmental economy, a curtailment of the standard of living for the people, and an amalgamation of banks and industry.[81]

This policy, however, proved impossible to execute completely, politically disastrous so far as it was put into effect, and in the end a great failure. Domestic and foreign developments were now rapidly combining to produce an economic panic in Japan. From the latter part of 1925 on, industrial profits plunged downward at an accelerated rate; unemployment increased. And in the spring of 1927 the nation underwent a major banking crisis; beginning in March of that year, some fifty banks closed their doors, headed by the important Bank of Taiwan.[82]

In the midst of this panic, the Wakatsuki cabinet resigned when, as will be recalled, the Privy Council refused to allow the government to grant relief funds by means of an Imperial edict. However, the economy policy of the government had long been unpopular with the military, with the masses of destitute people, and with most of the business class.

And even in these most critical times, there were several notorious scandals which further detracted from the popularity of the parties and party government. Chief among these was the Matsushima Scandal, which touched all three parties—the Kenseikai, the Seiyukai, and the Seiyuhonto.[83] Various party members had collected an enormous sum in bribes from Osaka businessmen, on the promise that the government would authorize a certain new area in Osaka as the licensed brothel quarters and thus make that particular land extremely valuable.

Premier Wakatsuki himself was probably not implicated, but one of the veteran Kenseikai members, who had been in the Diet since its opening, was involved, and in defending himself he accused Wakatsuki of perjury, thus casting a shadow of doubt in

---

tional debt had increased from ¥2,584 million in 1913 to ¥4,680 million in June, 1924 (all domestic loans); state expenditures had increased during the same period 240 per cent; the aggregate surplus of imports over exports since 1919 amounted to ¥2,771 million, thus rapidly depleting reserves built up during the war. *Ibid.*, pp. 230–231.

[81] *Ibid.*, p. 231.

[82] For some details, see Takahashi Kamekichi, *Nihon kogyo hatten ron*, p. 46. This compared in magnitude to the American banking crisis of March, 1933.

[83] For accounts, see Royama Masamichi, *Seiji shi (Political History)*, in Gendai Nihon bummei shi (History of Contemporary Japanese Civilization Series), Tokyo, 1940, p. 380; *JC*, November 18, 1926, pp. 600–602.

the public mind. Tokonami, head of the Seiyuhonto, was openly accused of having received some of the money,[84] and several Seiyukai members were definitely involved. It was another affair which lent support to the growing disgust with party corruption and rottenness.

Almost at the same time, Tanaka, the new president of the Seiyukai, was being accused of sins past and present. There had long been various accusations against him for his conduct during the Siberian expeditionary campaign; it was alleged that he had appropriated a large part of the Secret Service Fund for personal uses. Along with the airing of this charge, it was now alleged that he had solicited some ¥3,000,000 from a Kobe millionaire industrialist by making certain promises. There were several versions of these alleged promises: one was that Tanaka had agreed that the donor would be allowed to purchase some land on which a military arsenal would subsequently be built; and another was that Tanaka had agreed to get the donor a contract from Marshal Chang Tso-lin for the purchase of arms. This latter version was presented to the Diet on March 4, 1926, when a Kenseikai member read a printed statement to that effect by Lieutenant General Ishimitsu.[85] The Diet (with Kenseikai and Seiyuhonto support) passed a motion to investigate these charges. Although they were never proven, they were readily believed by a large part of the Japanese press and public. Tanaka's reputation did not augur well for the future of political purity.

Despite the cloud which hung over the Seiyukai, however, its return to power in 1927 was greeted with considerable enthusiasm by a nation weary of a "negative" policy. As early as October 4, 1925, the Seiyukai had brought forth its new "positive" economic policy based on protecting key industries, raising protective tariffs, embarking on a public works program centered around communications expansion, and working for "self-sufficiency" in food production by exploiting to the maximum the agricultural poten-

---

[84] Tokonami was accused of taking ¥30,000 as hush money. This he vehemently denied, but his accuser, who did get some money, was at the time chairman of the Party Affairs Committee of Tokonami's party. *JC*, November 18, 1926, p. 607.

[85] See speech by Nakano Masataka, House of Representatives, March 4, 1926, reported in *JC*, March 11, 1926, p. 308. Nakano read both a statement by Lieutenant General Ishimitsu and also a document compiled by an ex-paymaster of the army charging Tanaka with irregularities as Minister of War in the Hara and Takahashi cabinets.

tialities of the country. It was a policy of economic nationalism produced largely by Japan's plight in a depression-ridden world, enthusiastically supported by a great number of the hard-pressed businessmen and dovetailing with the ideas of the militarists. Like all the major party proposals, of course, it contained little mention of direct aid to labor and tenant-farming groups.

This general program was partly put into practice during the Tanaka ministry, which was in power between April 20, 1927, and July 1, 1929. It had little immediate effect, however, in alleviating economic problems; many of these were very closely connected with international trends and with Japanese foreign policy. Tanaka's "strong" foreign policy had as one of its objectives the stabilization and expansion of Asian markets, but its first result was to reduce the China market seriously by provoking boycotts against Japan and open hostility. Moreover, self-sufficiency on any large scale was impossible, and the Seiyukai policy of keeping Japanese prices comparatively high had a detrimental effect on foreign markets, which already had greatly diminished.

The general result of the Seiyukai economic and foreign policy— even though it was a result partly dictated by world conditions— was to create a situation in which capital overexpansion in terms of marketing potentialities continued, relatively high prices underwritten by the government remained, and at the same time unemployment and agrarian debt mounted.[86] The times were ripe for increasing social and political unrest. The capitalist system was attacked with more vigor and greater assistance than ever before, and the major political parties were directly in the line of fire. To many, they were the symbols of "vested interests," whose influence seemed to guide the policies of each administration.

And if the Tanaka ministry could do little to popularize its party or the business community, it did a vast amount of harm to both, through a new crop of political scandals, the exposé of which occupied the major attention of the reading public. Certainly one of the most sensational acts was the appointment of a leading "political merchant," Kuhara, as Minister of Communications, despite the fact that he was heavily indebted to the government and had been involved in a number of questionable financial transactions.

---

[86] Hamaguchi's attack on the government was of course very sharp: "By pursuing the so-called positive policy wantonly and issuing loans incontinently, the Government is not only obstructing the work of financial readjustment, but is preventing the fall of prices."

The allegation was that Tanaka was under personal obligation to Kuhara, and the appointment aroused opposition even within the cabinet itself.[87]

This was but one *cause célèbre* among many, however, and it is probably no exaggeration to state that even a people somewhat indifferent to political corruption were shocked by certain events during the Tanaka regime. There were scandals involving land sales and monopoly privileges from Saghalien to Kyushu and Korea. There were publicized cases of the sale of meritorious service awards and of the buying of peerages. The minister of railways was accused of accepting bribes amounting to some ¥600,000. Whatever the exaggerations and false accusations involved, the general situation was an all-time low for party morality and popularity.

When Hamaguchi returned to the political scene as Premier on July 2, 1929, he inherited the accumulated problems of nine years of depression. The Hamaguchi program encompassed a balanced budget, a sharp reduction in administrative expenses, and the free movement of gold. His first major move was to lift the gold embargo, which had been in effect in Japan since the time of the Terauchi ministry. This action was followed by a sharp drop in prices, which provided some relief to consumers.[88] With the collapse of the American markets late in 1929, however, prices began to fall to new depths, especially raw silk prices. This, together with a further decline in the price of rice, created desperate conditions in agriculture, especially among the tenant-farmer groups.[89] The government was forced to revise its "negative" policy, and in the spring of 1930 it began a silk valorization program, instituted some public works, and made large loans. Nothing could rehabilitate the lost markets of the world during this period, however, and gold shipments continued to flow out in large quantities, with speculators buying dollars in anticipation of the fall of the yen. When Great Britain left the gold standard, Japan's fiscal position

---

[87] Minister of Finance Mitsuchi, a leading Seiyukai member, was violently anti-Kuhara. In openly attacking the prospect of the latter's appointment, he stated: "Mr. Kuhara has received much relief money from the government for his enterprises, and I disapprove of the idea of allowing a government debtor to join the Cabinet as a Minister." Quoted in *ibid.*, May 31, 1928, p. 666. After some confusion, Mitsuchi resigned.

[88] For one interpretation of the embargo removal and its economic effects, see Yamamuro Sobun, "Economic Depression and the Gold Embargo," in *Contemporary Japan*, June, 1932, pp. 52–61.

[89] For a more detailed account of agrarian conditions, see chapter viii.

grew even worse, and by the end of 1931 the gold reserves of the Bank of Japan were only ¥470 million, as compared to ¥1,072 million two years previously.[90]

These critical times were followed by the *hijo kikyoku* (extraordinary conditions), with the beginning of the "Manchurian Incident" in September, 1931. Now political and economic conditions were ripe for a major assault upon the alliances between parties and propertied interests, with certain military and agrarian elements acting as the moving spirit of the opposition. Public opinion, even in the urban areas, gave the major parties little reason for optimism. Weary of continuous depression, cynical about the parties and representative government, tending to put the blame for general economic conditions on the coalition of party and big business, most people were unconcerned about the fate of the parties, and some were attracted to a crusade which promised to purify and rededicate the Japanese spirit by wiping out the old structure.

The famous "dollar-buyer" episode which opened the final prewar party administration—that of Inukai and the Seiyukai—brought forth another shower of criticism. All during the latter part of the Wakatsuki cabinet's regime, the large financial and business houses had been buying quantities of American dollars, gambling on the possibility that the gold embargo might be reimposed. The second Wakatsuki cabinet had strenuously resisted its reëstablishment, but when the cabinet was finally wrecked by internal dissension, the new Seiyukai ministry immediately put back the gold embargo. Overnight, speculators profited, by millions of yen. One of the houses reaping the largest profit was Mitsui, and many voices raised the cry that Mitsui, in concert with the Seiyukai, had sabotaged the nation to enrich itself.[91]

Thus it was not difficult for most Japanese to listen with some sympathy and understanding to the story of a patriotic young man, as he revealed it in August, 1933:

"I was born in Aomori, so I know well the starving conditions of the petty farmers. It is all due to the impasse of Japanese capitalism. What interested me in the plot was my desire that by freeing the people of the shackles of capitalism, I would enable farmers to get adequate food and clothes." [92]

---

[90] George C. Allen, *A Short Economic History of Japan, 1867–1937,* London, 1936, p. 99.

[91] See the Proceedings of the Sixty-first Diet, as reported in *JC,* March 24, 1932, p. 424.

[92] See translation of court-martial testimony of Ito Kameshiro. *Ibid.,* August 24, 1933, p. 238. See speeches of other participants quoted in Maruyama

The speaker was Ensign Ito Kameshiro, on trial for his life before a court-martial board because of his part in the "May Fifteenth Affair" of 1932, which had cost the life of Inukai and signaled the end of party cabinets in prewar Japan. Although the May Fifteenth Affair symbolized a change of substantial proportions, it was not without its build-up. Inoue Junnosuke, Minister of Finance in the Wakatsuki cabinet, had been assassinated about a month earlier; Baron Dan, head of Mitsui, had been shot only ten days before; indeed, scores of other industrial and political leaders were scheduled for death. The schemes of murder, martial law, and a new order for Japan that were afoot will be discussed more fully later, in the context of Japanese military Fascism. Here, it need only be said that in their objectives of destroying the old parties, parliament, and "capitalist controls," the young plotters had the active or passive support of many Japanese. Democracy and the party system were now equated by many with political corruption, domination by vested interests, selfishness, and depression. As their strength ebbed away, the parties were powerless to withstand attack from without and disintegration from within.

It has been our purpose in this chapter to indicate the role that Japanese capitalism played in this unfolding tragedy, and in so doing, to lay out one very fundamental problem which Japanese democracy faced and to which no solution was found. The Japanese industrial revolution was borne on the wings of state power, making use of modern techniques developed and advanced by the West. That this was a most natural—indeed, indispensable—development was implicit in the whole timing of that revolution in relation to the Japanese past and the Western present. Herein a central problem of Japanese democracy was posed. Western democracy had followed a leisurely evolutionary development strongly shaped in the early modern period by the economic and political interests of the middle class. If the Western liberal societies experienced an initial period of mercantilism and extensive commercial dependency upon state power, important changes subsequently occurred. The increasing power of the business community made possible and demanded a transition to modified laissez faire. In part this increased business power was the product of the natural advantages of the society, such as resources, location, and labor supply; in major degree, it was the result of a head

Masao, "Nihon Fascism no shiso to undo" (Japanese Fascist Thought and Action), Sec. 2 in Sonjo shiso to zettaishugi (Revere the Emperor—Oust the Barbarian Thought and Absolutism), Tokyo, 1947, pp. 130–131.

start in the process of political and commercial-industrial modernization. Since these were factors that could quickly become operative, the transition was made possible at a time when the advance of industrial techniques had not been such as to stamp the mercantilist pattern indelibly upon the economic structure of the society. Consequently, a relatively great degree of competition could prevail under modified laissez faire (in the beginning stages at least), precluding rapid concentrations, broadening the base of commercial-industrial groups, and making the term "middle class" meaningful. And in the transition and the period which followed, the middle class expressed its philosophy in the concepts of limitations upon the power of government, representative supremacy in government, and individual dignity and rights. If in expressing these ideas it was voicing selected passages from the whole literature of Western political tradition, still their force and vitality came from the fact that they represented the living realities of immediate interest. Armed with this philosophy and the concessions won on behalf of it, the business community assumed an increasingly important position in shaping the institutions which governed the whole of its society. Moreover, the progress of industrialization over the decades, though not without its corrosive influences, gradually made the democratic creed meaningful to the lower economic classes and gave them the power to effectuate some of the premises of that creed. Then the state took on the role of adjuster of conflicting interests more or less adequately represented in the power balance.

In modern Japan, however, it was not possible to duplicate this historic process, nor to find, at least in the prewar period, a satisfactory substitute for it which would help to make democratic principles meaningful to the society, and effective. The modern Japanese business class was the product of much more than a set of traditions adverse to its acceptance of Western-style democracy; it was the result of a timing sequence which sustained many of these traditions and projected them in modern form. If the neomercantilist policy was essential to a goal of speedy industrialization in the late nineteenth and early twentieth centuries, it was also a policy not easily to be abandoned, especially in a society like Japan, and one which carried vast political, social, and economic implications. Even if the Japanese resource-population balance had been more favorable, or less aggravated by the impact of capitalism, there would have remained in some degree the continued pressure of the advanced industrial West, and one composed of such a myriad of advantages as to be not easily overcome. But even if this had been possible—and one cannot deny that in the 1930's it loomed as a possibility—there remained the supreme fact that the neomercantilist pattern of development, armed with the end product of Western technological evolution, would have already shaped the commercial-industrial structure to such a degree and in such a manner as to make its economic and political forms extremely difficult to remold, barring internal or external violence.

It was within these forms that the Japanese business class existed and developed its political creed and action. Out of its own structure, its relation to government, and its needs, came an organic theory of politics and society. The paternalism which was a part of Japanese tradition was revitalized in the public relations between business and government, and hence sustained in the private relations between employer and employee, businessman and official. Moreover, the concurrent development of nationalism and industrialization caused primary stress to be placed upon the responsibility of capitalism to the state, with its obligations to the individual considered a matter of secondary importance. The emphases on power over freedom, on the state over the individual, and on unity over a true recognition and representation of conflicting interests—all were derivatives from the central premises. That these—premises and derivatives alike—formed the underpinning for the political action of the prewar business community as a whole is demonstrated by the history of that action. Their activity on behalf of a completely integrated political force was perhaps the most revealing example.

To state these generalizations so baldly is of course to pay less attention than is necessary to developmental changes in the economic, social, and political position of commerce and the business class; but when one has uncovered and analyzed these, the generalizations can still be left basically unchanged. It is also true that in positing these conclusions, insufficient justice is being meted out to the individual exceptions and to the general conflict within almost all elements of the business community. That there were some who desired it otherwise, some whose ideals and philosophy rested solidly with those of Western democracy, is readily admitted; it is even more important to acknowledge the fact that varying degrees of ambivalence, contradiction, and tension were a very real part of the over-all political position of the business classes. Indeed, tension and conflict were present throughout the whole of modern Japanese society, despite its institutions and

292

goals, or perhaps because of them. One does not need to deny any of this nor try to draw the lines of morality and immorality, however, in order to establish the dominant traits of business politics, its causes, and its results.

One final aspect of the problem is to be noted. Japanese capitalism entered the world scene at a time when classical liberalism was close to its zenith and was producing its own social and economic problems. It was already under growing attack in the countries of its origins. Only in those Western nations which under the old system had enjoyed a maximum of advantages and a minimum of social ills, only in those whose traditions now rested firmly upon political liberalism, was there a certain resiliency to the revolutionary currents of the extreme left and right. This resiliency enabled certain nations to undertake experiments with new forms of mixed economies which would permit the retention of basic democratic values, experiments that are still proceeding. In Japan, capitalism created great social and economic problems, without building any solid liberal foundations in its society. It could produce neither spectacular improvements in mass living standards nor a dynamic, new political philosophy. Consequently, it operated under the threat of a revolutionary attack, with few of the circumstances present which would encourage democratic tactics or moderation. In its failures as well as in its strengths, Japanese capitalism was of too little service to the democratic cause. And in this connection the impact of the contemporary West was once again of direct and vital significance, for not only was it involved in the Japanese economic debacle, but also it was bringing a new type of message to the Japanese people—one of doubt in democracy and of faith in Fascism or in the "New Democracy" of Communism.

VIII

THE RISE AND DECLINE
OF THE LEFT

UNDER THE CIRCUMSTANCES of Japanese politics, the "left" had an important function to perform in Japan on behalf of democracy. To give meaning to political competition, to clarify ideological lines, and to provide the lower economic classes with some real stake and voice in representative government were vital challenges. Yet it was obvious that only that section of the left dedicated to parliamentarism could conceivably perform these functions adequately.[1] Moreover, the very conditions which created such a need for a left-wing democratic movement operated to restrict and defeat it. Despite some initially favorable signs, the left never secured more than a toe hold in prewar Japanese society, and its ultimate failure was far more overwhelming than that of the conservative parties. To analyze the factors present in that failure, however, is to discover some additional insights into the nature of modern Japan and its political problems.

The weaknesses of the Japanese parties came to a focus in their failure to gain any real interest, support, or confidence from the Japanese "common man." Without his interest, "representative government" was subject to all the evils of exclusiveness, corruption, and ultraconservatism; without his confidence or support, the parties were like frail reeds ready to be toppled by the first contrary wind. The philosophy and actions of the conservative parties seemed to suggest that their chances for building a broad

---

[1] The term "left" as used in this section applies to a wide range of movements based upon Western democratic socialism, Communism, Anarchism, Syndicalism, and varieties of these. I am well aware of the problems created by this orthodox but imprecise term, and although it will be used here, an attempt will be made to draw the proper contrasts and parallels.

popular movement were unpromising. In theory, such groups as the urban laborers, tenant farmers, and owners of small landholdings would find more appealing political movements elsewhere. Indeed, it was precisely this theory that gave the leaders of the Japanese left their hope. Their eyes were fixed securely upon that great majority of the population who wanted—or, in their opinion, needed—change. But though the leftists never ceased trying to appeal to the lower economic classes, their greatest successes were confined to an intellectual elite that was weak both in numbers and in power.

It is not surprising, of course, that the lack of political maturity, especially in the "common man," was a great and continuing barrier to any form of Japanese democracy. We have already sketched the premodern legacy of a people lacking or deficient in a spirit of individualism, personal responsibility, self-confidence, and, indeed, all the attributes considered important for the democratic citizen. We have also outlined certain key aspects of modernization which interacted with this tradition to protect and even enhance it.

Among the many products of this interaction, modern Japanese education and law had a sufficient effect upon democratic possibilities, and especially those of the left, to require further examination here. On the surface, it might seem a contradiction that a political elite which had accepted the concept of "popular enlightenment" as fully as the Meiji leaders had, should establish a system of secondary education so benumbing to the public mind. Yet this effect was inherent in the education program for the people which the government directed after 1890.[2] After full allowance has been made for the traditionalist contributions, there remain other fundamental causes for this development which were of at least equal importance. Foremost were the tendencies generated by the late emergence of nationalism in Japan. Japanese nationalism came to flower in an age dedicated to the concept of power through mass allegiance and possessed of the techniques to implement this theory.[3] One of the most potent weapons of the modern state has been mass indoctrination, and Japanese leaders were not

---

[2] For general studies on Japanese education, in Japanese, see Matsushita Takeo, *Kindai Nihon kyoiku shi* (*A History of Modern Japanese Education*), Tokyo, 1949; and Takahashi Shunjo, *Nihon kyoiku shi* (*A History of Japanese Education*), Tokyo, 1929. See also Robert Hall's study, in English, *Education for a New Japan*, New Haven, 1949.

[3] See chapter ix of the present study.

slow to make use of this instrument. To be sure, the early period was filled with confusion and contradictions. The young rulers were not completely sure of themselves or of their creed. In their eagerness to encourage rapid change and in their own frank admiration for Western power, they allowed and even encouraged a program of almost indiscriminate "Europeanization." Advice and ideas were solicited from everywhere, including the United States, England, and France.[4] In this atmosphere of experimentation, certain *keimo gakusha* (enlightened scholars) such as Fukuzawa emerged, delving deeply into liberal concepts of education and seeking to apply these in private schools.

By 1890, however, the government had accepted a far-reaching system of education patterned essentially after German concepts, a move entirely consistent with the trends governing Japanese evolution.[5] The powerful *Mombusho* (Department of Education) directed a program which tended increasingly to stress *hinsei toya* (character education), that is, the inculcation of traditional ethical values applied to state purposes. Only the *sagyo kyoiku* (vocational education) aspects of Western liberal training were incorporated in the curriculum. The essence of the new program was broadly set forth in the famed Imperial Rescript on Education issued October 30, 1890.[6] Therein were contained the Confucian concepts adjusted to serve a modern power state. As time passed, moreover, the emphasis on nationalist indoctrination became progressively more pronounced, and even the Diet aided its course. In February, 1896, the House of Peers resolved that primary materials on moral training were sufficiently important to be controlled by the state; a similar resolution was passed by the House of Representatives in 1898. After 1904, primary textbooks, with a few exceptions, were prepared by the Department of Education. They were character-

---

[4] The government in this period was even receptive to American influence. Mori Arinori, when Minister to Washington, sought the advice of American educators, and, as a result, Professor David Murray of Rutgers was invited to act in a consultant capacity to the Japanese government, serving between 1873 and 1878. However, the French centralized system of education was the first model adopted, since it was considered more suitable to Japan.

[5] The influence of German concepts was pronounced as early as 1886. Mori himself helped lead the way as Education Minister. German scholars were brought to Japan, including Professor Hausknecht, disciple of Herbart, and the latter's theories contributed to the concept of *hinsei toya*. See Takahashi Shunjo, *op. cit.*, p. 421.

[6] For one English translation, see *Education in the New Japan*, published by General Headquarters, Supreme Commander for the Allied Powers, Civil Information and Education Section, Tokyo, 1948, Vol. II, p. 75.

ized by subject matter emphasizing traditional ethics, Shintoism, and Japanese history, written in an extremely mythical and chauvinistic manner. It is natural that one professor of Waseda University would write in 1908, "The present system of education makes for the perpetuation of an Oriental type of despotic government; it is no preparation at all for the adoption of Constitutionalism of a Western type." [7]

Actually, however, there was much that was uniquely modern in the Japanese educational program. Above all else, it was directed at the masses. By 1894, 61.7 per cent of all eligible children were going to primary school; this figure reached 93.2 per cent by 1903 and soon became practically 100 per cent, with compulsory education lengthened to six years in 1907.[8] Further expansion of compulsory education aroused less enthusiasm, but a universal audience was vital at the all-important primary level. In this manner, several generations of young Japanese grew up scarcely trained to use such literacy as they attained for advancement toward democratic ideals. As on so many other vital issues, moreover, the major party spokesmen, with a few exceptions, seemed oblivious to this fundamental weakness. When the parties came to power, certain general promises were made, but no basic reform was even undertaken. Very revealing is an exchange between Premier Hara and Tanaka Sannai, Education Minister in the wartime Okuma cabinet. On January 27, 1921, Tanaka, then a member of the House of Peers, demanded a lengthening of the period of compulsory education and the inclusion of citizenship training, stating:

The Meiji education has been too anti-political. In framing an educational policy adapted for present-day Japanese, it is not enough to

---

[7] From Ukita Kazutami, "Three Great Questions Bearing on the Future of Japan," in *Taiyo*, January, 1908, as quoted in *JM*, February 8, 1908, p. 148. Another critic, Fujii Kenjiro, wrote in 1911: "The recently issued moral text books for 3rd Year Primary School pupils are certainly calculated to promote great narrow-mindedness among the scholars by the way in which they exalt the State at the expense of the individual. Personal culture and the development of individual powers are represented as of little value unless they can be devoted to state interests. The narrow-minded patriotism which is being preached far and wide in this country at the present time is responsible for the growth of a certain amount of antipathy to foreign thought. Of course, it is quite right to encourage among our students a high respect for all that is good in our national character and for the noble acts of Japanese performed in former ages, but the notion that we Japanese are superior to all other nations can only be entertained by ignorant people." Quoted from Fujii Kenjiro, *Dangerous Patriotism*, in *JM*, May 27, 1911, p. 628.
[8] See Takahashi Shunjo, *op. cit.*, pp. 425–431.

aim at the cultivation of the spirit of obedience, but it must at the same time try to instill the spirit of independence . . . The evils attending elections of various kinds arise from the fact that the Normal School [secondary school] education in this country has completely neglected imparting political knowledge to students. Lack of political knowledge among the nation may be productive of evil results in the event of universal suffrage being introduced.[9]

Hara's reply was largely an apologia for the old system. He first countered with the plea that the Meiji educational program had not been too inadequate and that it was still in the process of being put into effect. Then he remarked:

In support of his [Tanaka's] demand for an extension of the period of compulsory education, the interpellator cited the examples of foreign countries, but that is no reason why Japan should blindly follow foreign examples. It is true that there is a body of opinion favoring an extension of the period of compulsory education, but the Government has not formulated a definite policy in this respect.[10]

Although higher education held out increasing hope for those who had the opportunity to acquire it, the average student went to his life work stamped with the traits of complete reverence for the Emperor, unquestioning obedience to the state, and ignorance combined with fantasy concerning the social sciences. Nor did these traits characterize the common people only; for many reasons and in varying degree, they were to be found in the elitist elements as well.

The secondary education system was but one complicating factor which affected the struggle of the left with particular force. An additional obstacle of great proportions was the governmental attitude toward political freedom. In spite of the references to civil liberties in the Constitution, and in spite of advances subsequent to its adoption, restrictions and suppression continued to be very prominent features of Japanese politics. These were exemplified by the continuous series of "Peace Preservation Laws," widespread government censorship, and many flagrant violations of individual liberties, either through official action or unofficially at the hands of private "patriots," whose attacks seldom met with more than very slight punishment.

This subject is not one that can be treated with simplicity. As

[9] Interpellation of Tanaka Sannai in the House of Peers, January 27, 1921, as reported from the Diet Proceedings in *JC*, February 10, 1921, p. 178.

[10] Statement of Hara, House of Peers, January 27, 1921, as reported in *ibid.*, p. 178.

has been noted earlier, there was an element of violence implicit in the actions of all Japanese dissident groups. There was quite naturally an interactive effect between a tradition of paternalism and the unfamiliarity with peaceful change or political toleration. If this interaction was often projected into the modern period by governmental initiative, it is also true that there were often extenuating circumstances for the attitude of the government. The extraordinary tensions and rapid transformations present in modern Japanese society strained moderation and gradualness, and, by the same token, placed a premium upon the use of coercive power. The injection of the Western philosophies of Anarchism and Communism into this scene, moreover, gave Japanese extremism a new type of organization and faith, weakened the classical democratic approach to freedom, and helped to set in operation the chain of events which has so often produced authoritarian states in the modern world.

The use of legislation to restrict drastically many types of political action was well established by the Meiji government before the Constitution of 1889 came into operation. And both the Law on Political Associations and Meetings and the Peace Law of 1887 were still in effect in 1890, and they were used frequently thereafter, especially during the early, hectic election periods. The party men who were struggling against the bureaucracy during this period bitterly opposed the Peace Law, and finally, in 1898, it was repealed. Only two years later, however, the *Chian Keisatsuho* (Public Peace Police Law) was enacted, a law which duplicated the earlier statute in almost every respect and added a clause (article 17) making it practically impossible to organize and maintain legal labor unions.[11] This article remained on the statute books without alteration until 1926, although it was not always strictly enforced.

Until the passage of the Universal Manhood Suffrage Act of 1925, moreover, there had been certain important restrictions on the rights of suffrage and party membership. For instance, students of public and private schools, even if they met other qualifications, had not been able to vote. In addition, certain categories of individuals, such as priests, religious teachers, and teachers of elementary schools, had been prohibited from joining political associations. Such restrictions were modified by the 1925 legislation. For example, male students of age could vote, but were still pro-

---

[11] For a complete translation of the Chian Keisatsuho of 1900, see *JM*, May 5, 1900, p. 446.

hibited from participating in any political association. Priests and teachers were allowed to join political parties.[12] The early stipulations, whatever their justification, had operated to prevent the infusion of new blood into the party movement from important elitist elements, thus denying it certain sources of leadership. Indeed, the law had contributed to the indifference or outright hostility shown by some of these groups, who, legally proscribed from political participation, condemned parties and parliamentarism in general.

Such acts as the Universal Manhood Suffrage Act of 1925 indicated the pressure which had been developing behind the democratic movement. If this was pressure outside the major parties, in considerable measure, it was partly in consequence of certain currents astir in Japanese society after World War I.[13] There were other trends developing, however. The same Kato cabinet which sponsored the expanded suffrage legislation passed a new "Peace Preservation Law" known as the *Chian Ijiho.*

This law was directed primarily against the Communists and Anarchists,[14] but it could be used against the democratic socialists and, indeed, any group or person desiring to change "the Japanese way." Its first article read:

"Anyone who has formed a society with the object of altering the national polity [*kokutai*] [15] or the form of government [*seitai*]

---

[12] See Miyazawa Toshiyoshi, *Senkyo ho yori* (*The Essence of the Election Law*), Tokyo, 1930, pp. 71 and 91.

[13] When the old parties were minority elements fighting for greater power, they often chided the government for not reducing suffrage limitations, and in 1912, a universal manhood suffrage bill actually passed the lower house with Seiyukai support. The Hara ministry, however, opposed immediate universal suffrage, and even within the Kenseikai, opposition was present. Kato was pledged to its enactment, however, especially after the famous "Restore the Constitution" battle which had enlisted strong press and public support. But in the final analysis, the press, the intellectuals, and other diverse elements, mostly outside the major parties, were the real leaders in the fight for suffrage expansion.

[14] The attempted assassination of the Prince Regent (Hirohito) by an extremist on December 27, 1923, naturally gave great impetus to legislation controlling radicalism.

[15] The term *kokutai* defies exact translation. Even the Japanese admit that its meaning is vague. Those who made the charge of vagueness in opposing the bill were answered by Minister of Justice Ogawa when he asserted that it meant rule by the Emperor, as clearly stated in the Imperial Constitution. See House of Representatives Proceedings, March 7, 1925, as reported in *JC*, March 19, 1925, p. 370. Ogawa's definition, however, is far too restrictive, and perhaps "national polity" is as good a translation

or denying the system of private ownership, or anyone who has joined such a society with full knowledge of its objects, shall be liable to imprisonment with or without hard labor for a term not exceeding ten years." [16]

The implications of this law made it potentially as restrictive as any act promulgated since the Meiji Restoration. One interesting official interpretation of the law was actually offered in the course of the Diet discussions over its passage. When a member of the *Kakushin Club* (Reform Club) asked whether movements carried on outside the Diet for revision of the Constitution were punishable under this bill, the director of the Criminal Affairs Bureau replied that although it was proper, under the provisions of the bill, for the legislators to debate a constitutional amendment within the Diet, party or independent movements for advocating such a measure outside the Diet were punishable.[17] The vagaries of the act, moreover, placed in jeopardy persons holding any of a great range of opinions, and laid the act open to use against the press, academic institutions, or any movement critical of the status quo and dedicated to basic change. But in the face of these possibilities, it was not only sponsored by a ministry which had ridden the crest of the popular wave, but was passed in the Diet by an overwhelming majority, the second reading passing by a vote of 246 to 18. And if it was designed to control the Communists, it was subsequently used for much broader purposes.

Nor was repressive action confined to "Public Peace" legislation. Press censorship was remarkably prevalent, both before and during the era of party government. In certain respects, to be sure, the Japanese press was very free. The libel laws were extremely

---

as any, but in its usage, kokutai developed much of the emotionalism and mysticism implicit in such phrases as "the American way."

[16] One English translation appears in *ibid.*, February 26, 1925, p. 272. (The above translation is mine—R. A. S.)

[17] Transcriptions of the House of Representatives, Special Committee on the Peace Preservation Bill, February 27, 1925, as reported in *ibid.*, March 5, 1925, p. 306.

The government spokesman did not actually say that the House could propose amendments, and it is not clear whether he meant that they could discuss the advisability of amendments even if they had not been proposed by the Emperor or substitute new amendments for those he might propose. The constitutionality of the latter interpretation was raised in connection with the 1946 Constitution. In prewar Japan, no clear-cut test case on this issue ever arose, as we have noted. What was evident from the official's statement, however, was that no popular movement could advocate revision of the Constitution legally.

loose and the most scurrilous personal attacks upon public officials often passed unchallenged, especially since most officials considered it beneath their dignity to reply and were rarely much troubled by public opinion concerning their personal lives. When it came to political fundamentals which might affect the public mind, however, the press, and later the radio, motion pictures, and other communication organs were subjected to a rigorous censorship moderated only by doubts in the minds of some officials and by a certain degree of inefficiency. Nor did the party regimes differ greatly in these respects from the old bureaucratic ministries. Indeed, the Hara administration so flagrantly abused the press that representatives of the *Jiji, Tokyo Asahi, Yomiuri, Kokumin, Hochi,* and other leading newspapers met on February 28, 1921, and passed a declaration, of which the following paragraph is an excerpt:

The Government has . . . issued orders for the suppression of news very frequently of late, thereby interfering with the freedom of the press. It also has brought pressure to bear upon news organs by prosecuting them. In this manner, the Government attempts to carry out a "secrecy administration," refusing to take the nation into its confidence. Such an attitude on the part of the Government cannot be tolerated under a constitutional regime.[18]

The Seiyukai administrations were not the only ones so charged. The Hamaguchi Minseito administration of 1929–1931 was attacked in the following resolution, which was passed by journalists representing all the press clubs of Tokyo: "The Government suppression of the Press has been outrageous of late, and we strongly denounce the political police methods. We call upon the Government to make clear its responsibility without delay." [19]

That such strong resolutions could be voiced is indicative of a degree of freedom far greater than that in the years following 1932, but press freedom, like other freedoms, was extensively curbed even in the period when parties were at the height of their power. Similar restraints operated in the realm of individual rights. Some of the purely bureaucratic cabinets had been extremely oppressive. One illustration was the arrest of five students in Tokyo on February 2, 1918, during the Terauchi cabinet regime, for express-

---

[18] Translated in *JC*, March 10, 1921, p. 333.

[19] Journalists' Resolution of December 17, 1930, translated in *ibid.*, December 25, 1930, p. 713.

ing nonviolent but "dangerous" ideas. In his defense of the students, one Kenseikai member of the Diet revealed their offenses:

First, they advocate the adoption of universal suffrage so as to place the administration on a democratic basis. Second, they urge that the civil officials' appointment regulations be abolished so as to throw the way open to talent. Third, they demand the establishment of a genuine coalition Cabinet by all parties by eliminating the influence of the clan statesmen. Lastly, they aim at the overthrow of the present unconstitutional Ministry in order to carry out their objects. Is any one of these items destructive of public peace and order? [20]

It would be tedious to recall even a small proportion of the cases similar to this which occurred both before and after the advent of party cabinets. To be sure, the party administrations tended to be somewhat more lenient toward goals such as universal suffrage and the overthrow of "clanism," but when it came to attacks from any part of the left or any criticisms which might be taken as dangerous to a vaguely defined "Japanese way," they could take action equally as repressive as that of bureaucratic administrations, or at least acquiesce in such action.

These general trends in education and law quite naturally posed central obstacles to democracy, and especially to any movement like democratic socialism. However, one must make certain sharp distinctions between prewar Japan—even Japan after 1932—and the completely totalitarian state. Measured in terms of real totalitarianism, Japanese methods were incomplete and deficient. Certainly, they did nothing to cultivate the ground for a developing democracy, but neither did they reach the stern efficiency and comprehensiveness of Communist and Fascist techniques. In this as in other strands of her society, Japan was set apart somewhat by her traditions. An appreciation of the importance of the public mind did not produce in Japanese leadership an acceptance of all possible techniques for its control, either in indoctrination or in restraint. In the period before 1932, this was partly due to the impact of Western liberalism, which had reached a sizable part of the ruling elements, even if at less than its full strength and in

---

[20] Interpellation of Miki Takekichi (Kenseikai) in the House of Representatives, February 19, 1918, as reported in *ibid.*, February 28, 1918, p. 324. A year earlier, Tagawa Daikichiro, one of the Diet's most outspoken members, was arrested, prosecuted, and convicted under the Press Law for an article in which he had attacked the Terauchi ministry.

warped form. In addition, however, there was the fact that modern Japan could not wholly assimilate the precise Western forms of authoritarianism. In many respects, this was a difference of degree rather than kind, and it should not be allowed to obscure the fundamental similarities which existed. However, Western authoritarianism had to reckon with a greater amount of individualism implicit either in its society or in its philosophy. Modernization never completely atomized Japanese society, nor did it bring to power disciples of a philosophy like Marxism which was the product of atomization. Therefore, it was neither necessary nor possible in modern Japan to treat the individual as an isolated unit, and, achieving this, to direct toward him with scientific precision and all-consuming purpose the solitary force of the state. To traditionalist Japanese leaders, certain Western accretions mixed with Confucianism produced a pattern of control more compatible with their society and their own values. Among these men, the theory remained strong that the "superior" were not to descend into the lower tiers of the political arena to lead the throng personally. Indeed, the overwhelming majority of the Japanese elite never lost their disdain and fear of mass movements in any form. Consequently they did not seek to create and rigorously control such a movement. Indeed, they eschewed with vigor many techniques conducive to effective popular leadership; public audiences and mass demonstrations organized for state purposes were practically unknown. Oratory continued to be considered vulgar, and there was probably no group of modern political leaders who maintained such resolute silence in public as the Japanese statesmen.[21] Most leaders were comfortable only with the type of impersonalized and incomplete direction signified by the secondary education program and occasional written statements replete with moral maxims and exhortations.

When to the educational pattern is added the program of restraint through law, the mixed character of the Japanese state, especially before the 1930's, can best be understood. On the one hand, the civil liberties traditional to the democratic society were severely

---

[21] This included not only officials, but also leaders of the major parties and even those in the field of education. In the early period, there had been certain outstanding exceptions. Men like Itagaki and Okuma had used public speech as one of their most important techniques, despite the many obstacles which they faced. In later years, however, the seasoned bureaucratic leaders of the two parties rarely delivered public addresses.

restricted by law. This was ample evidence of the deeply rooted paternalism and made precarious the path of opposition. On the other hand, however, the arena of freedom was undeniably being enlarged, in some respects, until the sharp reaction of the militarist era, and this unsteady expansion was a product of the impact of Westernism and the ambivalent attitudes of new elitist groups.

Taken as a whole, this situation was such as to give the left a chance to emerge and even grow in the premilitarist period, and still to place it under extensive handicaps. Although these handicaps cannot be fully appreciated until certain additional factors have been mentioned, it should already be clear that Japanese leftism faced an uphill struggle in its attempts to break out of a purely intellectual and elitist environment and to make itself a popular movement.

Before we turn directly to a study of the first "proletarian parties," however, we should direct some attention toward the broad socioeconomic factors which affected the leftist movement, especially Japanese "proletariat" conditions, rural and urban. Everywhere in the Japanese scene, the seeming ingredients of revolution —tension, institutional sterility, and poverty—were present. The condition of the agrarian groups offers some particularly interesting examples.[22] The industrial revolution represented a frontal challenge to Japanese agrarian supremacy and to the traditional security of all agrarian classes. And perhaps of all groups in Japanese society, the tenant farmer and small landowner benefited least from the process of modernization in an economic sense, and underwent the greatest psychological pressures in that process. When combined, moreover, the tenant and small landowning classes represented a substantial part of the population. More than 90 per cent of the agrarian families possessing land owned less than three *cho* (7.35 acres) each, and nearly 50 per cent owned

---

[22] For certain sources on modern agriculture and agrarian politics, see Okutani Matsuji, *Kindai Nihon nosei shiron* (*An Historical Treatise on Modern Japanese Agrarian Policies*), Tokyo, 1938; Tsuchiya Takao and Ono Michio, *Kinsei Nihon noson keizai shiron* (*Historical Treatises on the Agrarian Economy of Modern Japan*), Toyko, 1933; Ono Takeo, *Noson shi* (*A History of Agriculture*), Tokyo, 1941, and *Kindai Nihon noson hattatsu shiron* (*An Historical Treatise on Modern Japanese Rural Development*), Tokyo, 1950; and Mori Kiichi, *Nihon nogyo ni okeru shihonshugi no hattatsu* (*The Development of Capitalism in Japanese Agriculture*), Tokyo, 1947.

less than five *tan* (1.225 acres).[23] In 1928, more than 68 per cent of the some five and one-half million farm families were either tenant or part owner, part tenant.[24] Nearly one-half of all cultivated land was tenant-cultivated.[25] These statistics suffice to illustrate an important fact. As opposed to a small number of affluent rural leaders, there was a vast group of tenants, semitenants, and small landowners who faced more or less common problems. For the purposes of political and even economic analysis, it is impossible to make any rigid distinctions within this group.

The very fact that Japanese farming and landholding in general remained small-scale indicates a good deal concerning the impact of the industrial revolution upon agriculture. Probably the chief reasons for a continuation of small-scale agriculture in Japan were the heavy population pressures on the available land, a general insufficiency of capital, greater investment possibilities elsewhere, and high agrarian labor and mechanization costs in comparison to profits. It is true that statistics would seem to indicate some alleviation of population pressures during the process of modernization. There were actually somewhat fewer persons employed in Japanese agriculture in 1920 than in 1872, and the amount of land under cultivation had increased slightly.[26] This signified that the

---

[23] Note the following table on the percentages of lands owned by agrarian households, grouped by size of holdings, with reference to the total amount of agrarian land owned:

Year	Below 5 *tan* *	From 5 *tan* to 1 *cho* **	1–3 *cho*	3–5 *cho*	5–10 *cho*	10–50 *cho*	Above 50 *cho*
1914	48.22	24.97	18.00	5.32	2.51	0.85	0.07
1919	49.14	24.28	18.27	4.77	2.50	0.95	0.09
1921	49.37	24.20	18.13	4.71	2.51	0.99	0.09
1926	49.87	24.44	17.81	4.60	2.28	0.92	0.08
1928	49.64	24.58	18.03	4.54	2.24	0.89	0.08

* 5 *tan* equals 1.225 acres.
** 1 *cho* equals 2.450 acres.

This table is based on one from Ono Takeo, *Kindai Nihon noson hattatsu shiron*, p. 54; it was compiled chiefly from official government statistics, and Okinawa was not included in these before 1917.

[24] See table in *ibid.*, p. 56.

[25] See *ibid.*, p. 55. The proportion of tenant-cultivated land in 1905 was 43.9 per cent; in 1919, 45.9 per cent; in 1930, 47.8 per cent.

[26] The population of Japan in 1872 was listed as 34,800,000, of which those engaged in an occupation numbered 19,663,142 (this figure was a statistical average of the years 1872 to 1876). Of the working population, 15,229,911, or 77.5 per cent, were engaged in agriculture.

By 1930, the Japanese population had reached 64,450,000, and 27,261,106 persons were listed as engaged in work, but only 14,128,360, or 50 per

tremendous increases in population were being fed into urban commerce and industry, a very natural development. The rural areas in particular served as the great reservoir of man power for the industrial revolution. Unfortunately, the race between the increase in production and the population increase was close enough to preclude sizable gains in terms of living standards, especially for the lower economic classes. Moreover, the small decrease in pressure upon the land indicated by statistics was in most respects illusory. In the first place, pre-Meiji pressure was very heavy, and to alter the situation basically a substantial decrease in agrarian population would have been required. But more important, the over-all population increase actually intensified pressure in many ways, especially in times of industrial crisis, when the urban discontented and unemployed competed for land. This factor of occupational fluidity pressed ever harder upon agrarian communities, which were being constantly forced to disgorge their excess population.

The paucity of agrarian capital was equally reflective of Japanese economic conditions. Capital shortage, as has been noted, was a general problem for modern Japan, and one never completely solved. It was natural, moreover, that governmental efforts should be directed mainly at capital accumulation for industrial purposes, and this included a program of relatively heavy agrarian taxation, as well as many incentives for capital investment in commerce and industry. The high profits to be made in urban enterprise attracted private capital and made for high interest rates on agrarian loans.

Already the outlines of the Japanese agrarian community begin to emerge. Some millions of peasants tilled their small plots, working with infinite care over every square yard and employing mainly traditional methods, which produced heavy yields only with the application of long hours of drudgery. Homage—often genuine—but in any case, formal—was paid to the village elite, who usually constituted the upper economic group by virtue of landholdings and district enterprise. The authority of the local elite in political and economic decisions was challenged only in unusual circumstances. None of this meant that peasant life was without its quota of happiness and even contentment. Desires were few, and relief from boredom was provided by a ready sense of humor, the joys of petty gossip, and the excitement created over festive

cent, were listed in agriculture; the working groups that had increased the most were those in manufacturing and mining (21.0 per cent of total population) and commerce (11.7 per cent). For statistics, see *ibid.*, pp. 28–29.

occasions. Superstition, conservatism, and the simple life were the peasant's stock in trade.

But the horizon grew increasingly beclouded, and the peasant watched, at first with mild concern, but gradually with a deeper sense of unrest and frustration; and in some measure he was joined in this by even the wealthier rural elements. The causes were complex. Some were basically economic, and of these, one of the foremost was the increasing dependency of agriculture upon a capitalist economy and the world market. By the Taisho era, this dependency had reached significant proportions. It had produced important changes in agrarian production and had drastically curtailed subsidiary income in rural handicraft industries; and, most important, it seemed clear that agrarianism was becoming increasingly subordinate to urban fiscal and market controls. The farmer not only sensed his loss of self-sufficiency and independence, but also decried the inequities in the process which seemed apparent to him. He resented the tax collector as much as always, and the more so since he felt that his taxes were going for projects not connected with his own interests. He was often bitter toward the middleman, who took his profits merely to act as a conveyer belt to the urban consumer. And above all, he was angered by the inexplicable depressions which struck just as his desires had been expanded and his standards seemed on the rise. Particularly was this true of the long-continuing depression of the 1920's which followed a period of relative prosperity. During this depression, the entire agrarian community struggled to make income equal production costs. The prices of agrarian products collapsed. At the depth of the depression, all agrarian groups were operating at a net loss, and an agrarian debt approaching five billion yen had been built up by 1931. Practically none of this debt was the result of outlay for improvement; it represented an operating loss, and there seemed little hope for the lower agrarian elements to regain their solvency.[27]

Political developments were also conducive to general agrarian unrest. As for the landowners, their clear supremacy in the national Diet was being challenged increasingly by urban power, as has already been noted. Of general importance was the great reduction of political autonomy for the districts which was accompanying economic trends. The centralization drive opened by the Restoration itself forged ahead through the decades, wearing down the independent power of the rural elites, and ultimately imping-

[27] See table in *ibid.*, pp. 230–232.

ing directly upon every farmer. The abandonment of many district institutions culminated in the abolition of the *gun,* the major district office. Centralized rules and regulations governed rural life, but the farmer was never sufficiently conditioned to this loss of local autonomy, either by education or by an awareness of its necessity, to accept it without opposition.

Nor was the stimulus for unrest merely economic or political. It would be a shallow analysis indeed which overlooked the fact that the Japanese industrial revolution and the total impact of the West were building up the broadest types of tension in the rural areas. Here, where the cultural values of traditionalism had their greatest meaning, and hence their greatest tenacity, the intrusion of new and foreign ideas could be particularly painful. Having given up a goodly measure of his economic security, the farmer still struggled to avoid losing that traditional way of life and set of values which had provided him with psychological security. He did not want to give up reverence for the ancestors who had worked the soil before him, the superstitions which had simplified life's mysteries, or the naïve faith in superiors and the acceptance at face value of their moral maxims. Neither did the state want him to give these up, but the thrusts of Westernized culture struck ever deeper into rural life. Whether in the field of techniques or in the realm of ideas—whether it came in youth or old age—the challenge was there. Especially in the districts close to urban centers was the conflict sharp. In each individual, deep-rooted tensions were set up as he twisted and turned to find or regain some inner peace. Here was a real revolutionary potential, needing only leadership, organization, and a faith to carry it forward.

All these troubles were sources of unrest which, in addition to affecting the agrarian community as a unit, operated with increasing potency in the relations among its various component elements. The Restoration had established the concept of private property rights, and with it, a series of agrarian classes, graduated down to the tenant. The tenant and semitenant groups faced problems beyond those which they shared with the agrarian class as a whole. The process of modernization had taken from them the kind of traditional safeguards which went with tilling the soil. New laws gave maximum protection to the owners of property and practically none to the tenants. Naturally, the tenants did not accept graciously the denial of what they considered their customary rights. Especially in periods of depression did this cleavage between the written law and premodern agrarian custom create explosive tensions. Although the tenant had lost his traditional protections, moreover, he continued to bear traditional responsibilities, and, in addition, he had certain new ones. Ordinarily, he continued to pay rental in kind, thus profiting less than other classes in times of agrarian price inflation, and suffering at least equally in periods of agrarian depression. Tenant rentals were high, amounting to nearly 50 per cent on paddy-field land.[28] The general increase of economic pressure on the landlord was naturally passed along to the tenant whenever possible. The struggle of the tenants to obtain land and of the semitenants to acquire more land was obstructed by heavy obligations and high prices which ground them down.

The general factors affecting the agrarian scene together with those relating specifically to the tenant made it natural that the scope of disputes between tenants and owners should expand, and that their nature should change. Until the period around the Russo-Japanese War, tenant disputes followed in general the traditional pattern. They were particularized, ephemeral, and occasioned mainly by bad crop years and the desire for temporary relief from rental charges. With the accelerating development of the industrial revolution in Japan, however, all the broader tensions in the agrarian society that have previously been mentioned began to appear. Some of these resulted from the introduction of new ideas and techniques. The old concept of the harmonious master-retainer relationship was jeopardized by trends which lent support to the doctrines of class consciousness, unionism, and broad social reform being propagated in the districts. The establishment of tenant class unions in considerable numbers did not occur until the period during and just after the First World War, but for a

---

[28] For one discussion of the problem of tenant rentals, see Mori Kiichi, *op. cit.*, chapter iii. Mori includes (p. 173) the following statistics from a survey of tenant rentals conducted in 1936, based upon the previous three-year average and contained in Motoyuki Keiki, *Nihon nogyo kozo ron* (*A Treatise on the Structure of Japanese Agriculture*), p. 58. The survey did not include Hokkaido and Okinawa.

(A) Paddy land. Payment in rice: one crop a year, 45.8 per cent; two crops a year, 49.8 per cent. Payment in cash: one crop a year, 49.4 per cent; two crops a year, 53.7 per cent.

(B) Dry land. Payment in kind: rice—31.28 per cent; soya—31.44 per cent; rye—23.71 per cent; wheat—25.41 per cent; barley and soya—38.52 per cent; wheat and soya—35.80 per cent. Payment in cash: rice—31.6 per cent; soya—38.2 per cent; rye—18.2 per cent; barley and soya—28.4 per cent.

time their growth was exceedingly rapid. By 1922 there were some 1,114 tenant unions, with more than 132,000 members.[29] Bolstered by such organizations and harassed by the troubled conditions of the period, tenants challenged landowners in greatly increased numbers, the recorded disputes in peak years involving more than 180,000 agrarian families a year.[30] Also, in many instances, the issues had become broader. By the World War I period, there was an insistence upon more basic and long-run remedial measures which would include permanent rights for tenant cultivators.[31] Now the cry of land redistribution was raised more frequently. And by the 1920's, Western-style leftism was present in some degree in the Japanese agrarian scene.

But in the entire situation there was little to suggest that Japanese leftism in any form could capture the obvious agrarian unrest and shape it into an organized political movement with capacities for victory. Wholly aside from the problem of leadership, there were powerful obstacles. The traditional conservatism of the peasant and his reluctance to enter organizations external to the family were greatly reinforced in Japan by the forms which modern education and law took, as well as by the strong caste-class heritage which interacted with these forms. The fact that only a small proportion of the total number of peasants entered the tenant union movement and, more importantly, the great fragmentation of the unions and the factionalism within each were reflective of these central problems. Another indication was the continuation of the great influence of the landed gentry over rural life and political expression. Despite all the trends likely to result in separation and conflict, the hold of the rural gentry over subordinate farmers remained exceedingly strong. In part, this pattern of paternalism was maintained through the same judicious use of compromise and even benevolence which, as we shall note, was a part of the urban labor-management relationship. In large measure, however, it was the result of the broader factors mentioned above. After the enactment of the Universal Manhood Suffrage Law, the power of the agrarian landowners was put to the test and demonstrated as effective, as it was able to produce smashing majorities for the candidates of the rural elite.

[29] See table in Ono Takeo, *Kindai Nihon noson hattatsu shiron*, pp. 86–87. The zenith membership in tenant unions was reached in 1927, when 365,332 members were claimed by 4,582 tenant unions. *Ibid.*, p. 87.

[30] *Ibid.*, pp. 66 ff.

[31] *Ibid.*, pp. 61 ff.

There was an even more important reason for leftist weakness among agrarian groups than any factors yet summarized. Implicit in the great cultural conflict motivating agrarian unrest was a strong predilection against the West in general and Western-style democracy in particular. The basis of agrarian discontent lay in considerable measure with the total impact of urban capitalism upon agrarian supremacy and the destruction threatened by foreign innovations to the traditional sense of cultural continuity and security. Although the antipathy toward capitalism might fit well into a Western leftist movement, the strong antiurban and antiforeign aspects of Japanese agrarianism made it far easier for unrest to be channeled down the path of an ultranationalism that seemed to promise deliverance from unwelcome foreign influences and possibly a way to restore agrarian supremacy. Because of both their innate proclivities and the particular circumstances of Japanese development, the farmers were very susceptible to ideas of "revolution from the right" and ill-equipped for democracy in any form.

The Japanese urban laboring class was not a much better source of support for the prewar left than the peasant class. There were good theoretical reasons, it is true, for expecting more substantial aid from this urban group. As active participants in the industrial revolution, the urban workers were more susceptible to certain ideas and actions closely connected with it. The idolization of primitivism and agrarian supremacy were clearly incompatible with the new position in which these workers found themselves. They shared with other urban classes the materialist drives which were the product of rising capitalism. The problems which they faced made Western leftism more applicable and of greater immediate meaning to them. This did not mean that the cultural conflict present in the agrarian class was absent in the urban laboring groups. It existed, spreading tension and thereby creating an even greater revolutionary potential. However, the leftists benefited by the fact that the conflict was weighted with some advantages to them. A traditional renaissance offered little to the laboring class. The worker was tied to the process of modernization, whatever political forms it might take, and there was some evidence that his desires were increasingly in accord with leftist polemics. In its potentialities for organization, also, urban labor seemed to have advantages over the peasant. Familial centralism had to compete with other centripetal forces indigenous to urban, industrial life. And frequently the industrial worker was a transplanted individual, torn away from the family and searching for compensating affiliations.

However, when these factors have been modified by the circumstances of modern Japan or pitted against them, the extraordinary weaknesses of the labor movement before World War II are not difficult to understand. In the first place, there was an omnipresent interrelation between peasant and laborer—farm and city—which often blurred "cultural" distinctions and gravely retarded urban labor power in a variety of ways. The overwhelming number of city workers were either first- or second-generation peasants, and their ties with ruralism were still strong. Indeed, as has been mentioned, in depression periods, many returned to seek sustenance from the overcrowded soil. This fluidity was a definite check upon the development of strong unions or political associations based upon compact labor support. New waves of rural "immigrants" were constantly flooding the labor market, especially in periods of prosperity. In addition to the difficulties of "indoctrinating" these raw recruits, they produced conditions of labor surplus which gravely affected the possibilities of bargaining opportunities or strong unionism. The unions conducted their greatest efforts in the almost continuous depression of the 1920's, confronting conditions in which every worker had to fight to maintain his job against the great numbers of unemployed. Although these circumstances made good material for the left, they were scarcely conducive to strong organizations, especially when the hostility of law and officialdom were also factors to be met.

At least equally as important as these obstacles, however, was the unique paternalism which characterized employer-employee relationships. Some of the background of this phenomenon has already been given. The particular nature of Japanese industrial development combined with tradition to establish a labor-management relation marked by many ties resembling those within the family. Employers conditioned by the paternalistic nature of business-government relations, as well as by the dominant values of their heritage, assumed the parental role to an extent sufficient to give the classical virtues of harmony, loyalty, and obedience some appeal, in spite of generally bad labor conditions. What this system cost in efficiency, as measured in Western terms, it paid in a degree of stability that would have been completely impossible had management not given evidence of accepting some responsi-

313

bility for its "flock." [32] In many respects the worker was particularly conditioned to receptivity toward such treatment. Not only was his background in conformity with this, but, as has been indicated, he felt in desperate need of a substitute for the family ties that were being broken. Thus, unionism, with its economic-political appeals, was met by a management paternalism which had in some measure replaced family centralism, capturing a part of its emotional appeal. Although not universal or completely effective, this paternalism was sufficiently embedded in the whole nature of Japanese society to have great power.

The *Nihon Rodo Sodomei* (Japanese Federation of Labor) expressed some of these problems in its declaration of October, 1925, when it stated:

Because the growth of Japanese capitalism has been very rapid, there has not been the general awakening of class consciousness among the proletariat. On the other hand, reactionary and deceptive ideas have been infused in them by adroit means, and these mistaken ideas have taken a firm lodgement in their minds. The result is that out of a total of four million labourers throughout the country, only 250,000 represent organized labour. Even in the case of organized labour, the majority are under the spell of the specious name of the "harmony" principle. Particularly regrettable is it that labour unions are conspicuously lacking among the workers at big factories and mines who ought to form the head and front of labour movements.[33]

After years of struggle, the labor union movement by 1929 could only claim somewhat more than 6 per cent of the industrial workers. Its 330,000 members were divided into many small factions, with poor coördination. The average membership in individual unions was only 524. The organized labor movement was in no position of political power, either numerically or in terms of ideological solidarity.

---

[32] Such practices as basing the amount of the wages on the number of dependents which the worker had, retention of superfluous labor, and giving end-of-work bonuses are a few examples of management practices attuned to paternalism.

[33] Declaration of the Nihon Rodo Sodomei, October, 1925, translated in *JC*, October 22, 1925, p. 525.

The forerunner of modern Japanese unions was the *Yuaikai* (Fraternal Association), organized by Suzuki Bunji in 1912. Its original members numbered less than 50. Various other small unions sprang up, and the first amalgamation occurred in 1919, with the establishment of the Nihon Rodo Sodomei, which then consisted of 71 unions with a total membership of 30,-000. Subsequently, as we shall note, there were several splits in the Sodomei.

These were some of the handicaps under which the Japanese left operated. There remained the intellectuals—the academicians, students, writers, and other assorted individuals who might be considered as belonging in this category. For the most part, these were the leaders of the left, and there were many examples among them of men who had not only ability, but also sincerity and courage. The intellectual contribution to Japanese leftism and the strengths and weaknesses of the Japanese intelligentsia can perhaps be best presented by weaving them into the broader tapestry of the development of the leftist movement. At the outset, however, we might suggest two generalizations of possible importance. The intellectuals were never able to overcome the deeply rooted anti-intellectualist forces in their society, nor, for the most part, were they able to cast off a sense of inferiority and uncertainty which did much to immobilize them. These factors served to keep the intellectuals separated from popular sentiment or from forward positions of leadership. Furthermore, the intellectuals were confronted with a panorama of developments in their own country and abroad which promoted the greatest ideological cleavages among them, making it completely impossible to present any united front. And these fundamental differences reflected one of the gravest weaknesses of Japanese leftism.

Indeed, there is no better point at which to begin a direct discussion of the left-wing movement than the early diverse trends in leftist political philosophy, trends which symbolized the expanding conflict within Japanese society. As has already been noted, the early liberal movement developed individualism largely as a subordinate tool for nationalism and, in the process, distorted many cardinal liberal values. After the unequal contest that ensued, the official philosophy of state was firmly established in a Constitution which rested primarily upon Imperial absolutism. The archaic form of this authoritarian philosophy, together with the institutional problems which it created, helped to fan the flames of intellectual discontent. The growing tension derivative from economic and social change, moreover, abetted this unrest, and a continuous flow of Western concepts gave it new modes of expression. By the 1890's, a small leftist movement had emerged. The general philosophic expression of the left, however, like that of the more conservative "liberal" forces, was deeply colored by a surfeit of nationalism and traditionalist concepts. Unlike Western leftist movements, the Japanese left was not developing out of a background of individualism. For this reason, there have been in Japan many cases of fusion between "left" and "right." Oi Kentaro and his *Toyo Jiyuto* (Oriental Liberal Party) constitute an excellent early example. Oi's small party combined a solicitude for the poor and a quasi-socialist program with an extreme nationalism which made it a forerunner, of sorts, to the later national socialist movement.[34] The threat posed to the doctrinal purity of democratic socialism in Japan during this period was at least equal to that facing classical liberalism. In some respects, indeed, the former was more susceptible to perversion, owing to its superficial similarities with Confucianism and subsequently to the rise of Western socialist theories which were antidemocratic and closer to the potentialities of Japanese society. As an example of the influence of Japanese Confucianism, one may note the *Kokka Shakaito* (National Socialist Society), organized in August, 1905. This small group keynoted its program with the following sentence: "Because in the olden days, our Imperial House was, in a certain sense, a practitioner of socialism, our nation-people [*kokumin*] should stop the arbitrariness of the wealthy." [35] One does not need to read much between these lines to discern the tendency toward an argument which fused the premodern antipathy toward commercialism with the new nationalism.

Implicit also in the radical movement of this period was a considerable element of violence, both in theory and in practice. As has been noted in connection with the early liberal movement, the legacy of military ethics, the obstacles to legal reform, the

---

[34] As has been noted briefly earlier, Oi and other "left-wing" ex-samurai formed the Toyo Jiyuto in protest to the growing conservatism of the Jiyuto. The Toyo Jiyuto, set up in August, 1892, pledged itself to seek protection for the poor and the working classes through stronger government control of general economic conditions. It published the *Azuma Shimbun* and the first labor magazine, called *Shin Toyo* (*The New Orient*). Also, it organized the Greater Japan Labor Society, the League to Petition for Universal Suffrage, and the Committee of Investigation on Tenancy Regulations. For a brief discussion, see Royama Masamichi (ed.), *Musanseito ron* (*Treatises on Proletarian Parties*), Vol. XI of Gendai seijigaku zenshu (Collected Works on Modern Political Science), Tokyo, 1930, pp. 424–425.

The Toyo Jiyuto is interesting for a variety of reasons. It gave an early illustration of the ways in which strong nationalism could be linked to a socialist movement; the overtones of antiforeignism and Japanocentrism were clearly present in the Toyo Jiyuto, and were to be carried forward by later organizations. In a different way, its concentration upon the lower economic groups and its attempt to unite tenant and urban labor classes foreshadowed the later activities of the socialist movement as a whole.

[35] See *ibid.*, p. 426.

lack of understanding of democratic theory, and the absence of conditions that would allow liberal theory to be translated immediately into practice—all combined to encourage the use of force. Given these conditions, Western extremism could have considerable effect upon the thought and actions of the early Japanese rebels. Western Anarchism in particular had its appeal to some circles within the intellectual class. The early Anarchist movement, like all left-wing activities of this period, had only a minute following, but it acquired widespread notoriety through the famous "Great Treason Case" of 1910. A small group of Anarchists whose mentor was Kotoku Denjiro plotted to assassinate the Emperor Meiji.[36] The scheme was discovered in advance, but the exposé brought a great shock to the Japanese people, stimulating government suppression and casting over the entire leftist movement a shadow from which it was never able to emerge.

A study of the early Japanese left-wing movements makes it clear that although they reflected an increasing stimulation from Western thought, their tradition and the current problems of their society combined to give extremism and antiparliamentary theories

---

[36] For a brief, sympathetic account of Kotoku by a veteran socialist leader, see Arahata Kanson, *Nihon shakaishugi undo shi* (*A History of the Japanese Socialist Movement*), Tokyo, 1948, pp. 236–243.

Kotoku, born in Tosa, absorbed the ideas of *jiyuminken* (popular rights) and was greatly stimulated by Nakae Chomin, whom he knew personally. Much later, he revealed his anarchistic faith in a series of letters written to his lawyers while in prison awaiting trial for the plot. After the 1880's, he had been increasingly influenced by the writings of Kropotkin, and had visited America, where, it is said, he became fascinated by the possibilities of an anarchistic society as revealed in San Francisco conditions following the 1906 earthquake. Among the interesting statements made in Kotoku's writings were the strong defense of "direct action," the condemnation of parliamentary efforts as useless, the necessity of meeting terror with terror, and the great idealism of a perfect society in which men would be truly free. As has been true of most Anarchists, Kotoku had no clear-cut plan of action for winning a revolution and establishing an anarchistic state. In one message he stated that what was needed was a band of fifty men with bombs to blow up rich men and politicians. This romanticism reveals the strong link between the Anarchists and the young agrarian-military extremists of the early 1930's.

Despite his philosophy and the prominence which he was accorded in connection with the Meiji plot, Kotoku was not the leader of the assassination scheme; and, according to evidence cited by Arahata, although he was aware of the plans in the beginning, in the end he completely withdrew and was not in sympathy with the plan. See *ibid.*, p. 239. However, Kotoku was publicly proclaimed the leader and was speedily executed after the trial, along with eleven others.

317

a definite advantage. One concrete illustration of this fact can be found in the *Nihon Shakaito* (The Japan Socialist Party), organized in February, 1906. This party represented a union of most of the diverse leaders and factions within the socialist movement.[37] The second general meeting, held in February, 1907, provoked the inevitable debate over fundamental policy, and its results are most interesting. Three alternatives were presented: the original motion sponsored by Sakai Toshihiko provided for tactics which would combine a proparliamentary policy with direct action for the socialist cause; a substitute proposal of the Kotoku forces opposed universal suffrage and advocated reliance solely upon direct action; a third program of Tazoe Tetsuzo supported a straight parliamentary policy. The Sakai motion passed with twenty-eight votes, but the Kotoku proposal got twenty-two votes, whereas the Tazoe motion obtained only two supporters.[38]

Certain trends, however, were beginning to strengthen the moderate left. Progress in social and philosophic thought was tending to give moderation firmer foundations and greater hope. In the first place, an intellectual ferment was growing, particularly in the universities and higher schools, but with manifestations in many other circles. What was perhaps its most modest expression was contained in the writings of Minobe Tatsukichi and his advancement of the *kikansetsu* (organic theory) of the Emperor. Minobe, Professor of Law at Tokyo University, was advancing the thesis that the Emperor was one of the organs of the state, possessing no authority over and above it. This theory had only limited value to the democratic creed, as has already been noted, but it challenged the striking weaknesses of the divine-right theo-

---

[37] Earlier, on May 20, 1901, such socialist leaders as Katayama Sen, Kotoku Denjiro, Kinoshita Naoe, Kawakami Kiyoshi, Nishikawa Kojiro, and Abe Iso had established the *Shakai Minshuto* (Social Democratic Party). However, it was outlawed the day it appeared, by the Ito cabinet. When the succeeding Katsura ministry came to power several months later, the same group tried to organize under the name *Nihon Heiminto* (Japan Commoner Party), but was again stopped. The Nihon Shakaito was organized by some workers in a Kanda poor hostel, including Nishikawa. It was not initially suppressed by the government, and shortly thereafter the Heiminto and other elements joined. Although the membership did not reach two hundred, it included men who were subsequently to be leaders in many branches of the leftist movement, and it was fairly active, especially through the *Heimin Shimbun* (*The Commoner Newspaper*).

[38] Royama (ed.), *op. cit.*, p. 427. This meeting was reported in the *Heimin Shimbun*, and the party was banned on February 22; the newspaper ceased operations in April of the same year, because of government pressure.

rists and was thus sufficiently heretical to stir up a major debate.[39] Minobe's concepts had the increasing support of business elements in Japanese society, and the overwhelming number of Japanese scholars were willing to go at least as far as Minobe. Gradually, moreover, a more profound academic assault was building up against authoritarianism. Onozuka Kiheiji, Professor at Tokyo University, pioneered in advancing the study of politics beyond the narrow strictures of legalism and statism and may be said to have been an early leader of this movement.[40] In a series of works the first of which was published in 1908, he blazed a trail of research that was to be carried on by many others, among them Yoshino Sakuzo. These new methodological approaches to political science, together with the stimulus of social change in Japan and the aura of world democracy, produced an intellectual climate conducive to the development of democratic thought in many forms. The new emphasis was to present liberalism without its old nationalistic overtones and urge the development of the individual for his own worth. The great plea was for *jiga ishiki* (self-consciousness); and with the individual conscience separated from the overpowering purposes of state, the democratic movement had more secure philosophic underpinnings than ever before.[41] Yoshino, together with his Tokyo University student group, typified one important strand of the movement for democracy in Japan in the

[39] In July, 1911, Minobe delivered to teachers in the Normal and Middle schools a series of lectures on the Japanese Constitution in which he expounded his thesis. By the next year, with the publication of his earliest major work, he had been challenged by Hozumi Yatsuka, Professor of Law, and later by Uesugi Shinkichi, disciple of Hozumi. Hozumi and Uesugi argued that Minobe's doctrines violated Imperial sovereignty and tended to make sovereignty jointly held by the Emperor and the people.

Minobe's concept, however, had great influence with the bureaucracy and with the business groups, whose interests, as we have noted, were tied with such a theory. Among Minobe's many works, see his early studies, *Nihon kokuhogaku soron* (*A General Treatise on Japanese National Law*), Tokyo, 1907; *Kempo oyobi kemposhi* (*The Constitution and Constitutional History*), Vol. II in Kokuhogaku shiryo (Materials on Public Law), Tokyo, 1908; and *Nihon kempo no kihon mondai* (*The Central Problems of Japanese Constitutional Law*), Tokyo, 1920.

[40] See Royama Masamichi, *Nihon ni okeru kindai seijigaku no hattatsu* (*The Development of Modern Political Science in Japan*), Tokyo, 1949, for a detailed study of this development and its implications.

[41] Says Sugiyama, "*jiga no kaiho* [the emancipation of self] and *kosei no soncho* [respect for the individual personality]—these were the mottos of that era." Sugiyama Hirosuke, "Shakai" (Society), in *Gendai Nihon shi kenkyu* (*A Study of Modern Japanese History*), Tokyo, 1938, p. 24.

period around the First World War. A prolific writer, lecturer, and political organizer, Yoshino was in many respects the great symbol of the moderate left. His articles, particularly those which appeared in the *Chuo Koron* (*The Central Review*) between 1916 and 1919, received wide publicity and comment.[42] Yoshino's philosophy met with rigorous criticism from the right and left alike. Moving far beyond Minobe, he took his position with democratic socialism. At the same time, however, he avoided use of the term *minshushugi* (literally, "people rule principle," the common term for democracy), referring instead to the traditional term *mimponshugi* (literally, "people basis principle," the classical Confucian term). To have used the former phrase would have been openly to attack Imperial sovereignty.

Yoshino's central views, however, reflected an important trend. Many of those who were advancing the frontiers of democratic theory in Japan during this period were adherents of democratic socialism. For the most part, the initiative in expanding the theoretical framework of democracy had been seized by the moderate left. This is not to say that the universal problems posed by an attempt to unite socialism with democracy were solved by those few Japanese who had newly come to the task. In some respects, indeed, Japan offered a particularly difficult context in which to work out such solutions. However, the moderate socialists had moved further than their conservative compatriots toward cutting themselves loose from the fetishes of Japanese tradition and accepting the core values of political democracy.

But whatever ideological banners it carried, the left was now to assume a more prominent position on the Japanese stage. At the close of the First World War, as we have noted, there were numerous internal and external factors conducive to this greater activity. The industrial revolution was in full swing, producing a larger laboring class, mounting tensions at all levels of society, and new techniques for making use of these tensions. Some political change was already under way, and this demonstrated the insecure nature of the old order and indicated the potentialities for much broader attack. Moreover, world trends, as always, were of

---

[42] For Yoshino Sakuzo's most important articles during this period, see "Kensei no hongi o toite sono yushu no bi o nasu no michi o ronzu" (Preaching the Essentials of Constitutional Government and Discussing the Road Toward Realizing Its Complete Perfection), *Chuo Koron*, January, 1916, pp. 17–114; "Mimponshugi—shakaishugi—kagekishugi" (Democracy, Socialism, and Extremism), *ibid.*, February, 1919.

vital importance. A war had just been fought "to make the world safe for democracy," and Wilsonian idealism made its impression upon many Japanese, especially of the younger generation. But a new phase of the great Western battle over such symbolisms as "democracy" had already been inaugurated by the Russian Revolution. The profound influence of this event upon the intellectuals and labor leaders of the Far East probably need not be emphasized. The influence of the Communist Revolution was due partially to its success, partially to the fact that it had occurred in a country which in its evolution and contemporary problems bore many striking similarities to the Far East, and partially to the appealing intellectual climate in which its leaders operated, particularly since the Communist elite, in sharp contrast to most Western democratic theorists, were making serious efforts to synthesize Marxism with social trends in the Far East.

By 1920, the Japanese leftist movement was beginning to expand its activities. For a little more than a decade thereafter, it struggled with some vigor to make itself heard and felt. But in this short period it could not overcome two central problems which were implicit in it and its society. It could not achieve any measure of unity, nor could it develop an effective popular basis of support. In the background study, an attempt has already been made to high-light some of the broad causes for these failures, but now they must be given additional meaning and color through an analysis of developments after 1919. The opening note was sounded with the establishment of the *Shakaishugi Domei* (Socialist League), in December, 1920.[43] The League had the flavor of a new era, but the problems of the old one. Its membership, though small, included both the old-line socialists and younger representatives from student groups, labor unions, and various "cultural associations." Its purpose was not only to study socialist ideology, but, more important, to plan a broad popular movement for political action. In less than a year, however, it had split apart and dissolved. The government did ultimately ban the organization, but it had previously been wrecked by internal ideological friction. The League had attempted to encompass all socialist elements, with the result that violent disputes over policy and action had arisen, especially between the Communists and the Anarchists.

[43] See, among other accounts of the Shakaishugi Domei, Arahata, *op. cit.*, pp. 284–287; Royama (ed.), *Musanseito ron,* pp. 428–429; and Yamamoto Katsunosuke and Arita Mitsuho, *Nihon kyosanshugi undo shi* (*A History of the Japanese Communist Movement*), Tokyo, 1950, pp. 42–44.

Already, in 1920, Japanese Communism had begun to take form under the direct tutelage of Russian leaders.[44] In that year, the Far Eastern Branch of the Comintern had been established in Shanghai, with the objective of promoting Chinese and Japanese Communism. Three Japanese leftists, Sakai Toshihiko, Yamakawa Hitoshi, and Osugi Sakae, made initial contacts.[45] Late in 1920, Kondo Eizo, recently returned from America, established the *Gyominkai* (The Association of Enlightened People), which served as the forerunner to a formal Communist party. Under its auspices, the *Gyomin Kyosanto* (Enlightened People's Communist Party) was set up in August, 1921, and a series of leaflets was distributed by it in the major cities in the next few months. This brought on the first mass arrests of leftists, in December, 1921.[46] In the meantime, delegates had been chosen to represent Japan in the Far Eastern Peoples' Conference, held in Moscow under Comintern auspices.[47] The conference opened in February, 1922, presenting the colorful spectacle of many diverse Asian radicals drawn together by the issues of imperialism and revolution. Shortly after the Japanese delegates returned home, the Japanese Communist party was reëstablished, in July, 1922. Takase Kiyoshi was then dispatched to

[44] Japanese language materials on the Japanese Communist movement have become increasingly numerous. For one valuable bibliography which has recently been prepared for Western students, see the *Bibliography on Japanese Communism*, by Roger Swearingen and Paul Langer, New York, 1950.

[45] The Comintern faced a major problem in making decisions about leadership of the Communist movement. Most of the old-line radicals in Japan were exponents of Anarchism or Syndicalism. It was necessary to cultivate some of these, seeking to convert them or at least establish "popular front" relations. Osugi, for instance, was a veteran Anarchist and remained so, but upon his return from Shanghai, he worked for a common front movement.

[46] Kondo Eizo had continued the contacts with Shanghai first established by Sakai and Yamakawa, receiving advice and funds from Comintern agents there. His Gyominkai formed the nucleus of the embryonic Communist party which distributed propaganda from September to November, 1921. Some of this was directed toward military units and included, for their consumption, material arguing against the Siberian expedition. Alarmed officials arrested Kondo late in November, and on December 2 some forty people were picked up. See Yamamoto and Arita, *op. cit.*, p. 47.

[47] In October, 1921, Chang T'ai-lei had come to Japan as a secret emissary from the Comintern and had met with Kondo, Yamakawa, and Sakai to select delegates. Of the nine official delegates, six were Anarchists. In addition, there were certain other Japanese delegates, including Katayama Sen, the famous socialist veteran, who came as delegates from the American Communist Party, Japanese Branch. Katayama subsequently served as a representative on the Comintern, keeping in close touch with developments in the Japanese Communist movement from the vantage point of Moscow.

the Fourth Comintern Meeting of November, to report the creation of the party. He returned, armed with the so-called "Bukharin Thesis of 1922," the first Russian program for Japanese Communists.[48] Some of Bukharin's ideas met with strong opposition within Japan; the struggle between accepting complete subserviency and risking the wrath of the Comintern had already begun in Japanese Communist ranks.[49] Actually, the 1922 Thesis was never formally ap-

---

[48] The 1922 meetings were intended to stimulate the establishment of Communist parties throughout the Far East and to shape their ideological and tactical policies in accordance with the current orthodoxies of Russian leaders. The capture of the Asian nationalist movement was a prime objective which reflected itself throughout the conferences. The exhortation to emancipate the Asian peoples from the yoke of Western imperialism was assured of a favorable response from all groups represented. Working from this base, Communist leaders, using the Leninist doctrine as a guide, proceeded to weave together nationalism and Marxian tactics in underdeveloped areas, thereby advancing the theory of the two-stage revolution: an initial broad popular front, on behalf of a "bourgeois democratic revolution," and the ultimate "proletarian revolution."

Japan presented a troublesome problem to the Communists, since both capitalism and nationalism were well advanced, and imperialism was a weapon directed not so much *against* as *by* that country. The famous "Bukharin Thesis of 1922," which became the initial "line" for the Japanese Communist party, attempted to resolve these difficulties, keeping Communist policy in Asia relatively uniform. The 1922 Thesis argued that despite the great advancement and power of capitalism in Japan, "feudal remnants" were omnipresent. These showed particularly in rural areas, but they were also present in the structure of power in the Japanese state. Hence, it was incumbent upon the leaders of the "revolutionary proletariat" to aid in the completion of the "bourgeois democratic revolution," together with other groups including the "liberal bourgeoisie." Only with the success of the bourgeois revolution could the stage be set for a climactic revolution of the proletariat.

At the same time that "popular front" and "parliamentary participation" theories were advanced, however, the now familiar stingers were attached. Whatever associations it formed for the sake of expediency, the Communist party was to retain its inner solidarity and discipline, attacking and undermining its temporary allies, seeking to wrest leadership from their hands, and constantly proclaiming itself as the only true party of the masses. Moreover, the principles of the Japanese Communist party were to contain ideas that violently assaulted all aspects of Japanese society, including the institution of Emperor, and were to emphasize the absolute necessity of an eventual Communist party dictatorship. For the text of the Japanese Communist party's Thesis of 1922, see *ibid.*, pp. 52–57.

[49] For two accounts of Japanese Communist resistance to the 1922 Thesis written by former Communists who turned against the party, see Sano Hiroshi, "Moscow to Nihon Kyosanto no kankei shi" (History of the Relationship of Moscow and the Japanese Communist Party), *Chuo Koron*, March, 1950 (pp. 96–103), p. 98, and Nabeyama Sadachika, *Watakushi wa Kyosanto o suteta* (*I Abandoned the Communist Party*), Tokyo, 1950, pp. 55–65.

proved; before such action could be taken, the arrests of June, 1923, completely disrupted the party. Among the "orthodox," however, it was recognized as the official basis for party action and theory.

While the Communists were organizing in great secrecy, various leftist leaders of more moderate persuasion were striving to forward the proletarian party and labor union causes. They worked under multiple handicaps. Government hostility toward all left-wing movements encouraged extremism and gave the Communists a positive advantage, both in terms of their appeal and in terms of their tactics. Moreover, despite the advances of social democratic theory, those of the social democratic persuasion faced strong opposition, not only from well-organized Communist cadres, but also from the retreating Anarchists and Syndicalists, who had long played a prominent role in the Japanese left wing. In addition, the moderates did not have the mixed blessings of foreign funds and experienced foreign leadership which could provide certain advice and discipline. Nor could they seem to develop the zeal of the small but dedicated Communist fanatic groups. A final problem existed in the fact that few of the moderates could be expected to understand the dangers of Communist infiltration. There were many in the socialist movement who had not clearly defined their ideology or the tactics which they felt to be desirable. Oppression and worsening conditions in Japan tended to move a considerable number of moderates to the leftward. With the need for unity so great and experience with Communist collaboration so limited, moreover, the idea of a "popular front" had sufficient appeal to split the non-Communist elements wide open.

Some of these problems were betrayed in the crucial period

The Thesis was criticized from a number of points of view. Some objected to alienating the masses by any frontal assault upon the Emperorship. Others felt that the analysis of Japanese history was in error and opposed the whole concept of a two-stage revolution, insisting that Japan was at the proper stage for a proletarian dictatorship. Many were resentful of the strong domination by foreign leadership and the "Made in Russia" tag which the Thesis bore.

As a part of the picture, of course, it should be remembered that the "Communist party" in Japan at this time contained many assorted leftists, and that, as a result, the currents of Anarchism, Syndicalism, and even social democracy were all present. In addition to ideological cleavage, moreover, personal factionalism was strong as a result of past and present developments and of the whole nature of Japanese society. Russian allocation of funds and power naturally intensified personal rivalries.

324

between 1921 and 1925. In 1921 and 1922, many of the battles centered in and about the Nihon Rodo Sodomei. Although the Japanese Labor Federation was woefully weak, it was logically a core for any socialist movement. The general conferences of the Sodomei during this period were the scene of violent debates. Such issues as the best type of unionism, desirable political principles, and successful political tactics were argued vehemently by spokesmen for the conflicting movements represented in the Federation. Communist influence in the Sodomei was clearly on the rise, especially at the district level. Moreover, on the outside, despite their small numbers, the Communists were moving ahead more rapidly than any other group to seize the initiative of the whole leftist movement. Yamakawa Hitoshi, then secret leader of the Communist party, wrote a very influential article in the summer of 1922 in the magazine *Zenei* (*Vanguard*).[50] Criticizing the elitist, decentralized nature of the proletarian movement, Yamakawa called for a turn toward the masses, in an appeal well calculated to gain support from many non-Communist circles. Armed with such polemics as this, the proponents of nation-wide organizations and centrally controlled mass unionism dealt the Anarchists and Syndicalists a heavy blow in the September, 1922, attempt to establish a General Federation.[51] Naturally, the social democrats were important supporters of the "centralized union" theory, and the victory was theirs as well as that of the Communists. In this period, unionism was growing rapidly and expanding its political activities; the Sodomei Central Committee established a political section in the union in November, 1922. From outside, various intellectual groups, such as the Japanese Fabian Society under Abe Iso, were also seeking to stimulate political activity. Leftist

---

[50] Yamakawa's so-called *hoko tenkan* (change of course) theory was in line with the slogan of the Third Comintern Conference, which was "Toward the masses." That it was an emphasis badly needed in the whole Japanese leftist movement was clear, however, if that movement were to succeed, and Yamakawa's criticisms were therefore well timed to win attention.

[51] Some 106 delegates, representing over 27,000 members and every possible leftist position, met on September 30, 1922, in an effort to establish a General Federation of Japanese Labor Unions. The great debate was over the issue of "centralized unionism" versus "autonomous organization," and Anarchist defeat marked the end of their influence in the labor and socialist movements. On October 1, the Sodomei opened their general convention in Osaka, and, on the 3rd, adopted a resolution proclaiming "central unionism" as the correct policy. The Anarchists continued to resist, issuing a counter-statement in the name of some nineteen organizations, but their influence was definitely on the wane.

325

activities among university students spread like wildfire. The Labor victory in England in 1923 greatly encouraged the moderate left. In that same summer, various intellectual and labor leaders organized the *Seiji Mondai Kenkyukai* (Society for the Study of Political Problems), to educate the proletariat, advance organizational activities, and prepare for a strong labor party.[52]

The left wing was beginning to make itself felt despite its very limited strength. Political demonstrations, sponsorship of peasant and worker protests and strikes, and a great volume of literature had an increased importance in a period of deepening depression. At the same time, however, government severity was growing, and the inevitable divisions in the leftist movement were broadening. On June 5, 1923, the government carried out mass arrests of Communists, taking in most of the active party members.[53] Publicity connected with this event probably contributed to the assaults on leftists which followed the disastrous Tokyo earthquake of September 1, 1923. First, large numbers of Koreans were massacred by highly excited mobs, and then, in the period of martial law which ensued, a number of radicals, including Osugi Sakae, were murdered by police.[54]

---

[52] In its initial stages, the Kenkyukai was a broadly based leftist organization, but the Communists joined it in considerable numbers and ultimately succeeded in largely controlling it, making it a subsidiary to the Hyogikai. The early leaders included Shimanaka Yuzo, Aono Suekichi, Suzuki Mosaburo, and Takahashi Kamekichi; and some twenty-seven organizations, including the Sodomei, were affiliated. Although the Kenkyukai was never a political party, at its zenith in 1925 it had fifty-three branch organizations and some 3,000 members. See Royama (ed.), *Musanseito ron*, pp. 429–430.

[53] The arrests of Communists followed disclosures made as a result of riots at Waseda University. Right- and left-wing student groups came to blows over the issue of military education. This led to an investigation of Sano Manabu, Waseda teacher, who was mentor to the left-wing students. Sano's possessions were searched, and materials were found relating to the personnel and policies of the Communist party, of which Sano was a prominent leader. Yamakawa, Sakai, and many other Communists were arrested, although Sano himself escaped by fleeing the country. See Yamamoto and Arita, *op. cit.*, pp. 64–65.

[54] Osugi, his wife, and his small nephew were murdered by a *Kempeitai* (Military Police) captain, Amakasu. In the so-called Kameto Affair, nine leaders of the Young Communist League were killed by police in their cells "for making too much noise"—they were singing revolutionary songs. The lock-up of "radicals" had been undertaken as a security measure.

The Korean massacres stemmed from many sources. Prejudice against the Koreans in Japan had been fairly strong. The Koreans were considered unruly elements and law violators. Under the circumstances of Korean annexation, moreover, nationalist movements were always afoot among some Koreans,

The events of 1923 produced important repercussions in the Japanese left-wing movement. Conflicts between moderates and Communists had been intensified in the aftermath of declining Anarchist-Syndicalist strength. And the June Communist arrests, together with the publicity on radicalism just after the September earthquake, contained some revelations that were startling to the moderate left. With Communist members exposed, the social democrats discovered that Communist participation in such organizations as the Sodomei had been far more extensive than many had imagined. Although on the one hand the moderates decried *Kempeitai* (Military Police) brutality, "government reactionarism," and suppression tactics, on the other hand they began to respond with greater alacrity to Communist attacks and the attempts of the Communists to control leftist organizations. The struggle within the Sodomei became increasingly sharper. In the 1924 general meeting of the Federation there were bitter disputes between anti-Communist central headquarters leaders and certain Communist district representatives. With the Communists weakened by the arrests and by their own internal dissension, the non-Communists secured firmer control. As a reaction to this, the left-wing elements within the Federation moved toward secession. In December, 1924, a few unions in the Tokyo area set up the separatist *Kanto Chiho Rodo Hyogikai* (Kanto District Labor Council) and began publication of an independent newspaper, the *Rodo Shimbun* (*Labor Newspaper*). In the Sodomei general meeting of 1925, the far leftists were overwhelmingly defeated, and, as a result, on April 13 of that year some 25 labor unions organized the *Nihon Sodomei Kakushin Domei* (The Japanese Federation Reform League), with headquarters in Osaka. Sodomei headquarters quickly excluded the unions participating in the League, and on May 25 the group changed its name to Rodo Hyogikai. The national labor movement, still extremely weak, was now split in half. The Sodomei retained some 35 unions with a membership of slightly more than 20,000; the Hyogikai was composed of 32 unions claiming approximately 12,500 members.

The labor split reflected a general development in the leftist

---

and after 1920 the Communists played heavily upon this theme. Thus in the panic of the earthquake, reports of Korean looting together with fears of subversion swept the emotion-laden Japanese mobs. Hundreds (some figures say several thousands) of Koreans were killed. The Japanese Communist party used this massacre by making September 1 an anniversary day against imperialism.

movement. The only other important organization which was broadly representative of all left-wing elements was the *Seiji Mondai Kenkyukai* (Society for the Study of Political Problems). By 1925, the friction within the Kenkyukai had reached the breaking point, and the moderates were ousted or resigned, leaving the Kenkyukai a unit auxiliary to the Hyogikai. Later, in May, 1926, the organization received headquarters orders to change its name to *Taishu Kyoiku Domei* (League for Mass Education).

In the meantime there had been some very interesting developments in the illegal Japanese Communist movement. The small Japanese Communist party had been heavily battered by the June, 1923, arrests; most of its leaders had been imprisoned. The scars of internal battle over the 1922 Thesis, moreover, remained, and there was dissidence from several sides. Thus the stage was set for the March, 1924, decision to dissolve the party. The March meeting could not, of course, be attended by those in prison, but the decision met with their overwhelming approval; only a very few, such as Arahata Kanson, appear to have opposed the move.[55] Yamakawa's support for dissolution was incorporated into his "natural development" theory, which argued that neither the times nor the stage of Japanese development were propitious for a Japanese Communist party. Yamakawa favored prior work in building up the labor movement and enlarging propaganda activities without jeopardizing radicals by encumbering them with membership in an illegal party. This position seemed desirable to the overwhelming majority of Japanese Communists, but the Comintern reacted violently to the news of dissolution. Initial representatives dispatched to Shanghai were greeted coolly, and despite certain pleas for reconsideration, the Comintern remained adamant. In a

---

[55] For various accounts of events leading up to dissolution of the first Japanese Communist party, see Nabeyama, *op. cit.*, pp. 69–80; Sano Hiroshi, *op. cit.*, p. 99; Ichikawa Shoichi, *Nihon Kyosanto shoshi* (*A Short History of the Japanese Communist Party*), Tokyo, 1947 ed., p. 51. (Ichikawa's work, first published in 1932, is the present official history and bible of the Japanese Communist party.)

Two leaders of the dissolution movement, Akamatsu Katsumaro and Suzuki Mosaburo, together with their followers, were already tending toward the social democrats. Actually, however, almost the whole membership favored at least temporary abandonment of a formal party. In addition to Yamakawa Hitoshi, first leader of the party, and Sakai, another veteran, this group also included Nozaka Sanzo. It is interesting to note that in this period, as in the future, prison walls were no barrier to communications with Communist members outside.

Shanghai meeting of January, 1925, Japanese representatives had to listen to a stinging rebuke to their past leadership and an order to reëstablish the party.[56] The new mantle of power was now falling to Watanabe Masanosuke, Arahata Kanson, Sano Manabu, and Tokuda Kyuichi, as such veterans as Yamakawa, Sakai, and others fell into disgrace or left the party. The new leaders first organized a "Bureau," and followed up this action, in August, 1925, by the creation of a "Communist Group." The new organization set up for itself three major duties: first, to drive the social democrats out of the proletarian movement; second, to support "class-mass parties whose emphasis was solely upon the interests and participation of the masses themselves"; third, to capture leadership in "truly left-wing" organizations and build Communist factions within suitable proletarian parties.[57]

Meanwhile, the lengthy struggle among those in the non-Communist left to create a unified legal party was continuing, but the efforts toward unification were hampered by the factional proclivities of Japanese society, government policies, Communist sabotage, and major differences among the non-Communist forces themselves. With the passage of the Universal Manhood Suffrage Act in 1925, one of the general objectives of the leftist movement had been accomplished and the establishment of a party organization had been made urgent. In the midst of the hectic disunity of 1925, a series of meetings was held in an effort to bring forth a labor-farmer party. The initiative in this was generally with the "leftists" within the proletarian movement. While the moderates were still exploring the best procedures, the *Nihon Nomin Kumiai* (Japan Farmers' Union), which had fairly strong Communist and "popular front" representation, quickly called a party organizational meeting in June, 1925. At first, almost all leftist elements

---

[56] Watanabe, Arahata, Sano, and Tokuda were told that past leaders had been "anti-Marxist-Leninists" who had no true understanding of Communism, having disobeyed Comintern orders, failed to develop mass affiliations, and maintained only individual connections. See Yamamoto and Arita, *op. cit.*, pp. 73–74. The vitriolic nature of this attack did not make it easy for those "in error" to humble themselves before Comintern authorities.

[57] The "Bureau" had adopted a Political and an Organizational Thesis based upon theses of the Fourth General Comintern Meeting of 1924. The emphasis of these was upon winning over the masses and following the Bolshevik pattern of party organization. The core of the party was to be the factory cell, with the familiar principle of "democratic centralism" binding the cells and the intermediate party units to policy and tactical decisions of the party high command.

participated, but in the final meeting of November 29, 1925, the Sodomei and most other moderate delegates withdrew over the question of allowing the extreme left to enter the party.[58] In the absence of these groups, the *Nomin Rodoto* (Farmer-Labor Party) was formally established on December 1, 1925, only to be banned thirty minutes later by government order. The official prospectus of the Nomin Rodoto showed clearly the influence of the Communists, although neither membership nor policy was exclusively in their hands.

Immediately after the ban, new attempts to achieve some unity in the leftist ranks were made. Nomin Kumiai and Sodomei leaders met together and, with other, outside representatives, set up principles for a new party which would disavow the Communist line. The result was the establishment of the *Rodo Nominto* (Labor-Farmer Party), on March 5, 1926. The party program had been substantially revised; it provided for a pledge to abide by "the conditions of our country," legal methods, and parliamentary reform.[59] Differences within the new party, however, were not long in appearing. Again the question of a "popular front" loomed large. Although the moderates insisted that the Hyogikai and its auxiliaries be banned from any participation, the Nomin Kumiai, itself badly divided, argued for excluding these elements from the organizational meetings only, that is, from the meetings which established the official party policy. Those who advocated the Nomin Kumiai position most strongly consisted of both Communists and certain non-Communists who believed in the necessity and possibility of total amalgamation. The issue came to a head in arguments over whether to recognize certain district branches which were quickly organized by extremist elements and demanded admission to the party. In less than seven months, the party had

---

[58] The entire series of meetings was marked by violent disputes among the Seiji Kenkyukai, the Hyogikai, and the Sodomei. The Sodomei insisted that the Kenkyukai (now predominately extremist) and the *Musan Seinen Domei* (Proletarian Youth League) be shunned as Communist front organizations.

[59] Three important principles of the new party were as follows: "1. In accordance with the national conditions of our country, we pledge the realization of the political, economic, and social emancipation of the proletarian class. 2. Through legal methods, we pledge the reform of the system connected with inequitable land and production distribution. 3. We pledge the overthrow of the established parties which represent only the interests of the privileged classes, and [we pledge] the fundamental reform of the parliament." Quoted in Royama (ed.), *Musanseito ron*, p. 432.

broken wide open, with almost all the moderates withdrawing as a result of the defeat of their efforts to exclude the far left.

With Oyama Ikuo as party president, the Rodo Nominto became the recognized "popular front" party and the organ through which the Communists channeled their political activities. In this connection, the Comintern-directed policy of the Japanese Communist party was most interesting. The Moscow order was to work through the Rodo Nominto and through three organizations which were to be made captive organs: the Hyogikai, the *Musan Seinen Domei* (Proletarian Youth League), and the Nihon Nomin Kumiai. Communists were ordered to enter all these organizations en masse and, through them, to combat the "social chauvinism" of the moderate left. At the same time, however, Communist party members were warned against considering these organs as end objectives or as being, in any way, a substitute for a formal Communist party. Not allowed to organize a legal party, the Communists were to operate through the Rodo Nominto, but their sole allegiance was to the Communist party, and the only binding instructions were to come from Communist party headquarters. And, as subsequent events will indicate, not even those non-Communists who clung most doggedly to the objective of a "popular front" could avoid bitter attacks from the Communists within their ranks when they deviated from the immediate Comintern line.

With the hope of unity shattered as a result of the experiences of 1925 and early 1926, the moderate elements within the left wing came forward with their own parties. In March, 1926, the right wing of the Nihon Nomin Kumiai withdrew because of leftist controls, and in October it proceeded to establish the *Nihon Nominto* (Japan Farmers' Party). The Nominto reflected the additional problem of agrarian separatism which confronted the left wing, and its politics reflected a strong conservative and nationalist bent. On December 5, 1926, the main social democratic elements combined to establish the *Shakai Minshuto* (Social Mass Party). The leadership of the Shakai Minshuto came from intellectuals such as Abe Iso, Yoshino Sakuzo, and Horie Kiichi, together with the major Sodomei leaders. The general position of the new party was expressed in three tenets, as follows:

1. Firmly believing that the basis for setting up healthy livelihood conditions for the nation-people lies in the creation of a political and economic system which has its base in the working class, we pledge the realization of this.

2. Recognizing that healthy livelihood conditions of the nation-

people are damaged by the production and distribution laws of capitalism, we pledge the reform of these by legal methods.

3. We reject both the presently-established political parties which
represent the privileged classes and the extremist parties which ignore
the process of social evolution.[60]

Probably the Shakai Minshuto, more than any other leftist party,
sought to carry the true banners of socialist democracy in the
prewar period. It never deviated from the principles of parliamentarism and legal reform. Hence its fate—or at least the fate
of the principles which it represented—would be a decisive factor
in measuring the relation between democracy and the left. Although some of its leaders were weak in character or political apti-
tude, it inherited the central growth of democratic socialist thought
which had ripened in the period during and immediately after
World War I. Yet one must record the fact that the Shakai Minshuto from the beginning betrayed most of the weaknesses of the
other Japanese parties in terms of organization and tactics. On
the one hand, its leaders fell far short of seizing all opportunities
for wooing popular support, and on the other hand, the general
problem of factionalism was potent in the Shakai Minshuto as
elsewhere, contributing its share to the difficulties of attracting
support from other like-minded groups.

Indeed, the fragmentation of the left wing did not stop with the
emergence of the Rodo Nominto, the Nominto, and the Shakai
Minshuto. Four days after the official organization of the Shakai
Minshuto, so-called center elements from the Sodomei and the
Nihon Nomin Kumiai set up the *Nihon Ronoto* (Japan Labor-
Farmer Party). Those responsible for the Nihon Ronoto were,
for the most part, men who favored continued efforts to build a
more broadly based united front, but who were not willing to be
parties to any Communist-dominated group. Many had vigorously
opposed the withdrawal of the Sodomei from the Rodo Nominto
and also had objected to the strength of conservative trade union-
ists in the Shakai Minshuto. The Nihon Ronoto program did not
differ much from that of the Rodo Nominto, but in reality the new
party occupied a position midway between the Shakai Minshuto
and the Rodo Nominto.

In addition to the four national leftist parties and the numerous
district parties now on the open horizon, moreover, the second
Communist party had been established formally in great secrecy
on December 4, 1926, just one day before the creation of the Shakai

[60] For the complete program of the Shakai Minshuto, see *ibid.*, pp. 455–
462.

332

Minshuto. For many months, the Communists had been receiving directions and funds from a Soviet agent called Janson, who operated from behind the title of Commercial Attaché in the Russian Embassy.[61] Once again, however, the Japanese Communists ran afoul of Comintern ideas. This time, moreover, they became unwittingly involved in the Stalin-Trotsky battle, which was just reaching its climax in the Soviet Union. A new heresy had arisen, "Fukumotoism." Fukumoto Kazuo was a young intellectual whose power in Japanese Communist circles had grown steadily since 1925. With most of the veterans either in prison or members of the dissident Yamakawa group, he dominated the December, 1926, organizational meeting. Fukumoto accepted the concept of an incomplete bourgeois revolution in Japan, but insisted that a worker-peasant front must fight "bourgeois democracy" in its Japanese forms. And he went on to argue the necessity of a separate warfare on behalf of "Marxist essentials," a warfare which would concentrate upon ideological clarity and purification on the part of all participants. Since these theories challenged the Stalinist line and since their author had run afoul of important Soviet figures, a showdown in Moscow was demanded.[62]

The result of the Special Committee meeting held in Moscow was the Thesis of July, 1927, which casts light upon both the Japanese Communist movement and the general problem of disunity in the leftist ranks. The Thesis contained a blast for both "Yamakawaism," which was labeled "right-wing opportunism," and "Fukumotoism," which was castigated as "left-wing extremism." [63] Those among the new leaders who were "tainted" by the latter deviation were relieved of their positions by Comintern order,

---

[61] For an account of Janson (also known as Jonson and Yanson), see Nabeyama, *op. cit.*, pp. 104–105.

[62] For an orthodox Communist analysis of Fukumotoism, see Yamamoto and Arita, *op. cit.*, pp. 111–113; also Ichikawa, *op. cit.*, pp. 101 ff.; see also Sano Hiroshi, *op. cit.*, pp. 100–101; Nabeyama, *op. cit.*, pp. 102 ff.
The rise of Fukumotoism was described by the Communists as a reaction to the "opportunism" of Yamakawa. Janson had been bitterly opposed to Fukumotoism, and, as a result, the Comintern insisted upon a Moscow hearing.

[63] The Thesis stated that the development of the Communist party as an independent organization had already been demonstrated to be absolutely necessary, and that the errors made by Comrade Hoshi (Yamakawa) must be corrected. At the same time, however, the errors of Comrade Kuroki (Fukumoto) were equally serious. Fukumoto's theories would lead to reducing the organization to a small intellectualized group, isolated from the masses and dedicated only to the rarefied atmosphere of theoretic debate, thus enabling the social democratic elements to capture the proletariat. For a complete text of the Thesis, see Yamamoto and Arita, *op. cit.*, pp. 84–102.

and these included Fukumoto himself, Sano Fumio, and several others. Sano Manabu, Ichikawa, Arahata, Watanabe, and Nabeyama were appointed as new members of the Japanese Communist party's Central Executive Committee. The greater part of the Thesis, however, consisted of a reëvaluation of Japanese society which was intended to correct past errors. In this, it was evident that since the promulgation of the 1922 Thesis the party line had undergone some modification. Heavy stress was now placed upon the menace of Japanese imperialism, and some interesting predictions were made.[64] The new thesis admitted the claim of the "leftists" that Japanese capitalism had shown extraordinary advances and was reaching its zenith point, and that, in many respects, the situation matched Lenin's objective conditions for a proletarian revolution.[65] Indeed, there was a noticeable backing away from the purely two-stage revolutionary theory as set forth in the 1922 Thesis. The theory that "any laws whatsoever" connected with the first-stage bourgeois revolution must be used in Japan was denounced as fantasy, and comparison with China for tactical purposes was called foolish.[66] Although the 1927 Thesis carried forward the former line in continuing to discuss the importance of a bourgeois democratic revolution, it differed in emphasizing a combined worker-peasant revolutionary alliance working to foment a socialist revolution against the "reactionary capitalist-landlord league." But according to the new thesis, the central problem was the political apathy and ignorance of the masses—the absence of what Lenin called the "subjective conditions" for revolution.[67] This ignorance was, of course, equated with a lack of acceptance of the Communist party as the only true representative of the common people.

[64] Japanese imperialism was declared to be a direct threat to the Chinese revolution and the Soviet Union. However, a struggle between Japan on the one hand and the United States and Great Britain on the other was described as unavoidable.

[65] See the second section of the 1927 Thesis, *ibid.*, pp. 84–90.

[66] The obvious contrasts between China and Japan were drawn. The conclusion was that except for the "petty bourgeois" elements who were rapidly falling into the proletarian class, the Japanese bourgeois were not only unfit for a common front but must be fought vigorously.

[67] The importance of the "bourgeois democratic" revolution to Marxian theory and tactics is revealed in the painful dilemma facing Russian theorists who were attempting to fix Communist policy for Japan. Originally, Marxian theory rested exclusively upon an analysis of Western society, and Marx had defined the proper stage for a proletarian revolution as that stage when political liberalism had matured sufficiently to permit mass political conscious-

The position taken on the question of a popular front was most interesting. In addition to insisting that the Communist party had to act as an independent organization with all-powerful control over its members, the Thesis dwelt extensively upon the need for complete warfare against the social democrats. The Shakai Minshuto was described as a party attempting "to poison the masses with opportunism, patriotism, and social Imperialism." [68] Described as equally dangerous was "left-wing social democracy," as represented in Japan by the Nihon Ronoto. This party was denounced as doing nothing more than using left-wing terminology in order to hide its opportunism from the laboring masses, a "false socialism" which must be fought vigorously.[69] Having viciously attacked every element of the Japanese left-wing movement except the Rodo Nominto, however, the Thesis writers then proceeded to criticize the Japanese Communists for splitting such organizations as the Sodomei and the Nomin Kumiai.[70] The ideal,

---

ness and a maximum amount of freedom from state power, while, at the same time, the economic structure had reached a position of great concentration, permitting an easy transition to complete nationalization. Although the Russian Revolution had followed no such pattern, Leninism followed in general the concept of the "bourgeois democratic state," partly because it enabled Communism to use the rising nationalist tide in the underdeveloped areas, but also because it offered the possibility of an economic and political stage which would serve to develop the instruments of a successful Communist revolution.

Japan, however, indicated the difficulties of reconciling this element of Leninist theory with the realities. The Japanese industrial revolution did not produce the mature liberal society in which Communist tactics could operate with little restraint upon an insecure people. Indeed, the production of a full-fledged Western-style "bourgeois democratic" revolution was quite impossible in the circumstances that prevailed in Japan. With much of the industrial-commercial class wedded to an organic concept of state, the Communists were opposed by a degree of state power that could overwhelm them and by strong currents of faith in certain symbols not conducive to a broad popular front concept. In this connection, the Japanese Communists were forced to fight the tide of nationalism rather than to use it, as they did in China. And although this would have been true in any case because of the timing and nature of the Japanese nationalist movement, it was brought home to the Japanese people (including the Communist leaders) in stark and dramatic fashion by the desperate efforts of the Comintern to guide each step—a necessity because the tenuous relation between Marxist-Leninist theories and the Japanese situation rendered many moves artificialities which depended upon complete allegiance to world Communism rather than moves in accordance with the forwarding of a Japanese Communist revolution.

[68] *Ibid.*, p. 95.

[69] *Ibid.*, pp. 95–96.

[70] At the time of the split in the Sodomei and the formation of the Hyogikai,

of course, was to wrest leadership rather than risk separation from the masses, however difficult this might be when the Communist party was expected to denounce all other elements as fools or knaves and sabotage them at every opportunity. For the future, the Communist party was to carry on through the Rodo Nominto, following an immediate policy of both "bourgeois democratic" and "proletarian revolution" objectives.[71]

The 1927 Thesis did not put a halt to the violent polemic debate within the Japanese Communist movement or stop the development of deviation. Disputes continued to rage over the question of the two-stage revolution. A group centering around Yamakawa, Sakai, and Inomata Tsunao, men now unfrocked by the Comintern, denied the concept that a two-stage process was necessary. Known as the *Rono ha* (Labor-Farmer Faction) because of their organ, the *Rono,* they argued that the bourgeois democratic revolution must be made synonymous with the proletarian revolution, and that all efforts must be made to attack the bourgeois and render the "petty bourgeois" powerless immediately. The orthodox Comintern-directed Communists lashed back through their organ *Marxshugi* (*Marxism*). Watanabe, Sano Manabu, and others wrote articles in 1927 and early 1928 attacking the Rono ha for its attempt to destroy the idea that the stage of the bourgeois democratic revolution was historically necessary.[72]

Meanwhile, the various non-Communist elements of Japanese socialism had been engaged in abortive attempts to achieve some greater measure of unity before the 1928 elections. Throughout 1927, many amalgamation meetings were planned, but always the personal differences and the different shadings of leftism represented respectively by the various groups proved formidable barriers. The centrist groups, particularly the Nihon Ronoto, were the most active, but these elements could be happy only with a three-way union which would include such diverse elements as the

---

Sano Manabu had been in Moscow and had received instructions that the Communist party was to oppose this move. Before he could return, however, the break had occurred and any reknitting was impossible.

[71] The Communist party program as outlined by the Comintern included the following points: continuous struggle against imperialist war; aid for the Chinese revolution and the Union of Soviet Socialist Republics; absolute rejection of colonies; dissolution of the Diet; abolition of the Emperor system; universal suffrage for all above eighteen years of age; rights of assemblage, meeting, and association; freedom of speech and press; removal of land from landowners, government, and temples; and progressive labor legislation.

[72] See *ibid.*, pp. 113–122.

Shakai Minshuto and the Rodo Nominto. This was quite impossible. Thus the first election conducted under the universal manhood suffrage rules found not one "proletarian party," but four, with a fifth working from under cover.[73] This combined with all the other factors mitigating against leftist success to make those election returns dismal reading to the hopeful socialists. Labor party disunity made it impossible for the parties to present an organized campaign and split what little resources and leadership were available,[74] and it made government restrictions easier to obtain and more effective. The savage attacks which the left-wing party candidates leveled against one another naturally tended to undermine all these parties in the estimation of the people. On the whole, the lower economic classes did not vote for the candidates of any labor party, and this was especially true of the tenant farmers.

Of the 88 candidates who ran under various proletarian party labels, only 8 were elected. Four of these were from the Shakai Minshuto (moderate), 2 from the Rodo Nominto (far left), and 1 each from the Nihon Ronoto (center) and a district labor party.[75] The vote for leftist party candidates totaled nearly 500,000, but this was small indeed compared to the 4,274,898 votes cast for official Seiyukai candidates and the 4,201,219 votes cast for official Minseito candidates.[76]

The 1928 elections clearly showed the desirability of leftist unity, and strenuous efforts were made during the next two years to join various factions together. The resulting failure was not due to any lack of appreciation for the value of unified action, or to blindness to the risks of continued disunity. At the root of the problem, however, were ideological and personal obstacles so great as to permit amalgamation only on the most precarious and short-term basis.

Among the numerous leftist groups, the one approaching the question of unity with the greatest caution and reserve was the Shakai Minshuto. There were many reasons for this. Some of its

---

[73] The official party membership of the socialist parties, as registered with the Home Office in 1928, was as follows: Shakai Minshuto, 47,267; Nihon Ronoto, 23,520; Nihon Nominto, 92,792; and Rodo Nominto (1927 figures —the party was banned in 1928), 15,374.

[74] Labor party funds came primarily from entrance fees (usually ¥1), voluntary subscriptions, and party rallies.

[75] See Royama, *Musanseito ron*, pp. 441–442.

[76] The total votes for the leftist parties were 492,221. Of these, the Rodo Nominto received 193,028; Shakai Minshuto, 128,756; Nihon Ronoto, 86,975; Nihon Nominto, 46,180; and the remainder was divided among local leftists parties. Figures from *ibid.*, p. 442.

leaders were inordinately jealous of their position and feared the struggle for leadership which might ensue, but this was a factor in all the proletarian parties. More important, the Shakai Minshuto had been subjected to a continual torrent of abuse and personal vilification from those further to the left, especially the far left. It was not easy to tolerate such epithets as "social chauvinist," "tool of the bourgeoisie," and all the customary slander that came with its "Made in Moscow" mark. But above all, the social democrats, wedded to their program of parliamentarism and evolutionary reform, could not be truly integrated with any group which had as its ultimate objective something vastly different. One could still legitimately debate the wisdom of temporary coalitions based strictly upon self-interest, but in the context of prewar Japan, the social democrats were increasingly drawn to the conclusion that coalition with the Communists and far-left fellow travelers was not to their own interest.[77]

It was again the center groups, such as the Nihon Ronoto, which fostered most of the unification moves, but the far-leftist Rodo Nominto also strove for union on terms acceptable to it. These efforts were stimulated, in a sense, by the mass arrests of March 15, 1928, which dealt another mighty blow to the Communists and assorted leftists.[78] This was followed on April 10 by the official banning of the Rodo Nominto. With the far leftists much weakened and with the Tanaka government, by its domestic and foreign policy, threatening the whole leftist movement, unification efforts were intensified. Spurred on by the Nomin Kumiai faction within the Nihon Ronoto, the leftists held numerous consultations, and finally, on December 20, 1928, the *Nihon Taishuto* (Japan Mass Party) was formed.

The Nihon Taishuto was the result of a two-year struggle to combine leftist strength, but it was scarcely a fitting monument

[77] The very obvious foreign control of Japanese Communism, the Communists' lack of real strength, and the interaction between their enforced tactics of illegal operation and governmental suppression made the benefits of any coalition extremely dubious.

[78] The bold activities of the Communists in the 1928 elections, such as electioneering on behalf of Rodo Nominto candidates (including such prominent Communist party members as Tokuda Kyuichi), extensive pamphleteering, and the creation of factory cells and factory newspapers, gave government secret police and spies an excellent chance to collect an abundance of information. The result was the arrest of well over a thousand radicals shortly after the election. In this great dragnet operation, Communist party leadership was again decimated, and very few escaped.

to the efforts toward unification, and in a short time it had been broken up by factional and doctrinaire quarrels. Even in the beginning, although it was widely heralded as a "seven-party coalition," it did not include the Shakai Minshuto or the greater part of the old Rodo Nominto. Unwilling to make the choice between a coalition with the moderates or a merger with the far left, it secured no substantial part of either. The "seven parties" were chiefly the Nihon Ronoto, the Nominto, and district labor parties, with a sprinkling of representation from the old Rodo Nominto. The Taishuto program was based on progressive socialist demands,[79] but the gnawing question of coalition-with-whom continued to plague and divide its members. Many desired to unite exclusively with the Shakai Minshuto, which would not consider a coalition with the far left. Meanwhile, an important faction of the disbanded Rodo Nominto objected to amalgamation with the new party, and this faction, led by Oyama Ikuo, reëstablished itself under the label *Ronoto* (Labor-Farmer Party) in November, 1929.[80] Below the surface, moreover, the Communist party was also reëstablished, though weakened and bereft of many veteran leaders.[81] Soon, the Nihon Taishuto, which had promised to de-

---

[79] For the Nihon Taishuto program, see *ibid.*, pp. 482–484. The chief planks included opposition to militarism, demands for the purification of Japanese politics and parties, the development of progressive labor and social legislation, universal suffrage to all above twenty years of age, land reform, and nationalization of basic industries.

[80] It is interesting to note that the official Communist line at this time was to oppose the reëstablishment of the old Rodo Nominto, and that Oyama, who had long worked with the Communists, was suddenly denounced by them with the usual epithets.

[81] After 1928 the Comintern depended heavily upon Moscow-trained students to pick up the pieces of organizational work in Japan. Much earlier, the Japanese Communists had agreed to send some thirty students per year to the Moscow Far Eastern University. Although this quota could not be maintained, about forty students in all were sent during the years 1924–1926. Certain Japanese helped operate the program, including Katayama Sen, and later, Yamamoto Kenzo and Nozaka Sanzo. When the veteran leaders were imprisoned in Japan, the Moscow graduates were entrusted with the mission of reëstablishing the party and its organs. Handicapped by a lack of experience, they nevertheless kept the Japanese Communist party officially alive, even after the mass arrests of April, 1929, which practically annihilated the remaining veterans. For an interesting account of this from the Communist point of view, see Yamamoto and Arita, *op. cit.*, pp. 160–170.
Communist party central headquarters in Japan were reëstablished in November, 1928. *Akahata* resumed publication in December. Sano Manabu, Yamamoto Kenzo, and Ichikawa Shoichi had been seated as representatives of

339

velop a solid leftist front, was reduced to little more than the faction from the old Nihon Ronoto, with some Nominto elements. And another split had occurred in labor ranks and resulted in the formation of yet another party. An element within the Sodomei which opposed the policies of Matsuoka Komakichi and Nishio Suehiro broke away from both the Federation and the Shakai Minshuto, to form the *Zenkoku Minshuto* (All-Nation Mass Party).

Thus a deeply divided leftist movement faced the crucial 1930 general election and went down to overwhelming defeat. Although the total leftist vote increased slightly over that of 1928, only five leftist candidates were elected to the Diet, as opposed to eight in their first campaign.[82] In addition to facing the usual disadvantages, the labor parties had run too many candidates and had campaigned against each other with unprecedented bitterness.[83] In the aftermath of the 1930 elections, discouragement was omnipresent in the leftist camp. The labor parties were still completely separated from the Japanese "common man" by the great barriers which Japanese society posed. Divisions were as potent in the unions as in the parties, and stemmed from the same basic causes. And now the entire left was under unprecedented attack. The Communists and other extremists were being rapidly eliminated by mass arrests. But the moderates were also being increasingly threatened by the government and by the forces of the extreme right. The right was emerging to challenge the left for popular

---

the Japanese Communist party in the Sixth General Comintern Meeting of the summer of 1928. However, party organizational efforts were barely under way again when the mass arrests of April 16, 1929, occurred, and this time every prominent Communist leader in Japan was seized, along with many non-Communist radicals.

[82] Of the four nationally established leftist parties, the Shakai Minshuto polled 170,385 votes and elected 2 of its 33 candidates; the Nihon Taishuto polled 165,297 votes and elected 2 of its 23 candidates; the Ronoto (the old Rodo Nominto) polled 78,538 votes and elected 1 of its 13 candidates; the Zenkoku Minshuto polled 19,695 votes and elected none of its 4 candidates. The district parties of the left polled 68,389 votes, but elected none of 21 candidates. The proletarian party votes totaled 502,304. Figures from Royama (ed.), *Musanseito ron,* pp. 443–444.

[83] Note the following remark, attributed to Oyama, leader of the leftist Ronoto, directed against the Shakai Minshuto: "The Social Democrats are feelers of the bourgeoisie stretched to the proletarian camp. They keep up their shameful existence and activities at the instigation of the bourgeoisie in order to guide and to divert the true proletarian movement represented by the left wing." Quoted in *JC,* August 28, 1930, p. 259.

support. Divided as it was, the right nevertheless had great advantages. It was moving with, not against, the trends, seeking to channel public unrest against democracy, Westernism, and internationalism. Its most dynamic elements were seeking to combine a program of drastic social and economic reform along socialist lines with a nationalist platform of race consciousness and foreign expansion. The thin veneer of individual and class consciousness which had been spread over a part of Japanese society by the leftist movement could not long withstand this assault. Many of the "leftists" themselves were not too far separated in history or in convictions from national socialism, and the irresistible tide swept some of them into that camp labeled "right."

After 1930, labor parties representing the left were being formed and dissolved with great rapidity, never establishing any stable foundations or attaining unified composition. The first important effort occurred in 1930, when the fusion of modern elements was attempted. The Shakai Minshuto tried to form a joint party with the center group, now reorganized as the *Zenkoku Taishuto* (All-Nation Mass Party). A majority of the latter party, however, was still interested only in a three-way amalgamation which would include the Ronoto. The attempt ended in failure. The fateful elections of February, 1932, held under the shadow of the Manchurian War, gave the parties of the left only 287,000 votes, just a little more than half their previous total. These parties, by restricting their support to fewer contestants, made it possible for the smaller number of votes to elect five candidates, thereby keeping the same total in the Diet, but the left was now clearly declining and its morale was at an all-time low ebb.

With another serious defeat behind them, the two labor parties containing the bulk of the leftist elements, the Shakai Minshuto and the *Zenkoku Rono Taishuto* (All-Nation Labor-Farmer Mass Party, a combination of center-left elements) finally joined together on July 24, 1932. The new party, the *Shakai Taishuto* (Social Mass Party), was to represent the moderate leftists and unions, in some fashion, until its dissolution eight years later. Its program was anticapitalist, anti-Communist, and anti-Fascist. It did not manage to adopt this program, however, without major dissension from those who were ready to swallow the new gospel of national socialism.

With insignificant exceptions, the extreme leftists were now in prison, in exile, or recanting. Although internal trends, especially state force, had greatly contributed to this situation, the Comintern had also continued to play an important role. In the spring of 1931 a "New Political Thesis" was drafted, with extensive Russian "aid." The 1931 draft thesis went a long way toward the old Rono ha position, supporting the concept that Japan was now an advanced capitalist nation ripe for a proletarian revolution, and further relegating the "bourgeois democratic revolution" to the dustbin.[84] The outbreak of the Manchurian Incident, however, turned Russian attention completely to the security threat facing her. It was now more necessary than ever to bring all foreign Communist party policies into line with the national interests of the Union of Soviet Socialist Republics, irrespective of the result.

Thus, even before the ink had dried on the so-called 1931 Thesis, alterations were demanded by Russian-Comintern sources. The confusion in Japanese Communist circles was understandable. They had been publicly rebuked, within the past few months, for a document which, to the best of their knowledge, was in complete conformity with Russian-Comintern views. Various international organs lashed out at them for "minimizing" the peasants in the revolutionary program and for underrating the dangers of the Imperial system. When the 1932 Thesis was handed down, it devoted central attention to the problem of Japanese expansion, and made its two major points the overthrow of the Emperor system and the struggle against Japanese imperialism.[85] But in the process of this rapid repudiation, the Japanese Communist party had suffered another heavy blow, for it was now evident beyond any doubt that shifts within Russia and changing factors affecting Russian national interests could dictate overnight ultimatums from Moscow. And these orders made Japanese Communists look like fools or traitors to their cause. Shortly thereafter, a group of Communist heroes headed by Sano Manabu and Nabeyama recanted from their prison cells in a sensational manner.[86] Even before these recantations, however, the Communist movement had dwindled to insignificance, although it lived on in the minds and hopes of a few individuals.

[84] For the 1931 Thesis, see Yamamoto and Arita, *op. cit.*, pp. 215–220. This document is an excellent case study of Communist methods of making a transition or abrupt change while appearing to conform with earlier pronouncements.

[85] For this important document and the various developments leading up to it, see *ibid.*, pp. 252–292; also Sano Hiroshi, *op. cit.*, p. 102.

[86] See the heavily censored statement of Sano Manabu entitled "Comintern to no ketsubetsu" (Parting with the Comintern), in the August, 1933, issue of *Kaizo*; see also Nabeyama, *op. cit.*, pp. 159 ff.

In and of itself, Communist collapse was no loss, but the failure of the moderate left sealed the fate of democracy in prewar Japan. For all the unsolved problems it carried which were meaningful to democratic philosophy, still, a strong social democratic movement was the *sine qua non* for any vitalization of Japanese democracy. The defeat suffered by the left in prewar Japan was not caused by a lack of revolutionary potential. That potential was in some respects the very essence of modern Japanese society. The development of great inequities and tensions was an inevitable concomitant of the Japanese industrial revolution. To play upon injustice and insecurity—to capture the dream of ending misery and frustration—would not seem difficult on the surface. And obviously Japan offered the leftists certain advantages unavailable elsewhere in the Far East. Here was a literate population, to be tapped by all the propaganda devices adjusted to popular movements. Here was a people who had felt the full impact of cultural collision as had few, if any, peoples in the modern world—a clash that was not merely represented by a foreign periphery in their land, but lay in themselves. And here also was a people with a sense of power—their own power—born out of science and energy, available for undertakings which could dwarf present accomplishments, but seemingly unexpendable and excess, awaiting a plan or a cause.

But when the left chased these tangible and intangible assets, they seemed always to be will-o'-the-wisps, enticing but far away. And once again, the timing and circumstances of Japanese "modernization" were crucial. Essentially, modern Japan was not the product of a gradual, evolutionary development, but was a result of an incredibly rapid succession of external stimuli which were put to constructive use. Since "industrial" Japan was separated by only a few decades from the Tokugawa era, however, the preindustrial heritage was certain to weigh heavily upon the entire society, and especially upon the lower economic classes. Moreover, as has been constantly reiterated, the processes of modernization required by the situation were themselves sustaining forces for certain key traditional techniques and values. Taken together, these circumstances accounted for the heavy agrarian influence, the weaknesses of popular political consciousness, the nature of state power, and the particular role of Japanese nationalism.

In seeking to build a popular base, the leftists were confronted with a people who, scarcely removed from semifeudal conditions, were now subjected to intensive state indoctrination. The magni-

343

tude of the task was especially devastating to those of the moderate left who, by the very nature of their philosophy, were dedicated to political procedures placing a premium upon popular enlightenment and rationality. The difficulties of reaching the peasant with such a movement of reason and initiative could hardly be exaggerated in any case, but with state efforts attuned in other directions, it was hopeless. And the growing urban labor forces, closely connected with the rural scene, were also molded by the economic and political circumstances of their society in such a manner as to be of little service to the social democratic cause. Thus there remained as the core of the movement a small group, mostly intellectuals, whose handicaps were many and whose internal cleavages multiplied with the moving tides of the Western world and with every new shift of conditions within Japan. Nothing was more natural than that many within this group would dismiss the social democratic movement as a complete utopianism.

Perhaps the problems of the Communists need to be analyzed apart from those of the social democrats, despite the many obstacles which the two groups faced in common. Fundamentally, the Communists did not require the same economic-political environment as that needed by the moderate left. Indeed, though they would scarcely admit it, the Communists could find much in the background of Japanese society and in its modern structure which was compatible with their tactics and goals. It is not difficult to see that a change to democracy in any form represented a more complete revolution than Communism. The qualities of authoritarianism and irrational faith inseparably connected with Communism, together with the particular forms of elitism which it supports, can find an operative base in both the heritage and the current necessities of modern Asia. Why then, one may ask, did the dominant Communist group insist upon a "bourgeois democratic" revolution? In part, this demand revealed the rigidity of Marxist doctrine in the hands of the Leninist-Stalinist forces. But it also reflected the desirability of an "open society" within which to operate. Modern Japan illustrated the fact that when the state uses effectively the psychological and physical power now at its disposal, internal opponents can be dealt a mighty blow. Communism never got off its knees in prewar Japan, and this was not so much because its basic tactics were unsuited to that society—which was partially true in the case of the social democrats—as because those tactics were being used with fair effectiveness by its adamant opponents. In this context, it is particularly interesting to note the relationship between Communism and Japanese nationalism. Whereas Communist movements elsewhere in Asia found nationalism most susceptible to their use, and a weapon which coupled them with the concept of necessary state power, in prewar Japan the Communists were forced to fight nationalism at every turn because it had become the deadly weapon of an anti-Communist elite. And as the Communists in this process revealed themselves to be completely dependent upon Russian directives, they added fuel to the nationalist fires which were also trapping and destroying the social democratic forces.

The West cannot be omitted from the picture of leftist decline. The social democrats obtained practically no support from foreign trends. Moderate socialism had suffered numerous setbacks in Europe and was regarded as an anathema almost equal to Communism by most Americans. The only active "assistance" for the left came from Russia and its Comintern. Naturally, Russian policy was deliberately injurious to the moderate left, and, whatever its intentions, disastrous for the Japanese Communists. But from all sources, the internationalist aspirations of the socialist movement were being buffeted by strong nationalist tides.

The collapse of the prewar "left" in Japan did not mean the end of radicalism or social reform movements, as the next chapter will show. The conflicts within modern Japan were too deep, the techniques of state control too loose, and the elitist elements too much divided to permit that. But these new movements had no more relationship to democracy than Communism had. The fate of democracy in prewar Japan was spelled out in the overwhelming failure of the moderate left.

IX

THE MILITARIST ERA AND
PARTY COLLAPSE

THE HISTORY of Japan after 1931 represented the logical culmination of previous trends—an era in which ultranationalism and militarism took a dominant position, easily breaking through such
negligible obstacles as were placed in their path. Although this
period was quite naturally marked by a distinctive Japanese pattern, still it was as inextricably connected with certain world trends
as the era which preceded it. Like every time of crisis and
upheaval, moreover, it was filled with complexities, contradictions, and confusion. Around the issues of internal change and
external expansion, blocs from the military, the civil bureaucracy, and the parties took their positions, alternately struggling
and compromising with varying degrees of fanaticism or uncertainty. The over-all trend toward increased authoritarianism, however, was the one pronounced characteristic which could not be
mistaken.

It did not require a fundamental revolution to push the democratic movement aside in Japan, and, indeed, no such event occurred. The truly revolutionary potentials of the early 1930's were
ultimately neutralized by a program combining sheer force with
certain accommodations to change. This was a program that
matched best with the capacities and interests of the conservative
military leaders, and after 1936 they were clearly the most powerful
elements in the country. In securing this power, to be sure, they
were indebted to the collaboration of many of the old economic
and political elites. Such collaboration was partially voluntary and
partially coerced, and a separation of the two elements is not easy.
On the one hand, the cumulative effect of recent events tended
to underscore the insecurity and fears of top civilian conservatives,

causing them to see in certain military groups and principles a possible shield against disaster. On the other hand, the lack of feasible alternatives and the growing pressure of military power forced even those with reservations into some measure of concurrence or conformity.

Conflict remained, however, at the top and at other levels of Japanese society. If Japanese aggression had been successful, undoubtedly the status quo would have faced internal challenges once peace had come. Many solutions to basic problems creating unrest had been postponed; elitist elements were still divided, with the parts retaining uncertain powers; and finally, no real mass basis of support had been built up. In some of these respects, Japanese militarism was weak when compared with Western totalitarianism.

Such internal challenges as might have been made, however, would not have come from any strong movement fitting the label "democratic." In addition to the obviously adverse trends which would have followed military victory, the failure of democracy would have been too recent and too complete. Long since weakened by its many shortcomings, the Japanese democratic movement was no more than a hollow shell by the 1930's. Its thin and wavering lines broke easily, with parliamentarians continuing to desert their creed and join the opposition at an accelerated rate. The parties which represented the only organized forces dedicated to political competition declined in power, in principles, and, despite a few rallies, in popularity. Their imminent collapse was for a time forestalled by political forces more powerful than they. A part of the bureaucracy, especially a section of the Inner Court officials, maneuvered in such a fashion as to delay their complete capitulation. This was not out of any profound regard for the existent parties, to be sure, nor did it change their ultimate fate. After years of increasing hopelessness, the old parties all dissolved more or less voluntarily in 1940. A new party was formed—*one* new party which, in its very title, signified that democracy, representative government, and the party movement based upon these had been assigned to oblivion.

Since our central concern is with democracy and parties, it is not possible to concentrate on a detailed study of Japanese nationalism, militarism, and "Fascism." Any attempt to assess the final phases of the failure of the attempt at democracy in Japan, however, must include some general analysis of these forces and their impact. On balance, Japanese nationalism was always of great disservice to the democratic cause. In this respect, it showed certain close parallels to late-developing nationalism elsewhere, and, by the same token, strong contrasts to the evolution of earlier nationalism. If the rise of nationalism in a society like that of England is recalled, it will be remembered that its development was largely in the hands of the monarchy and the commercial classes. These elements were joined in a struggle against the universality of the church on the one hand, and against feudal particularism on the other. In the initial process of meeting these opponents, the doctrines of monarchical absolutism were formulated and held sway. Absolutism, however, soon came under attack; and in its subsequent growth, early Western nationalism was closely connected with the advance of democracy.

This connection lay mainly in the element of power sharing, which became the symbol of both the nation-state and the democratic society. Power was often wrested from reluctant hands, to be sure, and in the beginning, the power base was extremely limited. Gradually, however, it expanded, with the initial political forms intact. New elements of society demanded and obtained inclusion in the political institutions, thereby enriching the significance of parties and parliaments. Later, liberal philosophers played upon the vast potentialities of a mass citizenry operating to advance the wealth, power, and wisdom of the state, while at the same time realizing the development of their own individual personalities. Nationalism and democracy, thus fused, were proclaimed to the world.

As the twentieth century was to show, however, this fusion was more a product of timing and circumstances than of natural proclivities. Paradoxically, nationalism could be more easily merged with Western-style democracy before the importance of the "common man" was fully realized and before the modern mass movement was attuned to him. The historical merger of these two forces, moreover, was closely related to the fact that both were instruments suitable, to a large degree, for a pioneer "middle class." The earliest Western nationalism was relatively exclusive and was directed primarily at and by this "middle class." Its development paralleled their rise and was fashioned to complement and advance the political-economic institutions which reflected their interests.

This process also involved the development of certain checks or counterforces against aspects of nationalism which were hostile

348

to democracy. The irrational tendencies innate to a nationalist movement were softened by institutions and theories emphasizing human rationality. In like measure, nationalist unity became "the unity of free men" and "the strength derived from competition." By such means, the democratic forces shaped nationalism sufficiently to partake of its obvious advantages without succumbing to its potentially dangerous forms.

It is interesting to observe the Japanese nationalist movement in the light of some of these factors. We have already noted that Japanese nationalism, contrary to that of the early West, was strongly dominated in its formulative period by agrarian-military elements, and not by a "middle class." In terms of true agrarian interests, this involved certain basic paradoxes, but it is understandable, given the conditions of Japanese history. At a time when the commercial class was weak in every respect except the economic, the Japanese agrarian forces raised up a nationalist movement to halt the inroads of commercialization by emphasizing the superiority of their own primitive institutions. Shintoism, the traditional Emperor high-priest system, the soldier-peasant union, and the primitive economic society became symbols of this early nationalism—symbols drawn from the auguristic-sacrificial stage of Japanese agrarian society.

Japanese nationalism never lost the underlying force of these symbols despite the variety of forms which it subsequently took. The most basic reason for this lay in the inability of the rising commercial-industrial groups in Japan to substitute the early Western "middle class" symbols. Indeed, the first attempts to combine Western democracy and Japanese nationalism were marked by heavy agrarian influence, as we have noted. Between the democratic forces and the agrarian-military elements, a certain curious relationship existed. In their struggle against the power of the national bureaucracy and against most other aspects of centralization, the farmers could find some value in theories of "self-government" and "popular rights." Even the left wing of the Western democratic movement could be approached superficially in their denunciation of capitalist oppression and in their demands for social justice. The antiforeign proclivities of these groups also could be related to the democratic creed by means of such slogans as "The Independence of Asia" and "Asia for the Asians." Under this guise, expansionism could assume a democratic mission, and here was one link between Japanese nationalism and democracy which remained potent abroad even after it had ceased to have any meaning at home.[1]

Under agrarian-military banners, however, the "popular nationalist" movement could not possibly effect that union between democracy and nationalism accomplished in some measure by the early Western "middle class." The denial of such cardinal democratic values as individualism and political competition, the strong proclivities toward irrationalism, and the basic tendency to reject modernism were innate to the Japanese agrarian classes, and their "democratic" movement showed all these trends. They themselves quickly perceived the incompatibilities, and there was a constant stream of desertions to other camps. These were stimulated by the increased urban capitalist influence in the parties, disillusionment with the corruption and ineffectiveness of parliamentary institutions, and a series of continual crises in the economic and political fields. Fundamentally, however, there was never any logical reason to expect agrarian nationalism to support a democratic movement in Japan.

By the early 1900's, the ties between the agrarian-military nationalists and the democratic movement had already loosened, though actually the old connections were never to disappear completely. At first, the union had been well displayed, not only in elements of the Jiyuto, but also in such an organization as the *Genyosha* (Sea of Genkai Society). The Genyosha was a Kyushu association combining the three principles of continental expansion, patriotic devotion to Emperor and country, and support for popular rights.[2] We have already seen the extent to which such principles could fit into the main stream of the early Japanese liberal movement. The real successor to the Genyosha was the *Kokuryukai* (Amur River Society), founded in 1900. By this time,

---

[1] One can trace this theme through Itagaki, Oi, Toyama, Kita, and many others. And although the slogan of "The Coprosperity Sphere" took priority over "Asia for the Asians," the tremendous contributions of Japanese nationalism to the anti-Western imperialist movement in modern Asia are too clear to need elaboration.

[2] The Genyosha, sometimes called the parent society of modern Japanese Fascism, was established in 1881 and stemmed from an earlier organization first formed in 1877. Its leaders were closely connected with the Satsuma Rebellion forces and were staunch supporters of Saigo. The name of the society itself connoted its principle objective—crossing the *Genkai nada* or *Genyo* (Sea of Genkai) to expand on the continent. However, many of its leaders, including Toyama Mitsuru, maintained initial contacts with the *jiyuminken* (popular rights) forces. See Kinoshita Hanji, *Nihon Fascism shi* (*A History of Japanese Fascism*), Tokyo, 1949, Vol. I, pp. 3–5.

the Meiji Constitution had been in operation for ten years, and in the Kokuryukai program of external expansion and internal reform, the dominant note of "Emperorism" was clearer, and the antipathy to Westernism sharper in some respects.[3] It was not difficult for this trend to continue during the next several decades, profiting from the mounting crises which marked the path of Japanese modernization and the successes achieved in two wars. Thus, in the aftermath of the First World War, the agrarian-military elements had new opportunities to capture and direct the "popular nationalist" movement with a program of anti-Westernism, anti-capitalism, and antidemocracy.

Inextricably connected with this development was the fact that the Japanese commercial-industrial elements were never able to produce any synthesis between nationalism and democracy which would support the latter. In a sense, these groups rested their case with the Meiji Constitution and upheld the official "state nationalism" which flowed from it. Although this "state nationalism" was not precisely attuned to all agrarian nationalist forms, it accommodated many of them and was incompatible with democracy at nearly every point. Yet, as we have noted, the leading urban groups paid homage to this "state nationalism"—to the absolutism, organic unity, and state priorities which it symbolized—because these were the sources of its own support. Thus there was little in the way of either democratic institutions or theory which the Japanese business class could pose to reorient Japanese nationalism. Instead, the problems of capitalism produced a new variant of nationalism which took the form of "national socialism." Japanese national socialism cast off some of the antiquarian economic-political aspects of agrarianism while still aligning itself closely with the rural-military forces. It was the Japanese counterpart of

---

[3] The Kokuryukai has been known popularly in English as the Black Dragon Society, because the characters for Amur River are "black dragon." The chief founder of the Kokuryukai was Uchida Ryohei. Its original program was contained in six points: 1. Exploring the road of Eastern culture and realizing a harmony between Eastern and Western civilization, Japan should become the leader for the prosperity of the Asian race. 2. Abolish the defects in a constitutional administration which has inclined toward formalism and abridges popular freedom, thus showing the skillful administration of the Emperor. 3. Expansion abroad and reform at home, including social welfare legislation to improve labor conditions. 4. Respect for the Emperor's Rescript to soldiers, promotion of universal conscription, and the strengthening of national defense. 5. The reform of the present Westernized education so as to base it upon the Japanese national polity and cultivate the virtue and knowledge of the Yamato race. *Ibid.*, pp. 7–10.

the Western Fascist philosophy, and it came from the same basic source springs.

One other general factor remains to be considered in this discussion of the different implications of nationalism to Japan. When nationalism emerged there, the end product of early Western nationalism was already unfolding, and to the Japanese leaders, the most impressive thing was the specter of state power through mass support. The West also conveyed to Japan certain techniques with which to cultivate this invaluable asset. With the application of these, nationalism could become the prime tool of a political elite seeking to gain the unqualified support and sacrifice of its people. By the same token, however, sharing power with them now became less necessary and less feasible. It was less necessary because advanced techniques of mass indoctrination could produce substitutes for it through the skillful manipulation of nationalist symbols. It was less feasible because the masses, who were now affected by the nationalist appeal, were separated from governing capacities by a much larger gap than that applying to the elitist groups, for whom early nationalism had been basically intended. These facts were of vital importance in modern Japan, even though Japanese leaders could not utilize all the tactics that were being developed in the West.

When one turns to the portentous developments in Japanese nationalism after the First World War, the inner significance of the factors suggested above becomes clear. The year 1918, which marked the establishment of the Hara cabinet, also witnessed the beginning of important trends in the nationalist movement. The two events were closely connected in more than chronology. The First World War and its immediate aftermath comprised a period of rapid internal change and external stimulus. The Japanese industrial revolution was reaching its mature phases, Western ideologies were making their strongest impact, and the spirit of internationalism was growing. The time was ripe for nationalist reactions to some or all of these developments which would harmonize old foundations with new dynamic forms. Among the new nationalist organizations, to be sure, many were merely dedicated to the preservation of the "Japanese spirit" against the threat of Bolshevism and were without any particular positive program. Numerous patriotic societies sprang up, to combat leftist student activities, labor-farmer unions, and Socialist-Communist groups.[4] These soci-

---

[4] Among these organizations, the following constitute a cross section of groups established in the first years after the war: the *Taisho Sekishin Dan*

eties acted as magnets, drawing together many conservatives from the business, landowning, and military classes.[5] A number of conservative party leaders were members. The programs put forth were characterized by abstractions, with the Confucianist state nationalism of the Meiji leaders representing the predominant theme. Perhaps the most important of such early organizations was the *Dai Nihon Kokusuikai* (Greater Japan National Essence Society), which had direct connections with the Hara government.[6]

There were other nationalist movements under way, however, posing much greater challenges to the status quo. On October 9, 1918, an organization calling itself the *Rosokai* (The Society of Mature Men) was established.[7] The Rosokai was a curious medley of many diverse radicals, but "leftist" suspicions of the organization were sufficient to give the "national socialists" the predominant control. The sole unifying factor, however, was the demand for immediate "reform." By 1921, this society had been fragmented into more homogeneous units. Perhaps the most important of these fragments was the *Yuzonsha* (Society to Preserve the National Essence).[8] Kita Ikki and Okawa Shumei, the two most

---

(Taisho True Heart Association) and the *Kodogi Kai* (Society for the Principle of the Imperial Way), established in 1918; the *Dai Nihon Kokusuikai* (Greater Japan National Essence Society) and the *Juo Club* (Universal Club), established in 1919; the *Yamato Minrokai* (Yamato People's Labor Society), founded in 1921; and the *Sekka Boshidan* (Association to Prevent Bolshevism), organized in 1922. See *ibid.*, pp. 16 ff.

[5] The influence of the construction industry people in some of these organizations was particularly strong, which is not surprising when the boss tactics that operated in this field are considered.

[6] See Maruyama Masao, "Nihon Fascism no shiso to undo" (Japanese Fascist Thought and Action), Sec. 2 in *Sonjo shiso to zettaishugi* (*Revere the Emperor—Oust the Barbarian Thought and Absolutism*), Tokyo, 1947, p. 105. I am greatly indebted to Professor Maruyama for his brilliant analysis of Japanese militarism and ultranationalism.

The Kokusuikai, founded in 1919, had among its main sponsors Tokonami Takejiro, Home Minister in the Hara cabinet. Its program included the following points: 1. To conduct government so as to make the Throne the center and unify the race. 2. To save Asia, which, despite the union of Korea and Japan, has been plagued with violence due to human misery. "This is the mission of Japan." . . . . 4. To advance faith in the Gods and ancestors, rectifying popular thoughts. 5. To stabilize the national livelihood by harmonizing the interests of labor and capital. See Kinoshita, *op. cit.*, Vol. I, pp. 18–21.

[7] See Kinoshita, *op. cit.*, Vol. I, pp. 39–41, for some details.

[8] The Yuzonsha took its name from a Buddhist phrase. Translated, the term *yuzon* means "still exists," and in this context it represented the founders'

353

prominent leaders of the Yuzonsha, were to become symbols of Japanese military Fascism. Kita himself has been called the "father of the Fascist movement." [9] His famous book, *Nihon kaizo hoan*

conviction that, despite the threat of Communism, the Japanese "national essence" would still exist. Thus one may translate *Yuzonsha* as "The Society to Retain the Japanese Essence." See *ibid.*, p. 42.

[9] The fascinating life of Kita Ikki has been presented in an excellent biography by Tanaka Sogoro, entitled *Nihon Fascism no genryu—Kita Ikki no shiso to shogai* (*The Source of Japanese Fascism—The Thought and Career of Kita Ikki*), Tokyo, 1949. Kita's background and personality combined to make him the closest Japanese approximation to a Western Fascist leader. The influences on him in his formative years came from such diverse sources as the Confucian classics, the early Japanese socialists, and the Chinese revolutionaries. In personality, he was extremely egocentric and very impetuous. From the beginning, his ambition was to establish his own socialism, fitted into the Japanese polity. In his first major work, *Kokutai ron oyobi junsei shakaishugi* (*Theories of the National Polity and Pure Socialism*), published in 1906, Kita attacked both "academic" and "state" socialism, insisting that the real socialism was to be found in the harmony of nationalism, individualism, and liberalism. In a grandiose attempt to create this "true socialism," Kita ranged over the fields of Western science and religion in badly confused fashion, seeking to develop an "evolutional explanation" of society and socialism. Despite his attack upon "national socialism," Kita was strongly under the spell of the concepts of cultural relativism and the primacy of the state. Indeed, in defending the latter, he even accepted the "organic" theory of the Emperor.

This work and subsequent writings revealed two very significant tendencies. Although Kita had been exposed to many influences, his concepts of revolution were fundamentally based on the Meiji Restoration, and his strongest impressions related to Japanese experience. And his writings were imbued with that heroic interpretation of history which was so important in Western Fascism. He played upon the thesis that an inspired man or group could change the history of a country and of the world. This belief unshackles its supporters from all elements of determinism, paving the way for the fullest use of irrationalism and romanticism. And it was cardinal to the creed of Kita and his followers.

Another important factor in the formulation of Kita's theories was his connection with the Chinese revolution. Like many other Japanese dissidents, Kita found an escape mechanism in the Chinese revolutionary movement. He was soon to break sharply with the Westernized Sun Yat-sen, however, and to condemn him bitterly as a traitor to China. But at the same time, advocating a "patriotic and independent" Chinese revolution, Kita also attacked Toyama and Inukai with the charge that they were only interested in Japanese power over China, not in China's revolutionary needs. From his work with the Chinese revolution, Kita absorbed two concepts which guided his subsequent plan for Japan. He correctly perceived the need for military power and a tightly knit elitist organization, if a revolution were to succeed. Both these principles played a prominent part in his new revolutionary program. See Tanaka, *op. cit.*, pp. 3–212.

taiko (*A General Outline of Measures for the Reconstruction of Japan*), served as the bible for countless young militarists and other radical nationalists.

In this far-reaching work, Kita outlined his Utopia, an Imperially directed "reform" safeguarded by military power. According to Kita's plan, the Emperor should suspend the Constitution for three years, dissolve the Diet, and declare martial law in order to establish the reform. By this act, he would make clear that he was the cornerstone of the nation and the supreme representative of the people. At the same time, a military junta should be established by the election of members from the Reserve Army Corps.[10] This group would participate in government directly, maintaining order and investigating private assets for the purpose of expropriating all those exceeding the limit to be granted to each household. This limit was to be set at ¥1,000,000 in total assets, and landholdings were to be limited to a valuation of ¥100,000. The excess was to go to the state without compensation in the case of total assets, and with compensation in the form of 3 per cent government bonds in the case of land. Such land was to be redistributed by the state to the landless on easy-payment terms. Simultaneously, the Privy Council was to be dissolved and all the Inner Court officials were to be dismissed, in order to revitalize the Imperial Court. In their place, an Advisory Board was to be established to assist the Emperor.[11] The cabinet and the Diet were also to be revised.[12] Following these basic changes, a reform program was to be undertaken

---

[10] See Tanaka, *op. cit.*, pp. 241–244.

[11] The Advisory Board was to consist of fifty members appointed by the Emperor. No member of this board was to be held responsible to the cabinet or Diet, but if these passed a nonconfidence vote against a member, he should be obliged to submit his resignation to the Emperor. *Ibid.*, p. 244.

[12] A "National Reform Cabinet," excluding the old financial and political cliques, was to be established by the Emperor. This cabinet would be enlarged by the addition of such ministries of "production" as those of banking, mining, shipping, and others, to permit the development of an intensively planned economy.

The peerage system would be abolished, and for the House of Peers, a *Shingi-in* (Deliberative Council) would be substituted. A part of the Shingi-in would be elected by and from an elitist group who had a record of "distinguished services to the state"; the remainder were to be members appointed from this group by the Emperor. The "Deliberative Council" could veto the decision of the lower house only once. The lower house, *Shugi-in* (Assembly Chamber), would continue to be chosen by universal manhood suffrage. Once selected, the "National Reform Diet" would meet with the understanding that it could not discuss the basic policies of the reform which had already been enunciated by the Emperor.

which would result in an extensive curbing of the Japanese "plutoc-racy" and an expansionist foreign policy.[13] It is no wonder that Kita's program had an appeal to many discontented elements in Japan. His work, which was first put out in 1919 through the aid of Yuzonsha members, was to go through many editions, serving as the chief inspiration of the young military reformers.

Kita's philosophy, however, was only one part of the radical nationalist movement. This period also saw the revitalization of a purely agrarian-centered nationalism which had striking parallels with certain aspects of the nationalist appeal in the early Meiji era. Spurred on by the rural crisis, agrarian reformers now came forth with renewed vigor, demanding the restoration of rural polit-ical and economic rights. The foremost spokesman for this move-ment was probably Gondo Seikyo, whose writings were a major stimulus to later attempts at revolution. In his *Jichi mimpan* (*Self-Government by the People*), and *Noson jikyu ron* (*A Treatise on Rural Self-Help*), Gondo called for a return to agrarian autonomy and an agrarian-centered economy. His works were another inter-esting illustration of how tenuous the connections were between the objectives of democracy and agrarian demands.[14] Attacking

---

[13] In addition to the "reforms" mentioned above, connected with asset and property limitations, Kita outlined a series of social measures to be ap-plied in every phase of society. Further limitations upon private capitalism included restrictions on corporation investment, with the limit placed at ¥10,000,000; all investments above this figure were to be state investments, and thus the greater proportion of basic industry would be nationalized. Broad measures for the protection of the working classes were included; old-age pensions, state support for the poor, compulsory education through the age of sixteen years, exclusion of English and use of Esperanto as a second language, abolition of all "imported sports" and the substitution of Judo, Japanese fencing, and so forth, protection of women's rights, and main-tenance of universal military conscription.

As a foreign policy, Japan was to undertake the task of fostering the im-migration of Chinese and Indians to Australia, and also of the Chinese and Koreans to Siberia. Eventually, the Japanese reform measures could be extended to these areas, and with the unification of races would come an equalization of standards. A special administrative structure would be used to carry out reforms overseas. Kita concluded his foreign policy section with the demand that Japan occupy Siberia and prepare a large-scale force against Russia "for the security of the Japan Sea, Korea, and China." This would be the logical conclusion of the Russo-Japanese War. But since Japan's objectives of helping India attain independence, maintaining the security of China, and occupation of the Southern Pacific islands would affront the West, particularly the United States, a large naval force was also justified. See *ibid.*, pp. 245–266.

[14] See Maruyama, *op. cit.*, pp. 121–123.

356

Prussian-style centralization and bureaucratic controls, Gondo demanded rural self-government and a completely decentralized society. He used such nationalist symbols as the Emperor, Japanese traditionalism, and doctrines of racial supremacy to assault the forces of urbanism, capitalism, and Westernism. Despite its paradoxical antinationalist features, here was agrarian nationalism in its most purely Japanese form. Gondo had established his *Jichi Gakkai* (Self-Government Institute) in 1920 to promulgate these doctrines. Partially through its influence, other associations dedicated to similar principles emerged in the rural districts. One of these was the later *Aikyojuku* (Institute for Local Patriotism), established by Tachibana Kosaburo. Although Tachibana was probably not as antiurban as Gondo, one of his remarks conveys much of the spirit behind the agrarian-centered radicals of this whole period:

"Even if grass were to grow on the roof of the Mitsukoshi Department Store, Japan would not fall, but if the rain leaked through the roofs of five million Japanese farmers' homes, what would become of Japan?" [15]

Thus, by the mid-1920's, three broad strains of Japanese nationalism were making themselves felt. The first was a conservative movement coalescing various party, bureaucratic, and military forces around the banners of the "national polity" and the Meiji Constitution, prepared to make only relatively minor changes in the status quo, but increasingly antidemocratic in general philosophy. Even within this group, however, there were many divergent opinions on such subjects as the regulation of capitalism, political reform, and the proper ratio of military power. The second and third strains of the nationalist movement were revolutionary in their implications, but divided in their emphasis between the Kita concept of a highly centralized, industrial-centered state and the Gondo concept of a decentralized agrarian society. Any absolute division between these strains is artificial, for, in reality, there was a great deal of fusion, especially between the latter two. Characteristic of Japanese society, moreover, the sources of disunity were

---

[15] Quoted from a speech by Tachibana in Tanaka, *op. cit.*, p. 329.

Maruyama maintains that Tachibana stood between Kita and Gondo on the question of a state system. In his *Nihon aikoku kakushin hongi* (*Fundamental Principles of a Patriotic Reform of Japan*), Tachibana showed his bias against centralization and urbanism. However, he advocated a system of industrial control by corporate national organizations operating on a decentralized basis. See Maruyama, *op. cit.*, pp. 127 ff.

not always ideological, for personality and group conflicts were as omnipresent in the nationalist as in other movements. Nevertheless, it is through a knowledge of these three forces that the rise of nationalism in this era can best be understood.

The period down to the Manchurian Incident of 1931 might be called the preparatory period of Japanese ultranationalism. From the early 1920's, the rightist movement gained momentum, riding the waves of urban depression, rural misery, leftist threats, party corruption, and foreign developments. Perhaps the complicated events of this period can be summarized in terms of three pronounced trends. The first of these was the proliferation of various "popular nationalist" societies among the people, and the partially successful efforts to unify these into broadly based national organizations. As we have noted, a large number of associations, representing every aspect of the nationalist movement, emerged after 1918. Three which developed somewhat after the first period may serve as representative types. In 1924, the *Gyochisha* (The Society to Realize the Way of Heaven on Earth) [16] was established by Okawa Shumei. Okawa, a student of Indian philosophy and a man with contacts in high military and bureaucratic circles, had broken with Kita and had left the Yuzonsha, chiefly because of personality differences.[17] Despite this fact, however, the Gyochisha, led by Okawa, Mitsukawa Kametaro, and others, had a policy based largely upon Kita's *Nihon kaizo hoan taiko,* though it also incorporated some of the agrarian-centered philosophy. Okawa himself was a scholar of considerable repute, and among his books *Nihon oyobi Nihonjin* (*Japan and the Japanese*) was perhaps most illustrative of his views. In one section, he issued the following attack on capitalism and socialism:

---

[16] It is impossible to convey the meaning of *gyochi* through a literal English translation. Okawa took the name of the society from the classical phrase *sokuten gyochi,* which might be translated, "to realize the way of Heaven on earth."

[17] The immediate cause for the break between Okawa and Kita was disagreement over the visit of the Soviet representative, Joffe, to Japan. Kita, who was violently anti-Russian, wrote an open letter to Joffe, attacking Russian imperialism. Okawa and Mitsukawa seem to have hoped to use Joffe to advance Japanese interests in northeast Asia. For details on the Joffe incident, see Tanaka, *op. cit.,* pp. 276–282.

The basic cause of the antipathy between the two men, however, was the completely egocentric, domineering attitude of Kita, which had produced Okawa's growing antagonism.

358

The war between capitalism and socialism is not a war of principle; since they rest upon the same principle, it is only a struggle concerned with the actual boundary of the principle. In capitalism the possessors of material wealth are few, limited to the small number known as the capitalist class, whereas socialism proclaims the division of wealth to the working masses—but both place supreme value upon materialism.[18]

Okawa's central theme was the restoration of the classical Japanese virtues of "idealism" and "spiritualism," and the need for Japan to spread these virtues to the world.[19] The Gyochisha, like many other nationalist organizations, established several educational programs and had its own publication. In connection with these activities, Okawa obtained the services of a number of prominent people as "councillors," including Makino Shinken (already Lord Keeper of the Privy Seal) and several army generals such as Araki Sadao and Watanabe Jotaro.

Another noteworthy organization to emerge was the *Kenkokukai* (The Society to Build the Country),[20] founded by an ex-Anarchist. The major principles of the Kenkokukai revolved around the themes of restoring the Japanese spirit, harmonizing all interests within the society, and strengthening the state. The Kenkokukai was less anticapitalist than many of its counterparts, and it had great influence among rightist groups. Among its councillors were Toyama Mitsuru, now the *doyen* of the "patriots," and Hiranuma

---

[18] Quoted in Maruyama, *op. cit.*, p. 117.

In both his writings and his organizational activities, Okawa seems to have straddled the issues which divided men like Kita and Gondo. As Professor Maruyama indicates, Okawa's Gyochisha gave considerable evidence of rejecting the industrial-capitalist economic structure and of seeking the creation of a state policy centering around agrarian industry, championing at the same time a movement away from centralization and toward district rights. The subsequent connections of Okawa, leading up to the May Fifteenth Incident, also show his affinity for the agrarian forces. At the same time, however, the national socialist principles of Kita continued to be important in Okawa's thinking, and parts of his writings would support the theme of a centralized, state-owned capitalistic structure. In truth, Okawa's position was one example of the attempt to reconcile these two divergent streams of the nationalist movement.

[19] The Gyochisha program included the following points: 1. The building of a "Restoration Japan." 2. Establishment of the nation-people concept. 3. *Liberty* in spiritual life. 4. *Equality* in political life. 5. *Fraternity* in economic life. (Note the new use of the old liberal terms borrowed from the French Revolution.) 6. The emancipation of the colored races. 7. The ethical unity of the world.

[20] For details on the Kenkokukai see *ibid.*, pp. 57–60.

Kiichiro, a prominent bureaucrat whose prestige was steadily rising. The Kenkokukai had as its first president Uesugi Shinkichi, the long-time reactionary scholar. After Uesugi's death, however, many of the national socialist elements left the organization because of its conservative position on matters of economic and political reform.

Perhaps the most important organ of the conservative nationalists, however, was the *Kokuhonsha* (National Foundation Society). Stemming from the growing concern about leftist activities, the Kokuhonsha was established in 1924 under the leadership of Hiranuma. Into this organization went some of the most important Japanese leaders. Bureaucrats from the Ministry of Justice who had long had connections with Hiranuma were well represented, and of those within the new organization one was Suzuki Kisaburo, soon to become president of the Seiyukai. Among the military members were Field Marshals Togo Heihachiro and Uehara Yusaku; Generals Ugaki Kazushige, Kato Kanji, Araki Sadao, Mazaki Jinzaburo, Koiso Kuniaki, and Hata Shinji; and Admirals Arima Ryokitsu and Saito Makoto. Zaibatsu representatives included the Mitsui general manager, Ikeda Seihin, Mitsui's legal counselor Hara Yoshimichi, and Yuki Toyotaro from Yasuda. In addition, numerous other government officials and a few university scholars were enrolled. The Kokuhonsha proclaimed its purposes to be those of "nourishing and developing the national spirit," expanding the "national foundation" movement, and emphasizing educational reform.[21]

The Kokuhonsha represented a "patriotic" organization with a membership that did not have a complete identity of interests or principles. Indeed, there were substantial personal and political cleavages between the various elements. Some of its members were marked for death by the radical nationalists, whereas a few others were affiliated with this very group; still others were working for a "middle road." More than any organization of its time, the Kokuhonsha symbolized the future power orientation of Japan.

While many of the elitist groups in Japan were thus moving closer to the ultranationalist cause, the radicals of the "right" were trying to unify their forces and attain mass proportions. These efforts were perhaps best exemplified in two organizations which emerged just before the Manchurian Incident. First to appear was the *Zen Nihon Aikokusha Kyodo Toso Kyogikai* (All-Japan Pa-

---

[21] See *ibid.*, pp ˋ50–155.

triots' United Struggle Council). The purpose of the Council was the amalgamation of as many national socialist organs as possible. Despite its eventual failure and the relative shortness of its life, it reflected the growing power of the radical nationalists. A short time later, the *Dai Nihon Seisanto* (Greater Japan Production Party) was established as a nation-wide organization. Among its leaders were Uchida Ryohei, president of the Kokuryukai, and many other old-time chauvinists. The Seisanto succeeded in drawing a large number of radical "rightist" societies into its fold, and claimed a membership of 100,000 soon after its creation in 1931. Both the Patriots' Council and the Seisanto had programs which were antiparliamentary, anticapitalist, and violently nationalist.[22]

Thus in years prior to 1932, the "rightist" movement was growing at many levels. Literally scores of new societies were being established every year. Inroads were being made in both the conservative parties and the ranks of the leftists. Between such groups

---

[22] The three major "pledges" announced by the Zen Nihon Aikokusha Kyodo Toso Kyogikai were: 1. "We pledge ourselves to the overthrow of subversive parliamentary politics and to the realization of direct Imperial rule." 2. "We pledge the overthrow of capitalism by establishing the supreme power of production." 3. "We pledge ourselves to overcome domestic class conflicts and to promote our national power throughout the world." Kinoshita, *op. cit.*, Vol. I, p. 86.

The 1932 Seisanto program announcement contained lengthy political, economic, and social sections. Among the political planks were pledges to work toward the following goals: complete extermination of those politicians who lacked the "national concept"; the destruction of plutocratic political power and of the plutocratic parties—the Seiyukai and Minseito; the annihilation of the Communists, the Rono Taishuto, and the Shakai Minshuto; the construction of government for the "mutual prosperity" of the people; the development of a "strong" foreign policy based upon the "Greater Japan" concept; the establishment of independence and reform for Manchuria and Mongolia; the guidance and development of China; the exclusion of aggressive Western powers and the reconstruction of a new Asia; the increase of "national defense" efforts, and opposition to "traitor-like armament reduction."

The economic program included the call for a basic revision or abolition of the "ruinous capitalist economic system"; a policy for industrial development; the state control of finance and industries; social legislation and relief for the working classes; and the reduction of taxes.

The organization's social policy included the promotion of the "one nation—one family" ideal; an attack upon class "egotism"; the promotion of familial ethics; a broad program of social security, including unemployment insurance and medical care; an expansion of free education; and the establishment of "self-governing" patriotic youth organizations. See *ibid.*, pp. 90–92.

as the Kokuhonsha and the Seisanto, both sides of the street were being worked. Under the aegis of the Seisanto and many similar organizations, "patriotic" labor unions were being formed and social activities on behalf of the poor conducted. The national socialists and agrarian radicals were making strenuous efforts to capture the common man. In this, however, they failed, as had the democratic-leftist forces before them. Even in its heyday, the radical "rightist" movement found relatively few active adherents among the masses. Its strongest sources of civilian support came from the "middle class," particularly the small industrialists, contractors, shop owners, small landowners, and lower-class officials, especially those in the rural areas.[23] The Japanese intelligentsia were overwhelmingly aloof or hostile.[24] Nor did the efforts to unify the nationalist movement meet with any great success. Despite certain attempts at unification, the gap between the radicals and the conservative elitist groups dedicated to the status quo remained well-nigh unbridgeable. Even within the radical groups, moreover, disagreements over national socialism were strong. None of these obstacles, however, prevented the nationalist tides from sweeping forward, strengthened by all the advantages of crisis and the inner disintegration of the old order.

A second trend of great importance during this era was the merging of civilian and military forces. The close association between certain top-ranking generals and admirals and the bureaucratic-party forces was neither new nor unusual. However, it partook of added significance in such societies as the Kokuhonsha. But a similar alliance between civilians and military men which was even more interesting, was developing in the radical nationalist movement. There were ample reasons for this trend. As various Japanese writers have pointed out, the "election districts" of the army were

---

[23] See Maruyama, *op. cit.*, pp. 148 ff.

[24] Professor Maruyama states that one of the chief reasons for intellectual aloofness was the fact that, unlike the German intellectuals, the Japanese scholars had not placed recent emphasis upon their own culture, but rather upon Westernism. Maruyama goes on to state, however, that this Westernism was primarily in their heads, and not in their life pattern, with the result that they were unable to resist the tides, being spiritless, powerless, and isolated—lacking the inner fortification to resist. *Ibid.*

Perhaps two other factors are also of some importance in explaining the general position of the intelligentsia. One is the long history of anti-intellectualism in Japan and the equally long history of intellectual timidity which this had fostered. The other is the extreme naïveté and primitivism implicit in the Japanese Fascist movement, even as compared with Western Fascism.

in the rural areas. Most army recruits were peasants. Moreover, the services—particularly the army—were highly exceptional among Japanese institutions in that they provided opportunities for the individual to rise on his own merits. Consequently, many of the officers, especially of the lower ranks, came from peasant families and had poignant memories of rural suffering. In addition, military life was Spartan, and the pay standards of even the high officers were extremely low in comparison with those of the commercial-industrial classes. Finally, military indoctrination played heavily upon the nationalistic theme, building up the "warrior ethic" of self-sacrifice, fanaticism, and worship of state and Emperor. Implicit in this program was the inculcation of bitter hatred toward those who sponsored disarmament, questioned Japanese invincibility, or revealed any liberal skepticism.

Thus it was natural for a number of men like Kita and Okawa to have influence and to establish personal contacts with the young officers in the army and navy. Okawa's contacts, indeed, were with men on a high level as well as with junior officers. He had made early connections with such men as Koiso Kuniaki, Araki Sadao, Itagaki Seishiro, and Doihara Kenji—all of whom subsequently became prominent military-political leaders.[25] Kita, on the other hand, worked almost exclusively with the younger officers. After the armament reduction move of 1925, he began his active association with the young militarists. Nishida Zei became his faithful follower, and his influence was extended to many other youthful military "reformers." The young officers were also influenced, however, by Okawa, Gondo, and Tachibana. Indeed, their movements and organizations showed an ill-digested mixture of centralized national socialism and pure agrarian revolt. Some of the young militarists were even in contact with the socialists of the left. These various associations illustrated, in different ways, both the confusion and the consistency which marked the path of the civilian-military group of radical nationalists.

The amalgamation of civilian and military elements into radical nationalist societies was clearly in evidence in Okawa's *Gyochisha* (The Society to Realize the Way of Heaven on Earth) and grew after 1924 in the form of many similar groups. These associations stimulated the "Young Officers' Movement," which had reached important proportions by the end of the 1920's. Undoubtedly the

---

[25] See the very interesting section in Tanaka, *op. cit.*, entitled "Kita to gun to no kankei" (The Connections Between Kita and the Military), pp. 313–319.

most famous of the young officers' associations was the *Sakurakai* (Cherry-Blossom Society), formed in September, 1930. About a score of persons, under the sponsorship of Lieutenant Colonel Hashimoto Kingoro, organized a "research society" dedicated to reform of both the army and the nation.[26] Membership was limited to officers on the active list with the rank of lieutenant colonel, or below. In its contacts, its program, and its subsequent actions, the Sakurakai was symbolic of the revolutionary tide which had risen in the lower military ranks. To be sure, this civilian-military collaboration was complicated by various factors. Not only were ideological lines often confused, but the "ideology" of many of the young officers was confined within the simple bounds of "relief from capitalist oppression" and "resistance to foreign policy appeasers." Moreover, friction within and between the services was at least as great as that existing in civilian radical groups, and interfered with more than one plan for a *coup d'état.* As always, army-navy rivalry and personal factionalism were formidable problems, affecting all levels. Despite these difficulties, however, the intricate network of civilian-military connections which had developed by 1931 covered the field of Japanese politics in such a way as to presage military dominance. On the one hand, the radical "right" was now strongly represented in military circles, with many youthful officers finding a new faith in its general appeal and willing to sacrifice themselves for its purposes. The rightist radicals also had the moral blessings and some direct assistance from certain high-ranking military elements. On the other hand, many conservatives were prostrating themselves before the symbols of "state nationalism" with increasing fervor and accepting military counsel and leadership in an effort to stem the radical tides. This was done with varying degrees of enthusiasm, as the price of protection and as an inescapable necessity. The conservatives were now on the defensive, both in their relations with the Japanese people and in terms of their own psychological attitude. In the face of domestic depression, a mounting revolutionary crisis in northeast Asia, the failure of the democratic movement, and world trends which paralleled these developments, such political responses on the part of the elitist elements were most natural.

The two trends discussed above culminated in a third trend which had begun to appear by 1931: the rise of terrorism and attempted revolution. Political assassination, of course, had always

---

[26] See IMTFE, Document No. 12, Exhibit No. 183. Also Kinoshita, *op. cit.,* Vol. I, pp. 101–114.

been expectable in Japan. Okubo, Hoshi, and Hara were leaders who had met death in this fashion. After the First World War, moreover, the leftists had come under similar attack, with Osugi and Yamamoto Senji, among others, being victims. By the late 1920's, however, individual violence was being coördinated with revolutionary plans and projected into large-scale programs. These began to come to light in 1931. Already, in 1930, a youthful member of an extremist group had shot Premier Hamaguchi because of the latter's defense of the London Naval Reduction Treaty. But the first big plot was the one uncovered in March, 1931, for the creation of a so-called "March Incident." In the center of the plot were Okawa, Hashimoto, and other members of the Sakurakai, together with various high military officers. The plan was to overthrow civilian rule by violence and to substitute military rule under General Ugaki Kazushige. Shortly before the *coup d'état* was to have been undertaken, however, it was abandoned because of opposition from certain high army circles.[27] Still, the era of attempted revolution had commenced.

The period from March, 1931, to the "5–15 Incident" of May 15, 1932, represented the opening stages of the militarist era. Despite their internal disagreements, the military moved forward on the home front and overseas, using subterfuge, persuasion, and their legal prerogatives. The parties began to crumble, their key figures deserting to the military banners out of fear, conviction, or hope of power. And those opposed to the trends could find no method of stopping the defections.

After the "March Incident," the army showed increased political activity on many fronts. A campaign to win public support was undertaken, with professional newspapermen hired to write publi-

---

[27] For some details on the "March Incident," see the following documents from the IMTFE: Document No. 11517, Exhibit No. 157 (Affidavit of Shimizu Konosuke); Document No. 11514, Exhibit No. 158 (Affidavit of Tokugawa Yoshichika); Document No. 11516, Exhibit No. 163 (Affidavit of Ugaki Kazushige); Defense Document No. 2231, Exhibit No. 3195 (Sworn Deposition of Hashimoto Kingoro).

Okawa engineered the plot with the active assistance of Hashimoto. Some three hundred bombs were obtained, and funds were given by Tokugawa Yoshichika. Koiso and Tojo were among the high military officers with knowledge of the plan, and Okawa had talked with Ugaki, urging him to accept the premiership. Afterward, Ugaki insisted that he had indignantly refused; some others who were involved maintained that after first showing some interest, he changed his mind. At any rate, disapproval from some high military elements caused the plans to be discarded. Koiso informed Okawa that it was a direct order from the army to give up the plot.

cations for general distribution. Military press censorship was also begun, and writers who displeased the army were threatened with violence.[28] One of the main drives was on behalf of increased armaments. The military were still smarting under the reductions of the mid-1920's and the London Naval Treaty of 1930. They were cognizant, moreover, of the fact that a fairly large proportion of the public, especially in the urban areas, had welcomed relief from the heavy expenditures. Thus it was important to play upon such themes as "patriotism," "crisis," and "the interest of the state." In addition to using their own facilities, the extremists in the army and navy encouraged the increased activity of the powerful *Zaigo Gunjinkai* (Reserve Association), which was composed of all military reserves. Through the Zaigo Gunjinkai, millions of ex-servicemen could be reached.

One sign of the times was the army press release of a speech by Minami Jiro, Minister of War, given to division commanders at the time of general maneuvers in August, 1932. In this speech, Minami bitterly attacked those who were attempting to "undermine the confidence of the nation in the army." It was an open political bid for popular support which contained thinly veiled threats against those within the government and the parties who opposed army demands. Against the angry protests of men like Foreign Minister Shidehara that this was a violation of the Emperor Meiji's injunction to military men to abstain from politics, Minami and the army sullenly stood their ground.

Meanwhile, young military radicals, both at home and in the Kwantung Army, were busily planning to force a "strong" foreign policy by perpetrating an "incident" in Manchuria. In this, they were being aided and encouraged, as always, by Okawa and other civilian extremists.[29] Rumors of an impending crisis flooded high government circles, but the civilian officials could devise no counterattack. Thus the news of the "Manchurian Incident" which broke on September 18, 1931, was no surprise to top civilian officials. From the beginning, they either knew or suspected strongly that the "Incident" was a hoax.[30] This fact, however, did not en-

---

[28] See IMTFE, Document No. 11500, Exhibit No. 140 (Affidavit of Maeda Tamon, editorial writer for the *Asahi Shimbun*, 1928–1938).

[29] See IMTFE, Document No. 11517, Exhibit No. 157 (Affidavit by Shimizu Konosuke). Once when Okawa was intoxicated, he told Shimizu that he had planned to bring about an incident in Manchuria with Colonels Komoto, Amakasu, and Itagaki, all members of the Kwantung Army.

[30] See Wakatsuki Reijiro, *Kofuan kaiko roku—Wakatsuki Reijiro jiden* (*Recorded Memoirs of Kofuan—The Autobiography of Wakatsuki Reijiro*),

able them to control the resulting situation. Premier Wakatsuki constantly sought advice from Saionji and the Inner Court circle. Pledges were exacted from the top military men that the war would be confined, that only a minimal number of troops would be used, and that "army discipline" would be restored. The Emperor himself admonished the military and gave such moral assistance as was possible to the cabinet.

The obstacles facing the government, however, were unsurmountable. The greater part of the army, including the key figures, were in sympathy with the "direct action" tactics. Even those with some qualms were under heavy pressure from subordinates and completely unable to control the situation.[31] Moreover, a growing number of younger officials in the Foreign Office were favorable to the army and sabotaged attempts at opposition. In addition, the cabinet itself was split, with certain Minseito men defending the military position. Thus in the stormy cabinet sessions which followed the outbreak of war, only Shidehara and Inoue Junnosuke, Minister of Finance, fought the War Office vigorously. Adachi, whose subsequent actions helped to bring down the Wakatsuki ministry, as we have noted, actively supported the Minister of War. And at each successive meeting, the cabinet was faced with a series of *faits accomplis*. The army even moved large numbers of troops contrary to its promises and without Imperial sanction; but Wakatsuki saw no alternative except to authorize payment for the expenditures incurred. The opposition Seiyukai was of course even more loaded with proexpansionists and supporters of the military.

In the midst of these crises, the "October Incident" was revealed. The same old forces that had planned the earlier "March Incident" had revived their plot, and this time had somewhat more concrete

Tokyo, 1950, pp. 375 ff. Also IMTFE, Document No. 2194, Exhibit No. 181. The following telegram was sent from Consul General Hayashi at Mukden to Shidehara, on September 19, 1931:

"It is reported that Tatekawa, Divisional Director of the General Staff, arrived here on the 18th by the 1 p.m. train. This is probably true, although the Army authorities keep it secret. According to the confidential information from Mr. Kimura, Director of the Southern Manchurian Railway Company, when trackmen were sent for repair work on the section reported to have been damaged by the Chinese, the Army authorities forbade them to approach the spot. Putting this and that together, it is considered that the recent Incident was wholly an action planned by the Army."

[31] The commanding general of the Kwantung Army had been virtually isolated by his subordinates, and this same type of situation prevailed elsewhere when necessary for the execution of the radical program.

plans. First, the entire cabinet was to be assassinated at once during a cabinet meeting. Following this, the Metropolitan Police Board Headquarters was to be occupied, and the War Ministry and chief of staff isolated until a military government could be installed under General Araki. Internal dissension among the plotters and opposition from certain military circles caused the exposure of the plans. As usual, however, the army excluded the government from the case, hushed up the incident, and meted out light sentences to only a few of the ringleaders.[32]

Indeed, the March and October plots enormously strengthened the hand of the army in many respects. Incipient terrorism frightened all but the most courageous opponents of the army conspirators. Such developments also lent themselves to making more persuasive the argument that only the military could control the military. This general theme took many forms. Hiranuma insisted to the Inner Court that only General Araki or General Mazaki Jinzaburo were suitable candidates for the premiership, because only these had the confidence of the young officers and thus the power necessary to restore order. Certain members of the Inner Court circle rationalized compromise with the "conservative" military leaders to prevent revolution. Even the Emperor was warned to adopt a more moderate tone, lest he antagonize the military (who followed in some measure the old Tokugawa policy of *gai-son nai-atsu,* "outward respect, inner oppression").

When the Wakatsuki cabinet fell, however, Saionji was prepared to override demands for a Hiranuma or Araki cabinet and recommended Inukai, leader of the opposition party. Actually, the Seiyukai was far more acceptable to the conservative militarists. Such Seiyukai leaders as Kuhara, Mori Kaku, and Suzuki Kisaburo had close connections with rightists or military leaders, and were defenders of their policies. Even Inukai played a double line. In private, he worked to control military power and prevent a further expansion of the Chinese War, and in some of his maneuvers he incurred great hostility from powerful military circles.[33] In public, however, he continued to voice a "strong" foreign policy stand which was in line with his own past and that of his party, and most conducive to military purposes. Note, for instance, the following

[32] Tanaka's work contains a fairly detailed account of this episode. See his *Nihon Fascism no genryu* . . . , pp. 322–325.

[33] See IMTFE, Document No. 11524, Exhibit No. 161 (Affidavit by Inukai Ken).

passage from his speech of November 10, 1931, delivered to Seiyukai Diet members shortly before he assumed the premiership:

"The need of the moment is for Japan to discard her apologetic
diplomacy and enter on a new phase of independent diplomacy.
With firm determination, she must pursue the traditional national
polity. With a single mind, all people, military and civilian, must
devote their whole energy to the restoration of order in Manchuria." [34]

Immediately after this speech, the Seiyukai Diet members had
passed three resolutions, including a foreign policy resolution of
which the following is a part:

"If the League of Nations shows itself incapable of seeing the
situation and continues to offer intervention or put coercion on
Japan instead of amending its present mistaken course, Japan
may well withdraw from the League." [35]

As we have seen, however, the rightist "radicals" wanted "reform" to accompany expansion. The assault upon the "vested
interests" and party government was to continue; violence had
only begun. Thwarted in earlier attempts, the radicals of the right
were now determined to succeed. The opening moves in 1932
were made by a fanatic band known as the *Ketsumeidan* (Blood
Oath Association). The Ketsumeidan, like all agrarian radical
societies, owed much to the earlier work of Gondo and Tachibana,
but its chief mentor was Inoue Nissho, a Buddhist priest of the
Nichiren sect. Inoue's fabulous career had included broad travel
experience in northeast Asia, intimate contacts with Kwantung
Army men, and service as a Japanese spy. His Ketsumeidan was
made up of a small group of young peasants who had pledged
their lives to remove the "ruling clique" responsible for agrarian
misery. The chief weapon was to be assassination, and after a
select list of leaders from the business-political world had been
prepared, each member chose his victim by lot! [36] The first blow
was struck on February 9, when a young peasant lad shot former
Finance Minister Inoue. This act was followed on March 5 by the
murder of Baron Dan Takuma, the chief director of Mitsui. Before

---

[34] Speech of President Inukai to Seiyukai Diet members, November 10,
1931, as reported in *JC*, November 19, 1931, p. 643.

[35] Seiyukai resolutions passed November 10, 1931, as reported in *ibid.*,
p. 649.

[36] For some information on the Ketsumeidan and its activities, see Kinoshita,
op. cit., Vol. I, pp. 169–178.

any more victims could be dispatched, however, the Ketsumeidan leaders were arrested, and Inoue confessed the details of the plot.[37]

Others were ready to take over the Ketsumeidan assignment. Indeed, since February, preparations for another *coup d'état* had been brewing, a plot which led directly to the famous "May Fifteenth Incident." Spearheading the conspiracy was a group of young naval officers deeply influenced by Gondo and Tachibana. The support of a small band of eleven army cadets was also enlisted. Civilian participants included Tachibana and elements from his Aikyojuku; Okawa, who acted as general coördinator; and two other active supporters, Homma Kenichiro and Toyama Hidezo, son of Toyama Mitsuru.[38] Supplied with arms and funds, the young band prepared "to save Japan from collapse" by striking at the zaibatsu, political parties, and men around the Throne. On May 15, 1932, deployed in three units, the small group attacked. One unit shot Inukai; another raided the residence of Count Makino, Lord Keeper of the Privy Seal; and the third assaulted Seiyukai headquarters. Then the three units came together and jointly attacked Metropolitan Police Headquarters, and one young lieutenant threw a grenade at the Bank of Japan!

The importance of this fantastic venture can only be appreciated in the light of past trends and developments. It was primarily the manifestation of agrarian unrest. The assailants were mostly young peasant boys striking blindly at what they considered to be great injustice. Its implications for increased military power and control, however, were far-reaching indeed. The parties were dangerously close to collapse. Thus, when Saionji was called upon to recommend a successor to Inukai, he placed the name of an admiral, Saito Makoto, before the Emperor. The selection of Saito was not a great surprise, for he had been under consideration as a possible premier for several months. Three major factors were in his favor. First, although he was not their own choice, the army leaders were willing to accept him, and their veto power over the premiership was now generally acknowledged. Secondly, the parties presented a spectacle of deep divisions and weaknesses too

---

[37] *Ibid.*, pp. 177–178.

[38] See Tanaka, *op. cit.*, pp. 325–331. Actually, both Gondo and Tachibana initially opposed the plan as "blind action" and unwise. Indeed, Tachibana made a special trip to dissuade Koga, the leading agitator. Koga protested so vigorously, however, that Tachibana finally agreed to aid the plans. This element of reluctance on the part of the more mature mentors was not unusual throughout the period. As we shall note, it also played a part in the February Twenty-sixth Incident.

great to enable them to counteract general unrest and military opposition. The dominant Seiyukai was completely factionalized, with its divided fragments attacking one another. Finally, the Inner Court circle, the leading financial groups, and some of the party men saw in Saito and the navy a third force, capable of balancing the conflicting political elites and preventing revolution or complete army control.

The Saito ministry stayed in power from May 26, 1932, until July 7, 1934, and it was followed by one representing a similar power balance under Admiral Okada Keisuke, who was Premier from July 8, 1934, until March 8, 1936. In both cabinets, the major parties were given some representation. The Saito cabinet contained four Seiyukai and three Minseito men, but one from each party came from the House of Peers. The Okada cabinet admitted five party men, but the three Seiyukai men were expelled from the party for entering the cabinet against the command of the party leadership. But the four years which marked the course of these cabinets were years of further decline for democracy and for the old parties. The growing impotence of the parties and the increasing power of the military clique were the two most important trends of the period. There was now practically no cohesiveness within the parties themselves. The Minseito was still headed by Wakatsuki, but he was not very popular with the rank and file. He retained the presidency largely because of the lack of a suitable successor. Adachi and his supporters had walked out to form the ultranationalist *Kokumin Domei* (Nationalist League). Inoue, one of the most able prospective leaders, had been assassinated. Egi, the third powerful figure, was very ill. One faction within the party sought General Ugaki for the presidency, but this plan did not materialize. Finally, in November, 1934, Wakatsuki resigned and assumed the role of elder statesman.[39] The office of Minseito president remained vacant for several months, and then Machida Chuji, an old party stalwart, took the post. Machida was to remain as president until the disbandment of the party in 1940, but without any great distinction. Increasingly, after 1932, Minseito men were drifting into the militarist camp.

The situation within the Seiyukai was infinitely worse. After Inukai's murder, the aged Suzuki Kisaburo, who was noted for his prorightist views, was elected party president. The Tokonami and Kuhara factions, however, continued strong, and all three factions within the party remained at arm's length. The Suzuki

---

[39] See Wakatsuki, *op. cit.*, pp. 391 ff., for some details on this period.

group continually tried to make its support of the Saito administration contingent upon Saito's early resignation. This was not out of any great regard for the principles of democracy, but rather because the Seiyukai leaders, having a heavy majority in the lower house, were determined to return to office. On more than one occasion, the Suzuki forces threatened to overturn the government, but they were held in check by Inner Court opposition, dissension within Seiyukai ranks, and the generally unfavorable atmosphere for a restoration of party government.

The extreme nationalism which now permeated the Seiyukai was best illustrated by its "new policy" of 1933. In the platform it was stated that the first line of Japanese defense must be Manchukuo and the mandated South Sea Islands. Policy sections dealing with "popular thought" asserted that "the spirit of the national foundations should be vindicated and developed," the educational system should be reformed with this in mind, and religious sentiment should be cultivated among the people.[40] The religion, of course, was Shinto. Within the Seiyukai, moreover, a genuine authoritarian movement was developing. Men like Kuhara were proclaiming the virtues of militarism, the "Imperial way," and the theory of one party with its basis in "Japanism." Matsuoka Yosuke, the noted diplomat, resigned from the party in 1933 to form an organization which he called the *Seito Kaisho Remmei* (Political Party Dissolution League).

Perhaps nothing could better indicate the trends within the major parties than their actions during the famous attack upon Professor Minobe, which started in earnest in February, 1935. Minobe's organic theory concerning the Emperor was neither new nor of great service to democracy. It had been the theme of three of his books, one of which had gone through twelve editions, guiding many aspirants to officialdom. The Professor had long been an honored member of the Peers and served as one of the examiners on the Civil Service Examination Board. Despite this record, however, the tide of ultranationalism swept over him, and suddenly he was vigorously attacked in the Diet as a traitor to the Imperial polity.

On February 25, 1935, Dr. Minobe tried vainly to defend himself in the House of Peers.[41] If sovereignty were a right held inherently in the person of the Emperor, irrespective of the state,

---

[40] Seiyukai platform of 1933, from *JC*, July 6, 1933, p. 19.

[41] See Minobe's speech in the House of Peers, February 25, 1935, as reported in *ibid.*, March 7, 1935, p. 306.

he argued, then it would be a right which the Emperor possessed for his own interests and for the accomplishment of his personal objects. If this sovereignty were unlimited, then the Meiji Constitution itself had no meaning. But Minobe's logic was to no avail; the chauvinists—civilian and military—were demanding his head. This would seem to have been an issue of vital significance to the future of the parties. The leaders of the major parties, however, were either silent or active as participants on the side of Minobe's accusers. The Minseito was almost completely quiet. The Seiyukai officially denounced the Minobe theory as a danger to the Japanese state. Kuhara and other Seiyukai leaders actually attempted to make the matter an issue for pulling down the Okada cabinet.[42]

The Okada administration sought at first to ignore the controversy, but under the pressure of the militarists and the Seiyukai, it finally issued several statements; the second one, put out on October 22, 1935, read:

Any theories which, merely copying examples or theories abroad, claim the subject of sovereignty is not the Emperor but the nation, and that the Emperor is an organ of the nation—such as the so-called organ or institutional theory—must be strictly eradicated, as they run counter to the sacred national constitution and do a great harm to its true conception.

All things, political and educational, everything in fact, must be based on the true principle of the national constitution of the Empire which is unparalleled throughout the world, and all efforts must be made for the exaltation of its spirit.[43]

In pursuance of this object, the government began a program of indoctrination on the Constitution directed at one hundred and fifty professors. The first lecture was given by Count Kaneko, the only survivor of the group that had drafted it.[44] As for Minobe, he

---

[42] On June 21, 1935, the directors of the Seiyukai agreed on the following confused policy: "1. Vindication of the national polity and the denunciation of the Minobe theory. 2. Establishment of responsible government. 3. Elimination of subservient foreign policy. 4. Strong defense and agrarian improvement through the pursuit of a positive financial policy." From *ibid.*, June 27, 1935, p. 825.

[43] Government statement, issued October 22, 1935, as transcribed in *ibid.*, October 24, 1935, p. 512.

[44] If the reports of his lecture given on July 18, 1935, were accurate, Kaneko went completely overboard in his recollections of the drafting. He is quoted as having said that after close studies of such constitutions as the British, French, *and German* ones, none was found suitable, and that consequently the Japanese Constitution was drafted *merely in accordance with the national polity and history.* See *ibid.*, July 25, 1935, p. 117.

373

was finally forced to resign his peerage, his professorship emeritus, and all other honors. Representative government had been struck its heaviest blow, but scarcely any open opposition was to be found. The greater proportion of party men had actively participated in the digging of their own graves.

Even the left wing of the party movement was seriously affected by the trend to the right, as we noted briefly earlier. It will be recalled that the *Shakai Minshuto* (Social Mass Party) and the *Rono Taishuto* (Labor-Farmer Mass Party) were the two leading labor parties in 1931 and from then until their amalgamation as the *Shakai Taishuto* (Social Mass Party) on July 24, 1932. When the Central Committee of the Shakai Minshuto met on April 15, 1932, just prior to the union, it was split wide open on the question of social democracy versus "national socialism." Adherents of the former creed garnered a slim majority, one crucial vote being 61 to 51 in their favor. Many of the dissenters thereupon left the party, some of them to join earlier ex-"leftists" as leaders of various national socialist organs. Since the Rono Taishuto had a similar split, it was in reality only the remnants of the two parties that formed the Shakai Taishuto. Even after the creation of the new party, attrition continued. As we have noted, a part of the "left" had been in contact with the young officers and other radical "rightists." Obviously, agreement upon internal reform—the abolition of capitalism, land reform, and the overthrow of the "ruling clique"—was implicit in the programs of the two groups. Increasingly, moreover, the "left" despaired of both democratic and evolutionary procedures in Japan, and world conditions caused many to turn away from the concepts of internationalism and pacificism. Economic nationalism was now on the rise everywhere, and the discriminations involved withered the old socialist hopes.[45]

The Shakai Taishuto itself was ultimately altered by these factors. Up to 1937, it continued to oppose Fascism, Communism, and capitalism. With the advent of the "Second China Incident" in 1937, however, it began to falter. It supported the war, albeit not too enthusiastically. Shortly thereafter, moreover, it suffered a basic split, and the majority of its former members joined the "unity" movement of 1940. The only recognized party to oppose

---

[45] Prominent among the reasons for recanting given by democratic socialists and Communists was their disillusionment with the "false" internationalism of democracy and Communism. They pointed to Russian and American discrimination against Japanese fishermen and workers, Western imperialism against the Asians, and Russian imperialism under the guise of the Comintern.

the 1937 war was a small leftist group calling itself the *Nihon Musanto* (Japan Proletariat Party). It was led by left-wing socialists (not Communists) such as Kato Kanju and Suzuki Mosaburo. The Nihon Musanto was forcibly disbanded by the government in the latter part of 1937, and with this action, the last faint embers of an organized "left wing" in Japan began to fade out. The Communist movement had been confined to a few scattered individuals since the sensational recantations of Sano, Nabeyama, and others in 1933.

Thus, the years after 1932 were bitter years for the entire party movement. The quarrelsome factionalism within the parties was played up by a controlled and generally hostile press. Day after day, the parties were ridiculed and condemned as the insignificant instruments of self-centered men. Over the months and years, these themes were conveyed to the Japanese public. There were, however, a few factors which helped to prevent complete collapse of the party system. The first of these lay in the position and attitude of the Inner Court circle. Saionji in particular was constantly hopeful of a revitalization of the party movement, and in his recommendations he protected the parties as much as possible. Indeed, his sympathies lay with the more antimilitarist elements of the major parties, and he maneuvered as best he could to ward off the advances of party men like Adachi and Kuhara. Thus the parties were given considerable support from behind the scenes. This attitude on the part of Saionji, certain colleagues in the Imperial Court, and even the Emperor reflected, among other things, a general appreciation of Westernism, a fear of revolution, and an apprehension lest Japan be isolated and ultimately defeated through a policy of aggressive militarism. These were also reactions which helped in some measure to draw the highest Japanese conservative elements together, including some elements from the armed forces.

Interestingly enough, another force that had often served as an opponent of the democratic movement was to prove of some small advantage to the parties during this period—the Constitution. When the radical right and the militarist group as a whole deified the Emperor, they could not easily assault the instrument bestowed in one of the foremost Imperial acts, the Meiji Constitution. Indeed, more than one crafty party man pointed out that the Diet and the parliamentary system had been granted to the people by the august word of the Emperor and were not to be abolished except by committing a sacrilegious act. This struck

375

a sensitive spot with the radical "rightists" in particular.[46] It gave impetus to the concept that "reform" should be constitutional, and, in a sense, was of at least temporary aid to the parties, as well as to other groups desirous of continuing the status quo. Indeed, the circumstances surrounding Japanese constitutionalism cannot be entirely overlooked in explaining why Japanese authoritarianism, even at its zenith, was never as total as that of the West.

There was a final factor operating which may have helped to give the parties a slim hold on life. Militarism, despite the attention its proponents paid to public relations, was not universally popular in Japan. As the militarist shadow lengthened, there was some tendency among the more articulate members of the society to regret current trends. Even the general public showed signs of growing weary of constant crisis, war, and exhortations. An indication of these developments can be seen in the elections of 1936 and 1937, as we shall note. However, given the background and current activities of the major parties and the nature of Japanese society, there could be no real ground swell of popular support. Few clear alternatives were provided in a period when the parties were drawing ever closer to the nationalist-militarist line and when most organs spoke with a uniform voice on basic issues. It would be inaccurate to suggest, moreover, that a public which had always exhibited great indifference to politics had suddenly changed. The average farmer and worker were somewhat happier over their slightly improved lot after 1932, often anxious about war, but not participants in any mass movement and certainly not interested in the restitution of party supremacy. Nevertheless, the parties had a type of negative asset in the degree of passivity, or even antagonism, toward militarism. This was strongest, of course, in

---

[46] Attempting to counteract such charges, many ultranationalist societies took a stand similar to the following position of the *Aikoku Seiki Domei* (Patriotic Banner League): "We must . . . focus our patriotic movement on the destruction of the political parties. . . . However, the destruction of the political parties does not mean our denial of the parliamentary system. Our struggle, on the contrary, is an aggressive effort to find means of ensuring the right functioning of parliament in every sense of the word which will be the materialization of the grand spirit enunciated by the great Emperor Meiji. Government by the Emperor, which it is our ultimate objective to establish, however, is far from being analogous to dictatorship. Emperor government must be a system which will encourage the expansion of the mind of the people and bring it into harmony with the Great Mind of the Throne." From the Aikoku Seiki Domei program, quoted in Baba Tsunego, "Towards Parliamentary Revival," *Contemporary Japan*, June, 1934, pp. 21–22.

the urban areas. If it was an asset which they could not fully utilize and, in many ways, hardly deserved, still the parties—especially the Minseito and the Shakai Taishuto—felt its benefits.

All these qualified advantages, however, were not sufficient to enable the parties to recoup their strength. The signs of military power were omnipresent. Appointments could not be made without military approval, and this applied to many offices besides that of premier. On budgetary matters, the military exercised their full power, forcing a man like Finance Minister Takahashi to capitulate almost completely before their demands. On behalf of both their general political and their budget interests, the military hammered on the theme of "the coming crisis." This talk began as early as 1933 and was meant to apply to the period 1935–1936. During the latter two years, Japan's resignation from the League of Nations would take effect, the London Naval Reduction Treaty would expire, and China would have the legal right to purchase the South Manchurian Railroad Company. The military insisted that there be complete unity, with no internal dissension, so that Japan could cope successfully with her "life or death" problems.

Nor did the military rest content with pressure exerted from behind the scenes. It entered politics directly in a variety of ways. The army began to organize political discussion groups for its officers and enlisted men, to acquaint them with army views. It openly encouraged the political ambitions of those office seekers who would support the army program. Beginning in 1934, moreover, it greatly increased its publication output, large quantities of pamphlets and general literature being distributed for both army and civilian consumption. These materials contained all the ultranationalist symbols. Most of them were devoted to arguments for heavy armament expenditures, defenses of army policy, and appeals for the martial spirit.[47]

Much shading, however, must be added to convey a more accurate picture of the general scene. The "military" was never a single unit, and within it, differences were many and complex.

[47] For some of these pamphlets, see *Hijoji to kokubo* (*Emergency Conditions and National Defense*), published by Army Press, 1935; *Tenkanki no kokusai josei to waga Nihon* (*The Transitional Period of International Conditions and Our Japan*), Army Press, February, 1936; *Nichi-Ro seneki no kaiko to warera kokumin no kakugo* (*Reflections on the Russo-Japanese War and the Resolution of Our People*), Army Press, March, 1936; *Manshu jihen man gonen* (*Five Years After the Manchurian Incident*), Army Press, September, 1936; *Rikugun gumbi no jujitsu to sono seishin* (*The Perfection of Army Preparedness and Its Spirit*), Army Press, November, 1936.

In certain respects, the separation between the military elite and the young firebrands widened after 1931. As this elite began to acquire increasing power, their sympathy for the radicals often appeared to diminish, though in regard to relationship with this elite the radicals had always taken too much for granted and most conservative civilians too little. Now, army elements began to polarize around two groups—the *Kodo ha* (Imperial Way Faction), composed predominantly of the young extremists, and the *Tosei ha* (Control Faction), with its nucleus in the top-ranking group of army officers. A few military men like Ugaki were alienated even from the Tosei ha, largely because they symbolized the previous era of military subordination. Ugaki's earlier acquiescence in armament reductions, his close ties with the Minseito, and his position in connection with the plot of March, 1931, made him anathema to the majority of military men of whatever faction. Increasingly, however, the real struggle was between the Kodo and Tosei factions. Although differences here were frequently ones of degree rather than of kind and were often obscured by bitter personal rivalries and innumerable shadings, still, the struggle for control within the army was fought along these two central lines. And that struggle was at its height in the years between 1932 and 1936. The young radicals were now completely captivated by the dream of total "reform" and were becoming disgusted with some of their early heroes, who soon seemed overly timid, compromising, and vague. In the absence of thorough "reform," radical plots continued. The so-called "*Shimpeitai* (Sacred Soldiers) Affair" was revealed in July, 1933, as a fairly large-scale plan to effectuate the objectives of the raid of May 15. Another scheme was thwarted in November, 1934.

Although the attitude of the so-called Tosei group toward these plots was still ambivalent, a solid core of opposition toward radical tactics and certain radical objectives was gradually developing. In consequence of the revelation of the November plot, the Tosei group removed General Mazaki as Inspector General of Military Education. Mazaki, together with Araki, had long been considered the military inspiration of the young officer cliques. The Kodo ha struck back in August, 1935, when a young colonel murdered one of the Tosei leaders, General Nagata Tetsuzan, who had been appointed to Mazaki's post.[48] The crisis within the army was build-

---

[48] For some details on the murder of General Nagata, see Tanaka, *op. cit.*, pp. 353–354.

ing up to the explosion of February, 1936, an event which, as we shall note, was uniquely suited to subsequent Tosei dominance within the army and expanded power in the whole political sphere.

In addition to internal army conflict, there was also a continuation of friction between the army and the navy. In some respects, this friction was intensified by the rise of army power. Although the navy was not without its extremists, and although it certainly was not vitally concerned with the protection of representative government, it was destined by its very nature to be a more moderate force.[49] Indeed, the choice of navy men to head the two cabinets which followed the Inukai ministry was, as we have seen, prompted by this consideration.

The divisions within military ranks, however, did not interfere seriously with the continued over-all growth of military power. In fact, these divisions represented to the political elite the probable range of alternatives from which choices would have to be made, and represented them in very graphic form. It was inevitable that the conservatives would become increasingly dependent upon the "moderate" militarists to prevent internal revolution and to carry forth the expansion policy abroad in which Japan was now deeply enmeshed.

It would be an oversimplification and even a distortion, however, to imply that strong and tight bonds of unity were forged among the "conservative" elements, or that a genuine merger of "capitalist" and "military" interests was attained. The situation was much more complicated, as any reading of the documents of this period will reveal. All the old factors were present to prevent any complete unification—the agrarian-urban clash, power rivalries between the various branches of government, strong personal ties and equally strong animosities, and different individual and group interests. A Kuhara could go so far as to consort with the radicals, but a Takahashi would continue boldly to affront even the "moderate" militarists on many issues. A Saionji would make each compromise with reluctance and hope for a brighter future, whereas a Makino would incline a willing ear toward prominent rightists, a Hiranuma typify the top militarists' ideal, and a Konoe, in his

---

[49] Not only does a navy operate primarily away from the homeland, but also it is more elitist and much smaller in personnel, and thus it does not have the same capacity for, or interest in, a social revolutionary movement or an authoritarianism based upon mass power. Moreover, the Japanese navy received little glory in the continental expansion, and it had great respect for Anglo-American sea power.

quests for harmony, appear to be all things to all men. This picture was reflected also in commercial-industrial circles. The process of accommodation might be initiated by one side or the other, and it might be concluded willingly, under great pressure, or, in a few situations, not at all. The older men of the zaibatsu were dunned for funds by some of the very forces who attacked them, and often they paid blackmail money in traditional fashion. The price exacted for continued existence and increasing profits consisted of certain strategic retreats in over-all political power, competition from a new crop of zaibatsu fostered by the militarist regime, and a more controlled economy than ever before, with some of the controls disagreeable. To this situation, an Ikeda Seihin would react somewhat differently from a Sumitomo.

Thus one can see a picture of unity and disunity, compounded of fear, uncertainty, and confusion. The rising Tosei men drove a hard bargain which left many conservatives resentful and potentially subversive. The Tosei men could do this because both the internal situation and the external situation confronting Japan gave them a whip hand, and also because many of them were sufficiently dedicated to the "new order" to make harsh demands. There were other elements, of course, contributing to the confusion of the Saito-Okada era, and one of the most pressing was the perennial problem of irresponsibility. Uppermost in the minds of the Inner Court advisers was the protection of the Emperor and the Imperial Household. They shied away from such devices as Imperial conferences, for fear that the Emperor might be caused to make a decision. Many of them worried about the "liberalism" which he displayed in his questions and advice, since they knew its effect upon military circles. Some actually feared that the Emperor might be forced out, in favor of one of the Imperial Princes who was dedicated to the military cause. But none of the Inner Court advisers was completely certain of what the Emperor should or might have to do; in truth, his powers and responsibilities in terms of practical politics remained undefined and the subject of both speculation and apprehension.

This was almost as true with regard to the role of the Inner Court circle. Saionji himself had long wished to lay down the duties of the Genro and establish the practice of Imperial consultation with the premier, but in a period of crisis and party decline, this solution seemed unfeasible. Finally, an informal group called the *Jushin* (Chief Retainers) was established, to continue the work of the Genro. The Jushin Council was composed of the Inner Court officials and former premiers, and was headed by the aged Saionji. It first operated in the selection of Okada as successor to Saito.[50] But the Jushin was like its predecessor, the Genro, in that it had no legally defined responsibility, and now the practical limitations upon the authority of such a council were very great. Its precarious existence was perpetuated largely because it never really defied stronger forces; flexibility and compromise were its governing principles.

Within each branch and division of government, moreover, the lack of defined and accepted responsibility played a definite part in the trends of the times. Particularly important was the situation within military circles. High army officers continuously promised to "restore discipline" in the lower ranks, but not until after 1936 was any great progress made along these lines, and even then, the strength of subordinate groups continued to be impressive on occasion. As has been mentioned, among the reasons for this was the fact that the top military men found it advantageous to use the young officers' movements as levers to advance their own control, and also they had some sympathy with the objectives of the radical rightists. But another very important reason was, of course, the fact that the whole nature of Japanese society had so obscured individual responsibility and so enhanced group power that the greatest confusion reigned in respect to the decisions of leadership and in respect to the acceptance of personal responsibility. A parallel situation existed in the civilian bureaucracy; there, in such branches as the Foreign Office, the lower echelons often operated in direct violation of superiors' wishes, or at least without their sanction.

The events of 1936 climaxed the varied trends which had been growing since the Manchurian Incident. As the year opened, the Seiyukai leaders laid aside their factional quarrels sufficiently to formulate a direct challenge to the Okada government. Counting on its heavy majority in the Diet, the party proposed a vote of no confidence in the ministry. A general election had not been held since 1932; hence the government decided to dissolve the Diet, and campaigning promptly got under way. The election results were in some respects surprising. To be sure, neither the militarists nor the national socialists had entered the party field on a large scale. The radical right had made some attempts, but such parties as the Dai Nihon Seisanto were extremely small. However, the

[50] See Wakatsuki, *op. cit.*, pp. 397 ff.

Seiyukai had expected an easy victory, especially since most of its members had kept abreast of the nationalist trend far more than the Minseito had, or, of course, the Social Mass Party. However, the election was a victory for the Minseito, which had used as one of its slogans, "What shall it be, parliamentary government or Fascism?" It garnered 4,456,250 votes and 205 seats, whereas the Seiyukai obtained a popular vote of 4,156,643 and dropped (from 303) to 174 seats.[51]

In terms of percentage gains, however, the best showing was made by the Shakai Taishuto. It collected 18 seats (the previous high for the labor parties combined was 8) and polled 518,360 votes, double the labor total of 1932.[52] The openly national socialist groups collected a total of less than 400,000 votes and elected only 6 men to the Diet. Certainly the ultramilitarists won no spectacular victory, and, indeed, some of the results proved encouraging to those opposing the authoritarian trend. However, optimism on this score had to be tempered by many considerations. For the most part, the election was characterized by a lack of clearly defined issues and by the greatest public apathy. The figures for absenteeism at the polls rose generally, especially in the urban areas.[53] This indicated the widespread conviction that parties and elections were unimportant. Moreover, the Minseito success (the party still did not obtain a clear majority of the Diet) was largely a vote for the Okada administration, not the party. Most of the Minseito men, and certainly the party headquarters, had done a good deal of fence straddling on fundamental issues, basing their main stand on support for Premier Okada, a nonparty man.[54] Nevertheless, out of a rather limited and certainly confusing choice, the voters (particularly the urban voters) had tended toward the more mod-

[51] Statistics from Foreign Affairs Association of Japan, *Japan Year Book, 1943–1944*, Tokyo, 1945, p. 168.

[52] *Ibid.*

[53] Note the following proportions of persons not voting in the election of 1936, expressed in per cent of the eligible electorate, and compare them with the 1932 figures in parentheses. The percentages given are those of the six largest cities: Tokyo, 27.4% (20.3%); Osaka, 41.1% (34.6%); Nagoya, 18.4% (30.3%), Kyoto, 40.0% (37.7%); Yokohama, 32.9% (29.7%); and Kobe, 30.2% (25.8%). From *JC*, February 27, 1936, p. 264.

[54] One contemporary writer, Taketora Ogata, intepreted the election as a sign that the average voter desired to better the system of party government. See his "The General Election and After" in *Contemporary Japan*, June, 1936. In his analysis, however, he gave some very logical reasons for the results which did not support this hypothesis.

erate elements. The vote for the Shakai Taishuto was perhaps the most heartening sign for supporters of democracy, although the party garnered only about 500,000 of the 11,000,000 votes cast.

An answer to this election, however, was forthcoming in less than a week, with the outbreak of the famous "February Twenty-sixth Incident." [55] On the morning of February 26, more than 1,400 soldiers under the command of young Kodo ha officers attacked in various parts of Tokyo. The Premier's residence was occupied and the Premier was reported killed. The former Premier and present Lord Keeper of the Privy Seal Saito Makoto was slain; the venerable Takahashi was fatally wounded; General Watanabe, Tosei ha leader and Inspector General of Military Education, was dead. Another Inner Court official, Admiral Suzuki Kantaro, Grand Chamberlain, was wounded. Others marked for death escaped, and subsequently it was learned that Okada himself had miraculously avoided assassination, the rebels having killed his brother-in-law by mistake.

For three days, the capital was in confusion, with the rebels barricaded in one section of the city and the high army authorities unwilling to precipitate open bloodshed. Pamphlets were distributed, explaining the objectives of the purge—the destruction of the old ruling cliques and the salvation of Japan under a "new order." Finally, the revolutionists surrendered, in the face of the Emperor's personal commands, negotiations between the young officers and Mazaki, whom they trusted, and the marshaling of formidable forces against them. The nation was stunned by the greatest domestic crisis since the Satsuma Rebellion of 1877.

After a long series of abortive plots, finally a major uprising had been staged. The army units involved were from the First Division, units whose officers had been closely associated with the Kita-Nishida group. The timing of the incident was mainly connected with the imminent departure of these units to Manchuria. Actually, Kita himself was not directly involved, and both he and Nishida had opposed the hasty decision.[56] The big military name involved

---

[55] For more details concerning the February Twenty-sixth Incident, see Tanaka, op. cit., pp. 339–385; also Maruyama, op. cit.

[56] Kita did not think the timing for a revolution was proper, and he did not take any direct part in it until after it had begun. Then he supported the objective of having Mazaki made Premier with financial assistance from Kuhara. Nishida was staying at Kita's residence during the Incident and co-operated in making contacts with the military radicals.

was again that of Mazaki, and the ambitious Seiyukai leader Kuhara had taken a prominent part in the plot.[57] As in earlier conspiracies, there was a considerable amount of disagreement among the participants, and the plan itself was extremely vague. The rebel choice for premier was narrowed down to either Mazaki or Admiral Yamamoto Eisuke; by this time, Araki was considered unacceptable because of earlier "failures."

The "February Twenty-sixth Incident" was an act of desperation, born of the profound discouragement over the lack of "reform" and the nature of current trends. It would have stood a better chance of success had it been staged earlier. Its failure marked the climax of attempts at revolution by the radical right. Now, men from the Tosei ha moved swiftly and dealt the Kodo ha and allied groups a series of heavy blows. Certain generals having past or present connections with the radicals were transferred to the reserves, including Mazaki and Araki. The young leaders of the plot were tried with record speed, and this time a minimum of sentimentality was allowed to pervade the court atmosphere. Thirteen army officers and four civilians, including both Kita and Nishida, were executed.[58] From this point on, the radicals had their strongest foothold overseas, where many had already been sent.

At the same time, however, the aftermath of the February Twenty-sixth Incident saw the further development of the garrison state in Japan. With internal friction now reduced, the controlling Tosei men exercised a total power over Japanese politics far greater than that during the Saito-Okada era, and a power which steadily increased. Men like Generals Terauchi Hisaichi, Tojo Hideki, Sugiyama Hajime, and Koiso Kuniaki became powerful figures, both within the army and in the general political scene. The Okada cabinet had resigned, and Konoe, whom the Jushin wanted, refused the premiership on grounds of ill health. Then, after ascertaining that he would be satisfactory to the military, they turned to former Foreign Minister Hirota Koki. When Hirota began to construct his cabinet, he was presented with a series of army ultimatums on both personnel and policies. One of these demands was that the number of party seats in the cabinet be reduced to two, but since Hirota had to deal with the Diet and had previously promised the major parties two seats apiece, on this one item he held fast and the army finally accepted his demand. Otherwise, however, Hirota gave way on every point and promised also to abide by an army

---

[57] Kuhara had given various sums of money to the young leaders, and promised further financial support in the aftermath of a successful coup.

[58] For Kita's last few months, see Tanaka, op. cit., pp. 386–394.

program which included armament expansion, augmented economic controls, and strengthened supervision over "information." When the new Diet convened, moreover, War Minister Terauchi took a more truculent position on the floor than had been seen since World War I. His creed was contained in the demands for a thorough "renovation" of government, the abandonment of "liberalism," and the establishment of a "controlled, unified state." [59] His contempt for the old parties was so open and his browbeating tactics so ruthless that some of the more courageous members of the Diet could not remain silent. This situation finally led to the famous incident in January, 1937, between Hamada Kunimatsu, Seiyukai Diet member, and the Minister of War. Hamada openly accused the military of foisting a dictatorship upon Japan, and in an emotion-laden exchange, the aging Diet member held his ground.[60]

Indeed, in the period of the Hirota cabinet and its successor, the Hayashi cabinet, the parties offered more resistance to the military than at any time since 1932. Behind this resistance lay several important factors. Soon after the February Twenty-sixth Incident the army had expanded its power very abruptly, less hindered by internal problems and less conciliatory toward outside interests. The price of compromise with the military was going up. Although the men of the Tosei faction were not strident revolutionaries and although they continued to be hated by Kodo ha remnants and various radicals,[61] they had adjusted to some of the radical demands. In the army program, there were many planks calculated to bring forth the antagonism of the commercial-industrial groups, and the challenge to any form of representative government was now inescapable. The parties, moreover, were somewhat strengthened by public reactions to the incident of February 26 and by the Emperor's rebuke to the military.[62] The 1936 elections had also provided encouragement.

None of these factors, to be sure, altered the basic weaknesses

---

[59] See Maruyama, *op. cit.*, p. 161.

[60] Hamada charged that army support for dictatorship would alienate the military from the Japanese people; when Terauchi demanded an apology for false accusations, Hamada stated that he would commit *seppuku* (slashing the abdomen) if his statements were proven false.

[61] Radical plots continued even after the February Twenty-sixth Incident, and Terauchi himself was among the intended victims of at least one of these.

[62] In his opening message to the new session of the Diet following the February affair, the Emperor came close to offering a public rebuke to the military, and the records from the Kido and Saionji memoirs reveal that he was much more positive in private.

affecting the parties, nor did they halt the march of military power. The next few months and years saw many changes. One of the earliest was the reëstablishment of the old rule allowing only active-service generals or admirals to serve as minister of war and minister of the navy. But for a brief while, it seemed that the parties and the forces supporting them might be revitalized and take the offensive. There was little unity in Japanese politics in the hectic years of 1936 and early 1937. Even the Seiyukai adopted a hostile position toward the Hirota government, and in the aftermath of Hamada's attack, Terauchi resigned and the cabinet fell. The Jushin helpfully nominated Ugaki, who had long been close to the Minseito and now represented the most conservative element within the army, a man who could be counted upon to coöperate with the business and party elements. Jushin plans failed, however, when not a single eligible general would take the post of minister of war. Ugaki was forced to report that he could not form a cabinet. Again the army had exerted its power, and, unable to meet the challenge, the Jushin finally nominated General Hayashi Senjuro, a man acceptable to the army leaders. Hayashi took a stronger antiparty stand than had been taken by any premier up to this time. He insisted that members of his cabinet discard any party affiliations, and in his first statement of policy he called for the abandonment of party government. Actually, Hayashi's ideas were far more in line with the old "transcendental" concepts of the Meiji Genro than with the revolutionary concepts of the radical right or the ultranationalist concepts of most of the elements now dominating the army. The parties, however, naturally protested the Hayashi position, and the government was forced to dissolve the Diet only a few months after it came into power.

The resultant election of April, 1937, was the last competitive election in prewar Japan. The outcome was striking in only one respect: the Shakai Taishuto captured 36 Diet seats (exactly double its number in 1936) and received more than 1,000,000 votes.[63] There could be no doubt that some of the urban classes were turning to the Social Mass Party. However, the two major parties each polled more than three times the number of Shakai Taishuto votes, with the Minseito receiving 3,666,067 votes and 179 seats, and the Seiyukai receiving 3,608,882 votes and 174 seats.[64] The military faced the same old problem that had plagued the early Meiji leaders. Without having their own party in the

---

[63] Election figures quoted from *JC*, May 6, 1937, p. 554.
[64] *Ibid.*

field, they could hardly win an election, and the elections of 1937 were considered a strong rebuke to Hayashi. Again, the electorate had leaned toward the moderates or progressives, and this time in even more decisive fashion, although absentee statistics were also higher.

Soon after the election, on June 3, 1937, the Hayashi cabinet resigned. The elder statesmen once more sought a candidate who would maintain in some fashion the balance of power between the army, the bureaucracy, and the parties, effecting such compromises as accorded with the requirements of the situation. This time, Konoe Fumimaro was finally persuaded to take the premiership. Konoe had long been a favorite of the army, but at the same time he had the general confidence of the Inner Court and of the party men. Konoe personalized the element of coöperation which existed among the conservative groups. In him were mirrored the confusions, the ambivalences, the drive for unity, the fear of radicalism, and the fatalism which were some of the ingredients of civilian capitulation and military power. And Konoe had been in office scarcely a month before the outbreak of the "Second China Incident." This was the beginning of Japan's last major crisis—one which expanded into global war and total defeat.

Even the façade of Japanese democracy was now doomed. It was only a question when and how the Diet and the old parties would be altered. Occasionally, the parties exercised their right of criticism vigorously enough to make trouble for some of the cabinets which followed that of Konoe. There were even a few outspoken individuals from party ranks who continued to defend effective parliamentary government. For the most part, however, the Diet members faithfully voted for government bills, maintained a discreet silence, and watched the growing international crisis with mixed hope and worry.

This crisis dealt the final blow to any efforts in the direction of restoring parliamentary rights and the prestige of the parties. The premium upon unity had never been greater. Now the military made concessions to the economic "pressure groups" in an effort to get maximum coöperation. Even without these concessions, however, the cleavages among the conservative groups which had shown up clearly in the 1936–1937 period would have diminished under the increasingly grave circumstances which Japan faced abroad. Complete harmony was never attained, but the war gave the military and their ideas additional priorities.

In their last few years, the old parties were torn apart by bitter

387

factional struggles. Seiyukai factionalism became so intense that the party finally split into three sections after the resignation of Suzuki; the two most important fragments were led by Kuhara and Nakajima Chikuhei, another veteran politician. When the Nakajima forces took possession of Seiyukai headquarters and refused admittance to Kuhara's adherents, it provided momentary news interest to a press and public, which had become largely indifferent to party activities. The Minseito had internal problems of an almost equally serious nature, though it did not formally split up until just a few months before its complete dissolution. Even the Shakai Taishuto was deeply divided after 1937, and one strong group sought to unite with the nationalist parties. The members of the other group, led by Katayama Tetsu, remained faithful, for the most part, to the principles of social democracy, but they were prevented from organizing their projected *Kinro Kokuminto* (Workers' Nationalist Party), in May, 1940, by government edict.

Plans for a single new party had long been discussed in various circles.[65] In some instances, these plans came from party men who saw in such a party the possibility of recouping political power or offering stronger opposition to authoritarianism. Increasingly, however, the idea of a new party focused on the theory of state unity and a controlled Diet. The most acceptable leader for a unity movement was Prince Konoe, and in the spring of 1940 he agreed to undertake the sponsorship of the new organization. Even before July 22, 1940, when his second cabinet was inaugurated, the old parties had begun to dissolve. The Shakai Taishuto went first, dissolving on July 3. The Kuhara faction of the Seiyukai followed, on July 16; the Kokumin Domei, on July 26; the Nakajima Seiyukai faction, on July 30; and, finally, the Minseito, on August 15. Various minor parties also went, and in slightly more than a month, the old parties had all left the political scene.

After the inevitable preliminary meetings, the *Taisei Yokusan Kai* (Imperial Rule Assistance Association) was inaugurated on October 12, 1940. The goal toward which many Japanese politicians of the past had striven now seemed to be realized. Japan had "one great party," dedicated to preserving internal unity, assisting the Emperor by formulating public opinion, and acting as a general propaganda outlet for the government. The new party was set up like a department, with various bureaus and with a

---

[65] At least as early as 1936, serious discussions were under way among various bureaucrats, militarists, and party leaders.

detailed national organization. The opening sections from the regulations of the Provincial Planning Committee give some idea of its objectives and philosophy:

This association strives to establish a strong national defense structure by imbuing its members with the consciousness of being subjects of this empire; through mutual help and remonstrance taking the lead to become the propelling force of the people and always cooperating with the government as a medium for transmitting the wishes of the government as well as of the people at large.

We endeavor to be faithful loyal subjects. That is, we believe in our national structure, which is the manifestation of matchless absolute universal truth, faithfully observe the Imperial Rescripts of the successive sovereigns, serve the country in our respective posts, and exalt the great Divine Way.[66]

The overwhelming majority of the old party leaders joined the Imperial Rule Assistance Association (IRRA), pledging themselves to work for its objectives. Actually, however, the "one great party" was not a spectacular success. The same old factionalisms, the same lack of mass appeal, the same problems of responsibility and leadership dogged its path. But parties based upon representative supremacy and political competition were a thing of the past, and they had left a legacy of failure not easily to be forgotten.

With this survey of the militarist era it is possible to draw together some of the threads of our study. In the period after 1931, the failure of the Japanese democratic movement was revealed in its entirety. Democratic philosophy and institutions were completely riddled by the sword thrusts of militarism and ultranationalism. But this was more an extension than a reversal of previous trends, and it was in accord with the predominant forces of modern Japanese society.

Japanese nationalism took most of its primary symbols from a mixture of primitivism and Confucianism, both because these were central to Japanese tradition and because the agrarian-military class played the major role in the shaping and projection of the modern nationalist movement. The commercial-industrial forces were weak in numbers and social standing, but most important, it was not in the interest of these groups to attempt any basic reorientation of the nationalist themes. The prerequisites of their success and security seemed to lie in the same paternalism, "organic unity," and anti-individualism that had characterized the

---

[66] Translation from IMTFE, Document No. 451, Exhibit No. 67, Regulations of the Provincial Planning Committee of the Imperial Rule Assistance Association.

initial nationalist creed. To some of these concepts, indeed, they gave new significance, revealing the paradoxes implicit in nationalism from the standpoint of agrarian interests. Thus the struggle against centralized, capitalist domination accounted in large part for the early rural leadership of the democratic movement and for some agrarian sorties toward the "left." But the movement found its logical culmination in the "agrarian radicalism" of the period immediately after World War I. This radicalism was an attempt to bring tradition back to the side of agrarian supremacy; it was filled with the ronin spirit, and the echoes of "Revere the Emperor—Oust the barbarian" rang out with resounding force. In its most central objective, of course, "agrarian radicalism" was defeated; it could not possibly succeed, since its major target was the industrial revolution. Yet it is not difficult to distinguish between the failure to attain its main objective and the success of its general themes, for in modified and extended form these themes had found general acceptance.

Moreover, they had been given additional potency by the techniques and ideas available to Japanese leadership after the Meiji Restoration. As has been noted, the drive for centralization in Japan was almost coincident with the full flowering of Western liberalism and its emphasis upon the common man. It was also practically coincident with the development of mass-media communications and education to reach that common man. The concept of elitist tutelage of the masses invariably emerged from these circumstances. But this was not necessarily an advantage for democracy. Indeed, as has been suggested, there were now new methods by which to avoid power sharing and additional reasons for so doing. Although the nature of modern Japanese society did not permit all these advanced techniques of mass control to be utilized, they were cultivated sufficiently through education and law to provide relative stability and canalize social unrest down a nationalist course. For nationalism in this setting could easily become the unifying force, the protector of elitist power, and the most logical compromise with the Western challenge.

These were the two great sources from which modern Japanese nationalism received its vitality, but there were a host of interrelated and additional factors which gave it tendency and power. Quite naturally, the measure of success in Japanese modernization, particularly the spectacular and unbroken chain of military victories (if one excepts Siberia), were important stimulants. The victory over Russia in 1904–1905 became the great nationalist

390

symbol. It was used for the purpose of expounding such varied themes as the superiority of spirit over resources, the perfidy of the West, the importance of absolute unity, and the duty to keep faith with those who had sacrificed themselves for the cause of the nation. In terms of military exploits abroad, there was little to destroy the myth of Japanese invincibility and superiority.

If one probes deeply, however, he discovers that the elements of doubt, conflict, and crisis in modern Japan were at least as important as those of success in influencing the nationalist movement. Despite superficial signs to the contrary, modern Japan was a society filled with fundamental conflicts and hence driven to push nationalism ever further in an effort to attain some greater measure of internal unity and to combat the divisive forces effectively. The scope of these conflicts was so broad as to defy description, but fundamentally almost all of them were connected with the problem of assimilating the industrial phase of Western evolution. They were intensified, moreover, by the extraordinary speed and particular timing which marked the process of assimilation, by the contradictory and transitional nature of the West itself, and by the growing world crisis which enveloped the twentieth century.

A virulent nationalism was a most natural product of these conditions. It was not only an attack upon the problems of the rising rural-urban cleavage and growing sense of class divisions; it was a counterattack against Western imperialism, discrimination, and attitudes of superiority or indifference. It was a psychological weapon against the corrosive tendencies of doubt, confusion, and an inferiority complex in a people under the greatest emotional tension. And given the nature of the contemporary world, it was an inevitable by-product of the profound economic and political problems which modernization had bequeathed to Japanese society. Nor was it unique. Its pendulum-like swing closely followed world tendencies, and both its causes and its results had striking parallels in such Western societies as that of Germany.

Thus Japanese nationalism reached its culmination in the 1930's and became the driving force in that era which has often been labeled "Military-Fascist." It is clear that there were some important differences between this Japanese "Fascism" and its Western counterpart. In the first place, the concept of *der Führer* was absent in Japan. There was a great difference between a Hitler and a Tojo, and this reflected the complete lack of individualism in Japanese society. Moreover, Japanese "Fascism," as was noted earlier, never approached a mass movement. Those national socialist elements dedicated to this end failed, just as they failed to effect a *coup d'état* in the fashion of the march on Rome. Here again, certain basic elements of modern Japan were revealed, for given the nature of that society, the difficulties of creating a mass movement were substantial. The failure of the "radical right" allowed a great measure of traditional elitism to dominate in the Japanese militarist era, and partially because of this, that era was never as completely authoritarian as the Nazi regime.

Yet, were these differences fundamental when compared with the similarities? In both cases, Fascism was a basic attack upon individualism, democracy, Marxism, and internationalism. It was profoundly anti-intellectual, emphasizing the myth, the hero, and action. It forwarded irrationalism to new heights. It found its foremost expressions in a glorification of war and of the racial spirit. Many of its roots were agrarian, and among its most primary supporters were elements of the rural classes. Thus it reflected within it much of the primitivism implanted in a preindustrial society. It built up its own *raison d'être* through an ever expanding campaign of foreign aggression, meanwhile retreating from its initial anti-capitalist position. Finally, the intensive emphasis of Fascism upon cultural uniqueness could not hide the fact that it was a common development among societies with widely different "cultural heritages" but with similar modern problems of timing and development.

X

THE PROBLEM OF JAPANESE
DEMOCRACY

THE IMPORTANCE of understanding the failure of democracy in prewar Japan has never been greater than it is today. As a result of complete military defeat, Japan has been thrust upon the pathway of democracy a second time, but the future is still uncertain. Meanwhile, social change is the order of the day throughout Asia, with political forces and ideologies reaching a crescendo in battle. Obviously authoritarianism has countless advantages in this struggle, especially when it takes the modernized, dynamic form of Communism. The crucial and unanswered question is whether democracy can remove its legacy of failure everywhere in the Far East and demonstrate some capacity to survive and develop.

As a first step in exploring this possibility, it is essential to seek out the basic causes for past failures. In this work, we have attempted to focus on this problem in the context of Japan. If our conclusions are valid, however, it is possible that they may have a certain applicability to a much wider area. Like any society, of course, Japan has differences which make any complete identification with other communities impossible; indeed, Japanese "uniqueness" has been so widely heralded that this point scarcely need be made. In view of this, however, if it can be shown that some of the major causative factors involved in the failure of Japanese democracy were the result not of "uniqueness" but of certain "similarities," then they assume an enhanced significance. There is another advantage in studying Japan in an effort to discern the most basic handicaps facing democracy in late-developing societies. In some respects, Japan resembles a "controlled experiment." The presumed prerequisites for a modern democratic society—the independent nation-state, industrialization, and mass literacy—were all attained by modern Japan. Thus one is not dealing with a society which lacked the elementary democratic "requirements." Furthermore, one is examining a society which reached goals now common to almost all "underdeveloped" areas and therefore a society which might represent in some degree their projected future.

Before seeking to relate the Japanese prewar experience with democracy to broader horizons, however, it is necessary to present some generalizations concerning that experience. Certainly there can be no doubt that democracy failed in prewar Japan, but our major effort throughout this study has been to find the most basic reasons for that failure. It is possible, of course, to argue that democracy was never really tried in Japan, but that is to beg the question. It received the only kind of trial which Japanese society was equipped to give it. It failed, moreover, in an atmosphere of world failure, with democracy losing ground in many diverse parts of the globe.

One "explanation" that frequently dominates an analysis of this problem is the "plot" thesis. In its overextended use, this thesis carries the implication that Japanese democracy was born with the promise of a long and fruitful life, but was throttled in its infancy by the machinations of evil men. One might remark in passing that the tendency to oversimplify and distort history in this manner has been most pronounced recently in nondemocratic circles. To the Communists, it represents a polemic weapon with just enough substance to make it most serviceable, despite certain contradictions which it poses to economic determinism. To the Fascists, it is in accord with the radical superman myth which discards all determinism. In any case, however, such an explanation for the failure of Japanese democracy can only be superficial. Japan, to be sure, had its full share of Machiavellian leaders and men of ill will. Moreover, as we have seen, some of her greatest and most dedicated statesmen were extremely clever at placing additional obstacles in front of democracy. But it is vital to realize that in the case of Japanese society, there were impersonal forces operating both within and outside in such a fashion as to establish a steeply graded table of probability with regard to social change. The more central explanation for the failure of the Japanese democratic movement must be found within these forces.

Perhaps the most orthodox and widely accepted explanation for the failure of democracy in Japan has revolved around Japanese tradition or culture. The incompatibility between Japanese tradition and democracy has been recognized in both the East and the West, and this theme has been expressed in a great variety of ways. Even the casual observer can see the differences between the West and Japan at the close of the nineteenth century. We have sought to portray their significance in the opening sections of this study, and we have never ceased to acknowledge the important part which the Japanese heritage played in the institutions and ideas of the modern period.

When one deals with "cultural differences," however, there are many questions to be asked and certain problems left unsolved. Some of these questions quite naturally go far beyond the subject of Japan or the Far East. Prominent among those cultural elements of the West to which the evolution of democracy has been attributed are Greek humanism, the Hebraic-Christian philosophy, and Roman law. There is very strong evidence to indicate that these played some role in the later development of modern democratic thought and institutions, although Western students are by no means agreed upon the precise contributions which each made. It is extremely interesting to note, however, that the "cultural differences" between the medieval West and the Far East of that same period did not preclude a similarity of basic values, with their respective major themes almost indistinguishable.

The medieval Western ideal was that of organic unity and the integration of all concepts into a single, harmonious whole. These themes predominated in medieval institutions and thought, despite certain clear evidences of pluralism, evidences which could of course be paralleled in the Far East. There was no place for nonconformity or individualism—no place for theories of accepted differences or competitive ideas. And scholarship reflected these facts, as one student of the medieval West has succinctly noted:

"The task of the medieval thinker was one of reconciliation, of synthesis rather than creation." [1]

The emphasis of the medieval West upon organic unity and its preoccupation with the search for complete synthesis was in substantial accord with the dominant themes of "the great harmony" and organic integration which prevailed in the Far East. There was no complete identity, to be sure, and there were stirrings in the West, most of them connected with the titanic struggle between

---

[1] C. R. S. Harris, in the chapter entitled "Philosophy," in C. G. Crump and E. F. Jacob (eds.), *The Legacy of the Middle Ages* (1942 ed.), Oxford, 1926, p. 228.

395

church and state, which had significant implications for the future. But the similarity of ideals between the West and East during this period cannot be denied, and behind this lay a similarity in political-economic institutions. In neither area were the dominant philosophical chords those of democratic theory, although it is possible to find some embryonic potentialities in both. And one should not forget that the medieval West had already had some considerable heritage of Greek humanism, Hebraic-Christian philosophy, and Roman law.

Then when did the profound differences between such societies as nineteenth-century England and Japan emerge, and what produced them? It seems obvious that whatever their seeds in the medieval period, they were centrally connected with the great developments which led up to and included the Western industrial revolution. The emergence of modern democracy cannot be separated from the early rise of capitalism within the framework of the nation-state. In England, this process was in operation from the Tudor period onward, although many stages were involved. And with this process was connected not only an increasing differentiation between West and East, but also one between various parts of the West.

The fact that it took something more than a cultural legacy of humanism, Roman law, and Hebraic-Christian philosophy to make modern democracy is revealed in a striking manner both by the medieval period of European history and by the evolution of the modern West itself. Western political evolution, indeed, offers some very important evidence relating to the Japanese problem. The readers of this study have seen the remarkable political parallels between the modern societies of Japan and Germany. Certainly these were not the result of a common cultural tradition in the sense in which this concept is usually understood. Germany had been subjected to the great forces of Western tradition mentioned above. The factor that connected Japan and Germany was not tradition but the timing of their "modernization."

This factor of timing not only helps to explain the similarities between these two societies, but also offers a central explanation for the failure of democracy in both. To retrace our steps somewhat, it seems clear that "cultures" change, at least if the central values of a society are any index to its culture. The differences between the dominant ideals of the Western medieval period and those of the Western liberal society of the nineteenth century were profound. Behind these differences was the change from feudalism to the modern capitalist state. It is undoubtedly true that the great forces in Western tradition played an important role in inducing this change. However, a host of other factors were involved, including many which were far from deterministic in character. As a result, certain areas which had shared the broadest traditions of the West lagged behind in this new phase. Where the lag was appreciable, it could produce very substantial differences in the political forms of modern industrial-centered societies. Essentially, these variations all reflected the rational interests of commercial-industrial classes. In short, the industrial revolution was conducive to more than one political expression, depending upon the timing and intensity of its development. In the case of many late arrivals, the doctrines of economic and political liberalism were not the most logical expression of industrialism. Thus many aspects of the preindustrial heritage were little changed, not only because of the speed of the transition but also because the newly emerging forces did not present a strong challenge.

How do these hypotheses apply to modern Japan? They certainly do not imply that the traditional heritage of that society was unimportant in the modern period, but they do suggest that its real force came from the degree to which it harmonized with the requirements of a late-developing industrial society. There is no need to summarize in any detail the evidence presented earlier in this study which supports such a thesis. As we have seen, the inability of Japanese capitalism to underwrite the cardinal principles of democracy was centrally connected with the timing of its development, as this related to conditions both in Japan and in the world. This fact, in turn, had a direct or indirect influence upon every facet of modern Japan. The power of agrarianism, the history of Japanese constitutionalism, the character of Japanese nationalism —all were vitally affected. The import of timing, incidentally, escaped the majority of Communists as well as many men fighting for democracy. The Communists continued to espouse as orthodox the thesis that a "bourgeois democratic" revolution would inevitably accompany the industrial revolution regardless of time. This was the philosophic basis of the two-stage revolutionary theory for Asia. Although the absence of this development plagued the Communists often with regard to policy, however, its really lethal effect was naturally upon the democrats.

If timing does represent the major explanation for the failure of democracy in Japan, the ramifications of this fact can be very broad. Western-style democracy is the product of an earlier evolution which cannot possibly be duplicated in the modern world. The "natural evolution" of the same forces which molded eighteenth- and nineteenth-century England and the United States will not produce parallel results in the twentieth century. But this does not necessarily mean that the democratic cause is lost. It does mean that new techniques and ideas will have to be applied in order to adjust democracy to the modern world.

First, this involves the acceptance of a concept of democracy which is not burdened with provincialism or an inelastic historic reference and yet incorporates the indispensable essence of the democratic system. Perhaps the definition of democracy given in the Preface of this study is serviceable in these respects. That definition established two criteria: (1) adherence to the concept of the innate dignity of man and recognition of his total development as the ultimate goal of the state; and (2) acceptance of choice as the fundamental qualification of democratic institutions, with positive protection for civil liberties, a competitive party system, and the other necessities of an "open society." Such a definition acknowledges by implication the need for economic-political experimentation and recognizes the diversity of existing types of democratic societies. It does not seek to confine democracy within the narrow strictures of a single economic or political mold, yet it establishes criteria which cannot be met by authoritarianisms, including the false "democracy" of Communism.

How democracy is defined and philosophically defended is tremendously important today, and especially in an area like the Far East. In many respects, this is an age attuned to faith, when men everywhere are searching for ideals and programs which will give them hope and courage and, at the same time, relate them and their society to the rest of the world. The fact that Communism has captured much of the democratic symbolism and dynamic appeal in certain parts of Asia and among certain Asian groups is in part a commentary upon the narrow and paradoxical connotations which some of its "supporters" have foisted upon democracy. Although this can never really be separated from questions of policy, still it is possible to isolate it for the moment as a "state of mind" which is grossly out of step with the trends and necessities of the modern world.

Once he is aware of the broader, more flexible potentialities of his creed, the democrat of today must defend his values and demonstrate both in theory and practice that they are inextricably connected in the long run with those democratic procedures which

398

such opponents as the Communists completely warp. But the argument must be joined squarely, not only with the assorted authoritarians, but also with those who use eclecticism to confuse and obscure vital differences. This is a particular challenge in the Far East, since the proclivities of the modern West for philosophical rigidity have been matched in Asia by the tendency to seek a harmonization of all ideas, including ones that are fundamentally incompatible. This again reflects our earlier discussion, for the latter tendency bears a resemblance to the philosophic bent of the medieval West. Modern democracy must symbolize the rejection of both complete rigidity and the misuse of eclecticism. It must display its flexibility in the working out of selective syntheses which are logical and feasible, and the joint products of minds from many societies.

If the preceding represents a conceptual framework for democracy in the modern world, that framework can take on vitality only as the proper techniques are found to support and develop it. In this respect, the most important challenge of today lies in the international sphere. The world has now reached a stage of interdependence which makes the democratic problem at its roots an international one. As we have seen, democracy in modern Japan could not emerge as a natural, "indigenous" development which followed the old patterns, given the interplay between internal and external conditions that prevailed in the period after 1850. And in this, Japan bears some relation to all late-developing societies. An external stimulus composed of imperialism or indifference and fraught with international economic and political crisis breeds authoritarianism. Thus if democracy is to have any future in our times, it is indispensable to put forward a long-range coöperative program of mutual aid and understanding between the "advanced" democracies and the so-called "underdeveloped" or late-developing societies. The program must operate in accordance with the new concepts of democracy, following tactics which will make its premises meaningful. It is not within the province of this work to examine the many hazards and obstacles involved, or to explore the countless difficulties that must be overcome. It is for us simply to assert that the necessity for such a program is the chief lesson to be drawn from the failure of democracy in prewar Japan.

GLOSSARY

JAPANESE TRANSLITERATIONS

安部磯雄	Abe Isō
阿部信行	Abe Nobuyuki
安達謙蔵	Adachi Kenzō
愛国旌旗同盟	Aikoku Seiki Dōmei (Patriotic Banner League)
愛国公党	Aikokukōtō (Public Party of Patriots)
愛国社	Aikokusha (Society of Patriots)
愛郷塾	Aikyōjuku (Institute for Local Patriotism)
赤旗	*Akahata (Red Flag)*
赤松克麿	Akamatsu Katsumaro
青森	Aomori
青野季吉	Aono Suekichi
荒畑寒村	Arahata Kanson
新井白石	Arai Hakuseki
新井章吾	Arai Shōgo
荒木貞夫	Araki Sadao
有馬良橘	Arima Ryōkitsu
有栖川親王	Arisugawa Shinnō [Prince Arisugawa]
朝日	*Asahi (Morning Sun)*
浅野	Asano
安土桃山	Azuchi-Momoyama
幕府	bakufu (military administration)
幕末	Bakumatsu (shogunate twilight period)
萬機公論	banki kōron ([decisions on] all issues by public opinion)
番頭	bantō (manager)

戌申倶楽部	Boshin Club
武家諸法度	buke sho hatto (Regulations for the Military Class)
部落	buraku (hamlet)
武士	bushi (warrior)
平等	byōdō (equality)
治安維持法	Chian Ijihō (Peace Preservation Law)
治安警察法	Chian Keisatsuhō (Public Peace Police Law)
秩父	Chichibu
地方官会議	Chihōkan Kaigi (Assembly of Prefectural Governors)
珍品五ツ	chimpin itsutsu (five rare articles)
町	chō (equals 2.45 acres)
勅任官	Chokuninkan (Imperially appointed officials)
町人	chōnin (merchant)
長州	Chōshū
朝野新聞	*Chōya Shimbun (The Newspaper of the Whole Nation)*
超然内閣主義	chōzen naikaku shugi (the principle of transcendental cabinet)
中央倶楽部	Chūō Club (Central Club)
中央公論	*Chūō Kōron (The Central Review)*
大日本国粋会	Dai Nihon Kokusuikai (Greater Japan National Essence Society)
大日本協会	Dai Nihon Kyōkai (Greater Japan Society)
大日本生産党	Dai Nihon Seisantō (Greater Japan Production Party)
大日本史	*Dai Nihon shi (History of Greater Japan)*
大同倶楽部	Daidō Club (Club of Like Thinkers)
大同團結	Daidō Danketsu (Union of Like Thinkers)
代議政党	Daigi Seitō (Representative Party)
大名	daimyō (feudal lords)

大審院	Daishin-in (Supreme Court)
太政官	Dajōkan (Council of State, or Chief Administrative Office)
團琢麿	Dan Takuma
太宰春台	Dazai Shundai
土肥原賢二	Doihara Kenji
独立倶楽部	Dokuritsu Club (Independent Club)
同志会	Dōshikai (Comrades' Association)
道徳国家	dōtoku kokka (ethical state)
同族	dōzoku (same family)
越前	Echizen
江戸	Edo
穢多	eta (outcast)
江藤新平	Etō Shimpei
府	fu (Metropolitan District)
譜代大名	fudai daimyō (hereditary lords)
藤原惺窩	Fujiwara Seika
復古	fukko (return to antiquity)
富国強兵	fukoku kyōhei (wealthy country, powerful soldiery)
福地源一郎	Fukuchi Genichirō
福本和夫	Fukumoto Kazuo
福島	Fukushima
福沢諭吉	Fukuzawa Yukichi
古河	Furukawa
古沢迂郎	Furuzawa Urō
外交調査会	Gaikō Chōsa Kai (Foreign Policy Deliberation Committee)
外尊内圧	gai-son nai-atsu (outward respect, inner oppression)
学閥	gakubatsu (University clique)
芸州	Geishū
元勲内閣	genkun naikaku (elder statesmen cabinet)
元老	Genrō (Elder Statesmen)
元老院	Genrō-in (Elder Statesmen's Council, or Senate)

元禄	Genroku
言論自由論	*Genron jiyū ron* (*Treatise on Freedom of Speech*)
玄洋社	Genyōsha (The Sea of Genkai Society)
議政	Gijō (Legislature, or legislative official)
議政官	Gijōkan (Legislative Office)
議会尚早	gikai shōsō (too soon for a representative assembly)
義務	gimu (duty)
偽党撲滅	gitō bokumetsu (Smash the false parties!)
権藤成卿	Gondō Seikyō [Nariaki]
後藤新平	Gotō Shimpei
後藤象次郎	Gotō Shōjirō
群馬	Gumma
郡	gun (county, or local district)
行地社	Gyōchisha (The Society to Realize the Way of Heaven on Earth)
暁民会	Gyōminkai (The Association of Enlightened People)
浜田国松	Hamada Kunimatsu
浜口雄幸	Hamaguchi Yūkō
藩閥	hambatsu (fiefal clique)
藩	han (fief)
羽織	haori (Japanese outer coat)
原敬	Hara Takashi [Kei]
原嘉道	Hara Yoshimichi
橋本欣五郎	Hashimoto Kingorō
秦真二	Hata Shinji
旗本	hatamoto (bannerets)
鳩山和夫	Hatoyama Kazuo
服部徳訳	Hattori Naritsugu
林羅山	Hayashi Razan
林銑十郎	Hayashi Senjūrō
林子平	Hayashi Shihei
林有造	Hayashi Yūzō
林田龜太郎	Hayashida Kametarō

404

平民	heimin (commoner)
平民新聞	*Heimin Shimbun* (*The Commoner News-paper*)
平民党	Heimintō (Commoner Party)
秀吉	Hideyoshi
非常時局	hijō jikyoku (extraordinary conditions)
品性陶冶	hinsei tōya (character education)
平沼騏一郎	Hiranuma Kiichirō
平田篤胤	Hirata Atsutane
広島	Hiroshima
広田弘毅	Hirota Kōki
肥前	Hizen
保安条例	Hoan Jōrei (Peace Preservation Law)
封地封建	hōchi hōken (fiefal feudalism)
報知新聞	*Hōchi Shimbun* (*The News-Dispatch*)
放火泥棒	hōka dorobō (fire-setting robber)
北海道	Hokkaido
方向転換	hōkō tenkan (change of course)
本間憲一郎	Homma Kenichirō
本多利明	Honda Toshiaki
本州	Honshū
堀江帰一	Horie Kiichi
星亨	Hoshi Tōru
保守派	Hoshu ha (Conservative Faction)
朋党	hōtō (faction)
保全主義	hozenshugi (conservatism)
穂積八束	Hozumi Yatsuka
伊庭想太郎	Iba Sōtarō
茨城	Ibaragi
一大政党	ichidai seitō (one great political party)
市川正一	Ichikawa Shōichi
池田成彬	Ikeda Seihin
一国一城	ikkoku ichijō (one country, one castle)
猪俣津南雄	Inomata Tsunao
井上準之助	Inoue Junnosuke
井上馨	Inoue Kaoru
井上日召	Inoue Nisshō

犬養毅	Inukai Tsuyoshi [Ki]
石本新六	Ishimoto Shinroku
板垣征四郎	Itagaki Seishirō
板垣退助	Itagaki Taisuke
伊藤博文	Itō Hirobumi
伊藤亀城	Itō Kameshiro
伊東巳代治	Itō Miyoji
岩倉具視	Iwakura Tomomi
岩崎彌之助	Iwasaki Yanosuke
岩崎彌太郎	Iwasaki Yatarō
邪宗	jashū (heretical sects)
自治学会	Jichi Gakkai (Self-Government Institute)
自治民範	*Jichi Mimpan (Self-Government by the People)*
自我意識	jiga ishiki (self-consciousness)
自我の解放	jiga no kaihō (the emancipation of self)
時事新報	*Jiji Shimpō (Current News)*
自助社	Jijosha (Self-Help Society)
人民	jimmin (public)
神武天皇	Jimmu Tennō [The Emperor Jimmu]
神祇官	Jingikan (Office of Deities)
人権新説	*Jinken shinsetsu (New Theories of Popular Rights)*
人力車	jinrikisha
自主	jishu (self-government)
実業同志会	Jitsugyō Dōshikai (Business Fellow Thinkers' Association)
自由新聞	*Jiyū Shimbun (Liberty Newspaper)*
自由民権	jiyūminken (popular rights)
自由党	Jiyūtō (Liberal Party)
自由党会員名簿	*Jiyūtō Kaiin Meibo (Official Register of the Jiyuto)*
情意投合	jōi tōgō (mutual understanding)
上奏案	jōsōan (resolution memorializing the Emperor)
縦横倶楽部	Jūō Club (Universal Club)

406

重臣	Jūshin (Chief Retainers)
樺山資紀	Kabayama Sukenori
荷田春満（東麿）	Kada Azumamaro
開国	kaikoku (Open the country)
改進党	Kaishintō (Progressive Party)
改善	kaizen (improvement)
革新倶楽部	Kakushin Club (Reform Club)
鎌倉	Kamakura
神風自由党	Kamikaze Jiyūtō (Divine Wind Liberal Party)
賀茂真淵	Kamo no Mabuchi
金子堅太郎	Kaneko Kentarō
官僚	kanryō (bureaucracy)
関東	Kantō (Eastern Provinces)
樺太	Karafuto (Saghalien)
霞ヶ関	Kasumigaseki (site of the Foreign Office in Tokyo)
片岡健吉	Kataoka Kenkichi
片山潜	Katayama Sen
片山哲	Katayama Tetsu
加藤弘之	Katō Hiroyuki
加藤寛治	Katō Kanji
加藤勘十	Katō Kanju
加藤高明	Katō Takaakira [Kōmei]
加藤友三郎	Katō Tomosaburō
桂太郎	Katsura Tarō
河上清	Kawakami Kiyoshi
川崎	Kawasaki
啓蒙学者	keimō gakusha (enlightened scholars)
慶応	Keiō
経済雑誌	*Keizai Zasshi* (*Economics Magazine*)
憲兵隊	Kempeitai (Military Police)
県	ken (Prefecture)
家人封建制度	kenin hōken seido (family feudal system)
建国会	Kenkokukai (The Society to Build the Country)

407

研究会	Kenkyūkai (Study Association)
権利	kenri (rights)
憲政擁護会	Kensei Yōgo Kai (Protect the Constitution Association)
憲政本党	Kenseihontō (Orthodox Kenseito)
憲政会	Kenseikai (Constitutional Association)
憲政党	Kenseitō (Constitutional Party)
血盟團	Ketsumeidan (Blood Oath Association)
木戸孝允	Kido Kōin
機関説	kikansetsu (organic theory)
近畿	Kinki (Inner Provinces [Osaka and Kyoto districts])
勤王家	kinnōka (Imperial loyalists)
木下尚江	Kinoshita Naoe
勤労国民党	Kinrō Kokumintō (Workers' Nationalist Party)
北一輝	Kita Ikki
清浦奎吾	Kiyoura Keigo
貴族院改革期成会	Kizokuin Kaikaku Kisei Kai (Association Pledged to Peerage Reform)
孝	ko (filial piety)
小林一雄	Kobayashi Kazuo
高知新聞	*Kōchi Shimbun* (*Kochi Newspaper*)
皇道派	Kōdō ha (Imperial Way Faction)
皇道義会	Kōdōgi Kai (Society for the Principle of the Imperial Way)
幸福安全会	Kōfuku Anzenkai (Happiness-Security Society)
公議与論	kōgi yoron (public opinion)
公議所	Kōgisho (Public Deliberation Chamber)
講組	kogumi (association)
小磯国昭	Koiso Kuniaki
国家社会党	Kokka Shakaitō (National Socialist Society)
国会期成同盟会	Kokkai Kisei Dōmeikai (Association for the Petitioning for a National Assembly)

国権	kokken (national rights)
石	koku (equals 4.96 bushels)
国法汎論	*Kokuhō hanron* (*A General Treatise on National Law*)
国本社	Kokuhonsha (National Foundation Society)
国民同盟	Kokumin Dōmei (Nationalist League)
国民自由党	Kokumin Jiyūtō (Nationalist Liberal Party)
国民党	Kokumintō (Nationalist Party)
黒龍会	Kokuryūkai (Amur River Society)
国粋会	Kokusuikai (National Essence Society)
国體	kokutai (national polity)
孝明天皇	Kōmei Tennō [The Emperor Kōmei]
小室信夫	Komuro Shinobu
近藤栄蔵	Kondō Eizō
工人	kōnin (artisan)
河野広中	Kōnō Hironaka
河野敏鎌	Kōno Toshikama
近衛文麿	Konoe Fumimaro
個性の尊重	kosei no sonchō (respect for the individual personality)
幸徳伝次郎（秋水）	Kōtoku Denjirō [Shūsui]
交友倶楽部	Kōyū Club (Fraternal Club)
公卿	kuge (court noble)
久原房之助	Kuhara Fusanosuke
国	kuni (nation)
君主専政	kunshu sensei (monarchical absolutism)
黒田清隆	Kuroda Kiyotaka
協調会	Kyōchōkai (Conciliation Society)
卿太夫	kyōdaifu (major official)
共同運輸会社	Kyōdō Unyu Kaisha (Joint Navigation Company)
京都	Kyōto
九州	Kyūshū
九州同志会	Kyūshū Dōshikai (Kyushu Fellow Thinkers' Association)

町田忠治	Machida Chūji
牧野伸顕	Makino Nobuaki [Shinken]
満州事変	Manshū Jihen (Manchurian Incident)
丸山作楽	Maruyama Sakura
松田正久	Matsuda Masahisa
松島剛	Matsujima Tsuyoshi
松方正義	Matsukata Masayoshi
松岡駒吉	Matsuoka Komakichi
松岡洋右	Matsuoka Yōsuke
真崎甚三郎	Mazaki Jinzaburō
明治日報	*Meiji Nippō* (*Meiji Daily*)
明治天皇	Meiji Tennō [The Emperor Meiji]
目附	metsuke (censors)
三重	Mie
三木武吉	Miki Takekichi
民本主義	mimponshugi (principle of the people as the basis [of the state])
南次郎	Minami Jirō
民会	minkai (people's assembly)
民権自由論	*Minken jiyū ron* (*Treatise on Popular Rights and Liberty*)
美濃部達吉	Minobe Tatsukichi
民政党	Minseitō (Popular Government Party, or Democratic Party)
民主々義	minshushugi (democracy)
民党	mintō (popular parties)
民約論	*Minyaku ron* (*Social Contract* [Rousseau])
味噌	miso (bean paste)
水戸	Mito
水戸光圀	Mito Mitsukuni
三菱	Mitsubishi
三井	Mitsui
満川亀太郎	Mitsukawa Kametarō
宮島誠一郎	Miyajima Seiichirō
水野寅次郎	Mizuno Torajirō
文部省	Mombushō (Department of Education)
森有礼	Mori Arinori

森恪	Mori Kaku
元田肇	Motoda Hajime
本居宣長	Motoori Norinaga
室町	Muromachi
無産青年同盟	Musan Seinen Dōmei (Proletarian Youth League)
武藤山治	Muto Sanji [Yamaji]
陸奥宗光	Mutsu Munemitsu
苗字帯刀御免の家柄	myōji taitō gomen no iegara (of families privileged to wear the sword and have a surname)
鍋山貞親	Nabeyama Sadachika
永井柳太郎	Nagai Ryūtarō
長崎	Nagasaki
永田鉄山	Nagata Tetsuzan
名古屋	Nagoya
内安外競	naian gaikyō (internal peace, external competition)
内地	Naichi (Home Provinces)
内閣	naikaku (cabinet)
内閣議決書	Naikaku Giketsusho (Cabinet Resolution Document)
中江兆民（篤介）	Nakae Chōmin [Tokusuke]
中江藤樹	Nakae Tōju
中橋徳五郎	Nakahashi Tokugorō
中島知久平	Nakajima Chikuhei
中上川彦二郎	Nakamigawa Hikojirō
成金	narikin (newly rich)
日々新聞	*Nichi Nichi Shimbun* (*The Daily News*)
日本概史	*Nihon gaishi* (*Outline of Japanese History*)
日本平民党	Nihon Heimintō (Japan Commoner Party)
日本改造法案大綱	*Nihon kaizō hōan taikō* (*Outline of the Measures for the Reconstruction of Japan*)
日本無産党	Nihon Musantō (Japan Proletariat Party)

411

日本農民組合	Nihon Nōmin Kumiai (Japan Farmers' Union)
日本農民党	Nihon Nōmintō (Japan Farmers' Party)
日本及日本人	*Nihon oyobi Nihonjin* (*Japan and the Japanese*)
日本労働総同盟	Nihon Rōdō Sōdōmei (Japanese Federation of Labor)
日本労農党	Nihon Rōnōtō (Japan Labor-Farmer Party)
日本政記	*Nihon seiki* (*Political Records of Japan*)
日本社会党	Nihon Shakaitō (The Japan Socialist Party)
日本総同盟革新同盟	Nihon Sōdōmei Kakushin Dōmei (The Japanese Federation Reform League)
日本大衆党	Nihon Taishūtō (Japan Mass Party)
西田税	Nishida Zei
西川光次郎	Nishikawa Kōjirō
西尾末広	Nishio Suehiro
農民	nōmin (farmer, peasant)
農民労働党	Nōmin Rōdōtō (Farmer-Labor Party)
農村自救論	*Nōson jikyū ron* (*A Treatise on Rural Self-Help*)
野坂参三	Nozaka Sanzō [Nosaka Sanzō]
沼間守一	Numa Moriichi
小川平吉	Ogawa Heikichi
荻生徂徠	Ogyū Sorai
大井憲太郎	Ōi Kentarō
大石正巳	Ōishi Masami
岡田啓介	Okada Keisuke
岡本健三郎	Okamoto Kensaburō
大川周明	Ōkawa Shūmei
岡崎邦輔	Okazaki Kunisuke
小久保喜七	Okubo Kishichi
大久保利通	Ōkubo Toshimichi
奥田義人	Okuda Yoshito
大隈重信	Ōkuma Shigenobu
大倉	Ōkura
恩	on (favors, or benefactions)

小野	Ono (the business house of Ono)
小野梓	Ono Azusa
小野塚喜平次	Onozuka Kiheiji
大阪	Ōsaka
大阪朝日	*Ōsaka Asahi* (*Osaka Morning Sun*)
大阪毎日	*Ōsaka Mainichi* (*Osaka Daily*)
大杉栄	Ōsugi Sakae
鷗渡会	Ōto Kai (Gull Society)
大浦兼武	Ōura Kanetake
尾張	Owari
大山郁夫	Ōyama Ikuo
大山巌	Ōyama Iwao
尾崎行雄	Ozaki Yukio
頼山陽	Rai Sanyō
歴史科学	*Rekishi Kagaku* (*Historical Science*)
列藩会議	reppan kaigi (powerful han conference)
立憲同志会	Rikken Dōshikai (Constitutional Fellow Thinkers' Association)
立憲改進党	Rikken Kaishintō (Constitutional Progressive Party)
立憲国民党	Rikken Kokumintō (Constitutional Nationalist Party)
立憲民政党	Rikken Minseitō (Constitutional Democratic Party)
立憲の常道	rikken no jōdō (true constitutional road)
立憲政體	rikken seitai (constitutional government)
立憲政體略	*Rikken seitai ryaku* (*Outline of Constitutional Government*)
立憲政友会	Rikken Seiyūkai (Friends of Constitutional Government Association)
立憲帝政党	Rikken Teiseitō (Constitutional Imperial Party)
臨時政務調査局	Rinji Seimu Chōsakyoku (Temporary Administrative Affairs Investigation Bureau)
臨時帝国議会事務局	Rinji Teikoku Gikai Jimukyoku (Temporary Imperial Diet Affairs Bureau)

立志社	Risshisha (The Society to Establish One's Ambitions)
労働評議会	Rōdō Hyōgikai (Labor Council)
労働農民党	Rōdō Nōmintō (Labor-Farmer Party)
労働新聞	*Rōdō Shimbun* (*Labor Newspaper*)
浪人	rōnin (masterless samurai)
労農派	Rōnō ha (Labor-Farmer Faction)
老壮会	Rōsōkai (The Society of Mature Men)
佐幕開国	sabaku kaikoku (Support the bakufu— Open the country)
作業教育	sagyō kyōiku (vocational education)
西郷隆盛	Saigō Takamori
西郷従道	Saigō Tsugumichi
左院	Sa-in (Chamber of the Left)
西園寺公望	Saionji Kimmochi
齊藤実	Saitō Makoto
堺利彦	Sakai Toshihiko
坂本龍馬	Sakamoto Ryūma
酒	sake (rice wine)
桜会	Sakurakai (Cherry Blossom Society)
侍	samurai (warrior)
三条実美	Sanjō Saneyoshi
三家三卿	sanke sankyō (the three families and the three nobilities)
参勤交代	sankin kōtai (alternate trips for service)
佐野文夫	Sano Fumio
佐野学	Sano Manabu [Gaku]
参与	Sanyo (Council, or Councillors)
佐々木高行	Sasaki Takayuki
薩摩	Satsuma
制度取調局	Seido Torishirabekyoku (Department for Institutional Investigation)
政府を転覆	seifu wo tempuku (Overthrow the government!)
征夷大将軍	Sei-i Tai Shōgun (Barbarian-subduing Generalissimo)
正院	Sei-in (Central Chamber)
政治問題研究会	Seiji Mondai Kenkyūkai (Society for the Study of Political Problems)

政論党派	seiron tōha (political argument faction)
政商	seishō (political merchants)
政體	seitai (political structure)
政體書	Seitaisho (The Organic Act)
政哲夢物語	*Sei-tetsu yume monogatari* (*Dream Stories of Western Philosophy*)
政党	seitō (political party)
政党解消聯盟	Seitō Kaishō Remmei (Political Party Dissolution League)
政友倶楽部	Seiyū Club (Political Friends' Club)
政友本党	Seiyūhontō (Orthodox Seiyu Party)
赤化防止團	Sekka Bōshidan (Association to Prevent Bolshevism)
仙石貢	Sengoku Mitsugu
切腹	seppuku (slashing the abdomen)
社会民衆党	Shakai Minshūtō (Social Mass Party)
社会大衆党	Shakai Taishūtō (Social Mass Party)
社会主義同盟	Shakaishugi Dōmei (Socialist League)
柴四朗	Shiba Shirō
渋沢栄一	Shibuzawa Eiichi
幣原喜重郎	Shidehara Kijūrō
四国	Shikoku
島田	Shimada (the business house of Shimada)
島田三郎	Shimada Saburō
島中雄三	Shimanaka Yūzō
島津	Shimazu
神兵隊	Shimpeitai (Sacred Soldiers)
進歩派	Shimpo ha (Progressive Faction)
進歩党	Shimpotō (Progressive Party)
新東洋	*Shin Tōyō* (*New Orient*)
品川彌二郎	Shinagawa Yajirō
審議院	Shingi-in (Deliberative Council)
士農工商	shi-nō-kō-shō (warrior-farmer-artisan-merchant)
神道	Shintō (Way of the Gods)
資産家	shisanka (men of means)
私党	shitō (private party)

士族	shizoku (second-stratum nobility, below kazoku)
諸侯	shokō (lord)
庶民	shomin (common people)
醤油	shōyu (soya sauce)
衆議院	Shūgi-in (Assembly Chamber)
主治者	shujisha (political leaders)
主権線	shuken sen (the sovereign line)
集権的封建制度	shūkenteki hōken seido (centralized feudal system)
主政者	shuseisha (political leaders)
副島種臣	Soejima Taneomi
則天行地	sokuten gyōchi (to realize the Way of Heaven on earth)
尊皇愛国	sonnō aikoku (Revere the Emperor; love the country)
尊皇攘夷	sonnō jōi (Revere the Emperor—Oust the barbarians [Westerners])
総裁	Sōsai (Office [or Officer] of Supreme Control)
壮士	sōshi (strong-arm men)
末広鉄腸	Suehiro Tetchō
杉山元	Sugiyama Hajime [Gen]
住友貴左衛門	Sumitomo Kizaemon
枢密院	Sūmitsu-in (Privy Council)
鈴木文治	Suzuki Bunji
鈴木貫太郎	Suzuki Kantarō
鈴木喜三郎	Suzuki Kisaburō
鈴木茂三郎	Suzuki Mosaburō
橘孝三郎	Tachibana Kōsaburō
田川大吉郎	Tagawa Daikichirō
対外硬派	Taigaikō ha (Strong Foreign Policy Group)
大化	Taika
大政翼賛会	Taisei Yokusan Kai (Imperial Rule Assistance Association)
大成会	Taiseikai (Great Achievement Society)
大詔	taishō (Imperial rescript)

416

大正維新	Taishō Ishin (Taisho Restoration)
大正赤心團	Taishō Sekishin Dan (Taisho True Heart Society)
大衆教育同盟	Taishū Kyōiku Dōmei (League for Mass Education)
大陽	*Taiyō* (*The Sun*)
高橋龜吉	Takahashi Kamekichi
高橋是清	Takahashi Korekiyo
高瀬清	Takase Kiyoshi
反	tan (equals 0.245 acre)
田中義一	Tanaka Giichi
田中参内	Tanaka Sannai
田添鉄三	Tazoe Tetsuzō
帝国農会	Teikoku Nōkai (Imperial Agricultural Society)
定律の政治	teiritsu no seiji (government of law)
帝政党	Teiseitō (Imperial Administration Party)
天賦人権辨	*Tempu jinken ben* (*Understanding Natural Rights*)
天地の公道	tenchi no kōdō (equitable principle of nature)
寺内寿一	Terauchi Hisaichi
寺内正毅	Terauchi Masatake [Seiki]
栃木	Tochigi
東郷平八郎	Tōgō Heihachirō
党派	tōha (factions)
東北	Tōhoku (northeast)
東条英機	Tōjō Hideki
東海暁鐘新報	*Tōkai Gyōshō Shimpō* (*The Tokai Morning Bell News*)
床次竹二郎	Tokonami Takejirō
徳田球一	Tokuda Kyūichi
徳川家康	Tokugawa Ieyasu
徳川慶喜	Tokugawa Keiki [Yoshinobu]
徳川義親	Tokugawa Yoshichika
東京朝日	*Tōkyō Asahi* (*Tokyo Morning Sun*)
東京横浜毎日	*Tōkyō-Yokohama Mainichi* (*Tokyo-Yokohama Daily*)

問屋	tonya (wholesale houses)
土佐	Tosa
統制派	Tōsei ha (Control Faction)
頭山秀三	Tōyama Hidezō
頭山満	Tōyama Mitsuru
東洋議政会	Tōyō Giseikai (Oriental Parliamentary Society)
東洋自由党	Tōyō Jiyūtō (Oriental Liberal Party)
東洋新報	*Tōyō Shimpō* (*The Oriental News*)
豊川良平	Toyokawa Ryōhei
外様大名	tozama daimyō (outer lords)
通義権利	tsūgikenri (rights)
内田良平	Uchida Ryōhei
内田康哉	Uchida Yasuya
植原悦次郎	Uehara Etsujirō
上原勇作	Uehara Yūsaku
植木枝盛	Ueki Emori
上杉慎吉	Uesugi Shinkichi
宇垣一成	Ugaki Kazushige
右院	U-in (Chamber of the Right)
浮田和民	Ukita Kazutami
海坊主退治	umi bōzu taiji (Destroy the sea monsters!)
若槻礼次郎	Wakatsuki Reijirō
早稲田	Waseda
渡辺錠太郎	Watanabe Jōtarō
渡辺国武	Watanabe Kunitake
渡辺政之輔	Watanabe Masanosuke
彌次	yaji (jeerers)
山鹿素行	Yamaga Sokō
山県有明	Yamagata Aritomo
山川均	Yamakawa Hitoshi
山本英輔	Yamamoto Eisuke
山本権兵衛	Yamamoto Gombei
山本懸蔵	Yamamoto Kenzō
山本達雄	Yamamoto Tatsuo
山本貞二郎	Yamamoto Teijirō

山内豊信	Yamanouchi Toyonobu
大和民労会	Yamato Minrōkai (Yamato People's Labor Society)
矢野文雄	Yano Fumio
八代六郎	Yashiro Rokurō
安田善次郎	Yasuda Zenjirō
翼賛	yokusan (to aid)
読売新聞	*Yomiuri Shimbun* (*The Readers' Newspaper*)
萬	*Yorozu* (*What's What*)
吉田松陰	Yoshida Shōin
吉野作造	Yoshino Sakuzō
友愛	yūai (fraternity)
友愛会	Yūaikai (Fraternal Association)
郵便報知新聞	*Yūbin Hōchi Shimbun* (*The Post-Dispatch Newspaper*)
結城豊太郎	Yūki Toyotarō
友好会	Yūkokai (Friends' Society)
由利公正	Yuri Kōsei
有司専制	yūshi sensei (official absolutism)
猶存社	Yūzonsha (Society to Preserve the National Essence)
財閥	zaibatsu (financial cliques [or their members])
在郷軍人会	Zaigō Gunjinkai (Reserve Association)
全日本愛国者共同斗争協議会	Zen Nihon Aikokusha Kyōdō Tōsō Kyōgikai (All-Japan Patriots' United Struggle Council)
前衛	*Zenei* (*Vanguard*)
全国民衆党	Zenkoku Minshūtō (All-Nation Mass Party)
全国労農大衆党	Zenkoku Rōnō Taishūtō (All-Nation Labor-Farmer Mass Party)
全国大衆党	Zenkoku Taishūtō (All-Nation Mass Party)
頭巾	zukin (hood)

安藤徳器，西園寺公望

青野昆堂，日本政党変遷史

荒畑寒村，日本社会主義運動史

荒木貞夫，體を捨ててこそ，戦争と国民の覚悟

吾妻光俊，労働法

深谷博治，初期議会条約改正，　　近代日本歴史講座

福尾武四郎，日本家族制度史

福武直，日本農村の社会的性格

現代日本史研究

原奎一郎（編纂），原敬日記

原種行，大正・昭和時代史，新講大日本史

原田熊雄，西園寺公と政局

BIBLIOGRAPHY

JAPANESE WORKS
Books

Andō Tokuki. *Saionji Kimmochi.* Tōkyō, 1938.

Aono Kondō. *Nihon seitō hensen shi* (*A History of Changes in Japanese Parties*). Tōkyō, 1935.

Arahata Kanson. *Nihon shakaishugi undō shi* (*A History of the Japanese Socialist Movement*). *Tokyō*, 1948.

Araki Sadao. *Karada o sutete koso: sensō to kokumin no kakugo* (*Sacrifice Yourself: War and the Resolution of the People*). Tōkyō, 1937.

Azuma Mitsutoshi. *Rōdō hō* (*Labor Law*). Tōkyō, 1950.

Fukaya Hiroji. *Shoki Gikai jōyaku kaisei* (*The First Diets: Treaty Revision*), in Kindai Nihon rekishi kōza (Modern Japanese History Series). Tōkyō, 1940.

Fukuo Takeshiro. *Nihon kazoku seido shi* (*A History of the Japanese Family System*). Tōkyō, 1947.

Fukutake Tadashi. *Nihon nōson no shakaiteki seikaku* (*The Social Character of the Japanese Rural Community*). Tōkyō, 1949.

Gendai Nihon shi kenkyū (*Studies of Contemporary Japanese History*). Tōkyō, 1938.

Hara Keiichirō (ed.). *Hara Takashi nikki* (*The Diary of Hara Takashi*). Tōkyō, 1950–1951. 9 vols.

Hara Taneyuki. *Taishō-Shōwa jidai shi* (*A History of the Taisho and Showa Eras*). Vol. VIII of Shinkō dai Nihon shi (Modern Studies in the History of Japan). Tōkyō, 1939.

Harada Kumao. *Saionji-Kō to seikyoku* (*Prince Saionji and the Political Situation*). Tōkyō, 1950——. 9 vols.

421

橋本欣五郎，橋本欣五郎宣言，大日本青年党発行

林田亀太郎，日本政党史

平野義太郎，日本資本主義社会の機構

本庄栄治郎，明治維新経済史研究

　　　日本経済思想史概説

堀江保蔵，日本経済史

　　　日本資本主義の成立

市川正一，日本共産党小史

池田成彬，故人今人

　　　財界回顧

今村武雄，評伝高橋是清

今中次麿，日本政治史新講

　　　日本政治史大綱

井野辺茂雄，維新前史の研究

石井良助，日本法制史要

石川幹明，福沢諭吉

板垣退助，自由党史

伊藤博文（編纂），秘書類纂，金子堅太郎・平塚篤
　　改訂

[Hashimoto Kingorō.] *Hashimoto Kingorō sengen* (*Declaration by Hashimoto Kingoro*). Tōkyō: Dai Nihon Seinentō (Greater Japan Youth Party), 1936.

Hayashida Kametarō. *Nihon seitō shi* (*History of Japanese Political Parties*). Tōkyō, 1927. 2 vols.

Hirano Yoshitarō. *Nihon shihonshugi shakai no kikō* (*The Mechanism of Japanese Capitalist Society*). Tōkyō, 1934.

Honjō Eijirō. *Meiji ishin keizai shi kenkyū* (*A Study of the Economic History of the Meiji Restoration*). Tōkyō, 1930.

―――. *Nihon keizai shisō shi gaisetsu* (*A General Summary of the History of Japanese Economic Thought*). (1948 ed.) Tōkyō, 1946.

Horie Yasuzō. *Nihon keizai shi* (*An Economic History of Japan*). Tōkyō, 1949.

―――. *Nihon shihonshugi no seiritsu* (*The Establishment of Japanese Capitalism*). Tōkyō, 1939.

Ichikawa Shōichi. *Nihon Kyōsantō shōshi* (*A Short History of the Japanese Communist Party*). (1947 ed.) Tōkyō, 1932.

Ikeda Seihin. *Kojin konjin* (*The Living and the Dead*). Tōkyō, 1949.

―――. *Zaikai kaiko* (*Reminiscences on the Financial World*). Tōkyō, 1949.

Imamura Takeo. *Hyōden Takahashi Korekiyo* (*A Critical Biography of Takahashi Korekiyo*). Tōkyō, 1948.

Imanaka Tsugimaro. *Nihon seiji shi shinkō* (*New Materials on Japanese Political History*). Tōkyō, 1947. 2 vols.

―――. *Nihon seiji shi taikō* (*Outline of Japanese Political History*). Tōkyō, 1936.

Inobe Shigeo. *Ishin zenshi no kenkyū* (*A Study of Pre-Restoration History*). Tōkyō, 1935.

Ishii Ryōsuke. *Nihon hōsei shiyō* (*An Historical Summary of Japanese Law*). Tōkyō, 1949.

Ishikawa Mikiaki. *Fukuzawa Yukichi*. Tōkyō, 1935.

Itagaki Taisuke. *Jiyūtō shi* (*History of the Jiyuto*). Tōkyō, 1913. 2 vols.

Itō Hirobumi (ed.). *Hisho ruisan—Teikoku Gikai shiryō* (*Collection of Private Papers—Imperial Diet Materials*). Rev. by Kaneko Kentarō and Hiratsuka Atsushi. Tōkyō, 1934. 26 vols.

伊藤正徳，加藤高明

岩淵辰雄，現代日本政治論

陸軍省，近代国防の本質と経済戦略，其の他

　　　　満州事変満五年

　　　　日露戦役の回顧と我等国民の覚悟

　　　　陸軍軍備の充実と其の精神

　　　　空の国防

　　　　転換期の国際情勢と我が日本

　　　　非常時と国防

加田哲二，日本国家主義の発展

川島武宣，日本社会の家族的構成

木下半治，日本フアツシズム史

　　　　日本国家主義運動史

北一輝，日本改造法案大綱

幸田露伴，渋沢栄一伝

黒板勝美，国体新論

松岡洋右，昭和維新

Itō Masanori. *Katō Takaakira* [Kōmei]. Tōkyō, 1929. 2 vols.

Iwabuchi Tatsuo. *Gendai Nihon seiji ron* (*Discussion of Modern Japanese Politics*). Tōkyō, 1941.

Japan. War Ministry. *Kindai kokubō no honshitsu to keizai senryaku sonota* (*The Principles of Modern National Defense, Economic Warfare, and Other Matters*). Tōkyō, 1934. 37 pp.

——. ——. *Manshū jihen man gonen* (*Five Years After the Manchurian Incident*). Tōkyō, 1936. 76 pp.

——. ——. *Nichi-Ro seneki no kaiko to warera kokumin no kakugo* (*Reflections on the Russo-Japanese War and the Resolution of Our People*). Tōkyō, 1936. 48 pp.

——. ——. *Rikugun gumbi no jūjitsu to sono seishin* (*The Perfection of Army Preparedness and Its Spirit*). Tōkyō, 1936. 96 pp.

——. ——. *Sora no kokubō* (*National Air Defense*). Tōkyō, 1935. 43 pp.

——. ——. *Tenkanki no kokusai jōsei to waga Nihon* (*The Transitional Period of International Conditions and Our Japan*). Tōkyō, 1936.

——. War Ministry Press Section. *Hijōji to kokubō* (*Emergency Conditions and National Defense*). Tōkyō, 1935. 210 pp.

Kada Tetsuji. *Nihon kokkashugi no hatten* (*The Development of Japanese Nationalism*). Tōkyō, 1938.

Kawashima Takeyoshi. *Nihon shakai no kazokuteki kōsei* (*The Familial Structure of Japanese Society*). Tōkyō, 1949.

Kinoshita Hanji. *Nihon Fascism shi* (*A History of Japanese Fascism*). Tōkyō, 1949. 3 vols., Vol. I.

——. *Nihon kokkashugi undō shi* (*A History of the Japanese Nationalist Movement*). Tōkyō, 1939.

Kita Ikki. *Nihon kaizō hōan taikō* (*A General Outline of Measures for the Reconstruction of Japan*). Tōkyō, 1919.

Kōda Rohan. *Shibuzawa Eiichi den* (*Biography of Shibuzawa Eiichi*). Tōkyō, 1939.

Kuroita Katsumi. *Kokutai shinron* (*New Theories on the National Polity*). Tōkyō, 1925.

Matsuoka Yōsuke. *Shōwa ishin* (*The Showa Restoration*). Tōkyō, 1938.

松下丈夫，近代日本教育史

松下芳男，日清戰爭前後，近代日本歷史講座

美濃部達吉，議会制度論，現代政治学全集

　　　　議会政治の検討

　　　　憲法及び憲法史，国法学資料

　　　　日本行政法

　　　　日本憲法の基本問題

　　　　日本国法学総論

民政党総覧

宮沢俊義，選挙法要理

森喜一，日本農業に於ける資本主義の発達

鍋山貞親，私は共産党を捨てた

野村兼太郎，概観日本経済思想史

　　　　徳川時代の社会経済思想概論

大井一哲，憲政を破壊する政党政治

岡義武，近代日本の形成

426

Matsushita Takeo. *Kindai Nihon kyōiku shi* (*A History of Modern Japanese Education*). Tōkyō, 1949.

Matsushita Yoshio. *Ni-Shin sensō zengo* (*The Period Around the Sino-Japanese War*), in Kindai Nihon rekishi kōza (Modern Japanese History Series). Tōkyō, 1939.

Minobe Tatsukichi. *Gikai seido ron* (*A Treatise on Parliamentary Systems*). Vol. VII in Gendai seijigaku zenshū (Collected Works on Modern Political Science). Tōkyō, 1930.

————. *Gikai seiji no kentō* (*A Study of Parliamentary Politics*). Tōkyō, 1934.

————. *Kempō oyobi kempōshi* (*The Constitution and Constitutional History*). Vol. II in Kokuhōgaku shiryō (Materials on Public Law). Tōkyō, 1908.

————. *Nihon gyōsei hō* (*Japanese Administrative Law*). Tōkyō, 1936.

————. *Nihon kempō no kihon mondai* (*The Central Problems of Japanese Constitutional Law*). Tōkyō, 1920.

————. *Nihon kokuhōgaku sōron* (*A General Treatise on Japanese National Law*). Tōkyō, 1907.

Minseitō sōran (*General Survey of the Minseito*). Tōkyō, 1931.

Miyazawa Toshiyoshi. *Senkyo hō yōri* (*The Essence of the Election Law*). Tōkyō, 1930.

Mori Kiichi. *Nihon nōgyō ni okeru shihonshugi no hattatsu* (*The Development of Capitalism in Japanese Agriculture*). Tōkyō, 1947.

Nabeyama Sadachika. *Watakushi wa Kyōsantō o suteta* (*I Abandoned the Communist Party*). Tōkyō, 1950.

Nomura Kentarō. *Gaikan Nihon keizai shisō shi* (*A General History of Japanese Economic Thought*). Tōkyō, 1949.

————. *Tokugawa jidai no shakai keizai shisō gairon* (*An Introduction to the Social and Economic Thought of the Tokugawa Period*). (1949 ed.) Tōkyō, 1934.

Ōi Ittetsu. *Kensei wo hakai suru seitō seiji* (*Political Party Politics—The Destruction of Constitutionalism*). Tōkyō, 1932.

Oka Yoshitake. *Kindai Nihon no keisei* (*The Foundation of Modern Japan*). Tōkyō, 1947.

427

奥谷松治，近代日本農政史論

小野武夫，維新農村社会史論

　　近代日本農村発達史論

　　日本産業発達史の研究

　　農村史

尾佐竹猛，維新前後に於ける立憲思想

　　明治維新，近代日本歴史講座

　　明治政治史点描

　　日本憲政史の研究

　　日本憲政史大綱

大津淳一郎，大日本憲政史

蠟山政道，日本に於る近代政治学の発達

　　日本に於る政治意識の諸様相

　　政治史，現代日本文明史

　　政党の研究

蠟山政道（編纂），無産政党論，現代政治学全集

佐治謙譲，日本学としての日本国家学

佐藤清勝，大日本政治思想史

Okutani Matsuji. *Kindai Nihon nōsei shiron* (*An Historical Treatise on Modern Japanese Agrarian Policies*). Tōkyō, 1938.

Ono Takeo. *Ishin nōson shakai shiron* (*An Historical Treatise on Agrarian Society at the Restoration*). Tōkyō, 1932.

———. *Kindai Nihon nōson hattatsu shiron* (*An Historical Treatise on Modern Japanese Rural Development*). Tōkyō, 1950.

———. *Nihon sangyō hattatsu shi no kenkyū* (*Studies in the History of the Development of Japanese Industry*). Tōkyō, 1941.

———. *Nōson shi* (*A History of Agriculture*). Tōkyō, 1941.

Osatake Takeshi. *Ishin zengo ni okeru rikken shisō* (*Constitutional Theories in the Period Around the Restoration*). Tōkyō, 1929.

———. *Meiji ishin* (*Meiji Restoration*), in Kindai Nihon rekishi kōza (Modern Japanese History Series). Tōkyō, 1949. 4 vols.

———. *Meiji seiji shi tembyō* (*Sketches in Meiji Political History*). Tōkyō, 1938.

———. *Nihon kensei shi no kenkyū* (*A Study of Japanese Constitutional History*). Tōkyō, 1943.

———. *Nihon kensei shi taikō* (*An Outline of Japanese Constitutional History*). Tōkyō, 1939. 2 vols.

Ōtsu Junichirō. *Dai Nihon kensei shi* (*A Constitutional History of Greater Japan*). Tōkyō, 1927–1928. 11 vols.

Rōyama Masamichi. *Nihon ni okeru kindai seijigaku no hattatsu* (*The Development of Modern Political Science in Japan*). Tōkyō, 1949.

———. *Nihon ni okeru seiji ishiki no shoyōsō* (*Various Aspects of Political Consciousness in Japan*). Tōkyō, 1949.

———. *Seiji shi* (*Political History*), in Gendai Nihon bummei shi (History of Contemporary Japanese Civilization Series). Tōkyō, 1940.

———. *Seitō no kenkyū* (*Study of Political Parties*). Tōkyō, 1948.

Rōyama Masamichi (ed.). *Musanseitō ron* (*Treatises on Proletarian Parties*). Vol. XI of Gendai seijigaku zenshū (Collected Works on Modern Political Science). Tōkyō, 1930.

Saji Kenjō. *Nihon gaku to shite no Nihon kokka gaku* (*The Science of the Japanese State as the Science of Japan*). Tōkyō, 1938.

Satō Kiyokatsu. *Dai Nihon seiji shisō shi* (*History of Political Thought in Greater Japan*). Tōkyō, 1939. 2 vols.

429

沢田謙，後藤新平一代記

下出隼吉，明治社会思想研究

信夫清三郎，後藤新平一科学的政治家の生涯

鈴木茂三郎，日本財閥論

鈴木安蔵，評伝伊藤博文

　　　自由民権

　　　自由民権憲法発布，近代日本歴史講座

田畑忍，加藤弘之の国家思想

高橋龜吉，株式会社亡国論

　　　日本工業発展論

高橋龜吉（編纂）日本コンツェルン全集

高橋龜吉・青山二郎，日本財閥論

高橋清吾，政治科学原論

高橋誠一郎，福沢諭吉一人と学説

高橋俊乘，日本教育史

滝川政次郎，日本社会史

田村栄太郎，近代日本農民運動史論

Sawada Ken. *Gotō Shimpei ichidaiki* (*The Career of Goto Shimpei*). Tōkyō, 1929.

Shimoide Hayakichi. *Meiji shakai shisō kenkyū* (*Studies on Social Thoughts in the Meiji Era*). Tōkyō, 1932.

Shinobu Kiyosaburō. *Gotō Shimpei—kagakuteki seijika no shōgai* (*Goto Shimpei—The Life of a Scientific Statesman*). Tōkyō, 1941.

Suzuki Mosaburō. *Nihon zaibatsu ron* (*A Treatise on the Japanese Financial Cliques*). Tōkyō, 1934.

Suzuki Yasuzō. *Hyōden Itō Hirobumi* (*Critical Biography of Ito Hirobumi*). Tōkyō, 1944.

———. *Jiyūminken* (*Civil Rights*). Tōkyō, 1948.

———. *Jiyūminken kempō happu* (*Civil Rights and the Promulgation of the Constitution*), in Kindai Nihon rekishi kōza (Modern Japanese History Series). Tōkyō, 1939.

Tabata Shinobu. *Katō Hiroyuki no kokka shisō* (*Kato Hiroyuki's Theory of the State*). Tōkyō, 1939.

Takahashi Kamekichi. *Kabushiki kaisha—bōkoku ron* (*A Treatise on Share Companies—The Ruin of the Country*). Tōkyō, 1930.

———. *Nihon kōgyō hatten ron* (*A Treatise on Japanese Industrial Development*). Tōkyō, 1936.

Takahashi Kamekichi (ed.). *Nihon concern zenshū* (*Collected Works on Japanese Concerns*). Tōkyō, 1937. 18 vols.

Takahashi Kamekichi and Aoyama Jirō. *Nihon zaibatsu ron* (*A Treatise on the Japanese Financial Cliques*). Tōkyō, 1938.

Takahashi Seigo. *Seiji kagaku genron* (*The Principles of Political Science*). Tōkyō, 1937.

Takahashi Seiichirō. *Fukuzawa Yukichi—hito to gakusetsu* (*Fukuzawa Yukichi—The Man and His Doctrines*). Tōkyō, 1947.

Takahashi Shunjō. *Nihon kyōiku shi* (*A History of Japanese Education*). Tōkyō, 1929.

Takikawa Masajirō. *Nihon shakai shi* (*A History of Japanese Society*). Tōkyō, 1940.

Tamura Eitarō. *Kindai Nihon nōmin undō shiron* (*An Historical Treatise on the Modern Japanese Agrarian Movement*). Tōkyō, 1948.

田中惣五郎，日本フアッシズムの源流—北一輝の思想と生涯

    日本現代史への反省

    日本社会運動史

土屋喬雄，維新経済史

    日本の財閥

    日本資本主義史上の指導者達

土屋喬雄（編纂），日本資本主義史論集

土屋喬雄・小野道夫，近世日本農村経済史論

内田繁隆，日本政治社会思想史

    日本社会経済史

鵜崎熊吉，犬養毅伝

若槻礼次郎，古風庵回顧録—若槻礼次郎自伝

渡辺幾治郎，文書より見たる大隈重信侯

    日本憲法制定史考

    大隈重信

山本勝之助—有田満穂，日本共産主義運動史

山浦貫一，非常時局と人物

Tanaka Sōgorō. *Nihon Fascism no genryū—Kita Ikki no shisō to shōgai* (*The Source of Japanese Fascism—The Thought and Career of Kita Ikki*). Tōkyō, 1949.

——. *Nihon gendai shi e no hansei* (*Reflections upon Modern Japanese History*). Tōkyō, 1949.

——. *Nihon shakai undō shi* (*History of Japanese Social Movements*). Tōkyō, 1949.

Tsuchiya Takao. *Ishin keizai shi* (*Economic History of the Restoration*). Tōkyō, 1942.

——. *Nihon no zaibatsu* (*The Japanese Financial Cliques*). Tōkyō, 1949.

——. *Nihon shihonshugi shijō no shidōshatachi* (*Leaders in the History of Japanese Capitalism*). (1941 ed.) Tōkyō, 1939.

Tsuchiya Takao (ed.). *Nihon shihonshugi shi ronshū* (*A Collection of Essays on the History of Japanese Capitalism*). Tōkyō, 1937.

Tsuchiya Takao and Ono Michio. *Kinsei Nihon nōson keizai shiron* (*Historical Treatises on the Agrarian Economy of Modern Japan*). Tōkyō, 1933.

Uchida Shigetaka. *Nihon seiji shakai shisō shi* (*History of Japanese Political and Social Thought*). (1938 ed.) Tōkyō, 1931.

——. *Nihon shakai keizai shi* (*Social and Economic History of Japan*). Tōkyō, 1941.

Uzaki Kumakichi. *Inukai Tsuyoshi den* (*Biography of Inukai Tsuyoshi*). Tōkyō, 1932.

Wakatsuki Reijirō. *Kofūan kaiko roku—Wakatsuki Reijirō jiden* (*Recorded Memoirs of Kofuan—The Autobiography of Wakatsuki Reijiro*). Tōkyō, 1950.

Watanabe Ikujirō. *Bunsho yori mitaru Ōkuma Shigenobu kō* (*Marquis Okuma Shigenobu as Seen in the Documents*). Tōkyō, 1932.

——. *Nihon kempō seitei shikō* (*An Outline History of the Establishment of Japanese Constitutional Law*). Tōkyō, 1939.

——. *Ōkuma Shigenobu*. Tōkyō, 1943.

Yamamoto Katsunosuke and Arita Mitsuho. *Nihon kyōsanshugi undō shi* (*A History of the Japanese Communist Movement*). Tōkyō, 1950.

Yamaura Kanichi. *Hijō jikyoku to jimbutsu* (*Extraordinary Times and Men*). Tōkyō, 1937.

433

山崎又次郎，帝国憲法論

吉村宮男，近世政治史，新日本史

吉野作造，枢府と内閣

吉野作造（編纂），明治文化全集

浅田江村，二大私党対立の趨勢，太陽

馬場恒吾，田中義一，中央公論

暴動事件の批判，中央公論

才三十一帝国議会を論ず，中央公論

藤村義夫，貴族院の内面観，太陽

現内閣と薩摩派，中央公論

議会前の政界，太陽

軍閥問題，中央公論

行政整理意見，太陽

原内閣に対する要望，中央公論

林田亀太郎，時代錯誤の党議制，太陽

岩淵辰雄，宇垣閣と荒木閣，改造

官業主義と民業主義，中央公論

Yamazaki Matajirō. *Teikoku kempō ron* (*A Treatise on the Imperial Constitution*). Tōkyō, 1937.

Yoshimura Miyao. *Kinsei seiji shi* (*Modern Political History*), No. 16 in Shin Nihon shi (History of New Japan Series). Tōkyō, 1936.

Yoshino Sakuzō. *Sūfu to naikaku* (*Privy Council and Cabinet*). (1950 ed.) Tōkyō, 1930.

Yoshino Sakuzō (ed.). *Meiji bunka zenshū* (*Collected Works of Meiji Culture*). Tōkyō, 1928–1930. 24 vols.

ARTICLES

Asada Kōson. "Ni dai shitō tairitsu no sūsei" (Trends in the Rivalry of Two Great Private Parties), *Taiyō*, February, 1915.

Baba Tsunego. "Tanaka Giichi," *Chūō Kōron*, August, 1928.

"Bōdō jiken no hihan" (Criticism of the Riot Incidents), a symposium in *Chūō Kōron*, September, 1918.

Dai sanju ichi Teikoku Gikai o ronzu" (Discussing the Thirty-first Imperial Diet), *Chūō Kōron*, Spring, 1914.

Fujimura Yoshio. "Kizokuin no naimenkan" (An Inside View of the House of Peers), *Taiyō*, May, 1921.

"Gen naikaku to Satsuma ha" (The Present Cabinet and the Satsuma Faction), *Chūō Kōron*, January, 1912.

"Gikai zen no seikai" (The Political World Before the Diet), *Taiyō*, December, 1920.

"Gumbatsu mondai" (The Militarist Problem), a symposium in *Chūō Kōron*, September, 1918.

"Gyōsei seiri iken" (Opinions on Administrative Readjustment), a symposium in *Taiyō*, March, 1912.

"Hara naikaku ni taisuru yōbō" (Demands upon the Hara Cabinet), *Chūō Kōron*, October, 1918.

Hayashida Kametarō. "Jidai sakugo no tōgi sei" (The Outmoded Party-Diet System), *Taiyō*, May, 1921.

Iwabuchi Tatsuo. "Ugaki batsu to Araki batsu" (The Ugaki Clique and the Araki Clique), *Kaizō*, January, 1933.

"Kangyōshugi to mingyōshugi" (The Principles of Government Enterprise and Private Enterprise), a symposium in *Chūö Kōron*, March, 1912.

丸山真男，超国家主義の論理と真理，世界

　　日本フアツシズムの思想と運動，尊攘思想と絶
　　対主義

松山忠二郎，政党道徳論，中央公論

美濃部達吉，政党政治に於る官僚，中央公論

長島隆二，難破せる研究会，太陽

大隈の内閣評判記，中央公論

尾佐竹猛・林茂，政治史，現代日本史研究

尾崎行雄，墓標の代りに，改造

佐野博，モスコーと日本共産党の関係史，中央公論

佐野学，コミンテルンとの袂別，改造

佐々弘雄，政党政治の崩壊過程，改造

政変一年後の眺望，中央公論

政界の中心人物たらんとする原敬氏と加藤男，中央
　　公論

島田三郎，私財を掠め，公金を横領し，政商と親し
　　む，太陽

田川大吉郎，三菱内閣，太陽

Maruyama Masao. "Chōkokkashugi no ronri to shinri" (The Theory and Psychology of Ultranationalism), *Sekai*, May, 1946.

———. "Nihon Fascism no shisō to undō" (Japanese Fascist Thought and Action), Sec. 2 in *Sonjō shisō to zettaishugi* (*Revere the Emperor—Oust the Barbarian Thought and Absolutism*). Tōkyō, 1949.

Matsuyama Chūjirō. "Seitō dōtoku ron" (Discussion of Political Party Morality), *Chūō Kōron*, February, 1914.

Minobe Tatsukichi. "Seitō seiji ni okeru kanryō" (The Bureaucracy in Party Politics), *Chūō Kōron*, August, 1931.

Nagashima Ryūji. "Nampa seru Kenkyūkai" (The Kenkyukai in Peril), *Taiyō*, April, 1921.

"Ōkuma no naikaku hyōban ki" (The Story of the Okuma Cabinet's Reputation), *Chūō Kōron*, January, 1915.

Osatake Takeshi and Hayashi Shigeru. "Seiji" (Politics), in *Gendai Nihon shi kenkyū* (*Studies of Contemporary Japanese History*). Tōkyō, 1938.

Ozaki Yukio. "Bohyō no kawari ni" (In Place of a Gravestone), *Kaizō*, January, 1933.

Sano Hiroshi. "Moscow to Nihon Kyōsantō no kankei shi" (History of the Relationship of Moscow and the Japanese Communist Party), *Chūō Kōron*, March, 1950.

Sano Manabu. "Comintern to no ketsubetsu" (Parting with the Comintern), *Kaizō*, August, 1933.

Sasa Hiroo. "Seitō seiji no hōkai katei" (The Process of Collapse of Party Politics), *Kaizō*, July, 1933.

"Seihen ichinen go no chōbō" (Views One Year After the Political Change), *Chūō Kōron*, February, 1914.

"Seikai no chūshin jimbutsu taran to suru Hara Kei shi to Katō Dan" (Mr. Hara Kei and Baron Kato Who Seek to Serve as the Leaders of the Political World), *Chūō Kōron*, Spring, 1914.

Shimada Saburō. "Shizai o kasume kōkin o ōryō shi seishō to shitashimu" (Taking Private Capital, Usurping Public Money, Being Friendly with Political Merchants), *Taiyō*, May, 1921.

Tagawa Daikichirō. "Mitsubishi naikaku" (The Mitsubishi Cabinet), *Taiyō*, August, 1924.

437

高橋龜吉，三井・三菱・住友，中央公論

戸田海一，社会主義と個人主義，太陽

植原悦次郎，専制に均しき立憲政治，太陽

浮田和民，内務省の宗教方針，太陽

　　総選挙の高等批評，太陽

渡辺幾治郎，犬養と大隈，中央公論

吉野作造，憲政の本義を説いて其の有終の美を済す
　の道を論ず，中央公論

　　民本主義，社会主義，過激主義，中央公論

　　選挙権拡張問題，中央公論

　　選挙と金と政党，中央公論

Takahashi Kamekichi. "Mitsui, Mitsubishi, Sumitomo," *Chūō Kōron,* February, 1930.

Toda Umiichi. "Shakaishugi to kojinshugi" (Socialism and Individualism), *Taiyō,* January, 1912.

Uehara Etsujirō. "Sensei ni hitoshiki rikken seiji" (Constitutional Government Which Is Equal to Absolutism), *Taiyō,* May, 1921.

Ukita Kazutami. "Naimushō no shūkyō hōshin" (The Religious Policy of the Home Ministry), *Taiyō,* March, 1912.

——. "Sōsenkyo no kōtō hihyō" (Advanced Criticism of the General Election), *ibid.,* April, 1915.

Watanabe Ikujirō. "Inukai to Ōkuma" (Inukai and Okuma), *Chūō Kōron,* October, 1932.

Yoshino Sakuzō. "Kensei no hongi o toite sono yūshū no bi o nasu no michi o ronzu" (Preaching the Essentials of Constitutional Government and Discussing the Road Toward Realizing Its Complete Perfection), *Chūō Kōron,* January, 1916.

——. "Mimponshugi—shakaishugi—kagekishugi" (Democracy, Socialism, and Extremism), *ibid.,* February, 1919.

——. "Senkyo ken kakuchō mondai" (The Problem of Expanding Suffrage Rights), *ibid.,* February, 1929.

——. "Senkyo to kane to seitō" (Elections, Money, and Political Parties), *ibid.,* June, 1932.

ENGLISH WORKS
BOOKS

Allen, George C. *Japanese Industry: Its Recent Development and Present Condition.* New York, 1940.

——. *A Short Economic History of Japan, 1867–1937.* London, 1946.

Benedict, Ruth. *The Chrysanthemum and the Sword.* Boston, 1946.

Borton, Hugh. *Japan Since 1931, Its Social and Political Development.* New York, 1940.

——. *Peasant Uprisings in Japan of the Tokugawa Period.* Vol. XVI of 2d series, *Transactions of the Asiatic Society of Japan.* Tokyo, 1938.

Colegrove, Kenneth. *Militarism in Japan.* Boston, 1936.

Crump, C. G., and E. F. Jacob (eds.). *The Legacy of the Middle Ages.* (1942 ed.). Oxford, 1926.

439

Embree, John F. *The Japanese Nation, a Social Survey.* New York, 1945.

———. *Suye Mura, a Japanese Village.* Chicago, 1939.

Fahs, Charles B. *Government in Japan, Recent Trends in Scope and Operation.* New York, 1940.

Fisher, Galen M. *Creative Forces in Japan.* New York, 1922.

Foreign Affairs Association of Japan. *Japan Year Book for 1905.* Tokyo, 1906.

———. *Japan Year Book for 1943–1944.* Tokyo, 1945.

Fujisawa Rikitaro. *The Recent Aims and Political Development of Japan.* New Haven, 1923.

Grew, Joseph C. *Ten Years in Japan.* New York, 1944.

Griffis, William E. *The Mikado's Empire.* New York, 1913.

Gubbins, J. H. *The Making of Modern Japan.* London, 1922.

———. *The Progress of Japan, 1853–1917.* Oxford, 1911.

Hall, Robert. *Education for a New Japan.* New Haven, 1949.

Hamada Kenji. *Prince Ito.* Tokyo, 1936.

Holtom, Daniel C. *Modern Japan and Shinto Nationalism.* Chicago, 1943.

———. *National Faith of Japan: A Study in Modern Shinto.* London, 1938.

———. *The Political Philosophy of Modern Shinto.* Part II of Vol. XLIX, *Transactions of the Asiatic Society of Japan.* Keio University, 1922.

Honjo Eijiro. *The Social and Economic History of Japan.* Kyoto, 1935.

Huggins, H. C. *The Great Fortunes of Japan.* Hayama, Japan, 1930. 11 vols.

Idditti, S. *The Life of Marquis Shigenobu Okuma, a Maker of Modern Japan.* Tokyo, 1941.

Ike Nobutaka. *The Beginnings of Political Democracy in Japan.* Baltimore, 1950.

Ishii Ryoichi. *Population Pressure and Economic Life in Japan.* London, 1937.

Ito Miyoji (trans.). *Commentaries on the Constitution of the Empire of Japan by Ito Hirobumi.* Tokyo, 1906.

Kawabe Kisaburo. *The Press and Politics in Japan.* Chicago, 1921.

Kawakami, K. K. (ed.). *What Japan Thinks.* New York, 1921.

Kiyooka, E. (trans.). *The Autobiography of Fukuzawa Yukichi.* Tokyo, 1934.

Legge, James (trans.). *The Chinese Classics.* ([Oxford] 1893 ed., as reprinted in China, 1939.) Hongkong, 1861. 7 vols., Vol. I.

McLaren, Walter W. *A Political History of Japan During the Meiji Era, 1867–1912.* London, 1916.

McLaren, Walter W. (ed.). *Japanese Government Documents, 1867–1889*. Part I of Vol. XLII of *Transactions of the Asiatic Society of Japan*. Tokyo, 1914. [*JGD*.]

Maki, John M. *Japanese Militarism, Its Causes and Cure*. New York, 1945.

Mitsui, The House of, a Record of Three Centuries. Tokyo, 1937.

Mounsey, Augustus H. *The Satsuma Rebellion*. London, 1879.

Murdoch, James. *A History of Japan*. London, 1925–1926. 3 vols.

Nasu Shiroshi. *Aspects of Japanese Agriculture, a Preliminary Survey*. New York, 1941.

———. *Land Utilization in Japan*. Tokyo, 1929.

Nitobe Inazo. *Japan: Some Phases of Her Problems and Development*. New York, 1931.

Norman, E. Herbert. *The Feudal Background of Japanese Politics*. [Mimeo.] Secretariat Paper No. 9 for the Ninth Conference of the Institute of Pacific Relations. New York, 1945.

———. *Japan's Emergence as a Modern State*. New York, 1940.

———. *Soldier and Peasant in Japan: The Origins of Conscription*. New York, 1943.

Okuma Shigenobu (ed.). *Fifty Years of New Japan*. London, 1910. 2 vols.

Orchard, John B. *Japan's Economic Position, the Progress of Industrialization*. New York, 1930.

Ostrogorski, M. *Democracy and the Organization of Political Parties*. New York, 1922. 2 vols.

Páske-Smith, M. *Western Barbarians in Japan and Formosa in Tokugawa Days, 1603–1868*. Kobe, 1930.

Quigley, Harold S. *Japanese Government and Politics*. New York, 1933.

Reischauer, Edwin O. *Japan, Past and Present*. New York, 1946.

———. *The United States and Japan*. Cambridge, 1950.

Reischauer, Robert K. *Japan: Government—Politics*. New York, 1939.

Russell, Oland D. *The House of Mitsui*. Boston, 1939.

Sait, Edward M. *American Parties and Elections*. New York, 1927.

Sansom, George B. *Japan, a Short Cultural History*. (1943 ed.) New York, 1931.

———. *The Western World and Japan*. New York, 1950.

Satow, Ernest M. *A Diplomat in Japan*. London, 1921.

Schumpeter, Elizabeth B. *The Industrialization of Japan and Manchukuo, 1930–1940, Population, Raw Materials and Industry*. New York, 1940.

Smith, Neil S. (ed.). *Materials on Japanese Social and Economic History: Tokugawa Japan (1)*. London, 1937.

Swearingen, Roger, and Paul Langer. *Bibliography on Japanese Communi, m.* New York, 1950.

Takekoshi Yosaburo. *Economic Aspects of the History of Civilization of Japan.* New York, 1930. 3 vols.

———. *Prince Saionji.* Kyoto, 1933.

Takeuchi Tatsuji. *War and Diplomacy in the Japanese Empire.* New York, 1935.

Tsuchiya Takao. *An Economic History of Japan.* Vol. XV of 2d series, *Transactions of the Asiatic Society of Japan.* Tokyo, 1937. Also published separately as *The Development of Economic Life in Japan.* Tokyo, 1937.

Tsurumi Yusuke. *Present-Day Japan.* New York, 1926.

Uyehara, George Etsujiro. *The Political Development of Japan, 1867–1909.* London, 1910.

Yanaga Chitoshi. *Japan Since Perry.* New York, 1949.

Young, A. Morgan. *Japan in Recent Times.* New York, 1929.

ARTICLES

Coleman, Horace E. "The Life of Shoin Yoshida," *Transactions of the Asiatic Society of Japan,* Vol. XLV, Part I.

Ike, Nobutaka. "Triumph of the Peace Party in Japan in 1873," *The Far Eastern Quarterly,* Vol. II, May, 1943.

Lay, A. H. "A Brief Sketch of the History of Political Parties in Japan," *Transactions of the Asiatic Society of Japan,* Vol. XXX, Tokyo, 1902.

Ono Yeijiro. "The Industrial Transition in Japan," *Publication of the American Economics Association,* Vol. V, No. 1, January, 1890.

Yamamuro Sobun. "Economic Depression and the Gold Embargo," *Contemporary Japan,* June, 1932.

Yoshino Sakuzo. "Fascism in Japan," *Contemporary Japan,* September, 1932.

MISCELLANEOUS

International Military Tribunal for the Far East. "Proceedings" and "Exhibits." [MS collections.] [IMTFE.]

The Japan Chronicle [JC], before 1918 called *The Kobe Chronicle [KC].*

The Japan Mail [JM].

The Kobe Chronicle [KC]. See *The Japan Chronicle.*

INDEX

Abe Iso: leader in early "left-wing" party movement, 318 n. 37; forms Japanese Fabian Society, 325; aids in organization of Shakai Minshuto, 331–332

Abe Nobuyuki, is appointed War Minister pro tem by Hamaguchi, 239 n. 91

Adachi Kenzo: becomes leader in Minseito, 238 n. 88; proposes coalition cabinet and forces resignation of second Wakatsuki ministry, 241–242; supports militarists, 367; leaves Minseito to form Kokumin Domei, 371

agriculture: land control under the Tokugawa, 9; Tokugawa policy, 15 n. 26; theoretical emphasis, 19 n. 34; relation to Tokugawa commercialism, 23, 25; Tokugawa primitivist theory, 26 and n. 47; uprisings prior to Satsuma Rebellion, 61 n. 50; ties with Jiyuto, 97–98 and nn. 9 and 10, 101–108 and nn. 19–21, 26, 31, 33, 34, and 37; connections with Japanese familial system, 121–124 and nn. 5, 7, 8, and 10–12, 127 and n. 16; political power in early Meiji era, 254–257 and nn. 17–20; production compared to industry in World War I period, 270 and n. 49; relief measures during Hara ministry, 276–278 and n. 60; "proletarian" conditions, 305–312 and nn. 23, 25, 26, 28, and 29; relation to nationalism, 349–352, 389–392. See also farmers; landowners; tenant farmers

Aikoku Seiki Domei (Patriotic Banner League), position on political "reform," 376 n. 46

Aikokukoto (Public Party of Patriots): choice of name, 5; establishment and party pledge, 45–49 and n. 9; salient features, 56–57

Aikokusha (Society of Patriots): establishment and proposals, 58–59; reorganization, 61–62; changes name to Kokkai Kisei Domeikai, 62

Aikyojuku (Institute for Local Patriotism), leading "right-wing" center, 357

Akahata (Red Flag), Communist party newspaper, 339 n. 81

Akamatsu Katsumaro, leaves the Communist party, 328 n. 55

Anarchism: impact upon problem of Japanese civil liberties, 299; strength in early left-wing movement, 317–318 and n. 36; relation to Communism, 321, 322 nn. 45 and 47; decline in leftist and labor movements, 325 and n. 51

Aono Suekichi, joins Seiji Mondai Kenkyukai, 326 n. 52

Arahata Kanson: opposes dissolution of first Japanese Communist party, 328; becomes leader in Communist movement, 329 and n. 56, 334

Arai Hakuseki, is opponent of foreign trade, 29 n. 49

Arai Shogo, helps plan Korean revolution scheme, 107 n. 35

Araki Sadao: councillor for Gyochisha, 359; member of Kokuhonsha, 360; connections with Okawa, 363; ties with "October Incident," 368; loses prestige with young radicals, 384; is transferred to reserves, 384

Arima Ryokitsu, is member of Kokuhonsha, 360

Arisugawa Shinno [Prince Arisugawa], made Sosai, 51 n. 24

army: institution of conscription, 43 n. 3; early Choshu control, 43 n. 4; power revealed in crisis in second Saionji cabinet, 191–197 and nn. 114, 121, and 123; reforms of first Yamamoto ministry, 203; influence on pre-1918 cabinets, 211 n. 23; position during Hara era, 216–217 and nn. 30–33; budget reduction under Kato coalition ministry, 229 and n. 65; role in Chang Tso-lin murder, 236–237 and nn. 89,

forms proposed by Kita Ikki, 355 and n. 12. See also *chozen naikaku shugi;* political parties; and entries on specific premiers

capitalism: emergence in Tokugawa era, 22–27 and n. 41, 42, 47, and 48; advancement in techniques, 24; relation to Restoration, 35–37; early Meiji trends, 98–102 and nn. 15, 17, and 18; connections with early Meiji liberalism, 110–112 and nn. 42 and 44, 114–115; and paternalism, 134; rise of Japanese industrial revolution and trends in political role of business class, 247–275 and accompanying notes; crisis of 1920 and aftermath, 275–277 and n. 55; events leading to crisis of 1927, 284–285 and n. 80; problems during Tanaka regime, 287; impact of world depression on, 288–289; assaulted by military-agrarian elements, 289–290 and n. 92; effect upon Japanese democratic parties summarized, 290–293, 396–398; and the "right wing," 352–361 and nn. 4, 5, 9, 12, 13, 15, 18, and 22; concepts of Okawa, 358–359. *See also* business class; commerce; merchants

Chang T'ai-lei, comes to Japan as Comintern emissary, 322 n. 47

Chang Tso-lin: supported by Hara administration, 216–217 and n. 32; key to Tanaka policy, 236; murdered by Kwantung Army men, 236–237 and nn. 85 and 86

chemical industry: early development, 248; expansion during World War I period, 269

Chian Ijiho (Peace Preservation Law): enacted, 300; nature, 300–301 and nn. 14 and 15

Chian Keisatsuho (Public Peace Police Law), enacted, 299

Chichibu. *See* violence

Chihokan Kaigi (Assembly of Prefectural Governors), established, 55

China: trade privileges in Tokugawa period, 18; is opposed by Tokugawa scholars, 19 and n. 34; Opium War and the bakufu, 28–29; Formosan expedition, 44 n. 7; familial system compared with that of Japan, 121–122 and n. 7, 124 n. 12, 129–130 and n. 17; Sino-Japanese War of 1894–1895, 169–170; as victim of Western imperialism, 173 and n. 66; Hara ad-

ministration policy, 216–217 and nn. 30, 32, and 33; Shidehara policy in first Wakatsuki ministry, 234; Tanaka policy, 236–237 and nn. 83, 85, and 86; economic effects of Sino-Japanese War of 1894–1895, 249–250; and Kita Ikki, 354 n. 9, 356 and n. 13; Manchurian Incident, 366–367 and nn. 29–31; outbreak of 1937 war, 387

chonin. *See* merchants

Choshu: political role in Bakumatsu, 29, 31–33 nn. 54 and 55; proposals for national assembly, 50–51 and n. 20; power as reflected in pre-1918 cabinets, 211 n. 23

chozen naikaku shugi (the principle of transcendental cabinet): supported by Kuroda, 153; defended by Ito, 153–154; demanded by Yamagata, 153–154 n. 8; opposed by liberals, 154; as echoed by Terauchi, 209 and n. 18

Christianity: impact on Tokugawa Japan, 17–18 and n. 31; continued restrictions, 27; connection with early Japanese liberals, 281 n. 70

Chuo Club (Central Club), is connected with Katsura and Doshikai, 193 and n. 117

civil rights: early press laws, 60 and n. 49; repression after the Satsuma Rebellion, 61–62 and nn. 51 and 53, 64–65; age of press freedom, 74 and n. 85; under the Meiji Constitution, 83–84 and nn. 116 and 117; connected with agrarian revolts of 1880's, 102–108 and nn. 23, 26, 31, 33, and 35; policies of Japanese government, 298–305 and nn. 13–15, 17, and 20

Comintern: aids in establishment of Japanese Communist party, 322–324 and nn. 45–49; directives concerning "mass" organizations, 331; special 1927 meeting on Japan problem, 333–336 and nn. 62–64, 66, 67, 70, and 71; policy toward Japan after 1928, 339–340 and nn. 80 and 81, 341–342 and nn. 84–86

commerce: development during Tokugawa era, 22–27 and nn. 41, 42, 47, and 48; development in the han, 23–24 and n. 42; general relation to the Restoration, 35–37; early Meiji trends, 98–102 and nn. 15 and 17–19. *See also* business class; capitalism; merchants

Communism: parallels with early Meiji liberal movement, 103 n. 21; certain

445

Communism—*Continued*
resemblances to Confucianism, 125;
effect on civil liberties problem, 299;
impact of Russian Revolution, 321;
struggle in Shakaishugi Domei, 321;
emergence in Japan, 322–326 and nn.
44–53; early influence in Sodomei, 325
and nn. 50 and 51; first mass arrests
of 1923, 326 and n. 53; young Communists murdered after Tokyo earthquake, 326 n. 54; dissolution of first
Japanese Communist party, 328 and n.
55; opposition of Comintern and shift
of leadership, 328–329 and n. 56; organization of "Bureau" and "Communist Group," 329 and n. 57; use of
captive organizations, 330–331 and n.
58; party reëstablished, 332–333;
1927 Moscow meeting on Japan problem, 333–336 and nn. 62–64, 66, 67,
70, and 71; Japanese Marxist debate,
336; 1928 election activities and mass
arrests, 338 and nn. 77 and 78; trends
after 1928, 339–340 and nn. 80 and
81, 341–342 and nn. 84–86; summary
of failure, 343–345; rightist reaction
to, 352–353 and n. 4; reasons for recanting, 374 n. 45; and an analysis of
modern Asia, 393, 394, 397–399
Confucianism: rise in Tokugawa era, 5–
6; rival schools, 6 n. 6; basic tenets,
6–7; Tokugawa adaptations, 7–8, 12;
inadequacies for commercial revolution, 18–19 and n. 34; relationship to
Tokugawa nationalism, 18–19 and n.
34; influence on Tokugawa economic
theories, 26–27 and n. 48; emphasis on
psychological power, 124–126; in
Meiji educational program, 296–298;
continuing influence on modern leaders, 303–304 and n. 21; relation to
"left-wing" movement, 316; revealed
in "rightist" organizations, 352–353
and nn. 4–6; influence on Kita Ikki,
354 n. 9
Constitution. *See* Meiji Constitution
corruption: Hokkaido colonization scandal, 67; in the First Diet, 157–158 and
n. 23; charges involving Hoshi, 167
and n. 52, 169; events in second Yamagata ministry, 176–177 and nn. 79 and
80; discussion of problem, by Okuma,
178 and n. 82; the Siemens Affair, 204
and n. 7; attempt to split Seiyukai in
second Okuma ministry, 206–207 and
nn. 12 and 13; as major problem in the

parties, 247; and the business class,
262–263 and n. 34; major scandals of
the Meiji and early Taisho periods,
263–266 and nn. 37, 38, 40, and 41;
scandals of Hara era, 278, 281 and nn.
62, 65, 66, and 69; the Matsushima
Scandal, 285–286 and n. 84; scandals
in Tanaka ministry, 287–288 and n. 87

Dai Nihon Kokusuikai (Greater Japan
National Essence Society), establishment and principles, 353 and nn. 4
and 6
Dai Nihon Kyokai (Greater Japan Society), nature and policy, 166–167
and nn. 50 and 52
Dai Nihon Seisanto (Greater Japan Production Party), organization and program, 361 and n. 22
Dai Nihon shi (*History of Greater
Japan*), compilation and significance,
20
Daido Club (Club of Like Thinkers):
organization and principles, 188 n.
106; changed to Chuo Club and
joined to Doshikai, 193 n. 117
Daido Danketsu (Union of Like Thinkers), establishment and issues, 113
and nn. 48 and 49
Daigi Seito (Representative Party), failure, 155 n. 12
daimyo (feudal lords): number and
types during Tokugawa, 8–9 and n.
11; control by Tokugawa, 8–11; problems under growing commercialism,
24–25; consulted by bakufu, 29–30
and n. 52; contact with Throne, 31–
33 n. 54; opposition to Restoration
policies, 42–45 and nn. 3 and 4; pensions, 42 n. 3; attendance at national
meetings, 49; role in Gijo, 51 n. 24; removed from central government, 55 n.
33; relation to post-Restoration economic developments, 94–96 and nn.
2–4, 97–102 and nn. 9, 15, and 17–
20. See also *bushi*
Daishin-in (Supreme Court), establishment and functions, 59–60
Dajokan (Council of State, or Chief Administrative Office): establishment
and function, 53–54 and nn. 28 and
31; rejects petition for a popular assembly, 63–64; replaced by cabinet
system, 82
Dan Takuma, is murdered by Ketsumeidan, 369

446

Dazai Shundai, a pioneer in promoting commercialism, 26 n. 47

democratic socialism. See social democrats; and entries for specific parties

democracy: historic Western process, 1–3; initial weaknesses in Meiji Japan, 37–39; as seen in the Aikokukoto, 45–49 and nn. 8, 9, 14, and 18; handicaps implicit in Meiji system, 57, 60; the general effect of Japanese constitutionalism on democratic movement, 243–245; and the Japanese business class, 266–268, 270–273, 290–293; and the "left wing," 294–295 and n. 1; and the agrarian groups, 312; and the democratic socialist movement, 318–320 and nn. 41 and 42; and Japanese nationalism, 347–352 and nn. 1–3; decline in the Saito and Okada eras, 370–377 and nn. 42 and 45; summary of impact of Japanese nationalism on democratic movement, 389–392; failure analyzed, 393–399

Diet: arguments for, by Aikokukoto, 46–49; Tokugawa antecedents, 49–51 and nn. 20–23; establishment pledged in Imperial Oath, 52–53 and n. 26; debate between Kato Hiroyuki and popular rights group, 55–56 and nn. 35 and 36; proposals of Risshisha, 57–58 and n. 39; results of Osaka Conference, 59–60 and n. 46; position of Kokkai Kisei Domeikai, 62–63; arguments of the liberal parties, 74–81 and n. 88; powers under Meiji Constitution, 84–85 and n. 121; first session, 154–159 and nn. 11–13, 16, 21–23, and 25; second session, 160–161 and n. 30; third session, 161–162 and nn. 34 and 35; fourth session, 164–166 and nn. 44 and 47; fifth and sixth sessions, 166–168 and nn. 49, 50, and 52; seventh and eighth sessions, 169; twelfth session, 172–173; sixteenth session, 183; seventeenth and eighteenth sessions, 183–186 and nn. 92–95; twenty-eighth session, 191; thirtieth session, 202–204 and nn. 4, 6, and 7; thirty-fifth session, 206–207 and nn. 12 and 13; developments under Hara ministry, 218–221 and nn. 38–42 and 44; forty-fifth session, 221–222 and nn. 46 and 47; under the Kato coalition ministry, 229–231 and nn. 67, 70, and 71; under Tanaka ministry, 235 and n. 81; events of Hama-

guchi ministry, 239–240 and nn. 92 and 93; occupational groupings in early Diets, 254–257 and nn. 17–20; corruption in Meiji and early Taisho eras, 262–266 and nn. 34, 37, and 38; corruption in "party era," 278–281 and nn. 65 and 66; reforms suggested by Kita Ikki, 355 and n. 12; after 1937 China War, 387–388

district political activities. See local political activities

Doihara Kenji, has connections with Okawa, 363

Doshikai, i.e., Rikken Doshikai (Constitutional Fellow Thinkers' Association): established, 193–194 and nn. 117 and 118; swallows up most of Kokuminto, 196; attracts bureaucratic support, 196; Kato Takaakira becomes president, 197; political power in Okuma administration, 205–207; changed to Kenseikai, 208 n. 16; supported by Mitsubishi funds, 262

dozoku (same family): as type of buraku, 122–124 and n. 11; favored by feudalism, 128–130 and n. 17

Dutch. See Netherlands

Echizen, position in new governmental structure of 1868, 51 n. 24

eclecticism: a dominant note in Japanese society as revealed in Meiji Constitution, 243–245; a problem for democratic movement, 399

Edo. See Tokyo

education: Meiji policy, 295–297 and nn. 2, 4, 5, and 7; attitude of major parties, 297–298; military policy, 377

elections: Law of 1890, 113–114 and nn. 51–53; of 1890, 154 n. 11, 155 and nn. 12 and 13; of 1892, 160–161 and nn. 31 and 32; of 1898, 172 and n. 14; of 1903, 184; of 1912, 191; of 1915, 207 and n. 14; of 1917, 209; of 1920, 220 and nn. 41 and 42; of 1924, 227 and n. 63; universal manhood suffrage bill enacted, 229; of 1928, 235; of 1930, 237 and n. 87; of 1932, 242; agrarian strength in early elections, 254–257 and nn. 17–20; the labor party record in the 1928 elections, 337 and nn. 73, 74, and 76; labor in the 1930 elections, 340 and nn. 82 and 83; labor in the 1932 elections, 341; of 1936, 381–383 and nn. 53 and 54; of 1937, 386–387

Emperor: position before 1600, 4; under the Tokugawa, 11–12 and nn. 20 and 21; increased emphasis upon, 19, 34; entrance into politics during Bakumatsu, 29–33 and nn. 52 and 54; and Aikokukoto pledge, 46; Imperial Oath of 1868, 52–53 and n. 26; Imperial order of 1875, 59–60; powers under Meiji Constitution, 85–86, 149; powers as revealed in First Diet, 157 and n. 21; used to strengthen Matsukata cabinet, 160 n. 27; use of, proposed by Ito, 162–163; injection into politics during Fourth Diet, 165–166 and nn. 44 and 47; used in Fifth Diet, 167; used by Ito in his third ministry, 181; relations with military, 192 and n. 114; use attacked by Ozaki, 194–195 and n. 121; defied by Seiyukai, 195 and n. 123; political intervention ceases, 195–196 and n. 124; the Communist position concerning, 323–324 nn. 48 and 49. *See also* Meiji Tenno; monarchical theories; Showa Tenno; Taisho Tenno

England: contacts with early Tokugawa Japan, 18; threats in late Tokugawa period, 28; counterattack against Japanese antiforeignism, 32 n. 54; influence on early Meiji liberalism, 45 n. 9, 48, 50 and n. 22, 66 n. 67, 73–74 and nn. 81 and 83, 77–81 and nn. 95 and 97; London Naval Reduction Treaty, 238–239 and n. 92; influence on early Meiji education, 296; influence through British Labor Party, 326; economic and political development contrasted with that of Japan, 396–398

eta (outcast), position under Tokugawa, 15 n. 26

Eto Shimpei: joins early liberal movement, 44–45; executed as rebel, 56

factionalism: Tokugawa opposition to, 4–5; Tokugawa political source springs, 12–13; as a general force in modern Japanese politics, 117–119; basic socioeconomic causes, 132–134; evidences in early Meiji parties, 139–142 and nn. 32 and 36; as seen in Kenseito, 175–176 and n. 76; in the Seiyukai, 187 n. 100; in the Okuma group, 190–191; in the han, 205 n. 8; in the Seiyukai during Takahashi ministry, 222–223; in all branches of

government after Manchurian Incident, 240–245

family structure: origins and basic characteristics in pre-Meiji Japan, 120–130 and nn. 5, 7, 8, 10–12, and 16–18; effects on Japanese political behavior, 130–134 and n. 19; summary of political effects, 143–144

Far Eastern Peoples' Conference, purpose and actions, 322–323 and n. 48

farmers: social status under the Tokugawa, 14; Tokugawa restrictions, 15 n. 26; growing class divisions, 25 and n. 45; as described by Kato Hiroyuki, 55; connections with Jiyuto, 97–98 and nn. 9 and 10, 101–108 and nn. 19–21, 26, 31, 33, 34, and 37; opposition to commercial interests, 253–254; conditions in modern Japan, 305–312 and nn. 23, 25, 26, 28, and 29; and "right-wing" nationalism, 349–352, 362–363, 389–392. *See also* agriculture; landowners; tenant farmers

Fascism: relation to agrarian primitivism, 26 and n. 47, 312; Japan differentiated from West in respect to, 303–304; connections with Japan, 351–352; as personified in Kita Ikki, 354–356 and nn. 9 and 11–13; poor showing in 1936 elections, 381–382 and nn. 53 and 54; and the February Twenty-sixth Incident, 383–384 and nn. 56 and 57; and the Japanese military era, 391–392. *See also* militarism

February Twenty-sixth Incident, events and significance, 383–384 and nn. 56 and 57

feudalism: divisions and types in Japan, 3–4 and n. 3; connections with Meiji Restoration, 35–37; connections with Japanese familial system, 126–130 and nn. 16–18

France: influence on early Meiji liberalism, 72–74 and n. 83, 77; demands recession of Liaotung peninsula, 169; influence upon Saionji, 182 n. 89; influence on early Meiji education, 296 and n. 4

fu (Metropolitan District): represented in Gijokan, 54 n. 29; assemblies established, 64

fudai daimyo (hereditary lords), definition and positions, 8. See also *daimyo*

Fukaya Hiroji, analyzes decline of Jiyuto as "popular party," 166

Goto Shojiro—*Continued*
Daido Danketsu, 113 and n. 49; is attacked by Kaishinto, 138 n. 28; exemplifies problems of Japanese leadership, 140–141 and n. 35; is criticized during fifth session of Diet, 167; has ties with Mitsui, 260–261 and nn. 29 and 31

Great Britain. *See* England

Gyochisha (The Society to Realize the Way of Heaven on Earth): establishment and program, 358–359 and nn. 16–19; connections, 363

Gyominkai (The Association of Enlightened People), established as forerunner to Communist party, 322 and n. 46

Hamada Kunimatsu, debates with War Minister Terauchi, 385 and n. 60

Hamaguchi Yuko: becomes leader in Doshikai, 197; assumes presidency of Minseito and becomes Premier—events of ministry, 237–240 and nn. 87, 88, and 91–93; is shot and resigns premiership and Minseito presidency, 240; supports "negative" economic policies as Finance Minister, 284–285 and n. 80; reëstablishes "negative" policies as Premier, 288–289

han (fief): economic dislocation, 13; administration in Tokugawa era, 16 n. 28; rise of commercialism, 23–24 and n. 42; politics during the Bakumatsu, 31 and n. 54; economic problems during the Bakumatsu, 31 n. 53; abolition, 42 n. 3; assemblies, 49–50 and n. 21; embers of factionalism long-lived, 205 n. 8

Hara Takashi [Kei]: emerges as Seiyukai leader, 186; biographical sketch of early life, 186 n. 99; joins first Saionji cabinet, 188; becomes president of Seiyukai, 197; joins first Yamamoto cabinet, 201; joins Terauchi's Foreign Policy Committee, 210 n. 21; becomes Premier—personality sketch and events of ministry, 210–221 and nn. 27–33, 35, 36, 38, 41, 42, and 44; is assassinated, 212; has connections with Furukawa, 261; economic policies and trends during premiership, 275–281 and nn. 55, 56, 58, and 60; corruption during premiership, 278–281 and nn. 65, 66, and 69; defends educational system, 297–298

Hara Yoshimichi, is member of Kokuhonsha, 360

Hashimoto Kingoro: is leader of Sakurakai, 364; is involved in "March Incident," 365 and n. 27

Hata Shinji, is member of Kokuhonsha, 360

hatamoto (bannerets), definition and position, 8

Hattori Naritsugu, translates Rousseau's *Social Contract*, 73

Hausknecht, Professor, aids in establishment of Japanese educational policy, 296 n. 5

Hayashi Razan: as an important Tokugawa scholar, 6 n. 6; writings on social class theory, 14 n. 23

Hayashi Senjuro: becomes Premier—basic ideas, 386; resigns, 387

Hayashi Shihei, nationalist theories of, 19 n. 34

Hayashi Yuzo: joins Aikokukoto, 45 n. 9; resigns from Kenseito cabinet, 176; leaves Seiyukai, 187 n. 100

Hayashida Kametaro, aids in trying to split Seiyukai during second Okuma ministry, 206–207 and nn. 12 and 13

Heimin Shimbun (*The Commoner Newspaper*), published as leading "left-wing" organ—banned, 318 nn. 37 and 38

hijo kikyoku (extraordinary conditions), term used after outbreak of Manchurian Incident, 289

hinsei toya (character education), as core of Meiji educational program, 296 and n. 5

Hiranuma Kiichiro: is councillor of the Kenkokukai, 359–360; supports military men for premiership, 368

Hirata Atsutane, a leader of Shinto revival, 20 and n. 36

Hirota Koki, becomes Premier—events of ministry, 364–386 and nn. 60–62

Hizen: political role in Bakumatsu, 29; hostility to Sat-Cho control, 43; reduced power in Meiji oligarchy, 44–45 and n. 7; strong provincialism, 135–137

Hoan Jorei (Peace Preservation Law): first established, 142–143 and n. 40; repealed, 299. See also *Chian Keisatsuho*

Hokkaido, colonization project, 67

Homma Kenichiro, is connected with the May Fifteenth Incident, 370

Honda Toshiaki: nationalist theories, 19 n. 34; proponent of foreign trade, 28 n. 49

Horie Kiichi, aids in organization of Shakai Minshuto, 331–332

Hoshi Toru: leads conservative wing of Jiyuto, 107; is banned from Tokyo, 143 n. 40; presents to Emperor a petition to impeach government, 165; becomes central leader of Jiyuto, 166; has close connections with certain government leaders, 166 and n. 49; is impeached, 167 and n. 52; attacked by Peers during third Ito ministry, 181 n. 88; connected with major scandals, 264–265; assassinated, 264–265 and n. 38

House of Representatives. See Diet

Hozumi Yatsuka, challenges Minobe's organic theory, 319 n. 39

Hyogikai. See Rodo Hyogikai

Iba Sotaro, assassinates Hoshi Toru, 264–265 and n. 38

Ichikawa Shoichi, is advanced to Communist leadership by Comintern, 334

Ikeda Seihin, is member of Kokukonsha, 360

imperialism: Western threats in early Tokugawa period, 17–18, and nn. 31 and 32; Western threats in late Tokugawa period, 28–29; Western inroads on China and political effect in Japan, 173 and n. 66; Communist analysis of, 334 and n. 64; the Communist type, 334–336 and nn. 67, 70, and 71, 341–342 and nn. 84–86; connected with Japanese rightism, 349–351 and nn. 1–3; 352–359 and nn. 4, 6, 9, 13, 17, and 19

industrial revolution. See capitalism

Inomata Tsunao, becomes member of Yamakawa anti-Comintern faction, 336

Inoue Junnosuke: opposes Adachi's coalition ideas, 241; protests militarist actions, 367; is assassinated, 369

Inoue Kaoru: prepares Osaka Conference, 59; opposes Okuma proposals for a constitution, 67; approves of Teiseito, 81; tries to influence Itagaki, 138 n. 28; heads Rinji Teikoku Gikai Jimukyoku, 152 n. 4; belongs to "civil" bureaucratic faction, 159; joins second Ito cabinet, 164; becomes bitterly anti-Seiyukai, 205 n. 8; has close connections with Mitsui, 260–261 and nn. 27–29

Inoue Kowashi: proposes plan for oligarchy, 67 n. 69; opposes Ito's plan for use of Emperor, 162–163

Inoue Nissho, is mentor of the Ketsumeidan, 369–370

intellectuals: restrictions on political activities, 64–65; represented in the Jiyuto, 69–71 and nn. 72 and 73; influence of Western ideas in early Meiji era, 71–83 and nn. 76, 79, 81, 83, 84, 88, 95, and 97; activity on behalf of Meiji democracy, 115–116 and n. 54; Tokyo University dominance in bureaucracy, 156; anticapitalist predilections, 253–254; connection with "left-wing" movement, 315, 325–326 and nn. 52 and 53; and the "right wing," 362 and n. 24

Inukai Tsuyoshi [Ki]: emerges as Keio liberal, 78; leads Protect the Constitution Association, 192–193; joins Terauchi's Foreign Policy Deliberation Committee, 210 n. 21; attacks major parties, 224 and n. 54; joins Yamamoto cabinet, 226 and n. 60; joins in three-party "save the Constitution" movement, 227; dissolves Kakushin Club and joins Seiyukai, 232–233 and n. 77; becomes president of Seiyukai, 238 n. 88; supports military against Hamaguchi ministry, 239 and n. 92; becomes Premier—events of ministry, 242–243; assassinated, 243; attacks Meiji business indifference to liberalism, 258; is charged with being subsidized, 262; is opposed by Kita Ikki, 354 n. 9; plays double role toward militarism, 368–369

iron and steel industries, beginnings, 250; expansion during World War I period, 269–270

irresponsibility. See responsibility

Ishimoto Shinroku, dies while serving as War Minister, 192

isolation: causes, in Tokugawa era, 17–18 and n. 31; results, 18–21; increasingly threatened, 27–29

Itagaki Seishiro, has connections with Okawa, 363

Itagaki Taisuke: supports overthrow of Tokugawa, 33 n. 55; breaks with Meiji government and establishes Aikoku-koto, 43–46 and nn. 8 and 9; expresses nationalist line, 49 n. 18; sits on Sei-in, 55 n. 33; participates in answer to

and nn. 11 and 12; supports resolution against Matsukata government, 161; tries to impeach second Ito cabinet, 164–166 and nn. 44 and 47; effect of failure upon character of party, 166; splits with Kaishinto, 166; Hoshi becomes central figure, 166; support for Ito foreign policy, 166–167 and n. 49, 169–170; first alliance with Ito faction, 169–171 and nn. 57–60; alliance with Ito breaks down, 172–173 and nn. 64 and 66; becomes Kenseito, 173; later becomes Seiyukai, 179–180

Joffe, visits Japan and is attacked by Kita, 358 n. 17

joi togo (mutual understanding), as applied to Katsura-Saionji era, 189

Jonson. *See* Janson

Juo Club (Universal Club), established as a nationalist society, 353 n. 4

Jushin (Chief Retainers): establishment and function, 380–381; plans to appoint Ugaki Premier, 386; appoints Hayashi Premier, 386; selects Konoe for his first premiership, 387

Kabayama Sukenori, coöperates with Okuma forces, 170

Kada Azumamaro, a leader of Shinto revival, 20 n. 36

kaikoku (Open the country): relation to economic debate of Tokugawa era, 26 and n. 47; as a support for bakufu, 31; as symbol of final nature of the Restoration, 37

Kaishinto, i.e., *Rikken Kaishinto* (Constitutional Progressive Party): establishment, 68; basic philosophy, 77–81 and nn. 95, 97, and 104, 88–90; sources of early support, 108–111 and nn. 38–42; retrenchment, 111; as a sectional party, 137; battles with Jiyuto, 137–139 and nn. 28 and 29; organizational structure and problems, 140–141; strength in First Diet, 154–155 and nn. 11 and 12; supports resolution against Matsukata government, 161; aids in impeachment of second Ito cabinet, 164–166; splits with Jiyuto and attacks Ito foreign policy, 166–167; helps impeach Hoshi, 166 and n. 52; becomes Shimpoto, 170

Kakushin Club (Reform Club): formed out of Kokuminto, 224–225 and n. 57; dissolved, with major elements joining Seiyukai, 232–233 and n. 77

Kamikaze Jiyuto (Divine Wind Liberal Party), principles, 88 n. 132

Kamo no Mabuchi, a leader of Shinto revival, 20 and n. 36

Kaneko Kentaro: translates Burke's *Reflections on the Revolution in France*, 74 and n. 84; goes overseas to study parliamentary institutions, 152 n. 4; joins Seiyukai, 181 n. 87; gives lectures on the Constitution, 373 n. 44

kanryo. *See* bureaucracy

Kanto (Eastern Provinces), as stronghold of Meiji oligarchy, 135

Kanto Chiho Rodo Hyogikai (Kanto District Labor Council), as forerunner to Rodo Hyogikai, 327

Kasumigaseki clique (Foreign Office clique), control over diplomatic appointments, 218 n. 36

Kataoka Kenkichi: joins Aikokukoto, 45 n. 9; goes to Tokyo with petition, 62; leaves Seiyukai, 187 n. 100

Katayama Sen: aids in early "left-wing" party movement, 318 n. 37; is delegate to Far Eastern Peoples' Conference and becomes Japanese representative on the Comintern, 322 n. 47; helps operate Moscow training program, 339 n. 81

Katayama Tetsu: remains a social democrat, 388; seeks to form Kinro Kokuminto, 388

Kato Hiroyuki: opposes immediate representative government, 55–56 and n. 35; lectures and writes from German sources, 71–72 and n. 79

Kato Kanji, is member of Kokuhonsha, 360

Kato Kanju, leads Nihon Musanto, 374–375

Kato Takaakira [Komei]: becomes president of Doshikai, 197; is Foreign Minister in second Okuma cabinet, 205 n. 8; struggles with Genro, 205 n. 8, 206; refuses to reënter Okuma cabinet, 207; challenges Genro, 208 and n. 16; forms Kenseikai, 208 n. 16; opposes Terauchi's Foreign Policy Deliberation Committee, 210 and n. 21; joins in three-party "save the Constitution" movement, 227; becomes Premier of coalition cabinet—personal sketch and events of ministry, 228–233 and nn. 65, 67, 70, and 71; forms new all-Kenseikai ministry—events of ministry, 233–234; dies, 234; has close

Kato Takaakira—*Continued*
relationship with Mitsubishi, 262; opposes railroad nationalization, 264 n. 37; is involved in *"chimpin itsutsu"* affair, 279 and n. 65; supports Hamaguchi "negative" economic policies, 284–285

Kato Tomosaburo, accepts premiership—events of ministry, 223–225; dies, 225

Katsura Taro: is War Minister in Kenseito cabinet, 175 and n. 73; is connected with corrupt practices of second Yamagata cabinet, 177 n. 80; becomes Premier—events of first Katsura ministry, 182–188 and nn. 92–94, 97, 101, 105, and 106; gets support from Seiyukai, 186–188 and nn. 100 and 101; has connections with Daido Club, 188 n. 106; forms second ministry—events, 190–191; is chosen Premier a third time—events of third ministry, 192–196 and nn. 115, 117, 118, 121, 123, and 124; forms Rikken Doshikai, 193–194 and nn. 117 and 118; dies, 196

Kawakami Kiyoshi, aids early "leftwing" party movement, 318 n. 37

Kawasaki, as a part of the zaibatsu, 252

Kawashima Takeyoshi, emphasizes importance of "adopted-son" principle, 122 n. 8

Keio University, as a bulwark of early Meiji liberalism, 73 n. 81, 78

Kellogg antiwar pact, opposed in Japan, 235 and n. 81

Kempeitai (Military Police), brutality after Tokyo earthquake, 326–327 and n. 54

ken (Prefecture): represented in Gijokan, 54 n. 29; establishment of conferences of prefectural governors, 55; organization of assemblies, 64, 104–105 n. 27

Kenkokukai (The Society to Build the Country), organization and purposes, 359–360

Kenkyukai (Study Association), faction of House of Peers: alliance with Hara, 215–216 and nn. 28 and 29; supports Kato Tomosaburo, 224 and n. 51; participates in alliance with Kato's all-Kenseikai ministry, 233; alliance continued with Wakatsuki ministry, 234 and n. 78

Kenkyukai, leftist organization. See *Seiji Mondai Kenkyukai*

Kensei Yogo Kai (Protect the Constitution Association), formed to fight third Katsura ministry, 192–193

Kenseihonto (Orthodox Kenseito): established by Okuma faction, 177; remains aloof from bureaucratic sponsorship, 179; impotence, 182; proexpansionist position, 184 and n. 92, 187–188 and n. 102; agitation for alliance with bureaucracy, 190–191; dissolution of party and formation of Kokuminto, 190–191

Kenseikai (Constitutional Association): established, 208 n. 16; supports universal manhood suffrage, 222; seeks to take over ministry after Takahashi resignation, 223–224 and nn. 50 and 51; joins in three-party coalition, 227–233 and nn. 65, 67, and 70; coalition broken and all-Kenseikai ministry formed, 233; new coalition with Kenkyukai and Seiyuhonto, 233; Wakatsuki succeeds Kato as party president, 234 and n. 78; becomes the Minseito, 235; is involved in Matsushima Scandal, 285–286

Kenseito (Constitutional Party): established by Jiyuto and Shimpoto, 173; failure of Okuma-Itagaki cabinet and split in party, 173–177 and nn. 69, 72, 73, and 75–78; becomes Seiyukai, 179–181

Ketsumeidan (Blood Oath Association), participants and actions, 369–371

Kido Koin: aids in formation of antibakufu coalition, 33 n. 54; goes on Iwakura mission, 43; resigns from government, 44 n. 7; sits on Sei-in, 55 n. 33; participates in Osaka Conference, 59; submits proposal for a constitution, 66 n. 67; is influenced by Montesquieu, 72–73

kikansetsu. *See* organic theory of state

Kinki (Inner Provinces [Osaka and Kyoto districts]), as center of early party movement, 135 and n. 22

Kinoshita Naoe, aids in early "left-wing" party movement, 318 n. 37

Kinro Kokuminto (Workers' Nationalist Party), organization banned, 388

Kita Ikki: is father of Japanese "Fascist" movement—biographical sketch, 354 and n. 9; outlines political program, 354–356 and nn. 11–13; conflict with agrarian nationalists and with Okawa, 357–358 and nn. 15 and 17; has many

454

military connections, 363; is implicated in February Twenty-sixth Incident and is executed, 383–384 and nn. 56 and 58

Kiyoura Keigo: is unable to form ministry after first Yamamoto cabinet resigns, 205 n. 8; becomes Premier after second Yamamoto ministry—events of ministry, 226–227

Kizokuin Kaikaku Kisei Kai (Association Pledged to Peerage Reform), establishment, 230 n. 67

ko (filial piety), in Japanese familial system, 128–129

Kobayashi Kazuo: helps plan Korean revolution, 107 n. 35; represents revolutionary element in Jiyuto, 108

Kochi, as birthplace of Risshisha, 57

Kodo ha (Imperial Way Faction): nature and position, 378–379; and February Twenty-sixth Incident, 383–384 and nn. 56 and 57

Kodogi Kai (Society for the Principle of the Imperial Way), established as a nationalist society, 353 n. 4

Kofuku Anzenkai (Happiness-Security Society), establishment and policies, 45

Kogisho (Public Deliberation Chamber), establishment and functions, 54

kogumi (association), as a type of buraku, 122–124 and n. 11

Koiso Kuniaki: is member of Kokuhonsha, 360; has connections with Okawa, 363; is connected with "March Incident," 365 n. 27; becomes an important political figure, 384

Kokka Shakaito (National Socialist Society), establishment and principles, 316

Kokkai Kisei Domeikai (Association for the Petitioning for a National Assembly): organized, 62; philosophy, 62–63

Kokuko hanron (*A General Treatise on National Law*), as a pioneer work in developing Japanese political ideas and terminology, 71 and n. 78

Kokuhonsha (National Foundation Society), organization and purposes, 360

Kokumin Domei (Nationalist League): formed by Adachi, 371; dissolved, 388

Kokumin Jiyuto (Nationalist Liberal Party), position in the First Diet, 155 n. 13

Kokuminto, i.e., *Rikken Kokuminto* (Constitutional Nationalist Party): established from old Kenseihonto, 190–191; Oishi faction joins Katsura's Doshikai, 193–194; remaining group fights Katsura, 194; mostly swallowed up by Doshikai, 196; supports universal manhood suffrage and restrictions on military, 222 and nn. 46 and 47; dissolves to form Kakushin Club, 224–225 and n. 57

Kokuryukai (Amur River Society), establishment and program, 350–351 and n. 3

Kokusuikai. See *Dai Nihon Kokusuikai*

kokutai (national polity): connection of concept with early Meiji liberalism, 77; use of term in Chian Ijiho, and definition, 300–301 and n. 15

Komuro Shinobu, joins Aikokukoto, 45 n. 9

Kondo Eizo, is leader in early Japanese Communist movement, 322 and nn. 46 and 47

konin. See artisans

Kono Hironaka: goes to Tokyo with petition, 62; leads Jiyuto, 69; opposes Fukushima Governor, 104–105; defends coalition with Ito faction, 170–171 and nn. 58 and 60; forces Diet dissolution, 187 n. 101

Kono Toshikama, resigns as Kaishinto vice-president, 111

Konoe Fumimaro: is politically ambivalent, 379–380; assumes first premiership, 387; leads Taisei Yokusan Kai, 388–389

Korea: issue of Japanese-Korean war in 1873, 43–44 and n. 6; revolutionary plan of Oi Kentaro, 107 n. 35; Japanese agrarian opposition to importation of Korean rice in the 1920's, 277–278; Korean massacre after Tokyo earthquake and Communist use of event, 326–327 and n. 54

Kotoku Denjiro [Shusui]: is connected with "Great Treason Case," 317; biographical sketch, 317 n. 36

Kuhara Fusanosuke: becomes leader in the Seiyukai, 238 n. 88; favors unification of Seiyukai and Minseito, 241–242; struggles for control of Seiyukai, 242; is appointed Minister of Communications in Tanaka cabinet, 287–288 and n. 87; has "rightist" connections, 368, 379; is connected with

Kuhara Fusanosuke—*Continued*
February Twenty-sixth Incident, 383–384 and n. 57; leads Seiyukai faction into dissolution, 388
kunshu sensei. *See* monarchical theories
Kuroda Kiyotaka: heads Hokkaido colonization project, 67; is Premier—events of ministry, 152–153 and nn. 4 and 5; stands for nonparty cabinets, 153; resigns, 154 n. 10; belongs to "military" bureaucratic faction, 159; joins second Ito cabinet, 164
Kwantung Army: elements murder Chang Tso-lin, 236–237 and nn. 82, 85, and 86; build-up for Manchurian Incident, 366–367 and nn. 30 and 31
Kyochokai (Conciliation Society), establishment and function, 277
Kyodo Unyu Kaisha (Joint Navigation Company), established by Meiji government, 138
Kyoto: position during Tokugawa era, 12, 23 n. 41; increasing political importance during Bakumatsu, 29, 31–33 and n. 54
Kyushu, as stronghold of provincialism, 135–137 and n. 23
Kyushu Doshikai (Kyushu Fellow Thinkers' Association), as sectional party, 136

labor: rise of industrial labor force, 269–270 and nn. 48 and 49; lack of sympathetic legislation in "party era," 277 and n. 58; establishment of Kyochokai, 277; under the Chian Keisatsuho, 299; general problems and emergence of labor movement, 312–314 and nn. 32 and 33; labor and politics, 325 and n. 51, 327–328, 330–332 and n. 58; Comintern opposition to 1925 split, 335–336 n. 70; basic political weaknesses, 343–345; overtures of nationalists to, 361–362. *See also* labor unions
labor unions: tenant-farmer problems and the emergence of tenant unions, 309–311 and nn. 28 and 29; beginnings of Japanese labor unions, 314 and n. 33; ideological struggle within Sodomei, 325 and n. 51; organization of Hyogikai, 327–328; unions and party developments, 330–332 and n. 58; Comintern opposition to 1925

split, 335–336 n. 70. *See also* labor; *Rodo Hyogikai;* Sodomei
laissez faire: seeds in Tokugawa era, 27 n. 48; basic rejection by modern Japanese business class, 271–273; as exemplified in the Jitsugyo Doshikai, 281–282 and nn. 70, 71, and 73
landowners: political connections with Jiyuto, 97–98 and nn. 9 and 10, 101–102 and nn. 19 and 20, 107–108; voting strength and political position in early Meiji era, 114–115 and n. 52, 254–257 and nn. 17–20; political position in "party era," 277–278 and n. 60, 283–284; general agrarian conditions, 305–312 and nn. 23, 25, 26, 28, and 29. *See also* agriculture; farmers; tenant farmers
Law of Public Meetings: establishment and major provisions, 64–65; amendments, 103–104 and n. 23
leadership: as a major problem of Japanese politics, 117–119 and n. 2; effect of Japanese familial system and feudalism, 132–134; problem shown in early Meiji parties, 139–142 and nn. 35, 36, and 38; techniques in modern Japan, 303–304 and n. 21
"left wing": definition, 294 n. 1; function in Japanese democratic movement, 294–295; opening stages of activities, 315–318 and nn. 34 and 36–38; emergence after World War I, 324–326 and nn. 44–54; the struggle for unification and control, 327–341 and nn. 55–58, 62, 67, 70, 73, 76–78, 80, 82, and 83; summary of failure, 343–345; affected by "rightist" trend, 374–375 and n. 45
liberalism. *See* democracy
Liberal party. *See Jiyuto*
local government: reforms of 1878, 64; establishment of prefectural assemblies, 104 n. 27
local political activities: spread of popular rights movement, 58–59, 61–62, 73; riots of the 1880's, 104–107 and n. 31; loss of local autonomy, 308–309
Locke, John, influence on Kaishinto, 73 n. 81
London Naval Reduction Treaty, causes political struggle in Japan, 238–239 and nn. 91 and 92; continues to be resented by the military, 366
loyalty, as a political force in Japanese society, 117–119

457

tical activities, 252–253 and n. 15, 261–262; opposes railroad nationalization, 264 n. 37; contributions to Kenseikai, and the so-called "Mitsubishi cabinet," 282–284 and nn. 74 and 75

Mitsui: position during Restoration period, 98, 101 and n. 18; payment for Itagaki-Goto European trip, 110 n. 44; attacked by Kaishinto, 137–138 and n. 28; scope of operations, 252; political activities in Meiji era, 252–253, 260–261 and nn. 27–29 and 31; ambivalence toward business politics, 281 n. 70; contributions and power in party cabinets, 283–284 and n. 75; connected with "dollar buyer" episode, 289; connections with Kokuhonsha, 360

Mitsukawa Kametaro, aids in organization of Gyochisha, 358 and n. 17

Miyajima Seiichiro, proposes a constitution, 66 n. 67

Mizuno, Torajiro: leaves Risshisha, 74; leads Teiseito, 111 n. 46

monarchical theories: in late Tokugawa period, 19, 34, 36–37; relation to early Meiji liberalism, 46–47; position of Risshisha, 58; as seen in 1875 Imperial order, 59–60; connected with Kokka Kisei Domeikai petition, 62–63; attacked by Ueki, 70–71; contradictions in Jiyuto, 74–77 and nn. 88 and 91; expressions of Kaishinto, 79–81; as interpreted by Ito, 85–86; conflict in the Meiji Constitution concerning, 150; relation to theory of transcendental cabinets, 153–154 and n. 8; relation to Japanese educational program, 296–298 and nn. 5 and 7; debate over Minobe's organic theory, 318–319 and n. 39; and early nationalist societies, 350–351 and nn. 2 and 3; of Kita Ikki, 354–356 and nn. 9 and 11–13; and the Minobe issue, 372–374 and nn. 42 and 44. See also Emperor

Montesquieu: influences Kido, 72–73; influences Ono, 78 n. 95

Mori Arinori, helps to formulate Meiji educational program, 296 nn. 4 and 5

Mori Kaku, has connections with "right wing," 368

Moscow Far Eastern University, as training center for Japanese Communist leaders, 339 n. 81

Mosse, Albert, assists in drafting Meiji Constitution, 83

Motoda Hajime: joins Seiyukai, 201 and n. 1; refuses to resign from Takahashi cabinet, 222; joins Seiyuhonto, 227

Motoori Norinaga: a leader of Shinto revival, 20 and n. 36; spokesman for anticommercial theories, 26 n. 47

Murray, David, serves as consultant to Meiji government on educational policy, 296 n. 4

Musan Seinen Domei (Proletarian Youth League), established as Communist front organization, 330–331 and n. 58

Muto Sanji [Yamaji]: has strong Western ties, 281 n. 70; establishes Jitsugyo Doshikai, 281–282 and nn. 70, 71, and 73; attacks Japanese business politics, 282 and n. 71

Mutsu Munemitsu: opposes Shinagawa's policies, 160 n. 29; has connections with Furukawa, 261

Nabeyama Sadachika: advanced to Communist leadership ranks by Comintern, 334; recants Communism, 342 and n. 86

Nagai Ryutaro, attacks Hara and Seiyukai, 280

Nagata Tetsuzan, is murdered, 378

naian gaikyo (internal peace, external competition), motto coined by Fukuzawa, 109 n. 40

naikaku. See cabinet

Nakae Chomin [Tokusuke], acts as intellectual spokesman for Jiyuto, 68 and n. 72

Nakae Toju: an important Tokugawa scholar, 6 n. 6; his concept of class divisions, 15 n. 26

Nakahashi Tokugoro: refuses to resign from Takahashi cabinet, 222; joins Seiyuhonto, 227; is accused of unethical practices as a minister in Hara cabinet, 278–279

Nakajima Chikuhei, leads Seiyukai faction, 388

Nakamigawa Hikojiro, antagonizes Meiji oligarchs by actions as Mitsui general manager, 260 n. 29

narikin (newly rich): emergence in World War I period, 269; political role, 273, 283

national socialism. See Fascism

nationalism: Tokugawa source springs, 13, 18–21 and nn. 34–36; connections with agrarian primitivism, 26 and n. 47, 36; modified through the Restoration, 36–37; connected with early Meiji liberalism, 46–49 and n. 18; expressed by Kato Hiroyuki, 56 and n. 35; shown in Risshisha political program, 58; shown in Kokka Kisei Domeikai petition, 62–63; connected with emerging major parties, 75–81 and nn. 88 and 91; reaction to Western imperialism, 83 n. 115; summary of relation to popular rights movement, 88–91; connection with Daido Danketsu, 112–113 and nn. 48 and 49; relationship to provincialism, 136–137; relationship to Meiji business class, 253 and n. 16, 273; as a political tool for a modern elite, 295–296; in the Japanese educational program, 295–298 and nn. 4, 5, and 7; as a modern agrarian movement, 312; connected with early "left-wing" movement, 316 and n. 34; and the Communist movement, 322–324 and nn. 48 and 49, 334–335 n. 67; supports rightists, 340–341; summary of effect upon leftist movement, 343–345; broad relation to Japanese democracy, 347, 352 and nn. 1–3; developments in Japan after World War I, 352, 358–365 and nn. 16–19, 22, and 24; summary of effect, 389–392. *See also* militarism

navy: early control by Satsuma in Meiji era, 43 n. 4; continued control by Satsuma, 191, 196; opposes third Katsura ministry, 192; budget reductions under Kato coalition ministry, 229 and n. 65; opposition to London Naval Reduction Treaty, 238–240 and nn. 89, 91, and 92; and Siemens Affair, 265–266 and n. 41; connection with May Fifteenth Incident, 370 and n. 38; role in the Saito and Okada eras, 371, 379 and n. 49. *See also* militarism

Netherlands: Tokugawa trading privileges, 18; information to bakufu, 18 n. 32, 27, 28, 50 n. 22

newspapers. *See* press

Nihon Heiminto (Japan Commoner Party), attempted establishment and leaders—banned by Katsura, 318 n. 37

Nihon kaizo hoan taiko (*Outline of the Measures for the Reconstruction of*

Japan): as the bible for the young militarists, 354–355; main concepts, 354 n. 9, 355–356 and nn. 11–13

Nihon Musanto (Japan Proletariat Party), opposes China War, 374–375

Nihon Nomin Kumiai (Japan Farmers' Union), political activities, 329–332 and nn. 58 and 59

Nihon Nominto (Japan Farmers' Party): establishment and principles, 331; membership, 337 n. 73; 1928 election vote, 337 n. 76; joins in Nihon Taishuto, 339–340

Nihon oyobi Nihonjin (*Japan and the Japanese*), expresses Okawa's basic ideas, 358–359 and n. 18

Nihon Rodo Sodomei. *See* Sodomei

Nihon Ronoto (Japan Labor-Farmer Party): organization and policy, 332; is attacked by 1927 Communist Thesis, 335; seeks for leftist unification, 336–337; 1928 elections, 337 and nn. 73, 74, and 76; takes lead in formation of Nihon Taishuto, 338–339 and n. 79

Nihon Shakaito (Japan Socialist Party): establishment and policy, 318 and n. 37; banned, 318 n. 38

Nihon Sodomei Kakushin Domei (Japanese Federation Reform League): establishment, 327; becomes Rodo Hyogikai, 327

Nihon Taishuto (Japan Mass Party): organization and policies, 338–339 and n. 79; divided by political differences, 339–340

Nishida Zei: is follower of Kita Ikki, 363; is connected with February Twenty-sixth Incident and executed, 383–384 and n. 56

Nishikawa Kojiro, aids in early "left-wing" party movement, 318 n. 37

Nishio Suehiro, faces "left-wing" opposition in Sodomei, 340

nomin. *See* farmers; landowners; tenant farmers

Nomin Rodoto (Farmer-Labor Party): organized by the far left, 329–330 and n. 58; banned by government, 330

Nosaka Sanzo. *See* Nozaka Sanzo

Noson jikyu ron (*A Treatise on Rural Self-Help*), upholds agrarian autonomy, 356

Nozaka Sanzo: favors dissolution of first Japanese Communist party, 328 n. 55;

460

helps operate Moscow training program, 339 n. 81

Numa Moriichi: urges creation of Kaishinto, 108 n. 38; leads the *Tokyo-Yokohama Mainichi* faction of Kaishinto, 109 and n. 41

"October Incident," purpose and leaders, 367–368

Ogyu Sorai, an exponent of agrarian primitivism, 26 n. 47

Oi Kentaro: leads "left-wing" Jiyuto, 103, 107; plans Korean revolution, 107 n. 35; represents revolutionary element in Jiyuto, 108; forms Toyo Jiyuto, 316 and n. 34

Oishi Masami: leads "probureaucratic" faction of Kenseihonto, 190–191; aids in formation of Doshikai, 195; is charged with being subsidized with Mitsubishi funds, 262

Oka Yoshitake, states reasons for oligarchs' retreat from assembly concept, 54

Okada Keisuke: testifies on events preceding Manchurian Incident, 236 nn. 82 and 84–86; becomes Premier, 371; escapes death in February Twenty-sixth Incident, 383

Okamoto Kensaburo, joins Aikokukoto, 45 n. 9

Okawa Shumei: organizes Yuzonsha, 353–354; breaks with Kita and establishes Gyochisha, 358–359 and nn. 16 and 17; expounds basic ideas, 358–359 and nn. 18 and 19; has many military connections, 363; is involved in "March Incident," 365 and n. 27; has connection with Manchurian Incident, 366 and n. 29; is connected with May Fifteenth Incident, 370 and n. 38

Okubo Kishichi, interprets Oi's Korean plans, 107 n. 35

Okubo Toshimichi: leads antibakufu faction of Satsuma, 33 n. 54; goes on Iwakura mission, 43; leads oligarchy, 44 n. 7; plans new governmental structure in 1867, 51 n. 24; participates in Osaka Conference, 59; is assassinated, 62 and n. 53; submits proposal for a constitution, 66 n. 67; is impressed with Germany, 72

Okuda Yoshito, joins Seiyukai, 201 and n. 1

Okuma Shigenobu: serves as Hizen representative in the oligarchy, 44; sits

on Sei-in, 55 n. 33; splits with government, 66–67 and n. 67; leads Kaishinto, 77–78 and n. 94; expresses liberal philosophy, 78–79 and n. 97; builds Kaishinto from urban groups, 108–111; forms close ties with Mitsubishi, 109–110 and n. 42; resigns as president of Kaishinto, 111; attacks oligarchy and Jiyuto, 137; exemplifies problems of Japanese leadership, 140–141 and n. 38; is injured by assassin, 154 n. 10; pledges coalition with Jiyuto, 161; forms Shimpoto and aligns party with Matsukata, 170–172 and nn. 59 and 62; resigns from second Matsukata cabinet and breaks alliance, 172; helps form Kenseito and heads new ministry, 173–176 and nn. 69, 72, 73, and 75–78; resigns and leads Kenseihonto, 176–177; discusses political corruption, 178 and n. 82; returns to political power as Premier—events of ministry, 204–207 and nn. 8, 9, 12, and 14; dies, 223 n. 49; is charged with being subsidized by Mitsubishi, 261–262 and n. 32

Okura, as a part of the zaibatsu, 252

oligarchy. *See* Meiji oligarchy

on (favors, or benefactions), as part of Japanese familial system, 128–129

Ono, the business house of, position during Restoration period, 98

Ono Azusa: plays important role in Kaishinto and liberal movement, 78–79 and nn. 95 and 97; remains Imperial loyalist, 80

Onozuka Kiheiji, advances study of politics in Japan, 319 and n. 40

organic theory of state: as dominant philosophy of business class in Japan, 271–272; as set forth by Minobe, 318–319 and n. 39; challenged by Hozumi and Uesugi, 319 n. 39

Osaka: nature in Tokugawa era, 23 and n. 41; as center of early party movement, 135 and n. 22

Osaka Conference, purpose and results, 59–60

Osugi Sakae: is Anarchist participant in early Communist movement, 322 and n. 45; is murdered by Kempeitai, 326 and n. 54

Oto Kai (Gull Society), organization and political position, 109 and n. 39

Oura Kanetake: has connections with Katsura and the Chuo Club, 193 n.

popular rights movement: beginnings, 45–49 and nn. 8 and 9; handicaps, 57; effects of Satsuma Rebellion on, 61; actions and philosophy after Satsuma Rebellion, 61–64; repressive measures by government, 64–65; emergence of new issues, 67–68; climax of philosophic debate with opponents, 68–82 and nn. 73, 76, 79, 81, 83, 84, 88, 91, 95, 97, and 104; ties with antiforeignism, 83 n. 115; foundations broadened, 96–97 and n. 7; decline after 1885, 111–112; connection with treaty revision issue, 112–113 and nn. 48 and 49

Portugal: contacts with sixteenth-century Japan, 17 and n. 31; ouster, 18 and n. 32

Prefecture. See *ken*

press: laws of 1873 and 1875, 60 and n. 40; debates over political theory in early Meiji period, 74 and n. 85; pro-Jiyuto newspapers, 97 n. 8; pro-Kaishinto papers, 109 and n. 41; pro-Teiseito press, 111 and n. 46; debate between Jiyuto and Kaishinto newspapers, 137–138 and nn. 28 and 29; opposition to first Katsura ministry, 188; support for Kenseikai after Takahashi resignation, 223–224 and n. 50; approach of major parties to press, 301–302; military censorship, 366; military publications,. 377

Privy Council: established, 82–83; topples first Wakatsuki ministry, 234 and n. 79; attacks Tanaka ministry, 235; attacks London Naval Reduction Treaty and Hamaguchi ministry, 238–239; reforms proposed by Kita, 355 and n. 11

Prussia. See Germany

Rai Sanyo, historical writings and their importance, 20 and n. 35

railroads: early development, 248, 249–250 and n. 10; nationalization, 264 n. 37

reppan kaigi (powerful han conference): origins, 29–30 and n. 52; use by antibakufu forces, 32 n. 54; philosophic base, 50

representative government. See Diet

responsibility: as central problem in Japanese politics, 118–119; effect of Japanese familial system, 131–132; problem as exemplified in early Meiji parties, 140–141 and n. 38; problem intensified by Meiji Constitution, 150–151; attempted solution through Foreign Policy Deliberation Committee, 210 and n. 21; problem as revealed after outbreak of Manchurian Incident, 240–245, 381

revolution: ingredients present in modern Japan, 305; relation to militarist era, 346–347; ideas of Kita Ikki, 354–356 and nn. 9 and 11–13; attempts of the "right," 364–365 and n. 27, 378; the February Twenty-sixth Incident, 383–384 and nn. 56 and 57; events after February Twenty-sixth Incident, 385 and n. 61

rice riots of 1918, political results, 210

Rikken Doshikai. See Doshikai

Rikken Kaishinto. See Kaishinto

Rikken Kokuminto. See Kokuminto

Rikken Minseito. See Minseito

Rikken seitai ryaku (*Outline of Constitutional Government*), relation to development of early Meiji political ideas and terminology, 71–72 and n. 79

Rikken Seiyukai. See Seiyukai

Rikken Teiseito. See Teiseito

Rinji Seimu Chosakyoku (Temporary Administrative Affairs Investigation Bureau), established under Itagaki, and results, 175

Rinji Teikoku Gikai Jimukyoku (Temporary Imperial Diet Affairs Bureau), established, 152 n. 4

Risshisha (The Society to Establish One's Ambitions): organization and political principles, 57–59 and nn. 38 and 39; activities after Satsuma Rebellion, 61–62 and n. 51; use of French revolutionary theories, 73–74; economic functions, 95–96 and n. 7

Rodo Hyogikai (Labor Council): organized, 327–328; Seiji Mondai Kenkyukai becomes a branch organ, 328; moves into Rodo Nominto, 330–331; relation to Communist party, 331, 335 n. 70

Rodo Nominto (Labor-Farmer Party): establishment and internal political cleavages, 330 and n. 59; as a captive party of the Communists, 335–336; membership, 337 nn. 73 and 74; 1928 elections, 337 and n. 73, 74, and 76; banned by government, 338 and n. 78;

Rodo Nominto—Continued
  reëstablishment as Ronoto despite
  Communist opposition, 339 and n.
  80
Rodo Shimbun (*Labor Newspaper*),
  published as organ of far left, 327
Roessler, Hermann, assists in drafting
  Meiji Constitution, 83
ronin. See *samurai*
Rono ha (Labor-Farmer Faction), established by Yamakawa, Sakai, and
  others, 336
Ronoto (Labor-Farmer Party), creation
  from old Rodo Nominto ranks, 339 and
  n. 80
Rosokai (The Society of Mature Men):
  establishment and sponsors, 353; fragmented, 353; Yuzonsha organized
  from one element of, 353–354
Royama Masamichi: analyzes Ono's role,
  78 n. 95; discusses Fukuzawa's Throne
  theory, 80; points up Tokyo University power in the bureaucracy, 156;
  analyzes "Taisho Change," 199
Rousseau, serves as patron saint of
  Jiyuto, 73–76 and nn. 84 and 88
Russia: expansion toward Hokkaido, 28;
  early Meiji controversy over Saghalien, 44 n. 6; Nihilist currents in early
  Meiji popular movement, 77; demands
  recession of Liaotung peninsula, 169;
  Russo-Japanese War, 187–188 and nn.
  102 and 105; Hara administration Siberian policy, 216–217 and nn. 30, 31,
  and 33; economic effects of Russo-
  Japanese War, 268; impact of Russian
  Revolution on Japan, 321; Comintern
  establishes Japanese Communist
  party, 322–324 and nn. 45–49; relations with Japanese Communist movement, 331, 333–336 and nn. 62–64, 66,
  67, 70, and 71, 339–340 and nn. 80
  and 81, 341–342 and nn. 84–86; and
  Kita's program, 356 n. 13; actions
  charged in Japanese recantations of
  Communism, 374 n. 45
Russo-Japanese War: internal political
  effects on Japan, 187–188 and nn. 102
  and 105; economic effects, 268

sabaku kaikoku. See *kaikoku*
Saigo Takamori: leads antibakufu faction of Satsuma, 33 n. 54; breaks with
  new Meiji government, 44–45 and n.
  8; plans new governmental structure
  in 1867, 51 n. 24; sits on Sei-in, 55 n.

33; dies in Satsuma Rebellion, 61;
  establishes samurai school, 95–96
Saigo Tsugumichi: belongs to "military"
  bureaucratic faction, 159; is Minister
  of the Navy in Kenseito cabinet, 175
Sa-in (Chamber of the Left): establishment and powers, 54 n. 31, 55 and n.
  33; replacement by Genro-in, 59 and
  n. 46
Saionji Kimmochi: biographical sketch
  of early life, 182 n. 89; represents Ito
  faction, 182; becomes president of
  Seiyukai, 186; coöperates with Katsura
  faction, 186–188 and nn. 100 and
  103; forms first ministry, 188; resigns,
  189 and nn. 107, 109, and 111; accepts second premiership—events
  during second ministry, 191–192 and
  n. 114; reports Emperor's request to
  Seiyukai, 195 and n. 123; declines
  premiership after first Yamamoto ministry, 205 n. 8; is sympathetic to party
  government, 227–228; recommends
  Hamaguchi to succeed Tanaka as
  Premier, 237; turns to Inukai and the
  Seiyukai following Minseito fall, 242;
  is connected with Sumitomo through
  brother, 262 n. 33; approves railroad
  nationalization in 1908, 264 n. 37;
  recommends Saito to succeed Inukai,
  370–371; maintains proparty position, 375
Saito Makoto: is member of Kokuhonsha, 360; becomes Premier—events of
  ministry, 370–371; is killed in February Twenty-sixth Incident, 383
Sakai Toshihiko: proposes combined
  Diet and direct action policy for socialists, 318; leader in early Japanese
  Communist movement, 322 and nn.
  45–47; is arrested in mass arrests of
  1923, 326 n. 53; falls into disgrace
  with the Comintern, 329 and n. 56;
  joins Rono ha, 336
Sakamoto Ryuma, helps plan Tokugawa
  abdication, 33 n. 55
Sakurakai (Cherry Blossom Society):
  formation and nature, 364; involved
  in "March Incident," 365 and n. 27
samurai (warrior, warriors): social position in Tokugawa era, 14–16 and n.
  26; education, 16; political experience,
  16 and n. 28; numbers in Tokugawa
  era, 16 n. 29; worsening straits in late
  Tokugawa period, 24–25, 30–31 and
  n. 53; class splits over early Meiji

policies, 40–45 and nn. 3, 4, 6, and 7; pensions, 42 n. 3; position in Sanyo, 51 n. 24; economic and social problems after the Restoration, 94–96 and nn. 2–4, 97–102 and nn. 9, 15, and 17–20. See also *bushi; daimyo*

Sanjo Saneyoshi: active in overthrow of Tokugawa, 33 n. 55; leader in new era, 34, 51 n. 24; heads Sei-in, 55 n. 33

sankin kotai (alternate trips for service), description, 10; as aid to commercialism, 23; weakening, 32 n. 54

Sano Fumio, is demoted by Comintern as a "Fukumotoist," 334

Sano Manabu [Gaku]: leads left-wing students and active in Communist party, 326 n. 53; advances in power in Japanese Communist ranks, 329 and n. 56, 334; receives instructions to prevent labor union split, 335 n. 70; writes for *Marxshugi*, 336; recants, 342 and n. 86

Sanyo (Council, or Councillors), establishment, 51 n. 24

Sasaki Takayuki, writes concerning Ito's party plans, 163

Satsuma: political role in Bakumatsu, 29, 31–33 n. 54, 33 n. 55; proposals for national assembly, 50–51; position in initial governmental structure of 1868, 51 n. 24; strong provincialism, 135–137 and n. 23; faction aligns itself with Okuma forces, 170–172 and nn. 59, 62, and 63; decline in political power, 191; alliance with Seiyukai, 192; power as reflected in pre-1918 cabinets, 211 n. 23

Satsuma Rebellion: outbreak and results, 61 and nn. 50 and 51; relationship of Genyosha to, 350 n. 2

scandals. *See* corruption

sectionalism: as basic party weakness, 117; feudal background, 133–134; as force in early Meiji politics, 134–139 and nn. 22, 28, and 31

Seido Torishirabekyoku (Department for Institutional Investigation), establishment and purposes, 82

Seihiro Tetcho, writes political novels, 115 n. 54

Sei-i Tai Shogun (Barbarian-subduing Generalissimo): as Tokugawa title, 4; symbol taken over by Emperor, 32 n. 54

Sei-in (Central Chamber), establishment and position, 55 and n. 33

Seiji Kenkyukai. See *Seiji Mondai Kenkyukai*

Seiji Mondai Kenkyukai (Society for the Study of Political Problems): establishment and purposes, 326 and n. 52; changes name to Taishu Kyoiku Domei, 328; becomes Communist front organization, 330–331 and n. 58

Seitaisho (The Organic Act), establishment, 53

Sei-tetsu yume monogatari (*Dream Stories of Western Philosophy*), published as exposé of sources of Meiji Constitution, 83

Seito Kaisho Remmei (Political Party Dissolution League), organized by Matsuoka, 372

Seiyu Club (Political Friends' Club), personnel and activities, 202–203 and nn. 3 and 4

Seiyuhonto (Orthodox Seiyu Party): formed from Seiyukai split, 226–227; alliance with Kato and the Kenseikai, 233; alliance continued under Wakatsuki, 234 and n. 78; joins new Minseito, 235; connected with agrarian interests, 283–284; is involved in Matsushima Scandal, 285–286 and n. 84

Seiyukai, i.e., *Rikken Seiyukai* (Friends of Constitutional Government Association): established, 179–181 and nn. 84 and 87; position taken on Imperial powers, 179–180 and n. 84; party strategy under Ito's leadership, 183–185 and nn. 93–95; leadership transferred to Saionji, 185–186 and nn. 98 and 99; supports Katsura, 186–188 and nn. 100 and 101; events of first Saionji cabinet, 188–189 and nn. 107 and 109; defies third Katsura ministry and order from the Throne, 194–196 and nn. 121 and 123; forms alliance with Satsuma clique, 196; role in first Yamamoto ministry, 201–204 and n. 1; attempted split and election defeat, 206–207 and nn. 12–14; position in Terauchi ministry, 209–210 and n. 21; position during Hara's premiership, 212–221 and nn. 35, 41, 42, and 44; cleavages during Takahashi ministry, 222–223; support for Kato Tomosaburo ministry, 223–224; splits into two parties, 226–227; Tanaka succeeds Takahashi as president, 231–232 and nn. 75 and 76; Inukai joins party, 232–233 and n. 77; ceases to coöperate

465

Showa Tenno [The Emperor Showa]: opposes Kwantung conspirators, 237 n. 86; warns military after Manchurian Incident, 367–368; is pro-Western, 375; is considered in jeopardy, 380; decries February Twenty-sixth Incident, 385 and n. 62. See also Emperor; monarchical theories

Shugi-in (Assembly Chamber), establishment and powers, 54

Siberian expedition: Hara administration policy, 216–217 and nn. 30, 31, and 33; irregularities charged, 286 and n. 85; opposed in Japanese Communist leaflets, 322 and n. 46

Sino-Japanese War of 1894–1895: political effects on Japan, 169–170; economic effects, 249–250

social classes: divisions in Tokugawa era, 14–15 and nn. 23 and 26; Tokugawa social policy, 15–16 and n. 27; changes in late Tokugawa period, 22–25 and n. 45

social democrats: early movement and problems, 316–318 and nn. 34, 37, and 38; movement of World War I period, 318–320 and nn. 40–42; general problems during "party era," 324–325; increasing struggle with Communism, 327–328; the struggle to create a unified party, 329–332 and nn. 58 and 59, 336–341 and nn. 73, 74, 76–80, 82, and 83; summary of failure, 343–345. See also "left wing"

Sodomei, i.e., Nihon Rodo Sodomei (Japanese Federation of Labor): outlines union problems, 314; establishment, 314 n. 33; ideological cleavages, 325 and n. 51; major split in 1925, 327–328; withdraws from Nomin Rodoto, 330 and n. 58; participates in establishing Rodo Nominto, but later withdraws, 330–331; aids with creation of Shakai Minshuto, 331–332; suffers further political split, 332

Soejima Taneomi: joins early Meiji liberal movement, 44–45; participates in answer to Kato Hiroyuki, 56

sonno-joi (Revere the Emperor—Oust the barbarians [Westerners]): emergence, 19 n. 34; relation to Bakumatsu economic problems, 30–31 and n. 53; as dominant note of the Restoration, 36–37

Sosai (Office [or Officer] of Supreme Control), establishment, 51 n. 24

soshi (strong-arm men): used in early Meiji era by government, 104 n. 26; used in first Diet session, 157; used by major parties, 219

Spain: contacts with sixteenth-century Japan, 17; ouster, 18 and n. 32

Spencer, Herbert, influences early Meiji liberal movement, 73 n. 81

spinning industry, early development, 248 and n. 5, 249–250 and n. 10

Stein, Lorenz von: source of influence, 72 and n. 79; meetings with Ito, 82

suffrage. See elections

Sugiyama Hajime [Gen]: insists upon civilian noninterference with army discipline, 236–237; becomes an important political figure, 384

Sumitomo, the business house of: as a part of the zaibatsu, 252; political ties with Seiyukai, 262 and n. 33

Sumitomo Kizaemon: is president of Sumitomo and brother of Saionji, 262 n. 33; is threatened by extremists, 280

Sumitsu-in. See Privy Council

Sun Yat-sen, is opposed by Kita Ikki, 354 n. 9

Suzuki Bunji, forms Yuaikai, 314 n. 33

Suzuki Kantaro, is wounded in February Twenty-sixth Incident, 383

Suzuki Kisaburo: when Home Minister in Tanaka cabinet, impeached by Diet, 235; is leader in Seiyukai, 238 n. 88; struggles for control of the party, 242; is member of Kokuhonsha, 360; has connections with rightists, 368; becomes Seiyukai president, 371–372; resigns presidency, 388

Suzuki Mosaburo: joins Seiji Mondai Kenkyukai, 326 n. 52; leans toward social democrats, 328 n. 55; leads Nihon Musanto, 374–375

Syndicalism: power in early Japanese leftist movement, 322 n. 45, 323 n. 49; decline in labor and leftist movement, 325 and n. 51. See also Anarchism; "left wing"

Tachibana Kosaburo: represents agrarian nationalism, 357 and n. 15; has influence over young officers, 363; is connected with May Fifteenth Incident, 370 and n. 38

Tagawa Daikichiro, is arrested under Press Law, 303 n. 20

Yamamoto Eisuke, is connected with February Twenty-sixth Incident, 384

Yamamoto Gombei: leads Satsuma faction in navy, 191; strengthens Seiyukai stand against Katsura, 195 n. 123, 196; assumes premiership—events of ministry, 201–204 and nn. 1, 3, 4, 6, and 7; returns to politics—events of second ministry, 225–226

Yamamoto Kenzo, helps operate Moscow training program, 339 n. 81

Yamamoto Senji, is assassinated by rightists, 365

Yamamoto Tatsuo: joins Seiyukai, 201 and n. 1; joins Seiyuhonto, 227; urges industrial "rationalization," 276; is accused of unethical practices, 278

Yamamoto Teijiro, connects Mitsui and Seiyukai, 261

Yamato Minrokai (Yamato People's Labor Society), established as nationalist society, 353 n. 4

Yano Fumio: works on Okuma draft of a constitution, 67; plays important role in Kaishinto, 78, 79 n. 97; writes political novel, 115 n. 54

Yanson. *See* Janson

Yashiro Rokuro, refuses to reënter Okuma cabinet, 207

Yasuda, the business house of: as part of the zaibatsu, 252; connections with Kokuhonsha, 360

Yasuda Zenjiro, is murdered by "rightwing" extremists, 280 and n. 69

Yorozu (*What's What*), attacks "ruling class," 246

Yoshida Shoin, an Imperial patriot, 21

Yoshino Sakuzo: criticizes major parties, 246; leads intellectual democratic socialist movement, 319–320 and nn.

41 and 42; aids in organization of Shakai Minshuto, 331–332

"Young Officers' Movement": main elements, 363–364; the "March Incident," 365 and n. 27. *See also* army; Fascism; militarism; nationalism

Yuaikai (Fraternal Association), organized, 314 n. 33

Yuki Toyotaro, is member of Kokuhonsha, 360

Yuri Kosei, joins Aikokukoto, 45 n. 9

Yuzonsha (Society to Preserve the National Essence), organized from an element of Rosokai, 353 n. 8, 354

zaibatsu (financial cliques [or their members]): formation, 251–253; political ties in early Meiji period, 258–263 and nn. 25 and 27–34; political philosophy, 270–273; ambivalence toward Japanese business politics in "party era," 281 n. 70; role in "party era," 282–284 and nn. 74 and 75; and the militarists, 380

Zaigo Gunjinkai (Reserve Association), importance in military plans, 366

Zen Nihon Aikokusha Kyodo Toso Kyogikai (All-Japan Patriots' United Struggle Council), organization and program, 360–361 and n. 22

Zenei (*Vanguard*), published as leading Communist magazine, 325

Zenkoku Minshuto (All-Nation Mass Party), organized by Sodomei "left wing," 340

Zenkoku Rono Taishuto (All-Nation Labor-Farmer Mass Party), represents center-left elements of labor parties, 341

Zenkoku Taishuto (All-Nation Mass Party), represents centrist group, 341